MAINE STATE LIBRARY

# Virginia
# Legislative Petitions

Bibliography, Calendar, and Abstracts
from Original Sources
6 May 1776 – 21 June 1782

*Compiled by*
Randolph W. Church

Virginia State Library
Richmond

Published by authority of
THE LIBRARY BOARD

David F. Thornton, *Chairman*
Salem, Virginia

A. Gordon Brooks
Richmond, Virginia

Mrs. Warren B. French, Jr.
Edinburg, Virginia

Dr. Alyce O. Klussman
Alexandria, Virginia

Murray D. Rosenberg
Henrico County, Virginia

Mrs. Virginius R. Shackelford, Jr.
Woodberry Forest, Virginia

Ruth Anne M. Brooks
Richmond, Virginia

Mrs. Charles W. Harris
Wise, Virginia

M. O. Roache
Richmond, Virginia

Library of Congress Cataloging in Publication Data
Church, Randolph W. (Randolph Warner), 1907–
  Virginia legislative petitions

  Includes index.
  1. Petition, Right of—Virginia—Abstracts. 2. Virginia—Genealogy. 3. Virginia—History—Revolution, 1775-1783  I. Title.
KFV2420.C48  1984    016.328755′01    83-6646
ISBN 0-88490-114-9

Standard Book Number: 0-88490-114-9
© Virginia State Library 1984. All rights reserved.
Virginia State Library, Richmond, Virginia.
Printed in the United States of America.

# Contents

Symbols and Abbreviations ................................... vi
Introduction .................................................... vii
    *Editorial Apparatus*............................................. viii
    *Limits to this Bibliography* ......................................... x
    *The Manuscript Files* ............................................ x
    *Chronological Arrangement* ..................................... xiii
    *Entries* ........................................................ xiv
    *Acknowledgments* ............................................. xv
Virginia Legislative Petitions,
    6 May 1776–21 June 1782 .............................. 1
Index to Petitioners and Signers ............................. 509
Index to Subjects ............................................ 549
Geographic Index ........................................... 569

# Symbols and Abbreviations

| | |
|---|---|
| * | Manuscript once in the State Library but now missing |
| † | No record of manuscript except by reference in printed journal |
| C | Claim |
| CJ | Committee for Courts of Justice |
| GA | General Assembly |
| H | William Waller Hening, ed., *The Statutes at Large; Being a Collection of all the Laws of Virginia, from the First Session of the Legislature in the Year 1619.* . . . (Richmond, Philadelphia, and New York, 1809–1823) |
| HD | House of Delegates |
| JC | Journal of the Fifth Revolutionary Convention (6 May–5 July 1776) |
| JHD | *Journal of the House of Delegates* |
| JS | *Journal of the Senate* |
| M | Memorial |
| MHD | Manuscript minutes of the House of Delegates in the collections of the Virginia State Library |
| P | Petition |
| PC | Committee of Public Claims |
| PE | Committee of Privileges and Elections |
| PG | Committee of Propositions and Grievances |
| Prop. | Proposition |
| R | Committee for Religion |
| R | Representation (e.g., 106-R-†) |
| Rem. | Remonstrance |
| S | Senate |
| SC | Committee on the State of the Colony, Committee on the State of the Country, or Committee on the State of the Commonwealth (each of these was a committee of the whole) |
| T | Committee of Trade (October 1776) |

# Introduction

THE right of citizens and others to petition governing authorities was for many years a jealously guarded one. While recognized only indirectly in Magna Carta, it was reaffirmed in the English Bill of Rights of 1689. Originally petitions were for the purpose of asking favors or redressing wrongs, but they came to serve many other purposes. In Virginia petitions appear as early as the first session of the General Assembly in 1619 and increase in frequency during the ensuing years of both the colony and the commonwealth. They vanish from the Virginia scene, except for very particular purposes, shortly after the Civil War. Curiously enough, the right of petition was not mentioned in George Mason's Declaration of Rights or in Virginia's Constitution of 1776. The First Amendment to the United States Constitution, however, specifically enshrined it in the Bill of Rights. There is no compulsion now for legislative bodies to consider petitions independently since it has been ruled that an acknowledgment of receipt of them fulfills the constitutional requirement.

This bibliography begins with the Fifth Virginia Revolutionary Convention, which met from 6 May 1776 to 5 July 1776, with occasional references to earlier conventions or meetings of the House of Burgesses. It includes such associated documents as claims, memorials, and propositions—the difference between these and petitions not being easily ascertainable. It has been compiled by a close reading and indexing of the printed journals of the convention and later of the House of Delegates and Senate. Every manuscript, when found, has been compared with the printed record and annotated. Unfortunately, the early manuscript sources have been sadly depleted.

By tradition of the House of Burgesses, one must assume, all petitions and associated documents were introduced in the House, read, and referred to

## Introduction

appropriate committees. The committees reported back, and the House voted on the committees' recommendations. If rejected there was no further recourse; if approved or amended, the documents were forwarded to the upper house, where the procedure was similar. Many petitions were enacted into law.

Historians have not sufficiently recognized the importance of petitions, largely because there has been no easy method of locating them or the action taken on them, the legislative journals not having been indexed. Those who have taken the time to explore have often found the results rewarding. In truth, petitions were the basis of early legislation, and much more time was spent on them than on bills that were introduced without the written opinions of constituents. Petitions often were virtual referenda that could significantly affect legislative decisions. This is not to say, however, that occasional doubts were not expressed; one notes, for example, the phrase in a Henry County petition (965-P) that "it is well known that it is an easy matter to induce the ignorant multitude to sign anything."

### Editorial Apparatus

Because the legislative routine after the introduction and initial reading of a petition was highly repetitive, a standardized format with many abbreviations has been adopted to present this information. On the first line of each abstract (in **boldface type**) is the serial number assigned to the petition, memorial, claim, or other document, followed immediately by a letter or symbol code and the identification of the petitioner(s). Thus, **1-P** means that item one is a manuscript petition in the collections of the Virginia State Library. An asterisk (*) indicates that the manuscript once was in the library's collections but is now missing; such information comes largely from notations on empty folders. A dagger (†) indicates that the only evidence of the item was found in a legislative or convention journal entry.

For the convenience of researchers, the editor has included, beneath the boldface item number, the number that was assigned to the abstracted document if it was listed in either of the following partial bibliographies of manuscript petitions:

Eck-## is the number assigned by Hamilton J. Eckenrode in his *Calendar of Legislative Petitions, Arranged by Counties: Accomac-Bedford* (Richmond: Virginia State Library, 1908). Eckenrode listed manuscript petitions dating into the 1860s and sometimes later; his list is uneven in

## Editorial Apparatus

character with no attempt to trace the legislative histories of petitions; he generally limited his transcription of signatures to five.

Rob-## is the number assigned by James Rood Robertson in his *Petitions of the Early Inhabitants of Kentucky to the General Assembly of Virginia, 1769 to 1792* (Louisville: John P. Morton and Company, 1914). Robertson's book provided the full texts of all manuscript petitions he located, although some relevant items in this bibliography are missing from his list. He tried to decipher and index all manuscript signatures. He did not trace the legislative histories of petitions.

In addition to Eckenrode's and Robertson's compilations, historical journals have printed the texts of many individual petitions. A spot-check has been made of a number of these printings, but it has not seemed worthwhile to attempt to trace them all, as they often were published without significant dates and they sometimes have been badly transcribed.

At the left on the second line is the date on which the item is first noted in the appropriate printed journal or other source:

JC: 6 May 1776 refers to a 6 May 1776 entry in the journal of the Fifth Revolutionary Convention (6 May–5 July 1776).

JHD: 8 Oct. 1776 refers to an 8 October 1776 entry in the *Journal of the House of Delegates.*

MHD: 6 May 1782 refers to a 6 May 1782 entry in the manuscript minutes of the House of Delegates in the collections of the Virginia State Library.

At the right margin of the second line is the geographic area (if it can be determined) from which the petition came. Sometimes this information appears in the body of the petition, sometimes it is well known, and sometimes it may be inferred from a manuscript endorsement showing who introduced the petition to the convention or House. This designation does not include other places that may be mentioned in the petition, but all these related places (as in the case of a ferry from one county to another) are included in the geographic index, which begins on page 569.

Below these elements of the heading come the abstract itself, notes about the manuscript when applicable, and transcriptions of as many as the first five signatures on the document. Then follows the petition's known legislative history: its referral to a committee, the action of the committee, and the final action of the legislative body. If the petition resulted in the passage of a statute or ordinance, a reference is made to the published text. Citations to William Waller Hening, ed., *The Statutes at Large; Being a Collection of all the Laws of*

# Introduction

*Virginia, from the First Session of the Legislature in the Year 1619.* . . . (Richmond, Philadelphia, and New York, 1809–1823) are in concise form: "9H317" means volume 9 of Hening, ed., *Statutes*, page 317.

## Limits to this Bibliography

The commonwealth's archives contain, perhaps, many items bearing on petitions that have not been examined (such as petitions addressed to the governor, committee reports, drafts of bills, or court decisions). Locating and correlating all such items would have been virtually impossible. Indeed, owing to the early-twentieth-century rearrangement of the petitions, as described below, it is doubtful that all manuscript petitions from the revolutionary era have been located.

The manuscript petitions are both signed and unsigned. In some cases the signatures run into thousands of names and appear on duplicate petitions. These duplicates are listed, when found, but a notation of the names of signers is made from the first copy only. Throughout this bibliography, the signatures of a maximum of five persons (whose names were taken from the left column of the manuscript) have been printed. It is by no means certain that these were the first who signed, for the signatures are usually in several columns, often on many pages, and some are illegible. A fairly large number of signatures are by mark (X) only.

Because the abstracts of the petition text are condensed to print only the most salient matter, users of this volume are urged to refer to the manuscripts and journals for many important and informative details. The form of the manuscript petition was highly standardized. Customarily a petition opened with a salutation ("To the honourable the President and gentlemen of the House of Delegates of the Commonwealth now assembled. The petition of ———— humbly showeth . . .") and ended with a formal closing (". . . and your petitioners, as in duty bound, shall ever pray, etc."). Salutations and closings were not printed in the journals, and they are omitted in this bibliography.

## The Manuscript Files

As far as can be determined, the petition collection held in the Virginia State Library was in the hands of the secretary of the commonwealth during the nineteenth century. With the establishment of The Library Board under the Constitution of 1902, state agencies and institutions were authorized to transfer their archival records to the State Library. The legislative petitions

The abstract of this three-page 1776 petition from the "German Congregation" of Hebron Lutheran Church (157-P) is printed on page 47.

# To the Honourable the LEGISLATORS of the Commonwealth of VIRGINIA.

*The* ADDRESS *of sundry inhabitants of the county of* _____ *all adult persons.*

GENTLEMEN,

CONSCIOUS that nothing, in this critical situation of public affairs, when liberty, life, and all are at stake, ought to take up much of your valuable time, but matters of indispensable obligation, we therefore beg your attention only a few moments.

The undue means taken to overthrow the established church, by imposing upon the credulity of the vulgar, and engaging infants to sign petitions handed about by dissenters, have, it seems, so far succeeded as to cause a dissolution of the usual mode of her support, where we would choose it should rest in the present exigency of affairs, rather than, by strenuously insisting upon the rectitude of an establishment, throw this State in particular into commotion, and thereby prejudice the common cause, which we are resolved shall receive no detriment from us by any means whatsoever. If only withholding from a competent number of ministers of the gospel fixed salaries is the most likely means to make men unanimous in the defence of liberty, as has been urged, we should be very sorry indeed if there could be one found of that reverend order who would repine at the success of the measure. For even an unwillingness to sacrifice a part of our private property to the good of our country, much more an absolute refusal of it, is a poor argument indeed of our disinterested zeal for the commonwealth. Wherefore we would by no means wish to see Churchmen adopt the principles of Dissenters, withhold their concurrence in the common cause until their particular requests are granted, for by such a conduct all may be lost. Notwithstanding we think an established church in any State, under proper limitations and restrictions, and founded upon the warranty of holy scripture, is one of the great bulwarks of liberty, the cement of society, the bond of union, and an asylum for the persecuted to fly to; yet, as this is a controverted point, we are heartily willing it should be debated at a time when you have nothing of more importance to engage your attention.

The abstract of this 1777 printed address from the citizens of Mecklenburg County (337-Address) is printed on page 100.

## The Manuscript Files

were among the first record groups affected by this change. In time, records were located and transferred from various storage areas, including the attic of the Capitol. When the Capitol was being remodeled early in the twentieth century, however, some records were discarded. William G. Stanard, secretary of the Virginia Historical Society, salvaged as many of them as he could and transported them to the society's offices, where they remained until arrangements were made to transfer the records back to public custody. Between July 1949 and March 1951 approximately three thousand items, including 363 antebellum petitions, were transferred from the Virginia Historical Society to the State Library.

It is clear from statements made in early printed reports of The Library Board that the petitions had been folded in legal fashion, endorsed across the back, and filed chronologically (probably in boxes) by date of introduction within each session of the legislature. Sometime before 1930 a decision was made to alter this arrangement. Several years were spent unfolding the petitions, filing them flat in manila folders, and arranging them chronologically by counties and cities of origin. Their historical relationships to other state records were thus lost. A sad result of this endeavor was that for approximately two thousand petitions the county or city of origin could no longer be identified. These were gathered into a miscellaneous file group along with another, much larger, number of petitions whose dates and origins could not be established without a tedious reading of many unindexed legislative journals. These problems remain unresolved, and a new one was caused by the creation of subject files on such matters as religion and slavery.

Under the original direction of the late William J. Van Schreeven, state archivist from 1939 to 1969, a great deal of remedial work was done: the petitions were removed from deteriorating folders and filed in acid-free folders and archival boxes. Many have been restored by the W. J. Barrow Restoration Shop. Contents of the subject files were microfilmed and then reincorporated into the main corpus of papers, but no attempt can be made to duplicate the original filing sequence. Problematic files still remain. In them there may be manuscript petitions that are omitted from or listed as missing in this bibliography, but it would take many years to research these matters thoroughly.

*Chronological Arrangement*

In archival theory, a statute may be filed either under the date of its final approval or under the date it takes effect. Generally the legislative history of

## Introduction

bills eventually passed or defeated is not a primary filing objective. On the other hand, a file of legislative bills themselves may well be arranged by their dates of introduction.

Petitions, memorials, and the like are more similar to statutes than to any other legislative record—indeed many became acts—but to list petitions by date of final action would obscure their historical importance. For example, Richard Henderson's memorial on Transylvania (97-M) was introduced on 15 June 1776 but final action was not completed until 12 December 1778. To list the memorial under the latter date would throw it out of context. Items are listed in this bibliography either by the date of introduction noted in the journals or by the earliest date endorsed on the manuscript.

### Entries

An attempt has been made to establish a system of entries upon the following seven principles:

(1) For a petition from a single individual, the entry is the surname and given name.
   Thus: the entry for William Criddle is *Criddle, William.*

(2) For a petition from a group of individuals named in its preamble, the entry comprises all surnames and given names.
   Thus: the entry for George Wray, John Jones, Alexander Graham, George Graham, and Henry Sinclair is *Wray, George; Jones, John; Graham, Alexander; Graham, George; and Sinclair, Henry.*

(3) The entry for a petition from a group of residents of a county or corporation—irrespective of whether they term themselves "inhabitants," "freeholders," "citizens," or the like—gives the name of the locality followed by the word *citizens*, and sometimes *committee*, even if the petitioners may not have been an official county committee.
   Thus: the entry for "the petition of the Committee of the County of Norfolk in behalf of themselves, & their constituents the Freeholders of the said County" is *Norfolk County—Citizens (Committee).*

(4) For a petition from a specified group but with no personal names in the body of the petition, the entry gives the name of the group.
   Thus: the entry for "a Petition of the inspectors at Cabin Point" is *Tobacco Inspectors—Cabin Point Warehouse.*

(5) If the petition is from a parish, the parish name is followed by the county and the word *citizens.*
   Thus: the entry for "the Petition of the Sundry Inhabitants of the Parish of Newport in the County of Isle of Wight" is *Newport Parish, Isle of Wight County—Citizens.*

**Entries**

(6) For a petition from an unspecified group of dissenters from the Church of England, the entry is the word *Dissenters*, followed by their locality (if known).
(7) For a petition from a specific denomination, the entry is the name of the church, the county (if known), and the word *members*.

> Thus: the entry for "the petition of a Baptist Church at Occaqon, Prince William County" is *Baptist Church, Prince William County—Members (Occaqon [Occoquan])*.
>
> Entries for general denominational petitions are *Church of England, Baptist Association, Presbyterians, Quakers*, and the like.

## Acknowledgments

Outside of the abstracting of the petitions, the most meticulous part of this compilation was the indexing of the legislative and convention journals from the time of the introduction of the petitions to final action upon them. In this I was ably served by W. Thomas Baird, Jr., who diligently read all the early journals and noted references to the petitions. Marianne Withers completed this reading and worked with me in jointly abstracting the petitions and in assigning and filing index entries for petitioners, areas, and subjects. She also typed the complete manuscript and made many invaluable suggestions. Her work was indispensable. Charles Cella, Jr., aided in abstracting petitions of later sessions, and John W. Dudley rendered valuable services. Emily J. Salmon and Susan Bracey Sheppard, of the library's Publications Branch, guided the manuscript into print. To all of these I am most grateful. Errors of omission and commission are the sole responsibility of the compiler.

*Richmond, Virginia*                         RANDOLPH W. CHURCH

# Virginia
# Legislative Petitions
## 6 May 1776 – 21 June 1782

**1-P**   **Norfolk County—Citizens (Committee)**
    JC: 6 May 1776                                    Norfolk County
For designating time and place for holding elections for delegates to this convention since courthouse has been destroyed by enemy.
   Manuscript signed by: Jas. Holt, John Wilson, Danl. Sandford, Matt. Godfrey, Goodrich Boush, and fifteen others.
6 May 1776: Resolution passed by convention that sheriff, mayor, or clerk of county or borough may appoint time or place, publish notice, and hold elections for delegates to serve for one year.
27 May 1776: First appointment of delegates to committees.
15 June 1776: Election of delegates from Norfolk County and borough of Norfolk confirmed.

**2-P-†**   **Criddle, William**
    JC: 7 May 1776                                         Not known
Compensation for loss of right arm in battle at Norfolk in January 1776.
7 May 1776: Referred to special committee.
9 May 1776: Resolution passed by convention that he be allowed £10 for present and £10 per annum for life.

**3-P-†**   **Chesterfield County—Citizens**
    JC: 7 May 1776                                    Chesterfield County
For relief from musters of militia every fortnight.
7 May 1776: Laid on table.
10 May 1776: To PG.

## Virginia Legislative Petitions

15 June 1776: PG reports reasonable and is directed to prepare amended ordinance.
  For amended ordinance see Ordinances of Convention, chapter XII, which among other things provides for musters not more often than once every four weeks in each county and corporation.

**4-P-†**   **Ballendine, John**
  JC: 8 May 1776                                              Henrico County
                                                          Buckingham County
For free use of slaves now in public jail in working on canal from Westham to Richmond and in ironwork further up the James River.
8 May 1776: To PG.
16 May 1776: PG recommends rejection.
  Convention rejects.

**5-P-†**   **Corbin, John Tayloe**
  JC: 9 May 1776                                                  Not known
For release from imprisonment in guardhouse on charges of disloyalty, and clearance from these charges. Charges were based on a letter to Charles Neilson, of Urbanna, said to contain disloyal statements. Regrets that letter was so interpreted.
9 May 1776: To PE.
11 May 1776: PE recommends that Corbin be released, but that he be confined to that part of Caroline County between Pamunkey and Mattaponi rivers; that he not move from there without permission; that he be allowed fifteen days to raise a bond of £10,000; and that he not aid or assist enemy.

**6-P-†**   **Turner, James and Terry, William**
  JC: 9 May 1776                                              Halifax County
For pay for military service at the direction of Colonel Armistead Watlington, of Halifax, to assist North Carolina against insurgents at Cross Creek. Discharged at Hillsborough after service of five days.
9 May 1776: To PC.
14 May 1776: PC notes these persons did not see action in Orange County, N.C., but recommends that Turner be allowed £22 3s. 6d., and Terry be allowed £23 10s. 7d. for themselves, their men, and for waggonage, provisions, and ammunition.
  Convention agrees.

## 8 – 9 May 1776

**7-P-†**   **Boush, Samuel**
JC: 9 May 1776                                                    Norfolk County
Compensation for Negro slave, Mercury, apprehended for felony, sent to Williamsburg for trial by Committee of Safety on direction of Colonel Charles Scott and associates, but died before trial.
9 May 1776: To PC.
   Carried over to October 1776 session of GA.
9 Nov. 1776: PC of HD notes slave had defected to Lord Dunmore, and if found guilty would have been transported to West Indies for sale. PC recommends payment of £55.
   House agrees.
18 Dec. 1776: Senate agrees, JS.

**8-P-†**   **Boush, Samuel and Boush, Goodrich (Executors of Samuel Boush, deceased)**
JC: 9 May 1776                                                    Norfolk County
Compensation for Negro slave, Cuffey, who was said to have defected to Lord Dunmore, was sent to Williamsburg, but died before trial.
9 May 1776: To PC.
   Carried over to October 1776 session of GA.
9 Nov. 1776: PC of HD notes that evidence shows that the slave had not been active on Dunmore's behalf and was to have been returned to owner.
   PC recommends rejection.
   House rejects.

**9-P-†**   **Boush, Arthur**
JC: 9 May 1776                                                    Norfolk County
Compensation for Negro slave, Harry, who fled to Lord Dunmore in December 1775, was captured, sent to Williamsburg, and died in jail before trial.
9 May 1776: To PC.
   Carried over to October 1776 session of GA.
9 Nov. 1776: PC of HD recommends payment of £65.
   House agrees.
18 Dec. 1776: Senate agrees, JS.

**10-C-*** **Smith, William**
JC: 9 May 1776                                                    Not known
Compensation for Negro man slave who refused to surrender to troops in

3

## Virginia Legislative Petitions

December 1775 and was shot by Lieutenant William Sandford and killed. The slave was valued at £80.

9 May 1776: To PC.
    Carried over to October 1776 session of GA.
5 Dec. 1776: PC of HD recommends rejection since slave gave no armed resistance.
    House rejects.

### 11-P-†    Chesterfield County—Citizens
    JC: 10 May 1776      Chesterfield County

For the removal of the exemption from militia duty now allowed overseers.
10 May 1776: To PG.
15 June 1776: PG reports reasonable and is directed to prepare amended ordinance.
    For amended ordinance see Ordinances of Convention, chapter XII, which among other things removes exemption of overseers from militia duty.

### 12-R-†    Augusta County—Citizens (Committee)
    JC: 10 May 1776      Augusta County

For making an independent confederacy of the united colonies.
10 May 1776: To SC.
    Never reported in any separate form.

### 13-P    Lunenburg County—Citizens
    JC: 11 May 1776      Lunenburg County

For the removal of the exemption from militia duty now allowed overseers.
    Manuscript signed by: Lodowick Farmer, John Elam, Robert Dixon, Wm. DeGraffenreid, John Ragdale, and about 175 others, some names illegible.
11 May 1776: To PG.
15 June 1776: PG reports reasonable.
    For action see 11-P-†.

### 14-P-†    Bachelor (Batchelor?), Thomas
    JC: 11 May 1776      Norfolk County

For aid to the poor of Portsmouth Parish for whom the vestry has made him responsible. The four assigned him are about to perish.
11 May 1776: To PG.
    Carried over to October 1777 session of GA.

## 10 - 13 May 1776

3 Jan. 1778: PC of HD recommends rejection.
    House rejects.

**15-P-***    **Dixon, John, Jr.**
    JC: 11 May 1776                                                                      Not known

Compensation for loss of vessel and cargo on outbound voyage, February 1776, to secure military supplies with approval of Committee of Safety. The vessel was apprehended off Virginia capes by British and taken to Antigua where vessel and cargo were confiscated. Dixon escaped to Saint Eustatia where he had credit and friends and sailed back to Virginia with army supplies valued at £4,000.

11 May 1776: To PG.
    Carried over to October 1777 session of GA.
3 Jan. 1778: PG of HD recommends rejection.
    House rejects.
    See 69-M.

**16-P-***    **Hendricks, Humphrey**
    JC: 11 May 1776                                                                      Not known

For additional allowance for dressing and sighting rifles for Captain Cooke's company. Had been allowed £8 by Committee of Safety.

11 May 1776: To PC.
14 May 1776: PC recommends £1 12s. 3d. additional.
    Convention agrees.

**17-P**    **Wormeley, Ralph, Jr.**
    JC: 13 May 1776                                                                    Not known

For release from confinement for disloyalty. Cites letter he wrote to John Grymes, which apparently raised the indignation and odium of country. Expresses sorrow over differences of opinion on separation from England. Gives word he will conduct himself properly.

Manuscript is undated and unsigned.

13 May 1776: To PE.
15 May 1776: PE recommends that he be released under bond of £10,000 and sent under guard to his father's estate in Berkeley County, that part of which lies next to Frederick County. Guard to be furnished by General Lewis at Wormeley's expense, to leave in twenty days, not to leave his father's land or give aid to enemy.
    Convention agrees.

## Virginia Legislative Petitions

**18-P-***     **Stewart, Alexander**
         JC: 13 May 1776                                            Not known

    For annual allowance in addition to lump sum of £20 allowed him by commissioners for wound received in service of Captain George Moffat's company on Ohio River in late expedition against Indians.
13 May 1776: To PC.
14 May 1776: PC recommends £5 per year for four years.
         Convention agrees.

**19-P-***     **Lonsdale, William**
         JC: 13 May 1776                                            Not known

    Compensation for wound received in the late Indian expedition while serving in Captain George Moffat's company.
13 May 1776: To PC.
19 June 1776: PC recommends £5 per annum for four years.
         Convention agrees.

**20-**
**Prop.-†**     **Reveley, John**
         JC: 13 May 1776                                            Not known

    For erecting iron foundry for casting cannon. Presented by Mr. Digges of Committee of Safety.
13 May 1776: To PG.
         Apparently never reported but see 24-P-*.

**21-P-†**     **Henrico County—Citizens**
         JC: 13 May 1776                                      Henrico County

    To allow citizens to supply goods to army in lieu of payment of taxes in scarce paper money.
13 May 1776: To PG.
         Apparently never reported.

**22-P-†**     **Wray, George; Jones, John; Graham, Alexander; Graham, George; and Sinclair, Henry**
         JC: 16 May 1776                            Elizabeth City County

    Compensation for vessels taken by committee of safety of Elizabeth City County and sunk in channel of Hampton River to protect Hampton from enemy.
16 May 1776: To PC.

## 13 – 18 May 1776

21 May 1776: PC recommends £240 5s. for George Wray.
        Convention agrees.
14 June 1776: PC recommends £160 to John Jones, £40 to Henry Sinclair, and £125 to Alexander and George Graham.
        Convention agrees, but stipulates the amounts were not to be paid to the Grahams (who were natives of Great Britain) until further order.
        This order not found.

**23-P-†   Bucktrout, Benjamin**
        JC: 16 May 1776                         Williamsburg
  Offering a completed powder mill in Williamsburg to the convention on terms to be decided.
16 May 1776: To PG.
        Carried over to October 1777 session of GA.
3 Jan. 1778: PG of HD recommends rejection.
        House rejects.

**24-P-\*   Ballendine, John and Reveley, John**
        JC: 16 May 1776                       Buckingham County
  For financial assistance in mining iron and coal and establishing a blast furnace and foundry at a point below Seven Islands, one mile from James River, on Phelps's Creek, on a site for which they have contracted.
16 May 1776: To PG.
22 May 1776: PG recommends that the foundry be erected on the public account, but that the blast furnace be erected by Ballendine and Reveley on an advance of not more than £5,000 from the public, such funds to be disbursed by trustees and repaid in five equal payments, the lands of Ballendine and Reveley being held as security. Pig iron is to be sold to public at £7 10s. per ton.
        Convention agrees.
25 May 1776: Richard Adams, Nathaniel Wilkinson, and Turner Southall appointed commissioners for erecting foundry.
14 June 1776: George Carrington, John Nicholas, and William Cabell appointed trustees for blast furnace.

**25-R-†   Lynch, Charles**
        JC: 18 May 1776                          Bedford County
  For use of imprisoned slaves in mining saltpeter in "upper parts of country." Presented by Mr. Mercer of Committee of Safety.

## Virginia Legislative Petitions

18 May 1776: Convention, without referral to a committee, orders slaves to be delivered to Lynch. Allows an advance of £50 to him with authority to draw up to £500 from treasurer with bond. Powder to be provided at 6s. per pound and to be delivered to New London if required. Slaves that can be spared are to be sent under guard to lead mines.

**26-P-†    Transylvania—Citizens**
JC: 18 May 1776                         Western Lands South of Ohio River

For relief from increase in the cost of land grants by Colonel Henderson from 20s. to 50s. and increases in fees for entries and surveying. Cites deed of Six Nations to Sir William Johnson at Fort Stanwix in 1768 for lands south of Ohio River. Cherokees doubt validity of Henderson's claim. The petitioners wish to be part of Virginia, and if convention cannot adjudicate, the matter should go to Congress.

28 May 1776: To SC with attachments.

24 June 1776: Convention considers this and several similar petitions and resolves that citizens settled in this area should hold lands without payment of fees to private persons until matter is considered by legislature of this country. They further resolve that no purchases of Indian lands in chartered limits of Virginia be made without approval of Virginia legislature.

For a study of this subject see W. S. Lester, *The Transylvania Colony* (Spencer, Ind., 1935).

**27-P-*    Adams, Robert**
JC: 18 May 1776                                                    Not known

For a subsidy of £1,700 for manufacture of linen and sailcloth.

18 May 1776: To a special committee to bring in an ordinance to encourage this type of manufacture.

Committee did not report, and there is no ordinance or later act on the subject.

**28-P-†    Finnie, William**
JC: 20 May 1776                                                 Williamsburg

For additional compensation, as keeper of the magazine, for collecting arms for the country.

20 May 1776: To PC.

## 18 – 21 May 1776

14 June 1776: PC recommends additional allowance of £10 over and above allowance of £25 already granted by Committee of Safety. Convention agrees.

29-P  **Mecklenburg County—Citizens**  Mecklenburg County
    JC: 20 May 1776

For the removal of the exemption from militia duty now allowed overseers.
Manuscript signed by: William Lucas, Lewis Parham, John Lucas, Richard Howard, John James, and thirty-two others.
20 May 1776: To PG.
15 June 1776: PG reports reasonable.
    For action see 11-P-†.

30-P-*  **Chapman, William and Slaughter, George**  Not known
    JC: 20 May 1776

For full pay as captains in 1774 expedition against Indians, despite depletion of their companies by desertion.
20 May 1776: To PC.
21 May 1776: PC recommends rejection.
    Convention rejects.

31-P-†  **Preston, William**  Fincastle County
    JC: 21 May 1776

For compensation, 24 May to 7 November 1774, for raising and embodying militia in Fincastle County, under 24 May order of Lord Dunmore, and for sending expedition against Shawanese Indians.
21 May 1776: To PC.
28 June 1776: PC recommends rejection.
    Convention rejects.
    See 109-M.

32-P-†  **Wilson, Matthew**  Not known
    JC: 21 May 1776, for action

For additional pay as ensign in militia in late expedition against Indians.
Date unknown: To PC.
21 May 1776: PC recommends rejection.
    Convention rejects.

33-P  **Hansford, Edward**  Norfolk Borough
    JC: 21 May 1776

## Virginia Legislative Petitions

Additional compensation for his daughter, Elizabeth Hansford, in the amount of £132 7½d., for balance claimed due on loss of house and goods in burning of Norfolk. Cites £10 paid by Committee of Safety and use of wagons.
Manuscript unsigned.
21 May 1776: To PG.
>Apparently not reported or carried forward.

### 34-P-†    Fincastle County, Pendleton District—Citizens
JC: 21 May 1776                                             Fincastle County
For complete incorporation as part of the colony of Virginia and protesting seizure of property by John Carter and Robert Lucas of neighboring Washington District.
21 May 1776: To SC.
>Apparently never reported.

### 34A-P    Fincastle County, Pendleton District—Citizens
JC: 21 May 1776                                               Fincastle County
For complete incorporation as part of the colony of Virginia even though situated west of part of Fincastle County and even though some of their lands lay outside those the government had purchased from Indians. Cites formation of a committee similar to county committees.
Manuscript signed by John Coulter, chairman.
Manuscript has attached a copy of a recommendation of Fincastle County committee stating petition is reasonable even though lands lay west of Donaldson's (Donelson's) line. Signed by William Preston, chairman, and Abraham Trigg, clerk.
21 May 1776: To SC.
>Apparently never reported.

### 35-R-*    Wattaugh and Holstein Rivers—Citizens (owning lands there)
JC: 23 May 1776                                             Western Frontier
For being recognized as part of colony of Virginia. Pledges aid and obedience to instructions.
23 May 1776: To SC.
>Apparently never reported.

### 36-P-†    Hanover County—Citizens
JC: 25 May 1776                                                Hanover County
For dissolution of county committee and election of new one, claiming

## 21 – 27 May 1776

fraud in election of present one. Asks for ordinance incapacitating for public office those guilty of breach of faith or abuse of power.
25 May 1776: To PG.
        Apparently never reported.

**37-P-†**    **Hanover County—Citizens**
        JC: 27 May 1776                      Hanover County
For relief from payment of taxes by allowing each county to furnish to the army, in proper proportion, provisions that it has for the army.
27 May 1776: To PG.
        Apparently never reported.

**38-P-\***    **Tompkins, Bennett**
        JC: 27 May 1776                      York County
Compensation for two Negro slaves, Amy and Rachel, who attempted to escape to Lord Dunmore in November 1775, were captured with stolen goods, remanded to Williamsburg jail, where Amy died of jail fever. Rachel apparently was still held in November 1776 as witness.
27 May 1776: To PC.
        Carried over to October 1776 session of GA.
30 Nov. 1776: PC of HD finds reasonable and recommends £60 as recompense for Amy.
        House rejects on second reading.

**39-P-†**    **Smelly, John and Cutchin, Joseph**
        JC: 27 May 1776                    Isle of Wight County
For repayment for six hogsheads of tobacco containing 6,212 pounds valued at 20s. per 100, stolen from Smithfield's and Fulgham's warehouses where they were inspectors.
27 May 1776: To PC.
29 June 1776: PC recommends rejection since at time of theft warehouses had no doors.
        Convention rejects.

**40-P-\***    **Coulter, Michael**
        JC: 27 May 1776                      Not known
For additional compensation as a carpenter in the Indian expedition. Employed at Greenbrier by Colonel Charles Lewis.
27 May 1776: To PC.

19 June 1776: PC recommends £1 16s. above allowance already made.
Convention agrees.

### 41-P-*  Lyle, John
JC: 27 May 1776                            Not known

For additional pay as master drover in late expedition against Shawanese Indians. Was to receive 7s. 6d. per day. Allowed 5s. for forty-eight days and 6s. for fourteen days.
27 May 1776: To PC.
19 June 1776: PC recommends £7 1s. extra.
Convention agrees.

### 42-P-†  Tobacco Inspectors—Cabin Point Warehouse
JC: 28 May 1776                        Surry County

For disposition of tobacco in their warehouse for over one year. Warehouse not in proper order for safekeeping.
28 May 1776: To PG.
Apparently never reported.

### 43-P  Norfolk County—Citizens
JC: 28 May 1776                        Norfolk County

For rescinding action of convention requiring citizens to move from area bounded by south side of western branch of Elizabeth River, northeast side of road leading from head of branch to Great Bridge, east side of road leading from Great Bridge to Northwest Landing.

Manuscript signed by: John Wilson, Bassett Moseley, Thomas Talbot, Arthur Boush, Amos Etheridge, and about 200 others.
28 May 1776: To SC.
>SC immediately recommends that previous action be rescinded for Norfolk and Princess Anne counties except for those persons inimical to America.
>Convention agrees.

### 44-P  Smith, John
JC: 28 May 1776                        Norfolk Borough

For compensation of £1,500 for loss of houses in second burning of

## 27 – 28 May 1776

Norfolk on 6 February 1776, and for two slaves who deserted to Lord Dunmore.
  Manuscript unsigned.
28 May 1776: To PG.
    Apparently never reported.

**45-P-†  Crocket, Walter; Herbert, William; Russell, William; Harwood, James; Bledsoe, Anthony; and Campbell, William**
    JC: 28 May 1776, for action                Not known
  Additional compensation for them and their subalterns in late expedition against Indians.
Date unknown: To PC.
28 May 1776: PC recommends rejection.
    Convention rejects.

**46-P-†  Shelby, Evan**
    JC: 28 May 1776, for action                Not known
  Additional compensation for himself and officers in late expedition against Indians.
Date unknown: To PC
28 May 1776: PC recommends rejection.
    Convention rejects.

**47-P-†  Waterson, Henry**
    JC: 28 May 1776, for action                Not known
  Compensation for horse purchased from colony that died a few days later from worms.
Date unknown: To PC.
28 May 1776 PC recommends rejection.
    Convention rejects.

**48-P-†  Stephens, John**
    JC: 28 May 1776, for action                Not known
  Compensation for pay during illness incurred after return home from late expedition against Indians.
Date unknown: To PC.
28 May 1776: PC recommends rejection.
    Convention rejects.

## Virginia Legislative Petitions

**49-P-†   Lucas, Robert**
JC: 28 May 1776, for action                                    Not known
Compensation for horse, valued at £32, impressed to help carry troops from Fincastle County to Williamsburg. Horse died at Bedford courthouse.
Date unknown: To PC.
28 May 1776: PC recommends payment of £30.
   Convention rejects on second reading.

**50-P-*   Moffat (Moffett?), George**
JC: 28 May 1776                                                Not known
For relief of charge of £9 deducted from his pay in late expedition against Indians, for a horse that was not his. States that Andrew Irwin, a soldier in his company, should have been paid for forty-one rather than thirty days. Claims two packhorse drivers should be given additional pay.
28 May 1776: To PC.
19 June 1776: PC recommends £9 should be reimbursed for horse, and that Andrew Irwin should be paid 16s. 6d. extra. Recommends no extra pay for packhorse drivers.
   Convention agrees.

**51-P   Calvert, Christopher**
JC: 28 May 1776                                                Norfolk Borough
Compensation for losses of houses and timber during the two burnings of Norfolk.
Manuscript unsigned. Endorsed as being referred to PG, and later (date not known) to committee to examine report of commissioners for ascertaining losses of inhabitants of Norfolk.
28 May 1776: To PG, but see above.
   Apparently never reported.

**52-P-*   Calvert, Christopher**
JC: 29 May 1776                                                Norfolk Borough
Compensation for slave, Davy, suspected of planning to escape to Lord Dunmore, sent to Williamsburg jail, and now employed in public work.
29 May 1776: To PC.
29 June 1776: PC recommends rejection since petitioner is being paid for hire of slave by public.
   Convention rejects.

## 28 May – 1 June 1776

**53-P-†**    **Craig, John**
        JC: 30 May 1776               Western Lands South of Ohio River

For relief from regulations of proprietors of Transylvania, particularly those requiring residents to sign papers establishing area as an independent authority.

30 May 1776: To SC.
        Apparently never reported separately, but see 26-P-† for action.

**54-P**    **Laurel Hill—Citizens**
        JC: 1 June 1776               Virginia–Pennsylvania Boundary

For settlement of Virginia–Pennsylvania boundary dispute since it is a source of friction and the laws of neither state can be enforced.

    Manuscript signed by: Geo. Carmick, Francis McKenny, William Campbell, Amos Blood, Moses Blackman, and 179 others.

1 June 1776: To SC
        Apparently never reported.
        The boundary was not settled until 1784.
        For appointments of commissioners, see JHD, 9 December and 12 December 1778.

**55-P-†**    **Chesterfield County—Citizens (Committee)**
        JC: 1 June 1776               Chesterfield County

For repayment of money subscribed for gunpowder at 1s. per poll and paid to treasury, the powder being in hands of militia.

1 June 1776: The convention, as a whole, resolves that powder be taken and
        paid for by public at cost price if county committees can spare it. Persons to be reimbursed. Committee of Safety or executive power may allow ammunition to remain in localities as needed. When expended cost to be reimbursed to public.

**56-P**    **Port Royal, King George County, Caroline County, and Westmoreland County—Citizens**
        JC: 1 June 1776               Port Royal

For establishment of a ferry from town landing at Port Royal to Gibson's in King George County. Cites general dissatisfaction with present ferry from Gibson's to Roy's landing in Caroline County.

    Manuscript signed by: Francis Conway, William Johnston, Henry Lightburne, John Jones, Richard Lightburne, and 113 others.

1 June 1776: To PG.
        Carried over to October 1776 session of GA.

## Virginia Legislative Petitions

16 Nov. 1776: PG of HD recommends approval.
>House agrees and Senate agrees later.
>For act concerning this and other ferries see 9H233.

### 57-P  Great Britain—Natives and Merchants' Assistants
JC: 1 June 1776    Not known

For permission to embark to their native country. States that Committee of Safety has granted permission, but the vessel on which they were to embark was detained.

Manuscript signed by: Chas. Galbraith, Jas. Cranstone, John Hamilton, John Samuel, R. Summervill, and thirteen others.

1 June 1776: To PG.
>Apparently never reported but see 104-P-† for similar petition and action.

### 58-P-†  Lush, Andrew
JC: 3 June 1776    Portsmouth

Compensation for doctor's bill incurred for treatment of wife and son severely wounded by Lord Dunmore's men on 21 December 1775.

3 June 1776: To a special committee.
1 July 1776: Committee recommends £45.
>Convention rejects.

### 59-P-†  Halifax County—Citizens
JC: 3 June 1776    Halifax County

For removal of courthouse to center of county, south of Banister River. Cites survey and application to governor and Council in past that had been denied.

3 June 1776: To PG.
>Carried over to October 1776 session of GA.

5 Nov. 1776: PG of HD recommends approval.
>House agrees and orders bill drawn.

25 Nov. 1776: Bill passed by House.
28 Nov. 1776: House agrees to Senate amendments.
>For this act see 9H229.

## 1 – 4 June 1776

**60-C-***    **Cabell, Joseph**
        JC: 3 June 1776, for action           Pittsylvania County
                                                    Augusta County
                                                    Botetourt County
                                                     Fincastle County
                                                      Bedford County

    For extra pay of £93 8s. 6d. for work as commissioner to pay claims for military service of those from above counties who served in the late expedition against Indians.
Date unknown: To PC.
3 June 1776: PC recommends £21 15s. 6d.
19 June 1776: Convention agrees to £10 17s. 9d. only.

**61-C-†**    **Bachelor, Thomas**
        JC: 3 June 1776, for action                Norfolk Borough
   For compensation for houses and other property burned and destroyed by this country's troops in Norfolk.
Date unknown: To PC.
3 June 1776: PC resolves it is a matter of Continental concern.
        Apparently not taken up.

**62-P**    **Amelia County—Citizens and Militia**
        JC: 4 June 1776                                   Amelia County
   For the removal of the exemption from militia duty now allowed overseers.
   Manuscript (copy in same hand) signed by: Vivion Brooking, Philip Jones, Pleasant Roberts, Thomas G. Peachey, John Wilson, and 257 others.
4 June 1776: To PG.
15 June 1776: PG reports reasonable.
        For action see 11-P-†.
        Printed in full in 15V19, but with signatures rearranged.

**63-P-†**    **Price, Thomas**
        JC: 4 June 1776                                       Not known
   Compensation for wound received in 1774 expedition against Indians at Kanawha in Captain John Lewis's company.
4 June 1776: To PC.
19 June 1776: PC recommends £25 and price of lost rifle.
        Convention agrees.

## Virginia Legislative Petitions

**64-P-†** Jones, Joseph; Campbell, Joshua; Ferebee, James; and Burgess, William

JC: 4 June 1776            Not known

For compensation from the estate of John Goodrich, Sr., of £1,149 16s. 10d. in North Carolina currency for loss of sloop and cargo captured by Goodrich in Ocracoke Inlet and delivered to British.

4 June 1776: To PG.

    Carried over to October 1776 session of GA.

12 Nov. 1776: PG of HD recommends payment of £962 3s. 6d. of North Carolina currency from Goodrich's effects in this country.

    House agrees.

20 Nov. 1776: Senate agrees.

**65-P-*** Goodrich, Margaret

JC: 5 June 1776            Not known

Asks that her husband, John Goodrich, Sr., be allowed to stay at some plantation near at hand, rather than be sent to the back country.

5 June 1776: Laid on table; then to PE.

10 June 1776: Goodrich remanded to public jail.

11 June 1776: PE, citing 64-P-† with further details, resolves that Goodrich has borne arms against the country, and is subject to the penalties therefore. Recommends that Committee of Safety take action to recover Goodrich's debts from his assets; that a reasonable provision be made for his wife and children; that he be sent under strong guard to Charlottesville, but not until his health improves; and that in the meantime he be allowed use of a room in the dwelling of the keeper of the public jail, under guard.

**66-P-†** Mecklenburg County—Citizens

JC: 5 June 1776            Mecklenburg County

Protesting action of vestry of Saint James's Parish in laying levy in money rather than tobacco.

5 June 1776: To PG.

    Carried over to October 1776 session of GA.

11 Nov. 1776: PG of HD reports reasonable and directed to draw bill.

18 Nov. 1776: Bill to include other parishes in similar circumstances.

3 Dec. 1776: Bill presented also including Amherst Parish.

10 Dec. 1776: Bill passed by House and sent to Senate.

13 Dec. 1776: Senate agrees.

    For act see 9H238.

## 4 – 8 June 1776

**67-P-***     **Elligood, Mary**
JC: 5 June 1776                            Not known

For allowance out the estate of Jacob Elligood, her husband. He had been found inimicable to the liberties of America, and his estate had been confiscated.
5 June 1776: To PE
        Apparently never reported.

**68-R**     **Lewis, Andrew**
JC: 7 June 1776                            Not known

For increasing pay and allowance of John Stadler, as engineer, above those made by Continental Congress.

Manuscript unsigned. Has attached a signed statement by John Stadler as to his duties and present pay.
7 June 1776: Convention acts immediately without referral.
        Approves pay of 10s. per day including pay from Congress and traveling expenses beyond this sum. Also allowed theodolite and chain, together with a servant and horse to carry those instruments. His rations are to be those of a captain, and forage is to be allowed two horses. Pay to commence 4 May 1776.

**69-M**     **Aylett, William**
JC: 7 June 1776                            Not known

Reply to allegations that soldiers are charged more for goods out of public store than merchants charge.

Manuscript unsigned.
7 June 1776: To special committee on depreciation of currency.
2 July 1776: Committee reports that goods in public store have been sold at proper rates and in a proper manner. Prices vary on exchange rates. Convention agrees.

**70-P**     **Loudoun County—Citizens**
JC: 8 June 1776                           Loudoun County

For relief from land taxes for tenants paying high rents because of decline of grain and flour trade in Alexandria.

Manuscript signed by: John Minor, Patrick Leslie, Jacob Shields, Daniel Maloney, Adam Shouse, and sixty-eight others.
8 June 1776: To PG.

## Virginia Legislative Petitions

        Carried over to October 1776 session of GA.
7 Dec. 1776: To SC of HD.
        Apparently never reported.
        For later act concerning this and other items in general see 9H349.

**71-P-†**    **Tobacco Inspectors—Warrasqueake Bay Warehouses**
        JC: 8 June 1776                                  Isle of Wight County
For relief for theft of four hogsheads of tobacco, two weighing 2,157 pounds (on 19 March 1775) and two additional ones weighing 1,652 pounds (on 13 July 1775).
8 June 1776: To PC.
Date unknown: Carried forward to October 1776 session of GA.
24 Oct. 1776: PC of HD recommends £42 1s. on testimony of witnesses for
        Samuel Wilson and John Hodges here identified as the inspectors.
        House agrees.
7 Nov. 1776: Senate agrees, JS.

**72-C-***     **Darke, William and Beale, Isaac**
        JC: 8 June 1776                                              Not known
For expenses incurred in supporting two companies of riflemen from the time they were embodied to passage of ordinance authorizing the raising of them.
8 June 1776: To PC.
        Carried over to October 1776 session of GA.
9 Dec. 1776: PC of HD submits a detailed report, which was not printed.
        House rejects that portion of claim relating to pay for officers and soldiers prior to passage of ordinance, but agrees to a number of claims for provisions furnished in this period. These were not presented originally as separate items, but are listed below.
        Adam Bishop, ──────
        John Blair, £16 8s. 6d.
        Cornelius Connoway, 4s. 2d.
        Philip Coon, £1 19s. 7d.
        Daniel Culp, £2 15s. and £1 11s. 3d.
        William Dark(e), £1 2s. 2½d. and 14s. 4½d.
        John Hyser, £2 10s. 4½d. and £6 10s. 2d.
        John and William Ingles, £4 1s. 3d. and £2 7s.
        Isaac Israel [Christian], £17 14s. 3d. and £45 1s. 8d.
        Isaac Taylor, £10
        Henry Yeager, 12s. ½d.

## 8 June 1776

12 Dec. 1776: Senate agrees.
12 Dec. 1776: House agrees:
    Adam Bishop, £1 10s. 7½d.
17 Dec. 1776: Senate agrees.

**73-P     Potter, Thomas**
    JC: 8 June 1776                                       Halifax County
Asking for trial on allegation of horse stealing, or release with others from "loathsom" jail. Wishes to enter military service.
    Manuscript unsigned.
    Others include Manasses M'Gahey, on charge of murder, who petitioned separately (see 74-P) and the following for whom separate petitions do not exist: Thomas M'Cluskey and his wife, Elizabeth, on charge of burglary; Benjamin Higgins, charged with robbery; Habakkuk Pride, charged with murder; Samuel Flanagin, charged with horse stealing; and Mary Howell, on her way from Berkeley County, charged with murder.
8 June 1776: To a special committee.
11 June 1776: Committee recommends that Thomas and Elizabeth M'Cluskey, Thomas Potter, and Benjamin Higgins all be released from custody.
        Convention agrees.
        Committee recommends that a trial be held for Samuel Flanagin, Manasses M'Gahey, Habakkuk Pride, and Mary Howell.
        Convention lays on table.
12 June 1776: Convention agrees that a pardon, signed by president of convention, be issued to Samuel Flanagin and Manasses M'Gahey since they had long been detained without trial.
        Convention agrees that trial should be held for Habakkuk Pride and Mary Howell.
        For special court for trial of prisoners see 9H172.

**74-P     M'Gahey, Manasses**
    JC: 8 June 1776                                       Loudoun County
Asking for a speedy trial on charge of murder.
    Manuscript unsigned.
8 June 1776: To a special committee.
12 June 1776: Convention orders that he be pardoned.
        For details see 73-P.

Virginia Legislative Petitions

**75-P**
Rob-Not
found     **Fincastle County—Citizens (Western Part)**
     JC: 10 June 1776                                      Fincastle County
For division of the county or creation of a separate district for western part.
   Manuscript signed by: Charles Cummings, Andrew Coleville, Saml. Newel, George Blackburn, John Logan, and 223 others, some names being illegible. From surviving lines at top of some signatures in manuscript there were at least three identical petitions.
10 June 1776: To PG.
       Carried over to October 1776 session of GA.
24 Oct. 1776: To SC.
30 Oct. 1776: To special committee of the treasurer, Mr. Braxton, and Mr. Jefferson to draw bill making Kentucky one distinct county.
19 Nov. 1776: Bill amended and read third time.
26 Nov. 1776: House rejects.

**76-P-†**     **Fincastle County—Citizens (Western Part)**
     JC: 10 June 1776                                      Fincastle County
For relief from claims of persons who contend they own certain lands under old land grants and are demanding large sums of money for lands.
10 June 1776: To PG.
       Apparently not reported.

**77-P**     **Newport Parish, Isle of Wight County—Citizens**
     JC: 10 June 1776                                  Isle of Wight County
For dissolution of vestry and election of new one. Of those chosen last in 1756, many are dead, some resigned, and only one left.
   Manuscript signed by: Willis Wills, Samuel Wills, Thomas Fearn, Thomas Turner, William Turner, and seventeen others.
10 June 1776: To PG.
       Carried over to October 1776 session of GA.
12 Oct. 1776: PG of HD discharged. To R of HD.
       R reports reasonable.
       Carried over to May 1777 session of GA.
16 May 1777: HD authorizes bill also to include Stratton Major Parish of King and Queen County and Christ Church Parish of Middlesex County.

## 10 – 12 June 1776

2 June 1777: House amends, passes, and sends to Senate.
3 June 1777: Senate agrees.
    For this act see 9H317.

### 78-P-*   Ballendine, John
    JC: 11 June 1776                                                            Henrico County

For repayment of gunpowder, stored for construction of canals on James and Potomac rivers, which he had advanced to county committees at 2s. 6d. per pound.
11 June 1776: To PG.
15 June 1776: PG recommends rejection.
    Convention rejects.

### 79-P-*   Talbot, William
    JC: 12 June 1776                                                            Charles City County

Compensation for surgeon's fees for treatment of wounds, by Dr. William Rickman, incurred in an engagement with enemy's tenders off Sandy Point on 18 April 1776.
12 June 1776: To PC.
24 June 1776: PC recommends £16 13s. 6d.
    Convention agrees.

### 80-P-†   Botetourt County—Citizens (Western Waters)
    JC: 12 June 1776                                                            Botetourt County

For authority to appoint a county committee, to be permitted to vote for representatives in General Assembly, and for protection against Indians.
12 June 1776: To PG.
5 July 1776: PG recommends that permission be granted to vote for members
    of new GA.
    Convention agrees.

### 81-P
### Eck-A2   Accomack County—Citizens (Gingoteague [Chincoteague] Island)
    JC: 12 June 1776                                                            Accomack County

For rescinding 21 May 1776 order of convention requiring removal of livestock to escape ravages of enemy.

Manuscript says island has twenty families, an unspecified number of cattle, and 400 sheep, all in bad condition from unfavorable winter, but it could support stock from Wallop's and Assateague islands.

## Virginia Legislative Petitions

Manuscript signed by: Henry Custis, Tugley R. Wise, Jno. Burton, John Watts, John Barker Barnes, and two others.

12 June 1776: Convention as a whole directs order to be rescinded for all but Watt's Island.

No ponies mentioned.

### 82-P     Spotsylvania County—Citizens
JC: 12 June 1776                   Spotsylvania County

For militia musters to be held in center of county and not at Fredericksburg, which requires twenty or thirty miles travel.

Manuscript is fragmentary, with no signatures. Journal indicates there were several petitions.

12 June 1776: To PG.

> Apparently not reported, but similar new petitions were presented to October 1776 session of GA.
> See 230-P.

### 83-P-†     Caroline County—Citizens
JC: 12 June 1776                         Caroline County

For the removal of the exemption from militia duty now allowed overseers.

12 June 1776: To PG.

15 June 1776: PG reports reasonable.

> For action see 11-P-†.

### 84-P-*     Archer, Edward
JC: 14 June 1776                              Not known

For permission to take a stock of Lord Dunmore's wines as compensation for a seized vessel and Negro slave.

14 June 1776: To PG.

> Apparently not reported.

### 85-P-†     Packer, Augustine
JC: 14 June 1776, for action                   Not known

For extra pay as butcher in late expedition against Indians.

Date unknown: To PC.

14 June 1776: PC recommends £3.

> Convention agrees.

### 86-P-†     Johnson, William
JC: 14 June 1776, for action                  Caroline County

## 12 – 15 June 1776

Compensation for Negro slave, Gloster, who was convicted of burglary on 3 July 1775, in Caroline County, sentenced to be hanged, but broke out of jail and vanished.
Date unknown: To PC.
14 June 1776: PC recommends £75.
    Convention agrees.

**87-M    Cary, Wilson Miles**
    JC: 15 June 1776                             Not known
Compensation for boat and two slaves seized by Lord Dunmore, who, as governor, wrote on 14 October 1775, from ship *William*, for books of entry and clearance. Cary reluctantly sent books on boat with slaves, the latter being the property of John Jones. Jones demanded indemnity after boat and slaves were seized.
  Manuscript unsigned.
15 June 1776: To PG.
    Carried over to October 1776 session of GA.
22 Oct. 1776: PG of HD recommends £240 from effects of Lord Dunmore in
    proportion with other creditors.
    House agrees.
29 Oct. 1776: Senate agrees, JS.

**88-P-*    Crookshanks, John**
    JC: 15 June 1776                             Not known
For further allowance for boarding men in Campbell's and Clark's companies, Edward Snickers, the commissary, having allowed him only 6d. per day, per man.
15 June 1776: To PC.
    Carried over to October 1776 session of GA.
18 Dec. 1776: PC of HD recommends rejection.
    House rejects.

**89-P-*    Pritchett, Lucretia and Churchill, William (Executors of Joseph Pritchett, deceased)**
    JC: 15 June 1776                             Not known
Compensation for loss of a Negro man slave, Minny, in a heroic action

against a British tender in the Rappahannock River while voluntarily serving under Hugh Walker.
15 June 1776: To PC.
28 June 1776: PC recommends £100.
   Convention agrees.

### 90-P-*  Barnes, Thomas
  JC: 15 June 1776             Fincastle County

Compensation for services as assistant to Colonel William Ingles in late expedition against Indians. Services as assistant commissary included collecting and selling horses and cattle from 25 December 1774 to 6 February 1775, and in adjusting accounts in brigade book of Colonel Ingles.
15 June 1776: To PC.
   Carried over to October 1776 session of GA.
18 Dec. 1776: PC of HD recommends £10.
   House agrees.
   Senates agrees, JS.

### 91-P  Johnson, James
  JC: 15 June 1776             Lunenburg County

For repayment of cost of grog or toddy used to aid in recruitment of minute-men. Appointed to recruit by committee of Mecklenburg County.
 Manuscript unsigned.
15 June 1776: Convention rejects without referral to a committee.

### 92-P  Stratton Major Parish, King and Queen County—Citizens
  JC: 15 June 1776             King and Queen County

For dissolution of vestry and appointment of new one. Cites two former petitions to House of Burgesses, which did not hear the case. No vestry meeting since 21 December 1775. Vestry must meet to establish tobacco payments.
 Manuscript dated 2 May 1776.
 Manuscript signed by: Geo. Lyne, John Lyne, Hum. Garrett, Geo. Dillard, Spencer Boyd, and fifty-two others.
15 June 1776: To PG.
   Carried over to October 1776 session of GA.
12 Oct. 1776: PG of HD discharged. To R of HD.
7 Dec. 1776: R reports reasonable.
   House agrees.
   Carried over to May 1777 session of GA.

## 15 June 1776

16 May 1777: House authorizes bill.
    See 77-P for further action.
    For this act see 9H317.

### 93-P-*   Boot, Joseph
    JC: 15 June 1776                                   Not known

Compensation for disabling wounds received in last war (against Indians)
15 June 1776: To PC.
24 June 1776: PC recommends £5 for immediate relief and £1 per annum for life.
    Convention agrees.

### 94-P-*   Becket, George
    JC: 15 June 1776                                   Not known

Compensation for injury received in lifting wood while serving in Captain Lee's company of the 3d Virginia Regiment.
15 June 1776: To PC.
24 June 1776: PC recommends £5 per annum for life.
    Convention agrees.

### 95-P-†   Wilson, Peter
    JC: 15 June 1776                                   Augusta County

For additional pay for serving in Augusta militia under Captain John Lewis during Shawanese expedition. Left off payroll for seventy-five days ending 15 November 1774.
15 June 1776: To PC.
24 June 1776: PC recommends £5 12s. 6d.
    Convention agrees.

### 96-P-†   Travis, Champion
    JC: 15 June 1776                                   Jamestown

Compensation for spoilage or destruction of dwelling and offices used as guardhouses by Virginia troops at Jamestown.
15 June 1776: To PC.
    Carried over to October 1776 session of GA.
9 Nov. 1776: PC of HD discharged. To SC.
    Apparently never reported.

### 97-M-†   Henderson, Richard; Hart, Thomas; Hart, Nathaniel; Williams, John; Johnson, William; Luttrall, John; Hogg, James;

## Virginia Legislative Petitions

### Hart, David; and Bullock, Leonard Hendly
JC: 15 June 1776             Western Lands South of Ohio River

Respecting their right to hold property privately acquired by treaty with Cherokee Indians, negotiations for which were begun in the fall of 1774 and completed on 17 March 1775. This property lay on the Ohio River and its branches, westward of a line run by Colonel Donelson [or Donaldson] between Virginia and the Cherokee nation, part of which had settlements on the Kentucky or Louisa River and was called Transylvania. Comments on petitions of inhabitants, particularly John Craig, (see 53-P-†, as well as 26-P-†). Denies right of convention to abrogate private property rights, and claims no thought of setting up a separate government. (Apparently printed in full in journal of above date.)

15 June 1776: To SC. No action except on 26-P-†.

19 Nov. 1777: House revives memorial and several petitions relating to it. A special group of commissioners were to take depositions.

24 Nov. 1777: Postponed.
    See also an act passed this session for taxation of present lands, 9H355.

26 Oct. 1778: House considers memorial, along with invited members of Senate.
    Postponed.

29 Oct. 1778: Apparently an accompanying memorial presented by Henderson. House lays on table.

4 Nov. 1778: House and Senate participate further in joint hearing. House agrees (1) that all private purchases from Indians within charted boundaries of Virginia are void. Sent to Senate. House agrees (2) that purchases of land from Cherokee Indians within the commonwealth are void, but that Henderson should have compensation for the money and trouble involved. Sent to Senate. House agrees (3) that a special committee be appointed to consider compensation. Special committee appointed.

17 Nov. 1778: House requests Senate to form also a special committee on compensation (3). Senate agrees.

23 Nov. 1778: House special committee recommends that Henderson be allowed a special tract of land as compensation for trouble under restrictions by GA. House agrees.
    House special committee recommends 800,000 acres. House recommits to special committee.
    House special committee recommends boundaries of special tract

as defined by areas around Green River. House recommits to special committee.
30 Nov. 1778: House special committee recommends 400,000 acres.
>House agrees.
>House special committee deletes certain land around Green River. House agrees.
>Bill to be drawn by special committee.
1 Dec. 1778: Bill presented.
7 Dec. 1778: Bill to committee of whole.
8 Dec. 1778: Bill approved by committee.
9 Dec. 1778: House passes bill and sends to Senate.
10 Dec. 1778: Senate amends and House disagrees.
12 Dec. 1778: Senate recedes from amendments.
>For this act see 9H571.
>For a study of this subject see W. S. Lester, *The Transylvania Colony* (Spencer, Ind., 1935).

### 98-P-†    Hite, Abraham, Jr.
JC: 17 June 1776            Not known

For additional allowance as commissary of provisions in Hampshire County from July to November 1774, in Indian war at behest of county lieutenant (probably Abraham Hite, Sr., his father). Commissioners had allowed 5s. per day.

17 June 1776: To PC.
27 June 1776: PC recommends £6 10s. exclusive of allowance already made.
>Convention agrees.

### 99-P-†    Ritson, Thomas
JC: 18 June 1776            Norfolk Borough

Compensation for brig and cargo of salt commandeered by Colonels Howe and Woodford and not contracted for as provided by the convention. A letter from Howe was attached.

18 June 1776: To PC.
>Carried over to October 1776 session of GA.
25 Oct. 1776: PC of HD recommends rejection.
>House rejects.

### 100-P-†    Frederick County—Citizens (Committee)
JC: 19 June 1776            Frederick County

To require Quakers and Menonists to pay assessments when they refuse to

## Virginia Legislative Petitions

bear arms under the exemption provided in chapter II of Ordinances of Convention of July 1775. Also to require them to be drafted or provide substitutes at musters, or else be fined.
19 June 1776: To PG.
> Apparently not separately reported, but see Ordinances of Convention, chapter XII, which among other things requires Quakers and Menonists to serve in militia but not to attend general or private musters.

**101-P-†  Cowper, Edward**
> JC: 19 June 1776                                                                                  Hampton

Compensation for loss by fire, of stock, houses, and corn at Hampton River following engagement on 26 October 1775, between Captain Squires and Captains Lyne and Nicholas.
19 June 1776: To PC.
24 June 1776: PC recommends rejection since it is not a public claim.
> Convention rejects.

**102-P-†  Gilmore, Robert; Backley, John; Campbell, Alexander; Cooper, Thomas; and Skean, Jonathan**
> JC: 19 June 1776, for action                                                        Not known

For pay as rangers in late Indian expedition.
Date unknown: To PC.
19 June 1776: PC recommends 16s. 6d. to Robert Gilmore, 16s. 6d. to Jonathan Skean, £2 11s. to John Backley, £4 4s. to Alexander Campbell, and £2 6s. 6d. to Thomas Cooper.
> Convention agrees.

**103-P-†  Peyton, Ephraim**
> JC: 19 June 1776, for action                                                        Not known

Compensation for horse lost in late expedition against Indians.
Date unknown: To PC.
19 June 1776: PC recommends £10.
> Convention agrees.

**104-P-†  Great Britain—Natives**
> JC: 19 June 1776                                                                              Not known

To allow them to purchase and fit out a vessel, apply for passports from commander of British fleet, and depart colony for England. Declare themselves friendly, but cannot bear arms against their country.

## 19 - 21 June 1776

19 June 1776: To PG.
28 June 1776: PG finds reasonable and recommends that petitioners take oath not to bear arms against America, or give intelligence. Not to take out more than £50 each nor more provisions than needed for voyage. Every package and article taken aboard shall be searched by two members of county committee from which area they embark.
Convention agrees, and gives authority to Committee of Safety or executive to permit petitioners and others thus to depart.
See 57-P.

### 105-P  Baptist Church, Prince William County—Members (Occaqon [Occoquan])
JC: 20 June 1776                                   Prince William County

For religious privilege to worship God in their own way, to maintain own ministers and no others, and to be married, buried, and the like without paying parsons of other denominations.

Manuscript is fragmentary. Signed 19 May 1776 by: John Peak, John Hampton, Nickolas Anderson, James Peak, Edward Williams, and forty-five others.
20 June 1776: To PG.
Carried over to October 1776 session of GA.
12 Oct. 1776: PG of HD discharged. To R.
Apparently never reported.
This petition was reconstructed and printed in 18V38 with some variations in text and names.

### 106-R-† Isle of Wight County—Court Justices
JC: 20 June 1776                                       Isle of Wight County

Desire to be informed whether they have the power to commit and hold courts for examination of persons apprehended for criminal offenses.
20 June 1776: To SC.
Apparently not reported.

### 107-P-* Cocke, Anne
JC: 21 June 1776                                                 Jamestown

Compensation for impressed slave who, on 7 November 1775, helped to ferry 2d Virginia Regiment from Jamestown to Edwards's landing below

## Virginia Legislative Petitions

Cobham, and was captured by Lord Dunmore's forces.
21 June 1776: To PC.
       Carried over to October 1776 session of GA.
23 Nov. 1776: PC of HD recommends £75.
30 Nov. 1776: House agrees.
4 Dec. 1776: Senate agrees, JS.

### 108-P-*   Lyell, Fenwick
    JC: 21 June 1776                                       Not known

For investigation of his dismissal from naval service by court-martial while under command of Captain John Calvert, and restoration to his office.
21 June 1776: Convention rejects by refusal to refer to a committee.

### 109-M   Christian, William
    JC: 22 June 1776, for action                     Fincastle County

Compensation for himself, William Preston, and Arthur Campbell, for service at the request of Lord Dunmore, in organizing the frontier after May 1774 in the late Indian war.

Manuscript unsigned. It was presented on 3 January 1776 to the convention of December 1775, and ordered carried forward to the next convention.
Date unknown: To PG.
22 June 1776: PG recommends £14 3s. 6d. for Christian.
       Convention agrees.
       PG recommends rejection of Campbell's claim.
       Convention rejects.
       PG discharged from further consideration of Preston's claim.
       See 31-P-†.
       Reprinted in 17V169 without dates and with editorial changes.

### 110-P-*   Hughes, Thomas
    JC: 22 June 1776                                       Not known

Compensation for slave purchased by him as a servant for £20, who was trained as a soldier and served with spirit in many skirmishes, but who deserted to Lord Dunmore's forces on 19 January 1776.
22 June 1776: To PC.
1 July 1776: PC recommends £8 17s. 4d. for services.
       Convention rejects.

### 111-P-†   Shank, James
    JC: 24 June 1776, for action                         Not known

## 21 June – 8 October 1776

Compensation for service of thirty-eight days as packhorse manager in late expedition against Indians.
Date unknown: To PC.
24 June 1776: PC recommends £4 15s.
    Convention agrees.

**112-C-†  Haynes, Joseph; Smith, Daniel; and Smith, John**
    JC: 24 June 1776, for action      Not known

For additional pay for commanding forces in expedition against Shawanese Indians on South Branch of Potomac River in June 1774 under direction of Colonel Abraham Smith, of Augusta County.
Date unknown: To PC.
24 June 1776: PC recommends £4 15s. to Joseph Haynes, £2 17s. to Daniel Smith, and £6 13s. to John Smith.
    Convention agrees.

**113-P-†  Prichard, Samuel**
    JC: 24 June 1776      Not known

For reimbursement of £8 James River banknote (Virginia currency) destroyed in fire that consumed his dwelling house and grist mill.
24 June 1776: To PC.
28 June 1776: PC recommends reimbursement of £8.
    Convention agrees.

**114-P-*  Captains, 1st and 2d Regiments of the Virginia Line**
    JC: 5 July 1776      Not known

Asking convention to represent their right of promotion on the basis of seniority to the Congress, pointing out they received their appointments from districts rather than counties and had long experiences in campaigns, and those with less service were placed over their heads.
5 July 1776: Convention, without referral, resolves to recommend that delegates to the Congress endeavor to have promotions based on seniority.

**115-P**
Rob-2  **Fincastle County—Citizens (Western Part)**
    JHD: 8 Oct. 1776      Fincastle County

For admission of John Gabriel Jones and George Rogers Clark as duly elected delegates to the May 1776 convention, and protesting the authority attempted to be exercised by the proprietors of Transylvania, and questioning

## Virginia Legislative Petitions

their land purchases from the Cherokee Indians. States that they have elected twenty members to a committee.

Manuscript is dated at Harrodsburg, 7-15 June 1776, and signed by Abraham Hite, Jr., clerk, by order of the inhabitants.

8 Oct. 1776: HD lays on table.
11 Oct. 1776: To SC.
> Admission of Jones and Clark denied, but creation of a new county recommended.

This petition was sent to Williamsburg by Jones and Clark, but they arrived too late to present it to the convention, which had adjourned. Hence it was presented to the October 1776 session of the General Assembly. It was accompanied by a petition from the above mentioned committee, 116-P, which see.

### 116-P

Rob-3 **Fincastle County—Citizens (Committee for Western Part)**
JHD: 8 Oct. 1776                             Fincastle County

For being legally a part of the colony and for the creation of new counties. Cites the election of John Gabriel Jones and George Rogers Clark as their representatives. Deplores the actions of the proprietors of Transylvania.

Manuscript lists members of the committee present as: John Gabriel Jones, chairman, John Bowman, John Cowen, William Bennett, Joseph Bowman, John Crittenden, Isaac Hite, George Rogers Clark, Silas Harland, Hugh McGary, Andrew McConnel, James Herrod, William McConnel, and John Maxwell. Says they have sent James Herrod and Garret Pendergrass to confer with Delaware Indians. Manuscript signed by J. G. Jones, chairman, and Abraham Hite, Jr., clerk, and is dated at Harrodsburg, 20 June 1776.

8 Oct. 1776: HD lays on table.
11 Oct. 1776: To SC.
> A special committee appointed (the treasurer, Mr. Braxton, and Mr. Jefferson) to draft a bill for formation of new county. This committee was augmented from time to time.

25 Nov. 1776: Bill presented, amended, and read third time.
> The amendments provided for a division of Fincastle into three distinct counties and the parish of Botetourt into four distinct parishes and was passed and sent to Senate.

28 Nov. 1776: Senate amends.
5 Dec. 1776: House recedes from some Senate amendments but in turn amends others.

## 8 – 9 October 1776

7 Dec. 1776: Senate recedes and bill is passed.
  [For note on transmittal, see 115-P.]
  For this act see 9H257.
  By this act Kentucky, Washington, and Montgomery counties were formed and Fincastle County became extinct. Also Montgomery, Washington, and Kentucky parishes formed and Botetourt parish reduced to Botetourt County. Act to take effect 31 December 1776.

117-P
Eck–
A830  **Liviston, John**
  JHD: 8 Oct. 1776                              Amherst County
  Compensation for wounds received in 1758 in battle with Indians.
  Manuscript is dated 4 September 1776 at Amherst County and is signed by: Dan Gaines, Ambrose Rucker, James McNees, Sr., William Whitsitt, and Benjamin Meenes.
8 Oct. 1776: To special committee.
9 Oct. 1776: Committee finds reasonable and recommends £15 for present and £8 per annum for life.
  House agrees.
11 Oct. 1776: Senate agrees, JS.

118-P  **Corbin, John Tayloe**
  JHD: 9 Oct. 1776                              Caroline County
  For release from confinement in Caroline County by order of the convention on 11 May 1776. Cites the rigor of his life, and again expresses sorrow for his action.
  Manuscript has attached to it the first report of PE on 11 October 1776, noted below, and a recommendation for release signed by: Walker Taliaferro, Jn. Jones, Cy. Guy, Robt. Mickleburrough, Richard Johnston, and three others.
9 Oct. 1776: To PE.
11 Oct. 1776: PE reports and petition is recommitted to it.
19 Oct. 1776: PE again reports, and recommends that Corbin be released upon a bond, with security for £10,000, with the stipulation that

## Virginia Legislative Petitions

he not give intelligence to, or in any manner, aid or assist the enemy.

House agrees.

Senate apparently not required to act.

See 5-P-†.

**119-P     Pittsylvania County—Citizens**
JHD: 9 Oct. 1776                                              Pittsylvania County

For the division of the county along certain designated lines.

Manuscript signed by: Jeduthen Carter, Samuel Thompson, Jacob Kaufman, Samuel Hurly, Philip Debo, and 119 others.

9 Oct. 1776: To PG.

14 Oct. 1776: PG recommends division along different lines and is authorized to draw bill making two distinct counties.

15 Oct. 1776: Bill presented.

17 Oct. 1776: House passes bill. Sent to Senate.

23 Oct. 1776: Senate passes bill.

> For this act see 9H241. This establishes Henry County, effective 31 December 1776, and leaves part of Pittsylvania County separate.
>
> For a related act establishing places for holding courts in these counties see 9H242.

**119 A-P-†Pittsylvania County—Citizens**
JHD: 9 Oct. 1776                                              Pittsylvania County

For the division of the county.

> This is noted as a second petition in the journal, and in all probability was identical to 119-P.

**120-P-†   Lawson, Daniel and Garland, George**
JHD: 9 Oct. 1776                                              Richmond County

For reconsideration of their petition to House of Burgesses, denied 15 June 1775, for compensation for theft of hogshead of tobacco, weighing 1,065 pounds, stolen from Totuskey warehouse where they were late inspectors.

9 Oct. 1776: To PC.

9 Nov. 1776: PC recommends rejection, but House recommits.

23 Nov. 1776: PC, upon further consideration, recommends £10 13s.

House agrees.

26 Nov. 1776: Senate agrees, JS.

## 9 – 11 October 1776

### 121-P  Garland, Griffin and Barber, Charles
JHD: 9 Oct. 1776                                      Richmond County

For requiring the court of Richmond County to hear their case, pending since January 1776, on breach of peace. They had been arrested on the complaint of Charles Carter to Landon Carter, a justice, who had issued a warrant to the sheriff. The complaint was for trespass on the lands of Charles Carter on their way to survey adjoining waste land under a land warrant from Lord Fairfax. On refusal to give security for keeping the peace they had been placed in custody of the jailor. Garland was surveyor for Richmond County and Barber was interested in the land.

Manuscript unsigned.

9 Oct. 1776: To PG.

25 Oct. 1776: PG reports that the matter is remediable in courts of common law, and the petitioners should follow this course.
    House agrees.
    Apparently no Senate action required.

### 122-P-†  Blakely, William
JHD: 9 Oct. 1776                                        Pittsylvania County

Compensation for injury to a horse impressed to take the Cookes (Cooks?) counterfeiters to Williamsburg.

9 Oct. 1776: To PC.

3 Dec. 1776: PC recommends 40s.
    House agrees.

6 Dec. 1776: Senate agrees.
    For probable reference to same counterfeiters, see 145-P-* and 376-P-†.

### 123-P  Webley, Mary
JHD: 11 Oct. 1776                                      Norfolk Borough

Compensation for leg broken by cannon ball from British warship. Cites destruction of all effects in burning of Norfolk and that her husband had lost his right arm twenty years before and is unable to support her and three children.

Manuscript unsigned.

11 Oct. 1776: To a special committee.

12 Oct. 1776: Committee recommends £10 for her immediate relief.
    House agrees.

17 Oct. 1776: Senate agrees.

## Virginia Legislative Petitions

**124-P     Dissenters—Prince Edward County**
        JHD: 11 Oct. 1776                                    Prince Edward County
   For disestablishment of Church of England.
   Manuscript dated 24 September 1776 and signed by: Rich. Lankey, Hugh Porter, Charles Richey, Saml. Baker, George Skillideay, and 157 others, many in the same hand.
   11 Oct. 1776: To R.
        Committee apparently did not report.

**125-P**
Rob-4   **Slaughter, Thomas**
        JHD: 11 Oct. 1776                                    Kentucky Area
   For defense of area near Kentucky from Indian attacks.
   Manuscript signed by Thomas Slaughter for himself and other unspecified inhabitants. (This was before creation of Kentucky County.)
   11 Oct. 1776: To SC.
        Committee apparently did not report.

**126-P-†   Cunes, Jacob**
        JHD: 12 Oct. 1776                                    Not known
   Compensation for work done as armorer in Norfolk in November 1775 by order of Committee of Safety. He has no detailed accounts.
   12 Oct. 1776: To PC.
   21 Oct. 1776: PC reports but petition is recommitted.
   22 Oct. 1776: PC recommends rejection.
        House rejects.

**127-P-*   Campbell, Colin**
        JHD: 12 Oct. 1776                                    Not known
   Compensation for service as adjutant of militia in southern district since April 1775. Had refused to go aboard Lord Dunmore's ship to apply, and now there is no authority for payment.
   12 Oct. 1776: To PC.
   15 Oct. 1776: PC recommends rejection.
        House rejects.

**128-P     Halifax County—Citizens**
        JHD: 12 Oct. 1776                                    Halifax County
   Against removal of courthouse from present location.
   Manuscript is a consolidation, all in the same hand, including signatures, of

## 11 – 12 October 1776

four petitions. Originally signed by: Epa. White, Josiah Maxey, John Royall, Andrew Wade, Thomas Vaughan, and 527 others. Manuscript has attached the first and third of the original petitions.
12 Oct. 1776: To PG.
5 Nov. 1776: PG recommends rejection.
> House rejects.
> (In opposition to 59-P-†, which see.)

**129-P    Bouram, John**
JHD: 12 Oct. 1776                                         Halifax County
For location of Halifax County courthouse on his land, which he claims is centrally located.
Manuscript unsigned, but the name is spelled "Bouram" in the heading.
12 Oct. 1776: To PG.
> The act locating the courthouse on his land, 9H229, spells the name "Boram." For passage see 59-P-†.

**130-P    Watkins, George**
JHD: 12 Oct. 1776                                         Halifax County
For location of Halifax County courthouse on his land.
Manuscript signed: Geo. Watkins.
12 Oct. 1776: To PG.
24 Oct. 1776: Manuscript endorsement shows it was postponed to 4 November 1776.
> Rejected by act locating courthouse on John Boram's land. See 59-P-† and 129-P.

**131-P-†    Isle of Wight County—Citizens**
JHD: 12 Oct. 1776                                         Isle of Wight County
For sale of undisposed lands in undeveloped town of Patesfield by trustees, for benefit of county.
12 Oct. 1776: To special committee for preparation of a bill.
24 Oct. 1776: House passes bill and sends to Senate.
29 Oct. 1776: Senate passes bill, JS.
> For this act see 9H240.

## Virginia Legislative Petitions

**132-P**
Eck–
A831    **Amherst County and Bedford County—Citizens**
JHD: 12 Oct. 1776                                   Amherst County
                                                    Bedford County

For establishment of a ferry across Fluvanna (James) River from Henry Trent's land on north side to Nicholas Davies's land on south side.

Manuscript signed by: Thos. Gillenwaters, Thomas Lumpkin, James Franklin, Joseph Marys, John Dillard, and fifty-six others.

12 Oct. 1776: To PG.
19 Oct. 1776: PG finds reasonable and is directed to draw a bill.
24 Oct. 1776: Bill presented.
4 Nov. 1776: Several additional ferries added.
5 Nov. 1776: An additional ferry added.
30 Nov. 1776: Bill passed by House and sent to Senate.
6 Dec. 1776: Senate passes bill, JS.
>This ferry was being requested by petition as early as 14 May 1774 when it was carried forward to 7 June 1775, but not acted on. See manuscript, Eck–A829.
>
>For this act including several ferries see 9H233.

**133-P**    **Henley, Charles**
JHD: 14 Oct. 1776                                   Princess Anne County

For release from confinement as British sympathizer. Will take loyalty oath and move out of Princess Anne County. (Originally confined to Charlottesville jail on 22 July 1776, by order of Council, for giving intelligence to enemy.)

Manuscript unsigned.
14 Oct. 1776: To PE.
19 Oct. 1776: PE reports reasonable.
>House agrees.
>Senate action apparently not necessary.

**134-P-*** **Wilson, William**
JHD: 14 Oct. 1776                                               Not known

Compensation for wound received in battle with Ohio Indians, October 1774.
14 Oct. 1776: To PC.
16 Oct. 1776: PC recommends £25 for immediate relief.
>House agrees.

## 12 – 15 October 1776

17 Oct. 1776: Senate agrees, JS.

**135-P-†   Steward, Walter**
    JHD: 14 Oct. 1776                     Not known

Compensation for horse lost at battle of Point Pleasant, valued at £14. Steward was adjutant for Botetourt and Fincastle troops.

14 Oct. 1776: To PC.
16 Oct. 1776: PC recommends £14.
       House agrees.
17 Oct. 1776: Senate agrees.

**136-P-†   Jacobs, Thomas and Bailey, Edmund**
    JHD: 14 Oct. 1776              Accomack County

For return of five slaves who were captured in an attempt to escape to Lord Dunmore, and sent to lead mines. Claims their services needed by petitioners.

14 Oct. 1776: To PG.
15 Oct. 1776: PG reports reasonable.
       House agrees. Asks governor to return at public expense.
       Senate action apparently not necessary.
       These were the five slaves sent to lead mines by order of convention, 7 June 1776.

**137-P   Unwon, William; Jackson, Francis; Myatt, Peter; and Habit, Richard**
    JHD: 15 Oct. 1776                   Not known

For necessary clothing, which they as British prisoners of war from the 14th Regiment of the British regulars do not have and are unable to obtain.

Manuscript unsigned, but spelling of names is taken from heading. Addressed to House of Burgesses.

15 Oct. 1776: To SC.
       Committee apparently did not report.

**138-P**
Eck–Not
found    **Tyger's (Tygart's) Valley—Citizens**
    JHD: 15 Oct. 1776            East Augusta District

For retention of their area in East Augusta, and not transferring it to West Augusta. Gives present line of division.

Manuscript signed by: George Westfall, Daniel Deane, Daniel McLane,

## Virginia Legislative Petitions

John McLane, Raleigh Stewart, and fifty-nine others. Some signatures in same hand.

15 Oct. 1776: To PG.

8 Nov. 1776: PG discharged. To SC.

    Committee apparently did not report.

**139-P**
Eck–
A1092   **Tyger's (Tygart's) Valley—Citizens**
    JHD: 15 Oct. 1776               East Augusta District

For furnishing three companies of rangers to protect area of Tygart's Valley from depredation of Indians.

Manuscript is dated 26 September 1776, and is signed by: Benjamin Wilson, Moses Thomson, Jessee Hamilton, George Westfall, Peter Cassity, Jr., and sixty-five others. Many signatures in same hand.

15 Oct. 1776: To SC. Manuscript endorsement says to PG.

    Committee apparently did not report.

**140-P**   **Stafford County—Citizens**
    JHD: 15 Oct. 1776               Stafford County

To define the boundaries between King George and Stafford counties according to report of commissioners. (These commissioners acted under two bills of the House of Burgesses, 19 May 1774 and 12 June 1775, neither of which had become laws because the first was passed in a session prorogued by Lord Dunmore, and the second after his flight.)

Manuscript signed by: F. Thornton, John Washington, Henry Fitzhugh, William Hooe, Jn. James, and 107 others.

15 Oct. 1776: House directs a special committee to bring in a bill.

16 Oct. 1776: Committee presents bill.

18 Oct. 1776: House passes bill and sends to Senate.

24 Oct. 1776: Senate passes bill.

    For this act see 9H244.

    For attendant act on places of holding courts see 9H227.

**140 A-P**   **King George County—Citizens**
    JHD: 15 Oct. 1776               King George County

Identical with 140-P except in name of King George County.

Manuscript signed by: John Thornton, J. Skinker, John Paradise, Will Boon, Geo. White, and forty-five others.

    For action see 140-P.

## 15 – 16 October 1776

**141-P     Dissenters**
JHD: 16 Oct. 1776                Commonwealth as a Whole

For disestablishment of Church of England and freedom from taxation for religious purposes. (There are fragments of two petitions extant, but originally there must have been a large number, widely circulated.)

Manuscript has approximately 10,000 signatures. Signed on first sheet by: William Pigg, James Pigg, William Handley, James Hack, John May, and others. Many signatures illegible.

16 Oct. 1776: To R.
     Committee apparently never reported.

**142-P     Dunmore County—Citizens (Committee)**
JHD: 16 Oct. 1776                         Dunmore County

For requiring those who have conscientious scruples against bearing arms (notably Quakers and Menonists) to attend musters or else pay an annual sum for their absence.

Manuscript signed by: Joseph Pugh, chairman, and Francis Ravenhill, clerk.

16 Oct. 1776: To PG.
7 Nov. 1776: Committee reports reasonable, but apparently no action taken
         by House or Senate.
     The first act found concerning this matter appears to be in October 1777 session of General Assembly, 9H345.

**143-P-*     Craig, John**
JHD: 16 Oct. 1776                                   Not known

Compensation for death of horse, valued at £25, on hire to the country.

16 Oct. 1776: To PC.
24 Oct. 1776: Committee recommends rejection.
     House rejects.

**144-P-*     Pritchard, Samuel**
JHD: 16 Oct. 1776                                   Not known

Compensation for two tracts of land sold Lord Dunmore for £100, the balance, due and not paid on 3 August 1774, amounting to £61 2s. 3d. Requests that balance, in due proportion, be taken from Lord Dunmore's estate.

16 Oct. 1776: To PC.
24 Oct. 1776: PC recommends payment.
     House agrees.
7 Nov. 1776: Senate agrees, JS.

## Virginia Legislative Petitions

### 145-P-*  Cox, John
JHD: 16 Oct. 1776                  Pittsylvania County

Compensation for horse, impressed to apprehend counterfeiters of Virginia currency, which died from severe usage. Counterfeiters were Benjamin Cook and others.

16 Oct. 1776: To PC.
24 Oct. 1776: PC recommends £6.
      House agrees.
7 Nov. 1776: Senate agrees, JS.
      For probable reference to same counterfeiters, see 122-P-† and 376-P-†.

### 146-P  Mitchell, Joseph
JHD: 17 Oct. 1776                  Berkeley County

Offering to sell to the commonwealth 1,000 acres of land in West Augusta containing large quantities of saltpeter.

Manuscript signed: Joseph Mitchell.
17 Oct. 1776: To PG.
21 Oct. 1776: PG recommends rejection.
      House rejects.

### 147-P-†  Woolfolk, John George
JHD: 17 Oct. 1776                  Caroline County

Reimbursement of £2 18s. 6d. paid to a doctor for treatment of illness while serving as a volunteer with the militia.

17 Oct. 1776: To PC.
24 Oct. 1776: PC recommends payment.
      House agrees.
7 Nov. 1776: Senate agrees, JS.

### 148-P-†  Moseley, Edward Hack, Jr.
JHD: 18 Oct. 1776                  Not known

Compensation for slave who defected to Lord Dunmore, was captured, and ordered transported to West Indies. The ship in which he was being transported was captured by the British and the slave seized. He was valued at £85.

18 Oct. 1776: To PC.
24 Oct. 1776: PC recommends £85 less £10 7s. 6d. transportation charge,
      leaving £74 12s. 6d.
      House agrees.
7 Nov. 1776: Senate agrees, JS.

16 – 21 October 1776

**149-M** **Randolph, Harrison; Selden, Miles; Carr, Garland; Lewis, Addison; and Craig, Adam**
JHD: 18 Oct. 1776                                          Williamsburg
Compensation for their support and maintenance as "writers" in Williamsburg court under anticipation that they would be appointed as clerks in vacant Virginia county courts when the new government was formed.
Manuscript unsigned.
18 Oct. 1776: To PG.
24 Oct. 1776: PG discharged and petition withdrawn by permission of House.

**150-P**
Rob-Not
found      **Jones, John Gabriel and Clark, George Rogers**
JHD: 19 Oct. 1776                                          Kentucky Area
Asking for relief for the "County of Kentuck" by sending forces to give protection from Indians. (Kentucky County was not formed until 30 December 1776.)
Manuscript unsigned, and Rogers spelled "Rodgers."
19 Oct. 1776: To SC.
           Committee apparently did not report.

**151-C-†** **Todd, Samuel; Lindsay, John; and Micou, Paul**
JHD: 19 Oct. 1776                                          Not known
Compensation for unspecified claims for their action as commissioners, under order of last convention, in selling vessels, slaves, and appurtenances captured by Captain Taylor.
19 Oct. 1776: To PC, which was empowered to make a reasonable allowance.

**152-P-†** **Wooding, Robert**
JHD: 19 Oct. 1776                                          Halifax County
Asking postponement of removal of Halifax courthouse from land where it now stands, such land being owned by an orphan whom he represents.
19 Oct. 1776: To PG.
           See 59-P-†, 129-P, and 130-P for other action.
3 Jan. 1778: PG recommends rejection.
           House rejects.

**153-P-†** **Amherst County and Amherst Parish—Citizens**
JHD: 21 Oct. 1776                                          Amherst County

## Virginia Legislative Petitions

Asking for dissolution of vestry, which settled tobacco payments of the parish contrary to ordinance of convention.
21 Oct. 1776: To R.
> Vestry was not dissolved, but see 66-P-† for action requiring levy in tobacco.
> For act see 9H238.

**154-P-*  Maupin, Gabriel**
JHD: 21 Oct. 1776                                    Williamsburg
Compensation as keeper of military stores in city of Williamsburg from 30 October 1775 to 30 October 1776.
21 Oct. 1776: To special committee.
26 Oct. 1776: Committee recommends £50.
> House agrees.
1 Nov. 1776: Senate agrees, JS.

**155-P   Dissenters—Albemarle, Amherst, and Buckingham Counties**
JHD: 22 Oct. 1776                                    Albemarle County
                                                     Amherst County
                                                     Buckingham County
For disestablishment of Church of England. Object to supporting their church and Church of England as well. Claim every denomination should be on an equal footing.
Manuscript signed by: Jona. Lewis, Jr., John Coles, Victor Wooding, Thos. Napier, Charles L. Lewis, and seventy-one others.
22 Oct. 1776: To R.
9 Nov. 1776: R discharged and referred to SC.
> Committee apparently did not report.
> See 155 A-P.

**155 A-P   Dissenters—Albemarle, Amherst, and Buckingham Counties**
JHD: 22 Oct. 1776                                    Albemarle County
                                                     Amherst County
                                                     Buckingham County
Same in substance as 155-P, which see, but some changes in wording, and in a different hand.
Manuscript signed by seventy-three persons.

## 21 – 23 October 1776

**156-P     North Farnham Parish, Richmond County—Citizens**
JHD: 22 Oct. 1776                                                    Richmond County
For dissolution of the vestry of the parish.
  Manuscript is dated 14 June 1775, and was presented to the House of Burgesses 15 June 1775, where no action was possible because of proroguement. Manuscript signed by: Wm. Smith, N. B. Earnes, William Miskell, John Hammond, Newman Miskell, and 204 others.
22 Oct. 1776: To R.
Dec. 1776: Referred to next session of GA (manuscript endorsement) but no
     record found.
         A new petition was presented 19 October 1778 (678-P).
         For act dissolving vestry see 9H525.

**157-P     Lutheran Church [Hebron], Culpeper County—Members**
JHD: 22 Oct. 1776                                                    Culpeper County
For exemption from parochial charges except for the support of their own denomination.
  Manuscript is headed "German Congregation" and many signatures are in German script. Transliteration, in typed form with some history of the congregation, was prepared by B. C. Holtzclaw some years ago, and is attached. From this it is found that the manuscript is signed by: Adam Gaar, Adam Wayland, Johannes Jaeger, Andreas Carpenter Johannes Weber, and 113 others.
22 Oct. 1776: To R.
         Committee apparently did not report.

**158-P-†    Millyard, Sarah and Dixon, Jane**
JHD: 22 Oct. 1776                                                    Norfolk Borough
  Compensation for loss of dwelling and furniture in burning of Norfolk.
22 Oct. 1776: To PC.
2 Nov. 1776: PC recommends £10 each for present relief.
         House agrees.
7 Nov. 1776: Senate agrees, JS.

**159-P-*    Calvert, John**
JHD: 23 Oct. 1776                                                    Not known
  Compensation for loss of £38 by robbery in conducting business of the galley, *Norfolk's Revenge*, which he built and operated for Committee of Safety.
23 Oct. 1776: To PC.

## Virginia Legislative Petitions

25 Oct. 1776: PC recommends rejection.
   House rejects.

### 160-P Presbyterian Church (Hanover Presbytery)—Members
  JHD: 24 Oct. 1776      Hanover County and Surroundings
 For disestablishment of Church of England. (The extent of Hanover Presbytery is not defined.)
 Manuscript signed by: John Todd, moderator, and Caleb Wallace, clerk.
24 Oct. 1776: To R.
   Committee apparently did not report.

### 161-P-† Burwell, Lewis, Jr.
  JHD: 24 Oct. 1776         James City County
 Compensation for destruction of ferry-house, outhouses, and garden by Virginia troops occupying them as a guardhouse.
24 Oct. 1776: To PG.
15 Nov. 1776: PG discharged. Referred to SC.
   Committee apparently did not report.

### 162-P-* Goodrich, John, Jr.
  JHD: 24 Oct. 1776           Not known
 Compensation for goods furnished William Aylett for the country in the amount of £1,093. Release from sentence of convention of January last that public should have no further dealings with him.
24 Oct. 1776: To PG.
2 Nov. 1776: PG reports reasonable.
   (1) House recommits portion dealing with balance owed by Aylett.
   (2) House agrees that prohibition against dealing with petitioner by public be rescinded.
20 Dec. 1776: Both (1) and (2) agreed to by Senate, JS.

### 163-R-† West Augusta District—Citizens (Committee)
  JHD: 24 Oct. 1776        West Augusta District
 Protesting memorial (97-M-†) for laying off land west of Allegheny Mountains as a new government, and asking that it be laid off in four distinct counties.
24 Oct. 1776: To SC.
28 Oct. 1776: SC recommends (1) that representation be sent to Virginia
      members of Congress; (2) that proper measures should be taken
      against those who attempt to set up a separate government; (3) that

limits of West Augusta District should be ascertained, and that it be divided into three distinct counties; and (4) that representation be sent to Senate.

(1), (2), and (4) were agreed to by House and sent to Senate.

(3) was agreed to by House and a special committee was appointed to prepare a bill.

1 Nov. 1776: Bill was passed by House for setting up three counties and for ascertaining dividing line between these and Augusta County.

6 Nov. 1776: Senate amends bill and House agrees.

For this act see 9H262. The act defines the boundary, and sets up counties of Ohio, Yohogania, and Monongalia effective 8 November 1776.

**164-P    Dissenters—Berkeley County (Tuscarora Congregation)**
JHD: 25 Oct. 1776                                        Berkeley County

For disestablishment of Church of England, since required support of it is against petitioners' consciences.

Manuscript signed by: Hugh Varner, Wm. Patterson, Hugh Lyle, Dougall Campbell, Jn. Snodgrass, Sr., and 147 others. Signatures are all in same hand and include members of Back Creek Congregation.

25 Oct. 1776: To R.

19 Nov. 1776: In consideration of this and similar petitions R recommends and House agrees that (1) those desiring it should be free from taxes and contributions to any denomination; (2) denominations should be properly regulated; (3) acts making provision for support of clergy should be repealed, but vestries should have a right to raise funds; and (4) that all properties of the established church should be inviolate.

House orders bill to be brought in by special committee on these four items.

23 Nov. 1776: Quorum of special committee reduced to five.

30 Nov. 1776: Special committee discharged, and bill ordered to include only (1) right of dissenters to be exempt from supporting established church; (2) salaries of incumbents, including arrears, be provided for, and vestries empowered to comply with contracts; (3) provision for poor to be made; (4) clergy to be regulated; and (5) county courts to appoint members to make list of tithables. Special committee presents bill.

2 Dec. 1776: Referred to and discussed in SC.

3 Dec. 1776: Discussed in House and continued until next day.

## Virginia Legislative Petitions

4 Dec. 1776: Amended and passed by House.
5 Dec. 1776: Engrossed bill read a third time, passed, and sent to Senate.
9 Dec. 1776: Amended by Senate.
    Amendments agreed to by House.
    For this act see 9H164. This suspends until the end of the next session of the General Assembly a prior act making provision for the support of the clergy of the established church.

### 164 A-P-†Dissenters
    JHD: 25 Oct. 1776                       Not known
The journal notes two petitions of this date, but this second one is not identified. It must have been similar to 164-P, which see.

### 165-P-†   Brandon, David
    JHD: 26 Oct. 1776, for action            Halifax County
    To establish a ferry across the Dan River from his land to that of John Lawson.
    This petition was originally presented to the House of Burgesses on 10 June 1775, but no action was possible because of proroguement.
Date unknown: To PG.
26 Oct. 1776: PG reports reasonable and House orders incorporated in
    general ferry bill.
    For this act see 9H233.

### 166-P-†   Halifax County—Citizens
    JHD: 26 Oct. 1776, for action            Halifax County
    For establishing a ferry across the Dan River from the land of John Boyd to that of Patrick Boyd.
    This petition was originally presented to the House of Burgesses on 16 May 1774 and again on 10 June 1775, but no action was possible because of proroguement.
Date unknown: To PG.
26 Oct. 1776: PG reports reasonable and House orders incorporated in
    general ferry bill.
    For this act see 9H233.

### 167-P-†   Botetourt Parish, Botetourt County—Vestry
    JHD: 26 Oct. 1776, for action            Botetourt County
To sell land purchased for glebe, and use funds to purchase another site.
This petition was originally presented to the House of Burgesses on 6 June

## 25 – 28 October 1776

1775, but no action was possible because of proroguement.
Date unknown: To R.
26 Oct. 1776: R reports reasonable and House directs bill to be drawn.
20 Nov. 1776: Bill presented.
11 Dec. 1776: House passes bill and sends to Senate.
>This bill was not acted on until May 1777 session when it became part of a bill to dissolve the vestry. See 9H318.

### 168-M-† Blair, John and Randolph, Edmund (Trustees for Sale of Lord Dunmore's Property)
JHD: 26 Oct. 1776                              Williamsburg

A report of their findings and actions on Lord Dunmore's estate in and around the city of Williamsburg, including both real and personal property, made under an order of the last convention. Several books and papers attached.
26 Oct. 1776: To PC.
>Carried over to May 1777 session of GA.

26 June 1777: PC reports in detail the transactions and recommends approval of the report.
>House agrees.

27 June 1777: Senate agrees.
>See 260-M-†.

### 169-P Hanewinkel, Alexander
JHD: 26 Oct. 1776                              Fredericksburg

Requesting a public subsidy to enable him, with his partner, John Atkinson, to pursue the business of spinning, weaving, and rope making from hemp.
Manuscript signed: A. Hanewinkel. Attached is a memorial estimating the initial cost as £500.
26 Oct. 1776: To PG.
6 Nov. 1776: PG recommends rejection.
>House rejects.

### 170-P-† Crawley, John
JHD: 28 Oct. 1776                            Northumberland County

Compensation for damages suffered by being dispossessed from his home by soldiers stationed there, who also damaged his property.
28 Oct. 1776: To PG.
22 Nov. 1776: PG discharged. Referred to SC.
>Committee apparently did not report.

## Virginia Legislative Petitions

**171-P-†   Orange County—Citizens**
   JHD: 28 Oct. 1776                                Orange County
Requesting reduction of fees allowed county officials: secretary, court clerks, and surveyors.
28 Oct. 1776: To PG.
7 Dec. 1776: PG recommends that petition be deferred to next session of GA.
   House agrees.
12 Oct. 1778: PG discharged.
   No further action found.
   See 217-P-†.

**172-P-†   Lithgow, Alexander**
   JHD: 28 Oct. 1776                           Prince William County
Compensation for liquors and biscuits furnished militia at Quantico Creek upon request of commanding officer. Petitioner had expected to be paid by the public, but the governor said he needed the sanction of the House. The claim was for £28 15s.
28 Oct. 1776: To PC.
2 Nov. 1776: PC recommends rejection.
   House rejects.

**173-P   Methodist Church—Members of Convention**
   JHD: 28 Oct. 1776                                     Not known
Opposing disestablishment of Church of England. States they are not dissenters, and that their membership is about 3,000 persons.
   Manuscript signed: Geo. Shadford.
28 Oct. 1776: To R.
   Committee apparently did not report.

**174-C-†   Selden, Joseph**
   JHD: 28 Oct. 1776                            Elizabeth City County
Compensation for liquors furnished laborers in saltworks in the county.
28 Oct. 1776: To PC.
   Committee apparently did not report.

**175-P-†   Suggett, James**
   JHD: 28 Oct. 1776                                     Not known
Compensation for impressed horse, valued at £20, which died of hard usage.
28 Oct. 1776: To PC.

## 28 – 31 October 1776

2 Nov. 1776: PC recommends rejection.
    House rejects.

**176-P-\***   **Sandford, Daniel**
    JHD: 30 Oct. 1776                           Norfolk County
Compensation for rent of house taken over by militia at Great Bridge and damages to it.
30 Oct. 1776: To PC.
6 Nov. 1776: PC discharged. Referred to PG.
7 Nov. 1776: PG discharged. Referred to SC.
    Committee apparently did not report.

**177-P-\***   **M'Guire, John and Porterfield, Charles**
    JHD: 30 Oct. 1776                                Not known
Compensation for service in Arnold's siege of Quebec, where they were taken prisoners, suffered hardships, and lost preferment in the Continental army.
30 Oct. 1776: To PC.
1 Nov. 1776: PC recommends that pay of £37 5s. 6d. be awarded each plus
        £25 for expenses, and that delegates in Congress be applied to for
        reimbursement to Virginia of £66 5s. 4d., the amount of pay under
        Continental establishment.
    House agrees.
11 Nov. 1776: Senate agrees, JS.

**178-P**   **Brent, George and Brent, Robert**
    JHD: 30 Oct. 1776                              Stafford County
Compensation for labor of two slaves in lead mines, who had been convicted of a felony, pardoned by the late convention, but then attempted to escape to enemy. Suggests state may wish to purchase them.
    Manuscript unsigned.
30 Oct. 1776: To PC.
6 Nov. 1776: PG recommends that money due for labor be paid, and governor
        take proper measures to return slaves at public expense.
    House agrees.
    Apparently no action required by Senate.

**179-P-\***   **Brown, John; Woodruff, John; and Johnson, Tandy**
    JHD: 31 Oct. 1776                                Not known
Compensation for doctor's fees for treatment of illness incurred at James-

## Virginia Legislative Petitions

town while in military service in July 1775, in the amount of £5 7s. 6d.
31 Oct. 1776: To PC.
2 Nov. 1776: PC recommends £1 7s. 3d. to Brown, £1 1s. 6d. to Woodruff, and £2 18s. 9d. to Johnson.
    House agrees.
7 Nov. 1776: Senate agrees, JS.

### 180-P   Sussex County—Citizens
JHD: 31 Oct. 1776                                   Sussex County
Asking removal of milldams on Nottoway River that prevent passage of fish.
Manuscript is partially missing.
31 Oct. 1776: To PG.
    Carried over to May 1777 session of GA.
7 May 1777: PG recommends rejection.
    House rejects.

### 181-P   Lunenburg and Mecklenburg Counties—Citizens
JHD: 31 Oct. 1776                               Lunenburg County
                                                          Mecklenburg County
Asking for removal of milldams and other obstructions in Meherrin River that prevent passage of fish.
Manuscript signed by: Thomas Moody, Robt. Singleton, Wm. Fischer, Thos. Wright, Wm. Johnston, and 153 others.
31 Oct. 1776: To PG.
18 Nov. 1776: Postponed until third Monday of next session of GA.
7 May 1777: PG recommends that a sluice twelve feet wide be placed below fork of South Meherrin, but that the rest of the petition be rejected.
    House agrees, and PG to prepare bill.
    There is no record of this bill in JHD, JS, or Hening.

### 182-P   Davies, David
JHD: 31 Oct. 1776                                     Fairfax County
For advancement of sum of £500 to enable him with his own funds to erect works for the manufacture of linen and woolen cloth.
Manuscript signed: David Davies.
31 Oct. 1776: To PG.
9 Nov. 1776: PG recommends rejection.
    House rejects.

## 31 October – 1 November 1776

**183-P   Dissenters—Albemarle County and Amherst County**
JHD: 1 Nov. 1776                                                                   Amherst County
                                                                                              Albemarle County
Asks that all denominations be put on an equal footing. States that it is against petitioners' consciences to support established church.
   Manuscript signed by: Charles Lewis, Charles Lewis, Jr., Geo. Gilmer, Jno. Cole, John Marks, and 166 others, all in the same hand.
1 Nov. 1776: To R.
   Committee apparently did not report, but see 164-P for legislation concerning dissenters.

**184-P   Cowley, Abraham**
JHD: 1 Nov. 1776                                                                   Richmond Town
Compensation for wood furnished prisoners of 14th Regiment at Richmond in February 1776, while quartered in his house.
   Manuscript unsigned.
1 Nov. 1776: House rejects by refusing to refer to a committee.

**185-P   Bruce, William**
JHD: 1 Nov. 1776                                                                   King George County
Compensation for tobacco stolen from Morton's and Gibson's warehouses where he and the late William Harrison were inspectors, for which the proprietors had charged them.
   Manuscript has attached five depositions, all dated in May 1774, certifying to the robbery.
1 Nov. 1776: To PC.
19 Dec. 1776: Manuscript endorsement says not reported.
5 Jan. 1778: Manuscript endorsement says to remain in "status quo" until next session of GA.
8 Dec. 1778: PC recommends that it be deferred to next session of GA.
   House agrees.
   No further record found.

**186-P-†   Hewitt, Richard and Hore, Elias**
JHD: 1 Nov. 1776                                                                   Stafford County
Compensation for nine hogsheads of tobacco damaged by the flood of 1771 while stored in Aquia warehouse of which they were the late inspectors.
1 Nov. 1776: To PC.
9 Nov. 1776: PC recommends rejection.
   House rejects.

## Virginia Legislative Petitions

**187-P-*  Helphinstine, Peter**
        JHD: 1 Nov. 1776                               Not known

Compensation for horse, valued at £20, that died on Charleston, South Carolina, expedition and for expenses of petitioner for his return home after his resignation from army.

1 Nov. 1776: To PC.
2 Nov. 1776: PC recommends rejection since the matter is one in which the continent alone was interested.
       House rejects.

**188-P  Light, Peter**
        JHD: 1 Nov. 1776                             Berkeley County

Asking for an advance of public funds to enable him to erect a slitting mill for making slit iron and nails.

Manuscript is unsigned, and is directed to the convention of May 1776. Attached is a recommendation of the committee of Berkeley County, dated 15 June 1776, and is also directed to the convention. (It was never considered by the convention.)

1 Nov. 1776: To PG.
6 Nov. 1776: PG recommends rejection.
       House rejects.

**189-P  Prince William County—Citizens**
        JHD: 2 Nov. 1776                        Prince William County

Asking that landlords and creditors be required to accept produce of land, rather than scarce money, for debts due to them.

Manuscript signed by: Henry Peyton, John Ewell, Ja. Ewell, T. Blackburn, Richd. Graham, and ninety-nine others.

2 Nov. 1776: To SC.
       Apparently never reported.

**190-P-†  Pendleton, Philip and Myler, James**
        JHD: 2 Nov. 1776                        King and Queen County

Compensation for stolen tobacco taken from the Walkerton warehouses in 1774 and valued at £7 0s. 4d.

2 Nov. 1776: To PC.
9 Nov. 1776: PC recommends rejection.
       House rejects.

## 1 – 2 November 1776

**191-P-†   Cornick, Joel, Jr.; Banks, Thomas; Cornick, Lemuel; and Haynes, William**
JHD: 2 Nov. 1776                                                                  Not known
Compensation for slaves captured in Lord Dunmore's service, and sent by Committee of Safety to West Indies in ship of John Dixon that was captured by British and slaves seized.
2 Nov. 1776: To PC.
9 Nov. 1776: PC recommends that value of slaves less transportation be paid: £74 12s. 6d. to Joel Cornick, £42 5s. to Thomas Banks, £46 17s. 6d. to Lemuel Cornick, and £60 15s. to William Haynes.
   House agrees.
11 Dec. 1776: Senate agrees, JS.

**192-P-†   Keeling, Jacob**
JHD: 2 Nov. 1776                                                                  Not known
Compensation for slaves captured in Lord Dunmore's service, and sent by Committee of Safety to West Indies in ship of John Dixon that was captured by British and slaves seized.
2 Nov. 1776: To PC.
9 Nov. 1776: PC recommends that value of slaves less transportation be paid in the amount of £112 5s.
   House agrees.
11 Dec. 1776: Senate agrees, JS.

**193-P   Berkeley County—Citizens (Warm Springs Area)**
JHD: 2 Nov. 1776                                                              Berkeley County
For remedying the situation in the area, property of Lord Fairfax, so that they may cut timber for housing and fuel to accommodate the many persons using the springs for health purposes.
  Manuscript signed by: Alex. Williamson, W. Boxen, Will. Sydebotham, James Hoggar, Henry Rozer, Jr., and 249 others. Manuscript dated 15 August 1776.
2 Nov. 1776: To PG.
6 Nov. 1776: PG recommends that fifty acres be laid off for town. Directed to prepare bill.
16 Nov. 1776: Bill presented.
28 Nov. 1776: Bill amended.
   House passes bill.
30 Nov. 1776: Senate amends.
5 Dec. 1776: House amends Senate amendments.

## Virginia Legislative Petitions

6 Dec. 1776: Senate agrees.
    Senate passes bill.
    For this act see 9H247.

**194-P-***   **West, John, Jr.**
    JHD: 2 Nov. 1776                       Loudoun County
                                              Fairfax County
  Asking that Henry Bennett, of Great Britain, the heir to lands, slaves, and property of John Colville, after several generations, have appointed for him commissioners to look after his interests.
2 Nov. 1776: To PG.
    Carried over to October 1777 session of GA.
3 Jan. 1778: PG recommends rejection.
    House rejects.

**195-M**
Eck–
A1093   **Tandy, Smith**
    JHD: 4 Nov. 1776                       Augusta County
  For public assistance in establishing a mill for bleaching and manufacturing linen in Staunton, estimated at £310.
    Manuscript unsigned. Estimate attached at one time is missing.
4 Nov. 1776: To PG.
6 Nov. 1776: PG recommends rejection.
    House rejects.

**196-P**   **Criminals—Public Jail (Williamsburg)**
    JHD: 4 Nov. 1776                             Not known
  Protesting lack of prompt trials and of necessities, and asking their cases be expedited.
    Manuscript signed "The Criminals."
4 Nov. 1776: To PG.
11 Nov. 1776: PG reports reasonable.
    House requests that a bill be brought in, and that clothing and blankets be furnished prisoners.
    For a general act on the trial of prisoners see 9H172.

**197-P**   **Edwards, Andrew**
    JHD: 5 Nov. 1776                       Stafford County
  Opposing the erection of houses for naval stores at Cave's warehouses and

## 2 – 5 November 1776

using existing buildings for this purpose, and citing the loss of land and funds this would occasion him.

Manuscript signed: Andw. Edwards. Manuscript endorsement says that it is not to be considered, and that action was determined by that on Mr. Hunter's petition (198-P), which was rejected.

5 Nov. 1776: To PG, but see above.

    For act establishing warehouses at Cave's see 9H235.

### 198-P   Hunter, James
JHD: 5 Nov. 1776                    Stafford County

Asking, as contractor with the commissioners of the navy, to rent warehouses at Cave's for naval supplies, or to build at the public expense or his own, a new warehouse for which he would pay rent.

Manuscript unsigned.

5 Nov. 1776: To PG.
7 Nov. 1776: PG recommends rejection.
    House rejects.
    See 197-P.

### 199-P   Cumberland County—Citizens
JHD: 5 Nov. 1776               Cumberland County

Requesting that Cumberland County be divided into two distinct counties.

Manuscript signed by: Archer Alden, Saml. Alden, W. Townes, Stepn. Woodson, Charles Cox, and sixty-two others.

5 Nov. 1776: To PG.
9 Nov. 1776: PG reports reasonable and House directs that a bill be drawn.
22 Nov. 1776: Bill introduced and sent back to PG.
3 Dec. 1776: PG introduces amended bill.
5 Dec. 1776: House passes bill and sends to Senate.
9 Dec. 1776: Senate defeats bill.
    See 199 A-P and 199 B-P.

### 199 A-P   Cumberland County—Citizens
JHD: 5 Nov. 1776               Cumberland County

Text is identical with 199-P, which see.
Manuscript signed by forty-nine persons.

### 199 B-P   Cumberland County—Citizens
JHD: 5 Nov. 1776               Cumberland County

## Virginia Legislative Petitions

Text is identical with 199-P, which see.
Manuscript signed by eighty-five persons.

### 200-P-* Bean, Richard
JHD: 5 Nov. 1776                                        Not known

Asking for back pay for thirty-seven days as a soldier, his name having been omitted from the roll.

5 Nov. 1776: To PC.
23 Nov. 1776: PC recommends pay of £2 9s. 4d.
       House agrees.
29 Nov. 1776: Senate agrees, JS.

### 201-P Prince William County—Militia (Court-martial)
JHD: 5 Nov. 1776                                    Prince William County

Protesting the requirement that men of the militia who appear at musters without arms should be fined. (Treated as a proposition.)

Manuscript is a copy of the proceedings of 17 October 1776, signed by Evan Williams. Attached is a letter also protesting, signed by T. Blackburn.

5 Nov. 1776: To PG.
7 Nov. 1776: PG recommends rejection.
       House rejects.

### 202-P-* Brown, Elizabeth
JHD: 6 Nov. 1776                                        Not known

Compensation for death of husband, Coleman Brown, and loss of his equipment in expedition against Ohio Indians in 1774.

6 Nov. 1776: To PC.
9 Nov. 1776: PC recommends £20.
       House agrees.
       Senate action not found. It is likely that it agreed.

### 203-P-* Brooks, William
JHD: 6 Nov. 1776                                        Not known

Compensation for paper currency, in the amount of £9 4s., that was either lost or destroyed.

6 Nov. 1776: To PC.
23 Nov. 1776: PC recommends rejection.
       House rejects.

## 5 – 6 November 1776

**204-P**
Eck–A1  **Upshur, Arthur**
JHD: 6 Nov. 1776                                                Accomack County

For relief from £100 fine levied against him by committee of Accomack for sailing his schooner, laden with corn, to West Indies, after restriction was placed on such sailings by Continental Association, and also for relief from having been advertised in the *Virginia Gazette* as an enemy of the country. Claims loyalty to America and ignorance of restriction.

Manuscript signed: Arthur Upshur. Manuscript has attached extracts from the Accomack committee's minutes for 2 October 1775, 8 January, and 30 March 1776, and a letter from Upshur to the committee dated 30 January 1776, together with his orders to the ship's captain.

6 Nov. 1776: To PE
28 Nov. 1776: PE reports Upshur unquestionably a friend of American cause, and that the sailing was through ignorance of the restriction. Recommends the fine be returned and Upshur restored to his rights.
House agrees.
4 Dec. 1776: Senate agrees.
6 Dec. 1776: Senate directs action to be published in *Virginia Gazette*.

**205-P**  **Smith, Isaac**
JHD: 6 Nov. 1776                                                Not known

Asking to be allowed £63 16s. ½d. from the estate of Lord Dunmore due him as surviving partner in firm of Bowdoin and Eyre.

Manuscript unsigned, but has attached to it a detailed statement of the account.

6 Nov. 1776: To PG.
12 Nov. 1776: PG recommends payment in proportion with other creditors.
House agrees.
23 Nov. 1776: Senate agrees, JS.

**205.1-P-† Hobday, John**
JHD: 6 Nov. 1776                                                Gloucester County
                                                                 York County

Objecting, as manager of saltworks between Rappahannock and York rivers and also between York and James rivers, to deduction of payments to him by the Council for hire of laborers and soldiers and for provision of one gill of spirits a day to the workers.

6 Nov. 1776: To special committee on saltworks.

## Virginia Legislative Petitions

20 Nov. 1776: Committee recommends (1) allowance for spirits is reasonable, (2) allowance for extra pay for white persons should be rejected, and (3) allowance for extra pay for slaves should be rejected.
House rejects (2) and sends (1) and (3) back to committee.
22 Nov. 1776: Committee recommends amount paid for spirits, £46, 10s., is reasonable. Also recommends amount paid for slave labor, £124 11s. 6d., is reasonable.
House agrees.
28 Nov. 1776: Senate agrees, JS.

**206-P-*   Garland, Edward**
JHD: 7 Nov. 1776                                                                 Not known
Compensation for doctor's fees and medicines made necessary by his military service, and his inability to receive proper treatment or secure a place in army hospitals. The latter forced him to pay for private room and board.
7 Nov. 1776: To PC.
23 Nov. 1776: PC recommends £37 6s. 6d. for these services.
House returns petition to PC.
28 Nov. 1776: PC recommends £37 5s.
House rejects.

**207-P-†   Foster, Elizabeth**
JHD: 7 Nov. 1776                                                          Gloucester County
Compensation for death of husband, John Foster, who was fatally wounded in an engagement with Lord Dunmore's men on Gwynn's Island.
7 Nov. 1776: To PC.
26 Nov. 1776: PC recommends £20.
House agrees.
28 Nov. 1776: Senate agrees, JS.

**208-P   Parsons, James**
JHD: 7 Nov. 1776                                                          Hampshire County
Compensation for buying cattle at the time of Lord Dunmore's expedition against the Indians in 1774.
Manuscript unsigned.
7 Nov. 1776: To PC.
23 Nov. 1776: PC recommends £3 15s.
House agrees
29 Nov. 1776: Senate agrees, JS.

## 7 November 1776

**209-P-†  Whiting, Kemp**
  JHD: 7 Nov. 1776                                                Gloucester County
Compensation for damages to houses and property inflicted by soldiers while the property was being used as a hospital.
7 Nov. 1776: To PG.
8 Nov. 1776: PG discharged. To SC.
  Committee apparently did not report.

**210-P-†  Marchant, Daniel; Marchant, Elisha; Powell, Henry; Peed, Philip; Shipley, Joseph; and Shipley, John**
  JHD: 7 Nov. 1776                                                Gloucester County
Compensation for houses and property destroyed on Gwynn's Island by American soldiers.
7 Nov. 1776: To PG.
8 Nov. 1776: PG discharged. To SC.
  Committee apparently did not report.
  See 219-P-†.

**211-P-*  Savage, Nathaniel Littleton**
  JHD: 7 Nov. 1776                                                York County
Compensation for damage to houses and property in town of York by American soldiers.
7 Nov. 1776: To PG.
8 Nov. 1776: PG discharged. To SC.
  Committee apparently did not report.

**212-P  Smith, Isaac; Bowdoin, Preston; and Smith, Thoroughgood (Executors of John Bowdoin, deceased)**
  JHD: 7 Nov. 1776                                                Northampton County
For return of two slaves, sent to lead mines after having been captured in an attempt to escape to Lord Dunmore.
  Manuscript unsigned.
7 Nov. 1776: To PG.
9 Nov. 1776: PG recommends return and petitioners paid for hire. Governor is asked to take proper measures.
  Senate action apparently not needed.

**213-P  Hunter, James**
  JHD: 7 Nov. 1776                                                Not known
Asking release from a bond, posted for purchase of a slave captured in the

## Virginia Legislative Petitions

Rappahannock River, in the amount of £90. Slave was later killed by a shot from an American ship.
   Manuscript unsigned.
7 Nov. 1776: House rejects by refusal to refer to a committee.

### 214-P-†    M'Farlin, William
      JHD: 7 Nov. 1776                                 Not known
Compensation for service in expedition against Indians under Lord Dunmore in 1774.
7 Nov. 1776: To PC.
3 Dec. 1776: PC recommends £11 18s. 6d.
      House agrees.
6 Dec. 1776: Senate agrees, JS.

### 215-P-†    Waggoner, Andrew
      JHD: 7 Nov. 1776                                 Not known
Compensation for a horse he hired, when his own broke down, in carrying dispatches from Fort Pitt to Williamsburg. The hired horse died and owner required £30 in payment.
7 Nov. 1776: To PC.
30 Nov. 1776: PC recommends £30.
      House rejects recommendation.

### 216-P
Eck–A2    **Peck, Benjamin**
      JHD: 8 Nov. 1776                              Accomack County
Compensation for boat, valued at £6, that was lost in ferrying slaves at saltworks.
   Manuscript unsigned.
8 Nov. 1776: To PC.
22 Nov. 1776: PC discharged. To special committee on saltworks.
      Carried over to May 1777 session of GA.
9 May 1777: Special committee recommends £6.
      House agrees.
14 May 1777: Senate agrees, JS.

### 217-P-†    Culpeper County—Citizens
      JHD: 8 Nov. 1776                              Culpeper County
Protesting high fees paid to clerks of county courts and General Court, and asking provision that clerks be required to reside in their respective counties.

## 7 – 8 November 1776

8 Nov. 1776: To PG.
7 Dec. 1776: PG recommends that petition be deferred to next session of GA.
    House agrees.
12 Oct. 1778: PG discharged.
    No further action found.
    See 171-P-†.

**218-M**    **Church of England—Clergy**
    JHD: 8 Nov. 1776                            Not known
Against the abolition of the Church of England as proposed in certain petitions. Is apprehensive of commotions that may result and asks the matter be postponed.
    Manuscript unsigned, but petition refers to "a considerable number."
8 Nov. 1776: To R.
    Committee apparently did not report.

**219-P-†**    **Hudgins, William; Peed, Philip; Parrot, Robert; Shipley, John; Shipley, Ralph; Hudgins, Mary; Shipley, Joseph; Longest, Anne; Billups, Humphrey; Marchant, Elisha; Window, Thomas; Window, John; and Marchant, Daniel**
    JHD: 8 Nov. 1776                         Gloucester County
Compensation for destruction of corn fields, potato, and cotton patches by American soldiers.
8 Nov. 1776: To SC.
    Committee apparently did not report.
    See 210-P-†.

**220-C-***    **Morgan, Daniel**
    JHD: 8 Nov. 1776                              Not known
Claim for "sundry articles" due him on account of the expedition against the Indians in 1774. (Articles may well have been plunder from Indian towns.)
8 Nov. 1776: To special committee.
    No further action found in JHD.
    See 262-[M]-†.

**221-M**
Eck–Not found    **Augusta County—Citizens (Committee)**
    JHD: 8 Nov. 1776                          Augusta County
Asking that they not be required to support the Church of England since

### Virginia Legislative Petitions

they also support their own denominations.
    Manuscript signed by: Thos. Lewis, Samp. Matthews, Saml. McDowell, A. Thompson, Mich. Boney, and ten others.
8 Nov. 1776: To SC.
        Committee apparently did not report.

**222-P   Smyth, Adam**
    JHD: 11 Nov. 1776                       Botetourt County
Compensation for several years' service as rector of Botetourt Parish. Has not been paid due to inattention of vestry.
    Manuscript unsigned.
11 Nov. 1776: To SC.
        Committee apparently did not report.

**223-P-*   Emery, William**
    JHD: 12 Nov. 1776                       Norfolk Borough
Compensation for impressed ferryboat that was captured and destroyed by British.
12 Nov. 1776: To SC.
18 Nov. 1776: SC discharged. To PC.
23 Nov. 1776: PC recommends £20 5s. 6d.
        House agrees.
4 Dec. 1776: Senate agrees.

**224-P-*   Holliday, Hezekiah**
    JHD: 12 Nov. 1776                       Not known
For return of slave who escaped to Lord Dunmore in January 1776, was captured, sent to Williamsburg and then to lead mines.
12 Nov. 1776: To PG.
18 Nov. 1776: PG recommends slave be returned, together with his hire.
        House agrees and asks governor to arrange return.
18 Dec. 1776: Senate agrees, JS.

**225-P-†   Mayo, John**
    JHD: 12 Nov. 1776                       Not known
Compensation for a runaway slave taken by Lord Dunmore at Norfolk.
12 Nov. 1776: To PG.
        Carried over to October 1777 session of GA.
8 Jan. 1778: Carried over to October 1778 session of GA.

## 11 – 14 November 1776

13 Oct. 1778: PG recommends rejection, but states that subject matter is cognizable before a court of law.
House agrees.

### 226-P-* Pinkney, John
JHD: 12 Nov. 1776            Not known
Compensation for garden pales burned by Virginia soldiers.
12 Nov. 1776: To SC.
Committee apparently did not report.

### 227-P-† Woolford, Frederick
JHD: 12 Nov. 1776            Dunmore County
Compensation for housing and boarding troops in town of Woodstock.
12 Nov. 1776: To PC.
18 Dec. 1776: PC recommends rejection since amounts had been properly paid.
House agrees.

### 228-P-† Henrico County—Citizens (Committee)
JHD: 12 Nov. 1776            Henrico County
Compensation for repairs to church at Richmond (Saint John's Church) in order to accommodate the convention of July 1775.
12 Nov. 1776: To PC.
Committee apparently did not report, but an unidentified petition from Henrico was carried forward to the May 1778 session of the GA on 8 January 1778. It does not appear then or later.

### 229-P Manchester—Trustees
JHD: 14 Nov. 1776            Chesterfield County
Asks for an act to allow trustees or others to remove buildings or other obstructions that are or may be erected on the passage from the town to the river.
Manuscript unsigned.
14 Nov. 1776: To PG
12 Dec. 1776: PG recommends rejection since the matter is cognizable before a court of law.
House agrees.

### 230-P Spotsylvania County—Citizens
JHD: 14 Nov. 1776            Spotsylvania County

## Virginia Legislative Petitions

Asking that general musters of militia be held in center of the county rather than in Fredericksburg.

Manuscript signed by: Joseph Herndon, William Chiles, William Masters, Benja. Masters, John Craig, and thirty-five others.

14 Nov. 1776: To PG.

16 Nov. 1776: PG reports reasonable.

    House directs the special committee on the militia to incorporate the matter in a general bill. This bill did not become an act until 1777.

    See 82-P.

    For the general act see 9H268.

### 230 A-P  Spotsylvania County—Citizens
JHD: 14 Nov. 1776                      Spotsylvania County
Text is identical with 230-P, which see.
Manuscript signed by forty-nine persons.

### 230 B-P  Spotsylvania County—Citizens
JHD: 14 Nov. 1776                      Spotsylvania County
Text is identical with 230-P, which see.
Manuscript signed by forty-nine persons.

### 230 C-P  Spotsylvania County—Citizens
JHD: 14 Nov. 1776                      Spotsylvania County
Text is identical with 230-P, which see.
Manuscript signed by fifty-five persons.

### 230 D-P  Spotsylvania County—Citizens
JHD: 14 Nov. 1776                      Spotsylvania County
Text is identical with 230-P, which see.
Manuscript signed by thirty-five persons.

### 230 E-P  Spotsylvania County—Citizens
JHD: 14 Nov. 1776                      Spotsylvania County
Text is identical with 230-P, which see.
Manuscript signed by thirty-four persons.

### 230 F-P  Spotsylvania County—Citizens
JHD: 14 Nov. 1776                      Spotsylvania County

## 14 – 15 November 1776

Text is identical with 230-P, which see.
Manuscript signed by thirty-one persons.

**231-P-†  Savage, William**
  JHD: 14 Nov. 1776            Not known

Compensation for boat and sails impressed in the summer of 1776 by Colonel George Mason.

14 Nov. 1776: To PG.
7 Dec. 1776: PG reports that depositions should be taken, and matter carried
  over to October 1777 session of GA.
  House agrees.
8 Jan. 1778: House carries over to next session of GA.
3 Dec. 1778: House carries over to next session of GA.
19 Oct. 1779: PG recommends that (1) payment of £24 for sails is reasonable
  and that interest should be paid from 1 June 1776, and (2) that
  payment for boat be rejected.
  House agrees.
21 Oct. 1779: Senate agrees to (1).

**232-P  Nowlen, David**
  JHD: 14 Nov. 1776          Pittsylvania County

Compensation for impressed horse that was injured in transporting Joseph Ray, a criminal, to public jail in Williamsburg.

Manuscript unsigned. Has attached two depositions as to value of horse, and an assignment, signed by David Nowlen of value, to Samuel Calland & Co.

14 Nov. 1776: To PC.
23 Nov. 1776: PC recommends 40s.
  House agrees.
29 Nov. 1776: Senate agrees, JS.

**233-P-†  Southall, Turner**
  JHD: 15 Nov. 1776           Richmond Town

Compensation for thirty-two cords of wood furnished Abraham Cowley for use of British prisoners, valued at £16.

15 Nov. 1776: To PC.
3 Dec. 1776: PC recommends £16.
  House agrees.
6 Dec. 1776: Senate agrees, JS.

## Virginia Legislative Petitions

**234-P** **Trebell, William and Moody, William (Executors of Frederick Bryan, deceased)**
JHD: 15 Nov. 1776                                                       Not known

Asking for payment out of Lord Dunmore's estate in the amount of £52 12s. due on account.
Manuscript unsigned. Has attached an itemized bill for 1774 and 1775.
15 Nov. 1776: To PC. (Manuscript endorsement says PG.)
  Carried over to October 1778 session of GA, without reference.
13 Oct. 1778: PG recommends rejection since the matter is cognizable before a court of law.
  House agrees.

**235-P-*** **Watkins, Robert**
JHD: 15 Nov. 1776                                                       Not known

Compensation for additional days served in Indian expedition of 1774.
15 Nov. 1776: To PC.
23 Nov. 1776: PC recommends rejection since accounts show he has been fully paid.
  House agrees.

**236-P-*** **Brunswick County, Lunenburg County, and Mecklenburg County—Citizens**
JHD: 15 Nov. 1776                                                       Brunswick County
                                                                         Lunenburg County
                                                                         Mecklenburg County

Requesting that land taxes be on value of land and not on acreage owned, and that personal as well as real property be on value also.
15 Nov. 1776: To PG.
  Carried over to October 1777 session of GA.
3 Jan. 1778: PG recommends as reasonable.
  House agrees and sends to Senate.
  No Senate action found.
  For revision of tax laws see 9H349.

**237-P-***
Eck–Not
found   **Alexandria—Citizens**
JHD: 15 Nov. 1776                                                       Alexandria

Request for fortifying the town including purchase of cannon and forges and the formation of a garrison of militia.

## 15 – 16 November 1776

15 Nov. 1776: To SC.
6 Dec. 1776: SC finds reasonable and recommends that a clause be inserted covering Alexandria in a general bill providing for internal security and defense.
    For general bill see 9H192.

**238-P    Fambrough, Thomas**
    JHD: 16 Nov. 1776                           Halifax County
Compensation for damage to impressed horse used by sheriff to transport Thomas Potter to Williamsburg jail, he having been charged with stealing a bay mare belonging to John Wilson.
    Manuscript unsigned. Attached is a deposition, dated 9 April 1776, appraising the value of Fambrough's horse at £7.
16 Nov. 1776: To PC.
23 Nov. 1776: PC recommends 40s.
        House agrees.
29 Nov. 1776: Senate agrees, JS.

**239-P    Haynes, Joseph**
    JHD: 16 Nov. 1776                           Halifax County
Compensation for damage to impressed horse used by sheriff to transport John Johnson to Williamsburg jail in July 1775, he having been charged with murder. Haynes was assignee of John Dudgeon who originally owned the horse.
    Manuscript unsigned. Has attached two depositions as to value of horse.
16 Nov. 1776: To PC.
23 Nov. 1776: PC recommends 40s.
        House agrees.
29 Nov. 1776: Senate agrees.

**240-P-†    Lester, Dionysius**
    JHD: 16 Nov. 1776                         James City County
Compensation for ferry impressed at Jamestown for use of American troops in November 1775.
16 Nov. 1776: To PC.
30 Nov. 1776: PC recommends £12.
        House agrees.
4 Dec. 1776: Senate agrees, JS.

## Virginia Legislative Petitions

### 241-P-*   Galt, Patrick
JHD: 16 Nov. 1776                                   Not known

Compensation for service as surgeon to three companies of troops from 1 February 1776 to 28 April 1776.

16 Nov. 1776: To PC.

    Committee apparently did not report.

### 242-P   Culpeper County—Citizens
JHD: 16 Nov. 1776                               Culpeper County

Protesting the sale of liquors to soldiers at exorbitant prices, and citizens' inability to secure appointments as suttlers. Claims they can sell at lower prices.

Manuscript signed by: Ambrose Powell, James Collins, Jacob Ward, Munford Stevens, Humphrey Gaines, and 216 others.

16 Nov. 1776: To PG.

7 Dec. 1776: PG recommends rejection.

    House rejects.

### 243-P   Norfolk Borough—Mayor, Aldermen, Councilmen, and Citizens
JHD: 16 Nov. 1776                                 Norfolk Borough

Asking for relief from their distress occasioned by being driven from their homes in poverty by hostilities, and by having the greatest part of the town burned in the first conflagration by provincial troops, despite the denial of this fact by the Committee of Safety.

Manuscript unsigned.

16 Nov. 1776: To SC.

    Carried over to May 1777 session of GA.

15 May 1777: House orders consideration by committee of whole.

6 June 1777: Committee recommends (1) that commissioners be appointed to ascertain the number, and cause estimates to be made of houses and goods destroyed in Norfolk and suburbs in January 1776, distinguishing between those destroyed before and after 15 January and which property may have belonged to enemies of America, and (2) that reparation ought to be made by public for houses of friends of America burned by Colonel Howe.

    House agrees, and orders bill to be brought in by special committee for (1), and (2) to be sent to Senate.

    For the act containing the substance of (1) and (2) see 9H328. This

## 16 – 18 November 1776

act was continued and amended from time to time in subsequent sessions. See particularly 9H427 and 9H465.

### 244-P-* Hampden-Sidney [Hampden-Sydney] Academy—Trustees
JHD: 16 Nov. 1776                      Prince Edward County

Asking for public support to provide accommodations for students and to make the board a corporate body.

Manuscript was not located in an inventory of 1940.

16 Nov. 1776: To PG.
        Carried over to May 1777 session of GA.
31 May 1777: PG discharged. To committee of whole.
12 June 1777: Committee of whole discharged and permission given to withdraw petition.
13 June 1777: Permission given to introduce a bill permitting academy to hold a lottery.
        For the act providing a lottery see 9H321.

### 245-P-† Lawson, Thomas
JHD: 18 Nov. 1776                      Prince William County

Compensation for death of two oxen by drowning while carrying supplies for militia.

18 Nov. 1776: To PC.
18 Dec. 1776: PC recommends £12.
        House agrees.
18 Dec. 1776: Senate agrees, JS.

### 246-P-† Knibb, John and Renard, Richard
JHD: 18 Nov. 1776                      Henrico County

Compensation for tobacco stolen from Bermuda Hundred warehouses where they were inspectors.

18 Nov. 1776: To PC.
6 Dec. 1776: PC recommends £22 3s. 11½d. for tobacco stolen in October 1771 and on 11 July 1772.
        House agrees.
9 Dec. 1776: Senate agrees, JS.

### 247-P-† Knibb, John
JHD: 18 Nov. 1776                      Henrico County

Compensation for tobacco stolen from Bermuda Hundred warehouse in July 1770 where he and Thomas Stratton, deceased, were inspectors.

## Virginia Legislative Petitions

18 Nov. 1776: To PC.
    Apparently carried over several times without record.
1 Dec. 1778: PC recommends £3 12s. 8d.
    House agrees.
8 Dec. 1778: Senate agrees.

### 248-P    Hobday, John
    JHD: 18 Nov. 1776             Gloucester County

Compensation for invention of threshing machine run by horsepower, avoiding the waste and unsanitary conditions of treading out grain by horses and other animals. (Hobday had been awarded £100 by House of Burgesses on 20 May 1774, but this did not take effect since this assembly was prorogued. His machine was widely used.)
    Manuscript unsigned.
18 Nov. 1776: To PG.
23 Nov. 1776: PG recommends rejection.
    House rejects.

### 249-P-†    Tyson, Nathaniel
    JHD: 18 Nov. 1776            Northampton County

Compensation for loss of 540 paper dollars from his pocket in Philadelphia where he had been sent by Northampton committee to purchase cannon and other military stores.
18 Nov. 1776: To PG.
25 Nov. 1776: PG recommends rejection.
    House rejects.

### 250-P-*    Carrington, Joseph
    JHD: 18 Nov. 1776            Not known

Compensation of £9 5s. spent in raising minutemen for Amelia, Chesterfield, and Cumberland counties.
18 Nov. 1776: To PG.
    Carried over to October 1777 session of GA.
3 Jan. 1778: PG recommends rejection, but House agrees to £9 5s.
19 Jan. 1778: Senate agrees.

### 251-P-*    Ambler, Jacquelin
    JHD: 18 Nov. 1776            York County

Compensation for destruction of and damage to houses in town of York, used as a barracks by Virginia troops during the winter of 1775.

## 18 November 1776

18 Nov. 1776: To SC.
    Committee apparently did not report.

**252-P-†**   **Savage, Nathaniel Littleton**
    JHD: 18 Nov. 1776                               Norfolk Borough

Compensation for destruction of distillery and molasses in Norfolk in which he had an interest. Destroyed by Colonel Howe; valued at £800. Asks for appointment of persons to place valuation.

18 Nov. 1776: To SC.
    Carried over to October 1777 session of GA.
12 Dec. 1777: SC discharged. To special committee on losses at Norfolk.
    Committee apparently did not report.
    For a new petition on same subject see 674-P.

**253-P**   **Grayson, Spence**
    JHD: 18 Nov. 1776                                 Loudoun County

Asking that vestry of Cameron Parish appoint tobacco collectors in order for his salary to be paid for 1775, and that the court appoint persons to collect tithes for his salary in 1776.
    Manuscript unsigned. (It has interesting notes on reverse.)
18 Nov. 1776: To R.
    Committee apparently did not report.

**254-P-†**
Eck-Not
found   **Upshur, Arthur**
    JHD: 18 Nov. 1776                                 Accomack County

For payment of £100 contracted for with John Goodrich, Sr., on behalf of the country for sending an express vessel in October 1775 to Saint Eustatia to warn the captains of two of Goodrich's vessels that Lord Dunmore was prepared to capture and confiscate the ships and their cargoes of gunpowder to be bought from France at £5,000. Upshur's vessel was to bring back gunpowder. William, John Goodrich's son, countermanded order and fell into hands of Lord Dunmore.

18 Nov. 1776: To lie on table.
19 Nov. 1776: To PG.
25 Nov. 1776: PG reports reasonable and that £100 should be paid by public.
    House agrees.
28 Nov. 1776: Senate agrees.

## Virginia Legislative Petitions

**255-P-†  Roberts, William**
JHD: 18 Nov. 1776                                                Halifax County
For discontinuance of a ferry over Dan River from his land to that of Henry Gaines, the latter now being the property of Roger Shackleford.
18 Nov. 1776: To lie on table.
19 Nov. 1776: To PG.
22 Nov. 1776: PG reports reasonable.
>House agrees and directs that it be incorporated in general ferry bill.
>For general ferry act see 9H233.

**256-P-\*  Higgin, James**
JHD: 18 Nov. 1776                                                Not known
For repayment of amount of physician's fees he incurred while taken ill in military service.
18 Nov. 1776: To lie on table.
19 Nov. 1776: To PC.
3 Dec. 1776: PC recommends rejection.
>House rejects.

**257-P-†  Bousman, Jacob**
JHD: 18 Nov. 1776                                                Yohogania County
For establishing a ferry across Monongahela River from his land to town of Pittsburgh.
18 Nov. 1776: To lie on table.
19 Nov. 1776: To PG.
22 Nov. 1776: PG recommends as reasonable.
>House agrees and directs that it be incorporated in general ferry bill.
>For general ferry act see 9H233.

**258-P-\*  Zane, Isaac**
JHD: 18 Nov. 1776                                                Not known
To be allowed £21 19s. 6d. out of Lord Dunmore's estate for a debt that had not been paid.
18 Nov. 1776: To lie on table.
19 Nov. 1776: To PG.
>Carried over to October 1777 session of GA.
8 Jan. 1778: PG recommends £21 19s. 6d. in proportion with other creditors.
>House agrees.

## 18 – 29 November 1776

19 Jan. 1778: Senate agrees.

**259-M-\* Field, Henry, Jr.**
    JHD: 18 Nov. 1776                        Prince William County
                                                      Fauquier County
                                                      Culpeper County

For redress in collection of quitrents from tenants on the property of Lord Fairfax. The appeal is made under the direction of Lord Fairfax, who considers himself a true Virginia citizen.

Manuscript unsigned.
18 Nov. 1776: To lie on table.
19 Nov. 1776: To PG.
22 Nov. 1776: PG discharged. To SC.
       Committee apparently did not report, but in the October 1777 session of GA an act was passed that, among other things, detailed the matter of taxation on quitrents.
    For general act see 9H349.

**260-M-† Washington, Samuel; Rutherford, Robert; and Booth, William (Trustees for Sale of Lord Dunmore's Property)**
    JHD: 18 Nov. 1776                                 Berkeley County

Reporting on their actions under appointment by convention of May 1776, and showing sales of slaves and property amounting to £1,118 5s. 2d., and rental of farm, Mount Charlotte, to Edward Snickers.
18 Nov. 1776: To PC.
       Carried over to May 1777 session of GA.
26 May 1777: PC recommends speedy collection for sales.
       House agrees and instructs treasurer to collect.
27 June 1777: Senate agrees.
    See 168-M-†.

**261-P Cumberland County—Citizens**
    JHD: 29 Nov. 1776                               Cumberland County
Opposing the division of Cumberland County.

There are six manuscripts of this petition, all not exactly alike. Of these, two went to the House and four to the Senate, which referred them to the House. This particular one went to the House and is signed by: Fleming Palmoni, Hezekiah Carter, Shadrick Carter, Wm. Lawless, John Furlong, and fifty-four others.

## Virginia Legislative Petitions

29 Nov. 1776: To PG.
    Committee did not report, but see 199-P for other action.

### 261 A-P   Cumberland County—Citizens
JHD: 29 Nov. 1776                                                      Cumberland County
Text is similar to 261-P, which see. This petition went to House.
Manuscript signed by thirty-four persons.

### 261 B-P   Cumberland County—Citizens
JHD: 29 Nov. 1776                                                      Cumberland County
Text is similar to 261-P, which see. This petition went to Senate.
Manuscript signed by twenty-one persons.

### 261 C-P   Cumberland County—Citizens
JHD: 29 Nov. 1776                                                      Cumberland County
Text is similar to 261-P, which see. This petition went to Senate.
Manuscript signed by thirteen persons.

### 261 D-P   Cumberland County—Citizens
JHD: 29 Nov. 1776                                                      Cumberland County
Text is similar to 261-P, which see. This petition went to Senate.
Manuscript signed by eighteen persons.

### 261 E-P   Cumberland County—Citizens
JHD: 29 Nov. 1776                                                      Cumberland County
Text is similar to 261-P, which see. This petition went to Senate.
Manuscript signed by thirty-five persons.

### 262-[M]-†Harvie, John and Neaville, Joseph
JHD: 9 Dec. 1776, for action                                Not known
Concerning disposition of plunder captured in raids on Shawanese and Seneca Indian towns in 1774, which Lord Dunmore had promised Virginia troops. This plunder had been sold to troops by commanding officers at a total value of £341 6s. 3½d. (While this is not specifically termed a memorial, it is so listed because of its nature and the claims which resulted.)
Date unknown: To a special committee.
9 Dec. 1776: Committee recommends that, upon sworn testimony of commanding officers, those men who served under them should receive their proportionate share of the total sum from the public treasury.

29 November 1776 – 10 May 1777

House agrees to this and approves "the book of publick claims" to which it added several additional claims.
9 Dec. 1776: Senate agrees.
House agrees to following claim not presented originally as separate item: John Hardin, for wound, £20.
11 Dec. 1776: Senate agrees.
11 Dec. 1776: House rejects following claim not presented originally as a separate item: George Vallendigham, for extra pay.
11 Dec. 1776: House agrees to following claim not presented originally as a separate item: Joseph Bowman, for reimbursement for amounts paid out to deserters, £24 2s. 5d.
13 Dec. 1776: Senate agrees, JS.

### 263-[P]-† Thomas, Isaac
JHD: 14 Dec. 1776            Not known

Compensation for services in warning settlers of Indian raids, he being a resident in Cherokee towns; also for compensation for his personal losses. (This is called a "resolution" in the text, but it is in the nature of a petition.)
14 Dec. 1776: To a special committee.
18 Dec. 1776: Committee recommends £100 for services, but delays any grant for personal losses.
18 Dec. 1776: Senate agrees under name of "Jacob Thomas," JS.
The question of compensation for personal losses was the subject of a new petition in the May 1777 session of the General Assembly. See 370-P-†.

### 264-P-† St. George, Hamilton Usher
JHD: 10 May 1777            Not known

Compensation for a slave who died from jail fever contracted while imprisoned at Williamsburg. St. George had been tried and acquitted by a court as a British sympathizer, but two of his slaves had been seized and jailed before his trial. Both had been returned.
10 May 1777: To PC.
31 May 1777: PC recommends rejection.
House rejects.

### 265-P Cumberland County—Citizens
JHD: 10 May 1777            Cumberland County

Requesting that Cumberland County be divided on the line separating Littleton Parish from Southam Parish.

## Virginia Legislative Petitions

There are six copies of this petition, but all not exactly identical. This particular one is signed by: William Walker, Barlet Angella, Barren Angle, Miller Woodson, Nathan Glen, and forty-six others.
10 May 1777: To PG.
13 May 1777: PG recommends as reasonable and is directed to prepare a bill.
19 May 1777: Amended bill is passed by House.
3 June 1777: Senate passes bill.
    See 265 A-P, 265 B-P, 265 C-P, 265 D-P, and 265 E-P.
    For this act establishing Powhatan County as of 1 July 1777, see 9H322.

### 265 A-P  Cumberland County—Citizens
JHD: 10 May 1777                      Cumberland County
Text is similar to 265-P, which see.
Manuscript is signed by forty persons.

### 265-B-P  Cumberland County—Citizens
JHD: 10 May 1777                      Cumberland County
Text is similar to 265-P, which see.
Manuscript is signed by forty-one persons.

### 265 C-P  Cumberland County—Citizens
JHD: 10 May 1777                      Cumberland County
Text is similar to 265-P, which see.
Manuscript is signed by fifty-two persons.

### 265 D-P  Cumberland County—Citizens
JHD: 10 May 1777                      Cumberland County
Text is similar to 265-P, which see.
Manuscript is signed by fifty-one persons.

### 265 E-P  Cumberland County—Citizens
JHD: 10 May 1777                      Cumberland County
Text is similar to 265-P, which see.
Manuscript is signed by eighty-two persons.

### 266-P-†  Cumberland County—Citizens
JHD: 10 May 1777                      Cumberland County
Opposing division of Cumberland County. (There were several petitions, but the exact number is not known.)

## 10 May 1777

10 May 1777: To PG.
    Committee did not report, but see 255-P for other action.

**267-P-†  Charlotte County—Citizens**
    JHD: 10 May 1777                                                                                               Charlotte County
Requesting that a post rider be employed at public expense to serve areas south and west of Manchester. One is now being paid for privately.
10 May 1777: To PG.
13 May 1777: Carried over to next session of GA.
8 Jan. 1778: PG recommends rejection.
    House rejects.

**268-P  Dixon, Jane**
    JHD: 10 May 1777                                                                                              Norfolk Borough
Seeking full recovery of the estate of her husband, James Dixon, deceased, a portion of which is being held for the other possible heirs, none of which has been found.
    Manuscript unsigned.
10 May 1777: To a special committee.
16 May 1777: Special committee reports that allegation is true. Recommitted to same committee.
20 May 1777: Special committee recommends that the matter should be handled by a court of law.
    House agrees.

**269-P  Anderson, William**
    JHD: 10 May 1777                                                                          Cumberland County
Additional compensation for a slave found guilty of murder and executed.
10 May 1777: Rejected by refusal to refer to a committee.

**270-P-†  Carter, John Jarret**
    JHD: 10 May 1777                                                                                    Not known
Compensation for physical disorder brought on himself by hard duty after meritorious service in 1776.
10 May 1777: To PC.
16 May 1777: PC recommends £15 for present relief.
    House agrees.
19 May 1777: Senate agrees.

## Virginia Legislative Petitions

**271-P-†  Garner, Joseph**
JHD: 12 May 1777                  Not known
Compensation for accidental wound received in military service.
12 May 1777: To PC.
19 May 1777: PC recommends £5 per annum for life.
    House agrees.
22 May 1777: Senate agrees.

**272-P**
Eck–
A163    **Albemarle County—Citizens**
JHD: 12 May 1777               Albemarle County
For division of county into two counties.
  Manuscript has map attached and is signed by: W. Henry, J. Burton, George Duncan, Wm. Oglesby, Wilson Miles Cary, and 127 others.
12 May 1777: To PG.
13 May 1777: PG reports reasonable.
14 May 1777: PG directed to bring in a bill with specified clauses relating to parishes. Bill presented.
19 May 1777: House passes bill and sends to Senate.
3 June 1777: Senate passes bill.
    For act establishing Fluvanna County and Fluvanna Parish, effective 1 July 1777, see 9H325.

**273-P  Charlotte County and Lunenburg County—Citizens**
JHD: 12 May 1777               Charlotte County
                                            Lunenburg County
For adding a small portion of Charlotte County to Lunenburg County.
  Manuscript signed by: Abner Wells, Josiah Whitlock, Thos. Chappell, Sr., Thos. Chappell, Jr., Seth Farley, and sixty-one others.
12 May 1777: To PG.
13 May 1777: PG reports reasonable. Special committee directed to prepare bill.
19 May 1777: Bill presented.
2 June 1777: House passes bill.
4 June 1777: Senate makes amendments for parish purposes.
    House agrees to Senate amendments.
    For this act, including lines for Cornwall Parish and Cumberland Parish, effective 1 October 1777, see 9H327.

## 12 – 13 May 1777

**274-P-†   Miles, Joseph**
          JHD: 12 May 1777                              Not known
  Compensation for loss of eyesight suffered while on military duty in 1776.
  12 May 1777: To PC.
  7 June 1777: PC recommends £30 for present relief and £15 per annum until
          sight is restored.
          House agrees.
  9 June 1777: Senate agrees.

**275-P-†   Roy, Richard and Catlett, John**
          JHD: 12 May 1777                              Caroline County
  Compensation for tobacco, valued at £36 13s, stolen from Roy's warehouse
  in 1772 and 1773 where they were inspectors.
  12 May 1777: To PC.
  12 June 1777: PC recommends rejection.
          House rejects.

**276-P-†   Smith, Isaac and Bowdoin, Preston (Executors of John Bowdoin, deceased)**
          JHD: 13 May 1777                              Not known
  For return of Negro slave sent to lead mines by order of convention.
  13 May 1777: To PC.
  16 May 1777: PC finds reasonable and recommends estate be paid £8 per
          annum for hire from 15 June 1776.
          House agrees.
  19 May 1777: Senate agrees.

**277-P-†   Campbell, John**
          JHD: 13 May 1777                              Not known
  Recompense for the robbery of his partner, James O'Hara, by unfriendly
  Indians, on an expedition to Sanduskey to purchase powder under direction of
  Committee of Safety on 5 January 1776. Goods were valued at £69 4s.,
  redemption of saddle at £3 6s., and time for O'Hara and four horses at £23 5s.
  for thirty-one days of travel.
  13 May 1777: To PC.
  15 May 1777: PC finds reasonable.
          House agrees.
  16 May 1777: Senate agrees.

## Virginia Legislative Petitions

### 278-P     Martinsburg—Citizens
JHD: 14 May 1777               Berkeley County
For legal establishment of Martinsburg as a town.
Manuscript signed by: Michal Bowland, Robt. Cockburn, An. Siling, George Wollenback, Isaac Taylor, and thirty-three others.
14 May 1777: To PG.
16 May 1777: PG finds reasonable and is directed to prepare bill.
> For some reason this bill was not enacted into law until the October 1778 session of General Assembly.
> For this act see 9H569.

### 279-P-†   Coke, Sarah
JHD: 14 May 1777               Not known
Asking for payment of agreed rent of £45 per annum for her house, taken over as a barracks on 18 November 1775, and also compensation for damage done to it.
14 May 1777: To PC.
> Committee apparently did not report.

### 280-P     Mecklenburg County—Citizens
JHD: 14 May 1777               Mecklenburg County
Asking that the resolution concerning British factors be extended to married as well as single persons, that they be required to accept paper money for debts, and that those not showing a friendly disposition to the American cause be required to leave.
Manuscript signed by: Bennett Goode, Thos. Mitchell, John O'Connor, James Bilbo, Wm. Lawrence, and 186 others.
14 May 1777: To PG.
16 May 1777: PG discharged. To SC.
> Committee apparently did not report.

### 281-P-†   M'Kenny, John
JHD: 15 May 1777               Not known
Additional compensation for wounds received in military service in 1774. Has received £30, and £10 per annum.
15 May 1777: To PC.
22 May 1777: PC recommends an additional £5 per annum.
> House agrees.
28 May 1777: Senate agrees.

## 14 – 15 May 1777

**282-M-†  Baker and Hardy**
  JHD: 15 May 1777                                                    Not known

Compensation for rations furnished troops under contract with the Committee of Safety, dated 26 January 1776. This long and involved claim, printed in full with depositions, in various journals, hinges on the apparent fact that the firm was obliged to furnish rations for far more men than was anticipated, and that rising prices and spoilage had caused them great financial loss. Memorial had been presented to governor and Council who referred it to General Assembly.

15 May 1777: To PC.
16 May 1777: PC recommends commissioners be appointed to take depositions.
  House agrees.
24 June 1777: PC recommends £737 17s. 4½d. for flour and pork.
25 June 1777: Senate refers to special committee.
28 June 1777: Senate discharges special committee and carries matter over to next session.
8 Dec. 1777: Baker and Hardy petition House for action on their memorial. To PC.
  Carried over to October 1778 session of GA.
17 Nov. 1778: PC recommends £925 7s. 4½d.
  House agrees.
28 Nov. 1778: Senate agrees.

**283-P-†  Shinn, Levi**
  JHD: 15 May 1777                                                    Not known

Compensation for impressed horse killed by Indians in 1774.

15 May 1777: To PC.
28 May 1777: PC recommends rejection.
  House recommits to same committee.
31 May 1777: PC recommends £15.
  House agrees.
3 June 1777: Senate agrees.

**284-P-†  Smith, Thoroughgood, and Company**
  JHD: 15 May 1777                                                    Not known

For payment of debt of £27 10s. owed by Lord Dunmore.

15 May 1777: To PC.

## Virginia Legislative Petitions

16 June 1777: PC finds reasonable and directs that proportionate part be paid out of sale of Lord Dunmore's effects.
House agrees.
18 June 1777: Senate agrees.

285-P-†
Eck–Not
found **Hickman, George**
JHD: 16 May 1777                            Accomack County
Compensation for rations and lodging for soldiers and for four prisoners of war quartered with him in 1775.
16 May 1777: To PC.
26 May 1777: PC recommends £7 9s. for rations, and recommends that part relating to lodging of soldiers be rejected.
House agrees.
28 May 1777: Senate agrees to £7 9s. for rations.

286-P-† **Washburn, Charles**
JHD: 16 May 1777                            Not known
Additional compensation for service in militia in 1774.
16 May 1777: To PC.
19 May 1777: PC recommends £23 2s.
House rejects.

287-P-† **Cottrell, Anne and Powers, John**
JHD: 16 May 1777                            Not known
Compensation for use of two horses impressed in 1774.
16 May 1777: To PC.
19 May 1777: PC recommends 18s. 9d. for each.
House agrees.
21 May 1777: Senate agrees.

288-P-† **Warner, Daniel**
JHD: 16 May 1777                            Not known
Additional compensation for serving as scout on Virginia frontiers in 1774.
16 May 1777: To PC.
19 May 1777: PC recommends rejection.
House rejects.

## 16 May 1777

**289-P-†    Rose, John**
    JHD: 16 May 1777                                         Not known
Compensation for three hogsheads of tobacco out of twenty swept away by flood of 1771. The three were recovered and sold for benefit of country. They had been stored at Westham.
16 May 1777: To PC.
18 May 1777: Carried over to October 1777 session of GA.
7 Jan. 1778: Carried over to next session of GA.
8 Dec. 1778: PC recommends £7 4s.
    House agrees.
12 Dec. 1778: Senate agrees.

**290-P-†    Wilkins, Willis**
    JHD: 16 May 1777                                         Norfolk County
Asking that order of county committee for his removal from the county for refusing to take loyalty oath be rescinded. Says a "scruple of conscience" is responsible for his refusal, and that he is a friend of America.
16 May 1777: To PG.
20 May 1777: Carried over to next session of GA.
3 Jan. 1778: PG recommends rejection.
    House rejects.

**291-P-†    Orange County—Citizens**
    JHD: 16 May 1777                                         Orange County
Asking that the election of Charles Porter to the House of Delegates be voided because he made use of bribery and corruption.
16 May 1777: To PE.
17 May 1777: PE requests permission to secure depositions.
    House agrees.
9 June 1777: PE recommends rejection.
    House rejects.
    Senate action not required.

**292-P**
Eck-
A832    **Amherst County and Buckingham County—Citizens**
    JHD: 16 May 1777                                         Amherst County
                                                             Buckingham County
To discontinue ferry over Fluvanna (James) River from land of Benjamin Howard in Buckingham County to land of Neil Campbell in Albemarle

County, and to establish a new ferry from each side of the mouth of Rockfish River in counties of Amherst and Albemarle, from lands of William Howard to land of Thomas Anderson in Buckingham.

Manuscript has map attached and is signed by: Richd. Tankersley, William Loving, Ezekiah Bailey, Peter Bibee, George Cockburn, and fifty others.
16 May 1777: To PG.
2 June 1777: PG finds reasonable and is directed to prepare bill.
  For general ferry bill including above, see 9H334.

**293-P**
Eck–
A832  **Amherst County—Citizens**
  JHD: 16 May 1777                               Amherst County
To establish a ferry over Rockfish River from land of William Howard in Amherst County to his land in Albemarle County.

Manuscript signed by: Richd. Tankersley, William Loving, Peter Bibee, James Brown, George Cockburn, and forty-three others.
16 May 1777: To PG.
2 June 1777: PG finds reasonable and is directed to prepare bill.
  For general ferry bill including above, see 9H334.

**294-P-†  Harris, Charles**
  JHD: 17 May 1777                                    Not known
Additional compensation for wound received in Shawanese expedition. Had been originally awarded £17 10s.
17 May 1777: To PC.
23 May 1777: PC recommends additional £7 10s.
  House agrees.
28 May 1777: Senate agrees.

**295-P-†  Lambert, Jonathan and Baker, Christopher**
  JHD: 17 May 1777                                    Not known
Compensation for service in militia, their names having been omitted from the militia roll.
17 May 1777: To PC.
26 May 1777: PC recommends £1 5s. 6d. for Lambert and £9 18s. for Baker.
  House agrees.
28 May 1777: Senate agrees.

## 16 – 17 May 1777

**296-P  Crutcher, Leonard**
　　　　JHD: 17 May 1777　　　　　　　　　　　　　　Not known
　Compensation for robbery of £63 cash from ship chartered by Bridger Goodrich, partner of John Goodrich, Sr., as well as £20 worth of wearing apparel owned by John Mayo. This action took place in April 1776, and the ship was destroyed by fire set by robbers.
　Manuscript unsigned.
17 May 1777: To PG.
　　　　Carried over to October 1778 session of GA.
8 Jan. 1778: Carried over to next session of GA.
13 Oct. 1778: PG recommends rejection of claim of £60 from estate of John Goodrich, Sr., since the subject is cognizable before a court of law.
　　　　House rejects.

**297-P-†  Girty, Simon**
　　　　JHD: 17 May 1777　　　　　　　　　　　　　　Not known
　Additional compensation for services as interpreter in Indian towns in 1775. He had been allowed 5s. per day.
17 May 1777: To PC.
31 May 1777: PC recommends rejection.
　　　　House rejects.

**298-P  Voss, Edward**
　　　　JHD: 17 May 1777　　　　　　　　　　Spotsylvania County
　Additional compensation for Negro slave, tried and executed for burglary.
　Manuscript unsigned and addressed to "Convention."
17 May 1777: Rejected by refusal to refer to a committee.

**299-P-†  Fear, Hamner**
　　　　JHD: 17 May 1777　　　　　　　　　　　　　　Not known
　Compensation for wound accidentally received in 1776 from a guard.
17 May 1777: To PC.
26 May 1777: PC recommends £20 for present relief.
　　　　House agrees.
28 May 1777: Senate agrees.

**300-P-†  Lewis, Thomas**
　　　　JHD: 17 May 1777　　　　　　　　　　　Nansemond County
　Compensation for broken leg received by horse while in military service.
17 May 1777: To PC.

89

## Virginia Legislative Petitions

26 May 1777: PC recommends rejection of £14 19s. for surgeon's fees and board.

House disagrees and recommits to same committee.

20 June 1777: PC recommends £9 19s. for fees and board.

House agrees.

23 June 1777: Senate amends.

No record found of House agreeing to Senate amendment.

301-P
Eck–
A833 **Hay, Charles; Johnson, William; Horsley, Robert; Magann, Merritt; Woodroof, John; Brown, John; Floyd, Mitchell; Smith, Thomas; Pendleton, Edmund; Shelden, Thomas; Welt, George; Wade, Pearce; and Guttery, John**
JHD: 17 May 1777            Amherst County

Compensation for surgeon to treat violent disorders incurred in military service in June and July 1776, in the amount of £17 15s. 2d.; for John Guttery, £3 9s. 6d.

Manuscript unsigned, but has a list of accounts due.

17 May 1777: To PC.

26 May 1777: PC recommends (1) £2 0s. 9d. for Hay, £1 0s. 6d. for Johnson, 8s. 9d. for Horsley, £1 12s. 6d. for Magann, £1 17s. 4d. for Woodroof, £1 0s. 6d. for Brown, £1 0s. 6d. for Pendleton, and £1 15s. 9d. for Wade; and (2) recommends rejection of Floyd, Smith, Shelden, Welt, and Guttery.

House agrees to (1) and (2).

28 May 1777: Senate agrees.

302-P-† **M'Clannahan, William**
JHD: 17 May 1777            Not known

Compensation for lighter (ship) impressed in June 1776, which has not been returned and is presumed to be lost.

17 May 1777: To PC (PG?).

20 May 1777: Carried over to October 1777 session of GA.

7 Jan. 1778: Carried over to May 1778 session of GA.

20 Nov. 1778: PG recommends rejection.

House rejects.

303-P    **Long, Robert**
JHD: 17 May 1777            Culpeper County

## 17 May 1777

Compensation for disability incurred while serving in militia in 1775. Manuscript unsigned.
17 May 1777: To PC.
20 June 1777: Carried over to October 1777 session of GA.
19 Nov. 1777: PC recommends £30.
   House agrees.
21 Nov. 1777: Senate agrees.

### 304-P-†   Mayle, Lydia
  JHD: 17 May 1777              Norfolk County

Compensation for damage to houses and estate of her late husband, Dr. Charles Mayle, located at Great Bridge, by Virginia troops stationed there from 28 November 1775 to 28 June 1776.
17 May 1777: To SC.
   Committee apparently did not report.

### 305-P-†   Truss, Gideon
  JHD: 17 May 1777              Norfolk County

Compensation for damages to his houses at Great Bridge from Virginia troops stationed there from 30 November 1775 until 12 July 1776.
17 May 1777: To SC.
   Committee apparently did not report.

### 306-P-†   Truss, Josiah
  JHD: 17 May 1777              Norfolk County

Compensation for damages to his houses and property at Great Bridge from Virginia troops stationed there from 5 February to 12 July 1776.
17 May 1777: To SC.
   Committee apparently did not report.

### 307-P-†   Smith, William
  JHD: 17 May 1777              Norfolk County

Compensation for damage to his house and property at Great Bridge from Virginia troops stationed there from 28 November 1775 to 12 July 1776.
17 May 1777: To SC.
   Committee apparently did not report.

### 308-M   Marine Officers
  JHD: 17 May 1777                Not known

For preservation of their rank on equal terms as those of the minute officers.

## Virginia Legislative Petitions

Manuscript signed by: John Allison, James Quarles, Ben. Pollard, Thos. Meriwether, Thos. Hamilton, and two others.

17 May 1777: Referred to special committee.

21 May 1777: Special committee recommends that marine officers now in land service have same rank as minute officers.

    Petition recommitted to same committee and committee augmented.

    For action see 310-M.

### 309-P   Humphreys, Joshua; Parry, Joshua; Simpson, Alexander; and Garbert, Jacob
JHD: 19 May 1777                          Not known

Requesting a subsidy to manufacture firearms.

Manuscript is signed by petitioners as listed above.

19 May 1777: To PG.

18 June 1777: PG recommends rejection.

    House rejects.

### 310-M   Army Officers
JHD: 19 May 1777                          Not known

Objecting to marine officers, with less service, having the same rank as minute officers.

Manuscript apparently at one time had a list of those signing, but this is now missing.

19 May 1777: To special committee.

21 May 1777: Committee recommends that marine officers in land service have the same rank as minute officers.

    Petition recommitted to same committee and committee augmented.

27 May 1777: Committee recommends that this memorial, along with 308-M, be referred to governor and Council.

### 311-P-*
Eck–Not found   **Bedford County and Henry County—Citizens**
JHD: 20 May 1777                    Bedford County
                                          Henry County

Asking for a division of Bedford County.

From notes in the manuscript files it would appear petitions both for and against some division of the county were presented, but it does not appear how

## 19 – 20 May 1777

many there were in each category. These petitions were once extant, but they cannot now be found.
20 May 1777: To PG.
   Committee apparently did not report.

**312-P-\***
Eck–Not
found  **Bedford County and Henry County—Citizens**
   JHD: 20 May 1777      Bedford County
                   Henry County
  Against a division of Bedford County.
   See 311-P-\*.

**313-P-†** **Price, Thomas**
   JHD: 20 May 1777      Norfolk Borough
Compensation for five cannons impressed by the military for use at Kemp's landing and captured by British.
20 May 1777: To PC.
12 June 1777: PC recommends £20 for cannon and carriages and 15s. for
   canvas bags.
   House agrees.
14 June 1777: Senate agrees.

**314-M** **Bruton Parish, York County and James City County—**
    **Wardens and Vestry**
   JHD: 20 May 1777      York County
                   James City County
  Relief from uneven obligations imposed upon them for support of poor and vagrants and establishment of workhouses for persons coming into the parish from other areas.
  Manuscript unsigned.
20 May 1777: To PG.
31 May 1777: PG finds reasonable.
   House directs PG to prepare bill for relief for several parishes.
   Bill apparently not presented.

**315-P** **Campbell, Arthur and Edmondson, William**
   JHD: 20 May 1777      Washington County
  Seeking to invalidate the elections of Anthony Bledsoe and William Cocke

as members of the House of Delegates on charges of voting irregularities, bribery, and corruption.
Manuscript unsigned.
20 May 1777: To PE.
2 June 1777: PE recommends rejection, a long report of which is printed in JHD.
    House rejects.
    Senate action not required.

**316-P-†**   **Woodie, James**
JHD: 21 May 1777                            Norfolk County
                                                Princess Anne County
Compensation for removal of citizens of Norfolk and Princess Anne counties to interior, and removal of rope works from Norfolk to Warwick in Chesterfield County.
21 May 1777: To PC.
23 May 1777: PC recommends £48 14s.
    House agrees.
28 May 1777: Senate agrees.

**317-P**   **Alexander, James; Gwin, James; Hanley, James; Tincher, Francis; and Blanton, William**
JHD: 21 May 1777                           Greenbrier County
Requesting that General Andrew Lewis be required to sell them titles to land that they had settled and improved between 1770 and 1773.
Manuscript signed by: Robert Thomson, Samuell Calwell, John Cincade, William Craig, Archld. Handley, and three others.
21 May 1777: To SC.
    Committee apparently did not report.

**318-P**   **Lunenburg County—Court and Citizens, and Cumberland Parish—Vestry**
JHD: 21 May 1777                           Lunenburg County
To allow collections of levy for parish to be paid in money rather than tobacco.
Manuscript signed by: Thomas Tabb, John Ragsdale, Wm. Taylor, Lodowick Farmer, Everard Dowsing, and forty-one others.
21 May 1777: To PG.
2 June 1777: PG recommends rejection.
    House rejects.

## 21 – 23 May 1777

**319-P-†   Wilkinson, Mills**
          JHD: 21 May 1777                              Not known
  Compensation for escaped slave, captured, and sent to West Indies by order of Committee of Safety in January 1776. John Dixon's ship was captured by British, and slave lost.
21 May 1777: To PC.
20 June 1777: Carried over to October 1777 session of GA.
7 Jan. 1778: Carried over to next session of GA.
          No further action found.

**320-P    Cumberland County—Citizens**
          JHD: 21 May 1777                         Cumberland County
  For maintaining established church and allowing certain privileges to dissenters.
  Manuscript signed by: Zach. Hendrick, John Hendrick, Jno. Griffin, George Pollard, Cliffinden Woodroof, and seven others.
21 May 1777: House carries over to next session of GA.
6 Nov. 1777: To R.
          Carried over to next session of GA.
4 Dec. 1778: R recommends rejection.
          House rejects.

**321-P-†   Rowe, Hansford**
          JHD: 22 May 1777                              Not known
  Compensation for slave who escaped to Lord Dunmore in December 1775, was held in Williamsburg jail for deportation, and there died.
22 May 1777: To PC.
20 June 1777: PC recommends rejection.
          House rejects.

**322-P    Ellis, John**
          JHD: 23 May 1777                              Williamsburg
  As agent of William Lee of London, requesting compensation for damages done to buildings in Williamsburg, owned by Lee, and used as barracks and hospitals by Virginia troops. Damage estimated at £500.
  Manuscript unsigned.
23 May 1777: To PC.
9 June 1777: PC discharged. To SC.
          Committee apparently did not report.

## Virginia Legislative Petitions

**323-M**
Eck–Not
found   **Lynch, Charles**
JHD: 24 May 1777                                           Bedford County
   Asking that rates be established for hire of slaves from public jail for manufacture of saltpeter and gunpowder, and price to be paid for gunpowder.
   Manuscript unsigned.
24 May 1777: To PG.
7 June 1777: PG recommends (1) that following to be paid: £7 to estate of Andrew Sprowle, £10 to Charles Stewart, £7 to John Saunders, £4 again to John Saunders, £10 to Charles Mifflin, £10 to John Goodrich, £3 to estate of John Dunn, £5 to Anthony Warwick, £10 to Miss Keeling, such hire to begin 1 July 1776 and terminate 30 November 1778; and (2) that powder be paid for at rate of 6s. per pound until 31 December 1778.
   House agrees to (1).
12 June 1777: House agrees to (2).
14 June 1777: Senate agrees to (1) and (2).

**324-P**   **Botetourt County, Washington County, and Montgomery County—Citizens**
JHD: 24 May 1777                                           Botetourt County
                                                           Washington County
                                                           Montgomery County
   For relief from exorbitant prices charged for land by proprietors of large land grants made to private companies.
   Manuscript signed by: Charles Allison, John Rodgers, Edward Smith, William Thornton, Charles Bowen, and 144 others.
24 May 1777: To SC.
   Committee apparently did not report.

**325-P**   **Smith, William and Bressie, Henry**
JHD: 26 May 1777                                           Norfolk County
   Compensation for depredations by British troops.
   Manuscript unsigned. Has attached a list of goods and provisions stolen and burned by British troops.
26 May 1777: Rejected by refusal to refer to a committee.

**326-P-†**   **Montgomery County—Citizens**
JHD: 26 May 1777                                           Montgomery County

For altering the boundary line between Montgomery and Washington counties. (There were several petitions of this nature, but the exact number is not known.)
26 May 1777: To PG.
    PG reports reasonable and is directed to prepare a bill.
21 June 1777: Bill presented. Referred to ad hoc committee.
26 June 1777: Committee amends.
    House agrees.
27 June 1777: Senate agrees.
    For this act, effective 1 September 1777, see 9H330.

**327-P-†**   **Washington County—Citizens**
    JHD: 26 May 1777                       Washington County
Opposing the altering of the boundary line between Montgomery and Washington counties. (There were several petitions of this nature, but the exact number is not known.)
26 May 1777: To PG.
    Committee did not report.
    See action on 326-P-†.

**328-P**   **Riddick, Constantine**
    JHD: 27 May 1777                             Hanover County
Compensation for ship and cargo seized by Lord Dunmore in September 1775.
Manuscript unsigned, but has a price list attached.
27 May 1777: Rejected by refusal to refer to a committee.

**329-P**   **Harrison, Charles**
    JHD: 27 May 1777                                   Not known
Requesting permission, on orders from George Washington, to have his regiment inoculated for smallpox.
Manuscript unsigned.
27 May 1777: Laid on table.
    Apparently never taken up.
    For act in October 1777 session concerning inoculation for civilians, see 9H374.

**330-P-†**   **Langley, Robert**
    JHD: 27 May 1777                                   Not known

## Virginia Legislative Petitions

Seeking return of a slave captured in Lord Dunmore's service and sent to lead mines. Also seeking payment for his hire.
27 May 1777: To PC.
16 June 1777: PC recommends (1) rejection of return of slave, and (2) hire to be set at £12 per annum from 3 April 1776.
> House agrees.

17 June 1777: Senate agrees.

**331-P-†  Keeling, William; Hancock, John; Jones, Mary; Henley, John; and Keeling, William, Jr.**
JHD: 27 May 1777                                   Not known

Seeking return of slaves captured in Lord Dunmore's service and sent to lead mines. Also seeking payment for hire.
27 May 1777: To PC.
16 June 1777: PC recommends (1) rejection of return of slaves, and (2) payment for hire: £12 to Keeling, £12 to Hancock, £15 to Henley, £10 to Keeling, Jr. (all the above from 12 February 1776), £12 to Jones, £12 less £4 already paid again to Jones (all the above from 20 March 1776).
> House agrees.

17 June 1777: Senate agrees.

**332-P-†  Westmoreland County and King George County—Citizens**
JHD: 27 May 1777                              Westmoreland County
                                                                          King George County

Seeking the addition of a part of Westmoreland County to King George County. (There were several petitions of this nature, but the exact number is not known.)
27 May 1777: To PG.
> Carried over to October 1777 session of GA when various counter petitions were presented on 18 November 1777.

25 Nov. 1777: PG recommends that a counter petition from King George County be rejected.
> House agrees.

25 Nov. 1777: PG recommends that part of Westmoreland be added to King George County and part of King George be added to Westmoreland County. Bill to be drawn.
18 Jan. 1778: Bill passed and sent to Senate.
21 Jan. 1778: Senate amends.

## 27 – 28 May 1777

23 Jan. 1778: House agrees to Senate amendments.
For this act, effective 20 March 1778, see 9H432.

**333-M  College of William and Mary—Rector, Visitors, and Governors**
JHD: 28 May 1777                                             Williamsburg
Requesting that a fund be established by the General Assembly for support of the college. Contains a detailed account of the college's income and expenditures over a ten-year period and its mounting expenses.
Manuscript unsigned, but has accounts attached and a statement of the facilities available, including the library.
28 May 1777: To SC.
12 June 1777: SC discharged and no further action taken.
See 488-P and 791-P-†.

**334-P-†  Newell, Elizabeth**
JHD: 28 May 1777                                             Not known
Compensation for death of her husband, Samuel Newell, who was killed by Indians in January 1777 while carrying dispatches to the Cherokees.
28 May 1777: To PC.
2 June 1777: PC recommends £20 for current relief, and £10 per annum for three years to be paid out by Walker Crocket and John Montgomery for her and her children.
House agrees.
4 June 1777 Senate agrees.
See 335-P-†.

**335-P-†  Newell, James (Administrator of Samuel Newell, deceased)**
JHD: 28 May 1777                                             Not known
Compensation for horse, rifle, saddle, saddlebags, and clothes taken by Indians who killed Samuel Newell.
28 May 1777: To PC.
2 June 1777: PC recommends £58 15s.
House agrees.
4 June 1777: Senate agrees.
See 334-P-†.

**336-P-†  Hampshire County—Citizens**
JHD: 28 May 1777                                             Hampshire County
For establishment of town of Moorefield, to be named for Conrad Moore.

## Virginia Legislative Petitions

28 May 1777: Permission granted for a bill to be prepared.
        Carried over to October 1777 session of GA.
        For act establishing Moorefield, see 9H425.

### 337-
**Address   Mecklenburg County—Citizens**
    JHD: 29 May 1777                        Mecklenburg County

For maintaining the Church of England, and postponing debate on the subject until quieter times.

Manuscript signed by: Robert Larkin, Austin Wright, Ephraim Andrew, Jno. Cardan, Edw. Waller, and seventy-three others, some illegible. (The body of this address is printed, and this is the first example so found.)

29 May 1777: To R.
        Manuscript endorsement says referred to next session of GA, but it apparently was carried over to the October 1778 session.

4 Dec. 1778: Again carried over, but no further action found.

### 338-P   Fairfax County—Citizens
    JHD: 29 May 1777                                Fairfax County

Requesting a new election of delegates from Fairfax to General Assembly because smallpox was raging on 21 April 1777 in Alexandria, the polling place, and only about 60 of 300 freeholders voted.

Manuscript is addressed to House of Burgesses and is signed by: Thomas Lester, Daniel Jenkins, John Hurst, Phillip Grimes, Benja. Southard, and 128 others.

29 May 1777: To PE.
31 May 1777: PE recommends rejection.
        House rejects.

### 339-P-† Wilkinson, Cary (Agent for John Paradise, of London)
    JHD: 30 May 1777                                    Not known

Compensation for bill owed by Lord Dunmore, in amount of £182 2s.

30 May 1777: To PC.
16 June 1777: PC recommends that an amount, proportionate to other creditors, be paid from sale of Lord Dunmore's effects.
        House agrees.

18 June 1777: Senate agrees.

### 340-P-† Elliot, Elizabeth
    JHD: 30 May 1777                                    Norfolk County

## 29 – 30 May 1777

Compensation for warehouse at Kemp's landing, burned through negligence of Virginia troops quartered there.
30 May 1777: To PC.
12 June 1777: PC recommends rejection.
    House rejects.

**341-P    Hansborough, Peter**
    JHD: 30 May 1777                    Stafford County
Compensation for slave held for five months in Stafford County jail on suspicion of administering poison, who could not be tried for want of a court. He became frostbitten, lost a leg, and, after release, he died.
    Manuscript unsigned.
30 May 1777: To PC.
18 June 1777: Carried over to next session of GA.
7 Jan. 1778: Carried over to next session of GA.
8 Dec. 1778: Carried over to next session of GA.
    There is no further record.

**342-P    Dix, John**
    JHD: 30 May 1777                    Pittsylvania County
For discontinuing ferry over Dan River from his land to land of Robert Payne, and establishing a ferry, in about the same spot, to land he had purchased on Payne's side of the river.
    Manuscript unsigned, but dated 29 May 1777 on endorsement.
30 May 1777: To PG.
2 June 1777: PG finds reasonable and is directed to prepare a bill, which was
    approved by House and Senate.
    For this act see 9H334.

**343-P-†    Roane, Sarah**
    JHD: 30 May 1777                    Not known
For return of slave who was captured on way to join Lord Dunmore and was sent to lead mines. Also asks for hire.
30 May 1777: To PC.
16 June 1777: PC recommends rejection of return of slave, but recommends
    hire be set at £12 per annum from 16 July 1776.
    House agrees.
17 June 1777: Senate agrees to hire.

## Virginia Legislative Petitions

**344-P-†   Daniel, George (Guardian of William Murray)**
JHD: 30 May 1777                                                    Not known
For return of slave who was captured on way to join Lord Dunmore and was sent to lead mines. Also asks for hire.
30 May 1777: To PC.
16 June 1777: PC recommends rejection of return of slave, but recommends hire be set at £12 per annum from 16 July 1776.
   House agrees.
17 June 1777: Senate agrees to hire.

**345-P   Love, Phillip; Rowland, James; Rowland, Thomas; Barnes, Thomas; and Armstrong, John**
JHD: 30 May 1777                                                    Botetourt County
As remaining members of vestry of Botetourt Parish, they cite their inability to direct the affairs of the parish since it has been divided, for some members have resigned, others now reside outside of the parish, and the rector has not been paid for three years.
Manuscript signed by all of the petitioners.
30 May 1777: To R.
18 June 1777: R recommends that vestry be dissolved and a new one be elected.
   House agrees and incorporates this resolution in a bill allowing the vestry to sell the glebe and purchase a new one.
23 June 1777: Bill amended and passed.
26 June 1777: Senate passes bill.
   For this act see 9H318.

**346-P-†   Christian, William**
JHD: 30 May 1777                                                    Not known
Additional compensation for service in Cherokee expedition as commander of two battalions.
30 May 1777: To PC.
31 May 1777: PC recommends additional pay of £57 7s. 6d.
   House agrees.
3 June 1777: Senate amends, substituting pay of £38 2s. 6d.
   House disagrees.
   Senate insists on amendments.
9 June 1777: House recedes and approves Senate amendments.

## 30 May 1777

**347-P-†  Simpson, Southey**
JHD: 30 May 1777                                                   Not known
Compensation for transporting sulphur and gunpowder on Eastern Shore for shipping to Williamsburg; also for the purchase of 267½ pounds of lead.
30 May 1777: To PC.
2 June 1777: PC recommends £30 7s. 7½d.
    House agrees.
4 June 1777: Senate agrees.

**348-P   Collis, Thomas**
JHD: 30 May 1777                                         Prince William County
Compensation for loss of furniture and crops used by militia at his houses. Manuscript unsigned.
30 May 1777: To PC.
18 June 1777: Carried over to next session of GA.
7 Jan. 1778: Carried over to next session of GA.
20 Nov. 1778: PC recommends rejection.
    House rejects.

**349-P-†  Taylor, James**
JHD: 30 May 1777                                                Norfolk County
Compensation for two slaves who were removed to Great Bridge to help prepare fortifications and there died; also for cattle and sheep driven from his plantation and lost.
30 May 1777: To PC.
2 June 1777: PC recommends (1) compensation for slaves be rejected, and (2) that £27 10s. be paid for lost cattle and sheep.
    Recommitted to PC.
9 June 1777: PC discharged. To SC.
    SC did not report.
30 Oct. 1778: Petition again presented. To PC.
5 Nov. 1778: PC recommends £110 for slaves, £9 10s. for sheep, and £18 for cattle.
    House agrees.
23 Nov. 1778: Senate agrees.

**350-P-†  Norfolk Borough—Citizens**
JHD: 30 May 1777                                              Norfolk Borough
For laying out and rebuilding Norfolk borough in a more convenient plan, and for compensation for those who may be sufferers thereby.

## Virginia Legislative Petitions

30 May 1777: To a special committee.
5 June 1777: Committee finds reasonable, and recommends that commissioners be appointed to lay out the borough and to determine compensation.
    House agrees and directs committee to prepare a bill.
27 June 1777: Bill passed. Senate amends.
    House agrees.
    For this act see 9H314.

**351-P-†    M'Cue, William**
    JHD: 31 May 1777, for action        Not known
Compensation for loss of left hand by bursting of a rifle while he was stationed on Staten Island.
Date unknown: To PC.
31 May 1777: PC recommends £20 for current relief and £10 per annum for life.
    House agrees.
7 June 1777: Senate agrees.

**352-P-†    Smith, James**
    JHD: 31 May 1777, for action        Not known
Additional compensation for services as a sergeant in Shawanese expedition.
Date unknown: To PC.
31 May 1777: PC recommends £6 14s.
    House agrees.
6 June 1777: Senate rejects, JS.

**353-P-†    Philips, Thomas**
    JHD: 31 May 1777, for action        Not known
Compensation for impressed smooth-bored gun that was lost.
Date unknown: To PC.
31 May 1777: PC recommends £2 15s.
    House agrees.
7 June 1777: Senate agrees.

**354-P-†    Gilmore, John and Moore, John**
    JHD: 31 May 1777, for action        Not known
Compensation for additional military service in expedition against Shawanese in 1774.
Date unknown: To PC.

## 31 May 1777

31 May 1777: PC recommends £1 10s. for Gilmore and £2 5s. for Moore.
    House agrees.
7 June 1777: Senate agrees.

**355-P-†  Lyle, John**                                          Not known
    JHD: 31 May 1777
    Compensation for horse employed in expedition against Shawanese that appeared to be injured and died.
Date unknown: To PC.
31 May 1777: PC recommends rejection.
    House rejects.

**356-P-†  Rollin, James**                                Not known
    JHD: 31 May 1777, for action
    Compensation for extra time served in militia.
Date unknown: To PC.
31 May 1777: PC recommends £1 4s. 6d.
    House agrees.
7 June 1777: Senate agrees.

**357-P-†  Barnaby, Elias**                                Not known
    JHD: 31 May 1777
    Compensation for loss of services of five indentured servants, serving as shoemakers, who enlisted in the Continental service.
31 May 1777: To PC (PG?).
20 June 1777: Carried over to next session of GA.
7 Jan. 1778: Carried over to next session of GA.
20 Nov. 1778: PG recommends rejection.
    House rejects.

**358-P-†  Saint Anne's Parish, Essex County—Citizens**
    JHD: 31 May 1777                            Essex County
    Asking dissolution of vestry of parish for irregular proceedings.
31 May 1777: Carried over to next session of GA.
    No further record found.

**359-P  Jett, Thomas**
    JHD: 31 May 1777                          Westmoreland County

## Virginia Legislative Petitions

Asking for removal of Bray's tobacco warehouse from town of Leeds to his adjoining property.
Manuscript unsigned.
31 May 1777: House orders clause for removal to be inserted in general tobacco warehouse act.
For general act see 9H331.

### 360-P-* Sydnor, Giles
JHD: 31 May 1777                                  Richmond County
Recompense for money he received as bounty for enlisting in Continental service, of which he was robbed.
31 May 1777: To PC.
7 June 1777: PC recommends rejection.
   House rejects.

### 361-P-† Maxwell, James
JHD: 31 May 1777                                  Not known
Compensation for slave who joined Lord Dunmore's forces, was captured, and died in jail.
31 May 1777: To PC.
16 June 1777: PC recommends rejection.
   House rejects.

### 362-P Cooper, John
JHD: 31 May 1777                                  Norfolk County
Compensation for a slave who, in an attempt to join her husband who had defected to Lord Dunmore, was taken aboard the ship belonging to Andrew Sprowle, where her husband was. Sprowle refused to return her, and she accompanied Dunmore's fleet to Gwynn's Island where Sprowle died. The slave had never been found.
Manuscript unsigned.
31 May 1777: To PG.
7 June 1777: PG recommends payment of £55 from Sprowle's estate.
   House agrees.
23 June 1777: Senate agrees.

### 363-P-† Washington County—Citizens
JHD: 31 May 1777                                  Washington County
Seeking a new boundary line between Washington and Ohio counties. (There were several petitions, but the exact number is not known.)

## 31 May – 2 June 1777

31 May 1777: To PG.
> Committee did not report, and there is no record of a boundary change.

**364-P-†   King George County—Citizens**
   JHD: 2 June 1777                                      King George County
Opposing alteration of county lines as proposed by citizens of Westmoreland and Stafford counties. (There were several petitions, but the exact number is not known.)
2 June 1777: To PG
> See 332-P-†.

**365-P-†   Essex County—Citizens**
   JHD: 2 June 1777                                      Essex County
For reestablishment of Bowler's tobacco warehouse since the new Piscataway warehouse is inconvenient.
2 June 1777: To PG.
7 June 1777: PG recommends rejection.
> House rejects.

**366-P-†   Harrison, Burr**
   JHD: 2 June 1777                                      Not known
Compensation for money and provisions lost by the accidental sinking of his bateaux in the Ohio River in December 1776 when he, as paymaster and contractor, was trying to provision troops.
2 June 1777: To PG.
7 June 1777: PG recommends that commissioners be appointed to take depositions from witnesses, and that further consideration be carried over to the next session of GA.
> House agrees.

14 June 1777: Senate agrees.
8 Nov. 1777: PG recommends, after examining depositions, that Harrison be reimbursed £724 4s. for money lost, and £134 3s. 6d. for flour and salt damaged and lost.
> House agrees.

14 Nov. 1777: Senate agrees.

**367-M   Hazard, Ebenezer**
   JHD: 2 June 1777                                      Williamsburg

## Virginia Legislative Petitions

Asking that all postal workers be exempt from military duty and not be required to furnish a substitute.
Manuscript unsigned, but dated 2 June 1777.
2 June 1777: House lays on table.
> Apparently no further action taken, but for militia act that, among other things, exempts postmasters, see 9H267.

368-P-†     **Eaton, Amos; Shelby, Evan; Kincannon, James; Richardson, Abel; Beaty, John; M'Gaffock, James; Getwood, David; Aylett, James; Sawyers, William; Barnett, Robert; and Dunlop, Ephraim**
           JHD: 2 June 1777                          Not known

Compensation for destruction of cornfields, oat fields, meadows, and other property by troops on Cherokee expedition in August 1776.
2 June 1777: To PC.
12 June 1777: PC recommends (1) that Eaton be paid £52 10s. and (2) that
> petitions of Shelby, Kincannon, Richardson, Beaty, Getwood, Aylett, Sawyers, Barnett, Dunlop, and M'Gaffock be rejected.
> House agrees to (1).

14 June 1777: Senate agrees to (1).
6 Dec. 1777: PC, on reconsideration, recommends £20 for Barnett, £13 for
> Kincannon, £15 for Shelby, and £12 for Sawyers.
> House agrees.

13 Dec. 1777: Senate agrees.

**369-M**
Eck–
A1094     **Matthews, Sampson and Sinclair, Alexander**
           JHD: 2 June 1777                          Staunton

Requesting subsidy of £2,500 for purchase of Negroes to work in a linen and sail duck manufactory that had been authorized by General Assembly.
Manuscript unsigned.
2 June 1777: To PG.
20 June 1777: PG recommends rejection.
> House rejects.

370-P-†     **Thomas, Isaac**
           JHD: 2 June 1777                          Not known

Compensation for goods lost and a slave drowned by Indians when he fled Cherokee country to warn frontiers of the planned war.

## 2 – 3 June 1777

2 June 1777: To PG.
8 Jan. 1778: Carried over to next session of GA.
13 Oct. 1778: PG recommends rejection.
      House rejects.

**371-P-†   Cocke, William**
      JHD: 2 June 1777                             Not known
Compensation for destruction of cornfields by troops in late expedition against Cherokees in September 1776.
2 June 1777: To PC.
12 June 1777: PC recommends £99 10s.
      House agrees.
14 June 1777: Senate agrees.

**372-P-†   Owen, William; Owen, John; Ripley, Thomas; and Ripley, Andrew**
      JHD: 2 June 1777                             Not known
Compensation for extra expenses for illness contracted while on military duty.
2 June 1777: To PC.
20 June 1777: PC recommends rejection.
      House rejects.

**373-P-†   Duncom, Elizabeth**
      JHD: 2 June 1777                             Not known
Compensation for death of husband in Cherokee expedition, she being a cripple with five helpless children.
2 June 1777: To PC.
16 June 1777: PC recommends £20 for present relief and £5 per annum for five years to be administered by Anthony Bledsoe and William Cocke.
      House amends, changing £5 to £10, and agrees.
18 June 1777: Senate agrees.

**374-P-†   Ballard, William**
      JHD: 3 June 1777                           Norfolk County
Compensation for impressed lumber used to build forts at Great Bridge.
3 June 1777: To PC.
9 June 1777: PC discharged. To SC.
      Committee apparently did not report.

## Virginia Legislative Petitions

**375-P   Northumberland County—Citizens**
JHD: 3 June 1777                                         Northumberland County
For establishing tobacco warehouses on both sides of Wicomico River under separate inspections.
Manuscript signed by: Thos. Gaskins, J. Eustace, Wm. Taylor, Willson Nutt, John Leland, and 103 others.
3 June 1777: To PG.
7 June 1777: PG recommends as reasonable and CJ directed to add to tobacco inspection bill a clause to this effect.
For general tobacco inspection bill including above, see 9H331.

**376-P-†   Avery, Billy Haley and Grubb, James**
JHD: 3 June 1777                                         Pittsylvania County
Compensation for apprehending counterfeiters, Benjamin Woodward and the Cooks, transporting them to Williamsburg, and returning them to Pittsylvania County.
3 June 1777: To PC.
16 June 1777: PC recommends Avery receive £25 and Grubb receive £35. House agrees.
18 June 1777: Senate amends by reducing amount to Avery by deducting £13 13s. that had already been paid.
26 June 1777: House agrees to Senate amendments.
For probable reference to same counterfeiters, see 122-P-† and 145-P-*.

**377-M   Presbyterian Church (Hanover Presbytery)—Members**
JHD: 3 June 1777                                 Hanover County and Surroundings
For exemption of dissenters of every denomination from levies to support any church whatsoever. (Refers to 160-P. The extent of Hanover Presbytery is not defined.)
Manuscript dated Timber Ridge, 25 April 1777, and is signed: Richd. Tankey, moderator.
3 June 1777: House carries over to next session of GA.
8 Jan. 1778: This may have been carried over to the next session of GA, but the entry is not clearly identified.
No further action found.

**378-P   Sayer, Charles**
JHD: 3 June 1777                                         Norfolk County (?)
For return of slave, with hire, who was captured in service of Lord Dunmore

## 3 June 1777

and sent to lead mines, where he later escaped from the hospital, but was probably recaptured and returned.
 Manuscript unsigned.
3 June 1777: To PC.
16 June 1777: PC recommends rejection.
  House recommits to PC.
  Carried over to next session of GA.
7 Jan. 1778: Carried over to next session of GA.
8 Dec. 1778: Carried over to next session of GA.
  No further action found.

**379-P-†**   **Watson, Christopher**
  JHD: 3 June 1777             Not known
 Compensation for illness contracted in Indian expedition of 1776 from which it seems likely he will not recover.
3 June 1777: To PC.
12 June 1777: PC recommends £20.
  House agrees.
14 June 1777: Senate agrees.

**380-P**
**Eck-A4**   **Arbuckle, James**
  JHD: 3 June 1777            Accomack County
 Compensation for selecting site and building saltworks in Accomack County.
 Manuscript unsigned.
3 June 1777: To special committee on saltworks.
9 June 1777: Special committee recommends £33 7s. 3d.
  House agrees.
14 June 1777: Senate agrees.

**381-P-†**   **Tomer, Thomas; Brannum, John; Tredley, Michael; Burnett, Mary; Bannerman, Benjamin; Thompson, Isaac; Miller, James; Hodges, Ferebee; Scott, John; and Blake, Richard**
  JHD: 3 June 1777             Portsmouth
 Compensation for damages to their houses in Portsmouth, which were seized for barracks by Virginia troops.
3 June 1777: To PC.
9 June 1777: PC discharged. To SC.
  SC apparently did not report.

## Virginia Legislative Petitions

**382-P-†    Powell, Seymour**
JHD: 3 June 1777                                          Yorktown
Compensation for damages to his houses, pastures, and timber from Virginia troops quartered there. He has moved his residence to the town of Hanover.
3 June 1777: To SC.
    SC apparently did not report.

**383-P    Willoughby, John, Jr.**
JHD: 3 June 1777                                          Norfolk County
Compensation for eighty-seven slaves located on property of his late father, John Willoughby, at Willoughby Point. The slaves escaped to Lord Dunmore and have not been recaptured.
Manuscript unsigned, and has a list of slaves attached.
3 June 1777: House rejects by refusal to refer to a committee.

**384-M    Indiana—Proprietors**
JHD: 3 June 1777                                          Ohio River Lands
Expressing the hope that no act will be passed impeaching or prejudicing their titles to lands paid for by treaty with Indians and in recompense for depredations committed by them. The boundaries of the memorialists' lands are given and the lands valued at £85, 916 10s. 6d.
Manuscript dated at Fort Pitt on 12 March 1777 and unsigned. There are two copies, the larger of which has attached the Indian treaty of 1769. An additional copy of a memorial on the same subject presented by J. Thomas Wharton, vice-president of the company, and dated at Philadelphia, 1 October 1776, is also attached. This has wax seal of Pennsylvania. Indian signatures are by signs.
3 June 1777: To SC.
    Committee apparently did not report.
    For a discussion of the Indiana claims, see Thomas Perkins Abernathy, *Western Lands and the American Revolution* (New York, 1937).

**385-P    Rachel and Rachel, Jr.—(Slaves)**
JHD: 3 June 1777                                          Northumberland County
To restrain Zachariah Barr, administrator of John Barr, deceased, from holding by force their persons and property, and refusing to emancipate them under the terms of the will of John Barr.
Manuscript signed for Rachel and Rachel, Jr. It was originally directed to

## 3 June 1777

Governor Patrick Henry, but he and his Council referred it to the General Assembly on 2 June 1777. Colonial law had provided that requests for emancipation had to clear through the colonial governor, but the flight of Lord Dunmore had made this impossible.

Accompanying the petition, as listed below, is a wealth of manuscript material giving a full account of various transactions and providing a documentary history of the case, which may well be unique:

(1) the will of John Barr, drawn 13 March 1776, witnessed by William Brown, Joseph Rosson, and William Rosson, and a codicil of the same date with the same witnesses providing that Barr held no claim to title or interest in Rachel or Rachel, Jr., and directing his brother, Zachariah Barr, to set aside twenty-five acres of his land and build a house for Rachel and Rachel, Jr., for their sole use and profit. (The implication nowhere fully stated, is that Rachel, Jr., was probably John Barr's daughter, she being termed a mulatto.) The will was probated 13 May 1776, but the two executors named by John Barr, namely William Brown and Ezekial Hudnall, refused to qualify, and Joseph Hudnall was appointed administrator. On 9 September 1776, Zachariah Barr, with the consent of Joseph Hudnall, was appointed administrator in his place.

(2) a bill of complaint of Rachel against Zachariah Barr (probably in October 1776) addressed to the justices of Northumberland County giving among other things an inventory of her clothing that had been held by Barr.

(3) an order from Thomas Gaskins, one of the justices, dated 25 October 1776, requiring the constable to summon Barr and witnesses for a hearing on 2 November 1776.

(4) a copy of the original summons, which Barr destroyed.

(5) a copy of a new summons dated 1 November 1776.

(6) a long and rambling reply to the bill of complaint by Zachariah Barr defending his actions and the institution of slavery, received by Thomas Gaskins on 28 November 1776. (Action on this bill is not among the papers.)

(7) a restraining order from Thomas Ludwell Lee, a justice of Stafford County, dated 9 February 1777, requiring all persons to allow Rachel and Rachel, Jr., to pass without molestation to the house of William David Boyd in Northumberland County, where they had found asylum. Rachel and her child had fled there pre-

viously, but had been seized and removed to Stafford County by Zachariah Barr for sale as slaves.

3 June 1777: To PG.

7 June 1777: PG reports reasonable and is directed to prepare a bill.

24 June 1777: House passes bill.

26 June 1777: Senate passes bill.

    For act emancipating Rachel and Rachel, Jr., and allowing them to take and hold property devised or bequeathed to them, see 9H320. This act was not to be a precedent except under precisely similar circumstances. (The future careers of Rachel and Rachel, Jr., have not been found.)

### 386-M-†   Hunter, James

    JHD: 5 June 1777, for action                 Stafford County

For locating himself on 200 acres in Stafford County where he hoped to discover iron ore on an old furnace tract.

Date unknown: This memorial, originally presented to the governor, was referred to a special committee.

5 June 1777: Committee finds reasonable and is directed to prepare a bill.

24 June 1777: Bill presented.

26 June 1777: Bill amended and passed by House.

28 June 1777: Senate passes bill.

    For this act see 9H303.

### 387-C-†   Keeney, John

    JHD: 7 June 1777, for action                     Not known

For damages to crops and other items by erection of forts on his land.

Date unknown: To PC.

7 June 1777: PC recommends £17 12s. 6d.

    House agrees.

9 June 1777: Senate agrees.

### 388-C-†   Blackburn, Arthur

    JHD: 7 June 1777, for action                     Not known

Compensation for wounds, he having been scalped twice, in defending frontier crops from Indians.

Date unknown: To PC.

7 June 1777: PC recommends expenses of surgeon be paid, and petitioner be paid £20 for immediate relief and £6 per annum for life.

    House agrees.

## 5 – 10 June 1777

9 June 1777: Senate agrees.

### 389-P-† M'Kay, Jonathan (Administrator of Joel Cornick, deceased)
JHD: 11 June 1777, for action                  Not known

Compensation for slave captured in Lord Dunmore's service, and sent by Committee of Safety to West Indies in ship of John Dixon that was captured by British, and slave seized.

Date unknown: To PC.

11 June 1777: PC recommends £37 12s. 6d., this being the balance after deducting £7 7s. 6d. for transportation.
House agrees.

12 June 1777: Senate agrees.

### 390-P Rowland, Thomas
JHD: 10 June 1777, for action                Botetourt County

Compensation for himself and his military company for use of their own horses in their march to the frontiers of Fincastle County to protect inhabitants from enemy.

Manuscript fragmentary, but appears to have been presented 4 June 1777.

4 June 1777(?): To PC.

10 June 1777: PC recommends for the service of their horses as follows:

Thomas Rowland, for seventeen days, at 1s. 3d. per day,
£ 1    1s. 3d.

James Robinson, Henry Cartmill, James Alcom, Martin Baker, George Huchinson, John Wood, Reverend Adam Smith, Thomas Bowyer, William Astin, James Leatherdale, William Leatherdale, John Crawford, Robert Woods, David Wallace, Edward Gulliford, James Bryant, Josiah Bryant, William Bryant, John M'Farrin, Robert Fenley, Jacob Kimerland, Elijah Vinsant, Robert Birdwell, John Moor, Thomas Howell, Thomas Eagnew, and Samuel Blair, the same, £1 1s. 3d. each,            £28 13s. 9d.

Isaac Richardson, David Harbinson, James Nicholas, Jonathan Wood, William Crawford, Joseph Titus, William Kyles, William Ritchey, Martin M'Farrin, Joseph Kyles, James Espey, Samuel M'Clure, and Samuel M'Farran, fifteen days each, 18s. 9d. each,
£12    3s. 9d.

Patrick Lockhart, George Rutledge, John Mills, jun., William Calbert, Henry Smith, Edward Carbin, James Gaunt, Samuel M'Roberts, Joseph Carrol, Thomas Peage, John Jones, Stephen Hoalston, Henry Walker, William Henry, John Burks, George

## Virginia Legislative Petitions

Givens, Thomas Arbuckle, James Cloyd, David Lawrence, Isaac Lawrence, Patrick Lawrence, William Wills, John Fragor, James M'Cuown, and William Ross, 14 days each, 17s. 6d. each,

£21 17s. 6d.
£63 16s. 3d.

House agrees.
12 June 1777: Senate agrees.

**391-P-†  Deborax, Charles**
JHD: 12 June 1777, for action                      Montgomery County
Compensation for timber used for building fort, guardhouse, and magazine at lead mines, and for the loss of a horse.
Date unknown: To PC.
12 June 1777: PC recommends rejection of claim for horse and recommends
    £5 for timber.
House agrees to £5.
14 June 1777: Senate agrees.

**392-P-†  Fitzgerald, Jarret**
JHD: 12 June 1777, for action                      Not known
Compensation for horse that died while escorting Cherokees to Williamsburg.
Date unknown: To PC.
12 June 1777: PC recommends rejection.
House rejects.

**393-P-†  Watson, Christopher**
JHD: 12 June 1777, for action                      Halifax County
Compensation for expenses incurred in transporting his son, who had become ill in military service at Long Island, on Holstein River, to Halifax.
Date unknown: To PC.
12 June 1777: PC recommends £20.
House agrees.
14 June 1777: Senate agrees.

**394-P-†  Berry, Thomas**
JHD: 16 June 1777, for action                      Not known
Compensation for wound inflicted by Indians.
Date unknown: To PC.

## 12 – 16 June 1777

16 June 1777: PC recommends rejection.
    House rejects.

**395-P-†    Berry, George, Jr.**
    JHD: 16 June 1777, for action    Not known
Compensation for wound inflicted by Indians.
Date unknown: To PC.
16 June 1777: PC recommends rejection.
    House rejects.

**396-P-†    Hart, George**
    JHD: 16 June 1777, for action    Not known
Compensation for horse, which was lost or stolen while Hart was serving as surgeon at Long Island, on Holstein River, during Cherokee expedition.
Date unknown: To PC.
16 June 1777: PC recommends rejection.
    House rejects.

**397-P-†    Jones, Joshua**
    JHD: 16 June 1777, for action    Not known
Compensation for wound received in service at battle near Long Island, on Holstein River.
Date unknown: To PC.
16 June 1777: PC recommends £10 for present relief.
    House agrees.
18 June 1777: Senate agrees.

**398-P-†    Douglas, Samuel**
    JHD: 16 June 1777, for action    Not known
Compensation for knife wound accidentally received.
Date unknown: To PC.
16 June 1777: PC recommends £10.
    House agrees.
18 June 1777: Senate agrees.

**399-P-†    Latham, John**
    JHD: 16 June 1777, for action    Not known
Compensation for field of corn cut down for erection of fort at Long Island, on Holstein River.
Date unknown: To PC.

## Virginia Legislative Petitions

16 June 1777: PC recommends £3.
    House agrees.
18 June 1777: Senate agrees.

### 400-P-†   Downman, Raleigh
    JHD: 16 June 1777, for action                             Not known
For return of four slaves captured while trying to escape to Lord Dunmore and sent to lead mines; also for their hire.
Date unknown: To PC.
16 June 1777: PC recommends rejection of return of slaves, but recommends hire of £12 a year for each from 16 July 1776 and same rate for one who had died.
    House agrees to rate of hire.
18 June 1777: Senate agrees.

### 401-P-†   Finley, John
    JHD: 20 June 1777, for action                             Not known
Compensation for wound received in battle with Cherokee Indians near Long Island, on Holstein River, on 20 July 1776.
Date unknown: To PC.
20 June 1777: PC recommends £10.
    House agrees.
21 June 1777: Senate agrees, JS.

### 402-P
Eck–Not
found     **Woodward, Chesley**
    JHD: 20 June 1777, for action                         Bedford County
Compensation for return of horse and wagon, in service of military from Norfolk to Bedford County.
    Manuscript unsigned.
Date unknown: To PC.
20 June 1777: PC recommends 12s. 6d. per day for a total of £8 2s. 6d.
    House agrees.
26 June 1777: Senate agrees.

### 403-P   Coleman, Rebecca
    JHD: 20 June 1777, for action                             Not known
Compensation for expenses incurred for nursing of son who became ill in

## 16 – 26 June 1777

United States service and died at home of Martha Hodges, in Henrico County.
Date unknown: To PC.
20 June 1777: Carried over to next session of GA.
7 Jan. 1778: Carried over to next session of GA.
5 Nov. 1778: PC recommends £7 4s. to be charged to account of commonwealth against United States.
    House agrees.
23 Nov. 1778: Senate agrees.

**404-Misc.**
**Claims-**† JHD: 26 June 1777, for action                    Not known
    The following miscellaneous claims were not presented separately, and apparently went to PC without a prior reading on the floor of the House. They are listed as they were approved in the journals and are indexed under name and subject.
Date unknown: To PC.
26 June 1777: PC recommends approval.
    House agrees.
28 June 1777: Senate agrees.

404.1      To Solomon Porch, for his Negro man Tom, who was condemned and executed, and by the court of the county of Sussex valued at £100 0s. 0d.

404.2      To Robert Harris, for his Negro man slave Pritch, who was condemned and executed, and by the court of the county of Hanover valued at £50 0s. 0d.

404.3      To John Jones, assignee of John Mayo, for his Negro slave James, who was condemned and executed for felony, and by the court of the county of York valued at £55 0s. 0d.

404.4      To Anne Cocke, ferry keeper at Swan's Point, for ferriage of sheriff and guards with a criminal, 8s. 9d.

404.5      To Bryant O'Cannon, his pay as a soldier in Captain Marshall's company, forty-seven days at 1s. 6d.; £3 10s. 6d.

404.6      To Nicholas Smith for 647 weight of beef, at 2d. per pound, for Captain Long's company of militia when stationed at Tygart's Valley, £5 7s. 10d.

404.7      To Hybert Brink, for two sheep for the use of Captain Parson's company, £1 4s. 0d.

404.8      To James Griffin, a further allowance of eleven days as a private in Captain Moffett's company, 16s. 6d.

## Virginia Legislative Petitions

| | |
|---|---|
| 404.9 | To Patrick Lowry, for pasturage of forty horses, thirty-six hours each, at 6d.; £1 0s. 0d. |
| 404.10 | To William Cage, for going express from Monongahela to Winchester, 140 miles, at 6d. per mile, deducting 12s. of his pay, which he drew as a soldier at that time, £2 18s. 0d. |
| 404.11 | To James Wood, for amount paid Thomas Craig for transcribing five copies of Colonel Mason's remarks on the necessary evidence against Henderson and others, £2; and for the expenses of sundry witnesses at Fort Pitt, £1 11s. 2d.; for a total of £3 11s. 2d. |
| 404.12 | To Charles Simms, for amount paid David Ferguson for going express to George Croghan, Esquire, £1 16s. 0d. |
| 404.13 | To James Wood, for his trouble in taking depositions respecting the claims of Mr. Henderson and the Indiana Company, nine days, at 25s. per day, £11 5s. 0d. |
| 404.14 | To Abraham Hite, the same, fourteen days, £17 10s. 0d. |
| 404.15 | To Benjamin Dodd Wheeler, a wounded soldier in Captain Nicholas Lewis's company of minutemen, to reimburse him the expense of a doctor, £2 3s. 0d. |
| 404.16 | To David Dalton, ditto, £1 15s. 0d. |
| 404.17 | To Isaac Wood, ditto, 8s. 6d. |
| 404.18 | To William Burton, for his Negro Tom, who was condemned and executed for felony, and by the court of the county of Amherst valued at £100 0s. 0d. |
| 404.19 | To John Lewis, for his Negro woman slave Jenny, who was condemned and executed for conspiracy, and by the court of the county of James City valued at £50 0s. 0d. |
| 404.20 | To Bartholomew Carrel, for a bay mare lost in the Shawanese expedition, appraised at £5 15s. 0d. |
| 404.21 | To Conrod Smith, for a roan mare, ditto, £7 10s. 0d. |
| 404.22 | To Hannah Hubbard, for the use of her horse taken by the sheriff to convey Ridley Young, a criminal, to the public jail, £2 0s. 0d. |
| 404.23 | To Thomas Tambrough, for the use of his horse to convey Thomas Potter, a criminal, to the public jail, £2 0s. 0d. |
| 404.24 | To Stephen Neil, for ditto to convey John Chapman to the public jail, £1 10s. 0d. |
| 404.25 | To John Wiley, a further allowance on sixty-three days' horse hire in 1774, over and above the sum allowed him by the commissioners, £1 12s. 1d. |
| 404.26 | To Francis Berry, a soldier in Captain John Floyd's company on |

## 26 June 1777

the Shawanese expedition, for 105 days, at 1s. 6d., omitted in the roll, £7 17s. 6d.

404.27 To William Anderson, for his Negro man slave John, who was condemned and executed for murder, and by the court of the county of Cumberland valued at £95 0s. 0d.

404.28 To James Robinson, for a gray horse, appraised at £12 2s. 6d., and a brown horse at £9, lost in the Shawanese expedition; £21 2s. 6d.

404.29 To Thomas Pate, for ironwork for the public jail, £37 18s. 6d.

404.30 To Richard Harrocks, for a dozen mahogany chairs, with hair bottoms, for the use of the Senate, at 50s. each, £30 0s. 0d.

404.31 To Daniel M'Kenzie, for a horse, appraised at £3; one horse at £9; one mare, £10; one saddle, £1; one blanket, 8s.; one halter and pack saddle, 6s. 3d.; and three bells, 10s. 6d.; all lost in the Cherokee expedition, £24 4s. 9d.

404.32 To Andrew Wallace, for one black horse eleven years old, £15; one horse three years old, £21; total value, £36 0s. 0d.

404.33 To Christopher Irwin, for one horse, £13 0s. 0d.

404.34 To Humphrey Hoggins, for seventy-nine days hire, at 1s. 3d. per day, £4 18s. 9d.

404.35 To John Cochran, for a bay horse, which died in the public service, appraised at £13 0s. 0d.

404.36 To James Sawyers, for a roan horse lost, £14; one saddle and bridle lost, £2 5s.; total value, £16 5s. 0d.

404.37 To John Young, for a bay mare drowned in crossing the Tennessee River, saddle and bridle lost, £9 10s. 0d.

404.38 To William Crawford, for two horses, appraised at £43. Deduct for forty days hire of said horses, each at 1s. 6d. per day, which was allowed by the auditors, £6; £37 0s. 0d.

404.39 To James Buford, for four horses appraised at £69 10s. Deduct for hire of two horses, forty-one days each, at 1s. 6d. per day, which was allowed by the auditors, £6 3s.; £63 7s. 0d.

404.40 To William Meade, for a horse appraised at £11. Deduct for thirty-nine days hire, 1s. 6d. per day, £2 18s. 6d.; total to be paid, £8 1s. 7d.

404.41 To David Wallace, for a horse appraised at £6. Deduct for seventeen days hire, at 1s. 3d. per day, £1 1s. 3d.; total to be paid, £4 18s. 9d.

404.42 To Joshua Rentfro, for a gray horse, bridle and saddle, £15; a bay horse, £10; £25 0s. 0d.

## Virginia Legislative Petitions

404.43    To Stephen Holstein, for one ditto, appraised at £15. Deduct for fourteen days hire, at 1s. 3d. per day, 17s. 6d.; total to be paid, £14 2s. 6d.
404.44    To William Hugart, for a sorrel horse, £21 0s. 0d.
404.45    To Patrick Murphey, for a bay ditto, £10 10s. 0d.
404.46    To Ephraim Dunlop, for two ditto at £27 and £16; £43 0s. 0d.
404.47    To Isham Talbot, for a dark bay ditto £16 6s. 0d.
404.48    To Michael Ocheltre, for a roan ditto, £15 0s. 0d.
404.49    To James Campbell, for a chestnut ditto and bell, £14 6s. 0d.
404.50    To Benjamin Thomas, for a sorrel ditto, £11 0s. 0d.
404.51    To Matthew Scott, for a roan ditto, £11 0s. 0d.
404.52    To John Wood, for a sorrel mare, £11; one brown ditto, £7; and a gray horse, £10; total to be paid, £28 0s. 0d.
404.53    To Robert Boggs, for a bay mare, £8 0s. 0d.
404.54    To Thomas Logwood, one mare, £4 0s. 0d.
404.55    To Robert Finley, for a bay horse, £21 15s. 0d.
404.56    To Robert Preston, for one ditto, £13 10s. 0d.
404.57    To William Wills, Jr., for a gray ditto, £15 0s. 0d.
404.58    To Jacob Gender, for a roan ditto, £13 0s. 0d.
404.59    To Jacob Anderson, for a dark bay mare, £12 12s. 0d.
404.60    To William Markland, for a white horse, £7; one bay ditto, £5 10s.; total to be paid, £12 10s. 0d.
404.61    To Joseph M'Cormick, for a bright bay mare, £20 0s. 0d.
404.62    To John Adair, for a bay horse, £12 5s. 0d.
404.63    To William Hall, for a roan ditto, £16 10s. 0d.
404.64    To James M'Cockle, for a bay ditto, £25 0s. 0d.
404.65    To James Robinson, for a sorrel horse, £8; and a black ditto, £13; total to be paid, £21 0s. 0d.
404.66    To Joseph Russel, for a black ditto, £6 10s. 0d.
404.67    To William Hicks, for a black ditto, £11 10s. 0d.
404.68    To Jonathan Martin, for a black ditto, £15 0s. 0d.
404.69    To David Getgood, for a black mare, £9 0s. 0d.
404.70    To Gideon Morris, for a sorrel horse, £12; one brown ditto at £10; and a white ditto at £9 10s.; total to be paid, £31 10s. 0d.
404.71    To Samuel Gay, for one horse, £16 0s. 0d.
404.72    To William Ingram, for a bright bay ditto, £8 0s. 0d.
404.73    To Isaac Riddle, for a blue roan ditto, £12 0s. 0d.
404.74    To Robert Stewart, for a bald eagle ditto, £15 0s. 0d.
404.75    To David Smith, for a bay ditto, £5 10s. 0d.
404.76    To James Berry, for a white ditto, £9 10s. 0d.

## 26 June 1777

| | |
|---|---|
| 404.77 | To John Smith, for a bay ditto, £26 0s. 0d. |
| 404.78 | To Edward Ross, for one horse, £7 10s. 0d. |
| 404.79 | To Daniel Smith, for a black horse, £12 0s. 0d. |
| 404.80 | To Gideon Faris, for a gray ditto, £11 10s. 0d. |
| 404.81 | To William Haynes, for a horse, £9 0s. 0d. |
| 404.82 | To Jesse Womack, for one ditto, £12; and one ditto, £11; total, £23 0s. 0d. |
| 404.83 | To John M'Clanahan, for one ditto, £5 0s. 0d. |
| 404.84 | To John Furhran, for three ditto, £32 10s. 0d. |
| 404.85 | To John Phelps, for one ditto, £6 11s. 0d. |
| 404.86 | To William Frogg, for a bay ditto, £4 0s. 0d. |
| 404.87 | To Absalom M'Clanahan, for one horse, £4 0s. 0d. |
| 404.88 | To Archibald Graham, for a gun, £2 0s. 0d. |
| 404.89 | To William Milum, for two horses, £21 0s. 0d. |
| 404.90 | To James Arnold, for a black mare, £12 0s. 0d. |
| 404.91 | To Lance Woodward, for one horse, £4 0s. 0d. |
| 404.92 | To Hanhrist Carlock, for a white mare, £10 0s. 0d. |
| 404.93 | To Francis Katharine, for a sorrel ditto, £9 0s. 0d. |
| 404.94 | To Daniel Henderson, for a bay horse, £10 0s. 0d. |
| 404.95 | To Thomas Berry, for a black ditto, £7 0s. 0d. |
| 404.96 | To Michael Rowland, for a bald eagle ditto, £12 0s. 0d. |
| 404.97 | To Amos Heaton, his pay as lieutenant, ninety-three days, at 4s. per day for a total of £18 12s. 0d. |
| 404.98 | John Latham, sergeant, for thirty-five days, at 2s. per day for a total of £3 10s. 0d. |
| 404.99 | Henry Rice, ditto, for ninety-three days, at ditto per day for a total of £9 6s. 0d. |
| 404.100 | David Rounceval, ditto, for ninety-three days, at ditto per day for a total of £9 6s. 0d. |
| 404.101-404.103 | William Ramsay, William Mitchell, and James Bradley, privates, fifteen days, at 1s. 4d. each per day; 20s. each for fifteen days; total, £3 0s. 0d. |
| 404.104-404.117 | William Henson, William Lane, Lambert Lane, Charles Rice, John Rice, William Rice, Jesse Henson Philip Mulhey, Sr., Philip Mulhey, Jr., Joab Springer, Jonathan Mulhey, Philip Williams, Onsbey Carney, and Moses Winters, fifty-nine days each, £3 18s. 8d. each; total, £55 14s. 0d. |
| 404.118-404.121 | Lewis Crane, John Crane, John Harris, Sr., and James Harris, fifty-nine days each, £3 18s. 8d. each; total, £15 14s. 8d. |
| 404.122- | Benjamin Drake, James Beets, Isaac Lindsay, Benjamin Rice, and |

## Virginia Legislative Petitions

404.126    John M'Farland, forty-nine days each, £3 5s. 4d. each; total, £16 6s. 8d.

404.127-    Arthur Onsby, David Irwin, Nicholas Edwards, Nicholas Rice,
404.150    Samuel Martin, George Miller, James Kelley, William Nettles, Thomas Ramsey, James Richardson, James M'Clern, Thomas Fowler, James Hamilton, John Harris, Jr., Thomas Smith, John Nowland, James Smith, George Coon, James Williams, William Lane, William Rice, Sr., Henry Whitner, Lewis Whitner, and Isaac Rounceval, ninety-three days each, £6 4s. each; total, £148 16s. 0d.

404.151    Henry Richardson, ninety-three days, £6 4s. 0d.

404.152    David Hunter, fifty-three days, £3 10s. 8d.

404.153    To James M'Farland, for a bay horse, appraised at £11 0s. 0d.

**405-P and M-†**    **Fluvanna County—Citizens**
     JHD: 30 Oct. 1777            Fluvanna County

Asking for an inquiry into the election of William Henry, Jesse Benton, and Roger Thompson as justices of the peace for the county, and John Cobbs as clerk of the peace, accusing them of bribery and corruption.

30 Oct. 1777: Laid on table.

3 Nov. 1777: To PG.

12 Nov. 1777: PG recommends that the attorney general prosecute these persons as soon as the General Court is established.
     House agrees.
     Apparently no Senate action required. Disposition of these cases not found.
     See 623-P. For final action see 1132-P.

**406-P**    **Bohon, Benjamin**
     JHD: 30 Oct. 1777            Orange County

Compensation for nursing his three sons, John, Benjamin, and William, and their companion, William Twisdell, all of whom were taken ill while in military service.

Manuscript unsigned.

30 Oct. 1777: To PC.

14 Nov. 1777: PC recommends £23 13s. 4d.
     House agrees.

18 Nov. 1777: Senate agrees.

## 30 – 31 October 1777

**407-P  Boling, Anne**
JHD: 30 Oct. 1777                                              Orange County
Compensation for nursing three sons in military service, William, Jesse (who died), and John, and Thornsberry Boling (who was in Continental service).
Manuscript unsigned, but has deposition on reverse.
30 Oct. 1777: To PC.
19 Nov. 1777: PC recommends £7 2s. 6d. for services to William, Jesse, and John, but recommends rejection for services to Thornsberry.
House amends by allowing £6 5s. 0d. for services to Thornsberry to be charged to account of commonwealth against United States of America.
House agrees to recommendation and amendment.
21 Nov. 1777: Senate agrees to both.

**408-P  Morton, Richard**
JHD: 30 Oct. 1777                                              Orange County
Compensation for nursing his son, Jarot Morton, who was taken ill in military service.
Manuscript unsigned.
30 Oct. 1777: To PC.
11 Nov. 1777: PC recommends £16 9s. 2d.
House agrees.
18 Nov. 1777: Senate agrees.

**409-P-†  Washington County Court—Members**
JHD: 30 Oct. 1777                                           Washington County
Asking that court date be set on third Tuesday of each month.
30 Oct. 1777: House directs a bill be drawn by special committee.
Bill was passed by House and Senate.
For this act see 9H439.

**410-P-†  Brown, John**
JHD: 31 Oct. 1777                                                 Not known
Additional compensation for rations furnished Virginia troops.
31 Oct. 1777: To PC.
11 Nov. 1777: PC recommends rejection.
House rejects.

### 411-P   Beckford Parish, Dunmore County—Vestry
JHD: 31 Oct. 1777   Dunmore County

To require a levy from Frederick Parish and Norborne Parish for proportional part of cost of two churches built in these two parishes when they were part of Beckford Parish.

Manuscript unsigned.

31 Oct. 1777: To R.

2 Jan. 1778: R recommends rejection.

   House rejects.

### 412-P-*   Saint Patrick's Parish, Prince Edward County—Vestry
JHD: 31 Oct. 1777   Prince Edward County

To sell present glebe and purchase a more convenient one.

31 Oct. 1777: House directs special committee to prepare a bill.

5 Nov. 1777: Bill presented.

18 Nov. 1777: House passes bill.

21 Nov. 1777: Senate passes bill.

   For this act see 9H440.

### 413-P   Gambel, Margaret
JHD: 1 Nov. 1777   Not known

Compensation for death of her husband, James Gambel, in Continental service.

Manuscript unsigned, but has certificate of Thomas Nelson attached.

1 Nov. 1777: To PC.

18 Nov. 1777: PC recommends rejection. Recommitted to PC.

22 Nov. 1777: PC recommends £30 to be charged to account of commonwealth against United States of America.

   House agrees.

29 Nov. 1777: Senate agrees.

### 414-P   Terrell, William
JHD: 1 Nov. 1777   Norfolk County

Compensation for horse, which died while petitioner was transferring arms from Suffolk to Norfolk.

Manuscript unsigned, but has certificate of value attached.

1 Nov. 1777: To PC.

1 Dec. 1777: PC recommends £40.

   House agrees.

5 Dec. 1777: Senate agrees.

## 31 October – 3 November 1777

**415-P    Orange County—Citizens**
    JHD: 3 Nov. 1777                                                    Orange County
For levying taxes on value of land and not on size of acreage.
    Manuscript signed by: Robert Sandford, Benjamin Benson, John Pemberton, John Furnis, Charles Walker, and thirty-eight others.
3 Nov. 1777: To SC.
        Committee apparently did not report.
        See 415A-P.

**415 A-P    Orange County—Citizens**
    JHD: 3 Nov. 1777                                                    Orange County
Text is identical with 415-P, which see.
Manuscript signed by forty-three persons.

**416-P    Douglass, Margaret**
    JHD: 3 Nov. 1777                                                    Orange County
Compensation for nursing her son, George Douglass, who became ill in military service while at Williamsburg and was taken by her to her home in Orange County.
    Manuscript unsigned.
3 Nov. 1777: To PC.
11 Nov. 1777: PC recommends £6 7s. 6d. for nursing and £2 for transferring
    him.
        House agrees.
18 Nov. 1777: Senate agrees.

**417-P    Finnill, Thomas**
    JHD: 3 Nov. 1777                                                    Orange County
Compensation for nursing two sons, John Finnill and Reuben Finnill, who became ill while in military service. Reuben was in Continental service.
    Manuscript unsigned.
3 Nov. 1777: To PC.
19 Nov. 1777: PC recommends (1) the sum of £8 15s. for nursing John, and
    (2) that claim for Reuben be rejected.
        House agrees to (1), recommits (2) to PC.
21 Nov. 1777: Senate agrees to (1).
22 Nov. 1777: PC recommends for (2) that the sum of £8 15s. be allowed and
    that it should be charged in the account of commonwealth against
    United States of America.
        House agrees to (2).

29 Nov. 1777: Senate agrees to (2).

**418-P  Johnson, Thomas, Jr.**
JHD: 3 Nov. 1777                                                    Louisa County
   Reimbursement of £12 12s. for death of two steers he hired from Charles Yancey to transfer military supplies in Shawanese expedition, together with £2 13s. 6d. court costs.
   Manuscript unsigned.
3 Nov. 1777: To PC.
11 Nov. 1777: PC recommends £15 5s. 6d.
   House agrees.
18 Nov. 1777: Senate amends by reducing amount to £12 12s.
1 Dec. 1777: House postpones Senate amendments stating that Senate has no
   authority to amend or alter resolutions "in nature of a money bill,"
   and that it may only reject or approve. Requests Thomas Jefferson
   to notify Senate that a conference is desired and appoints a committee to present the case.
4 Dec. 1777: Jefferson presents a brief report on the House's opinion.
   House agrees, appoints a conference committee.
   Senate agrees to conference, which is begun. Senate requests a full
   statement.
9 Jan. 1778: Jefferson prepares and presents for the committee a long and
   reasoned history of English parliamentary practice on money bills,
   generally regarded as one of his first major political papers.
19 Jan. 1778: Senate agrees to further conference.
23 Jan. 1778: Jefferson reports Senate insists on amendments.
   House postpones action on this report.
   Johnson presents a new petition on this same subject on 13 May
   1778, which see (569-P).

**419-P  Campbell, Robert**
JHD: 3 Nov. 1777                                              Washington County
   Compensation for accidental wound received while in military service in Shawanese expedition of 1774.
   Manuscript unsigned, but has attached to it a certificate of the Washington County court and a certificate of three citizens.
3 Nov. 1777: To PC.
22 Nov. 1777: PC recommends £10 for his present relief and £10 per annum
   for life.
   House agrees.

## 3 – 4 November 1777

29 Nov. 1777: Senate agrees.

**420-P   Duncan, James; Reeves, Richard; and Grills, William**
   JHD: 4 Nov. 1777                                    Frederick County
   Compensation for clothing and rifles lost when their boat carrying provisions from Fort Pitt to Fort Randolph was accidentally sunk.
   Manuscript unsigned, but has a deposition attached to it as to the value of the articles.
4 Nov. 1777: To PC.
19 Nov. 1777: PC recommends £5 to Duncan £6 to Reeves, and £8 16s. to Grills.
   House agrees.
21 Nov. 1777: Senate amends by adding that amounts should be charged to account of commonwealth against United States of America.
   House probably agrees to amendment but record not found.

**421-P   Donnan, David**
   JHD: 4 Nov. 1777                                    Dinwiddie County
   Compensation for two runaway slaves killed by a fire in the Prince George County jail on 15 February 1775. Donnan was guardian of five orphan children, and their father had owned the slaves. A similar petition had been rejected by the House of Burgesses on 13 June 1775.
   Manuscript unsigned.
4 Nov. 1777: Rejected by refusal to refer to a committee.

**422-P-†   Mecklenburg County—Citizens**
   JHD: 4 Nov. 1777                                    Mecklenburg County
   For changing the location of ferry at Royster's on Roanoke River to avoid additional fording of a creek.
4 Nov. 1777: To PG.
8 Nov. 1777: PG recommends as reasonable.
   House agrees and sends to Senate.
   There is no record of Senate action, and the change is not found in Hening.

**423-P-†   Dunn, James**
   JHD: 4 Nov. 1777                                    Not known
   Return of slave who escaped to Lord Dunmore, was captured, and was sent to lead mines or saltpeter works. Also asks for payment for hire.
4 Nov. 1777: To PC (PG?).

## Virginia Legislative Petitions

7 Jan. 1778: Carried over to next session of GA.
20 Nov. 1778: PG recommends rejection.
>House rejects.

### 424-P  Lawson, William
JHD: 4 Nov. 1777                                   Halifax County

Additional compensation for wagon impressed for militia service. Had received 15s. per day.

Manuscript unsigned, but has certificate attached.
4 Nov. 1777: To PC.
11 Nov. 1777: PC recommends 5s. extra per day.
>House agrees.

19 Nov. 1777: Senate rejects, JS.

### 425-P-†  Suffolk—Citizens
JHD: 4 Nov. 1777                                          Suffolk

For appointment of commissioners to determine value of damage done by Virginia soldiers in 1775 to houses and gardens used as barracks.
4 Nov. 1777: To PC.
9 Dec. 1777: PC reports as reasonable.
>House agrees.
>Senate action not found.

### 426-P  Culpeper County—Citizens
JHD: 4 Nov. 1777                                   Culpeper County

For levying taxes on value of land and not on size of acreage.

Manuscript signed by: John Strother, John Erhardt Oelschagel, Alexander Baxter, John Slaughter, James Gaines, and sixty-four others.
4 Nov. 1777: To committee of whole on a motion for a supply for the public exigencies.
>For the act for raising money for public exigencies, including, among many items, taxation on value of land, see 9H349.

### 427-P-*  Montgomery County and Washington County—Citizens
JHD: 5 Nov. 1777                                Montgomery County
                                                Washington County

For laying off townships along and near the Ohio River for trading purposes and as a barrier against Indians.
5 Nov. 1777: To PG.
>Carried over to next session of GA.

## 4 – 5 November 1777

16 Oct. 1778: PG recommends rejection.
    House rejects.

**428-P-†**   **Augusta County and Botetourt County—Citizens**
    JHD: 5 Nov. 1777                                         Augusta County
                                                                                           Botetourt County

For the formation of a new county out of Augusta and Botetourt counties. (There were several petitions of this nature, but the exact number is not known.)
5 Nov. 1777: To PG
26 Nov. 1777: PG finds reasonable. House attempts, unsuccessfully, to postpone until next session of GA.
8 Dec. 1777: PG directed to prepare bill for forming several counties.
10 Dec. 1777: PG directed to have bill include formation of new parishes in new counties.
12 Dec. 1777: PG directed to have bill change name of Dunmore County.
16 Dec. 1777: Bill presented and referred to special committee.
24 Dec. 1777: Special committee suggests amendment, which was agreed to. House passes bill.
10 Jan. 1778: Senate makes several amendments, which were finally reconciled between House and Senate.
    The act as finally passed added part of Augusta County to Hampshire County; formed Rockingham County and Rockingham Parish out of Augusta County; formed Greenbrier County and Greenbrier Parish out of Botetourt and Montgomery counties; formed Rockbridge County and Rockbridge Parish out of Augusta and Botetourt counties; established town of Lexington; dissolved the vestry of Augusta Parish; provided for election of vestries in parishes of Rockingham, Augusta, Rockbridge, Botetourt, and Greenbrier; and changed name of Dunmore County to Shanando (Shenandoah).
For this act, effective 1 March 1778, see 9H420.

**429-P**   **Botetourt County—Citizens**
    JHD: 5 Nov. 1777                                         Botetourt County

For the division of Botetourt County and extension of boundary to Greenbrier River; also for confirmation of titles to lands.
    Manuscript signed by: John Stewart, Charles O'Hara, John Rodgers, John Archer, William Kreggar, and seventy others
5 Nov. 1777: To PG.

## Virginia Legislative Petitions

19 Nov. 1777: Reported and recommitted to PG.
25 Nov. 1777: PG reports reasonable, but recommends rejection of extension of boundary.
> This petition appears, in most part, to be covered in 428-P-†, which see.

### 430-P    Botetourt County—Citizens
JHD: 5 Nov. 1777                                               Botetourt County
Opposing division of county.
Manuscript signed by: Joshua Wilson, Benjamin Stoff, Cornelius Reed, John Wilson, Stephen Storey, and 115 others.
5 Nov. 1777: To PG.
26 Nov. 1777: PG recommends rejection.
> House rejects.
> See 428-P-†.

### 430 A-P    Botetourt County—Citizens
JHD: 5 Nov. 1777                                               Botetourt County
Text is similar to 430-P, which see.
Manuscript signed by fifty persons.

### 430 B-P    Botetourt County—Citizens
JHD: 5 Nov. 1777                                               Botetourt County
Text is similar to 430-P, which see.
Manuscript signed by thirty-six persons.

### 430 C-P    Botetourt County—Citizens
JHD: 5 Nov. 1777                                               Botetourt County
Text is similar to 430-P, which see.
Manuscript signed by twenty-two persons.

### 430 D-P    Botetourt County—Citizens
JHD: 5 Nov. 1777                                               Botetourt County
Text is similar to 430-P, which see.
Manuscript signed by forty-six persons.

### 430 E-P    Botetourt County—Citizens
JHD: 5 Nov. 1777                                               Botetourt County
Text is similar to 430-P, which see.
Manuscript signed by forty-five persons.

## 5 – 6 November 1777

**431-P     Marrs, Henry Munday**
JHD: 5 Nov. 1777                                           Not known
Compensation for horse killed in October 1776 while Marrs was employed in service of country at Fort Henry. He has been paid 18s. 9d. for hire.
Manuscript unsigned, but has certificate attached.
5 Nov. 1777: To PC.
22 Nov. 1777: PC recommends additional £6 1s. 3d.
    House agrees.
29 Nov. 1777: Senate agrees.

**432-P     Bristow, William**
JHD: 6 Nov. 1777                                           Not known
Compensation for illness contracted while in military service at Great Bridge in 1775.
Manuscript unsigned.
6 Nov. 1777: To PC.
19 Nov. 1777: PC recommends rejection since Bristow was in Continental service.
    Recommitted to PC.
22 Nov. 1777: PC recommends £15 to be charged to account of commonwealth against United States of America.
    House substitutes £20.
29 Nov. 1777: Senate amends.
    There is no record that House agreed to Senate amendments. These may have altered money amounts to which House objected. See 418-P.

**433-P**
Eck-
A1096     **Tyger's (Tygart's) Valley—Citizens**
JHD: 6 Nov. 1777                                           Augusta County
For the creation of a new county including lands in the Valley and on Buchanan's Creek and west fork of Monongalia River.
Manuscript signed by: Wm. Westfall, Wm. Currants, John Casaday, Wm. Casaday, George Westfall, and 167 others.
6 Nov. 1777: To PC.
19 Dec. 1777: PG recommends that it be carried over to next session of GA.
    House agrees.
26 Nov. 1778: PG recommends rejection.
    House rejects.

## Virginia Legislative Petitions

**434-P-†**   Bailey, Joshua; White, John; and Cornwell, Samuel
JHD: 6 Nov. 1777                                                                Not known
For exemption from military service of those employed in their proposed mill for manufacturing cotton and wool.
6 Nov. 1777: To PG.
8 Nov. 1777: PG recommends rejection.
    House rejects.

**435-P-†**
Rob–Not
found     **Kentucky County—Citizens**
JHD: 6 Nov. 1777                                                          Kentucky County
Compensation for wounds received in defending Kentucky from Indians.
6 Nov. 1777: To PG.
    Committee apparently did not report.
    This is probably 470-P, which see.

**436-P**   **Washington County—Citizens**
JHD: 6 Nov. 1777                                                         Washington County
For locating courthouse in center of the county, and adjusting line between Montgomery and Washington counties.
    Manuscript signed by: Saml. Scott, Ja. Thompson, George Scott, Evan Shelby, Jr., Pleasant Lockett, and 278 others.
6 Nov. 1777: To PG.
    Carried over to next session of GA.
15 Oct. 1778: PG recommends rejection.
    House rejects.

**436 A-P**   **Washington County—Citizens**
JHD: 6 Nov. 1777                                                         Washington County
Text is similar to 436-P, which see.
Manuscript signed by sixty persons.

**436 B-P**   **Washington County—Citizens**
JHD: 6 Nov. 1777                                                         Washington County
Text is similar to 436-P, which see.
Manuscript signed by twenty-three persons.

## 6 November 1777

**436 C-P   Washington County—Citizens**
  JHD: 6 Nov. 1777                                   Washington County
  Text is similar to 436-P, which see.
  Manuscript signed by seventy-six persons.

**437-P   Washington County and Montgomery County—Citizens**
  JHD: 6 Nov. 1777                                   Washington County
                                                     Montgomery County
  In opposition to moving courthouse to center of Washington County. (There were several petitions, but the exact number is not known. They included petitions from militia and county court of Washington County.)
  Manuscript signed by: Wm. Edmidson, Jno. Black, John Berry, John Kinkead, John Dunkin, and eighteen others. (There are sixty-three others, comprising loose signatures, which may have been attached to this petition.)
  6 Nov. 1777: To PG.
  8 Nov. 1777: Carried over to next session of GA and again referred to PG.
  23 May 1778: Manuscript endorsement says rejected, 23 May 1778.

**437 A-P   Washington County and Montgomery County—Citizens**
  JHD: 6 Nov. 1777                                   Washington County
                                                     Montgomery County
  Text is similar to 437-P, which see.
  Manuscript signed by an indeterminate number of persons. Many signatures loose and undecipherable.

**437 B-P   Washington County and Montgomery County—Citizens**
  JHD: 6 Nov. 1777                                   Washington County
                                                     Montgomery County
  Text is similar to 437-P, which see.
  Manuscript signed by an indeterminate number of persons.

**438-P   Washington County and Montgomery County—Citizens**
  JHD: 6 Nov. 1777                                   Washington County
                                                     Montgomery County
  For having land surveyors elected by citizens or appointed by county courts, and requiring them to reside in their respective counties.
  Manuscript signed by: James Depart, Geo. Martin, Wm. Conner, John Beatey, Robert Beaker, and twenty-five others.
  6 Nov. 1777: To PG.

## Virginia Legislative Petitions

12 Nov. 1777: PG discharged and petition laid on table.
Apparently no further action taken.

### 438 A-P  Washington County and Montgomery County—Citizens
JHD: 6 Nov. 1777                                   Washington County
Montgomery County

Text is similar to 438-P, which see.
Manuscript signed by fifty-seven persons.

### 439-P  Venable, Nathaniel
JHD: 6 Nov. 1777                                     Prince Edward County

Additional compensation for two wagons and teams impressed in 1776 for public service.

Manuscript unsigned, but has account and certificate of verification attached.

6 Nov. 1777: To PC.

1 Dec. 1777: PC recommends (1) additional compensation for one wagon and team be rejected, and (2) additional compensation be allowed for another wagon and team in amount of 15s.
House rejects (1), agrees to (2).

5 Dec. 1777: Senate agrees to (2).

### 440-P  Western Lands—Citizens
JHD: 6 Nov. 1777                                     Western Lands

Asking that inquiry be made into land grants allowed by the king to certain persons and companies, and to determine which are void, particularly those made to Ohio Company and Walker's Company.

Manuscript signed by: Alexr. Montgomery, John Walker, James Alley, Joseph Moon, James Black, and 108 others.

6 Nov. 1777: To PG.

12 Nov. 1777: Manuscript endorsement says PG discharged and petition laid on table. There is no record in JHD.
Apparently no further action taken.

### 441-P-†  Montgomery County—Citizens
JHD: 6 Nov. 1777                                     Montgomery County
Greenbrier County

Asking that portions of the north corner of Montgomery County be added to new Greenbrier County.

## 6 – 8 November 1777

6 Nov. 1777: To PG.
      See 428-P-† for action.

**442-P**   **Fuqua, Randolph**
      JHD: 7 Nov. 1777                       Not known
  Claiming reward for apprehending George Gray, convicted of horse stealing. Reward had been denied him by court.
  Manuscript unsigned.
7 Nov. 1777: To PC.
14 Nov. 1777: PC recommends £10.
      House agrees.
18 Nov. 1777: Senate agrees.

**443-P**   **Hodges, Martha**
      JHD: 8 Nov. 1777                     York County
  Additional compensation for wagon and team impressed to move baggage of militia.
  Manuscript unsigned.
8 Nov. 1777: To PC.
14 Nov. 1777: PC recommends additional compensation of £6 15s.
      House agrees.
18 Nov. 1777: Senate agrees.

**444-P-†**   **Augusta County—Citizens**
      JHD: 8 Nov. 1777                     Augusta County
  For a division of Augusta County into two counties.
8 Nov. 1777: To PG.
      See 428-P-† for action.

**445-P-†**   **Bedford County—Citizens**
      JHD: 8 Nov. 1777                   Bedford County
                                                  Henry County
  For the formation of a new county out of parts of the counties of Bedford and Henry. (There were several such petitions, suggesting varying divisions, but the exact number is not known.)
8 Nov. 1777: To PG.
9 Dec. 1777: PG recommends a particular division, and recommends that two different divisions be rejected.
      House agrees to first recommendation and directs PG to prepare bill.

## Virginia Legislative Petitions

24 Dec. 1777: Bill amended by House.
26 Dec. 1777: House passes bill and sends to Senate.
1 Jan. 1778: Senate refers to committee of whole and after debate rejects it, JS.

### 446-P  Spotsylvania County—Citizens
JHD: 8 Nov. 1777                                  Spotsylvania County
For moving courthouse from Fredericksburg to center of county.
Manuscript signed by: O. Towles, Z. Lewis, Thomas Towles, William Davenport, Phil. Bud Johnson, and 494 others. Has attached the distance each petitioner lived from Fredericksburg.
8 Nov. 1777: To PG.
2 Dec. 1777: PG recommends that it be carried over to next session of GA. House agrees.
28 Oct. 1778: PG finds reasonable and bill is presented and passed.
Senate later agrees.
For act removing courthouse to some other place near the center, see 9H558.

### 447-P-† Spotsylvania County—Citizens
JHD: 8 Nov. 1777                                  Spotsylvania County
Opposing the moving of the courthouse to center of county. (First noted on 2 December 1777 when it is carried over, along with 446-P, to next session of GA.)
8 Nov. 1777: To PG.
2 Dec. 1777: Carried over to next session of GA.
28 Oct. 1778: PG recommends rejection.
House rejects.
See 455-P.

### 448-P  Washington County Court—Members
JHD: 8 Nov. 1777                                  Washington County
For establishment of a town (Abingdon) and courthouse there for the county.
Manuscript signed by: Geo. Blackburn, Wm. Campbell, James Montgomery, John Campbell, Thos. Masten, and five others.
8 Nov. 1777: To PG.
Apparently a bill was prepared and carried over to next session of GA where it was passed by both houses in October 1778 session. For act establishing Abingdon, see 9H555.

## 8 – 10 November 1777

**449-P**
Eck-
A1097 **Cogar, Jacob**
JHD: 8 Nov. 1777                            Augusta County
Compensation for military service in Indian expedition in 1776.
Manuscript unsigned, but has affidavit attached.
8 Nov. 1777: To PC.
7 Jan. 1778: Carried over to next session of GA.
26 Nov. 1778: PC recommends £4 9s. 4d.
      House agrees.
4 Dec. 1778: Senate agrees.

**450-P**   **Ewin, Samuel**
JHD: 10 Nov. 1777                              Not known
Asking for a reward, on behalf of John Blankenship, James M'Call, and himself, for securing information about proposed actions of Cherokee Indians west of Long Island, on Holstein River. They were originally commissioned to bring back a Cherokee Indian for interrogation, but claimed they secured the necessary information without bringing in a prisoner.
Manuscript unsigned.
10 Nov. 1777: To PC.
19 Nov. 1777: PC recommends £100.
      House agrees.
20 Nov. 1777: Senate sends to special committee.
21 Nov. 1777: Senate rejects, JS.

**451-P**   **Williams, Thomas**
JHD: 10 Nov. 1777                              Charlotte County
Additional compensation for provisions he purchased for his company of militia.
Manuscript unsigned.
10 Nov. 1777: To PC.
18 Nov. 1777: PC recommends an additional amount of £7 9s. 5d.
      House agrees.
21 Nov. 1777: Senate agrees.

**452-P**   **Gorman, William**
JHD: 10 Nov. 1777                                Not known
Compensation for wound received while transporting gunpowder and military stores from New Orleans to Pittsburgh in April 1777.

Manuscript unsigned, but carries an endorsement from Governor Patrick Henry that General Assembly should act. Accounts are also attached. It would appear that Gorman was a resident of New Orleans.
10 Nov. 1777: To PC.
14 Nov. 1777: PC recommends £10 for surgeon's fees and £40 for present relief.
    House agrees.
15 Nov. 1777: Senate agrees, JS.

**453-P**    **Irvine, Margaret**
    JHD: 10 Nov. 1777        York County
Compensation for illness and death of her husband, Abraham Irvine, while in Continental service.
Manuscript unsigned, but has certificate of death attached.
10 Nov. 1777: To PC.
1 Dec. 1777: PC recommends £35 for support of herself and her children to be charged to account of commonwealth against the United States of America.
    House agrees.
5 Dec. 1777: Senate agrees.

**454-P**
Eck–
A1663    **Ruffin, Edmund, Jr.**
    JHD: 10 Nov. 1777        Bedford County
Compensation for slave who attempted to escape to Lord Dunmore in 1775, was captured and jailed in Williamsburg, where he was booked for transportation to West Indies, but presumably escaped.
Manuscript unsigned, but has attached to it the minutes of the Committee of Safety of 24 December 1775 listing other slaves of Ruffin who attempted to escape to Lord Dunmore together with a list of slaves belonging to others.
10 Nov. 1777: To PC.
22 Nov. 1777: PC recommends £60.
    House recommits to PC.
24 Dec. 1777: PC recommends £15, it appearing that the slave was delivered to Captain Eustace, with others, for transportation to West Indies, but their disposition had never been determined.
    House agrees.
1 Jan. 1778: Senate agrees.

## 10 – 12 November 1777

**455-P  Spotsylvania County—Citizens**
  JHD: 11 Nov. 1777                              Spotsylvania County
  To postpone consideration of moving Spotsylvania County courthouse (446-P) until next session of General Assembly.
  Manuscript unsigned.
  11 Nov. 1777: To PG.
  2 Dec. 1777: PG recommends postponement.
    House agrees.

**456-P-†  Peed, John**
  JHD: 11 Nov. 1777                              Not known
  Compensation for wound accidentally received in military service.
  11 Nov. 1777: To PC.
  19 Nov. 1777: PC recommends rejection.
    House rejects.

**457-P  Moon, Gideon**
  JHD: 11 Nov. 1777                              Mecklenburg County
  Compensation for wound accidentally received in military service.
  Manuscript unsigned.
  11 Nov. 1777: To PC.
  1 Dec. 1777: PC recommends £10 for current relief and £5 per annum for three years.
    House agrees.
  5 Dec. 1777: Senate agrees.

**458-P  Goodrich, John, Sr.**
  JHD: 12 Nov. 1777                              Not known
  For release from Albemarle County jail to which he had been taken from Williamsburg.
  Manuscript unsigned.
  12 Nov. 1777: House lays on table.
  14 Nov. 1777: House being informed that Goodrich had escaped from Albemarle County jail, it is ordered that attorney general prosecute him as soon as General Court is established and opened.

**459-P-†  Bailey, James Wallace**
  JHD: 12 Nov. 1777                              King William County
  Compensation for slave convicted for felony and sentenced to be hanged, who escaped from King William County jail to the British.

## Virginia Legislative Petitions

12 Nov. 1777: To PC.
9 Dec. 1777: PC recommends that it be carried over to next session of GA.
6 Nov. 1778: PC recommends £90.
    House agrees.
23 Nov. 1778: Senate agrees.

### 460-P    Bucktrout, Benjamin
    JHD: 14 Nov. 1777        Williamsburg

Compensation for impressed horse that died by falling into a well.
Manuscript unsigned, but has certificate of value attached.
14 Nov. 1777: To PC.
1 Dec. 1777: PC recommends £30.
    House agrees.
5 Dec. 1777: Senate agrees.

### 461-P-†    Stroud, Joseph
    JHD: 14 Nov. 1777        Not known

To be engaged by the commonwealth in the making of salt.
14 Nov. 1777: To committee on saltworks.
    Committee apparently did not report.

### 462-P    Vanbibber, Abraham
    JHD: 15 Nov. 1777        Not known

Compensation for his apprehension and imprisonment by the British because of his having secured and shipped war supplies by subterfuge from Saint Eustatia Island. He had been informed upon by the captain of a state vessel.

Manuscript unsigned, but has attached a copy of a letter to the U.S. provisional congress.
15 Nov. 1777: To an ad hoc committee.
    Committee apparently did not report and no further record found.

### 463-P-†    Blackburn, Benjamin
    JHD: 15 Nov. 1777        Not known

Compensation for loss of fifty pounds of gunpowder from a leaky cask in transportation from Williamsburg to Botetourt County.
15 Nov. 1777: To PC.
7 Jan. 1778: PC recommends rejection.
    House rejects.

## 14 – 18 November 1777

**464-P        Frazer, William**
        JHD: 17 Nov. 1777                      King William County
To remove Quarles's tobacco warehouse to a more convenient location on his land.
    Manuscript unsigned.
17 Nov. 1777: To PG.
8 Jan. 1778: Carried over to next session of GA.
23 Oct. 1778: PG recommends approval.
        House lays on table.
        No further action found.

**465-P        Orange County—Citizens**
        JHD: 17 Nov. 1777                           Orange County
For a division of the county.
    Manuscript signed by: Rowland Thomas, Reuben Daniel, George Moor, William Stevenson, Nehemiah Roswell, and 128 others.
17 Nov. 1777: To PG.
        Manuscript endorsement says carried over to next session of GA.
30 May 1778: PG recommends rejection.
        House rejects.

**466-P-†     King George County—Citizens**
        JHD: 18 Nov. 1777                      King George County
                                                            Stafford County
For adjusting of military quotas between Stafford County and that part of King George County that was formerly part of Stafford County.
18 Nov. 1777: To PG.
21 Nov. 1777: PG reports reasonable.
        House rejects.

**467-P-\***    **King George County—Citizens**
        JHD: 18 Nov. 1777                      King George County
Concerns the transferring of land between King George and Westmoreland counties.
18 Nov. 1777: To PG.
        For action on this, see 332-P-†.

**468-P-\***    **Stafford County—Citizens**
        JHD: 18 Nov. 1777                            Stafford County
                                                            King George County

## Virginia Legislative Petitions

Asking that military quotas between King George County and that part of Stafford taken from King George County not be adjusted.
18 Nov. 1777: To PG.
21 Nov. 1777: PG recommends rejection.
    House rejects.

**469-P**    **Ballendine, John and Reveley, John**
JHD: 18 Nov. 1777                  Buckingham County
Asking an additional subsidy for completing the iron furnace in Buckingham County over the £5,000 already granted.
Manuscript unsigned, but has attached accounts of funds expended, and a statement from George Carrington for himself and other trustees.
18 Nov. 1777: To PG.
21 Nov. 1777: PG recommends an additional £2,500
    House agrees.
24 Nov. 1777: Senate agrees.

**470-P**
Rob–Not found    **Epperson, Richard and Jones, Catlet**
JHD: 18 Nov. 1777, for action          Kentucky County
Compensation for wounds received in protection of Kentucky from Indians.
Manuscript signed by Richard Epperson, Catlet Jones, and Daniel Boone.
Date unknown: To PG. (Probably 435-P-†, which see.)
18 Nov. 1777: PG recommends £10 for present relief and £5 per annum for
    life for Epperson and Jones.
    Recommitted to PG.
22 Nov. 1777: PG recommends £10 for present relief and £5 per annum for
    life for Epperson, and £20 for present relief and £10 per annum for
    life for Jones.
    House agrees.
29 Nov. 1777: Senate amends, but House apparently did not agree for Epperson presented a new petition on 26 November 1778 (896-P-†), and Jones did the same on 15 October 1778 (662-P-†).

**471-P**    **Gist, Nathaniel**
JHD: 19 Nov. 1777                           Not known
Asking that treaty with Cherokee Indians be confirmed, and that an island in

## 18 – 21 November 1777

Holstein River that was granted to him by the Cherokee Indians in 1761 or 1762 also be confirmed.

Manuscript unsigned.

19 Nov. 1777: House lays on table.

       Apparently no further action taken.

### 472-P
Eck-A6    **Smith, Thoroughgood (Administrator of Patrick Galt, deceased)**

    JHD: 19 Nov. 1777                      Accomack County

Compensation for services of Patrick Galt as surgeon to Virginia troops before he was officially appointed to the office.

Manuscript signed: Thoroughgood Smith. A letter from Galt, dated at Onancock, 27 December 1776, is attached, together with four depositions.

19 Nov. 1777: To PC.

7 Jan. 1778: Carried over to next session of GA.

8 Dec. 1778: Carried over to next session of GA, but no further record found.

### 473-P    Lewis, William

    JHD: 19 Nov. 1777                    Northumberland County

Compensation for damages done to boat and horse, both impressed.

Manuscript unsigned, but has certificate at bottom.

19 Nov. 1777: To PC.

7 Jan. 1778: Carried over to next session of GA.

20 Nov. 1778: PC recommends rejection.

       House rejects.

### 474-P-†    Ballendine, John

    JHD: 21 Nov. 1777                          Henrico County

Asking that an act be passed vesting in him the powers of subscribers and directors that were given by an act of 1772 allowing him to construct a canal around the falls of the James River at Westham. Also asking for increases in tolls.

21 Nov. 1777: To PG.

22 Nov. 1777: PG reports reasonable.

       House agrees and orders bill or bills drawn.

29 Dec. 1777: Bill presented and sent to special committee.

1 Jan. 1778: Bill amended, but postponed according to JHD until 10 March

## Virginia Legislative Petitions

1778 when the GA was not in session. (There are many later petitions by Ballendine.)
No act found in Hening.

**475-P  Lewis, Edward**
JHD: 21 Nov. 1777                                     Lunenburg County
Compensation for accidental wound received while serving in militia.
Manuscript unsigned.
21 Nov. 1777: To PC.
1 Dec. 1777: PC recommends £20 for present relief and £10 per annum for life.
   House agrees.
5 Dec. 1777: Senate agrees.

**476-P-†  Spotsylvania County—Citizens**
JHD: 21 Nov. 1777                                     Spotsylvania County
Supporting a petition of Orange County that part of Spotsylvania County be added to Orange County.
21 Nov. 1777: To PG.
   Committee apparently did not report.

**477-P-†  Hommel, Peter**
JHD: 21 Nov. 1777                                     Not known
Compensation for supporting James Evans, a soldier in the militia, who had been wounded in 1775.
21 Nov. 1777: To PC.
1 Jan. 1778: PC recommends rejection.
   House rejects.

**478-P-†  Lee, Lewis**
JHD: 21 Nov. 1777                                     Not known
Compensation for indentured servant, Jesse Kelley, a mulatto, who enlisted in military service.
21 Nov. 1777: To PC.
8 Dec. 1777: PC recommends rejection.
   House rejects.

**479-P  Caroline County—Citizens**
JHD: 21 Nov. 1777                                     Caroline County

## 21 – 23 November 1777

For universal fishing rights in Rappahannock River, which had been denied by landholders on western side.

Manuscript signed by: Richd. Roy, William Kidd, John McClean, Thomas Broaddus, James Daniel, and 115 others.

21 Nov. 1777: House rejects by refusal to refer to a committee.

**480-P-†  Aimes, John**
　　JHD: 21 Nov. 1777　　　　　　　　　　　　　　　　Not known

Compensation for indentured servant, a mulatto, who enlisted in the military service.

21 Nov. 1777: To PG.
8 Dec. 1777: PG recommends rejection.
　　House rejects.

**481-P  Nelson, Thomas**
　　JHD: 21 Nov. 1777　　　　　　　　　　　　　　Fauquier County

Compensation for an apprentice, George Bullitt, who enlisted in the military service.

Manuscript unsigned.

21 Nov. 1777: House rejects by refusal to refer to a committee.

**482-P-†  Culpeper County—Citizens**
　　JHD: 21 Nov. 1777　　　　　　　　　　　　　　Culpeper County

For adding part of Culpeper County to Orange County. (There were several such petitions, but the exact number is not known.)

21 Nov. 1777: To PG.
　　Carried over to next session of GA.
30 May 1778: PG recommends rejection.
　　House rejects.

**483-P-†  Reveley, John**
　　JHD: 22 Nov. 1777　　　　　　　　　　　　　　Henrico County

Regarding his finding a special clay near the coal pits on the James River for manufacturing brick for foundry at Westham. He claims the firebricks have proved themselves, and asks that his wages and future service be determined.

22 Nov. 1777: To PG.
1 Jan. 1778: Carried over to next session of GA, but no further record found.
　　There are later petitions from Reveley, some of which relate to this matter.

## Virginia Legislative Petitions

**484-P   Virginia Infantry and Artillery Officers**
  JHD: 22 Nov. 1777                                                    Not known
To allow expenses for forage for their horses, as is done in Continental service.
  Manuscript signed by: James Quarles, Edward Moody, William Long, John McElheny, Will Lawson, John Dualey, and James Moody.
  22 Nov. 1777: To committee of whole on state of army.
           Committee apparently did not report.
           For general act stipulating that Virginia troops should receive same bounty, pay, rations, and clothing as those in Continental service, see 9H337.

**485-P   Row, Frances**
  JHD: 22 Nov. 1777                                                    Not known
Compensation for death of her husband, Benjamin Row, in military service.
  Manuscript unsigned.
  22 Nov. 1777: To PC.
  5 Jan. 1778: PC recommends £30 for her present support to be charged to account of commonwealth against the United States of America.
           House agrees.
  9 Jan. 1778: Senate agrees.

**486-P-†   Burwell, Anne**
  JHD: 22 Nov. 1777                                                    Not known
Compensation for slave who was accidentally drowned while transporting ammunition for use of Virginia troops in December 1776.
  22 Nov. 1777: To PC.
  5 Jan. 1778: PC recommends £120 to be charged to commonwealth account against the United States of America.
           House agrees.
           Senate probably agrees, but record not found.

**487-P-†   Tobacco Inspectors—Rocky Ridge Warehouse, Cary's Warehouse, John Bolling's Warehouse, Bollingbrooke Warehouse, Osborne's Warehouse, Crutchfield's Warehouse, Page's Warehouse, and Meriwether's Warehouse**
  JHD: 22 Nov. 1777                                        Chesterfield County,
                                                     Hanover County, and others
Stating that salaries are inadequate and asking for salaries commensurate with their services.

## 22 – 24 November 1777

22 Nov. 1777: To PG.
24 Dec. 1777: PG recommends rejection.
    House rejects.

**488-P    Sussex County—Citizens**
    JHD: 22 Nov. 1777                            Sussex County

Complaining of payment made to College of William and Mary for tobacco lands leased from the college, stating that rent paid in tobacco or sterling money was too high, and asking that rents be paid in tobacco at current prices in Sussex County or in current money of the commonwealth.

Manuscript signed by: Aug. Claiborne, William Chamblis, Jesse Peebles, James Hall, Jr., Wm. Dunn, Sr., and eleven others. Manuscript has attached a printed indenture between Augustine Claiborne and College of William and Mary, with what appears to be the seal of the college attached.

22 Nov. 1777: To PG.
24 Dec. 1777: Carried over to next session of GA, but no further record
        found.
    See 333-M and 791-P-†.

**489-P    Matthews, Anne**
    JHD: 24 Nov. 1777                                Not known

Compensation for death of husband, Owen Matthews, who died in military service in New York.

Manuscript unsigned.
24 Nov. 1777: To PC.
9 Dec. 1777: PC recommends £20 to be charged to account of commonwealth
        against the United States of America.
    House agrees.
17 Dec. 1777: Senate agrees.

**490-P-†    Hays, Ann**
    JHD: 24 Nov. 1777                                Not known

Compensation for death of her husband, Daniel Hays, who died in military service.

24 Nov. 1777: To PC.
6 Dec. 1777: PC recommends £20 for immediate relief, and £5 per annum for
        three years.
    House agrees.
13 Dec. 1777: Senate amends.
    It does not appear that House approved Senate amendments.

## Virginia Legislative Petitions

These may involve money changes, which were in controversy. No further record found.

**491-P-†  Milby, Ellinah**
JHD: 24 Nov. 1777                                         Not known
Compensation for death of her husband, James Milby, who died in military service.
24 Nov. 1777: To PC.
1 Dec. 1777: PC recommends £20, to be charged to account of the commonwealth against the United States of America.
  House agrees.
5 Dec. 1777: Senate agrees.

**492-P-†  Stewart, Ralph**
JHD: 24 Nov. 1777                                         Not known
Compensation for slave who ran away in 1774 and joined the Shawanese expedition, during which he was killed.
24 Nov. 1777: To PC.
1 Jan. 1778: PC recommends rejection.
  House rejects.

**493-P-†  Fluvanna County—Citizens**
JHD: 24 Nov. 1777                                    Fluvanna County
To move courthouse to lands of Wilson Miles Cary.
24 Nov. 1777: To PG.
4 Dec. 1777: PG finds reasonable. House orders PG to prepare bill.
  For a related petition see 527-P-†.
  For act providing that justices of Fluvanna County appoint a new place for courthouse, and that Cumberland County justices do likewise, and repealing establishment of town of Effingham in Cumberland County, see 9H438.

**494-P-†  Fluvanna County—Citizens**
JHD: 24 Nov. 1777                                    Fluvanna County
In opposition to removing courthouse from present location.
24 Nov. 1777: To PG.
4 Dec. 1777: PG recommends rejection.
  House rejects.
  See 493-P-†.

## 24 – 25 November 1777

**495-M and P**
Eck–
A834 **Wilcox, Edmund**
JHD: 24 Nov. 1777                        Amherst County

Compensation for surgeon's fees for attending George Witt, Thomas Sheldon, Thomas Smith, John Guttery, Thomas Akins, and James Burns, all in Continental service.

Manuscript unsigned, but has accounts attached to it.
24 Nov. 1777: To PC.
1 Dec. 1777: PC recommends £24 14s. 10c. to be charged to account of commonwealth against the United States of America.
House agrees.
5 Dec. 1777: Senate agrees.

**496-P**    **Chiles, Thomas**
JHD: 25 Nov. 1777                        Caroline County

Compensation for damage to his horse, and expenses for his upkeep, in transporting John Goodrich, Sr., from Williamsburg to New London, Bedford County, whence Goodrich was transported to Botetourt County, but the horse was left at New London.

Manuscript unsigned, but has accounts of Chiles attached together with three depositions.
25 Nov. 1777: To PC.
9 Dec. 1777: PC recommends £3 in returning horse to public, and £9 13s. 10d. for expenses.
House agrees.
15 Dec. 1777: Senate agrees.

**497-P-†**    **Griffin, John Tayloe and Griffin, Mary**
JHD: 25 Nov. 1777                        Brunswick County

Concerns real and personal property devised by Philip Lightfoot in his will to John Lightfoot, his son. If John died without heirs, the property would revert to Armistead Lightfoot and his heirs. Mary Lightfoot Griffin is the sole heir, and under age. Asks that certain property in Brunswick County be sold and proceeds used to purchase slaves.
25 Nov. 1777: House directs special committee to prepare bill.
5 Dec. 1777: Bill presented and referred to enlarged committee.
1 Jan. 1778: Proposed bill amended and reported.
6 Jan. 1778: House agrees to amended bill.
8 Jan. 1778: Senate rejects on second reading, JS.

## Virginia Legislative Petitions

**498-P**
Rob-6 **Kentucky County—Citizens**
    JHD: 25 Nov. 1777                              Kentucky County
For erection of saltworks on property now owned by individuals.
   Manuscript signed by: Saml. Campbell, James Brown, Azariah Davies, David Kerr, Bartholomew Thornton, Daniel Boone, and eighty-four others.
25 Nov. 1777: To PG.
        Carried over to next session of GA.
16 Oct. 1778: PG recommends rejection.
        House rejects.

**499-P-†**   **Adams, Anne**
    JHD: 27 Nov. 1777                                    Not known
Asks for allowance of £20 sterling, which she had been awarded as widow of British officer for many years before the present conflict, and which she cannot now receive from Great Britain.
27 Nov. 1777: To PC.
1 Jan. 1778: PC recommends rejection.
        House rejects.

**500-P-†**   **Augusta County—Citizens**
    JHD: 27 Nov. 1777                                 Augusta County
For adding part of Augusta County to Hampshire County.
27 Nov. 1777: To PG.
8 Dec. 1777: PG recommends as reasonable and is directed to prepare bill.
        House and Senate agree to act.
        For this act see 9H420.

**501-P-†**   **Yohogania County—Citizens**
    JHD: 27 Nov. 1777                                Yohogania County
Protesting the appointment of militia officers for the county by the governor and Council when proper nominations had been made by the court of Yohogania and delivered to a messenger for transmittal to Williamsburg. Asking for proper authority to settle land title disputes. Protesting penalties for not reading on Sundays, after divine services, certain laws that were required to be read since it interfered with their modes of worship.
27 Nov. 1777: To PG.
17 Dec. 1777: PG recommends rejection of (1) requests for authority to settle

## 25 – 28 November 1777

land titles and (2) removing penalties for not reading laws on Sundays.

House agrees.

17 Dec. 1777: PG finds reasonable the protest over appointment of militia officers and states "that the Governor and Council had no authority to appoint a county lieutenant for Yohogania, other than Dorsey Penticost, who was at that time county lieutenant for the district of West Augusta, and resided in the said county."

House rejects the phrase about Penticost.

House also rejects an amended resolution that removes phrase about Penticost.

**502-P-†   Stephens, Richard, Jr.**
JHD: 28 Nov. 1777                                                                   Augusta County

Claiming a reward for apprehending Joseph Hadley, a horse thief, who was tried and convicted by the court, but the judges refused to give Stephens a certificate since his only witness was Charles Morehead, who had been drafted into the militia and sent to headquarters.

28 Nov. 1777: To PC.
1 Jan. 1778: Carried over to next session of GA.
29 Oct. 1778: PC recommends £20.
31 Oct. 1778: House agrees.
25 Nov. 1778: Senate agrees.

**503-P   Purdie, Alexander**
JHD: 28 Nov. 1777                                                                   Williamsburg

Compensation for extra services performed as public printer in printing sundry copies of test act, certificates, militia act, and others.

Manuscript unsigned.
28 Nov. 1777: To PC.
7 Jan. 1778: PC recommends £95.
    House agrees.
9 Jan. 1778: Senate agrees.

**504-P   Christ Church Parish, Lancaster County—Citizens**
JHD: 28 Nov. 1777                                                                   Lancaster County

For dissolution of the vestry.

Manuscript signed by: Richard Ball, John Taylor, Samuel Kent, Joseph Hubbard, Minetree Jones, and two others.

28 Nov. 1777: To R.

## Virginia Legislative Petitions

5 Dec. 1777: R recommends as reasonable and is directed to prepare a bill.
12 Dec. 1777: Bill presented.
30 Dec. 1777: House passes bill.
5 Jan. 1778: Senate passes bill.
    For this act see 9H439.

**504 A-P  Christ Church Parish, Lancaster County—Citizens**
    JHD: 28 Nov. 1777                    Lancaster County
Text is identical with 504-P, which see.
Manuscript signed by forty persons.

**504 B-P  Christ Church Parish, Lancaster County—Citizens**
    JHD: 28 Nov. 1777                    Lancaster County
Text is identical with 504-P, which see.
Manuscript signed by seventy persons.

**504 C-P  Christ Church Parish, Lancaster County—Citizens**
    JHD: 28 Nov. 1777                    Lancaster County
Text is identical with 504-P, which see.
Manuscript signed by fifty-six persons.

**504 D-P  Christ Church Parish, Lancaster County—Citizens**
    JHD: 28 Nov. 1777                    Lancaster County
Text is identical with 504-P, which see.
Manuscript signed by thirty-five persons.

**505-P-†  Christ Church Parish, Lancaster County—Citizens**
    JHD: 28 Nov. 1777                    Lancaster County
Opposing dissolution of vestry.
28 Nov. 1777: To R.
5 Dec. 1777: R recommends rejection.
       House rejects.
       See 504-P.

**506-P-†  Pittsylvania County—Citizens**
    JHD: 28 Nov. 1777                    Pittsylvania County
Objecting to new location of courthouse, stating that it is not in center of county.
28 Nov. 1777: To PG.
       Carried over to next session of GA.

16 Oct. 1778: PG recommends rejection.
    House recommits.
19 Oct. 1778: PG again recommends rejection.
    House rejects.

**507-P-†**   **Cantrell, Christopher; Scott, John; and Scott, Joseph**
    JHD: 28 Nov. 1777                        Hampshire County
                                                        Augusta County

    Protesting actions of Andrew Tamboro in claiming land that contained saltpeter that the petitioners discovered, and asking that rights of discoverers be vested in them if on unclaimed land, and they, after paying damages, have the right to work claimed land if the owner refuses to do so.
28 Nov. 1777: To PG.
19 Dec. 1777: PG recommends that right to work unclaimed land is reasonable.
    House rejects.
19 Dec. 1777: PG recommends that right to work claimed land be rejected.
    House rejects.

**508-P-†**   **Cammock, Henry**
    JHD: 28 Nov. 1777                               Not known
    Compensation for accidental wound received in military service.
28 Nov. 1777: To PC.
6 Dec. 1777: PC recommends rejection since petitioner is fit for duty.
    House rejects.

**509-P**
Eck–Not
found   **Devore, James**
    JHD: 29 Nov. 1777                               Augusta County
                                                        Yohogania County

    For establishment of ferry across Monongahela River to western bank, which had been allowed by county court.
    Manuscript unsigned.
29 Nov. 1777: To PG.
24 Dec. 1777: Carried over to next session of GA.
15 Oct. 1778: PG recommends as reasonable.
    House agrees and orders bill drawn.
Date unknown: House and Senate pass bill.
    For general ferry act, including this one, see 9H546.

## Virginia Legislative Petitions

**510-P-†   Zenesburg—Citizens**
  JHD: 29 Nov. 1777          Not known
 Compensation for homes and property abandoned because of attacks of Indians, the petitioners having fled to Fort Henry.
29 Nov. 1777: To PG.
19 Dec. 1777: PG recommends rejection.
  House rejects.

**511-P-†   Carmack, John; Smith, Ezekiel; Looney, John; and Drake, Jonathan**
  JHD: 29 Nov. 1777          Not known
 Compensation for collecting lost cattle and horses and returning them to central point after late Cherokee expedition. Auditors have refused to make payment.
29 Nov. 1777: To PC.
9 Dec. 1777: PC recommends £182 19s. for Carmack, £66 for Smith, £105 16s. for Looney, and £147 5s. for Drake.
  House rejects for want of sufficient proof.
10 Dec. 1777: House appoints commissioners to examine these accounts and authorizes treasurer to pay certified findings and sends resolution to Senate.
23 Dec. 1777: Senate amends resolution.
  House probably agrees to Senate amendments, but no further record found.

**512-P   Rawlings, Margaret**
  JHD: 1 Dec. 1777          Not known
 Compensation for nursing Absalom Wasper, a sick soldier, on his march to New York.
 Manuscript unsigned, but endorsement says rejected 19 November 1778.
1 Dec. 1777: To PC.
7 Dec. 1777: Carried over to next session of GA.
20 Nov. 1778: PC recommends rejection.
  House rejects.

**513-P-†   Bennett, James**
  JHD: 1 Dec. 1777          Not known
 For payment of balance due him for military service, withheld by Charles Collier.
1 Dec. 1777: To PC.

## 29 November – 2 December 1777

5 Jan. 1778: PC recommends matter be determined by courts.
    House amends and rejects for want of proof.

**514-P**
Rob-5    **McGary, Hugh**
    JHD: 1 Dec. 1777        Kentucky County
  Compensation as express rider from Kentucky to Pittsburgh to carry list of 200 horses, with their markings, captured by the Cherokees in March and April 1777.
  Manuscript unsigned, but has two certificates attached.
1 Dec. 1777: To PC.
5 Jan. 1778: PC recommends £28 2s. 6d.
    House agrees.
9 Jan. 1778: Senate agrees.
    See 548-P-†.

**515-P-†**    **Tobacco Inspectors—Crutchfield's Warehouse, Page's Warehouse, and Meriwether's Warehouse**
    JHD: 1 Dec. 1777        Hanover County
  Asking for larger and more certain salaries.
1 Dec. 1777: To PG.
    Committee apparently did not report.

**516-P**
Eck-A5    **Coleburn, Robert**
    JHD: 1 Dec. 1777, for action        Accomack County
  Compensation for 310 pounds of beef furnished militia in October 1777 at 9d. per pound.
  Manuscript unsigned, but has certificate attached dated 8 October 1777.
Date unknown: To PC.
1 Dec. 1777: PC recommends £11 12s. 6d.
    House amends and agrees to £7 15s.
5 Dec. 1777: Senate agrees.

**517-P-†**    **Casson, Charles**
    JHD: 2 Dec. 1777        Portsmouth
  Compensation for medicinal rum and wine furnished Portsmouth hospital for use of Samuel Harris, a surgeon.
2 Dec. 1777: To PC.

9 Dec. 1777: PC recommends rejection.
   House rejects.

### 518-P-† Benton, Lazarus
JHD: 2 Dec. 1777                                            Not known
  Compensation for the death of four sons and a son-in-law killed by the Indians, thus leaving him unable to support himself.
2 Dec. 1777: To PC.
6 Dec. 1777: PC recommends £20 per annum for life.
   House agrees.
13 Dec. 1777: Senate agrees.

### 519-P-† Stewart, John
JHD: 2 Dec. 1777                                            Not known
  Compensation for wound received in campaign against Indians in Shawanese expedition of 1774.
2 Dec. 1777: To PC.
21 Jan. 1778: PC recommends £20 for current relief.
   House agrees.
21 Jan. 1778: Senate agrees.

### 520-P  Caroline County—Citizens
JHD: 5 Dec. 1777                                        Caroline County
  Asking that certain fixed sums in tithes be levied for ministers of all denominations, leaving it to the payer as to what denominations he chooses to support.
  Manuscript signed by: Walker Taliaferro, Jn. Jones, Roger Quarles, John Minor, Wm. Marshall, and fifty-five others.
5 Dec. 1777: To R.
2 Dec. 1778: Carried over to next session of GA.
   No further record found.

### 520 A-P  Caroline County—Citizens
JHD: 5 Dec. 1777                                        Caroline County
  Text is identical with 520-P, which see.
  Manuscript signed by thirty-three persons.

### 520 B-P  Caroline County—Citizens
JHD: 5 Dec. 1777                                        Caroline County

## 2 - 5 December 1777

Text is identical with 520-P, which see.
Manuscript signed by fifty-one persons.

**521-P Terry, Stephen**
    JHD: 5 Dec. 1777                                       Not known
Compensation for military wound received in battle of Brandywine.
Manuscript unsigned.
5 Dec. 1777: To PC.
9 Dec. 1777: PC recommends £25 for present relief and £10 per annum for life to be charged to the account of this commonwealth against the United States of America.
       House amends, deleting £10 per annum for life, and agrees.
17 Dec. 1777: Senate agrees to amended resolution.

**522-P Buckingham County—Citizens**
    JHD: 5 Dec. 1777                              Buckingham County
Asking that part of Buckingham County be added to Cumberland County.
Manuscript signed by: Natl. Anderson, Wm. Anderson, Matthew Anderson, Richd. Ford, Joseph Price, and fifty-seven others.
5 Dec. 1777: To PG.
       Manuscript endorsement says reasonable.
       Apparently no further action taken, but this may have been carried over as 695-P-†, which has been entered separately for lack of proof. A somewhat different portion of Buckingham County was added to Cumberland County in 1778.
       For this act see 9H559.

**523-P-† Gist, Nathaniel**
    JHD: 5 Dec. 1777                                         Not known
Compensation for bringing in chiefs of Cherokee Indians to Big Island to discuss treaty and possibly enlist some in Continental service.
5 Dec. 1777: To special committee.
21 Jan. 1778: Committee recommends £50.
       House agrees.
21 Jan. 1778: Senate agrees.

**524-P Owens, John**
    JHD: 5 Dec. 1777                                  Pittsylvania County
For a new ferry over Dan River to land of Sylvester Adams.
Manuscript unsigned.

## Virginia Legislative Petitions

5 Dec. 1777: To PG.
22 Dec. 1777: Carried over to next session of GA.
8 Jan. 1778: Carried over to next session of GA.
3 Dec. 1778: PG finds reasonable and is authorized to prepare bill.
    House and Senate approve bill.
    For general ferry bill, including this one, see 9H585.

**525-P-†  Parker, Nicholas**
    JHD: 5 Dec. 1777                                      Not known
Compensation for illness and death of his son, Nicholas Parker, Jr., while in military service.
5 Dec. 1777: To PC.
7 Jan. 1778: Carried over to next session of GA.
29 Oct. 1778: PC recommends £25 4s. 3d. for board of his son and £18 5s. for expense of physician.
    Recommitted to PC.
31 Oct. 1778: PC recommends deletion of item for board, but recommends £18 5s. for expense of physician, such amount to be charged to the account of the commonwealth against the United States of America.
    House agrees to amended resolution.
23 Nov. 1778: Senate agrees to amended resolution.

**526-P  Orange County—Citizens**
    JHD: 5 Dec. 1777                                    Orange County
To restrain production of tobacco and emphasize raising and manufacturing of necessary articles for prosecution of war.
    Manuscript signed by: James Taylor, Ben. Porter, Thos. Chew, Andrew Stephen, John Terrill, and 101 others.
5 Dec. 1777: House rejects by refusal to refer to a committee.

**527-P-†  Cumberland County—Citizens**
    JHD: 5 Dec. 1777                                 Cumberland County
                                                              Fluvanna County
Asking for repeal of act laying off town of Effingham as county seat of Cumberland County, and that justices consider a new site for the courthouse.
5 Dec. 1777: To PG.
19 Dec. 1777: PG finds reasonable and is directed to prepare bill.
24 Dec. 1777: Bill reported and referred to special committee with directions to allow Fluvanna County to select new courthouse site.

1 Jan. 1778: Revised bill presented.
3 Jan. 1778: House passes bill.
9 Jan. 1778: Senate passes bill.
    For related petition see 493-P-†.
    For this act see 9H438.

**528-P-†  Fox, John**
    JHD: 5 Dec. 1777                        Gloucester County
To establish a ferry from his land to Cappahosic Ferry and mouth of Stanhope Creek, across York River.
5 Dec. 1777: To PG.
24 Dec. 1777: Carried over to next session of GA.
    No further action found, but a new petition was presented 9 November 1778 (793-P).

**529-M  Continental Army—Field Officers**
    JHD: 6 Dec. 1777                               Not known
Asking for relief for widow and family of Lieutenant Colonel Seayers, a Continental officer who was killed at Germantown in October 1777.
    Manuscript signed by: Wm. Woodford, Chas. Scott, Ro. Lawson, Will Heth, John Nevill, and ten others.
6 Dec. 1777: To a special committee.
10 Dec. 1777: Committee recommends £200 to be charged to the account of
        the commonwealth against the United States of America, and that
        the situation be represented to Congress.
    House agrees.
20 Dec. 1777: Senate agrees.

**530-P-†  Cumberland County—Citizens**
    JHD: 6 Dec. 1777                          Cumberland County
For maintaining courthouse at present location.
6 Dec. 1777: To PG.
23 Dec. 1777: PG recommends rejection.
    House rejects.
    For related petition see 527-P-†.

**531-P-†  Baker, Benjamin**
    JHD: 8 Dec. 1777                          Nansemond County
For official recognition of tobacco warehouse erected at South Quay.
8 Dec. 1777: Special committee to prepare bill.

## Virginia Legislative Petitions

House and Senate include this in general warehouse act. For this act see 9H400.

### 532-P-† Smith, James
JHD: 8 Dec. 1777                                         Not known

Compensation for nursing two sons who were taken ill in Continental service.

8 Dec. 1777: To PC.

7 Jan. 1778: PC recommends £23 8s. 4d. for nursing and £4 for medicines to be charged to the account of the commonwealth against the United States of America.

    House agrees.

9 Jan. 1778: Senate agrees.

### 533-P-† Pearson, Moses
JHD: 8 Dec. 1777                                   Pittsylvania County

Compensation for illness contracted in military service.

8 Dec. 1777: To PC.

5 Jan. 1778: PC recommends £10.

    House agrees.

9 Jan. 1778: Senate agrees.

### 534-P
Eck–Not found    **Amelia County—Citizens**

JHD: 8 Dec. 1777                                        Amelia County

Asking for division of county along parish lines.

Manuscript signed by: Jeremiah Walker, Sam. Holden, John Fowlkes, Griffin Smith, David Ball, and twenty-eight others.

8 Dec. 1777: Carried over to next session of GA.

15 Oct. 1778: PG recommends rejection.

    House rejects.

    See 666-P-†.

### 534 A-P
Eck–Not found    **Amelia County—Citizens**

JHD: 8 Dec. 1777                                        Amelia County

Text is similar to 534-P, which see.

Manuscript signed by ninety-four persons.

## 8 December 1777

**534 B-P**
Eck–Not
found    **Amelia County—Citizens**
        JHD: 8 Dec. 1777                  Amelia County
    Text is similar to 534-P, which see.
    Manuscript signed by fifty-three persons.

**535-P**    **Hopkins, Jonathan**
        JHD: 8 Dec. 1777               Princess Anne County
    Claim for £13 15s. worth of wheel timber furnished garrison at Portsmouth.
    Manuscript unsigned, but has two certificates and one account attached.
8 Dec. 1777: To PC.
5 Jan. 1778: PC recommends £13 15s.
        House agrees.
9 Jan. 1778: Senate agrees.

**536-P-†**    **Gibson, Abraham**
        JHD: 8 Dec. 1777                       Portsmouth
    Compensation for damages to houses and lots used by Virginia troops as a garrison.
8 Dec. 1777: To PC.
        Committee apparently did not report.
        See note on 545-P.

**537-P-†**    **Fulgham, Charles**
        JHD: 8 Dec. 1777                        Not known
    Compensation for salvage and court costs paid for slave taken by John Goodrich, Sr., to North Carolina, where he was recaptured and returned.
8 Dec. 1777: To PG.
8 Jan. 1778: PG recommends £44 17s. 6d.
        House agrees.
19 Jan. 1778: Senate agrees.

**538-P-†**    **Buckingham County—Citizens**
        JHD: 8 Dec. 1777                  Buckingham County
    Opposing any alteration of lines between Buckingham and Cumberland counties.
8 Dec. 1777: To PG.
        Committee apparently did not report.
        See 522-P.

## Virginia Legislative Petitions

**539-P-†　Kidd, Daniel**
　　　JHD: 8 Dec. 1777　　　　　　　　　　　　　　Not known
　Protesting underpayment for linen and other necessaries purchased for use of the Cherokee expedition.
　8 Dec. 1777: To PC.
　5 Jan. 1778: PC recommends rejection.
　　　House rejects.

**540-P-†　Morris, Richard**
　　　JHD: 9 Dec. 1777　　　　　　　　　　　　　　Not known
　For death of his own horse during military service in 1776, he being unable to hire one.
　9 Dec. 1777: To PC (PG?).
　1 Jan. 1778: Carried over to next session of GA.
　20 Nov. 1778: PG recommends rejection.
　　　House rejects.

**541-P　Savidge, Mourning**
　　　JHD: 9 Dec. 1777　　　　　　　　　　　　　　Surry County
　Compensation for death of husband, Philip Savidge, in military service.
　Manuscript unsigned.
　9 Dec. 1777: To PC.
　5 Jan. 1778: PC recommends £20 to be charged to the account of the commonwealth against the United States of America.
　　　House agrees.
　9 Jan. 1778: Senate agrees.

**542-P　Williams, Mildred**
　　　JHD: 9 Dec. 1777　　　　　　　　　　　　　　Surry County
　Compensation for death of husband, Lewis Williams, in military service.
　Manuscript unsigned.
　9 Dec. 1777: To PC.
　5 Jan. 1778: PC recommends £25 to be charged to the account of the commonwealth against the United States of America.
　　　House agrees.
　9 Jan. 1778: Senate agrees.

**543-P　Moody, Hannah**
　　　JHD: 9 Dec. 1777　　　　　　　　　　　　　　Surry County

## 8 – 10 December 1777

Compensation for death of husband, Samuel Moody, in military service.
Manuscript unsigned.
9 Dec. 1777: To PC.
5 Jan. 1778: PC recommends £20 to be charged to the account of the commonwealth against the United States of America.
    House agrees.
9 Jan. 1778: Senate agrees.

**544-P    Archer, Edward**
    JHD: 10 Dec. 1777                                                 Not known
Compensation for ship and slave seized by Lord Dunmore. (Apparently Archer had seized a quantity of wine in retaliation.)
Manuscript unsigned.
10 Dec. 1777: To PC (PG?).
8 Jan. 1778: Carried over to next session of GA.
13 Oct. 1778: PG recommends rejection.
    House rejects.

**545-P    Veale, Thomas; Culpeper, Henry; Lello, John; and Butt, Arthur**
    JHD: 10 Dec. 1777                                                   Portsmouth
Compensation for damages to and rent for houses occupied by Virginia troops in Portsmouth.
Manuscript unsigned.
10 Dec. 1777: To PC.
    Committee apparently did not report.
    Veale petitioned again later (873-P-†).
    At this point there was no system of recompense for damages done by Virginia troops, but later such petitions were referred to the commissioners, reestablished in the October 1777 session of the GA, for determining not only loss by burning, but also damages by troops in Portsmouth, Suffolk, Great Bridge, and Norfolk County, as well as Norfolk borough. See 9H-27.

**546-P-†    Loudoun County—Citizens**
    JHD: 10 Dec. 1777                                           Loudoun County
Contesting the enlistment of apprentices in the military without granting exemptions to their masters.
10 Dec. 1777: To PG.

24 Dec. 1777: PG recommends rejection.
   House rejects.

### 547-P    Meriwether, Francis
JHD: 10 Dec. 1777                                     Spotsylvania County
Stating that in 1773 he agreed with Cunningham and Company, merchants of Glasgow, to purchase a tract of land for £300; that he had offered the purchase money, but had been refused title. Asking that he be allowed to pay £300 to commonwealth and receive title. (Meriwether petitioned again in November 1779 [1158-P].)
   Manuscript unsigned.
10 Dec. 1777: House rejects by refusal to refer to a committee.

### 548-P-†   Gould, David
JHD: 10 Dec. 1777                                           Kentucky County
For horse, valued at £50, which he sold Hugh McGary to ride express to Fort Pitt, and for which he has not received payment.
10 Dec. 1777: To PC.
5 Jan. 1778: PC recommends rejection.
   House rejects.
   See 514-P.

### 549-P    Littleton Parish, Cumberland County—Vestry
JHD: 10 Dec. 1777                                         Cumberland County
Asking what disposition should be made of balance of tithes collected and held after exemption of dissenters from paying such tithes, and whether the balance could be used to reduce the new levy or to improve the church.
   Manuscript signed by: Nathan Glen, Thomas Nash, Fredk. Hatcher, Adcock Hobson, Benja. Wilson, Geo. Carrington, Jr., Jos. Calland, and Jno. Langhorne.
10 Dec. 1777: To R.
   Carried over to next session of GA.
4 Dec. 1778: Attempt made to carry over, but recommitted to R.
16 Dec. 1778: R recommends rejection since matter is fully covered by law.
   House rejects.

### 550-P-†   Hamilton, Margrett
JHD: 10 Dec. 1777                                                 Not known
Compensation for death of husband, David Hamilton, in military service at battle of Brandywine.

10 Dec. 1777: To PC.
7 Jan. 1778: Carried over to next session of GA.
20 Nov. 1778: PG recommends rejection since matter had been handled by a
    county court.
        House rejects.

**551-P   Figg, Sarah and Buck, Diana**
        JHD: 10 Dec. 1777                                          Not known
Compensation for death of their husbands, James Figg and John Buck, in military service.
Manuscript unsigned, but has certificate of Thomas Nelson attached.
10 Dec. 1777: To PC.
7 Jan. 1778: PC recommends £20 each to be charged to account of commonwealth against the United States of America.
        House agrees.
9 Jan. 1778: Senate agrees.

**552-P**
Eck-A1534, under Bath County
        **Bledsoe, Anthony**
        JHD: 11 Dec. 1777                                       Bedford County
For extra compensation for hire of horses and wagons to convey baggage in Cherokee expedition, particularly for travel on Sunday.
11 Dec. 1777: To PC.
5 Jan. 1778: PC recommends £5 14s. additional for return of wagons to
    Bedford and £25 7s. 6d. for travel on Sundays.
        House agrees.
9 Jan. 1778: Senate agrees.

**553-**
**Address-† Lunenburg County—Citizens**
        JHD: 11 Dec. 1777                                      Lunenburg County
Protesting undue efforts by dissenters to secure signatures on petitions to overthrow the Church of England, they having secured signatures of minors and those unduly credulous.
11 Dec. 1777: To R.
        Committee apparently did not report.

## Virginia Legislative Petitions

**554-M-†  Penticost, Dorsey**
JHD: 11 Dec. 1777      Yohogania County
                       West Augusta District
Compensation for extra duties performed when he was county lieutenant for West Augusta District.
11 Dec. 1777: To PC.
7 Jan. 1778: PC recommends rejection.
    House rejects.

**555-P-†  Halifax County—Citizens**
JHD: 12 Dec. 1777      Halifax County
Asking for a division of the county along the Dan River. (There were several such petitions, but the exact number is not known.)
12 Dec. 1777: Carried over to next session of GA.
21 Oct. 1778: Supported by a new petition, 693-P-†.
    To PG.
28 Oct. 1778: PG recommends rejection.
    House rejects.

**556-P-†  Durley, Mary**
JHD: 24 Dec. 1777, for action      Not known
Compensation for impressed vessel.
Date unknown: To PG.
24 Dec. 1777: PG recommends £20.
    House agrees.
5 Jan. 1778: Senate agrees, JS.

**557-C-†  Military Officers and Soldiers**
JHD: 27 Dec. 1777      Not known
Asking that pay of those at Fort Pitt, Wheeling, Little Kanawha, and Point Pleasant be the same as that received from the commonwealth until they were enlisted in Continental service.
27 Dec. 1777: To PC.
1 Jan. 1778: PC recommends as reasonable.
    House agrees.
9 Jan. 1778: Senate agrees.

**558-C-†  Cooke, Adam, deceased (Estate)**
JHD: 2 Jan. 1778, for action      Not known

## 11 December 1777 – 5 January 1778

Compensation for articles taken from him by Indians while he was a spy in the country's service.
Date unknown: To PC.
2 Jan. 1778: PC recommends £10 2s. 0d.
> House agrees.
5 Jan. 1778: Senate agrees.

### 559-C-†   Coles, William
JHD: 2 Jan. 1778, for action           Not known

Compensation for articles taken from him by Indians while he was a spy in the country's service.
Date unknown: To PC.
2 Jan. 1778: PC recommends £19 9s.
> House agrees.
5 Jan. 1778: Senate agrees.

### 560-P-†   Tobacco Inspectors—Cabin Point Warehouse
JHD: 3 Jan. 1778, for action           Surry County

Asking for indemnification for any accidents to tobacco in storage before late inspection law took place.
Date unknown: To PC.
3 Jan. 1778: PC recommends rejection.
> House rejects.

### 561-P-†   Glass, Vincent
JHD: 5 Jan. 1778, for action           Not known

Compensation for horse hired from him for use of militia.
Date unknown: To PC.
5 Jan. 1778: PC recommends rejection.
> House rejects.

### 562-P-†   Logwood, Thomas
JHD: 5 Jan. 1778, for action           Not known

Compensation for hire of two horses for use of militia in Cherokee expedition.
Date unknown: To PC.
5 Jan. 1778: PC recommends rejection.
> House rejects.
> Logwood presented a new petition on 20 November 1778; see 840-P-†.

## Virginia Legislative Petitions

**563-P-†  Henderson, Nathaniel**
JHD: 5 Jan. 1778, for action                                    Not known
Compensation for price of horse, purchased from Ebenezer Wood, and expenses as express rider from Boonesborough to Fort Pitt.
Date unknown: To PC.
5 Jan. 1778: PC recommends rejection.
    House rejects.

**564-C  Mosby, Littlebury**
JHD: 7 Jan. 1778, for action                                    Powhatan County
Compensation for two horses, on hire to militia, that were lost or stolen. Manuscript unsigned, but has two certificates of value attached.
Date unknown: To PC.
7 Jan. 1778: PC recommends £50.
    House agrees.
9 Jan. 1778: Senate agrees.

**565-Remonstrance-†**
    **Military Officers**
JHD: 13 Jan. 1778                                               Not known
Complaining of high cost of clothing purchased from the public store.
13 Jan. 1778: To lie on table.
15 Jan. 1778: Referred to special committee to report to next session of GA.
    Apparently no further action taken.
    See 566-M-†.

**566-M-†  Aylett, William**
JHD: 13 Jan. 1778                                               Not known
Asking that his proceedings in running public store be investigated.
13 Jan. 1778: To lie on table.
15 Jan. 1778: To special committee to report to next session of GA.
    Apparently no further action taken. (See 565-Remonstrance-†.)
    Aylett also petitioned on 5 November 1778 for investigation.
    See 773-M-†.

**567-Misc. Claims-†**
JHD: 17 Jan. 1778, for action                                   Not known
The following miscellaneous claims were not presented separately, and apparently went to PC without a prior reading on the floor of the House. They

## 5 – 17 January 1778

are listed as they were approved in the journals and are indexed under name and subject.

Date unknown: To PC.

17 Jan. 1778: PC presents report. To lie on table.

20 Jan. 1778: Report read. PC recommends approval. House agrees.

23 Jan. 1778: Senate amends, rejecting the following claims for want of sufficient proof:

Michael Franciscoe (567.17), for one bay horse, £9; John Walker (567.24), for one black ditto, £12; James Tuttle (567.25), for one brown mare, £5; William White (567.26), for one black horse, £11; Meredith Reins (567.28), for one black mare, £10 10s.; John Craig (567.32), for one roan horse, £7 10s.; Samuel Campbell (567.36), for one bay ditto, £10 10s.; Peter Huff (567.47), for one mare, pack saddle, and one kettle, £13 7s. 6d.; William Edmondson (567.51), for one white mare, £6; Andrew Bransteter (567.66), for one dark brown ditto, £10 10s.; and Valentine Little (567.69) for a white ditto, £12.

24 Jan. 1778: House agrees to Senate amendments.

| | |
|---|---|
| 567.1 | To Henry Lawson, guardian of Sally Simmons, for her Negro man slave Daniel, who was condemned and executed for felony, and by the court of the county of Lancaster valued at £120 0s. 0d. |
| 567.2 | To James Garnett, for his Negro man slave Toney, who was condemned and executed, and by the court for the county of Essex valued at £150 0s. 0d. |
| 567.3 | To Thomas Beasley, for his Negro Ned, who was condemned and executed for felony, and by the court of Chesterfield County valued at £60 0s. 0d. |
| 567.4 | To Smith Blakey, for his Negro man Lewey, who was condemned and executed, and by the court of Hanover County valued at £130 0s. 0d. |
| 567.5 | To Joseph Martin, for a bay mare, appraised at £15, and a white horse at £12, lost at Fort Lee, in the country's service, £27 0s. 0d. |
| 567.6 | To Benjamin Dancey, of Craven County, North Carolina, assignee of Robert Hicks, for his Negro man slave Caesar, who was condemned and executed for felony and burglary, and by the court of Isle of Wight County valued at £55 0s. 0d. |
| 567.7 | To James Lyon, for a horse lost on the Cherokee expedition, appraised at £15 0s. 0d. |

## Virginia Legislative Petitions

| | |
|---|---|
| 567.8 | To James Abell, for hire of his horse to convey Richard Sampson, a criminal, from Prince William County to Williamsburg, 16s. 0d. |
| 567.9 | To William Martin, for ditto, 16s. 0d. |
| 567.10 | To John Ball, for ditto, a criminal, from Pittsylvania County to Williamsburg, £2 10s. 0d. |
| 567.11 | To Thomas Black, for ditto, £2 10s. 0d. |
| 567.12 | To Jesse Chilton, for ferriages of sheriffs and guards with criminals, £1 10s. 0d. |
| 567.13 | To Robert Brown, for five days hire of his horse conveying a criminal to the public jail, at 2s. per day, 10s. 0d. |
| 567.14 | To John Muldrough, for a bay horse lost on the late Cherokee expedition, £8 10s. 0d. |
| 567.15 | To William Calvert, for a sorrel ditto, £5 0s. 0d. |
| 567.16 | To William Ross, assignee of Adam M. Cormack, for one bay mare, £12 0s. 0d. |
| 567.17 | To Michael Franciscoe, for a bay ditto, £9 0s. 0d. |
| 567.18 | To Michael Ohair, for one black horse, saddle, and bridle, £9 0s. 0d. |
| 567.19 | To Philip Love, for one flea-bitten gray horse, £18 0s. 0d. |
| 567.20 | To James Mason, for a bay mare, £15 0s. 0d. |
| 567.21 | To Samuel Eason, for one dark bay horse, £14 10s. 0d. |
| 567.22 | To David English, for one sorrel mare, £14 0s. 0d. |
| 567.23 | To Solomon Hendrick, for one bay ditto, £22 0s. 0d. |
| 567.24 | To John Walker, for one black ditto, £12 0s. 0d. |
| 567.25 | To James Tuttle, for one dark gray mare, £6; one brown ditto, £5; for a total of £11 0s. 0d. |
| 567.26 | To William White, for one black horse, £11 0s. 0d. |
| 567.27 | To James M'Donald, for 428 pounds flour at 12s. 6d. per hundredweight, £2 13s. 6d. |
| 567.28 | To Meredy Reins, for one black mare, £10 10s. 0d. |
| 567.29 | To Charles Cocks, for one horse, £8 10s. 0d. |
| 567.30 | To Ebenezer Meads, for one sorrel ditto, £20 0s. 0d. |
| 567.31 | To Michael Gleaves, for one black mare, £10 10s.; one ditto, £16; £26 10s. 0d. |
| 567.32 | To John Craig, for one white mare, £8 10s.; one roan horse, £7 10s.; £16 0s. 0d. |
| 567.33 | To Samuel Montgomerie, for one bay horse, £21 0s. 0d.; 302 days horse hire, at 15d. per day, £18 17s. 6d.; for a total of £39 17s. 6d. |

## 17 January 1778

| | |
|---|---|
| 567.34 | To Christian Shultz, for one gray mare, £6 0s. 0d. |
| 567.35 | To Robert M'Nutt, for one sorrel horse, £5 0s. 0d. |
| 567.36 | To Samuel Campbell, for one bay ditto, £10 10s. 0d. |
| 567.37 | To Samuel Ingram, for one dun ditto, £27 10s. 0d. |
| 567.38 | To Jacob Sterns, for one black ditto, £11 0s. 0d. |
| 567.39 | To William Carr, for one black mare, £12 0s. 0d. |
| 567.40 | To James Newell, Jr., for one black horse, £11 0s. 0d. |
| 567.41 | To John Simpson, for one white ditto, £14 0s. 0d. |
| 567.42 | To Francis Hamilton, for one bay ditto, £7 10s. 0d. |
| 567.43 | To William Bennitt, for one bay mare, £6 0s. 0d. |
| 567.44 | To Thomas Price, for one gray mare, £14 0s. 0d.; one bald eagle ditto, £14 0d. 0d.; one bay horse, £9 17s. 6d.; for a total of £37 17s. 6d. |
| 567.45 | To John Gibson, for one bay mare, £10 10s. 0d. |
| 567.46 | To Littleton Brooks, one ditto, £12 10s. 0d. |
| 567.47 | To Peter Haff, for one mare, pack saddle, and one kettle, £13 7s. 6d. |
| 567.48 | To James Daugherty, for one sorrel horse and bit, £8 15s. 0d. |
| 567.49 | To James Walker, assignee of Absalom Stafford, for one gray horse, £16 10s. 0d. |
| 567.50 | To Frederick Fraily, for three horses, £16 10s. 0d. |
| 567.51 | To William Edmundson, for one white mare, and one roan ditto, £19 0s. 0d. |
| 567.52 | To Andrew Cowan, for one gray horse, £12 0s. 0d. |
| 567.53 | To David Carson, for one bay ditto, £15; and one bell, 6s.; £15 8s. 0d. |
| 567.54 | To John Adair, assignee of George Grey, for one gray horse, £16 10s. 0d.; pack saddle and rope, 6s.; bell, 4s.; halter, 1s.; the last four at 11s. 0d.; for a total of £17 1s. 0d. |
| 567.55 | To James M'Kain, for one dark brown mare, £10 10s. 0d.; pack saddle, 10s.; bell, 5s.; halter, 1s. 3d.; the last three at 16s. 3d.; for a total of £11 6s. 3d. |
| 567.56 | To James Cameron, for a black horse, £12 10s. 0d.; bell, 1s. 3d.; pack saddle, 4s.; the last two at 5s. 3d.; for a total of £12 15s. 3d. |
| 567.57 | To James Steel, for one bay horse, £18 10s.; one sorrel ditto, £8 10s.; for a total of £27 0s. 0d. |
| 567.58 | To George Scott, for one gray ditto, £19 0s. 0d. |
| 567.59 | To Robert Gambell, for one sorrel ditto, £8 0s. 0d. |
| 567.60 | To Joseph Perrin, for one ditto, £10 0s. 0d. |
| 567.61 | To Daniel M. Cormack, for one roan ditto, £5 10s. 0d. |

## Virginia Legislative Petitions

| | |
|---|---|
| 567.62 | To Nicholas Edwards, for one gray ditto, £12 0s. 0d. |
| 567.63 | To Jonathan Jennings, for one bay ditto, £17 0s. 0d. |
| 567.64 | To John Hounshel, for one brown ditto, £13 0s. 0d. |
| 567.65 | To George Parker, for one sorrel mare, £10 0s. 0d. |
| 567.66 | To Andrew Bransteter, for one dark brown ditto, £10 10s. 0d. |
| 567.67 | To William Peoples, for one gray horse, £15 0s. 0d. |
| 567.68 | To James Doran, for one black ditto, £10 0s. 0d. |
| 567.69 | To Valentine Little, for one white ditto, £12 0s. 0d. |
| 567.70 | To George Caldwell, for one bay ditto, £15 0s. 0d. |
| 567.71 | To Samuel Fair, for one bay ditto, £9; and one dark bay, £20; £29 0s. 0d. |
| 567.72 | To Jeremiah Rust, for one gun, powder horn, and shot bag, £6 10s. 0d. |
| 567.73 | To Alexander Butler, for damage done his gun, 6s. 0d. |
| 567.74 | To Robert Hardwick, for one blanket, £1 7s. 6d. |
| 567.75 | To William Brown, for damage done his gun, 5s. 0d. |
| 567.76 | To Joseph M'Reynolds, for ditto, 2s. 6d. |
| 567.77 | To Leonard Helm, for sixty-four rations, at 8d. each, £2 2s. 8d. |
| 567.78 | To Benjamin Logan, for two hundred and eighty-eight ditto for Captain Todd's company, £9 12s. 0d. |
| 567.79 | To James Greer, for work done on a granary, and other buildings, at Harrodsburg, and finding nails, £2 6s. 6d. |
| 567.80 | To Robert Cowden, for one black horse, £11 0s. 0d. |
| 567.81 | To Samuel Ewin, for one white ditto, £28 4s. 0d.; one gray ditto, £21; one brown ditto, £17; one bay mare, £12; three bells, 13s.; three bridles, 5s. 3d.; one bag, 7s. 6d.; for a total of £79 9s. 9d. |
| 567.82 | To Andrew Irwin, for two grubbing hoes and one axe, £1 10s. 0d. |
| 567.83 | To Richard Thomas, for one black horse, £10 0s. 0d. |
| 567.84 | To John Gordon, for one bay mare, £19 0s. 0d. |
| 567.85 | To Robert Stephenson, for an express, £1 10s. 0d. |
| 567.86 | To Thomas Goldsby, for one rifle gun, £6; and tomahawk, 3s.; for a total of £6 3s. 0d. |
| 567.87 | To Robert M'Elheney, additional allowance for horse hire, £2 18s. 9d. |
| 567.88 | To Peter Turney, assignee of Joseph Cole, for one bay horse, £9 0s. 0d. |
| 567.89 | To Anthony Bledsoe, for one bay horse and bit, £17 0s. 0d. |
| 567.90 | To John Swearenger, Sr., for the use of his pasture, and the damage he sustained while the tories were confined and tried at his house, £10 0s. 0d. |

## 17 January – 14 May 1778

567.91     To Joel Hatcher, for his Negro man slave Simon, who was tried for felony and sentenced to be hanged, and by the court of the county of Chesterfield valued at £80 (but prior to the day appointed for his execution, he set fire to the jail in which he was confined, and suffered so much in the flames that he died a few days later), £80 0s. 0d.

**568-P-†**     **Underhill, William**
JHD: 17 Jan. 1778                                        Not known
   Relating to payment of his account.
17 Jan. 1778: To PC.
                 Carried over to next session of GA.
30 May 1778: PC recommends £221 3s.
                 House agrees.
30 May 1778: Senate agrees.

**569-P**     **Johnson, Thomas, Jr.**
JHD: 13 May 1778                                    Louisa County
   Reimbursement of £12 12s. for death of two steers hired from Charles Yancey to transfer military supplies in Shawanese expedition, together with £2 13s. 6d. court costs. (This is identical with 418-P, which see.)
   Manuscript unsigned.
13 May 1778: To PC.
21 May 1778: PC recommends £15 5s. 6d.
                 House agrees.
30 May 1778: Senate amends, reducing amount.
                 House lays on table.
                 No further action taken.
                 Johnson presents a new petition, 832-P, on the same subject on 20 November 1778, which see.

**570-P**     **Payne, Archer**
JHD: 13 May 1778                                  Goochland County
   Compensation for slave imprisoned on suspicion of a felony in August 1777, who broke jail, refused to surrender, and was shot.
   Manuscript unsigned.
13 May 1778: Rejected by refusal to refer to a committee.

**571-P-†**     **Card-makers and Wire-drawers**
JHD: 14 May 1778                                    Not known

## Virginia Legislative Petitions

Asking for exemption from military service.
14 May 1778: To PG.
19 May 1778: PG recommends rejection.
    House rejects.

**572-P    Hooe, Gerard**
    JHD: 14 May 1778                    King George County
For increase in ferry tolls.
Manuscript unsigned.
14 May 1778: Rejected by refusal to refer to a committee.

**573-P-†    Halifax County—Citizens**
    JHD: 14 May 1778                    Halifax County
Opposing a division of the county.
14 May 1778: To PG.
    Carried over to next session of GA.
28 Oct. 1778: PG recommends rejection.
    House rejects.

**574-P-†    Timberlake, Philip**
    JHD: 15 May 1778                    Not known
Compensation for nursing of his son, John Timberlake, who became ill in the Continental service.
15 May 1778: To PC.
21 May 1778: PC recommends £10 to be charged in the account of this commonwealth against the United States of America.
    House agrees.
30 May 1778: Senate agrees.

**575-P    Badgett, Thomas**
    JHD: 15 May 1778                    Louisa County
Compensation for nursing of his son, John Badgett, who became ill in the Continental service.
Manuscript unsigned, but has certificate attached.
15 May 1778: To PC.
21 May 1778: PC recommends £3 15s. for nursing and 20s. for transportation to be charged in the account of this commonwealth against the United States of America.
    House agrees.
30 May 1778: Senate agrees.

## 14 – 15 May 1778

**576-P-†  Criddle, William**
          JHD: 15 May 1778                              Not known
Additional compensation for loss of arm in military service in 1776.
15 May 1778: To PC.
16 May 1778: PC recommends £8 for present relief and £2 additional for life.
          House agrees.
28 May 1778: Senate agrees.
          See 2-P-†.

**577-P-†  Fry, Benjamin**
          JHD: 15 May 1778                              Not known
Compensation for wound received at battle of Brandywine while in Continental service.
15 May 1778: To PC.
19 May 1778: PC recommends £30 for present relief and full pay as sergeant
          for life to be charged in the account of this commonwealth against
          the United States of America.
          House agrees.
30 May 1778: Senate agrees.

**578-P-†  Randolph, Beverley**
          JHD: 15 May 1778                         Cumberland County
Contesting the elections of Joseph Carrington and George Carrington as delegates to the House since, at time of election, they were commissioners of taxes for Cumberland County.
15 May 1778: To PE.
1 June 1778: PE reports that "memorial" is reasonable and that commissioners of taxes cannot sit in General Assembly.
          House carries over to next session of GA, but no further action
          found.
          Earl G. Swem and John W. Williams, *A Register of the General
          Assembly, 1776–1918* (Richmond, 1918), do not comment on this
          contest. They show Joseph Carrington and George Carrington as
          delegates for the two sessions in 1778, and George Carrington and
          Beverley Randolph as delegates for the two sessions in 1779.

**579-P**
Eck–Not
found      **Amelia County—Citizens**
          JHD: 15 May 1778                              Amelia County

177

## Virginia Legislative Petitions

Opposing a division of the county. (No petition for a division has been found.)
Manuscript signed by: James Collicot, Matthew Tucker, Jr., Sam. Wills, Edw. Munford, Joel Mottley, and twenty-three others.
15 May 1778: To PG.
        Committee apparently did not report, but endorsement on manuscript says "Reasonable."

### 579 A-P
Eck–Not
found    **Amelia County—Citizens**
       JHD: 15 May 1778                Amelia County
Text is identical with 579-P, which see.
Manuscript is signed by seventy-three persons.

### 579 B-P
Eck–Not
found    **Amelia County—Citizens**
       JHD: 15 May 1778                Amelia County
Text is identical with 579-P, which see.
Manuscript is signed by 114 persons.

### 579 C-P
Eck–Not
found    **Amelia County—Citizens**
       JHD: 15 May 1778                Amelia County
Text is identical with 579-P, which see.
Manuscript is signed by 349 persons.

### 579 D-P
Eck–Not
found    **Amelia County—Citizens**
       JHD: 15 May 1778                Amelia County
Text is identical with 579-P, which see.
Manuscript is signed by seventy-nine persons.

### 580-P-†   **Parker, Robert**
       JHD: 16 May 1778                Accomack County
Asking release from five-year prison sentence for being a British sympathizer.

## 15 – 18 May 1778

16 May 1778: To PG.
19 May 1778: PG recommends release.
      House rejects on second reading.

**581-P-†**   **Wallace, Hugh**
      JHD: 18 May 1778                                   Not known
Compensation for loss of a leg while in Continental service at battle of Brandywine.
18 May 1778: To PC.
19 May 1778: PC recommends £30 for present relief and full pay as sergeant during life to be charged in the account of this commonwealth against the United States of America
      House agrees.
30 May 1778: Senate agrees.
      See 1090-P-† and 1309-P-†.

**582-P-†**   **Dickenson, William**
      JHD: 18 May 1778                                   Not known
Compensation for loss of an arm while in Continental service at battle of Brandywine.
18 May 1778: To PC.
19 May 1778: PC recommends £30 for present relief and full pay as a soldier for life to be charged in the account of this commonwealth against the United States of America.
      House agrees.
30 May 1778: Senate agrees.

**583-P-†**   **Lumsdon, George**
      JHD: 18 May 1778                                   Louisa County
Compensation for horse impressed to carry runaway slave to jail because the horse died.
18 May 1778: To PC.
21 May 1778: PC recommends rejection, but House recommits to PC.
27 May 1778: PC recommends £35.
      House agrees.
27 May 1778: Senate agrees, JS.

**584-P-†**   **Hansford, Edward**
      JHD: 18 May 1778                                   Norfolk County

## Virginia Legislative Petitions

Compensation for debts owed him by Andrew Sprowle whose estate is in hands of commonwealth.
18 May 1778: House lays on table.
    No further record found.

**585-P-†  Starke, Joseph**
    JHD: 19 May 1778            Not known
Compensation for loss of his horse in Cherokee expedition.
19 May 1778: To PC.
27 May 1778: PC recommends rejection.
    House rejects.

**586-P-†  Carlyle, John, and others**
    JHD: 20 May 1778            Berkeley County
Asking for an extension of time for building on lots in town of Bath.
20 May 1778: To a special committee to prepare a bill.
21 May 1778: Bill presented.
22 May 1778: House passes bill.
28 May 1778: Senate amends bill.
    House agrees.
    For this act see 9H460.

**587-P-†  Doggett, George**
    JHD: 20 May 1778            Not known
Compensation for accidental wound received while in militia.
20 May 1778: To PC.
27 May 1778: Carried over to next session of GA.
15 Dec. 1778: Carried over to next session of GA.
    No further record found.

**588-P-†  Brown, John**
    JHD: 20 May 1778            Not known
Compensation for wound received in Continental service at Saratoga.
20 May 1778: To PC.
27 May 1778: PC recommends £30 for present relief to be charged in the account of this commonwealth against the United States of America.
    House agrees.
30 May 1778: Senate agrees.

## 19 – 21 May 1778

**589-P-†   Whitehead, Grizzel**
JHD: 20 May 1778                                             Bedford County
Compensation for horse impressed to move John Goodrich, Sr., from Bedford County to Charlottesville.
20 May 1778: To PC.
27 May 1778: PC recommends £30.
       House agrees.
30 May 1778: Senate agrees.

**590-P-†   Temple, John**
JHD: 20 May 1778                                                  Not known
Compensation for loss of eye in Continental service.
20 May 1778: To PC.
29 May 1778: PC recommends £30 for present relief to be charged in the account of this commonwealth against the United States of America.
       House agrees.
30 May 1778: Senate agrees.

**591-P-†   Davenport, James**
JHD: 21 May 1778                                                  Not known
Compensation for wound received while in Continental service at battle of Brandywine.
21 May 1778: To PC.
27 May 1778: PC recommends £30 for present relief and full pay as soldier for life to be charged in the account of this commonwealth against the United States of America.
       House agrees.
30 May 1778: Senate agrees.

**592-P-†   Wilson, John**
JHD: 21 May 1778                                           Hampshire County
Compensation for wound incurred while in militia and defending frontiers.
21 May 1778: To PC.
27 May 1778: PC recommends £30 to be charged in the account of this commonwealth against the United States of America.
       House agrees.
30 May 1778: Senate agrees.

## Virginia Legislative Petitions

**593-P-†   Watkins, William**
JHD: 21 May 1778                                     Dinwiddie County
Repayment for counterfeit $8 bill.
21 May 1778: To PC.
27 May 1778: PC recommends £2 8s. in discount money from treasury.
   House agrees.
30 May 1778: Senate agrees.

**594-P-†   Hambleton, John**
JHD: 21 May 1778                                              Not known
Compensation for illness incurred while on military duty.
21 May 1778: To PC.
23 May 1778: PC recommends £30 for present relief to be charged in the account of this commonwealth against the United States of America.
   House agrees.
30 May 1778: Senate agrees.

**595-P-†   Cullins, John**
JHD: 21 May 1778                                     Hampshire County
Compensation for wound incurred while defending frontier, and for nursing while he had smallpox.
21 May 1778: To PC.
27 May 1778: PC recommends £30 for present relief and £6 for expenses to be charged in the account of this commonwealth against the United States of America.
   House agrees.
30 May 1778: Senate agrees.

**596-P-†   Virginia Commissioners of the Navy**
JHD: 23 May 1778                                              Not known
Asking for an increase in salary for the clerk of the commission.
23 May 1778: To T.
   Committee apparently did not report.

**597-P-†   Caldwell, George**
JHD: 23 May 1778                                              Not known
For expenses in recovering his horse, impressed for Cherokee expedition of 1776.
23 May 1778: To PC.

29 May 1778: PC recommends rejection.
    House rejects.

**598-P-†  Edmondson, James Powell**
    JHD: 23 May 1778                                             Not known
    Compensation for loss of leg in military service.
23 May 1778: To PC.
27 May 1778: PC recommends £30 for present relief and full pay as soldier for
    life to be charged in the account of this commonwealth against the
    United States of America.
    House agrees.
30 May 1778: Senate agrees.

**599-P-*  Miles, Joseph**
    JHD: 23 May 1778                                          Sussex County
    Additional compensation for loss of eyesight suffered while on military
duty in 1776.
23 May 1778: To PC.
29 May 1778: PC recommends an additional amount of £9 6s. 8d. per annum
    for life, which will amount to full pay as soldier.
    House agrees.
30 May 1778: Senate agrees.
    See 274-P-†.

**600-P-†  Early, Jacob**
    JHD: 23 May 1778                                             Not known
    Compensation for loss of his horse on Cherokee expedition in 1776.
23 May 1778: To PC.
27 May 1778: PC recommends £12 10s.
    House agrees.
30 May 1778: Senate agrees.

**601-P-†  Kennedy, William**
    JHD: 23 May 1778                                             Not known
    Compensation for carrying letters to Cherokee chiefs in 1774 at request of
Andrew Lewis and William Preston.
23 May 1778: To PC.
27 May 1778: PC recommends £15.
    House agrees.
30 May 1778: Senate agrees.

## Virginia Legislative Petitions

**602-P-†  Pittsylvania County—Citizens**
JHD: 23 May 1778                                    Pittsylvania County
Opposing moving the courthouse to a new location.
23 May 1778: To PG.
    Carried over to next session of GA.
16 Oct. 1778: PG recommends approval.
    House recommits.
19 Oct. 1778: House approves.
    No Senate action required.

**602.1-P  Washington County—Citizens**
JHD: 23 May 1778                                    Washington County
Asks rejection of petition, now before House, that would alter boundary line between counties of Montgomery and Washington.
Manuscript signed by: Aaron Lewis, Robert Buchanan, John Jamison, Edward Jamison, James Crabtree, and fifty-four others. Endorsement says rejected 23 May 1778.
23 May 1778: To PG.
    House rejects.

**602.1 A-P**
    **Washington County—Citizens**
    JHD: 23 May 1778                              Washington County
Text is similar to 602.1-P, which see.
Manuscript signed by seventy-nine persons.

**602.1 B-P**
    **Washington County—Citizens**
    JHD: 23 May 1778                              Washington County
Text is similar to 602.1-P, which see.
Manuscript signed by forty-six persons.

**603-P-†  Tobacco Inspectors—Bolling's Warehouse, Cedar Point Warehouse, Blandford Warehouse, Boyd's Warehouse, Davis's Warehouse, and John Bolling's Warehouse**
JHD: 23 May 1778                                    Chesterfield County
Asking for an increase in salaries.
23 May 1778: To PG.
    Committee apparently did not report.

## 23 – 25 May 1778

**604-P-†  Montgomery County, Washington County, and Kentucky County—Citizens**
JHD: 23 May 1778
Montgomery County
Washington County
Kentucky County

Asking for a land law.
23 May 1778: Laid on table.
No further record found.

**605-P-†  Tucker, Robert**
JHD: 25 May 1778
Norfolk Borough
Norfolk County

Compensation for houses and mills burned by Virginia troops in Norfolk County and storehouses burned in Norfolk borough in 1775.
25 May 1778: To T.
27 May 1778: T reports reasonable.
Recommends £1,000 advance on property burned in Norfolk County until exact value is determined. Also recommends that commissioners for Norfolk report on valuation of property destroyed in Norfolk borough.
For act expanding authority of Norfolk commissioners to adjoining areas, see 9H427.

**606-P-†  Ballendine, John**
JHD: 25 May 1778
Henrico County
Buckingham County

Asking (1) that he be allowed the present market price for pig iron, rather than the £7 10s. per ton for which he had contracted; (2) that he be allowed to sell excess pig iron from Buckingham County not needed by public; (3) that he be allowed extra costs for labor and necessaries; (4) that he be allowed to dispose of extra pig iron not needed by public; and (5) that he be allowed to erect a forge and slitting mill at Westham.
25 May 1778: To PG.
28 May 1778: PG rejects (1).
PG recommends (2) that Ballendine must sell to public pig iron required, (3) that Ballendine should be allowed extra costs, and (4) that Ballendine should be allowed to sell extra pig iron not required by public.

## Virginia Legislative Petitions

PG recommends (5) that erection of forge and slitting mill be carried over to next session of GA.
House agrees to all of above.
30 May 1778: Senate agrees.
No further reference found to (5).

### 607-P-* Bedford County and Henry County—Citizens
JHD: 25 May 1778          Bedford County
                 Henry County
Asking that a new county be formed from parts of Bedford and Henry counties.
25 May 1778: To PG.
 Committee apparently did not report, but this may have been carried over as 969-P-†, which has been entered separately for lack of proof.

### 608-P-† Madison, Thomas
JHD: 25 May 1778              Not known
Compensation for himself and others for herding stocks of horses and cattle belonging to public after Cherokee expedition.
25 May 1778: To PC.
30 May 1778: PC recommends as follows:

| | |
|---|---|
| The commonwealth to John Carmack, | Dr. |
| To herding and taking care of the country cattle from 13 November 1776 to 11 June 1777, 212 days, at 6s. per day, | £ 63 12s. 0d. |
| To William Carmack, ditto from 13 November to 29 February, 109 days, at 3s. per day, | £ 16 7s. 0d. |
| To John Delaney, ditto 148 days, at 3s., | £ 22 4s. 0d. |
| To Stephen Richards, for ditto 209 days, at 3s., | £ 31 7s. 0d. |
| To Matthew Dean, for ditto 194 days, at 3s., | £ 29 2s. 0d. |
| To John Fulkerson, for ditto twenty-one days, at 3s., | £ 3 3s. 0d. |
| To Cornelius Carmack, for ditto twenty-five days at 3s., | £ 3 15s. 0d. |
| To Andrew Greer, for ditto thirty-two days at 3s., | £ 4 16s. 0d. |
| To Joseph Greer, for ditto thirty-two days, at 3s.; to three bells at 3s. 8d.; total at | |

## 25 May 1778

| | | |
|---|---|---|
| To John Nash, herding cattle sixty days, at 3s.; to three bell collars 5s.; total at | £ 9 | 5s. 0d. |
| To finding two horses, | | 10s. 0d. |
| | £189 | 8s. 0d. |

Cr.

| | | |
|---|---|---|
| By cash paid by Thomas Madison to Andrew and Joseph Greer, as per receipt 11 June 1977, | £ 9 | 12s. 0d. |
| Balance | £179 | 16s. 0d. |

7 June 1777 The commonwealth to Jonathan Drake     Dr.

| | | |
|---|---|---|
| To taking care of, and hunting for, the country horses from 26 October to 7 June, 225 days, at 5s. per day, | £ 56 | 5s. 0d. |
| To Isaac Drake, from 26 October to 15 March, 141 days, at 3s., | £ 21 | 3s. 0d. |
| To Benjamin Drake, the same, | £ 21 | 3s. 0d. |
| To Isaac Drake and Benjamin Drake, fifteen days more each at 3s., | £ 4 | 10s. 0d. |
| To Henry Hickey for ditto, from 29 January to 17 June, 129 days, at 4s., | £ 25 | 16s. 0d. |
| To John Drake, for ditto from 26 October to 15 March, 141 days, at 3s., | £ 21 | 3s. 0d. |
| To the hire of a horse, | £ 2 | 18s. 0d. |
| | £152 | 18s. 0d. |

Cr.

By six beef hides, at 8s., £2 8s. 0d.
By cash paid Isaac Drake, £2 5s. 0d.

| | | |
|---|---|---|
| | £ 4 | 13s. 0d. |
| Balance | £148 | 5s. 0d. |

December 1776 The commonwealth to John Looney     Dr.

| | | |
|---|---|---|
| For his services as bullock master, 120 days, at 6s. per day, | £ 36 | 0s. 0d. |
| To Samuel Looney, a drover, thirty days, at 4s., | £ 6 | 0s. 0d. |
| To Peter Looney, ditto, sixty-seven days, at 4s., | £ 13 | 8s. 0d. |
| To Peter Looney, Jr., ditto, thirty-three days, at 4s., | £ 6 | 12s. 0d. |
| To Peter Looney, ditto, fifty days, at 4s., | £ 10 | 0s. 0d. |
| To William M'Broon, ditto, 120 days, at 4s., | £ 24 | 0s. 0d. |
| To John Cox, ditto, sixty-six days, at 4s., | £ 13 | 4s. 0d. |
| | £109 | 4s. 0d. |

## Virginia Legislative Petitions

December 1777 The commonwealth to Ezekiel Smith  Dr.
For his services in taking care of the country
   horses, after the return of the army, seventy-
   eight days, at 5s. per day,   £19 10s. 0d.
To Henry Hickey, seventy-eight days, at 4s.,   £15 12s. 0d.
To Isaac Drake, seventy-eight ditto, at 3s.,   £11 14s. 0d.
To one Negro, thirty days, at 2s.,   £ 3 0s. 0d.
To Hugh Blair, thirty ditto, at 3s.,   £ 4 10s. 0d.
To Benjamin Drake, seventy-eight days, at 3s.   £11 14s. 0d.
                                            £66 0s. 0d.

30 May 1778: House agrees.
1 June 1778: Senate agrees.

### 609-P-† Powell, Jeremiah and Powell, Anne
JHD: 25 May 1778   Norfolk County
Compensation for impressed horse that was lost about the time of the battle of Great Bridge.
25 May 1778: To PC.
29 May 1778: PC recommends that estate of Francis Wright, father of Anne Powell, be paid £21.
   House agrees.
30 May 1778: Senate agrees.

### 610-P-† Haynes, John
JHD: 26 May 1778   Not known
Compensation for horse he hired for Cherokee expedition in 1776, which was lost.
26 May 1778: To PC.
29 May 1778: PC recommends £12 10s.
   House agrees.
30 May 1778: Senate agrees.

### 611-P-† Berry, Thomas
JHD: 26 May 1778   Not known
Compensation for messenger sent to bring home his son who had become ill in Continental service. His son was found dead.
26 May 1778: To PC.

## 25 – 26 May 1778

29 May 1778: PC recommends £22 10s.
    House rejects.

**612-P-†  Watkins, Joseph**
    JHD: 26 May 1778                                Not known
Compensation for loss of left arm in Continental service at battle of Brandywine.
26 May 1778: To PC.
29 May 1778: PC recommends £30 for present relief and half pay as soldier for life, to be charged in the account of this commonwealth against the United States of America.
    House agrees.
30 May 1778: Senate agrees.

**613-P-†  M'Kinney, Charles**
    JHD: 26 May 1778                                Not known
Compensation for impressed horse used for march to Kentucky and never returned.
26 May 1778: To PC.
29 May 1778: PC recommends £11 6s.
    House agrees.
30 May 1778: Senate agrees.

**614-P-†  Wilson, Archer**
    JHD: 26 May 1778                                  Not known
Compensation for loss of left arm while in Continental service at battle of Germantown.
26 May 1778: To PC.
29 May 1778: PC recommends £30 for present relief and full pay as soldier for life, to be charged in the account of this commonwealth against the United States of America.
    House agrees.
30 May 1778: Senate agrees.

**615-P-†  Henry County—Citizens**
    JHD: 26 May 1778                                Henry County
                                                                Bedford County
Opposing formation of a new county from parts of Henry and Bedford counties.

## Virginia Legislative Petitions

26 May 1778: To PG.
    Committee apparently did not report.

### 616-P-†   Goff, John
    JHD: 27 May 1778                           Not known
  Compensation for two horses impressed for Cherokee expedition and never returned.
27 May 1778: To PC.
29 May 1778: Carried over to next session of GA.
29 Oct. 1778: PC recommends £20.
    House agrees.
23 Nov. 1778: Senate agrees.

### 617-P   Payne, John, Jr.
    JHD: 27 May 1778                      Goochland County
  Compensation for impressed single chair and harness, badly damaged while being used to convey John Goodrich, Sr., from Bedford County to Williamsburg.
  Manuscript unsigned, but has two depositions attached to it, dated 28 September 1778.
27 May 1778: To PC.
    Carried over to next session of GA.
5 Nov. 1778: PC recommends £10 15s. over price for which they were sold.
    House agrees.
23 Nov. 1778: Senate agrees.

### 618-P   Dickenson, Arthur
    JHD: 27 May 1778                          York County
  Compensation for outlawed slave who was killed while trying to escape. (This may be related to 622.4-Misc. Claim, but the record is not clear.)
  Manuscript unsigned.
27 May 1778: House rejects by refusal to refer to a committee.

### 619-P-†   Ballendine, John
    JHD: 27 May 1778                       Henrico County
                                                  Buckingham County
  Asking that he be allowed to purchase, with annual payments, the foundry at Westham and the blast furnace in Buckingham County.
27 May 1778: To PG.

27 – 30 May 1778

28 May 1778: PG finds (1) petition is reasonable; (2) that commissioners be appointed to determine amounts of public money spent on foundry and, with proper security, transfer title to Ballendine; and (3) that commissioners do the same for the blast furnace in Buckingham County, conveying title to Ballendine and John Reveley. House rejects on second reading.

**620-P-†  Brett, George**
JHD: 28 May 1778                                              Not known
Requesting additional compensation for building a galley for the Navy Board, which had specified that the size be increased.
28 May 1778: To T.
29 May 1778: T finds reasonable and states that Navy Board should make justified increases in payment.
House agrees.
30 May 1778: Senate rejects, JS.

**621-P    Bryant, Thomas**
JHD: Not found [28 May 1778]                                  Not known
Protests the removal of William DeLoyent, and asks that there be training in the art of gunnery.
Manuscript, signed Thos. Bryant, is dated at Williamsburg, 28 May 1778, and is directed to House of Burgesses. Manuscript is endorsed as a petition and further states that it was rejected. (Bryant and DeLoyent have not been identified.)

**622-Misc. Claims-†**
JHD: 30 May 1778, for action                                  Not known
The following miscellaneous claims were not presented separately, and apparently went to PC without a prior reading on the floor of the House. They are listed as they were approved in the journals and are indexed under name and subject.
Date unknown: To PC.
30 May 1778: PC finds reasonable.
    House agrees.
    Senate agrees, JS.
622.1   To the estate of Samuel Newell, deceased, for a black horse, appraised at £12; to one ditto, black ditto, appraised at £16; £28 0s. 0d.

191

## Virginia Legislative Petitions

622.2     To John Gordon, for one dark bay horse impressed into the service of the country, and by means of severe usage died, appraised at £40 0s. 0d.

622.3     To Thomas Hammond, for a mare taken for the use of the militia on its march to Greenbrier, and lost, £6 0s. 0d.

622.4     To Arthur Dickinson, for his Negro man slave James, who was condemned and executed for a rape, and by the court of the county of James City valued at £150 0d. 0d.

622.5     To Adam Young, for a dark bay mare, £10; forty-six days hire of a horse, at 1s. 3d. per day, £2 17s. 6d.; £12 17s. 6d.

622.6     To Jonathan Dawson, for a horse, bell, and pack saddle, £5 15s. 0d.

622.7     To William Russell, Sr., for a bay horse, £12; ninety-five days hire of a horse at 1s. 3d. per day, £5 18s. 9d.; £17 18s. 9d.

622.8     To John Cox, for a gray horse, £18; five bells, 30s.; one roan horse, £14; total at £33 10s. 0d.

622.9     To Valentine Little, for a white horse, £12 0s. 0d.

622.10     To William Lane, for a bay mare, £6 16s. 6d.

622.11     To Henry Dougherty, for a white horse, £8 10s.; one chestnut sorrel, ditto; bell, pack saddle, and halter, £11 17s. 6d.; one bell, two halters, and two pack saddles, 9s. 6d.; total at £20 17s. 0d.

### 623-P    Thomson, Roger; Henry, William; Burton, Jesse; and Cobbs, John

JHD: 30 May 1778                          Fluvanna County

Asking that the charges of bribery and corruption of which they stand accused be heard by the House or else a prosecutor be appointed to pay the charges of a trial since they do not have funds to do so themselves.

Manuscript signed by petitioners. It also contains the names of those who brought the charges on 30 October 1777 (405-P and M-†) namely: John Ware, Elias Wells, Willis Wells, John Beckley, William Martin, Caleb Stone, Elijah Stone, Benja. Lee, William Pace, and William Taylor.

30 May 1778: Rejected by refusal to refer to a committee.

For final action see 1132-P.

### 624-C-†    Gibbs, John

JHD: 1 June 1778, for action                    Not known

Compensation for slave executed for a felony.

Date unknown: To PC.

## 30 May – 9 October 1778

1 June 1778: PC recommends £225.
> House agrees.
> Senate agrees.

### 625-P Shepherd, Abraham
JHD: 9 Oct. 1778                                           Berkeley County

To establish a ferry on his land near Mecklenburg town, in Berkeley County, over Potomac River to land of Thomas Swearingen in Maryland. Swearingen keeps his boats on Maryland side.

Manuscript unsigned.
9 Oct. 1778: To PG.
15 Oct. 1778: PG finds reasonable.
> House to incorporate in general ferry bill.
> This bill passed by House and Senate.
> For general ferry act, including this ferry, see 9H546.

### 626-P Manchester—Citizens
JHD: 9 Oct. 1778                                           Chesterfield County

Asking that an act be passed enlarging the powers of the trustees of Manchester town to prevent encroachment on the town's commons.

Manuscript signed by: Robert Goode, Wm. MacKenzie, Jno. McKeund, Jacob Rubsamen, John Puller, and sixteen others.
9 Oct. 1778: To PG.
15 Oct. 1778: PG finds reasonable but petition is recommitted to it.
20 Oct. 1778: PG recommends that trustees be allowed to sue those building on commons.
> House agrees and directs PG to prepare bill.
24 Oct. 1778: House passes bill.
28 Oct. 1778: Senate amends bill.
> House agrees to amendments.
> For this act see 9H578.

### 627-P Buckingham County—Citizens
JHD: 9 Oct. 1778                                           Buckingham County

Opposing a division of the county.

Manuscript signed by: George Damron, Stephen Gouret, Nicholas Morret, Wm. Gannaway, William Gripson, and 119 others.
9 Oct. 1778: To PG.
> Committee did not report since it was decided to divide the county.

## Virginia Legislative Petitions

For act adding part of Buckingham County to Cumberland County, see 9H559.

**628-**
**Address    Cople Parish, Westmoreland County—Citizens**
JHD: 9 Oct. 1778                                           Westmoreland County
Asking that established church be continued under proper regulations.
The text of the petition is printed but is signed by: Solomon Freelander, James Muse, Jr., James Muse, Patr. Tanford, Nicholas Muse, and 188 others.
9 Oct. 1778: To R.
4 Dec. 1778: Carried over to next session of GA.
   No further record found.

**629-P-†    Harwood, Christopher**
JHD: 9 Oct. 1778                                                        Not known
Compensation for loss of his own horse while he was in military service.
9 Oct. 1778: To PC.
19 Oct. 1778: PC recommends £100.
   House agrees.
29 Oct. 1778: Senate agrees.

**630-P-*    Berry, James**
JHD: 9 Oct. 1778                                             Washington County
Compensation for wound received 11 September 1777, while on Indian expedition.
9 Oct. 1778: To PC.
17 Oct. 1778: PC recommends £30 for present relief and one year's pay as a soldier.
   House agrees.
29 Oct. 1778: Senate agrees.

**631-P-†    Brown, Thomas**
JHD: 9 Oct. 1778                                                        Not known
Compensation for incapacity resulting from frostbite in both legs incurred while a prisoner in a British jail after battle of Germantown.
9 Oct. 1778: To PC.
19 Oct. 1778: PC recommends £30 for present relief and full pay as a soldier for life to be charged in the account of this commonwealth against the United States of America.
   House agrees.

## 9 – 10 October 1778

29 Oct. 1778: Senate agrees.

**632-P-†   Campbell, William, Jr.**
 JHD: 9 Oct. 1778                                                    Botetourt County
 Compensation for death of his horse while returning from Bedford County where Campbell had acted as guard for transferral of John Goodrich, Sr.
9 Oct. 1778: To PC.
29 Oct. 1778: PC recommends £45.
  Recommitted to PC.
31 Oct. 1778: PC again recommends £45.
  House agrees.
18 Nov. 1778: Senate rejects, JS.

**633-P   Brunswick County—Citizens**
 JHD: 10 Oct. 1778                                                    Brunswick County
 For relief from paying double taxes for failing to take the oath of allegiance, which had not been given to them because of inaction of county court.
 Manuscript signed by: William Short, Sr., Peter Wynne, Norman Wynne, Stith Wynne, John Turbyfill, Sr., and eighty-four others.
10 Oct. 1778: To PG.
15 Oct. 1778: PG finds reasonable and is directed to prepare a bill on 19 October.
  House and Senate pass bill as part of act for raising a supply of money for public exigencies. This part extended time to take oath to 1 May 1779 with treble taxes for failure.
  For this act see 9H547.

**634-P-†   Buford, John**
 JHD: 10 Oct. 1778                                                    Not known
 Compensation for gun stolen from him while on military march in 1776.
10 Oct. 1778: To PC.
29 Oct. 1778: PC recommends £10 15s.
  House recommits to PC.
31 Oct. 1778: PC again recommends £10 15s.
  House agrees.
18 Nov. 1778: Senate rejects, JS.

**635-P-†   Sandidge, Joseph**
 JHD: 10 Oct. 1778                                                    Not known
 Compensation for disabling wound received at battle of Brandywine.

## Virginia Legislative Petitions

10 Oct. 1778: To PC.
19 Oct. 1778: PC recommends £30 for present relief and full pay of soldier for three years, to be charged in the account of this commonwealth against the United States of America.
House agrees.
29 Oct. 1778: Senate agrees.

**636-P-†  Allen, Charles**
JHD: 10 Oct. 1778                                                              Not known

Compensation for illness contracted after discharge from military service, in order that he may repay Turner Patterson's expenses for nursing him.
10 Oct. 1778: To PC.
19 Oct. 1778: PC recommends £10 to be charged to be charged in the account of this commonwealth against the United States of America.
House agrees.
29 Oct. 1778: Senate agrees.

**637-P  Shenandoah County—Citizens**
JHD: 10 Oct. 1778                                                    Shenandoah County

For dissolution of the vestry of Beckford Parish.
Manuscript signed by: John Sheen, John North, Joseph Pugh, John Jackman, Darby Downey, and twenty-six others.
10 Oct. 1778: To R.
16 Oct. 1778: R reports reasonable.
House agrees and directs R to prepare a bill.
This bill was incorporated into a law regarding a number of vestries and was passed by House and Senate.
For this act see 9H525.

**638-P-†  Barnes, Isaiah**
JHD: 12 Oct. 1778                                                              Not known

Compensation for illness contracted in military service in 1776.
12 Oct. 1778: To PC.
19 Oct. 1778: PC recommends £30.
House agrees.
29 Oct. 1778: Senate agrees.

**639-P-†  Newman, Abner**
JHD: 12 Oct. 1778                                                              Not known

## 10 - 12 October 1778

Compensation for travel expenses in trying to locate two soldiers left ill in North Carolina. He found that they had died.
12 Oct. 1778: To PC.
17 Oct. 1778: PC recommends £12 5s. to be charged to the United States.
   House agrees.
28 Oct. 1778: Senate rejects, JS.

**640-P-†  Bramham, Spencer Thaddeus**
   JHD: 12 Oct. 1778                                                Not known
Compensation for nursing his son, Spencer Bramham, who became ill in military service in 1776.
12 Oct. 1778: To PC.
19 Oct. 1778: PC recommends £5 10s. 10d. to be charged in the account of this commonwealth against the United States of America.
   House agrees.
29 Oct. 1778: Senate agrees.

**641-P-†  Thomas, Joseph**
   JHD: 12 Oct. 1778                                                Not known
Compensation for nursing two sons who became ill in the Continental service.
12 Oct. 1778: To PC.
19 Oct. 1778: PC recommends £11 7s. 6d. to be charged in the account of this commonwealth against the United States of America.
   House agrees.
29 Oct. 1778: Senate agrees.

**642-P-†  Thornton, Daniel**
   JHD: 12 Oct. 1778                                                Not known
Compensation for nursing his son, Jesse Thornton, who became ill in the Continental service.
12 Oct. 1778: To PC.
17 Oct. 1778: PC recommends £4 1s. 8d. to be charged in the account of this commonwealth against the United States of America.
   House agrees.
29 Oct. 1778: Senate agrees.

**643-P-†  Jones, William**
   JHD: 12 Oct. 1778                                                Not known

Compensation for wound received at battle of Brandywine while he was in the Continental service.
12 Oct. 1778: To PC.
17 Oct. 1778: PC recommends £15 for present relief and full pay of a soldier for life to be charged in the account of this commonwealth against the United States of America.
House agrees.
29 Oct. 1778: Senate agrees.

**644-P**     **Buckles, James; Buckles, William; and Lewis, Jacob**
JHD: 12 Oct. 1778                      Berkeley County
Additional compensation for military service in expedition against Indians in 1778. They had been paid as sergeants rather than as officers.
Manuscript unsigned.
12 Oct. 1778: To PC.
19 Oct. 1778: PC recommends additional amounts of £36 to James Buckles, £17 to William Buckles, and £12 to Jacob Lewis, to be charged in the account of this commonwealth against the United States.
House agrees.
28 Oct. 1778: Senate rejects, JS.

**645-P-†**     **Baskervill, William**
JHD: 12 Oct. 1778                            Not known
Compensation for recruiting for Continental service even though his quota was not reached.
12 Oct. 1778: To PC.
14 Nov. 1778: Carried over to next session of GA.
No further record found.

**646-P**     **Moon, Jacob and Thornburg, Benjamin**
JHD: 12 Oct. 1778                      Berkeley County
Remission of a fine of £100 levied on each of them for not taking oath or affirmation as to value of their property for tax purposes. Claims that oath was not administered by assessors, and that they were ignorant of it.
Manuscript unsigned. It was directed to the governor, Patrick Henry, and carries his note that GA should act upon it.
12 Oct. 1778: To PG.
15 Oct. 1778: PG finds reasonable.
House lays it on table.
No further record found.

## 12 – 13 October 1778

**647-P-†  Mecklenburg Town (Shepherdstown)—Citizens**
    JHD: 12 Oct. 1778                                     Berkeley County
Asking for an act to forbid hogs being allowed to run at large.
12 Oct. 1778: To PG.
15 Oct. 1778: PG finds reasonable and is directed to prepare a bill.
20 Oct. 1778: House passes bill.
24 Oct. 1778: Senate passes bill.
        For this act see 9H560.

**648-P  Southampton County—Citizens**
    JHD: 13 Oct. 1778                               Southampton County
Asking for the dissolution of the vestry of Nottoway Parish.
Manuscript signed by: Jno. Burges, Willm. Urquhart, Benjn. Ruffing, Wil. King, John Boykin, and fifty-two others.
13 Oct. 1778: To R.
16 Oct. 1778: R finds reasonable and is directed to prepare a bill.
        This action is incorporated in a general vestry bill, which was passed by House and Senate.
        For the general act see 9H525.

**649-P-†  Bedford County—Citizens**
    JHD: 13 Oct. 1778                                     Bedford County
For a division of the county. (There were several petitions, but the exact number is not known.)
13 Oct. 1778: To PG.
24 Oct. 1778: PG finds reasonable and House directs that the committee appointed to form a new county out of Bedford and Henry counties insert a clause dividing Bedford County.
        The substance of this petition was combined with 650-P to form a bill that was passed by the House.
20 Nov. 1778: Senate rejects bill, JS.

**650-P  Botetourt County—Citizens**
    JHD: 13 Oct. 1778                                     Botetourt County
For adding parts of Botetourt County to the counties of Bedford and Henry.
Manuscript signed by: Joseph Rentfre, William Hungate, John Hale, Elijah Dickeson, John Loyd, and sixty others.
13 Oct. 1778: To PG.
22 Oct. 1778: PG finds reasonable.
        House recommits.

## Virginia Legislative Petitions

27 Oct. 1778: PG revises their resolution to provide that parts of Botetourt County be added to a new county to be formed out of Bedford and Henry counties.

House agrees and refers resolution to special committee on Bedford and Henry counties.

The substance of this petition was combined with 649-P-† to form a bill that was passed by the House.

20 Nov. 1778: Senate rejects bill, JS.

**651-P** **Falkner, Ralph; Burton, James; Cole, John; Garland, Peter; Apperson, Richard; Bell, John; Stubblefield, Beverly; Taylor, Richard; Hudson, William; Conway, Henry; Oliver, Drury; Boulding, Wood; Murray, Abraham; Eppes, William; Holland, George; Ewing, Alexander; Pointer, William; Trucker, William; and Jenkins, William**

JHD: 13 Oct. 1778                                                    Not known

For travel expenses to Williamsburg to direct recruiting for the Continental army at the direction of George Washington.

Manuscript unsigned.

13 Oct. 1778: To PC.

16 Oct. 1778: PC recommends £24 each "to be charged to the continent." House agrees.

22 Oct. 1778: Senate refers to a special committee.

28 Oct. 1778: Senate rejects, JS.

**651.1-P**
Eck–Not
found    **Amherst Parish and Amherst County—Citizens**

JHD: Not found [13 Oct. 1778]                           Amherst County

For a division of Amherst Parish and sale of glebe, the proceeds to be divided between the parishes.

Manuscript signed by: Matthew Harris, Wm. Loving, James Stevens, Dan. Gaines, John Wiatt, and four others. Endorsed by county court. Endorsement also shows it was referred on 13 October.

13 Oct. 1778: To R.

16 Oct. 1778: R finds reasonable and is directed to prepare bill.

29 Oct. 1778: Bill presented, including division of Camden Parish in counties of Pittsylvania and Henry, the latter resulting from 675-P-†, which see.

6 Nov. 1778: House passes bill.

## 13 - 14 October 1778

17 Nov. 1778: Senate passes bill.
    For this act see 9H567.

**651.2-P**
Eck–Not
found     **Amherst County—Citizens**
    JHD: Not found [13 Oct. 1778]      Amherst County
For a general assessment to support all parishes.
Manuscript signed by: Thomas Powell, Ambrose Rucker, William Tinsley, William Camden, John Penn, and sixty-two others. Endorsed by county court. Endorsement also shows it was referred on 13 October.
13 Oct. 1778: To R.
4 Dec. 1778: Carried over to next session of GA.
    No further record found.

**652-P-†**   **Fisher, Stephen**
    JHD: 14 Oct. 1778      Not known
Compensation for wound received from Indians in defense of Kentucky.
14 Oct. 1778: To PC.
19 Oct. 1778: PC recommends £30 for present relief and 3s. per day for three
    years, from 25 October 1777.
    House agrees.
29 Oct. 1778: Senate amends.
20 Nov. 1778: Senate recedes from its amendment.

**653-P-†**   **Gillock, Lawrence**
    JHD: 14 Oct. 1778      Not known
Compensation for bringing his sick son home and nursing him while the latter was in the Continental service.
14 Oct. 1778: To PC.
19 Oct. 1778: PC recommends £7 10s. for travel and £5 9s. 2d. for nursing to
    be charged in the account of this commonwealth against the
    United States of America.
    House agrees.
29 Oct. 1778: Senate agrees.

**654-P-†**   **Thomasson, William**
    JHD: 14 Oct. 1778      Orange County
Compensation for nursing his son, Turner Thomasson, and another soldier, Thomas Fleming, both of whom became ill in the Continental service.

14 Oct. 1778: To PC.
19 Oct. 1778: PC recommends rejection, but House recommits.
21 Oct. 1778: PC recommends £15 10s. to be charged to the United States of America.
>House agrees.
23 Nov. 1778: Senate agrees.

**655-P  Reveley, John**
>JHD: 14 Oct. 1778                                     Henrico County

Requesting payment for completion of foundry at Westham, for casting cannon and making pig metal, and for service in finding clay for firebricks.

Manuscript unsigned, but refers to four double stacks and eight air furnaces.
14 Oct. 1778: To PC.
19 Oct. 1778: PC recommends £578.
>House agrees.
17 Nov. 1778: Senate agrees.
>For additional resolutions concerning employment of workers at the foundry and purchase of pig iron, see JHD, 21 November, 28 November, 2 December, and 8 December 1778.

**656-P  Edwards, John**
>JHD: 14 Oct. 1778                                     Brunswick County

Compensation for horse, impressed by sheriff of Brunswick County to convey Jesse Briggs, a horse thief, to jail. The horse had been lost.

Manuscript unsigned.
14 Oct. 1778: To PC.
19 Oct. 1778: PC recommends rejection, but House recommits.
5 Nov. 1778: PC recommends £33.
>House agrees.
5 Dec. 1778: Senate agrees, JS.

**657-P-†  Pendleton, Henry**
>JHD: 15 Oct. 1778                                     Culpeper County

Compensation for death of impressed horse.
15 Oct. 1778: To PC.
29 Oct. 1778: PC recommends £20 to be charged in the account of this commonwealth to the United States of America.
>House agrees.
25 Nov. 1778: Senate agrees.

## 14 – 15 October 1778

**658-P-†   Britt, John**
JHD: 15 Oct. 1778                                                Southampton County
Compensation for nursing two of his sons who became ill in the Continental service.
15 Oct. 1778: To PC.
29 Oct. 1778: PC recommends £1 5s. for travel and £8 16s. 8d. for nursing one son, to be charged in the account of this commonwealth against the United States of America.
House recommits.
14 Nov. 1778: PC again recommends the above resolution.
House agrees.
28 Nov. 1778: Senate agrees.

**659-P-†   Hawkins, Joshua**
JHD: 15 Oct. 1778                                                            Not known
Compensation for wound not cared for while he was a British prisoner.
15 Oct. 1778: To PC
19 Oct. 1778: PC recommends £30 for his present relief to be charged in the account of this commonwealth against the United States of America.
House agrees.
29 Oct. 1778: Senate agrees.

**660-P-†   Voss, Edward**
JHD: 15 Oct. 1778                                                      Culpeper County
Compensation for death of a slave from castration, ordered by court after his attempt to ravish a white woman.
15 Oct. 1778: To PC.
23 Oct. 1778: PC recommends £300.
House agrees.
28 Oct. 1778: Senate agrees.

**661-P-†   Williams, John; Pickens, Samuel; Livingston, Samuel; Tolly, Daniel; Surmerman, George; Riley, Patrick; Allen, Samuel; and Worthington, Edward**
JHD: 15 Oct. 1778                                                            Not known
Compensation for loss of guns, ammunition, and other valuable personal articles upon the overturning of a canoe while returning from transporting salt for use of garrison at Salt Lick.
15 Oct. 1778: To PC.

## Virginia Legislative Petitions

5 Nov. 1778: PC recommends £20 to Williams, £12 15s. to Pickens, £15 10s. to Livingston, £8 11s. to Tolly, £10 18s. to Surmerman, £1 12s. to Riley, £12 16s. to Allen, and 12s. to Worthington.
House agrees.
23 Nov. 1778: Senate agrees.

**662-P-†  Jones, Catlet**
JHD: 15 Oct. 1778                                Kentucky County
Compensation for wound received in battle with Indians. (He had previously petitioned on 18 November 1777 [470-P].)
15 Oct. 1778: To PC.
21 Oct. 1778: PC recommends £20 for his present relief and £10 per annum for life.
House agrees.
28 Oct. 1778: Senate agrees.

**663-P**
Eck–
A724   **Coleman, Daniel**
JHD: 15 Oct. 1778                                Amelia County
For relief from double taxation for delinquency in not taking loyalty oath in the prescribed time.
Manuscript unsigned.
15 Oct. 1778: To PG.
19 Oct. 1778: PG to prepare a bill.
The substance of this petition was incorporated in a general tax bill and passed by House and Senate.
For general tax bill see 9H547.

**664-P   Tinsly, Joshua**
JHD: 15 Oct. 1778                                Essex County
For relief from double taxation for delinquency in not taking loyalty oath in the prescribed time.
Manuscript unsigned, but carries an attestation of the county court.
15 Oct. 1778: To PG.
19 Oct. 1778: PG to prepare a bill.
The substance of this petition was incorporated in a general tax bill and passed by House and Senate.
For general tax bill see 9H547.

## 15 – 17 October 1778

**665-P  Miller, Simon**
JHD: 15 Oct. 1778                                              Essex County
For relief from double taxation for delinquency in not taking loyalty oath in the prescribed time.
Manuscript unsigned.
15 Oct. 1778: To PG.
19 Oct. 1778: PG to prepare a bill.
> The substance of this petition was incorporated in a general tax bill and passed by House and Senate.
> For general tax bill see 9H547.

**666-P-†  Amelia County—Citizens**
JHD: 15 Oct. 1778, for action                                  Amelia County
Opposing division of county along parish lines.
Date unknown: To PG.
15 Oct. 1778: PG finds reasonable.
> No further action required.
> See 534-P.

**667-P-†  Davidson, Thomas**
JHD: 16 Oct. 1778                                              Not known
Compensation for partial loss of eyesight caused by smallpox while in Continental service.
16 Oct. 1778: To PC.
21 Oct. 1778: PC recommends £12 for traveling expenses, £30 for present relief and full pay as a soldier for three years to be charged in the account of this commonwealth against the United States of America.
> House lays on table.
2 Dec. 1778: House amends, substituting half pay as a soldier for six years.
> House agrees.
12 Dec. 1778: Senate agrees.

**668-P-†  Rogers, Ulysses**
JHD: 17 Oct. 1778                                              Not known
Compensation for wound received while in Continental service.
17 Oct. 1778: To PC.

## Virginia Legislative Petitions

21 Oct. 1778: PC recommends £30 for present relief and full pay as a soldier for three years to be charged in the account of this commonwealth against the United States of America.
Laid on table.
2 Dec. 1778: Amended to provide half pay as a soldier for six years.
House agrees.
12 Dec. 1778: Senate agrees.

**669-P    Portlock, Samuel**
JHD: 17 Oct. 1778                              Norfolk Borough
For readjusting the amounts allowed by commissioners for burning of houses by order of convention as opposed to that allowed for burning by state troops.
Manuscript unsigned.
17 Oct. 1778: Referred to commissioners.
13 Nov. 1778: Commissioners recommend an additional £759 12s. 6d.
House agrees.
19 Nov. 1778: Senate passes a general resolution.

**670-P-†    Wonycutt, Aphia**
JHD: 17 Oct. 1778                              Norfolk Borough
For readjusting the amounts allowed by commissioners for burning of houses (property of her deceased husband, Nicholas Wonycutt) by order of convention as opposed to that allowed for burning by state troops.
17 Oct. 1778: Referred to commissioners.
13 Nov. 1778: Commissioners recommend £493 and an additional amount of £65.
House agrees.
19 Nov. 1778: Senate passes a general resolution.

**671-P-†    Peyton, Craven**
JHD: 19 Oct. 1778                              Not known
To secure title to lands and slaves he had mortgaged to a British firm and which he has now sold at a profit. The firm's agent refuses to take mortgage money or give title. Asks that the petitioner may be allowed to place mortgage money in the state treasury and receive title.
19 Oct. 1778: To PG.
20 Oct. 1778: PG discharged.
No further action found.

## 17 - 19 October 1778

**672-P    Culpeper County—Citizens**
JHD: 19 Oct. 1778                                    Culpeper County

For requiring mill owners to enlarge openings in dams on Rapidan and Robertson rivers to twenty feet in width to enable passage of fish from 1 March to 20 May annually.

Manuscript signed by: Robert Terrill, James Powell, Charles Hume, Zachariah Gilder, Wm. Broskin, and eighty-three others.
19 Oct. 1778: To PG.
6 Nov. 1778: PG recommends rejection.
   House rejects.

**673-P    Orange County and Culpeper County—Citizens**
JHD: 19 Oct. 1778                                    Orange County
                                                     Culpeper County

To repeal an act forcing mill owners to open passages for fish in Rapidan and Robertson rivers.

Manuscript signed by: James Coleman, Uriah Proctor, John Hiatt, William Heath, John Collins, and forty-seven others.
19 Oct. 1778: To PG.
6 Nov. 1778: PG reports reasonable and is directed to prepare a bill.
   The House and Senate pass this bill for Rapidan River only.
   See 806-P.
   For this act see 9H579.

**673 A-P  Orange County and Culpeper County—Citizens**
JHD: 19 Oct. 1778                                    Orange County
                                                     Culpeper County

Text is identical with 673-P, which see.
Manuscript signed by 297 persons.
See also 806-P.

**674-P    Savage, Nathaniel Littleton**
JHD: 19 Oct. 1778                                    Norfolk Borough

Compensation for distillery, of which he was part owner, that was burned by order of convention.

Manuscript unsigned.
19 Oct. 1778: To committee appointed to examine report of commissioners
         on burning of Norfolk.
20 Nov. 1778: Committee recommends £500.
   House agrees.

### Virginia Legislative Petitions

24 Nov. 1778: Senate agrees.

**675-P-†  Pittsylvania County and Henry County—Citizens**
JHD: 19 Oct. 1778     Pittsylvania County
                      Henry County
For the division of Camden Parish and the sale of the glebe.
19 Oct. 1778: To R.
  For action on this petition, see 651.1-P.

**676-P  Portsmouth Parish, Norfolk County—Citizens**
JHD: 19 Oct. 1778     Norfolk County
For dissolution of vestry and appointment of a new one.
  Manuscript signed by: David Porter, Saml. Veale, Chas. Conner, Wm. Booker, John Norris, and thirty-six others. Endorsement is dated 21 October 1778.
19 Oct. 1778: To R.
22 Oct. 1778: R reports reasonable.
  This was incorporated in a general vestry bill and was passed by House and Senate.
  For general vestry act see 9H525.

**677-P  Elizabeth River Parish, Norfolk County—Citizens**
JHD: 19 Oct. 1778     Norfolk County
For dissolution of vestry and appointment of new one.
  Manuscript signed by: Richd. Jarvis, Lemuel Langley, James Wylden, James Jinnings, Basett Moseley, and sixty-one others. Endorsement is dated 21 October 1778.
19 Oct. 1778: To R.
22 Oct. 1778: R reports reasonable.
  This was incorporated in a general vestry bill and was passed by House and Senate.
  For general vestry act see 9H525.

**678-P  North Farnham Parish, Richmond County—Wardens**
JHD: 19 Oct. 1778     Richmond County
For dissolution of vestry and appointment of a new one.
  Manuscript signed by: Charles McCarty and John Sydnor. Has attached the minutes of the vestry dated 16 December 1777.
19 Oct. 1778: To R.

## 19 – 20 October 1778

11 Nov. 1778: Reports as reasonable (but calls it Northampton Parish).
　　　　　　Petition was incorporated in a general vestry bill and was passed by House and Senate.
　　　　　　For general vestry act see 9H525.

### 679-P-† Terry, Stephen
　　　　　JHD: 19 Oct. 1778　　　　　　　　　　　　　　Not known

Additional compensation for wound received at battle of Brandywine. (He had already received £25. See 521-P.)

19 Oct. 1778: To PC.
29 Oct. 1778: PC recommends full pay as a soldier for three years to be charged in the account of this commonwealth against the United States of America.
14 Nov. 1778: House amends to half pay as a soldier for six years and agrees.
28 Nov. 1778: Senate agrees.

### 680-P-† Madison, John
　　　　　JHD: 19 Oct. 1778　　　　　　　　　　　　　　Not known

Compensation for horse, impressed by express rider to carry message from Congress to governor. The horse died.

19 Oct. 1778: To PC.
29 Oct. 1778: PC recommends £60 to be charged in the account of this commonwealth against the United States of America.
　　　　　　House agrees.
23 Nov. 1778: Senate agrees.

### 681-P-† "Persons, Sundry"
　　　　　JHD: 19 Oct. 1778　　　　　　　　　　　　　　Not known

Asking for appointment of commissioners to buy up the necessaries of life and sell to the public at a moderate advance, the profits to be paid into the public treasury.

19 Oct. 1778: To T.
11 Dec. 1778: T recommends rejection.
　　　　　　House rejects.

### 682-P Fluvanna County—Citizens
　　　　　JHD: 20 Oct. 1778　　　　　　　　　　　　　Fluvanna County

For dissolution of county and returning parts of it to Albemarle, Louisa, and Goochland counties.

Manuscript signed by: John Strange, Benjamin Martin, Thos. Linthicum,

## Virginia Legislative Petitions

Tandy Rice, William Johnson, and thirty-two others. Several identical petitions follow from which a number of signatures have been clipped.
20 Oct. 1778: To PG.
13 Nov. 1778: PG recommends rejection.
    House rejects.

### 682 A-P   Fluvanna County—Citizens
    JHD: 20 Oct. 1778                         Fluvanna County
Text is identical with 682-P, which see.
Manuscript signed by twenty-seven persons.

### 682 B-P   Fluvanna County—Citizens
    JHD: 20 Oct. 1778                         Fluvanna County
Text is identical with 682-P, which see.
Manuscript signed by forty-nine persons.

### 682 C-P   Fluvanna County—Citizens
    JHD: 20 Oct. 1778                         Fluvanna County
Text is identical with 682-P, which see.
Manuscript signed by fifty-four persons.

### 683-P   Fluvanna County and Goochland County—Citizens
    JHD: 20 Oct. 1778                         Fluvanna County
                                            Goochland County
Asking that Fluvanna County not be dissolved. (In opposition to 682-P, which see.)
Manuscript signed by: William Woody, Spencer Haislip, Wm. Burges, Richd. Omohundro, Samuel Kidd, and 117 others.
20 Oct. 1778: To PG.
13 Nov. 1778: PG recommends no dissolution.
    House agrees.
    No further action required.

### 683 A-P   Fluvanna County and Goochland County—Citizens
    JHD: 20 Oct. 1778                         Fluvanna County
                                            Goochland County
Text is identical with 683-P, which see.
Manuscript signed by fifty-eight persons.

## 20 October 1778

**683 B-P Fluvanna County and Goochland County—Citizens**
JHD: 20 Oct. 1778　　　　　　　　　　　　Fluvanna County
　　　　　　　　　　　　　　　　　　　　　Goochland County
Text is identical with 683-P, which see.
Manuscript signed by thirty-six persons.

**683 C-P Fluvanna County and Goochland County—Citizens**
JHD: 20 Oct. 1778　　　　　　　　　　　　Fluvanna County
　　　　　　　　　　　　　　　　　　　　　Goochland County
Text is identical with 683-P, which see.
Manuscript signed by fifty-five persons.

**684-P-† Rockingham County—Court Justices**
JHD: 20 Oct. 1778　　　　　　　　　　　　Rockingham County
Protesting county boundaries made when Rockingham County was formed out of Augusta County. Asking (1) that boundaries be reformed; (2) that the glebe of Augusta Parish be sold; (3) that commissioners be appointed to value courthouse, jail, and churches in Augusta County and to determine proper amount due Rockingham County; and (4) that tobacco levied by Augusta County be divided with Rockingham County.
20 Oct. 1778: To PG
19 Nov. 1778: PG reports (2) as reasonable, but carried over to next session of GA and no further record found; (4) as reasonable, to which House agrees; (3) for rejection, but carried over to next session of GA and no further record found; (1) as reasonable, but carried over to next session of GA and no further record found—(1) was apparently both supported and objected to by citizens in the lower end of Augusta County, some of whom wished to be added to Rockingham County.

**685-P-† Augusta County—Citizens**
JHD: 20 Oct. 1778　　　　　　　　　　　　Augusta County
For adding lower part of Augusta County to Rockingham County.
20 Oct. 1778: To PG.
19 Nov. 1778: For action see 684-P-†.

**686-P　Hanover Parish and Washington Parish, Westmoreland County and King George County—Citizens**
JHD: 20 Oct. 1778　　　　　　　　　　　　Westmoreland County
　　　　　　　　　　　　　　　　　　　　　King George County

## Virginia Legislative Petitions

For adding part of parish of Hanover to parish of Washington, and part of parish of Washington to parish of Hanover, for dissolution of vestries, and for sale of glebe of parish of Washington.

Manuscript signed by: John Washington, John Martin, Wm. Piper, William Nelson, J. Bernard, and 141 others.

20 Oct. 1778: To R.

11 Nov. 1778: R recommends that exchanges of parts of parishes is reasonable.
Recommitted to R.

13 Nov. 1778: R recommends that (1) exchanges of parts of parishes is reasonable, (2) that dissolution of vestries is reasonable, and (3) that sale of Washington glebe is reasonable.
This was incorporated in a general vestry bill passed by House and Senate.
For general vestry act see 9H525.

**687-P-†  Bell, John**
JHD: 20 Oct. 1778                                    State of Delaware
Additional compensation for seizure of 220 bushels of salt for public use.
20 Oct. 1778: House rejects by refusal to refer to a committee.

**688-P  Stratton, John**
JHD: 20 Oct. 1778                                    Northampton County
Compensation for damages done to his property by soldiers.
Manuscript unsigned.
20 Oct. 1778: To PC.
8 Dec. 1778: Carried over to next session of GA.
No further record found.

**689-P-†  Dudley, Thomas**
JHD: 21 Oct. 1778                                    Not known
Compensation for 200 pounds of tobacco taken from Shepherd's warehouse in the summer of 1775 when he was inspector.
21 Oct. 1778: To PC.
8 Dec. 1778: PC recommends rejection.
House rejects.

**690-P-†  Marable, Matthew**
JHD: 21 Oct. 1778                                    Mecklenburg County
Compensation for serving as venire man in trial of Thomas Green. He claims

## 20 – 21 October 1778

570 pounds of tobacco, but was allowed only 123 pounds.
21 Oct. 1778: To PC.
29 Oct. 1778: Carried over to next session of GA.
   No further record found.

**691-P-†   Ingram, Samuel**
   JHD: 21 Oct. 1778                                                Not known
Compensation for wound received in engagement with Indians in July 1777.
21 Oct. 1778: To PC.
5 Nov. 1778: PC recommends £30 for present relief, £40 for surgeon's fees, and half pay as a soldier for four years.
   House agrees.
20 Nov. 1778: Senate amends, but agrees to sums.
5 Dec. 1778: House agrees to Senate amendments.

**692-P-†   Schofield, William**
   JHD: 21 Oct. 1778                                                Not known
Compensation for wound received at battle of Germantown.
21 Oct. 1778: To PC.
29 Oct. 1778: PC recommends £30 for present relief and full pay as a soldier for one year to be charged in the account of this commonwealth against the United States of America.
   House recommits to PC.
31 Oct. 1778: PC recommends as above, but changes to half pay as a soldier for two years.
   House agrees.
25 Nov. 1778: Senate agrees.

**693-P-†   Halifax County—Citizens**
   JHD: 21 Oct. 1778                                                Halifax County
For a division of the county.
21 Oct. 1778: To PG.
25 Oct. 1778: PG recommends rejection.
   House rejects.
   See 555-P-†, to which it refers.

**694-P**
Eck–
A1106   **Augusta County—Citizens**
   JHD: 21 Oct. 1778                                                Augusta County

## Virginia Legislative Petitions

Urging rejection or postponement of consideration of petition for adding part of Augusta County to Rockingham County. (There were several such petitions, but the exact number is not known.)
Manuscript signed by: Alexander McClennedain, George Mathews, Alexander Sinclair, Alexander Robertson, Thomas Husband, and 239 others.
21 Oct. 1778: To PG.
19 Nov. 1778: PG recommends rejection, but carried over to next session of GA.
   There appears to be no further action on this petition, but apparently it was again presented on 21 May 1779.
   See 943-P-† and 945-P-†.

**695-P-†   Buckingham County—Citizens**
      JHD: 21 Oct. 1778, for action          Buckingham County
For adding part of Buckingham County to Cumberland County. (This may be 522-P, but it is entered separately for lack of proof.)
Date unknown: To PG.
21 Oct. 1778: PG directed to prepare a bill.
22 Oct. 1778: Bill presented.
26 Nov. 1778: Bill amended.
27 Nov. 1778: House passes bill.
28 Nov. 1778: Senate passes bill.
   For this act see 9H559.

**696-P-†   Buckingham County—Citizens**
      JHD: 21 Oct. 1778                     Buckingham County
Opposing addition of part of Buckingham County to Cumberland County.
21 Oct. 1778: House rejects.

**697-P-†   Stephen, Adam and Noble, Anthony**
      JHD: 22 Oct. 1778                       Berkeley County
Compensation for seventy-five muskets and eight rifles furnished Berkeley County militia in its march to Fort Pitt in September 1778.
22 Oct. 1778: To PC.
24 Oct. 1778: PC recommends £590 12s. 6d. for muskets and £144 for rifles to be charged in the account of this commonwealth against the United States of America.
28 Oct. 1778: Resolution corrected in some manner.
      House agrees.
      Senate amends.

214

## 21 - 22 October 1778

17 Nov. 1778: House agrees to Senate amendments.

**698-P  James, Richard**
  JHD: 22 Oct. 1778                                   Cumberland County
  Asking for a fee, as sheriff of Cumberland County, for collecting a court judgment from William Smith, former sheriff, for collection of an arrearage of £312 8s. in quitrents.
  Manuscript unsigned.
22 Oct. 1778: To PC.
6 Nov. 1778: PC recommends rejection.
  House rejects.

**699-P-†  Petit, George**
  JHD: 22 Oct. 1778                                   Not known
  Compensation for wound received at battle of Germantown on 19 June 1778.
22 Oct. 1778: To PC.
29 Oct. 1778: PC recommends £30 for present relief and half pay as a soldier for life to be charged in account of this commonwealth against the United States of America.
  House recommits to PC.
31 Oct. 1778: PC still recommends £30, but only the half pay be charged in account of this commonwealth against the United States of America.
  House agrees.
23 Nov. 1778: Senate agrees.

**700-P-†  Blanks, David**
  JHD: 22 Oct. 1778                                   Not known
  Compensation for accident while getting timbers for gun carriages.
22 Oct. 1778: To PC.
29 Oct. 1778: PC recommends £30 for present relief and half pay as an artificer for three years.
  House agrees.
23 Nov. 1778: Senate agrees.

**701-P-†  Campbell, James**
  JHD: 22 Oct. 1778                                   Not known
  Compensation for wound received at battle near Piscataway while in Continental service.

## Virginia Legislative Petitions

22 Oct. 1778: To PC.
28 Oct. 1778: PC recommends £30 for present relief and half pay as a soldier for life from 15 April 1777, to be charged in the account of this commonwealth against the United States of America.
House agrees.
17 Nov. 1778: Senate agrees.

**702-P-†  Francis, William**
  JHD: 22 Oct. 1778                                                Not known
Compensation for paralytic illness contracted while in Continental service.
22 Oct. 1778: To PC.
29 Oct. 1778: PC recommends £30 for present relief and full pay as a soldier for three years to be charged in the account of this commonwealth against the United States of America.
Recommitted to PC.
31 Oct. 1778: PC recommends £30 for present relief, but the charge against the account to be only half pay as a soldier for three years.
House agrees.
25 Nov. 1778: Senate agrees.

**703-P-†  Compton, Archibald**
  JHD: 22 Oct. 1778                                                Not known
Compensation for wound received in military service at Germantown.
22 Oct. 1778: To PC.
5 Nov. 1778: PC recommends £30 for present relief and half pay as a soldier for life, the latter to be charged in the account of this commonwealth against the United States of America.
House agrees.
25 Nov. 1778: Senate agrees.

**704-P-†  Wroe, William**
  JHD: 22 Oct. 1778                                                Not known
Compensation for surgeon's fees paid by him when taken ill while on furlough.
22 Oct. 1778: To PC.
8 Dec. 1778: PC recommends £3 11s. to be charged in the account of this commonwealth against the United States of America.
12 Dec. 1778: Senate agrees.

## 22 October 1778

**705-P**
Eck-
A1664  **Quarles, John**
JHD: 22 Oct. 1778                               Bedford County
Compensation for three counterfeit $15 bills, valued at £13 10s., received back from officers who were advanced funds for recruiting.
  Manuscript unsigned, but has affidavits signed by Patrick Henry, Edmund Randolph, and others.
22 Oct. 1778: To PC.
10 Nov. 1778: PC finds reasonable.
  House agrees.
17 Nov. 1778: Senate rejects, JS.

**706-P**  **Frazer, William and Fleet, Henry**
JHD: 22 Oct. 1778                               King William County
                                                King and Queen County
For discontinuance of Fox's ferry and Fleet's ferry across Mattaponi River from both sides.
  Manuscript unsigned.
22 Oct. 1778: To PG.
27 Oct. 1778: PG finds reasonable and is directed to prepare bill.
  Bill was apparently not presented and no further record found.

**707-P-†**  **Bedford County and Henry County—Citizens**
JHD: 22 Oct. 1778, for action                   Bedford County
                                                Henry County
For forming a new county out of Bedford and Henry counties.
Date unknown: To PG.
22 Oct. 1778: PG reports reasonable and is directed to prepare a bill.
28 Oct. 1778: Bill presented.
  For the ramifications of this bill and related and combined ones, see 649-P-† and 650-P. The final bill was rejected by the Senate.

**708-P-†**  **Henry County—Citizens**
JHD: 22 Oct. 1778, for action                   Henry County
                                                Bedford County
Opposing the formation of a new county from Bedford and Henry counties.
Date unknown: To PG.
22 Oct. 1778: PG recommends rejection.
  House rejects.

## Virginia Legislative Petitions

**709-P-†   Ronaldson, Patrick**
JHD: 23 Oct. 1778                                                                      Not known
For relief from three-mile limit imposed upon him as a British prisoner of war. Claims he is in sympathy with American cause.
23 Oct. 1778: House rejects by refusal to refer to a committee.

**710-P-†   Robertson, George**
JHD: 23 Oct. 1778                                                                      Not known
For relief from censure for trip to England in June 1777 to visit an aged parent.
23 Oct. 1778: To committee to bring in a bill to expel and prevent return of British sympathizers.
   No further record found.
   For act concerning expatriation see 10H129.

**711-P   Virginia Artillery—Officers**
JHD: 23 Oct. 1778                                                                      Not known
Protesting the appointment by governor and Council of Captain Charles De Klauman as their superior.
Manuscript signed by: Wm. Jennings, Saint Blackwell, Richd. Booker, Gideon Johnson, Henry Marshall, and five others.
23 Oct. 1778: To PG.
26 Nov. 1778: PG recommends rejection, but House recommits to PG.
   Manuscript endorsement says to be heard again on 12 December 1778, but no record found.

**712-P   Goodrich, Margaret**
JHD: 23 Oct. 1778                                                             Nansemond County
Asking return of slaves of John Goodrich, Sr., her husband, from lead mines and elsewhere since she is unable to hire slaves or keep them.
Manuscript unsigned, is dated 16 October 1778, and has attached a copy of the order of Council on 23 August 1776 allowing her 150 acres in Nansemond County, 500 acres in Isle of Wight County, and £40 a year to hire slaves until further action of GA.
23 Oct. 1778: To PG.
8 Dec. 1778: PG recommends rejection.
   House rejects.

## 23 October 1778

**713-P**    Hampton—Citizens
      JHD: 23 Oct. 1778                        Hampton
                                     Elizabeth City County

    For expansion of the town's boundaries.
    Manuscript signed by: John Hunter, Roe Cowper, Jas. Barron, Miles King, Jacob W. Rae, and thirty-four others.
23 Oct. 1778: To PG.
         Manuscript endorsement says carried over to next session of GA, but no further action found.

**714-P**
Eck–
A1099    **Miller, Jean**
      JHD: 23 Oct. 1778                        Augusta County
    For transfer of her husband, Alexander Miller, from Augusta County jail to Rockingham County jail.
    Manuscript unsigned.
23 Oct. 1778: To PG.
19 Nov. 1778: PG recommends rejection.
         House rejects.

**715-P**    Saint Paul's Parish, Hanover County—Citizens
      JHD: 23 Oct. 1778                        Hanover County
    For dissolution of vestry.
    Manuscript signed by: S. Meredith, William Richardson, Johne Starke, Richa. Chapman, Wade Gooch, and 470 others, some indecipherable.
23 Oct. 1778: To R.
11 Nov. 1778: R recommends as reasonable and is directed to prepare a bill.
         This was incorporated in a general vestry bill passed by House and Senate.
    For general vestry act see 9H525.

**715 A-P**    Saint Paul's Parish, Hanover County—Citizens
      JHD: 23 Oct. 1778                        Hanover County
    Text, which is fragmentary, is similar to 715-P, which see.
    Signatures are missing.

**716-P-†**    **Norfolk County, Princess Anne County, and Nansemond County—Citizens**

## Virginia Legislative Petitions

JHD: 24 Oct. 1778
Norfolk County
Princess Anne County
Nansemond County

For some action against British sympathizers who are allowed to remain in the counties. There were two such petitions.

24 Oct. 1778: To committee to bring in a bill to expel and prevent the return of British sympathizers.
No further record found.
For act concerning expatriation see 10H129.

**717-P-†** **Tobacco Inspectors—South Quay Warehouse**
JHD: 24 Oct. 1778
Not known

For increases in allowances.
24 Oct. 1778: To committee for reviving several warehouses for inspection.
For general act concerning warehouses and allowances, see 9H482.

**718-P-†** **Tobacco Inspectors—Crutchfield's Warehouse, Page's Warehouse, and Meriwether's Warehouse**
JHD: 24 Oct. 1778
Not known

For increases in allowances.
24 Oct. 1778: To committee for reviving several warehouses for inspection.
For general act concerning warehouses and allowances, see 9H482.

**719-P-†** **Westmoreland County—Citizens**
JHD: 24 Oct. 1778
Westmoreland County

For placing Mattox warehouse and Bray's warehouse under one inspection.
24 Oct. 1778: To committee for reviving several warehouses for inspection.
Apparently not included in general act, 9H482.

**720-P-†** **Feston, John**
JHD: 24 Oct. 1778
Not known

Compensation for injury received from a wagon that overturned while he was in Continental service.
24 Oct. 1778: To PC.
27 Oct. 1778: PC recommends £15 for present relief and half pay as a soldier for two years, to be charged in the account of this commonwealth against the United States of America.
House agrees.
Not found in JS.

## 24 – 27 October 1778

**721-P-†  Tompkins, John and Tompkins, Bennett**
    JHD: 24 Oct. 1778                        Gloucester County
Compensation for public saltworks erected on their land.
24 Oct. 1778: To PC.
6 Nov. 1778: PC recommends rejection.
        House recommits to PC.
7 Nov. 1778: PC again recommends rejection.
        House rejects.

**722-P  Western Lands—Citizens**
    JHD: 24 Oct. 1778                           Western Lands
Asking for confirmation of titles to certain unappropriated lands on which they had settled.
       Manuscript signed by: Ishmael Abbott, Edw. Passons, Francis Farley, Jr., Francis Farley, Sr., Nat Farley, and 195 others.
24 Oct. 1778: To committee for establishing land office.
       Land office not established until 1779, see 10H35, 50.

**723-P-†  Purdie, Alexander**
    JHD: 24 Oct. 1778                            Williamsburg
Asking for liquidation of debt for paper used in public service, and that public blacksmith repair his presses.
24 Oct. 1778: To special committee.
24 Nov. 1778: House apparently agrees and Senate amends.
26 Nov. 1778: House agrees to Senate amendments.

**724-P-†  Walker, Thomas**
    JHD: 27 Oct. 1778                          Albemarle County
Asking for confirmation of titles for himself and others for lands surveyed for the Loyal Company beginning in 1753.
27 Oct. 1778: To committee of whole.
3 Nov. 1778: To PG.
11 Nov. 1778: PG recommends that titles be granted to lands surveyed before hostilities had commenced. (There is a long discussion of this in JHD.)
        House lays on table.
26 Nov. 1778: PG directed to prepare bill. (A further long discussion in JHD.)
7 Dec. 1778: House rejects bill.
        See 737-P-†.

## Virginia Legislative Petitions

### 725-P  Yohogania County—Citizens
JHD: 27 Oct. 1778                                    Yohogania County
For a division of the county.
Manuscript signed by: John Elliott, Charles Records, Henry Taylor, Jonathan Radors, James Patterson, and 182 others.
27 Oct. 1778: To PG.
30 Oct. 1778: PG recommends it be carried over to next session of GA.
    House agrees.
    No further action found.

### 726-P  Kirk, James
JHD: 27 Oct. 1778                                    Fairfax County
For the popular election of trustees of unincorporated towns, particularly Alexandria and Leesburg, rather than having them be self-perpetuating bodies.
    Manuscript unsigned.
27 Oct. 1778: To PG.
1 Dec. 1778: PG recommends as reasonable and to apply to all unincorporated towns.
    House agrees and directs PG to prepare a bill.
    This bill was passed by House and Senate.
    For this act see 9H560.

### 727-P-†  Hackett, Goldsbury
JHD: 27 Oct. 1778                                    Not known
Compensation for thirty stand of firearms impressed for military service.
27 Oct. 1778: To PC.
6 Nov. 1778: PC recommends £141.
    House agrees.
23 Nov. 1778: Senate agrees.

### 728-P  Galt, James
JHD: 27 Oct. 1778                                    Williamsburg
Additional compensation for himself as caretaker of hospital for mentally ill.
Manuscript unsigned, but has attached accounts of hospital and list of patients there.
27 Oct. 1778: To PC.
14 Nov. 1778: PC recommends £50 a year additional for Galt and £12 10s. a year additional for the matron.
    House recommits to PC.

20 Nov. 1778: PC recommends £100 a year additional for Galt and £25 a year additional for the matron.
House agrees.
1 Dec. 1778: Senate rejects, JS.
For final outcome, see 982-P.

729-P-† Calvert, Cornelius
JHD: 27 Oct. 1778   Norfolk Borough
Compensation for two cannons removed from his wharf by order of Norfolk committee, which were subsequently captured by British.
27 Oct. 1778: To PC.
6 Nov. 1778: PC recommends rejection.
House rejects.

730-P-† Sullivant, Thomas
JHD: 27 Oct. 1778   Not known
Compensation for loss of eyesight from inoculation for smallpox given while in military service.
27 Oct. 1778: To PC.
29 Oct. 1778: PC recommends £30 for present relief and half pay as a soldier for life, the latter to be charged in the account of this commonwealth against the United States of America.
House recommits to PC.
31 Oct. 1778: PC makes same recommendation.
House agrees.
23 Nov. 1778: Senate agrees.

731-M
Eck–
A1100  **Preston, William and Thompson, William (Executors of James Patton, deceased)**
JHD: 28 Oct. 1778   Augusta County
Asking confirmation of land grants made by governor and Council on 26 April 1745 to James Patton, deceased.
Manuscript unsigned.
28 Oct. 1778: To PG
17 Nov. 1778: PG recommends as reasonable and is directed to prepare a bill.
23 Dec. 1778: House rejects bill on third reading.

## Virginia Legislative Petitions

**732-P-†   Muter, George**
JHD: 28 Oct. 1778                                                                                    Not known
Reimbursement for expenses in saving the brig *Liberty* from falling into hands of enemy.
28 Oct. 1778: To PC.
29 Oct. 1778: PC recommends £52 to allow Colonel Muter and Colonel
    Moebelle to pay a bond.
    House recommits to PC.
31 Oct. 1778: PC makes same recommendation.
    House agrees.
27 Nov. 1778: Senate rejects, JS.

**733-P-†   White, John**
JHD: 28 Oct. 1778                                                                                    Not known
Compensation for his horse, stolen by a deserter and carried to the British.
28 Oct. 1778: To PC.
26 Nov. 1778: PC recommends rejection.
    House rejects.

**734-P     Stadler, John**
JHD: 28 Oct. 1778                                                                                    Not known
Compensation for travel expenses as army engineer.
Manuscript unsigned.
28 Oct. 1778: To PC.
5 Nov. 1778: PC recommends £83 6s. 9d.
    House agrees.
27 Nov. 1778: Senate rejects.

**735-P-†   Nowland, Thomas and Clapham, Josias**
JHD: 29 Oct. 1778                                                                                    Loudoun County
For discontinuing Clapham's ferry and establishing a new one across the Potomac River from land of Thomas Nowland to land of Arthur Nelson.
29 Oct. 1778: To PG.
17 Nov. 1778: PG finds reasonable and House directs it be incorporated in
    general ferry bill.
    This bill was passed by House and Senate.
    For general ferry act see 9H585.

**736-P-†   Minor, John**
JHD: 29 Oct. 1778                                                                                    Loudoun County

## 28 – 29 October 1778

Asking for increase in fees by increasing rates for tobacco; and allowing 1s. per day for feeding criminals, as sheriff of Loudoun Cuonty.
29 Oct. 1778: To PG.
3 Dec. 1778: PG recommends as reasonable.
> House agrees and refers to committee of whole for preparation of a bill.
> For the act regarding fees and tobacco rates, see 9H528.

**737-P-†** **"Persons, Sundry"**
JHD: 29 Oct. 1778                                                Western Lands
For confirmation of land titles for acreage purchased from Loyal Company.
29 Oct. 1778: To PG.
> For action on these claims see 724-P-†.

**738-M**
Eck–Not
found   **Walker, Thomas**
JHD: 29 Oct. 1778                                                Albemarle County
Asking confirmation of land grants to representatives of Peter Jefferson, deceased, and Thomas Meriwether, deceased, the original grant, lying on waters of New River, having been secured from the governor and Council in May 1748 by William Gray and Ashford Hughes. Asking also to survey the residue of this grant.
Manuscript unsigned, but carries endorsement to be carried over to next session of GA.
29 Oct. 1778: To PG.
13 Nov. 1778: PG recommends as reasonable.
> House recommits to PG.
> No further record found.

**739-P**   **Loudoun County—Citizens**
JHD: 29 Oct. 1778                                                 Loudoun County
For the establishment of a ferry across the Potomac River from the lands of Charles Slimmer to Maryland.
Manuscript signed by: Griffion Hammond, John Fawley, Junis Petters, Joseph Burgoyne, Jacob Dehaven, and fifty-six others.
29 Oct. 1778: To PG.

## Virginia Legislative Petitions

17 Nov. 1778: PG recommends as reasonable.
> This was incorporated in a general ferry act passed by House and Senate.
> For general ferry act see 9H585.

**740-P-†   Turner, John Farbush**
   JHD: 29 Oct. 1778                                        Not known
Compensation for impressed schooner that was captured by enemy.
29 Oct. 1778: To PC.
8 Dec. 1778: Carried over to next session of GA.
> No further record found.

**741-P   Wilson, Thomas**
   JHD: 29 Oct. 1778                                   Yohogania County
Compensation for military service allowance, which he requested John Pollock to receive for him, but Pollock was robbed, is now deceased, and has no estate.
Manuscript unsigned, but carries a certificate of a witness to the robbery.
29 Oct. 1778: To PC.
5 Nov. 1778: PC recommends rejection.
> House rejects.

**742-P   Keesell, George**
   JHD: 29 Oct. 1778                                  Rockingham County
Compensation for slave, under death sentence for murder, who escaped from jail and was shot.
Manuscript unsigned, but has attached certificate of court and description of sentence.
29 Oct. 1778: To PC.
5 Nov. 1778: PC recommends £225.
> House agrees.
23 Nov. 1778: Senate agrees.

**743-P-†   Durham, Amos**
   JHD: 29 Oct. 1778                                        Not known
Compensation for nursing a sick Continental soldier.
29 Oct. 1778: To PC.
11 Nov. 1778: PC recommends rejection.
> House recommits to PC.

## 29 – 30 October 1778

14 Nov. 1778: PC recommends £7 6s. to be charged in the account of this commonwealth against the United States of America.
    House agrees.
25 Nov. 1778: Senate agrees.

**744-P-†  Cureton, James**
    JHD: 29 Oct. 1778                                          Not known
Compensation for wound received near Amboy while in Continental service.
29 Oct. 1778: To PC.
5 Nov. 1778: PC recommends £30 for present relief and half pay as a soldier for life, the latter to be charged in the account of this commonwealth against the United States of America.
    House agrees.
23 Nov. 1778: Senate agrees.

**745-P  Presbyterians (Seceding)**
    JHD: 29 Oct. 1778                                          Not known
Asking that oath may be taken by raising right hand rather than by kissing Bible.
Manuscript signed by: Josiah Moffett, Alexd. Wilson, John Wilson, John Rodgers, Hamilton Rogers, and twenty-nine others.
29 Oct. 1778: To R.
2 Dec. 1778: R recommends as reasonable.
    House agrees.
    Not found in JS.

**746-P  Loyal, Paul; Taylor, James; Hutchings, John; and Phripp, Matthew (Executors of Joseph Hutchings, deceased)**
    JHD: 30 Oct. 1778                                Norfolk Borough
Compensation for costs of rebuilding Mason's Hall, which had been burned by order of convention. These petitioners had been omitted from the commissioners' lists of claims for Norfolk losses.
Manuscript signed by petitioners.
30 Oct. 1778: To PC.
13 Nov. 1778: PC recommends £1,200.
    House agrees.
14 Nov. 1778: Senate agrees, JS.

## Virginia Legislative Petitions

**747-P-†** **Tucker, Joanna**
JHD: 30 Oct. 1778                                    Norfolk Borough
Compensation for household and kitchen furniture destroyed in burning of Norfolk.
30 Oct. 1778: To committee to examine report of commissioners on destruction in Norfolk.
13 Nov. 1778: Committee defers for lack of proof.
    No further record found.

**748-P**
Eck-A7  **Parramore, Thomas**
JHD: 30 Oct. 1778                                    Accomack County
Requesting return from lead mines of slave who attempted to escape to Lord Dunmore and was captured. Also asks for hire.
    Manuscript unsigned, but dated 3 December 1778.
30 Oct. 1778: To PC.
8 Dec. 1778: PC recommends that it be deferred.
    No further record found.

**749-M-†** **Mental Hospital—Directors**
JHD: 30 Oct. 1778                                    Williamsburg
    Asking for additional support for the hospital.
30 Oct. 1778: To PG.
30 Nov. 1778: PG recommends further provision.
    House agrees. Bill to be prepared.
3 Dec. 1778: House passes bill.
8 Dec. 1778: Senate passes bill.
    For this act see 9H479.

**750-P** **Tobacco Planters and Merchants**
JHD: 31 Oct. 1778                                    Not known
Asking for amendments to tobacco laws, providing security for tobacco inspectors to prevent fraud and embezzlement.
    Manuscript signed by: Thomas Pleasants, Jr., Joseph Lewis, Thos. Adams, Parke Goodell, John Brooke, and fourteen others.
31 Oct. 1778: To committee of whole.
    Provisions in these matters were included in a general revision of tobacco laws, which was passed by House and Senate.
    For general act see 9H482.

## 30 October – 2 November 1778

**751-P-†  Goode, John**
JHD: 31 Oct. 1778                                              Not known
Compensation for nursing four sick soldiers in August 1776.
31 Oct. 1778: To PC.
11 Nov. 1778: PC recommends £9 13s.
     House agrees.
23 Nov. 1778: Senate agrees.

**752-P-†  Wilson, John**
JHD: 2 Nov. 1778                                         Norfolk County
                                                  Princess Anne County
For repayment of £100 reward he had offered for killing of a Negro slave who was abetting Josiah Phillips in terrorism. The slave was killed by Zadock Dailey.
2 Nov. 1778: To PC.
11 Nov. 1778: PC recommends reimbursement of £100.
     House agrees.
23 Nov. 1778: Senate agrees.

**753-P-†  Wilson, John; Jones, Solomon; Powell, Abraham; Lowery, Samuel; Miller, Anthony; and Representatives of Forman, William; Peterson, Edward; Powell, Benjamin; Johnson, Samuel; Harness, Isaac; Pugh, Jacob; Shivers, Elisha; M'Grew, Robert; River, Henry; and Viney, Bartholomew**
JHD: 2 Nov 1778                                        Hampshire County
Compensation for guns and blankets lost in battle with Indians in September 1777 on western frontiers where many of the militia were killed.
2 Nov. 1778: To PC.
6 Nov. 1778: PC recommends as reasonable and suggests (1) £9 10s. to John Wilson, (2) £1 10s. to Solomon Jones, (3) £2 to Abraham Powell, (4) £1 10s. to Samuel Lowery, and (5) £1 10s. to Anthony Miller. PC also recommends to the representatives of the following: (1) £11 for William Forman, (2) £11 for Edward Peterson, (3) £14 15s. for Benjamin Powell, (4) £10 for Samuel Johnson, (5) £12 for Isaac Harness, (6) £10 for Jacob Pugh, (7) £7 for Elisha Shivers, (8) £1 10s for Robert M'Grew, (9) £1 10s. for Henry River, and (10) £1 10s. for Bartholomew Viney.
PC recommends that the above ought to be charged in the account of this commonwealth against the United States of America.
     House agrees.

## Virginia Legislative Petitions

23 Nov. 1778: Senate agrees.

### 754-P    Moss, Frederick and Johnson, James
JHD: 2 Nov. 1778                                                Halifax County

Compensation for traveling expenses in guarding the criminals, Thomas Potter, Randolph Boush, and Robert Williamson, from Halifax County to public jail.
Manuscript unsigned.
2 Nov. 1778: To PC.
6 Nov. 1778: PC recommends £11 15s. for each.
  House agrees.
23 Nov. 1778: Senate agrees.

### 755-P-†    Boram, John; Robertson, William; and Moss, Frederick
JHD: 2 Nov. 1778                                                Halifax County

Compensation for impressed horses, used to transport the criminals, Thomas Potter, Randolph Boush, and Robert Williamson, from Halifax County to public jail.
2 Nov. 1778: To PC.
6 Nov. 1778: PC recommends £1 10s. for each.
  House agrees.
23 Nov. 1778: Senate agrees.

### 756-P-†    Estes, Elijah
JHD: 2 Nov. 1778                                                Not known

Compensation for wound received at battle of Brandywine.
2 Nov. 1778: To PC.
5 Nov. 1778: PC recommends £30 for present relief and half pay as a soldier for three years, the latter to be charged in the account of this commonwealth against the United States of America.
  House agrees.
23 Nov. 1778: Senate agrees.

### 757-P-†    Lane, Gilman
JHD: 2 Nov. 1778                                                Not known

Compensation for expenses for illness contracted while at Portsmouth in Continental service.
2 Nov. 1778: To PC.

## 2 – 3 November 1778

5 Nov. 1778: PC recommends £12 9s. 9d. to be charged in the account of this commonwealth against the United States of America.
House agrees.
23 Nov. 1778: Senate agrees.

**758-P    Bullitt, Cuthbert**
JHD: 2 Nov. 1778             Botetourt County
For establishment of a new town near Warm Springs.
Manuscript unsigned, but mentions Andrew Lewis and Thomas Lewis.
2 Nov. 1778: To PC.
23 Nov. 1778: PC recommends it be carried over to next session of GA.
     No further record found.

**759-M-†    Virginia Officers**
JHD: 3 Nov. 1778             Not known
Requesting that a sufficient amount of land be reserved for grants for those who served in Continental service.
3 Nov. 1778: To a special committee.
19 Dec. 1778: Committee recommends (1) that a tract of land bounded by Green River, Cumberland Mountains, North Carolina line, Tennessee River, and Ohio River, excluding land already granted and land belonging to Richard Henderson and Company, be reserved for officers and soldiers; (2) that officers and soldiers may locate their proper share of land on any vacant or ungranted lands; (3) that 200 acres of land, over and above the Continental bounty, be allowed all soldiers in Virginia line who serve three years or more; (4) that commissioned and non-commissioned officers have their land allotments increased in the same amounts as the above resolution; and (5) that general officers have their allotments increased. (Acreage not specified.)
House agrees to (1).
House lays (2), (3), (4), and (5) on table.
Senate amends (1) and House agrees.

**760-P    Manchester Parish, Chesterfield County—Citizens**
JHD: 3 Nov. 1778             Chesterfield County
For dissolution of the vestry.
Manuscript signed by: Daniel Branch, Jr., John Fowler, Jr., John Fowler, Hen. Bowles, Matthew Cheatham, and forty-six others.
3 Nov. 1778: To R.

## Virginia Legislative Petitions

11 Nov. 1778: R finds reasonable, and is directed to prepare a bill.
        This was incorporated in a general vestry bill, which was passed by House and Senate.
        For general vestry act see 9H525.

### 761-P-†   Bybee, Joseph
        JHD: 3 Nov. 1778         Not known

Compensation for wound received at battle of Brandywine.
3 Nov. 1778: To PC.
14 Nov. 1778: PC recommends £30 for present relief and half pay as a soldier for one year, the latter to be charged in the account of this commonwealth against the United States of America.
        House agrees.
25 Nov. 1778: Senate agrees.

### 762-P-†   Barrett, Amy
        JHD: 3 Nov. 1778         Not known

Compensation for death of husband, Jonathan Barrett, who was captured by British and died in a New York jail.
3 Nov. 1778: To PC.
20 Nov. 1778: PC recommends rejection since, under action of GA, county courts are supposed to make provision for support of widows.
        House rejects.

### 763-M-†   Wood, James
        JHD: 4 Nov. 1778         Not known

For better medical treatment of officers who become ill in the service.
4 Nov. 1778: To special committee.
        No further action found.

### 764-P-†   Hutchings, Leanna
        JHD: 4 Nov. 1778         Not known

Return or hire for slave who attempted to escape to Lord Dunmore and was captured. He is now employed in public works for the state.
4 Nov. 1778: To PC.
8 Dec. 1778: PC recommends that this matter be carried over to next session of GA.
        No further record found.

## 3 – 4 November 1778

**765-P-†  Gass, David**
JHD: 4 Nov. 1778                                                            Not known
Compensation for service as a lieutenant in Boone's company in defending frontier.
4 Nov. 1778: To PC.
14 Nov. 1778: PC recommends that this matter be carried over to next session of GA.
No further record found.

**766-P-†  Clarkson, David**
JHD: 4 Nov. 1778                                                       Fluvanna County
Additional compensation for team and wagon, impressed in September 1777.
4 Nov. 1778: To PC.
11 Nov. 1778: PC recommends rejection.
House rejects.

**767-P-†  Harrup, Elizabeth**
JHD: 4 Nov. 1778                                                      Brunswick County
Compensation for death of husband in battle of Brandywine. She has two sons in service and three small children. The county court has refused her an allowance.
4 Nov. 1778: To PC.
6 Nov. 1778: PC recommends county court should grant her £30 for her immediate relief.
House agrees.
23 Nov. 1778: Senate agrees.

**768-P-†  Braden, Joseph**
JHD: 4 Nov. 1778                                                            Not known
Compensation for horse, impressed for Continental service in 1777, that was never returned.
4 Nov. 1778: To PC.
14 Nov. 1778: PC recommends £22 to be charged in the account of this commonwealth against the United States of America.
House agrees.
25 Nov. 1778: Senate agrees.

**769-P  Fleming, William**
JHD: 4 Nov. 1778                                                      Botetourt County

## Virginia Legislative Petitions

Asking that county court be required to take care of poor since there is no chance of electing a vestry.

Manuscript unsigned.

4 Nov. 1778: To R.

4 Dec. 1778: R recommends that this matter is reasonable and is directed to prepare a bill to provide that the commissioners of tax supply funds for the poor.

This was incorporated in a general vestry bill, which was passed by House and Senate.

For general vestry act see 9H525.

**770-P-†   Kirk, James**
JHD: 4 Nov. 1778                                    Not known

Compensation for barrel of gin, impressed for Continental use.

4 Nov. 1778: Rejected by refusal to refer to a committee.

**771-P   Southampton County—Citizens**
JHD: 4 Nov. 1778                              Southampton County

For charging tolls on bridge to be rebuilt over Nottoway River.

Manuscript signed by: Wm. Blunt, Thos. Vaughan, Robert Williams, Kirby Bittle, Benja. Spivy, and forty-one others.

4 Nov. 1778: To PG.

17 Nov. 1778: PG reports reasonable and bill is directed to be drawn.

This matter was incorporated in a general ferry act, which was passed by House and Senate.

For general ferry act see 9H585.

**772-P-†   Woodford, William; Taliaferro, John; Lewis, John; and Washington, Samuel**
JHD: 5 Nov. 1778                                  Caroline County

For sale of property vested in various descendants of John Thornton, deceased.

5 Nov. 1778: House directs a bill to be drawn.

This bill was passed by House and Senate.

For this act see 9H575.

**773-M-†   Aylett, William**
JHD: 5 Nov. 1778                                    Not known

For appointment of committee to investigate alleged unwarranted profits from sale of articles to officers and soldiers.

## 4 – 5 November 1778

5 Nov. 1778: To T
    No further action found.

### 774-P    Jarrett, John
    JHD: 5 Nov. 1778                                             Surry County
For death of an ox that was employed in government service.
    Manuscript unsigned.
5 Nov. 1778: To PC.
26 Nov. 1778: PC recommends rejection for lack of proof.
    House rejects.

### 775-P-†    Aaron, Abraham
    JHD: 5 Nov. 1778                                         Pittsylvania County
Compensation for repairing guns for militia ordered out against Indians in June 1778.
5 Nov. 1778: To PC.
11 Nov. 1778: PC recommends rejection.
    House recommits to PC.
14 Nov. 1778: PC recommends £27 5s.
23 Nov. 1778: Senate rejects, JS.

### 776-P    Montague, William
    JHD: 5 Nov. 1778                                         Lancaster County
Asks that slave who attempted to defect to Lord Dunmore in Montague's yawl in 1776 and was captured be returned to him from lead mines with proper hire, together with value of boat.
    Manuscript unsigned.
5 Nov. 1778: To PC.
8 Dec. 1778: PC recommends that it be carried over to next session of GA.
3 May 1779: To T. Perhaps a new petition presented.
10 June 1779: T recommends (1) that petition for hire is reasonable; (2) that hire for 16 July 1776 to 1 January 1777 be paid at rate of £8 per annum, for 1777, £10 per annum, for year 1778, £20 per annum, and for year 1779, £60 per annum; and (3) that at end of 1779 the slave be returned to his master at expense of country.
    House agrees to all.
16 June 1779: Senate agrees to all.

### 777-P    Bland, William
    JHD: 5 Nov. 1778                                                 Williamsburg

## Virginia Legislative Petitions

For additional compensation for his position as ordinary of Newgate. (The ordinary of Newgate, a little known public official, was a chaplain of the public jail, charged with hearing confessions, and furnishing last rites. For his British counterparts see Horace Bleakley, *The Hangmen of England* . . . [London, 1929]. Bland was appointed to his position 28 December 1776, JS.)
Manuscript unsigned.
5 Nov. 1778: To PG.
3 Dec. 1778: PG recommends an additional £50 per annum. (On 28 June 1777 the treasurer had been authorized to pay Bland £50 a year so long as he was in office, JHD.)
House agrees.
No Senate action found, JS.
Bland petitioned again later. See 1137-P-†.

**778-P   Princess Anne County—Citizens**
JHD: 5 Nov. 1778                             Princess Anne County
For removal of county courthouse from New Town to Kemp's landing.
Manuscript signed by: Henry Gasking, Dim Corrick, John James, Jr., Horatio Corrick, James Edwards, and 155 others.
5 Nov. 1778: To PG.
8 Dec. 1778: PG finds reasonable and is directed to prepare a bill.
11 Dec. 1778: House passes bill.
12 Dec. 1778: Senate amends bill and House agrees to amendments.
For this act see 9H577.

**779-P   Chowning, John**
JHD: 5 Nov. 1778                                     Lancaster County
For changing location of his ferry from north side of Rappahannock River in Lancaster County to his land in Middlesex County, and for increasing ferriages.
Manuscript unsigned, but dated 31 October 1778.
5 Nov. 1778: To PG.
3 Dec. 1778: Carried over to next session of GA.
No further record found.

**780-P-†   Thornton, James**
JHD: 6 Nov. 1778                                           Not known
Compensation for indentured servant who enlisted in Virginia troops in 1777.
6 Nov. 1778: To PC.

## 5 – 6 November 1778

14 Nov. 1778: PC recommends rejection.
       House rejects.

### 781-P-†   Thornton, James
      JHD: 6 Nov. 1778                                        Not known

Compensation for nursing his brother, Jeremiah Thornton, who was wounded at battle of Brandywine, and for his travel expenses incurred in bringing his brother home.
6 Nov. 1778: To PC.
11 Nov. 1778: PC recommends £3 16s. 8d. for nursing only.
       Recommitted to PC.
       PC recommends rejection of travel expenses.
       House agrees to nursing and rejects travel.
5 Dec. 1778: House lays on table.
8 Dec. 1778: House agrees to £3 16s. 8d. for nursing and £11 1s. for travel.
12 Dec. 1778: Senate agrees.

### 782-P-†   Johnson, Richard
      JHD: 6 Nov. 1778                                   Caroline County

Compensation for forage for his horses and others and for loss of a drum while a major in Caroline County militia.
6 Nov. 1778: To PC.
14 Nov. 1778: PC recommends rejection of forage for his own horses but
       allows for other forage the sum of £4 19s., and £2 2s. for drum.
       House agrees.
25 Nov. 1778: Senate agrees.

### 783-P-†   Henderson, Nathaniel
      JHD: 6 Nov. 1778                                   Kentucky County

Compensation for travel to Williamsburg for ammunition, and death of slave killed by Indians.
6 Nov. 1778: To PC.
15 Dec. 1778: PC recommends £400 as compensation for slave.
       House agrees.
16 Dec. 1778: Senate agrees.

### 784-P
Eck-A8   **Simpson, Southey**
      JHD: 6 Nov. 1778                                   Accomack County

Compensation of £500 for supervising construction of two galleys under order of Naval Board.
Manuscript unsigned.
6 Nov. 1778: To PC.
7 Nov. 1778: PC recommends rejection for want of proof.
   House rejects.

**785-P  Goochland County—Citizens**
   JHD: 6 Nov. 1778                                        Goochland County
Opposing adding part of Fluvanna County to Goochland County.
Manuscript signed by: John Lewis, Elliott Lacy, John Stephen Woodson, Isham Woodson, Hugh Moss, and thirty-eight others.
6 Nov. 1778: Rejected by refusal to refer to a committee.

**786-P-†  Harris, William**
   JHD: 6 Nov. 1778                                            Bedford County
Requesting to sell by lottery twenty-nine acres of land since he is unable to pay required fees.
6 Nov. 1778: Rejected by refusal to refer to a committee.

**787-P-†  Downs, Henry; Blair, John; Willis, John; Taylor, George; Spencer, Edward; Slaughter, Robert; Jackson, William; Dunlop, Alexander; Edwin, James; and Fuller, Edward**
   JHD: 6 Nov. 1778                                             Western Lands
Asking permission to survey 50,000 acres of land west of Cowpasture or Greenbrier rivers under grant from king in 1745.
6 Nov. 1778: To PG.
1 Dec. 1778: PG recommends rejection.
   House rejects.

**788-P-†  Goochland County—Citizens**
   JHD: 6 Nov. 1778                                        Goochland County
In opposition to adding part of Fluvanna County to Goochland County.
6 Nov. 1778: To PG.
   Committee apparently did not report.

**789-P-†  Gautier, Nicholas**
   JHD: 7 Nov. 1778                                            Henrico County
Asking for the establishment of the office of notary in town of Richmond, and his appointment thereto.

## 6 – 9 November 1778

7 Nov. 1778: Rejected by refusal to refer to a committee.

### 790-P   Berry, Thomas
JHD: 7 Nov. 1778                         Charlotte County

Compensation for travel to find and return home his sick son, Bradley Berry, who was found dead. (Identical with 611-P-†.)

Manuscript unsigned, but has several certificates vouching for the facts.
7 Nov. 1778: To PC.
14 Nov. 1778: PC recommends £22 10s.
      House agrees.
23 Nov. 1778: Senate rejects, JS.

### 791-P-†   College of William and Mary—Rector, Visitors, and Governors
JHD: 9 Nov. 1778                       Williamsburg

Asking financial support from the commonwealth. (This is related to 333-M and 488-P.)
9 Nov. 1778: To a special committee.
3 Dec. 1778: Committee recommends rejection.
      House rejects.

### 792-M
Eck–Not
found   **Lynch, Charles**
JHD: 9 Nov. 1778                        Bedford County

Asking that payment of money, with interest, advanced to him by commonwealth, be repaid by him in money rather than powder, due to incursions of Indians.

Manuscript unsigned.
9 Nov. 1778: To PG.
3 Dec. 1778: Carried over to next session of GA.
12 Nov. 1779: PG reports as reasonable.
      Recommitted to PG.
17 Nov. 1779: PG recommends (1) that Lynch be released from his contract and allowed to repay balance of money, with interest, to commonwealth; (2) that Lynch should have credit for 150 pounds of powder stolen from him; and (3) that Lynch should repay to the

## Virginia Legislative Petitions

commonwealth the 250 pounds of powder sold by him, amounting to £450.

House rejects (2).

House agrees to (1) and (3).

19 Nov. 1779: Senate amends.

22 Nov. 1779: Senate recedes from amendments.

**793-P     Fox, John**
JHD: 9 Nov. 1778                                            Gloucester County

For establishment of ferry from York County across York River to Gloucester County.

Manuscript signed by: John Buckner, Jr., Wm. Duval, John Royston, John Cooke, John Dixon, and 120 others.

9 Nov. 1778: To PG.

3 Dec. 1778: PG recommends rejection.

House rejects.

**794-P-†     Cummins, Peter**
JHD: 9 Nov. 1778                                            Prince William County

Compensation for travel home from place of discharge from Continental service, he being ill.

9 Nov. 1778: To PC.

14 Nov. 1778: PC recommends £14 8s. to be charged in the account of this commonwealth against the United States of America.

House agrees.

25 Nov. 1778: Senate agrees.

**795-P     Maupin, Gabriel**
JHD: 10 Nov. 1778                                            Williamsburg

For increase in salary as keeper of the public magazine.

Manuscript unsigned.

10 Nov. 1778: To PC.

14 Nov. 1778: PC recommends as reasonable, and salary augmented to that of lieutenant colonel, he keeping the rank of captain.

Recommitted to PC.

20 Nov. 1778: PC recommends that salary be increased $75 a month and that he should not retain rank of captain.

House agrees.

2 Dec. 1778: Senate amends $75 to $50 and deletes portion about captain.

5 Dec. 1778: House agrees to Senate amendments.

## 9 – 11 November 1778

**796-P-†   Salmon, John**
        JHD: 10 Nov. 1778                                    Not known
   Compensation for injury to his horse that had been impressed.
10 Nov. 1778: To PC.
14 Nov. 1778: Carried over to next session of GA.
        No further record found.

**797-P**
Eck–Not
found   **Ward, John**
        JHD: 10 Nov. 1778                                    Bedford County
   To establish a ferry from his land in Bedford County across Staunton River to his land in Pittsylvania County.
   Manuscript unsigned.
10 Nov. 1778: To PG.
1 Dec. 1778: PG recommends as reasonable and is directed to prepare a bill.
        This was incorporated in a general ferry bill, which was passed by House and Senate.
        For general ferry act see 9H585.

**798-M   Hite, Thomas**
        JHD: 10 Nov. 1778                                    Berkeley County
   Asking for commissioners to arrange the sale of 257 acres of land that had been escheated from the property of Bryan Obanion for the benefit of his heirs. Obanion had two illegitimate children, Frances, who died as an infant, and Aaron, who had no children and died intestate. Bryan Obanion had left his property to these children or their heirs.
   Manuscript unsigned.
10 Nov. 1778: To a special committee.
13 Nov. 1778: Committee recommends as reasonable and House directs that it prepare a bill.
        This bill was passed by the House and Senate.
        For this act see 9H576, but see also 11H60 for repeal of act.

**799-P-†   Amherst County—Citizens**
        JHD: 11 Nov. 1778                                    Amherst County
   As volunteers for reinforcing the Continental army, they feel entitled to bounty and full pay.

241

## Virginia Legislative Petitions

11 Nov. 1778: To PC.
> Apparently found reasonable since it was incorporated in an act. For this act see 9H588.

**800-P-†   Wood, Leighton, Jr.**
JHD: 11 Nov. 1778                                                                Not known
Compensation for auditing accounts of William Aylett before the accounts were transferred to a Mr. Prentis.
11 Nov. 1778: To PC.
15 Dec. 1778: PC recommends £100.
> House agrees.
17 Dec. 1778: Senate agrees.

**801-P-†   Tyler, William**
JHD: 11 Nov. 1778                                                                Not known
Compensation for nursing at his home three Continental soldiers who were ill.
11 Nov. 1778: To PC.
20 Nov. 1778: PC recommends £11 6s. 6d. to be charged in the account of this commonwealth against the United States of America.
> House agrees.
25 Nov. 1778: Senate agrees.

**802-P-†   Field, Henry**
JHD: 11 Nov. 1778                                                                Not known
Compensation for his horse, impressed and lost in Continental service.
11 Nov. 1778: To PC.
14 Nov. 1778: PC recommends £12 to be charged in the account of this commonwealth against the United States of America.
> House agrees.
25 Nov. 1778: Senate agrees.

**803-P-†   Noe, Bazil**
JHD: 11 Nov. 1778                                                          Culpeper County
Compensation for his horse, impressed and lost in Continental service.
11 Nov. 1778: To PC.
14 Nov. 1778: PC recommends £20 to be charged in the account of this commonwealth against the United States of America.
> House agrees.
25 Nov. 1778: Senate agrees.

## 11 – 13 November 1778

**804-P-†   Thilman, Paul**
JHD: 11 Nov. 1778                                             Hanover County
To operate a ferry from Hanover County across Pamunkey River to Caroline County, in lieu of a bridge that was washed away.
11 Nov. 1778: To PG.
8 Dec. 1778: PG recommends rejection.
   House rejects.

**805-P-†   George (Slave)**
JHD: 12 Nov. 1778                                             Not known
Requesting an act for his emancipation, his former master, John Thornton, deceased, having assured him many times he would do so.
12 Nov. 1778: To a special committee.
14 Nov. 1778: Bill presented.
17 Nov. 1778: Bill to PG where it was amended to include other slaves, the property of Mrs. Joseph Bankes, deceased, and various slaves in general.
3 Dec. 1778: PG amends further.
   House lays on table.
   No further action found.

**806-P   Orange County and Culpeper County—Citizens**
JHD: 12 Nov. 1778                                             Orange County
                                                              Culpeper County
To repeal an act requiring mill owners to open passages for fish in milldams on Rapidan and Robertson rivers.
Manuscript signed by: Zack Herndon, Rodger Halsy, John Samuel, James Gordon, John Allphin, and thirty-eight others.
12 Nov. 1778: To PG.
3 Dec. 1778: PG recommends as reasonable, and House directs it to prepare a bill.
9 Dec. 1778: House passes bill for Rapidan River only.
12 Dec. 1778: Senate passes bill.
   See 673-P and 673 A-P.
   For this act see 9H579.

**807-P-†   Monongalia County—Court**
JHD: 13 Nov. 1778                                             Monongalia County
For use of fines collected to defray expenses of the administration of justice, and for not requiring a special levy.

## Virginia Legislative Petitions

13 Nov. 1778: To CJ.
3 Dec. 1778: CJ recommends rejection.
    House rejects.

**808-P    Yohogania County—Court**
    JHD: 13 Nov. 1778                  Yohogania County
For use of fines collected to defray the expenses of the administration of justice, and for not requiring a special levy.
    Manuscript unsigned.
13 Nov. 1778: To CJ.
3 Dec. 1778: CJ recommends rejection.
    House rejects.

**809-P-†    Peterson, Edward; Bleuw, John, Sr.; Williams, Richard, Sr.; Williams, Remembrance; Ross, John; Leston, Edward; Glaze, Windle; and Green, Thomas**
    JHD: 13 Nov. 1778                  Hampshire County
Allowance for services in guarding five deserters from Continental army from Hampshire County to Winchester.
13 Nov. 1778: To PC.
20 Nov. 1778: PC recommends £4 each to be charged in the account of this commonwealth against the United States of America.
    House agrees.
25 Nov. 1778: Senate agrees.

**810-P-†    Walker, Jeremiah**
    JHD: 14 Nov. 1778                  Chesterfield County
For remission of fines, in tobacco, imposed upon him for jail charges and imprisonment for preaching.
14 Nov. 1778: To R.
20 Nov. 1778: R recommends rejection.
    House rejects.

**811-P    Halifax County—Citizens**
    JHD: 14 Nov. 1778                  Halifax County
For rescinding recent action giving members of General Assembly a pay increase.
    Manuscript signed by: Wm. Terry, John Shackelford, William Hawkins, Nathl. Hunt, Eli Hunt, and twenty-one others. Dated 4 November 1778.
14 Nov. 1778: To PG.

## 13 – 16 November 1778

8 Dec. 1778: PG recommends as reasonable.
    House tables on second reading.

### 812-P    Prince William County—Citizens
    JHD: 14 Nov. 1778    Prince William County

For rescinding recent action giving members of General Assembly a pay increase.

Manuscript signed by: Lynarigh Helm, John Hooe, John Maximillian, Foushee Tebbs, Evan Williams, and ninety-four others.
14 Nov. 1778: To PG.
8 Dec. 1778: PG recommends as reasonable.
    House tables on second reading.

### 813-P    Walton, George; Walton, Joseph; Walton, Sherwood; Franklin, Thomas; Walton, William; and Williams, Joseph
    JHD: 14 Nov. 1778    Western Lands

For surveying lands on the Clinch River under a 1751 order of Council for 110,000 acres.

Manuscript unsigned, but has certificate showing that some lands had been surveyed.
14 Nov. 1778: To PG.
3 Dec. 1778: PG recommends rejection.
    House rejects.

### 814-P    Watkins, Thomas
    JHD: 14 Nov. 1778    Not known

For reimbursement of expenses in apprehending deserters from the Continental army.

Manuscript unsigned.
14 Nov. 1778: To PG.
26 Nov. 1778: PG recommends rejection.
    House rejects.

### 815-P    Fredericksburg—Citizens
    JHD: Not found [16 Nov. 1778]    Spotsylvania County

Opposing removal of courthouse of Spotsylvania County from Fredericksburg.

Manuscript signed by: Chas. Dick, Fielding Lewis, Chas. Washington, Chs.

Yates, J. S. Mercer, and two others. Manuscript endorsement says referred to committee of whole.
No further record found.

**816-P-†   Purdie, George**
JHD: 17 Nov. 1778                                          Isle of Wight County
Compensation for slave, indicted for burglary, who escaped jail in 1777 and has not been found.
17 Nov. 1778: To PC.
1 Dec. 1778: PC recommends rejection.
      House rejects.

**817-P-†   Tomlinson, Samuel; Reinhart, George; Smith, John; M'Clain, Joseph; Greathouse, Jacob; Boyd, John; Shepperd, William; and Grindstaff, Jacob—Representatives of**
JHD: 17 Nov. 1778                                                     Ohio County
Reimbursement for rifles and pouches taken by Indians when these men were killed in an engagement with the Indians.
17 Nov. 1778: To PC.
28 Nov. 1778: PC recommends the following to the representatives: (1) £11 for Samuel Tomlinson, (2) £16 2s. 6d. for George Reinhart, (3) £10 for John Smith, (4) £8 7s. 6d. for Joseph M'Clain, (5) £9 7s. 6d. for Jacob Greathouse, (6) £9 for John Boyd, (7) £14 15s. for William Shepperd, and (8) £6 17s. 6d. for Jacob Grindstaff.
      PC also recommends that the above payments ought to be charged in the account of this commonwealth against the United States of America.
      House agrees.
4 Dec. 1778: Senate agrees.

**818-P-†   Quakers**
JHD: 17 Nov. 1778                                                          Not known
Objecting to difficulties and sufferings from any legislation not recognizing that it is a tenet of their religion not to engage in war.
17 Nov. 1778: To committee of whole on bill to expel persons inimicable to liberties of America.
      No further record found, but Quakers and Menonists were allowed later to provide substitutes. See 10H257.

## 17 – 18 November 1778

**819-P-†  Blair, John, and Associates**
JHD: 17 Nov. 1778                                                  Western Lands
Citing grant of land given Blair's father for 160,000 acres of land in 1751 and asking for extension of time for surveying.
17 Nov. 1778: House orders to lie on table.
          No further action found.

**820-P-†  Winchester—Citizens**
JHD: 18 Nov. 1778                                                  Frederick County
For incorporating Winchester.
18 Nov. 1778: To PG.
1 Dec. 1778: PG reports reasonable and House directs it to prepare a bill.
8 Dec. 1778: Bill presented.
          Carried forward to next session of GA.
          This bill was not passed by House and Senate until 1779.
          For this act see 10H172.

**821-P-†  Robertson, William and Robertson, William, Jr.**
JHD: 18 Nov. 1778                                                  Culpeper County
For relief from judgment of Culpeper County court for conviction for certain offenses resulting in fines and imprisonment. These offenses were for statements about unjust drafts.
18 Nov. 1778: To PG.
3 Dec. 1778: PG recommends rejection.
          House rejects.

**822-P-†  Raines, John**
JHD: 18 Nov. 1778                                                  Dinwiddie County
Compensation for team and wagon, impressed to carry baggage from Petersburg to Wilmington, North Carolina.
18 Nov. 1778: To PC.
8 Dec. 1778: PC recommends rejection.
          House rejects.

**823-P-†  Humphreys, Sarah**
JHD: 18 Nov. 1778                                                  Not known
Compensation for death of her husband, John Humphreys, at battle of Quebec in Continental service, he having died intestate and leaving many debts.
18 Nov. 1778: To PC.

20 Nov. 1778: PC recommends £200 to be charged in the account of this commonwealth against the United States of America, and that the governor transmit a copy of the report to the Continental Congress.
House agrees.
24 Nov. 1778: Senate amends.
26 Nov. 1778: House agrees to Senate amendments.
3 Dec. 1778: Senate recedes from amendments and agrees.

**824-P-†  Phripp, Matthew and Tankard, Stephen**
JHD: 18 Nov. 1778                                          Norfolk Borough
Compensation for property destroyed in Norfolk borough by Virginia troops.
18 Nov. 1778: To committee to examine report of commissioners on examination of losses in Norfolk borough (after postponement from 13 November 1778).
20 Nov. 1778: Committee recommends that representatives of John Phripp, deceased, including Matthew Phripp, be allowed £2,130 13s., and that Stephen Tankard be allowed £1,204.
House agrees.
24 Nov. 1778: Senate agrees.

**825-P    Winslow, Benjamin**
JHD: 18 Nov. 1778                                          Orange County
For confirmation of land grant authorized in 1763.
Manuscript unsigned.
18 Nov. 1778: To lie on table.
1 Dec. 1778: To PG.
    Manuscript endorsement says carried over to next session of GA, but no further record found.

**826-P-†  Augusta County—Citizens**
JHD: 19 Nov. 1778                                          Augusta County
For a division of the county.
19 Nov. 1778: Carried over to the next session of GA.
    There is no further record of this petition, but many new petitions were presented in May 1779.

**826-A-P-†Augusta County—Citizens**
JHD: 19 Nov. 1778                                          Augusta County

## 18 – 20 November 1778

Text must have been identical with 826-P-†, which see.

### 827-P-† White, Robert
JHD: 19 Nov. 1778                                                                 Not known

Compensation for wound received in battle in the Jerseys.
19 Nov. 1778: To PC.
1 Dec. 1778: PC recommends £100 for current relief and full pay as a lieutenant for life, half of the latter to be charged in the account of this commonwealth against the United States of America.
House agrees.
8 Dec. 1778: Senate agrees.

### 828-M Simms, Charles
JHD: 19 Nov. 1778                                                              Augusta County

For confirmation of land purchase on Ohio River, secured from George Croghan who purchased land from the Six Nations of Indians, and allowing it for claims for officers and soldiers.
Manuscript unsigned.
19 Nov. 1778: To FG.
Carried over to next session of GA.
See 1028 1-M.

### 829-P-† Hook, John
JHD: 20 Nov. 1778                                                              Bedford County

Compensation for horse, impressed to convey John Goodrich, Sr., from Bedford County courthouse to Charlottesville, and not returned.
20 Nov. 1778: To PC.
1 Dec. 1778: PC recommends £65.
House agrees.
7 Dec. 1778: Senate agrees.

### 830-P-† Clarke, Thomas
JHD: 20 Nov. 1778                                                                 Not known

Compensation for wound received at battle of Brandywine.
20 Nov. 1778: To PC.
26 Nov. 1778: PC recommends £30 for present relief and full pay of sergeant for life, one half of latter to be charged in the account of this commonwealth against the United States of America.
House agrees.
4 Dec. 1778: Senate agrees.

## Virginia Legislative Petitions

**831-P-†  Bunch, James**
JHD: 20 Nov. 1778                                    Not known
Compensation for wounds received from Indians while defending frontier in Washington County in 1777.
20 Nov. 1778: To PC.
26 Nov. 1778: PC recommends £30 for present relief and half pay as a soldier for three years.
  House agrees.
4 Dec. 1778: Senate agrees.

**832-P  Johnson, Thomas, Jr.**
JHD: 20 Nov. 1778                                    Louisa County
Reimbursement of £12 12s. for death of two steers hired from Charles Yancey to transfer military supplies in Shawanese expedition, together with £2 13s. 6d. court costs. (This is identical with 418-P and 569-P, which see.)
Manuscript unsigned, but has abstract of Louisa County court decision attached.
20 Nov. 1778: To PC.
1 Dec. 1778: PC recommends £12 12s. and £2 13s. 6d. to be charged in the account of this commonwealth against the United States of America.
  House agrees.
7 Dec. 1778: Senate agrees without the amendments, which had been a matter of controversy, JS.

**833-P  Herrin, Jonathan, Sr.**
JHD: 20 Nov. 1778                                    Not known
Compensation for nursing son, Jonathan Herrin, Jr., who had become ill in Continental service.
  Manuscript unsigned.
20 Nov. 1778: To PC.
26 Nov. 1778: PC recommends £5 11s. 8d. to be charged in the account of this commonwealth against the United States of America.
  House agrees.
4 Dec. 1778: Senate agrees.

**834-P-†  Dillon, William**
JHD: 20 Nov. 1778                                    Not known
Compensation for nursing his son, Jesse Dillon, who became ill in July 1777 while on furlough from state service.

## 20 November 1778

20 Nov. 1778: To PC.
26 Nov. 1778: PC recommends £9 11s. 8d.
       House agrees.
4 Dec. 1778: Senate agrees.

**835-P-†   Sadler, Benjamin, Jr.**
      JHD: 20 Nov. 1778                         Not known
For funds to employ a surgeon to treat a broken leg resulting from a fall in a British jail after battle of Germantown.
20 Nov. 1778: To PC.
26 Nov. 1778: PC recommends £40.
       House agrees.
7 Dec. 1778: Senate agrees.

**836-P-†   Rogers, Benjamin; Rigdon, John; Ogle, Joseph; Moore, James; Andrew, James; Stephinson, Charles; Peatt, Robert; and Representatives of Mugg, Notley; Sterneighter, Henry; Atkinson, Matthew; Ogle, Jacob; and Hedges, Ezekiel**
      JHD: 20 Nov. 1778                         Not known
Compensation for guns, blankets, and other items, taken by Indians in 1777 who had killed many of these men's company members while they were defending frontiers in Ohio County.
20 Nov. 1778: To PC.
1 Dec. 1778: PC recommends £10 0s. 6d. for Rogers; 33s. each for Rigdon, Joseph Ogle, Moore, Andrew, Stephinson, and Peatt; for representatives of Mugg, £6 10s. 0d.; for Sterneighter, £5; of Atkinson, £8; of Jacob Ogle, £10 3s.; and of Hedges, £10 13s.
      PC also recommends that the above ought to be charged in the account of this commonwealth against the United States of America.
      House agrees.
8 Dec. 1778: Senate agrees.

**837-P-†   Duke, Sarah**
      JHD: 20 Nov. 1778                         Not known
Compensation for loss of gun, mare, and harness belonging to her husband, Francis Duke, who was killed by Indians in Ohio County in 1777. He was a commissary.
20 Nov. 1778: To PC.

## Virginia Legislative Petitions

26 Nov. 1778: PC recommends rejection.
    House rejects.

**838-P-†**    **Wilson, John**
    JHD: 20 Nov. 1778                  Not known
  Compensation for horse and harness, impressed by Matthew Atkinson, who was killed in Ohio County by Indians in 1777.
20 Nov. 1778: To PC.
26 Nov. 1778: PC recommends £25.
    House agrees.
9 Dec. 1778: Senate agrees.

**839-P-†**    **Weldie, William**
    JHD: 20 Nov. 1778                  Not known
  For funds to employ a surgeon for illness contracted in a British jail following the battle of Germantown.
20 Nov. 1778: To PC.
26 Nov. 1778: PC recommends £40.
    House agrees.
4 Dec. 1778: Senate agrees.

**840-P-†**    **Logwood, Thomas**
    JHD: 20 Nov. 1778                  Not known
Compensation for two horses lost on Cherokee expedition in 1776.
20 Nov. 1778: To PC.
26 Nov. 1778: PC recommends £21 10s.
    House agrees.
4 Dec. 1778: Senate agrees.
    See 562-P-†.

**841-P-†**    **Ramsey, Thomas**
    JHD: 20 Nov. 1778                  Not known
Compensation for nursing a soldier, Abraham Crabtree, taken ill on the Cherokee expedition.
20 Nov. 1778: To PC.
26 Nov. 1778: PC recommends £4 13s. 4d.
    House agrees.
4 Dec. 1778: Senate agrees.

## 20 November 1778

**842-P-†   Douglass, Edward**
          JHD: 20 Nov. 1778                               Not known
    Compensation for horse, impressed by John Douglass, which was killed by Indians in Cherokee expedition of 1776.
20 Nov. 1778: To PC.
26 Nov. 1778: PC recommends £16 10s.
          House agrees.
7 Dec. 1778: Senate agrees.

**843-P-†   Bourn, Eleanor**
          JHD: 20 Nov. 1778                               Not known
    Compensation for nursing her son, John Bourn, who became ill in Continental service. (Original entry under Leanor Bowen.)
20 Nov. 1778: To PC.
26 Nov. 1778: PC recommends £7 11s. 8d. to be charged in the account of this
          commonwealth against the United States of America.
          House agrees.
4 Dec. 1778: Senate agrees under name of Eleanor Brown.

**844-P   Upper Parish, Nansemond County—Citizens**
          JHD: 20 Nov. 1778                          Nansemond County
    For sale of workhouse and land in Suffolk, and for sale of glebe.
    Manuscript signed by: John Driver, Jno. Brickell, Henry Riddick, Josiah Riddick, Willis Riddick, and sixty-three others.
20 Nov. 1778: To R.
2 Dec. 1778: R recommends (1) that sale of glebe be rejected, and (2) that sale
          of workhouse and land be allowed.
          House rejects (1).
          House agrees to (2) and directs R to prepare a bill.
          This bill was approved by House and Senate and incorporated in a
          general bill.
    For general vestry act see 9H525.

**845-P**
Eck-Not
found   **Potomac River Lands—Citizens (owning lands there)**
          JHD: 20 Nov. 1778                             Augusta County
    For formation of a new county in the area between north and south fork of Potomac River.
    Manuscript signed (in same hand) by: James Dyer, John Wertmiller, Roger

## Virginia Legislative Petitions

Dyer, Thomas Hicks, Thomas Blizzard, and 337 others.
20 Nov. 1778: To PG.
26 Nov. 1778: PG recommends rejection.
    House rejects.

### 846-P-†    Staunton—Citizens
JHD: 20 Nov. 1778             Augusta County

Asking for an act to empower trustees to make special assessments to repair streets and furnish aqueducts.
20 Nov. 1778: To PG.
3 Dec. 1778: PG recommends as reasonable and is directed to prepare a bill.
8 Dec. 1778: House returns bill to PG.
    No further action found, but see a similar petition on 22 May 1779 (948-P).

### 847-P
Eck–
A457    **Fairfax County—Citizens**
JHD: 20 Nov. 1778             Fairfax County

As proprietors of lots adjoining the town of Alexandria, they request that lots be added to the town, two additional streets laid off, and time for making improvements be extended, all in conformity with the conveyance of John Alexander, deceased.

Manuscript signed by: Edward Ramsey, John Butcher, Wm. Knight, Adam Lynn, John Fitzgerald, and nine others.
20 Nov. 1778: To PG.
    Carried over to next session of GA.
30 Oct. 1779: PG recommends as reasonable.
    Recommitted to PG.
6 Nov. 1779: PG again recommends as reasonable and is directed to prepare a bill.
    This bill was passed by House and Senate.
    For this act see 10H192.

### 848-P
Eck–Not
found    **Alexandria—Trustees**
JHD: 20 Nov. 1778             Fairfax County

Concerning disposal of property rights in town of Alexandria.

## 20 November 1778

Manuscript signed by: Wm. Ramsay, Robert Adam, John Muir, Thomas Fleming, and Richd. Conway.
20 Nov. 1778: To PG.
    See 847-P for action.
    Property rights are covered in act, 10H192.

### 849-P-†   Ohio Company
JHD: 20 Nov. 1778                                       Western Lands
Requesting that members of company living in Maryland and Virginia may receive patents, as soon as the land office is established, for 200,000 of the 500,000 acres of land for which they had received grants in 1743.
20 Nov. 1778: To PG.
    No further action found.
    For prohibition of settlement in this area, see 10H159.

### 850-P   Field, Ezekiel
JHD: 20 Nov. 1778                                       Western Lands
For securing his claim for land on the Kanawha River, granted by royal proclamation to his father, John Field, for which no warrant had ever been issued.
Manuscript unsigned.
20 Nov. 1778: To PG.
    No further record found.

### 851-P-†   White, John
JHD: 20 Nov. 1778, for action                         Not known
Text not found.
Date unknown: To PC.
20 Nov. 1778: PC recommends rejection.
    House rejects.

### 852-P
Eck-
A1101   **Monongalia River Lands, Buckanan River Lands, Tyger's (Tygart's) Valley Lands—Citizens**
JHD: 20 Nov. 1778                                       Augusta County
Relief from penalties for not taking loyalty oath since there was no justice to administer it.
Manuscript signed by: Ralph Stewart, William Martin, Hugh Martin, Alexander Miller, Patr. Hamilton, and thirty-nine others.

20 Nov. 1778: Laid on table.
> For a general act that among other things revised time and penalties for not taking loyalty oath, see 9H547.

### 853-P-† Singleton, Elizabeth
JHD: 20 Nov. 1778     Not known
Compensation for accidental wound from a gun discharged by a soldier.
20 Nov. 1778: Rejected by refusal to refer to a committee.

### 854-P-† Thornton, George
JHD: 21 Nov. 1778     Not known
Compensation for horse, impressed for use by Continental troops in North Carolina.
21 Nov. 1778: To PC.
1 Dec. 1778: Committee recommends £55 to be charged in the account of this commonwealth against the United States of America.
> House rejects.

### 855-P-† Morgan, Daniel and Snickers, Edward
JHD: 21 Nov. 1778     Frederick County
Compensation for thirteen guns furnished militia for expedition into Ohio.
21 Nov. 1778: To PC.
8 Dec. 1778: PC recommends £50 to Morgan for ten guns and £15 to Snickers for three guns.
> House agrees.
12 Dec. 1778: Senate agrees.

### 856-P Morton, Sarah
JHD: 21 Nov. 1778     Not known
Relief for herself and child since her husband, Edmond Morton, a navy lieutenant, has never returned from a voyage, and she believes him a prisoner.
Manuscript unsigned.
21 Nov 1778: To PC.
8 Dec. 1778: PC recommends rejection.
> House rejects.

### 857-M de Sequeyra, John
JHD: 21 Nov. 1778     Williamsburg
Compensation for services as a physician in mental hospital.
Manuscript unsigned.

## 20 – 21 November 1778

21 Nov. 1778: To PC.
15 Dec. 1778: PC recommends £150.
      House agrees.
17 Dec. 1778: Senate agrees.

**858-P-†  Drake, Margaret**
      JHD: 21 Nov. 1778                            Not known
Compensation for three horses, the property of her husband, that were lost when he was killed by the Indians in Kentucky.
21 Nov. 1778: To PC.
26 Nov. 1778: PC recommends £350.
      House agrees.
4 Dec. 1778: Senate agrees.

**859-M-†  Buchanan, William**
      JHD: 21 Nov. 1778                          Montgomery County
Compensation for two horses carried off by Indians while he was employed in the defense of Kentucky.
21 Nov. 1778: To PC.
26 Nov. 1778: PC recommends £190.
      House agrees.
4 Dec. 1778: Senate agrees.

**860-P-†  South, John and Drake, Ephraim**
      JHD: 21 Nov. 1778                              Not known
Compensation for two horses, impressed for use of Kentucky militia and either lost or killed.
21 Nov. 1778: To PC.
26 Nov. 1778: PC recommends (1) £40 for South, and (2) that petition of
      Drake be rejected.
      House agrees to (1) and rejects (2).
4 Dec. 1778: Senate agrees to (1).

**861-P-†  Lyle, William**
      JHD: 21 Nov. 1778                              Not known
Requesting relief from the auditors' refusal to pass his accounts as commissary of militia at Fort Randolph. These accounts are mostly claims by a variety of persons for provisions, horses furnished, and equipment lost.
21 Nov. 1778: To PC.

## Virginia Legislative Petitions

15 Dec. 1778: PC recommends as follows:

    To Samuel Lyle, for eighty-five days hire of three horses, at 4s. per day, £17 0s. 0d.

    To ditto for pasturage for nine horses, ten days and nights, at 9d. each pasturage, £3 7s. 6d.; and ten diets for packhorsemen, at 2s. each, £1 0s. 0d.; for a total of £4 7s. 6d.

    To ditto for pasturage for twelve horses, two days and nights at 18s.; four diets for packhorsemen at 8s.; £1 6s. 0d.

    To John M'Mullen, for driving packhorses thirty-seven days, at 10s. per day; £18 10s. 0d.

    To James Malone (a soldier), for driving packhorses seven days, at 8s. 8d. per day, (he having been allowed soldier's pay), £3 0s. 8d.

    To John Davidson, for driving packhorses twenty-four days, at 10s. per day, £12 0s. 0d.

    To John Lyle, for thirty days horse hire, at 4s. per day, £6 0s. 0d.

    To James Boyle, for forty-two days, ditto, £8 8s. 0d.

    To John Evans, for thirty-two days, ditto, £6 8s. 0d.

    To John Robertson, for twenty-two days, ditto, £4 8s. 0d.

    To John Cummins, for thirty-eight days, ditto, £7 12s. 0d.

    To Henry Hysaw, for a horse lost, appraised at £35 0s. 0d.

    To Robert M'Elheny, for 2,262 pounds flour, at 20s. per hundredweight, £22 12s. 4¾d.

    To Captain David Gray, for ninety-nine days horse hire, at 4s. per day, £19 16s. 0d.

    To ditto ditto for a bell lost, 20s., £1 0s. 0d.

    To Alexander M'Lure, for thirty-eight days, horse hire, £7 12s. 0d.

    To Joseph Reid, for forty-four days, ditto, £8 16s. 0d.

    To Moses M'Lure, for twenty-one days, ditto, £4 4s. 0d.

    To William Ramsey, for twenty-one days, ditto, £4 4s. 0d.

    To Mary Mackey, for forty-two days, ditto, £8 8s. 0d.

    To Elizabeth Reid, for twelve days, ditto, £2 8s. 0d.; to a pack saddle, 15s., one black mare lost, appraised at £24; £24 15s. 0d.; to one bell, lost, appraised at 15s., £0 15s. 0d.; for a total of £27 18s. 0d.

15 Dec. 1778: PC also recommends rejection of that part of petition allowing for damage of horses and hire of those horses that were lost.

    House recommits to PC.

    No further action found.

## 21 November 1778

**862-M-†   Virginia Navy Officers**
       JHD: 21 Nov. 1778                                Not known
   Requesting a pay increase.
21 Nov. 1778: To special committee.
       Committee apparently did not report.


**863-M    King William County—Citizens**
       JHD: 21 Nov. 1778                          King William County
   Asking for a law to regulate salaries of clergy of Church of England.
   Manuscript unsigned.
21 Nov. 1778: To R.
4 Dec. 1778: R recommends it be carried over to next session of GA.
       While this memorial does not seem to have been acted on independently, see note below.
       For act further suspending salaries of clergy, see 10H111.


**864-P    Ellegood, Jacob**
       JHD: 21 Nov. 1778                          Princess Anne County
   Requesting that as a prisoner for sympathizing with loyalists, he be allowed to return to his Princess Anne County plantation.
   Manuscript signed: Jacob Ellegood, and dated 19 August 1778, at Blandford.
21 Nov. 1778: To PG.
3 Dec. 1778: PG recommends rejection.
       House rejects.


**865-P**
Eck–
A1665    **Bedford County and Amherst County—Citizens**
       JHD: 21 Nov. 1778                              Bedford County
                                                     Amherst County
   To establish a ferry across the Fluvanna (James) River from Battery Creek in Bedford County to Otter Creek in Amherst County on land of Nicholas Davis.
   Manuscript signed by: Thomas Logwood, Isaac Bannester, Simon Miller, Jr., Peter Forquesan, Sr., John Hook, and sixteen others.
21 Nov. 1778: To PG.
3 Dec. 1778: PG finds reasonable and is directed to prepare a bill.
       This was incorporated in general ferry act, which was passed by House and Senate.
       For general ferry act see 9H585.

## Virginia Legislative Petitions

**866-P-†   Grider, Martin and Grider, John**
JHD: 21 Nov. 1778                                               Not known
Asking for release from prison on charges of being British sympathizers, and saying they wish to take the loyalty oath and regain their citizenship.
21 Nov. 1778: To PG.
3 Dec. 1778: PG recommends rejection.
   House rejects.

**867-P-†   Lebo, Isaac**
JHD: 21 Nov. 1778                                        Washington County
For relief from judgment of court sentencing him to three months imprisonment (probably for being a British sympathizer).
21 Nov. 1778: To PG.
1 Dec. 1778: PG recommends rejection.
   House rejects.

**868-M   Robinson, John, deceased—Administrators**
JHD: 21 Nov. 1778                                               Not known
Asking that administrators continue to hold rights, to which they were party, in a grant of 100,000 acres of land on Greenbrier River made in 1753.
   Manuscript unsigned.
21 Nov. 1778: To PG.
1 Dec. 1778: PG recommends it be carried forward to next session of GA.
   House agrees.
   No further record found.

**869-P-†   Harwell, Richard**
JHD: 21 Nov. 1778                                               Not known
Subject not known. Presented on 21 November 1778, but apparently never read or referred. No further reference found.

**870-P-†   Archer, Edward**
JHD: 21 Nov. 1778                                          Norfolk Borough
Compensation for house burned in Norfolk borough by order of convention.
21 Nov. 1778: To committee appointed to review report of commissioners.
11 Dec. 1778: PC recommends £65.
   House agrees.
   Did not reach Senate in this session.

## 21 – 23 November 1778

27 May 1779: House revives and sends to Senate.
11 June 1779: Senate agrees.

### 871-P-† Mason, George
JHD: 23 Nov. 1778                           Fairfax County

For confirmation of land titles and surveys made by him for land on western waters granted him during British government. (Presented on 21 November 1778, but not read until 23 November 1778.)
23 Nov. 1778: To PG.
     Committee apparently did not report.

### 872-P Scott, James
JHD: 23 Nov. 1778                      Prince William County

Asking land grants for fifty-nine indentured servants imported from Scotland before the Revolution. (Presented on 21 November 1778, but not read until 23 November 1778.)
23 Nov. 1778: To PG.
     Committee apparently did not report.

### 873-P-† Veale, Thomas
JHD: 23 Nov. 1778                               Portsmouth

Compensation for rents of several houses in Portsmouth used by soldiers. (Presented on 21 November 1778, but not read until 23 November 1778.)
23 Nov. 1778: To committee appointed to review reports of commissioners.
     Committee apparently did not report.

### 874-P-† Craig, John
JHD: 23 Nov. 1778                                Not known

Compensation for horse, impressed for Cherokee expedition in 1776 and never returned. (Presented on 21 November 1778, but not read until 23 November 1778.)
23 Nov. 1778: To PC.
1 Dec. 1778: PC recommends £7 10s.
     House agrees.
8 Dec. 1778: Senate amends.
9 Dec. 1778: House agrees to Senate amendments.

### 875-P-† Williams, Evan and Daugherty, Michael (Assignees of William White)
JHD: 23 Nov. 1778                               Not known

## Virginia Legislative Petitions

Compensation for horse and harness, property of William White, that were impressed for Cherokee expedition of 1776. White had assigned his rights to the petitioners. (Presented on 21 November 1778, but not read until 23 November 1778.)
23 Nov. 1778: To PC.
1 Dec. 1778: PC recommends (1) £11 for horse, and (2) that claim for harness be rejected.
      House approves (1).
      House rejects (2).
7 Dec. 1778: Senate agrees on (1).

**876-P-†**   **Gass, David**
      JHD: 23 Nov. 1778                                 Not known
Compensation for two horses, impressed for use of Kentucky militia and not returned. (Presented on 21 November 1778, but not read until 23 November 1778.)
23 Nov. 1778: To PC.
26 Nov. 1778: PC recommends £80.
      House agrees.
4 Dec. 1778: Senate agrees.

**877-P-†**   **Martin, John**
      JHD: 23 Nov. 1778                                 Not known
Compensation for two horses, impressed for use of Kentucky militia and not returned. (Presented 21 November 1778, but not read until 23 November 1778.)
23 Nov. 1778: To PC.
28 Nov. 1778: PC recommends £90.
      House agrees.
4 Dec. 1778: Senate agrees.

**878-P-†**   **Seary, Bartlett**
      JHD: 23 Nov. 1778                                 Not known
Compensation for a horse, impressed for use of the Kentucky militia and not returned. (Presented on 21 November 1778, but not read until 23 November 1778.)
23 Nov. 1778: To PC.
26 Nov. 1778: PC recommends £25.
      House agrees.
4 Dec. 1778: Senate agrees.

23 – 24 November 1778

879-M-† Brett, John; Suttle, William; Murphey, Lewis; Florence, William; Wilder, George; Owens, Charles; Baremore, George; White, James; Cullens, Daniel; Hutchingson, William; Shaw, Thomas; Hazleky, Samuel; Davis, William; Johnson, Daniel; Ballenger, Wm.; Burnett, Thomas; Newman, Edmond; Holtsclaw, Nathan; Hughes, John; Bottom, John Side; M'Gregor, Walter; Leg, Wm.; Shadborne, Amos; Feagan, Wm.; Lashbrooks, John; Horton, Beverly; Wiggonton, John; Wiggonton, Abraham; French, John; Purcel, Thomas; and Matthews, Beverly

JHD: 24 Nov. 1778                      Not known

Asking for bounty for enlisting soldiers, and allowance for pay and rations for the period when this was legal. (Presented on 21 November 1778, but not read until 24 November 1778.)

24 Nov. 1778: To PC.

15 Dec. 1778: PC recommends (1) request for bounty be rejected, and (2) that pay and rations be allowed for the following:

    To John Brett, captain, for eleven days pay and rations, amounting to £6 1s. 0d.

    To William Suttle, a private, for eleven days pay and rations, £1 5s. 8d.

    To Lewis Murphey, William Florence, George Wilder, Charles Owens, George Baremore, James White, Daniel Cullens, William Hutchingson, Thomas Shaw, Samuel Hazleky, William Davis, Daniel Johnson, Wm. Ballenger, Thomas Burnett, Edmond Newman, Nathan Holtsclaw, John Hughes, John Side Bottom, Walter M'Gregor, Wm. Leg, Amos Shadborne, Wm. Feagan, John Lashbrooks, Beverly Horton, John Wiggonton, Abraham Wiggonton, John French, Thomas Purcel, and Beverly Matthews, the same pay and rations, each 25s. 8d., for a total of £37 4s. 4d.

15 Dec. 1778: House recommits to PC.

No further record found.

880-P-† Callaway, John

JHD: 24 Nov. 1778                      Bedford County

For increase in allowance for hire of wagon and team for transferring troops. (Presented 21 November 1778, but not read until 24 November 1778.)

24 Nov. 1778: To PC

## Virginia Legislative Petitions

8 Dec. 1778: Carried over to next session of GA.
No further record found.

### 881-P-† Brown, Sarah
JHD: 24 Nov. 1778                                         Not known
Relief for necessities of life since her four sons are in service and two are prisoners. (Presented 21 November 1778, but not read until 24 November 1778.)
24 Nov. 1778: To PC.
1 Dec. 1778: PC recommends £30 for present relief.
House agrees.
8 Dec. 1778: Senate agrees.

### 882-P-† Gwatkins, Charles
JHD: 24 Nov. 1778                                         Not known
Compensation for horse, impressed for use of militia in Kentucky. (Presented 21 November 1778, but not read until 24 November 1778.)
24 Nov. 1778: To PC.
8 Dec. 1778: Carried over to next session of GA.
No further record found.

### 883-P-† Davis, James
JHD: 24 Nov. 1778                                         Bedford County
Compensation for horse and harness, impressed by militia for march to Kentucky and never returned. (Presented 21 November 1778, but not read until 24 November 1778.)
24 Nov. 1778: To PC.
26 Nov. 1778: PC recommends £20.
House agrees.
4 Dec. 1778: Senate agrees.

### 884-P-† Forqueren, Peter
JHD: 24 Nov. 1778                                         Bedford County
Compensation for horse, impressed by militia for march to Kentucky. (Presented 21 November 1778, but not read until 24 November 1778.)
24 Nov. 1778: To PC.
8 Dec. 1778: Carried over to next session of GA.
No further record found.

## 24 November 1778

**885-P-†  Walker, John**
    JHD: 24 Nov. 1778                                    Not known
Compensation for his horse, lost on the Cherokee expedition of 1776. (Presented 21 November 1778, but not read until 24 November 1778.)
24 Nov. 1778: To PC.
1 Dec. 1778: PC recommends £12.
        House agrees.
8 Dec. 1778: Senate agrees.

**886-P-†  Tuttle, James**
    JHD: 24 Nov. 1778                                    Not known
Compensation for his horse, lost on the Cherokee expedition of 1776. (Presented 21 November 1778, but not read until 24 November 1778.)
24 Nov. 1778: To PC.
1 Dec. 1778: PC recommends £6.
        House agrees.
8 Dec. 1778: Senate agrees.

**887-P-†  Brumstreter, Andrew**
    JHD: 24 Nov. 1778                                    Not known
Compensation for his horse, lost on the Cherokee expedition of 1776. (Presented 21 November 1778, but not read until 24 November 1778.)
24 Nov. 1778: To PC.
1 Dec. 1778: PC recommends £10 10s.
        House agrees.
8 Dec. 1778: Senate agrees.

**888-P**
Rob-7   **Henderson, Nathaniel**
    JHD: 24 Nov. 1778                                    Kentucky County
Compensation for Negro slave, killed in defense of Fort Boone. (Presented 21 November 1778, but not read until 24 November 1778.)
    Manuscript unsigned.
24 Nov. 1778: To PC.
8 Dec. 1778: PC recommends rejection.
        House recommits to PC.
15 Dec. 1778: PC recommends £400.
        House agrees.
16 Dec. 1778: Senate agrees.

## Virginia Legislative Petitions

**889-P-†  Bogard, Abraham**
JHD: 26 Nov. 1778                                              Not known
Compensation for his horse, killed in the Shawanese expedition of 1774. (Presented 21 November 1778, but not read until 26 November 1778.)
26 Nov. 1778: To PC.
8 Dec. 1778: PC recommends £7 10s.
    House agrees.
12 Dec. 1778: Senate agrees.

**890-P-†  Priggett, Edward; M'Carty, James; and Vance, Jacob**
JHD: 26 Nov. 1778                                              Not known
Compensation for three horses, impressed for Cherokee expedition of 1776. (Presented 21 November 1778, but not read until 26 November 1778.)
26 Nov. 1778: To PC.
8 Dec. 1778: PC recommends (1) £7 for Priggett, (2) £6 6s. 6d. for M'Carty, and (3) £8 for Vance.
    House agrees.
12 Dec. 1778: Senate agrees.

**891-P-†  Jordan, Thomas, Jr.**
JHD: 26 Nov. 1778                                              Not known
Compensation for disability received by illness in Continental service. (Presented 21 November 1778, but not read until 26 November 1778.)
26 Nov. 1778: To PC.
8 Dec. 1778: PC recommends £30 for present relief and half pay for life, the latter to be charged in the account of this commonwealth against the United States of America.
    House agrees.
12 Dec. 1778: Senate agrees.

**892-P-†  Tucker, Robert**
JHD: 26 Nov. 1778                                              Norfolk Borough
Compensation for damage done his mill and other buildings in erecting a fort. (Presented 21 November 1778, but not read until 26 November 1778.)
26 Nov. 1778: To committee to examine report of commissioners.
2 Dec. 1778: Report of commissioners received.
    To lie on table.

## 26 November 1778

In May 1778 an act was passed specifically mentioning Robert Tucker's property.
No further record found.
For this act see 9H465.

**893-P-† Adams, James**
JHD: 26 Nov. 1778                                Bedford County
Compensation for horse, impressed by militia for march to Kentucky. (Presented 21 November 1778, but not read until 26 November 1778.)
26 Nov. 1778: To PC.
8 Dec. 1778: PC recommends £13 10s.
    House agrees.
12 Dec. 1778: Senate agrees.

**894-P-† Murphey, Michael**
JHD: 26 Nov. 1778                                Bedford County
Compensation for horse, impressed by militia for march to Kentucky. (Presented 21 November 1778, but not read until 26 November 1778.)
26 Nov. 1778: To PC.
8 Dec. 1778: PC recommends £10.
    House agrees.
16 Dec. 1778: Senate amends.
    House agrees to Senate amendments.

**895-P-† Boon, Squire**
JHD: 26 Nov. 1778                                Kentucky County
Compensation for horse stolen while Boon was riding express from Kentucky to Williamsburg. He traveled 150 miles on foot. (Presented 21 November 1778, but not read until 26 November 1778.)
26 Nov. 1778: To PC.
8 Dec. 1778: PC recommends rejection.
    House rejects.

**896-P-† Epperson, Richard**
JHD: 26 Nov. 1778                                Not known
Compensation for wound, received at battle of Boonesborough. (Presented 21 November 1778, but not read until 26 November 1778.) (Epperson had been denied a previous petition on 29 November 1777, 470-P.)
26 Nov. 1778: To PC.

8 Dec. 1778: Carried over to next session of GA.
No further record found.

### 897-P   Russell Parish, Bedford County—Citizens
JHD: 26 Nov. 1778                                                  Bedford County
Requesting permission to sell glebe. (Presented 21 November 1778, but not read until 26 November 1778.)
Manuscript unsigned.
26 Nov. 1778: To R.
2 Dec. 1778: R recommends rejection.
  House rejects.
  A new petition was presented 19 May 1779. See 940-P.

### 898-P-†   Little, Andrew
JHD: 26 Nov. 1778                                                           Not known
Compensation for three horses, impressed for Cherokee expedition and never returned. (Presented 21 November 1778, but not read until 26 November 1778.)
26 Nov. 1778: To PC.
8 Dec. 1778: Carried over to next session of GA.
  No further record found.

### 899-P
Eck-
A1098   **Cowpasture River Lands, Bullpasture River Lands, Jackson River Lands, and Back Creek Lands—Citizens**
JHD: 1 Dec. 1778                                                   Augusta County
                                                                                 Rockbridge County
For formation of a new county out of Rockbridge and Augusta counties.
Manuscript signed by: Samson Christian, William Jameson, James Crockett, John Dunlop, Peter Kinder, and 121 others. (Manuscript dated 15 April 1778, and noted as received on 30 November 1778.)
1 Dec. 1778: Carried over to next session of GA.
  No further action found.

### 899-A-P
Eck-
A1098   **Cowpasture River Lands, Bullpasture River Lands, Jackson River Lands, and Back Creek Lands—Citizens**

## 26 November – 3 December 1778

JHD: 1 Dec. 1778                                           Augusta County
                                                                           Rockbridge County

Text is identical with 899-P, which see.
Manuscript signed by same persons as in 899-P, but in different order.

**900-P-†   Goochland County—Citizens**
        JHD: 3 Dec. 1778, for action              Goochland County
For the division of Goochland County and the addition of parts of Louisa and Hanover counties to Goochland.
Date unknown: To PG.
3 Dec. 1778: PG recommends rejection.
        House rejects.

**901-P-†   Goochland County—Citizens**
        JHD: 3 Dec. 1778, for action              Goochland County
In opposition to dividing county.
Date unknown: To PG.
3 Dec. 1778: PG finds reasonable.
        No action required.
        See 900-P-†.

**902-P-†   Alexandria—Citizens**
        JHD: Not found [3 Dec. 1778]              Fairfax County
For incorporation of Alexandria and extension of the town's boundaries, and for mayor and recorder to be justices of Fairfax County.
Date unknown: To PG.
        Carried over to next session of GA.
12 Nov. 1779: PG finds (1) incorporation of town reasonable, and (2) that mayor and recorder be justices of Fairfax County be rejected.
        House rejects (2).
        House agrees to (1) and directs PG to prepare a bill.
29 Nov. 1779: House passes bill including town of Winchester.
2 Dec. 1779: Senate amends.
4 Dec. 1779: House agrees to Senate amendments.
        For this act see 10H172.

**903-P**
Eck–A458 (Subject in error)
        **Alexandria—Citizens**
        JHD: 3 Dec. 1778                              Fairfax County

## Virginia Legislative Petitions

Opposing incorporation of Alexandria (902-P-†).
Manuscript signed by: Samuel Simmons Power, James Collins Power, Thomas Reed, Mich. Gretter, Philip Jackson, and 101 others.
3 Dec. 1778: To PG.
    Committee apparently did not report.

**904-M-†  Indiana Company**
    JHD: 10 Dec. 1778, for action            Western Lands
Asking confirmation of lands purchased from "the Indians at the treaty held at Fort Stanwix, in the year 1768."
10 Dec. 1778: To be considered in May 1779 session. To be published for six
    successive weeks in *Virginia Gazette*.
    No further record found.
    For remonstrance of General Assembly on congressional action on
    Indiana and Vandalia lands, see JHD, 10 December and 15
    December 1779.

**905-P-†  Wilkinson, Edward**
    JHD: 15 Dec. 1778, for action                Not known
  Subject not known.
Date unknown: To PC.
15 Dec. 1778: Carried over to next session of GA.
    No further record found.

**906-P-†  Taliaferro, Richard; Ewers, Thomas; Crawford, John; Higginbotham, Benjamin; Davis, Richard; Tyler, Charles; Stevens, James; Bowman, Wm.; Dickerson, John; Brown, John; Masters, James; Brummet, William; Ingram, William; Ware, Edward; Davis, Richard; Bybee, Thomas; Page, William; Burden, Archibald; Ricketts, Stephen; Johnson, John; Tyler, Daniel; Steel, Francis; Masters, Edward; Bozwell, Reuben; Clark, John; Holman, Tandy; Allen, Wm.; Henderson, Robert; Ogleby, Thomas; M'Carty, Robert; Tyler, John; Austin, William; M'Knight, William; M'Lane, James; Horrell, James; Horrell, Wm.; Fortune, Benjamin; Smith, Johnston; and Scruggs, Brett**
    JHD: 15 Dec. 1778                              Not known
For bounty for recruiting soldiers, and for pay and rations until this practice was suspended.
Date unknown: To PC.

## 10 – 15 December 1778

15 Dec. 1778: PC recommends rejection of bounty claims.
House agrees.
PC recommends the following for pay and rations:
To Richard Taliaferro, captain, for fifty-one days pay, at £12 per month, and three rations per day, at 1s. each ration, £28 1s. 0d.
To Thomas Ewers, lieutenant, for fifty-one days, at £8 2s. per month, and two rations per day, £15 17s. 6d.
To John Crawford, sergeant, for fifty-one days, at 2s., and one ration per day, £7 13s. 0d.
To Benjamin Higginbotham, ditto, the same, £7 13s. 0d.
To Richard Davis, sergeant, for forty-eight days, at 2s., and one ration per day, £7 4s. 0d
To Charles Tyler, James Stevens, Wm. Bowman, and John Dickerson, privates, for fifty-one days, at 1s. 4d., and one ration per day, each £5 19s.; £23 16s. 0d.
To John Brown, for forty-eight days, at ditto, £5 12s. 0d.
To James Masters, for forty-seven days, at ditto, £5 9s. 8d.
To William Brummet, for forty-four days, at ditto, £5 2s. 8d.
To William Ingram, for the same, £5 2s. 8d.
To Edward Ware, for thirty-eight days, at ditto, £4 8s. 8d.
To Richard Davis, for thirty-six days, at ditto, £4 4s. 0d.
To Thomas Bybee, for thirty-two days, at ditto, £3 14s. 8d.
To William Page, for thirty-one days, at ditto, £3 12s. 4d.
To Archibald Burden, for twenty-two days, at ditto, £2 11s. 4d.
To Stephen Ricketts, for twenty-one days, at ditto, £2 9s. 0d.
To John Johnson, for nineteen days, at ditto, £2 4s. 4d.
To Daniel Tyler, Francis Steel, and Edward Masters, for ten days each at £1 3s. 4d.; £3 10s. 0d.
To Reuben Bozwell, John Clark, Tandy Holman, and Wm. Allen, for fifty-one days each at £5 19s.; £23 16s. 0d.
To Robert Henderson, for forty-eight days, £5 12s. 0d.
To Thomas Ogleby, for thirty-six days, £4 4s. 0d.
To Robert M'Carty, for thirty-four days, £3 19s. 4d.
To John Tyler, for thirty-two days, £13 14s. 8d.
To William Austin, for twenty-eight days, £3 5s. 4d.
To William M'Knight, for thirteen days, £1 10s. 4d.
To James M'Lane, for the same, £1 10s. 4d.
To James Horrell, Wm. Horrell, Benjamin Fortune, and Johnston Smith, for nine days each at 21s. each, £4 4s. 0d.

## Virginia Legislative Petitions

   To Brett Scruggs, for eight days, 18s. 8d.
15 Dec. 1778: Recommitted to PC.
   No further record found.

### 907-Misc. Claims-†

  The following miscellaneous claims were not presented separately, and apparently went to PC without a prior reading on the floor of the House. They are listed as they were approved in the journals and are indexed under name and subject.
   JHD: 15 Dec. 1778              Not known
Date unknown: To PC.
15 Dec. 1778: PC recommends approval.
   House agrees.
17 Dec. 1778: Senate agrees.

| | |
|---|---|
| 907.1 | That the claim of the said Abraham Cole is reasonable, and that the petitioner ought to be allowed £85 for the said horses, being the sum at which they were appraised, £85 0s. 0d. |
| 907.2 | To Isaac Hite, for a horse, lost in the service of the country in 1777, appraised at £30 0s. 0d. |
| 907.3 | To Joseph Pearson, for his Negro man slave Aaron, who was condemned and executed for felony, and by the court of the county of Northumberland valued at £200 0s. 0d. |
| 907.4 | To Edward Voss, for his Negro man slave March, alias Mark, who was condemned and executed for felony and burglary, and by the court of the county of Spotsylvania valued at £100 0s. 0d. |
| 907.5 | To Thomas Goodwin, for his Negro man slave Will, who was condemned and executed for felony, and by the court of the county of King William valued at £90 0s. 0d. |
| 907.6 | To the estate of John Decamp, deceased, for Bazil, a Negro man slave, who was condemned and executed for murder, and by the court of the county of Yohogania valued at £200 0s. 0d. |
| 907.7 | To Samuel Campbell, for a horse lost at Long Island, on the Cherokee expedition, appraised at £10 10s. 0d. |
| 907.8 | To James Harris, assignee of Andrew M'Ferrin, who was assignee of John Patterson, for a sorrel mare, valued at £11; and a bell, 3s., lost on the Cherokee expedition; £11 3s. 0d. |
| 907.9 | To Henly Moore, for a horse lost in the Cherokee war, appraised at £18 0s. 0d. |
| 907.10 | To Meredy Reins, for a black mare lost, £10 0s. 0d. |

## 15 December 1778 – 8 May 1779

| | |
|---|---|
| 907.11 | To James Newell, administrator of Samuel Newell, deceased, for riding express, £13 0s. 0d. |
| 907.12 | To John Martin, for a dark bay horse appraised at £25; and a bright bay ditto, at £18, lost in the service of this state in Kentucky; £43 0s. 0d. |
| 907.13 | To Joseph Cartwright, for a mare lost in the said service, appraised at £50 0s. 0d. |
| 907.14 | To William Poage, for a black mare appraised at £12; and a bay horse at £27, lost in the said service; £39 0s. 0d. |
| 907.15 | To Levi Todd, for a black horse lost in the said service, appraised at £35 0s. 0d. |
| 907.16 | To James Bullock, for his Negro man, Caesar, who was condemned and executed, and by the court of the county of Bedford valued at £144 0s. 0d. |
| 907.17 | To the estate of Lockey Collier, for the following slaves who were condemned and executed for murder, and by the court of the county of Elizabeth City valued at the following sums, to wit: Jack at £400, Davy at £500, Cain at £300, Mingo at £400, and Rachael, £250, for a total of £1,850 0s. 0d. |

(This claim is supported by a manuscript separately giving deposition of Elizabeth City County court and valuation of slaves.)

**908-P-†  Singleton, Henry**
JHD: 8 May 1779                                                         Norfolk Borough
  Asking for a certified substitution of the valuation of his property lost at Norfolk, the original having been lost.
8 May 1779: To special committee.
15 June 1779: Committee recommends acceptance of substitute, with valuation of £350 to be paid by treasurer.
          House agrees.
22 June 1779: Senate agrees.

**909-P-†  Wray, George**
JHD: 8 May 1779                                                                   Hampton
  Compensation for damages, estimated at £300, done to his houses in Hampton, which were occupied by Virginia troops in 1775.
8 May 1779: To special committee.
15 June 1779: Committee recommends as reasonable.
          House rejects.

## Virginia Legislative Petitions

**910-P**  **Dixon, John and Nicholson, Thomas**
JHD: 8 May 1779    Williamsburg
For appointment as public printers to succeed Alexander Purdie, deceased. Manuscript unsigned.
8 May 1779: Laid on table.
11 June 1779: House recommends appointment.
    Senate agrees.
    Apparently they superseded Clarkson and Davis.

**911-P**  **Clarkson, John and Davis, Augustine**
JHD: 8 May 1779    Williamsburg
For appointment as public printers to succeed Alexander Purdie, deceased. Manuscript unsigned.
8 May 1779: Laid on table.
5 June 1779: Joint committees of House and Senate recommend appointment as of May. (Apparently temporary.)
    House agrees.
    Senate agrees.

**912-P**  **Hunter, William**
JHD: 11 May 1779    Williamsburg
For appointment as public printer to succeed Alexander Purdie, deceased. He lacks certain types.
Manuscript unsigned.
11 May 1779: Laid on table.

**913-P-†**  **Anderson, John and Anderson, Mede**
JHD: 11 May 1779    Not known
Asking for encouragement in developing lead mines on property owned by state.
11 May 1779: To PG.
13 May 1779: PG recommends rejection.
    House rejects.

**914-P**  **Fox, John**
JHD: 11 May 1779    Gloucester County
For establishment of a ferry from Gloucester County to York County across York River.
Manuscript signed by: John Whiting, C. Armistead, Francis Tomkins, Jno. Hubard, Joseph Billups, Sr., and twenty-three others.

## 8 – 11 May 1779

11 May 1779: To PG.
18 May 1779: PG recommends as reasonable.
   Recommitted to PG.
25 May 1779: Carried over to next session of GA.
12 Dec. 1779: PG recommends as reasonable and is directed to prepare a bill.
20 Dec. 1779: Bill passed.
21 Dec. 1779: Bill rejected by Senate, JS.

**915-P-†   Clapham, Josias**
   JHD: 11 May 1779                           Loudoun County

For repayment of funds advanced in 1779 for bounty and subsistence of troops raised in Loudoun County. Clapham, upon advice of court-martial, following a recommendation of the governor, had dispatched William Stanhope to draw up to £9,000 from the treasury. Stanhope is said to have been robbed.
11 May 1779: To PG.
13 May 1779: PG recommends that Clapham be reimbursed for amounts he
   can prove he advanced, and that he be allowed expenses for his
   attendance of the GA on this business.
   House agrees.
14 May 1779: Senate agrees.
   See 916-P-†.

**916-P-†   Stanhope, William**
   JHD: 11 May 1779                           Loudoun County

For immunity from repayment of funds that he was carrying for Josias Clapham and of which he was robbed at Bowling Green.
11 May 1779: To PG.
18 June 1779: PG recommends (1) that three groups of state currency, $8,000
   each, be withdrawn from circulation as of 1 July 1779, (2) that
   anyone presenting these bills before 1 January 1780 be prosecuted
   unless they can show proper ownership, and (3) that Stanhope be
   allowed £214 8s. 8d., the amount that he was carrying.
   House agrees and directs a bill to be prepared for (1) and (2).
19 June 1779: Senate agrees.
   No special act found in Hening.
   See 915-P-†.

**917-M    Tucker, St. George**
   JHD: 11 May 1779                           Chesterfield County

## Virginia Legislative Petitions

For exporting food to the Bermudians who are attached to the American cause.

Manuscript unsigned.

11 May 1779: To special committee.
    Committee apparently did not report.

### 918-P    Culpeper County—Citizens
JHD: 12 May 1779        Culpeper County

For a division of the county into three distinct counties.

Manuscript signed by: Arm. Bohannan, Geo. Rowe, Elias Campbell, John Yowell, Wm. Kelley, and 284 others.

12 May 1779: To PG.
14 June 1779: Carried over to next session of GA.
23 Oct. 1779: PG recommends rejection.
    House rejects.

### 918 A-P    Culpeper County—Citizens
JHD: 12 May 1779        Culpeper County

Text is identical with 918-P, which see.

Manuscript signed by 228 persons.

### 919-P    Binn, Charles
JHD: 12 May 1779        Loudoun County

For repayment of surplus charged to him as clerk of Loudoun County for two different items claimed to be the same.

Manuscript unsigned.

12 May 1779: To special committee.
22 May 1779: Committee recommends payment of 40s.
    House agrees.
    Senate agrees.

### 920-P-†    Louisa County—Citizens
JHD: 12 May 1779        Louisa County

Asking that Thomas Mitchell, a former resident, now in the Bermudas, be allowed to return since he is friendly to the American cause.

12 May 1779: To PG.
25 May 1779: PG recommends rejection.
    House rejects.
    See 921-P-†.

## 12 – 15 May 1779

**921-P-†  Mitchell, Mildred**
JHD: 12 May 1779                                             Louisa County
Asking that her husband, Thomas Mitchell, be allowed to return to this country.
12 May 1779: To PG.
25 May 1779: PG recommends rejection.
       House rejects.
       See 920-P-†.

**922-P  Mecklenburg County and Halifax County—Citizens**
JHD: 13 May 1779                                          Mecklenburg County
                                               Halifax County
Establishment of a ferry across Roanoke River from lands of James Wilkins to those of Robert Munford.
Manuscript signed by: William Hall, Jas. Hall, Winkfield Hayes, Jno. Cruze, Natha. Cunningham, and 138 others.
13 May 1779: To PG.
20 May 1779: PG reports reasonable and is directed to prepare a bill.
       This bill was included in general ferry bill passed by House and Senate.
       For general ferry act see 10H124.

**922 A-P  Mecklenburg County and Halifax County—Citizens**
JHD: 13 May 1779                                          Mecklenburg County
                                               Halifax County
Text is identical with 922-P, which see.
Manuscript signed by 177 persons.

**923-P  Orange County—Citizens**
JHD: 13 May 1779                                             Orange County
Asking that "each person having property in the County" contribute "an equal part of the monies" toward the quota for raising recruits.
Manuscript signed by: Eliot Brown, William Brown, John Thomas, John Lanibrand, Joseph Clark, and twenty others.
13 May 1779: Rejected by refusal to refer to a committee.

**924-P-†  Selden, Elizabeth**
JHD: 15 May 1779                                           Norfolk Borough
Asking for interest on £815, awarded for property in Norfolk belonging to

277

her late husband, which had been destroyed, she having been late in applying for a certificate.
15 May 1779: Rejected by refusal to refer to a committee.

**925-P    Frederick Parish, Frederick County—Churchwardens and Vestrymen**
JHD: 15 May 1779                                    Frederick County
For dissolution of vestry.
Manuscript signed by: Marquis Calmes, Frederick Conrad, John Smith, Alex. White, Ed. Snickers, and Robt. Wood.
15 May 1779: To R.
>Committee apparently did not report.
>For dissolution of certain vestries, including Frederick, that were providing for poor, see 10H288.

**926-P    Tobacco Inspectors—Falmouth and Dixon's Warehouses, Royston's (Roiston's) Warehouse, Fredericksburg Warehouse, and Page's and Crutchfield's Warehouses**
JHD: 15 May 1779                                    Hanover County
                                                    Stafford County
                                                    Spotsylvania County
Asking for increases in allowances.
Manuscript signed by: John Richards, Karliel Williams, Andrew Glassell, and Mann Page.
15 May 1779: To special committee on tobacco warehouses.
>Incorporated in a general bill passed by House and Senate.
>For this act, which among other things increased fees, see 10H75.

**927-P    Tobacco Inspectors—Blandford Warehouse, Boyd's Warehouse, and Davis's Warehouse**
JHD: 15 May 1779                                    Prince George County
Asking for increases in allowances.
Manuscript signed by: Lessenby Williams, Robt. Birchill, John Hurall, John Watts, William Grammer, and Daniel Sturdivant. Dated 10 May 1779.
15 May 1779: To special committee on tobacco warehouses.
>Incorporated in a general bill passed by House and Senate.
>For this act, which among other things increased fees, see 10H75.

## 15 May 1779

**928-P**
Eck-
A164    **Charlottesville—Citizens**
JHD: 15 May 1779                                    Albemarle County
To compel proprietors of unimproved lots in Charlottesville to improve them or sell them to persons who will.
  Manuscript signed by: Samuel Taliaferro, Micajah Chiles, Benja. Collard, Jno. Jones, Richd. Harvie, and six others.
15 May 1779: To PG.
26 May 1779: PG recommends rejection.
    House recommits to PG.
14 June 1779: PG recommends (1) that clearing of lots is reasonable, and (2) that forced selling of lots should be rejected.
    House rejects forced selling.
    House finds (1) reasonable and is directed to prepare a bill.
    No further record found.

**929-P    Fredericksburg—Citizens**
JHD: 15 May 1779                                    Spotsylvania County
To establish a ferry over the Rappahannock River from the lands of Colonel Fielding Lewis to lands of William Fitzhugh.
  Manuscript signed by: Fra. Thornton, Fielding Lewis, Chas. Washington, Chas. Dick, Geo. Thornton, and sixty-two others.
15 May 1779: To PG.
18 May 1779: PG reports reasonable.
    House recommits to PG.
2 June 1779: PG recommends rejection.
    House rejects.
    A new petition was introduced on 23 October 1779 (1065-P).

**930-P-†    Allen, Richmond**
JHD: 15 May 1779                                    New Kent County
Questioning whether his election to the House of Delegates is legal since the sheriff stopped the voting when it was determined that one of the candidates, John Armistead, was a tax commissioner.
15 May 1779: To PE.
19 May 1779: PE finds election illegal, and recommends that a new writ for election be issued.
    House agrees and directs speaker to issue a new writ.
    Allen was properly elected at new election.

## Virginia Legislative Petitions

**931-P    Tillotson Parish, Buckingham County—Citizens**
    JHD: 17 May 1779                              Buckingham County
For dissolution of vestry and election of a new one.
Manuscript signed by: Robt. Smith, Joseph Childress, Gideon Crews, Jno. Finn, Robt. Childress, and forty-eight others.
17 May 1779: To R.
    Committee apparently did not report.

**932-P    Wicomico Parish, Northumberland County—Citizens**
    JHD: 17 May 1779                         Northumberland County
For dissolution of vestry and election of new one.
Manuscript signed by: John Gibbons, George Hunt, John Haynie, William Pitman, Rodham Angel, and 130 others (all in same hand).
17 May 1779: To R.
    Committee apparently did not report.

**933-P-†    Augusta County—Militia**
    JHD: 17 May 1779                                 Augusta County
For raising additional troops to defend the frontier.
17 May 1779: House directs that matter be referred to a special committee on militia, and bills be prepared.
    For act concerning this and other militia matters, see 10H18.

**934-P    Flood, Elizabeth**
    JHD: 17 May 1779                                Richmond County
Asking that her granddaughter and her granddaughter's father, Archibald M'Call, be allowed to return to Virginia from England where they had resided since before the war. The mother had died. M'Call was friendly to America, and his whole property lies in Virginia. Elizabeth Flood was the widow of Dr. Nicholas Flood, of Tappahannock.
Manuscript unsigned.
17 May 1779: To PG.
8 June 1779: PG reports reasonable.
    House refers to committee of whole.
    No further action found, but Elizabeth Flood petitioned again later, 1502-P-† and 1580-P.

**935-P    Todd, William**
    JHD: 17 May 1779                          King and Queen County
Asking repeal of act of 1772 docking entail on his land, and that the trustees

## 17 – 18 May 1779

who sold the real and personal property be directed to transfer funds to him.
   Manuscript unsigned.
17 May 1779: To PG.
20 May 1779: PG finds reasonable and is directed to prepare a bill.
27 May 1779: House passes bill.
8 June 1779: Senate passes bill.
   For this act see 10H103.

**936-P   Stafford County—Citizens**
   JHD: 17 May 1779                                    Stafford County
   To establish a ferry across the Rappahannock River from the lands of Colonel Fielding Lewis to lands of William Fitzhugh.
   Manuscript signed by: Tho. Vowle, Andrew Edwards, Alvin Mountjoy, Benjamin Batt, Geo. Burroughs, and fourteen others.
17 May 1779: To PG.
   For action see 929-P.

**937-P   Falmouth—Trustees**
   JHD: 18 May 1779                                    Stafford County
   In opposition to new ferry across Rappahannock River from the lands of Colonel Fielding Lewis to lands of William Fitzhugh.
   Manuscript signed by: Ch. Carter, Arthur Morson, David Braggs, William Love, Edward Moor, and one other.
18 May 1779: To PG.
2 June 1779: PG finds reasonable.
   For action see 929-P.

**938-P   Mercer, Hugh (deceased)—Trustees**
   JHD: 18 May 1779                                    Spotsylvania County
   In opposition to ferry across Rappahannock River from the lands of Colonel Fielding Lewis to lands of William Fitzhugh.
   Manuscript signed by: James Hunter, James Hunter, Jr., and G. Weedon.
18 May 1779: To PG.
   For action see 929-P.

**939-P   Culpeper County—Citizens**
   JHD: 18 May 1779                                    Culpeper County
   For imposition of higher taxes in order to restore credit of state currency.
   Manuscript signed by: Robt. Terrell, John Piner, Edgar Jett, David Cave, John Montague, and sixty-seven others.

## Virginia Legislative Petitions

18 May 1779: To committee for procuring equal assessment of taxable property.

This relates to act for laying a tax, payable in certain enumerated commodities, passed by House and Senate.

For this act see 10H79.

**940-P**
Eck–Not
found  **Russell Parish, Bedford County—Citizens**
JHD: 19 May 1779                                              Bedford County
For sale of present glebe and purchase of a new one.
Manuscript unsigned.
19 May 1779: To R.
26 May 1779: R reports reasonable and is directed to prepare a bill.
12 June 1779: House passes bill.
16 June 1779: Senate passes bill.

For this act see 10H109.

**941-P**  **Frederick County—Citizens**
JHD: 20 May 1779                                              Frederick County
For establishment of a ferry across Shenandoah River from land of T. B. Martin in Frederick County to land of Lord Fairfax.

Manuscript signed by: Jno. Hoge, Sam. May, F. Edmonson, Jr., Abrm. Bowman, Wm. Kincade, and forty others.
20 May 1779: To PG.
2 June 1779: PG finds reasonable and is directed to prepare a bill.

This was incorporated in a general ferry act passed by House and Senate.

For this act see 10H124.

**942-P**  **Vaughan, Craddock; Tomlinson, Benja.; Jordan, Saml.; Cureton, John, Jr.; Ingraham, Richard; Hobson, Nichs.; Broadnax, Edw.; DeGraffenreid, Wm.; Stokes, Hy.; Stokes, Hy., Jr.; and Farmer, Lodk.**
JHD: 20 May 1779                                              Lunenburg County
For increase in allowances to veniremen and witnesses summoned to court trials.

Manuscript unsigned.

## 19 – 21 May 1779

20 May 1779: To PG.
>Increases for witnesses were made in a general act passed by House and Senate.
>For general act see 10H127.

**943-P-†  Augusta County—Citizens**
>JHD: 20 May 1779                               Augusta County

For a division of the county.
20 May 1779: To PG.
14 June 1779: Carried over to next session of GA.
25 Nov. 1779: PG recommends rejection.
>House rejects.

**944-P-†  Johnson, William; Randall, Abel; and Poston, Elias**
>JHD: 21 May 1779                              Hampshire County

Request by three Hampshire County tax commissioners for an increase in allowance for their clerk.
21 May 1779: To committee of whole "for raising a supply of money."
>Made part of act 10H9.
>For increases in allowances for all clerks of tax commissioners, see 10H9.

**945-P-†  Augusta County—Citizens**
>JHD: 21 May 1779                               Augusta County

Opposing any consolidation with Rockingham County.
21 May 1779: To PG.
>Carried over to next session of GA.
>See 694-P and 943-P-† for action.

**946-P   Grayson, William**
>JHD: 21 May 1779                           Prince William County

For severance of several lots he owns in Dumfries from that town.
Manuscript signed by: Foushee Tebbs, Richd. Graham, Wm. Brent, Evan Williams, Reginald Graham, and eight others.
21 May 1779: To PG.
25 May 1779: PG recommends as reasonable and is directed to prepare a bill.
29 May 1779: House passes bill.
1 June 1779: Senate amends bill and House agrees to amendments.
>For this act see 10H102.

## Virginia Legislative Petitions

**947-P**   Moreton, John
JHD: 22 May 1779   Prince Edward County
For additional compensation as sheriff for bringing criminal to jail.
Manuscript unsigned.
22 May 1779: To PG.
    Committee apparently did not report.
    No further action found.

**948-P**
Eck–
A1102   **Staunton—Citizens**
JHD: 22 May 1779   Augusta County
To prevent swine from running at large, and to allow trustees to levy a tax to keep streets and aqueducts in repair.
Manuscript signed by: Samp. Mathews, Josa. Humphrey, Wm. Bowyer, Alexd. Sinclair, James Buchanan, and thirteen others.
22 May 1779: To PG.
12 June 1779: House passes bill on third reading.
16 June 1779: Senate amends bill.
18 June 1779: House passes amended bill.
Date unknown: Senate passes bill.
    See 846-P-†.
    For this act see 10H119.

**949-P**   **Orange County—Citizens**
JHD: 24 May 1779   Orange County
Asking that the county be divided into two districts for purposes of musters and courts-martial.
Manuscript signed by: William Cave, John Hiatt, Lawrence Egbert, James Coleman, John Collins, and 183 others.
24 May 1779: House lays on table.
    No further action found.

**950-M**   **Auditors of Public Accounts**
JHD: 24 May 1779   Williamsburg
Asking that salaries of clerks to auditors be increased.
Manuscript signed by: Thos. Everard, James Cocke, and Dun. Rose.
24 May 1779: To PG.
27 May 1779: PG recommends £500 for clerk and assistant clerk.
    House agrees and directs PG to prepare bill.

## 22 – 24 May 1779

This bill was passed by House and Senate at £800 each.
For this act see 10H107.

**951-P**
Eck–
A1667    **Bedford County—Citizens**
JHD: 24 May 1779                                Bedford County
For a division of the county.
Manuscript signed by: Anthony Pate, William Watts, Thomas Charters, Jesse Meador, William Drake, and forty others. Manuscript dated 25 May 1779.
24 May 1779: To PG.
26 May 1779: PG recommends rejection.
House rejects.

**951 A-P**
Eck–
A1667    **Bedford County—Citizens**
JHD: 24 May 1779                                Bedford County
Text is identical with 951-P, which see.
Manuscript signed by sixty-two persons. Dated 24 May 1779.

**951 B-P**
Eck–
A1667    **Bedford County—Citizens**
JHD: 24 May 1779                                Bedford County
Text is identical with 951-P, which see.
Manuscript signed by fifty-nine persons. Dated 22 May 1779.

**951 C-P**
Eck–
A1667    **Bedford County—Citizens**
JHD: 24 May 1779                                Bedford County
Text is identical with 951-P, which see.
Manuscript signed by sixty-three persons. Dated 22 May 1779.

**951 D-P**
Eck–
A1667    **Bedford County—Citizens**
JHD: 24 May 1779                                Bedford County

## Virginia Legislative Petitions

Text is identical with 951-P, which see.
Manuscript signed by 119 persons. Dated 22 May 1779.

**952-P**
Eck–
A1668 **Bedford County—Citizens**
JHD: 24 May 1779                                              Bedford County
Opposing a division of the county.
Manuscript signed by: Arthur Barnabas, Phil. Jacob Irion, Lewis Irion, Benjamin Johnson, William Owen, and 533 others.
24 May 1779: To PG.
26 May 1779: PG recommends as reasonable.
    House recommits to PG.
    No further action found.

**953-P**   **Henry County—Citizens**
JHD: 24 May 1779                                              Henry County
For the addition of part of Henry County to Bedford County.
Manuscript signed by: Caleb Tate, John Doughten, John Minefee, William Minefee, William Bartec, and 568 others. Some signatures are illegible.
24 May 1779: To PG.
    Manuscript endorsement says rejected.

**954-P**   **Stafford County—Citizens**
JHD: 24 May 1779                                              Stafford County
To have courthouse remain in its present location.
Manuscript signed by: Daniel Traverse, John Fitzhugh, William Fitzhugh, James Hunter, Thomas Fitzhugh, and 441 others, all in same hand.
24 May 1779: To PG.
1 June 1779: PG recommends rejection.
    House rejects.

**955-P**   **Stafford County—Citizens**
JHD: 24 May 1779                                              Stafford County
Opposing removal of courthouse from present location on land of William Garrard (954-P).
Manuscript unsigned.

## 24 – 25 May 1779

24 May 1779: To PG.
>Committee apparently did not report, but see 10H108 for act empowering justices of Stafford County to locate center of county as place for building courthouse.

**956-P**  **Washington, Bailey**
JHD: 24 May 1779   Stafford County

Asking that center of county be located as a place for courthouse.
Manuscript unsigned.
24 May 1779: To PG.
>This petition resulted in a bill passed by House and Senate for locating center of county.
>For this act see 10H108.

**957-P**  **Pittsylvania County—Citizens**
JHD: 25 May 1779   Pittsylvania County

For clearing the Banister River of stops and milldams to allow the passage of fish.

Manuscript signed by: John Short, John Horner, Ambrose Beuford, James Wade, Spencer Shelton, and twenty-three others. Some signatures are illegible.
25 May 1779: To PG.
2 June 1779: PG recommends rejection.
>House rejects.

**958-P-***
Eck–
A725  **Amelia County and Chesterfield County—Citizens**
JHD: 25 May 1779   Amelia County
   Chesterfield County

Asking that tolls be used to maintain two rebuilt bridges over Appomattox River: Beville's and Goode's.

Manuscript signed by: Stith Hardaway, John Booker, Jr., William Giles, Edward Booker, Jeremiah Walker, and forty-nine others. (From Eck.)
25 May 1779: To PG.
2 June 1779: PG recommends rejection.
>House rejects.

## Virginia Legislative Petitions

**959-P**
Eck–
A1104   **Augusta County—Citizens**
JHD: 25 May 1779                                          Augusta County
For a division of the county, and creation of Bath County.
Manuscript signed by: John Pollard, Wm. McClintog, Robt. Armstrong Turner, Thomas Muhollen, James Davis, and twenty-five others.
25 May 1779: To PG.
14 June 1779: Carried over to next session of GA.
25 Nov. 1779: PG recommends rejection.
   House rejects.
   Bath County was not created until 1791.

**959 A-P**
Eck–
A1104   **Augusta County—Citizens**
JHD: 25 May 1779                                          Augusta County
Text is identical with 959-P, which see.
Manuscript signed by twenty-three persons.

**959 B-P**
Eck–
A1104   **Augusta County—Citizens**
JHD: 25 May 1779                                          Augusta County
Text is identical with 959-P, which see.
Manuscript signed by six persons.

**960-P**
Eck–
A1103   **Augusta County—Citizens**
JHD: 25 May 1779                                          Augusta County
Asking that the portion of Monongalia County transferred to Augusta County be returned to Monongalia County.
Manuscript signed by: Wm. Taylor, William Robinson, Richard Moorefield, Daniel Stout, Thomas Bartlett, and 100 others.
25 May 1779: To PG.
14 June 1779: PG recommends as reasonable and is directed to prepare a bill.
16 June 1779: PG presents a bill, including the addition of part of Augusta
   County to Rockingham County. (See petition of 14 June 1779,
   998-P-†, from Rockingham County.)

## 25 – 27 May 1779

18 June 1779: House passes bill.
19 June 1779: Senate omits Rockingham portion and amends Monongalia portion.
House agrees to Senate amendments.
For this act see 10H114.

**961-P**    **Drysdale Parish, Caroline County and King and Queen County—Citizens**
JHD: 25 May 1779                        Caroline County
                                               King and Queen County

For a dissolution of the vestry.
Manuscript signed by: Thomas Laury, Thos. Coleman, Henry Samuel, Matthew Gayle, Jos. Gatewood, and 155 others.
25 May 1779: To R.
     Committee apparently did not report.
     New petitions were presented on 15, 16, and 22 October 1779. See 1027-P, 1027A-P, 1027B-P, 1027C-P, 1033-P, 1033A-P, 1033 B-P, and 1059-P.

**962-P-†**    **Burwell, Lewis, Jr.**
JHD: 26 May 1779                        James City County
Compensation for burning of ferry-house and outbuildings on James River in 1776 when Virginia troops were stationed there.
26 May 1779: To special committee.
4 June 1779: Committee recommends rejection.
     House rejects.

**963-P**    **Goodrich, Dorothy**
JHD: 26 May 1779                                Not known
Asking that she and two small children be allowed to join her husband, John Goodrich, Jr., on an enemy vessel.
Manuscript unsigned.
26 May 1779: To PG.
     Committee apparently did not report.

**964-P-†**    **Winchester—Citizens**
JHD: 27 May 1779                           Frederick County
To incorporate the town.
27 May 1779: To PG.
10 June 1779: PG reports reasonable and is directed to prepare a bill.

## Virginia Legislative Petitions

26 June 1779: Carried over to next session of GA.
        For action see 902-P-†.
        For act incorporating Alexandria and Winchester, see 10H172.

**965-P**    **Henry County—Citizens**
        JHD: 27 May 1779                                Henry County
Opposing a division of the county.
    Manuscript signed by: Will Tunstall, John Salmon, Edmd. Lyne, Mordecai Hord, Henry Lyne, and two others. (In reference to dividing Henry County it is noted in the petition: "It is well known that it is an easy matter to induce the ignorant multitude to sign anything.")
27 May 1779: To PG.
28 May 1779: Committee recommends rejection.
        House rejects.

**966-P**
Eck–
A1107    **Augusta County—Citizens**
        JHD: 27 May 1779                               Augusta County
Opposing a division of the county.
    Manuscript signed by: Andw. Hamilton, James Griffith, John Wright, Robert Owin, Robert Bratton, and sixty-one others.
27 May 1779: To PG.
14 June 1779: Carried over to next session of GA.
25 Nov. 1779: House rejects division (943-P-†).

**966 A-P**
Eck–
A1108    **Augusta County—Citizens**
        JHD: 27 May 1779                               Augusta County
Text is similar to 966-P, which see.
Manuscript signed by forty-five persons.

**967-P**    **Moody, Matthew**
        JHD: 27 May 1779                                    Not known
Asking for payment for services of court cryer to court of oyer and terminer.
    Manuscript unsigned.
27 May 1779: To PG.
        Committee apparently did not report.

## 27 – 31 May 1779

**968-P-†   Johnson, Winniford**
    JHD: 28 May 1779                              Not known
Compensation for death of son, John Johnson, from frostbite, for whom she had sent a messenger to bring him home from the Jerseys. He was found dead.
28 May 1779: To T.
4 June 1779: T recommends £135.
    House agrees.
10 June 1779: Senate agrees.

**969-P-†   Bedford County and Henry County—Citizens**
    JHD: 28 May 1779, for action              Bedford County
                                                                    Henry County
For forming a new county out of Bedford and Henry counties. (This may be 607-P-*, but it is entered separately for lack of proof.)
Date unknown: To PG.
28 May 1779: PG reports as reasonable and is directed to prepare a bill.
29 May 1779: Bill presented.
31 May 1779: Bill recommitted to PG.
3 June 1779: PG again presents bill.
4 June 1779: House rejects bill on third reading.

**970-P     Swearingen, Sarah**
    JHD: 31 May 1779                           Berkeley County
Asks repeal of act that established, in favor of Abraham Shepherd, a ferry across Potomac River to Maryland.
    Manuscript unsigned.
31 May 1779: To PG.
10 June 1779: PG reports as reasonable.
        Recommitted to PG.
        Apparently no further action taken, but Thomas Swearingen, Jr., presented a new petition on 15 October 1779 (1019-P).
    See 625-P and 9H456.

**971-P-†   Tucker, Travis**
    JHD: 31 May 1779                           Norfolk Borough
Protesting the decision of the commissioners not to award him the value of his property destroyed in Norfolk borough.
31 May 1779: To T.
4 June 1779: T recommends rejection.
        House rejects.

## Virginia Legislative Petitions

**972-P-†  Stafford County—Citizens**
JHD: 1 June 1779, for action                    Stafford County

Asking (1) that location of courthouse be changed, and (2) that commissioners be appointed from adjacent counties to locate the center of Stafford County. (This may refer to 956-P, but it is entered separately for lack of proof.)
Date unknown: To PG.
1 June 1779: PG finds (1) reasonable and is directed to prepare a bill.
    PG recommends rejection of (2).
    House rejects.
3 June 1779: PG presents bill for (1).
4 June 1779: Bill recommitted to PG.
10 June 1779: PG presents bill.
    House amends.
11 June 1779: House passes bill.
16 June 1779: Senate passes bill.
    See 954-P and 955-P.
    For this act see 10H108 authorizing justices to locate center of county.

**973-P  Frederick County and Berkeley County—Citizens**
JHD: 1 June 1779                    Frederick County
                                            Berkeley County

Protesting the fact that the present circulating currency has been refused for payment of bills, bonds, and mortgages.
Manuscript signed by: John Smith, Danl. Morgan, Benj. Berry, William Cochran, Nathll. Pitney, and forty-six others.
1 June 1779: To PG.
26 June 1779: May have been carried over to next session of GA.
    No further record found.

**973 A-P  Frederick County and Berkeley County—Citizens**
JHD: 1 June 1779                    Frederick County
                                              Berkeley County

Text is identical with 973-P, which see.
Manuscript signed by seventy-one persons.

**973 B-P  Frederick County and Berkeley County—Citizens**
JHD: 1 June 1779                    Frederick County
                                              Berkeley County

## 1 - 2 June 1779

Text is identical with 973-P, which see.
Manuscript signed by thirty-three persons.

### 973 C-P  Frederick County and Berkeley County—Citizens
JHD: 1 June 1779                                      Frederick County
                                                             Berkeley County

Text is identical with 973-P, which see.
Manuscript signed by fifty-one persons.

### 973 D-P  Frederick County and Berkeley County—Citizens
JHD: 1 June 1779                                      Frederick County
                                                             Berkeley County

Text is identical with 973-P, which see.
Manuscript signed by forty-two persons.

### 973 E-P  Frederick County and Berkeley County—Citizens
JHD: 1 June 1779                                      Frederick County
                                                             Berkeley County

Text is identical with 973-P, which see.
Manuscript signed by forty-nine persons.

### 974-P-†  Botetourt County and Montgomery County—Citizens
JHD: 2 June 1779                                   Botetourt County
                                                         Montgomery County

Asking formation of new county from upper end of Botetourt County and lower end of Montgomery County.
2 June 1779: To PG.
18 June 1779: Carried over to next session of GA.
        No further record found.

### 975-P  Kinkade, Robert
JHD: 2 June 1779                                      Rockbridge County

For relief from treble taxes for not taking loyalty oath by prescribed time.
     Manuscript signed by: James Montgomery, Henry James, Thomas Mitchell, Robt. Wilson, Jam. Hunter, and forty-one others attesting loyalty.
2 June 1779: To PG.
18 June 1779: PG finds reasonable and is directed to prepare a bill.
        For general act providing relief see 1JH194.

## Virginia Legislative Petitions

**976-P  Henderson, Richard, and Company**
JHD: 2 June 1779                                      Western Lands
For relief from burden of lands granted them by General Assembly between Ohio and Green rivers.
Manuscript unsigned.
2 June 1779: To special committee to bring in a bill on titles of different claimants to unpatented lands.
  No further record found.

**977-P-†  Hughes, William**
JHD: 2 June 1779                                      Not known
Compensation for injury received in military service in 1762.
2 June 1779: To T.
4 June 1779: T recommends rejection.
  House rejects.

**978-P-†  M'Roberts, Alexander**
JHD: 2 June 1779                              Prince Edward County
Additional compensation for work as clerk for commissioners of Prince Edward County.
2 June 1779: To T.
10 June 1779: T recommends rejection.
  House rejects.

**979-M  Penet, Wendel, and Company**
JHD: 2 June 1779                                              France
Desires to establish a manufactory of artillery and small arms in Virginia.
Manuscript unsigned.
2 June 1779: To a special committee of seventeen.
22 June 1779: Committee has four new members appointed. Quorum to consist of five members.
25 June 1779: Committee recommends (1) that the proposal is of great importance; (2) that the company have conveyed to them for full consideration the commonwealth's rights in canal, foundry, and other works at Westham; (3) that the governor and Council be empowered to purchase and convey to the company 3,000 acres of land for their works, together with a place near the James River convenient to ore, wood, and water, together with a coal mine, securing from the company security to repay funds advanced; (4) that the governor and Council appoint persons, with the company,

## 2 – 4 June 1779

to examine location of places on both sides of James River that may be proper for erecting the works, and if they find any other place except John Ballendine's, they shall report the same, and the governor is empowered to purchase it, as well as lands necessary to open a canal or road to Richmond or Manchester, and convey the same to the company with security; and (5) that the governor be empowered to contract with the company to use return of arms and military stores against their obligation, and he is empowered to contract for an annual return of arms.

House agrees.

25 June 1779: Senate agrees.

The effect of this resolution might well have removed John Ballendine from the scene, but the French government refused to allow Penet, Wendel, and Company to move from France.

For the proposed contract between Penet, and governor and Council, see JHD, 30 October, 11 December, and 15 December 1779.

**980-P   Owen, Richardson**
JHD: 3 June 1779                                          Montgomery County

For a grant of land adjacent to his ironworks on Cedar Creek and other encouragement.

Manuscript unsigned.

3 June 1779: To PG.

10 June 1779: PG recommends a grant of 5,000 acres provided works are completed by 1 June 1786 (?).

PG to prepare bill.

No further record found.

**981-P   Fluvanna County—Citizens**
JHD: 4 June 1779                                          Fluvanna County

Asking for a proportion of the glebe land for Fluvanna Parish that was formerly part of Saint Anne's Parish in Albemarle County.

Manuscript signed by: Armiger Lilly, Thos. Appleberry, Richd. Allen, Wm. Barnett, James Adams, and forty-eight others.

4 June 1779: To R.

14 June 1779: R recommends that glebe land and appurtenances be sold at public auction, and that funds be divided between the two parishes

## Virginia Legislative Petitions

in proportion to their tithables and be used for the purchase of new glebes.

R to prepare a bill.

18 June 1779: House passes bill.

19 June 1779: Senate passes bill.

For this act see 10H112.

The Reverend Charles Clay petitioned on 14 October 1779 regarding the change in his status by sale of glebe of Saint Anne's Parish (1017-P).

**982-P  Mental Hospital—Directors**
JHD: 5 June 1779                                     Williamsburg

Asking for an increase in salaries of keeper, James Galt, and matron. Both of them are about to resign.

Manuscript unsigned.

5 June 1779: To T.

14 June 1779: T recommends an additional £200 per year for keeper, and an additional £100 per year for matron.

House agrees.

16 June 1779: Senate agrees.

See 728-P.

**983-P-†  Howse, Lawrence**
JHD: 5 June 1779                                     Not known

For expenses of £11 5s. 6d. for apprehending deserters from Continental army.

5 June 1779: Laid on table.

No further record found.

**984-P  Culpeper County—Citizens**
JHD: 5 June 1779                                     Culpeper County

Asking that Culpeper County be divided into three distinct counties.

Manuscript signed by: William Allan, John Bartley, Robt. Adcock, Phil. Yancey, Jas. Barbour, and 124 others.

5 June 1779: To PG.

14 June 1779: Carried over to next session of GA.

23 Oct. 1779: PG recommends rejection.

House rejects.

## 5 – 9 June 1779

**984 A-P   Culpeper County—Citizens**                           Culpeper County
    JHD: 5 June 1779
    Text is identical with 984-P, which see.
    Manuscript signed by twenty-nine persons.

**985-P**
Eck–Not
found      **Croghan, George**                                   Augusta County
    JHD: 5 June 1779
    Asking to be heard on his claim to western lands.
    Manuscript unsigned.
5 June 1779: House agrees to hear him on 8 June.
    See 988-M.

**986-M-†   Virginia Artillery Officers**                         Not known
    JHD: 5 June 1779
    For redress of many disadvantages and inconveniences under which they labor. (There were several memorials and letters, but the exact number is unknown.)
5 June 1779: To SC.
    No further record found.

**987-P    Fox, John**                                            Gloucester County
    JHD: 5 June 1779
    Stating he purchased entailed land of John Rootes and Sarah Rootes, but has not received title since only one trustee survives.
    Manuscript unsigned.
5 June 1779: Special committee to bring in bill.
17 June 1779: House passes bill.
        Senate passes bill.
        For the act appointing new trustees and allowing any three of them to pass title, see 10H120.

**988-M**
Eck–
A1110      **Croghan, George**                                   Augusta County
    JHD: 9 June 1779
    Asking for confirmation of title to western lands purchased from Indians in 1753. In 1774, Lord Dunmore had Croghan's title proved and recorded.
    Manuscript unsigned.

9 June 1779: House lays on table.
> No further record found.
> See 985-P.

### 989-M-† Hite, Isaac
JHD: 10 June 1779                      Not known

Compensation for surgeon's fees in treating a wound received from Indians in defense of Boonesborough.

10 June 1779: To T.
14 June 1779: T finds reasonable and recommends £400.
> House agrees.
> No Senate action found.
> Hite repeated his memorial on 14 October 1779 (1015-P-†).

### 990-P Ballendine, John
JHD: 14 June 1779                     Henrico County

Citing his efforts to construct a canal at Westham, stating it has gone as far as his land reaches, and also stating he had spent up to £20,000 on the construction. Asks that his rights and privileges, formerly vested in trustees, be confirmed to him and his heirs. Also asks that tolls be allowed, and that boring mill be repaired.

Manuscript unsigned.

14 June 1779: To special committee.
25 June 1779: Committee recommends that governor and Council appoint proper persons to settle all matters and accounts between Ballendine and the commonwealth including lands and furnace in Buckingham County, and lands, works, and canal at Westham, and that necessary contracts be executed.
> House agrees.
> Senate agrees.
> See 979-M.

### 991-P-† Ellis, John
JHD: 14 June 1779                      Not known

As agent of William Lee asks compensation for damage done to houses and lots by Virginia troops.

14 June 1779: Carried over to next session of GA.
> No further record found.

## 10 – 14 June 1779

**992-P-†   Black, William**
    JHD: 14 June 1779                                                    Chesterfield County
  To establish a ferry across James River from his land in Chesterfield County to the land of Charles Lewis, in Henrico County.
  14 June 1779: Carried over to next session of GA.
    No further action found.
    Black presented a new petition on 20 October 1779 (1047-P).
    For final establishment of this ferry in November 1781, see 10H459.

**993-P-†   Randolph, Thomas Mann**
    JHD: 14 June 1779                                                          Henrico County
  For discontinuance of a ferry from his land at Varina in Henrico County, across James River to land of Richard Batte, in Chesterfield County.
  14 June 1779: Carried over to next session of GA.
    No further action found.
    Randolph presented a new petition on 20 October 1779 (1048-P-†).

**994-P-†   Tucker, Travis**
    JHD: 14 June 1779                                                         Norfolk Borough
  Asking compensation for house in Norfolk borough that had been destroyed. The valuation had been lost or mislaid.
  14 June 1779: To special committee.
    Committee apparently did not report.
    See 971-P-† for a similar petition.

**995-P-†   Love, Alexander**
    JHD: 14 June 1779                                                         Norfolk Borough
  States that he now has documents to prove his losses in Norfolk borough and Portsmouth, for which he will ask compensation. Also states he has erected a brewery and distillery, which he cannot operate because of a general law forbidding distilling of grain.
  14 June 1779: To a special committee.
    Committee apparently did not report, but see 10H112 for act repealing act forbidding distillation of grain.

**996-P-†   Frederick County—Citizens**
    JHD: 14 June 1779                                                          Frederick County
  To remedy abuses in law authorizing military substitutes.

299

## Virginia Legislative Petitions

14 June 1779: To PG.
18 June 1779: PG finds reasonable.
> Recommends that governor direct county lieutenant or commanding officer to examine carefully all exemptions granted for those using servants or apprentices for substitutes.
> House agrees.
> Senate action not found.

**997-M  Pendleton, Edmund and Lyons, Peter (Administrators of John Robinson, deceased)**
JHD: 14 June 1779                                    Not known
For a credit to Robinson's estate of £1,500 paid by Robinson personally, in 1758, to John Turnbull, agent for the Indian trade.
Manuscript not signed.
14 June 1779: To auditors.
16 June 1779: Auditors find request reasonable and suggest £1,500 and interest be paid to estate.
> House agrees.
17 June 1779: Senate agrees.

**998-P-†  Rockingham County—Citizens**
JHD: 14 June 1779, for action              Rockingham County
For adding part of Augusta County to Rockingham County.
Date unknown: To PG.
14 June 1779: PG finds reasonable and is directed to prepare a bill.
> See 960-P for action.

**999-P-†  Rockingham County—Citizens**
JHD: 14 June 1779, for action              Rockingham County
Opposing adding part of Augusta County to Rockingham County.
Date unknown: To PG.
14 June 1779: PG recommends rejection.
> House rejects.
> See 998-P-†.

**1000-P  Hyland, Frances**
JHD: 13 Oct. 1779                                    Henrico County
For appointment of her son, Robert Ormston, and herself as doorkeepers of the House of Delegates.
Manuscript unsigned.

## 14 June – 13 October 1779

13 Oct. 1779: HD immediately appoints the following: William Hicks, John Creagh, William Drinkard, and Daniel Hix.
House rejects Hyland and Ormston.

**1001-P-†  Hix, Daniel**
    JHD: 13 Oct. 1779                            Not known
  For appointment as doorkeeper to the House of Delegates.
13 Oct. 1779: House approves.
    See 1000-P.

**1002-P  Jones, John**
    JHD: 13 Oct. 1779                    Henrico County
  For appointment as doorkeeper to the House of Delegates. (This is a list of recommendations.)
  Manuscript signed by: Geo. Webb, Edm. Randolph, John Blair, and James Madison.
13 Oct. 1779: House rejects.
    See 1000-P.

**1003-P  Lafong, George**
    JHD: 13 Oct. 1779                       Williamsburg
  For appointment as doorkeeper to the House of Delegates.
  Manuscript unsigned.
13 Oct. 1779: House rejects.
    See 1000-P.

**1004-P  Lenox, Walter**
    JHD: 13 Oct. 1779                       Williamsburg
  For appointment as doorkeeper to the House of Delegates.
  Manuscript unsigned.
13 Oct. 1779: House rejects.
    See 1000-P.

**1005-P  Pate, Matthew**
    JHD: 13 Oct. 1779                       Williamsburg
  For appointment as doorkeeper to the House of Delegates.
  Manuscript dated 4 October 1779, and is a recommendation. Signed by: Jas. Jones, J. Ambler, and Edward Archer.
13 Oct. 1779: House rejects.
    See 1000-P.

## Virginia Legislative Petitions

**1006-P-†  Urie, William**
JHD: 13 Oct. 1779                                      Not known
For appointment as doorkeeper to the House of Delegates.
13 Oct. 1779: House rejects.
See 1000-P.

**1007-P   Prince William County—Tax Commissioners**
JHD: 14 Oct. 1779                          Prince William County
Relief for citizens (names not specified) who did not take the loyalty oath, and reimbursement of triple fines.
Manuscript signed by: Foushee Tebbs, Cuth. Bullitt, and John Murray.
14 Oct. 1779: To PG.
15 Oct. 1779: PG recommends that further time be allowed and that treble taxes be rescinded.
  PG directed to prepare a bill.
  These recommendations were incorporated in a general law passed by House and Senate.
  For this act see 9H194.

**1008-P   Nelson, John**
JHD: 14 Oct. 1779                                   Charlotte County
Relief for not taking loyalty oath, and reimbursement for triple fines.
Manuscript unsigned.
14 Oct. 1779: To PG.
15 Oct. 1779: PG reports reasonable.
  Recommitted to PG.
  For action see 1007-P.
  For this act see 9H194.

**1009-P   Holt, Joseph**
JHD: 14 Oct. 1779                                   Charlotte County
Relief for not taking loyalty oath, and reimbursement for triple fines.
Manuscript signed by: Thomas Reed, P. Carrington, and Wm. Morton.
14 Oct. 1779: To PG.
15 Oct. 1779: PG reports reasonable and is directed to prepare a bill.
  For action see 1007-P.
  For this act see 9H194.

**1010-P   Powell, John**
JHD: 14 Oct. 1779                                   Brunswick County

## 13 – 14 October 1779

Relief for not taking loyalty oath, and reimbursement for triple fines.
Manuscript unsigned.
14 Oct. 1779: To PG.
15 Oct. 1779: PG reports reasonable and is directed to prepare a bill.
    For action see 1007-P.
    For this act see 9H194.

**1011-P**
Rob-8   **Kentucky County—Citizens**
    JHD: 14 Oct. 1779                   Kentucky County
Protesting that the giving of 400 acres of land to each settler is inadequate compensation for those defending Kentucky.
    Manuscript signed by: James Estill, David Gass, John South, Sr., Stephen Hancock, Pemberton Rawlings, and fifty-one others.
14 Oct. 1779: To PG.
    The land office law provided more than 400 acres.
    For land office act see 10H50.

**1012-P**   **Prince William County—Citizens**
    JHD: 14 Oct. 1779                 Prince William County
For removal of courthouse from Dumfries, where tavern keepers flourish, to lands of John Randolph, at center of county.
    Manuscript signed by: Elijah Moore, Nelson Ware, William Hogan, Luke Hanks, Richard Thunley, and 277 others (all in same hand).
14 Oct. 1779: To PG.
16 Oct. 1779: Carried over to next session of GA.
17 May 1780: House rejects upon approving a petition in opposition to removal on 17 May 1780.

**1013-P**   **Brunswick County—Tax Commissioners, Assessors, and Sheriff**
    JHD: 14 Oct. 1779                   Brunswick County
For extension of time in making their returns due to unavoidable delays.
    Manuscript dated 1 October 1779 and signed by: Douglass Wilkins, Jr., Edmund Webb, Henry Walton, He. Eldridge, He. Harriss, and seven others.
14 Oct. 1779: To PG.
15 Oct. 1779: PG reports as reasonable.
    Recommitted to PG.
19 Oct. 1779: House rejects.

## Virginia Legislative Petitions

**1014-P**
Eck–
A165   **Albemarle County—Citizens**
JHD: 14 Oct. 1779                                   Albemarle County
Asking that every person purchasing unappropriated western lands be required to settle a free white man on every 400 or 500 acres within three years.
   Manuscript signed by: Mask Leak, R. Davenport, Nath. Garland, John Wharton, Robert Harris, and 118 others.
14 Oct. 1779: To PG.
22 Nov. 1779: PG recommends rejection.
   House rejects.

**1015-P-†  Hite, Isaac**
JHD: 14 Oct. 1779                                         Not known
Compensation for surgeon's fees, in amount of £400, for treating a wound received from Indians in defense of Boonesborough. (This is a repetition of 989-M-†.)
14 Oct. 1779: To T.
20 Oct. 1779: T recommends as reasonable.
   House agrees.
   No Senate action found.

**1016-P   Calvert, Maximillian**
JHD: 14 Oct. 1779                              Elizabeth City County
Compensation for ship impressed by Committee of Safety in 1776 and converted into an armed vessel.
   Manuscript unsigned, but has four depositions attached.
14 Oct. 1779: To T.
4 Nov. 1779: T reports as reasonable.
   Recommitted to T.
6 Nov. 1779: T recommends £3,000.
   House agrees.
9 Nov. 1779: Senate agrees.

**1017-P**
Eck–Not
found   **Clay, Charles**
JHD: 14 Oct. 1779                                    Albemarle County
For right of tenancy of Saint Anne's glebe, which had been divided, part

304

## 14 – 15 October 1779

going to Fluvanna County, and for payment of arrearage in tobacco for salary as a minister.
   Manuscript unsigned.
14 Oct. 1779: To R.
14 Dec. 1779: R recommends rejection.
>House rejects.
>See 981-P and 1077-P.

**1018-P   Galloway, David and Ashton, Burdit**
>JHD: 15 Oct. 1779            King George County

Stating they intermarried with Margaret Blair and Sarah Blair, daughters of James Blair, deceased, who died intestate, and that two additional daughters, Elizabeth Blair and Anne Blair, were not of age. Ask that Blair's lands be sold and money be distributed among heirs.
   Manuscript unsigned.
15 Oct. 1779: To PG.
20 Oct. 1779: PG recommends rejection.
>House rejects.

**1019-P   Swearingen, Thomas, Jr.**
>JHD: 15 Oct. 1779            Berkeley County

For repeal of an act establishing a ferry from the land of Abraham Shepherd across Potomac River to Maryland.
   Manuscript unsigned.
15 Oct. 1779: To PG.
22 Nov. 1779: PG reports as reasonable and is directed to prepare a bill including ferry across Kentucky River.
>These matters were included in a general ferry bill passed by House and Senate.
>For this act see 10H196.
>See 970-P.

**1020-P   Berkeley County—Citizens**
>JHD: 15 Oct. 1779            Berkeley County

Opposing discontinuance of Abraham Shepherd's ferry.
   Manuscript signed by: Saml. Oldham, B. Beeler, Robert Stephen, Wm. Chambers, Dave Hunter, and ninety-one others.
15 Oct. 1779: To PG.
>Rejected by passage of 1019-P, which see.

## Virginia Legislative Petitions

### 1021-P   Hite, Isaac and Wallace, Caleb
JHD: 15 Oct. 1779                                          Not known

For extension of time in redeeming Continental currency for exchange, used for acquisition of land on western waters under certificates.
Manuscript unsigned.
15 Oct. 1779: To PG.
16 Oct. 1779: PG recommends rejection.
   House recommits to PG.
18 Oct. 1779: PG recommends as reasonable and is directed to prepare a bill or bills, which were passed by House and Senate.
   For general act see 10H148.

### 1022-P   Charlotte County—Citizens
JHD: 15 Oct. 1779                                       Charlotte County

For forfeiture of all lands acquired by deserters from Continental army.
Manuscript signed by: Ja. Speed, Sackville Bremer, Ro. Rakestraw, James Cunningham, Richard Gaines, Jr., and fifty-six others.
15 Oct. 1779: To PG.
16 Oct. 1779: PG recommends rejection.
   House rejects.

### 1023-P-†   Caroline County—Citizens
JHD: 15 Oct. 1779                                        Caroline County

For repeal of an act passed at last session of GA on escheats and forfeitures of British subjects.
15 Oct. 1779: To PG.
19 Oct. 1779: PG discharged and petition referred to committee to amend the act.
   For amendment of act see 10H153.

### 1024-P
Eck-
A836   **Amherst County and Buckingham County—Citizens**
JHD: 15 Oct. 1779                                        Amherst County
                                                        Buckingham County

For repeal of act for levy on tobacco stored in public warehouses.
Manuscript signed by: Richd. Shelton, David Woodroof, William Allen, Notley Mattocks, Richd. Tankersley, and 230 others.
15 Oct. 1779: To PG.
22 Oct. 1779: PG finds reasonable and is directed to prepare a bill.

## 15 October 1779

See 10E180 for amendment of tobacco warehouse laws. This act does not mention levies for storage.

**1025-P**
Eck–
A837   **Amherst County, Albemarle County, and Buckingham County—Citizens**
JHD: 15 Oct. 1779                    Amherst County
                                              Albemarle County
                                              Buckingham County

For repeal of act laying a tax payable in certain enumerated commodities.

Manuscript signed by: Richd. Shelton, David Woodroof, William Allen, Notley Mattocks, Richd. Tankersley, and 237 others.

15 Oct. 1779: To PG.
20 Oct. 1779: PG recommends rejection.
        House rejects.

**1026-P**
Eck–
A838   **Amherst County—Citizens**
JHD: 15 Oct. 1779                      Amherst County

For a more equal division of the boundaries between Amherst and Lexington parishes.

Manuscript signed by: David Montgomery, Aaron Campbell, Henry Gilbert, Richd. Tankersley, Gabl. Penn, and sixteen others.

15 Oct. 1779: To R.
        Committee apparently did not report.
        A new petition was presented on 18 May 1780 (1216-P).
        For act changing boundaries see 10H369.

**1027-P**   **Drysdale Parish, King and Queen County and Caroline County—Citizens**
JHD: 15 Oct. 1779                King and Queen County
                                              Caroline County

For a division of the parish.

Manuscript signed by: Philip Johnston, Edward Anderson, John Long, Richd. Johnston, Wm. Johnston, and thirty-one others.

15 Oct. 1779: To R.
2 Nov. 1779: R reports as reasonable and is directed to prepare a bill.
6 Nov. 1779: House passes bill creating Saint Asaph's Parish.

## Virginia Legislative Petitions

12 Nov. 1779: Senate passes bill.
       For this act see 10H209.
       For act explaining and amending this act, see 10H213.

### 1027 A-P Drysdale Parish, King and Queen County and Caroline County—Citizens
JHD: 15 Oct. 1779            King and Queen County
                                              Caroline County

Text is identical with 1027-P, which see.
Manuscript signed by thirty-nine persons.

### 1027 B-P Drysdale Parish, King and Queen County and Caroline County—Citizens
JHD: 15 Oct. 1779            King and Queen County
                                              Caroline County

Text is identical with 1027-P, which see.
Manuscript signed by twenty-seven persons.

### 1027 C-P Drysdale Parish, King and Queen County and Caroline County—Citizens
JHD: 15 Oct. 1779            King and Queen County
                                              Caroline County

Text is identical with 1027-P, which see.
Manuscript signed by ninety-three persons.

### 1028-P Antrim Parish, Halifax County—Churchwardens and Vestry
JHD: 15 Oct. 1779                          Halifax County
For dissolution of vestry and sale of glebe.
    Manuscript signed by: Jno. Dickie, Mathew Sims, George Boyd, Walter Coles, Isaac Coles, and three others.
15 Oct. 1779: To R.
2 Nov. 1779: R recommends as reasonable and is directed to prepare a bill.
       Bill apparently was never presented.

### 1028.1-M
Eck-
A1111   **Simms, Charles**
JHD: 16 Oct. 1779                          Augusta County
Asks that title to 2,961 acres of land be confirmed, since having been in the

## 15 – 16 October 1779

Continental army since 1776, he has been unable to improve the lands as required by law.
   Manuscript unsigned.
16 Oct. 1779: To PG.
19 Oct. 1779: PG reports reasonable.
   House and Senate agree on a bill.
   See 828-M.
   For this act see 10H139.

### 1029-P-† Eppes, Peter
   JHD: 16 Oct. 1779                                         Not known
Presented on behalf of Elizabeth Ramsay, widow of Patrick Ramsay, and her five children. States that the whole family visited in England in June 1775, and she and her children are unable to return. Asks that her land not be escheated.
16 Oct. 1779: To PG.
   Committee apparently did not report.

### 1030-P
Rob–9   **Boonesborough (Boonesfort), Kentucky County—Citizens**
   JHD: 16 Oct. 1779                                    Kentucky County
For the establishment of Boonesborough as a town, and for division of lots.
   Manuscript signed by: William Hancock, Edward Nelson, John Bullock, James Berry, Joseph Doniphan, and twenty-eight others. It has attached a list of those killed and captured by Indians, 1775–1779.
16 Oct. 1779: To PG.
19 Oct. 1779: PG recommends (1) that establishment of town is reasonable,
   (2) that residents should not be allowed to draw lots for areas in the town. (3) that 640 acres be laid off, and (4) that every person holding a lot should have title confirmed.
   House rejects (2), the drawing of lots.
   House directs PG to prepare a bill for (1), (3), and (4).
25 Oct. 1779: Bill presented and amended.
26 Oct. 1779: House passes bill.
28 Oct. 1779: Senate passes bill.
   For this act see 10H134.

### 1031-P-† Admiralty Court—Justices
   JHD: 16 Oct. 1779                                       Williamsburg
For allowing the court to meet in its present location rather than moving to town of Richmond when capital is transferred from Williamsburg.

## Virginia Legislative Petitions

16 Oct. 1779: To PG.
21 Oct. 1779: PG reports as reasonable and is directed to prepare a bill.
   This bill was passed by House and Senate.
   For this act see 10H136.

**1032-P**
Eck–
A839 **Amherst County—Citizens**
   JHD: 16 Oct. 1779     Amherst County

Protesting unequal assessments for tax purposes.

Manuscript signed by: James Higginbotham, Ambrose Rucker, Moses Higginbotham, John Higginbotham, Frederick Higginbotham, and twenty others. Endorsement says certified by Council on 6 September 1779.

16 Oct. 1779: To PG.
30 Oct. 1779: PG recommends rejection.
   House rejects.

**1033-P Drysdale Parish, King and Queen County and Caroline County—Citizens**
   JHD: 16 Oct. 1779     King and Queen County
                          Caroline County

Opposing a division of the parish.

Manuscript signed by: Bland Vaughan, Jeremiah Pickett, John Moore, James Martin, Charles Blanton, and 105 others.

16 Oct. 1779: To PG.
   For action see 1027-P.

**1033 A-P Drysdale Parish, King and Queen County and Caroline County—Citizens**
   JHD: 16 Oct. 1779     King and Queen County
                          Caroline County

Text is identical with 1033-P, which see.
Manuscript signed by 137 persons.

**1033 B-P Drysdale Parish, King and Queen County and Caroline County—Citizens**
   JHD: 16 Oct. 1779     King and Queen County
                          Caroline County

Text is identical with 1033-P, which see.
Manuscript signed by twenty-two persons.

## 16 – 18 October 1779

**1034-P-†** Walker, Samuel; M'Farren, Martin; Logan, Hugh; M'Roberts, Samuel; M'Roberts, Alexander; Ritchie, William; Miller, William; George, William; Newman, Jonathan; and Kyle, Joseph

JHD: 18 Oct. 1779                          Botetourt County

For expenses incurred in apprehending counterfeiters of Continental currency.

18 Oct. 1779: To T.
20 Oct. 1779: T recommends £18 4s. for Walker, M'Farren, Logan, S. M'Roberts, A. M'Roberts, Ritchie, and Miller; £10 for George and Newman; and £28 for Kyle.
    House agrees.
27 Oct. 1779: Senate agrees.

**1035-P-†** Porter, Samuel

JHD: 18 Oct. 1779                               Not known

Compensation for surgeon's fees for treatment of wound received from Shawanese Indians.

18 Oct. 1779: To T.
20 Oct. 1779: T recommends £45.
    House agrees.
27 Oct. 1779: Senate agrees.

**1036-P-†** Hughes, John

JHD: 18 Oct. 1779                               Not known

Additional compensation for blindness resulting from inoculation for smallpox while in service of United States.

18 Oct. 1779: To T.
21 Oct. 1779: T recommends £70 for current relief.
    House agrees.
27 Oct. 1779: Senate agrees.

**1037-P** Loudoun County—Citizens

JHD: 18 Oct. 1779                              Loudoun County

Asks that proof for land claims, based on importation rights, be made under existing laws at the time the claim was first made, and that legal proof, as required by law establishing new land offices, not be required. Also asks for extension of time in making proof.

Manuscript signed by: John Weylie, Beinamin Brown, Wm. Thomas, John Whaley, John Cockeral, and 167 others.

## Virginia Legislative Petitions

18 Oct. 1779: To PG.
30 Oct. 1779: PG recommends that extension of time be allowed.
    House agrees.
    Senate action not found.
2 Nov. 1779: PG recommends that request for deleting legal proof be rejected.
    House rejects.

### 1037 A-P  Loudoun County—Citizens
JHD: 18 Oct. 1779                                         Loudoun County
Text is identical with 1037-P, which see.
Manuscript signed by 171 persons.

### 1038-P  Stafford County—Citizens
JHD: 18 Oct. 1779                                         Stafford County
For subject and action see 1037-P, with which this is identical.
Manuscript signed by: John Cooke, John Browne, Tho. Tarny, Elijah Threlkeld, John Mountjoy, and thirty-two others.

### 1039-P  Prince William County—Citizens
JHD: 18 Oct. 1779                                Prince William County
For subject and action see 1037-P, with which this is identical.
Manuscript signed by: Foushee Tebbs, T. Blackburn, Cuth. Bullitt, William Grayson, John Tyler, Jr., and seventy-four others (all in same hand).

### 1040-P  Tyler, Thomas G.
JHD: 18 Oct. 1779                                         Stafford County
As clerk of Stafford County and administrator of the estate of Henry Tyler, deceased, former clerk, asks for a payment of 4,546 pounds of tobacco earned by Henry Tyler for transcribing two official books of public records. The payment had been rejected by the county court.
Manuscript unsigned.
18 Oct. 1779: To PG.
22 Oct. 1779: PG recommends rejection.
    House rejects.

### 1041-P-† Jerdone, Sarah
JHD: 18 Oct. 1779                                               Not known
Asking for relief from the forfeiture of the estate of her two sons who had been sent to Great Britain for their education in 1775, and were unable to return. Her husband was Francis Jerdone, deceased.

## 18 – 19 October 1779

18 Oct. 1779: To PG.
  Committee apparently did not report.

### 1042-P-† Baylor, John
  JHD: 19 Oct. 1779                          Caroline County
Claims that he never was a British sympathizer, but has always been loyal to Virginia. Asks relief from the escheats of his property.
19 Oct. 1779: To a special committee appointed to amend the present law.
27 Oct. 1779: Committee finds that Baylor has always been a friend of America.
  For general act amending former act and exempting certain classes of persons from being declared British sympathizers, see 10H153.

### 1043-P Culpeper County—Citizens
  JHD: 19 Oct. 1779                         Culpeper County
Asking for increases in fines for those refusing to work on roads and highways.
  Manuscript signed by: Robert Nixon, Thos. Shaw, Jones Mannefee, Joseph Bradford, Benjamin Gaines, and forty others.
19 Oct. 1779: To PG.
21 Oct. 1779: PG finds reasonable.
  To special committee to bring in a bill on highways, milldams, and bridges.
  This bill was passed by House and Senate.
  For act increasing fines, see 10H164.

### 1044-P Boyd, George
  JHD: 19 Oct. 1779                           Halifax County
For relief from fines, costs, and damages imposed by General Court for advancing a considerable amount of public money to Walter Coles for use in recruiting soldiers in 1778.
  Manuscript unsigned.
19 Oct. 1779: House rejects by refusal to refer to a committee.

### 1045-P-† Culpeper County—Citizens
  JHD: 19 Oct. 1779                         Culpeper County
Asking for a law to curb excessive gambling with penalties of double taxes for those over fifty years of age, and of two years in military service for those under fifty years of age.

## Virginia Legislative Petitions

19 Oct. 1779: To a special committee to bring in a bill "to suppress excessive gaming."
Bill passed by House and Senate.
For general act see 10H205.

**1046-P   Henrico County—Citizens**
JHD: 20 Oct. 1779                                                   Henrico County
To increase punishment for horse stealing, and to increase reward for apprehending thieves.
Manuscript signed by: Nich. Seabrook, Edwd. Park, Elisha Price, James Price, Richard Hogg, and twenty-two others, some from adjacent counties.
20 Oct. 1779: To PG.
22 Oct. 1779: PG recommends rejection.
House rejects.

**1047-P   Black, William**
JHD: 20 Oct. 1779                                                Chesterfield County
To establish a ferry across James River from his land in Chesterfield County to the land of Charles Lewis in Henrico County.
Manuscript unsigned.
20 Oct. 1779: To PG.
21 Oct. 1779: PG recommends it be carried over to next session of GA.
19 Dec. 1780: Carried over to next session of GA.
No further action found.
For final establishment of this ferry in November 1781, see 10H459.

**1048-P-†   Randolph, Thomas Mann**
JHD: 20 Oct. 1779                                                   Henrico County
To discontinue ferry across James River from his land in Henrico County to the land of Richard Batte in Chesterfield County.
20 Oct. 1779: To PG.
Committee apparently did not report.
See 993-P-†.

**1049-P   Orange County—Citizens**
JHD: 20 Oct. 1779                                                    Orange County
For equalization of land tax, and for some uniform method of assessment.
Manuscript signed by: Thos. Bell, Andrew Shepherd, George Procter, Lewis Willis, Ben Winslow, and 104 others.

## 20 – 21 October 1779

20 Oct. 1779: Rejected by refusal to refer to a committee.

**1050-P**
Eck–Not
found    **Augusta County—Citizens**
    JHD: 20 Oct. 1779                                                      Augusta County
  To pass a bill, under a plan proposed by the House of Delegates, to establish certain privileges for several denominations and religious societies.
  Manuscript dated 29 September 1779, and signed by: Geo. Moffatt, Jas. Allen, Michaell Dickey, Wm. Johnston, Jno. King, and seventy-three others.
20 Oct. 1779: To special committee concerning religion.
        Committee apparently did not report.

**1051-P**    **Lancaster County—Citizens**
    JHD: 20 Oct. 1779                                                      Lancaster County
  To repeal certain acts recently passed concerning taxation on slaves and tithables, and to amend act on religious freedom, most of which they favor.
  Manuscript signed by: Jas. Ball, James Ball, Jr., Wm. Sydnor, John Bailey, Jas. Ewell, and forty-four others.
20 Oct. 1779: Rejected by refusal to refer to a committee.

**1052-P-†**  **Hutson, Eleanor**
    JHD: 21 Oct. 1779                                                          Not known
  Compensation for death of husband, John Hutson, who drowned while on military duty in Indian country.
21 Oct. 1779: To T.
30 Oct. 1779: T recommends £24 for present relief and £12 per annum during
       her widowhood.
       House agrees.
5 Nov. 1779: Senate amends.
       House agrees.

**1053-P**  **Brunswick County—Citizens**
    JHD: 21 Oct. 1779                                                   Brunswick County
  To have the state stock salt, iron, and wool cards so that individuals can purchase them.
  Manuscript signed by: Aaron Brown, Henry Nicolson, Eleck Dugger, Eleck Andrews, David Mays, and twenty-five others.
21 Oct. 1779: House rejects by refusal to refer to a committee.

## Virginia Legislative Petitions

**1054-P    Mayo, John**
JHD: 21 Oct. 1779                                           Chesterfield County
To establish a ferry from his land in Manchester to Sandy Bar on the opposite shore.
Manuscript unsigned.
21 Oct. 1779: To PG.
9 Nov. 1779: Carried over to next session of GA.
   No further action found.
   Mayo presented a new petition on 8 November 1780 (1288-P).

**1055-P-†    Culpeper County—Citizens**
JHD: 21 Oct. 1779                                               Culpeper County
Opposing the passage of a proposed bill on religious freedom.
21 Oct. 1779: To a special committee to bring in a bill concerning religion.
   No further action found.

**1056-P    Essex County—Citizens**
JHD: 22 Oct. 1779                                                  Essex County
Opposing the passage of a proposed bill on religious freedom.
Manuscript signed by: James Booker, W. Young, Luke Carrington, Willm. Edmonson, William Perkins, and 119 others.
22 Oct. 1779: To a special committee to bring in a bill concerning religion.
   No further action found.

**1057-P-†    Clarke, John**
JHD: 22 Oct. 1779                                                      Not known
Compensation for surgeon's fees in treating his son, Benajah Clarke, who became sick in service and died.
22 Oct. 1779: To T.
13 Nov. 1779: T recommends £58 6s.
   House agrees.
17 Nov. 1779: Senate agrees.

**1058-P    Ritchie, Archibald**
JHD: 22 Oct. 1779                                                  Essex County
For relief from act placing a deadline on land grants due from importation rights prior to Revolution.
Manuscript unsigned.
22 Oct. 1779: To PG.
   No further action found.

## 21 – 23 October 1779

**1059-P Drysdale Parish, King and Queen County and Caroline County—Citizens**
JHD: 22 Oct. 1779                  King and Queen County
                                                                            Caroline County

In opposition to a division of the parish.
Manuscript signed by: Thos. Coleman, Ambrose White, Edwin Motley, Chilion White, James Whalen, and 264 others.
22 Oct. 1779: To R.
2 Nov. 1779: R recommends rejection.
    House rejects.

**1060-P Harvey, Mungo and Dean, John**
JHD: 22 Oct. 1779                              Richmond County

Relates to a debt owed by them to Alexander and David Campbell of Glasgow, Scotland, and asks that the amount paid by them to state treasurer be refunded if this debt is paid personally to the Campbells.
Manuscript unsigned.
22 Oct. 1779: To a special committee.
6 Nov. 1779: Committee recommends rejection for want of proof.

**1061-P Thompson, Roger**
JHD: 22 Oct. 1779                                     Not known

Compensation for impressed horse, killed by wagoner.
Manuscript unsigned.
22 Oct. 1779: House rejects by refusal to refer to a committee.

**1062-P Seayers, Frances**
JHD: 23 Oct. 1779                                     Not known

Additional compensation for death of her husband, John Seayers, in order that their children can be educated.
Manuscript unsigned.
23 Oct. 1779: To PG.
30 Oct. 1779: PG recommends (1) that £500 be allowed for present relief, and
            (2) that her three sons should be educated at public expense.
    House amends and agrees to (1).
3 Nov. 1779: Senate agrees to (1).
30 Oct. 1779: House amends (2) and directs PG to prepare a bill.
5 Nov. 1779: House rejects the prepared bill (2).
10 Nov. 1779: House agrees that Congress should be asked to provide for (2).

## Virginia Legislative Petitions

12 Nov. 1779: Senate agrees to resolution on (2).
    See 529-M.

### 1063-P-* Camp, Mary
    JHD: 23 Oct. 1779                                               Williamsburg
Compensation for land taken in 1776 whereon a magazine was erected.
    Manuscript petition not extant. There are five depositions concerning the use of Mary Camp's property.
23 Oct. 1779: To PG.
24 Nov. 1779: PG seeks appraisal. Report to governor.
3 Dec. 1779: PG recommends £300.
    House agrees.
6 Dec. 1779: Senate refers to a special committee.
    No further action found.

### 1064-P-† Tobacco Inspectors—Falmouth Warehouse and Dixon's Warehouse
    JHD: 23 Oct. 1779                                               Stafford County
For increases in their salaries by amendment of tobacco law.
23 Oct. 1779: To PG.
30 Oct. 1779: PG finds reasonable and is directed to prepare a bill.
    This bill was passed by House and Senate.
    For general act see 10H180.

### 1065-P Stafford County and Spotsylvania County—Citizens
    JHD: 23 Oct. 1779                                               Stafford County
                                                                          Spotsylvania County
    To establish a ferry across the Rappahannock River from lower end of Falmouth, on land of Mr. Dixon, to lands of Fielding Lewis and then to town of Fredericksburg.
    Manuscript signed by: Hancock Lee, Thos. Seddon, Charles Martin, Battaley Bryan, John Bell, and twenty-five others. Survey attached.
23 Oct. 1779: To PG.
27 Oct. 1779: PG finds reasonable and is directed to prepare a bill.
    House agrees to bill substituting Garwin Lawson for Mr. Dixon.
6 Nov. 1779: Senate passes bill.
    For this act, including other ferries, see 10H196.

23 – 25 October 1779

**1065 A-P Stafford County and Spotsylvania County—Citizens**
  JHD: 23 Oct. 1779                                Stafford County
                                                   Spotsylvania County
 Text is identical with 1065-P, which see.
 Manuscript signed by thirty-three persons. Survey attached.

**1065 B-P Stafford County and Spotsylvania County—Citizens**
  JHD: 23 Oct. 1779                                Stafford County
                                                   Spotsylvania County
 Text is identical with 1065-P, which see.
 Manuscript signed by fifty-one persons. Loose signatures and two surveys attached.

**1066-P**
Eck–
A166   **Walker, Thomas, Jr.**
       JHD: 23 Oct. 1779                           Albemarle County
 For emancipation of William Beck, a mulatto slave, for exemplary service with Charles Lewis in several campaigns.
 Manuscript unsigned.
 23 Oct. 1779: To PC.
 30 Oct. 1779: PG reports reasonable.
        House agrees.
        Senate agrees.
        Bills passed by House and Senate.
        For act emancipating William Beck and other slaves, see 10H211.

**1067-P-† Peyton, Craven**
       JHD: 23 Oct. 1779                                Not known
 Acting for George William Fairfax whose lands had been escheated as a British sympathizer, and since Fairfax has been in Great Britain since 1773 and is unable to return, asks that act be amended to prevent escheat.
 23 Oct. 1779: To committee to bring in a bill amending escheat law.
        Such a bill was passed by House and Senate.
        For general act see 10H153.

**1068-P-† Fairfax County—Citizens**
       JHD: 25 Oct. 1779                                Fairfax County
 Stating that marine defense is insufficient, and that public debt needs adjustment. Suggesting that quotas for soldiers to United States forces be

## Virginia Legislative Petitions

made without emission of money, and that enacted laws be promulgated to the people.
25 Oct. 1779: To PG.
4 Nov. 1779: Carried over to next session of GA.
    No further record found.

### 1069-P
Eck–Not found (A459?)
    **Alexandria—Citizens**
        JHD: 25 Oct. 1779                           Fairfax County
  Protesting that naval office at mouth of Potomac River is inconvenient, and asking that it be established elsewhere, particularly in Alexandria.
  Manuscript signed by: Wm. McFarley, Richard Avell, Jacob Cox, Washer Blunt, Benja. Chapin, and thirty-one others.
25 Oct. 1779: To PG.
    PG recommends (1) that naval office be placed in Alexandria, and (2) that a deputy office be placed in Alexandria.
    House recommits (1) to PG.
    House agrees to (2) and directs PG to prepare bill.
    House and Senate pass bill for (1).
    For this act see 10H208.

### 1070-P    **Manchester—Citizens**
        JHD: 25 Oct. 1779                        Chesterfield County
  Asks for an act to prevent hogs and goats from running at large in the town.
  Manuscript signed by: James Lyle, John Murchie, Wm. Mackenzie, Samuel DuVal, Jr., Jacob Rubsamen, and three others.
25 Oct. 1779: To PG.
30 Oct. 1779: PG recommends rejection.
    House rejects.

### 1071-P
Rob–10   **Callaway, Richard**
        JHD: 25 Oct. 1779                          Kentucky County
  To establish a ferry across Kentucky River from the town of Boonesborough to the other shore.
  Manuscript unsigned.
25 Oct. 1779: To PG.

## 25 October 1779

30 Oct. 1779: PG reports reasonable and is directed to prepare a bill.
>This was included in a general ferry bill passed by the House and Senate.
>For a general ferry act see 10H196.

**1072-P**
Eck–
A726   **Eggleston, William and Eggleston, Joseph**
JHD: 25 Oct. 1779                                          Amelia County

Asking that tax commissioners for Amelia County be required to reduce their land assessments from £8 per acre to £5 per acre.

Manuscript signed by petitioners and by: Daniel Hardaway, Miles Bott, William Bott, and Field Mann.
25 Oct. 1779: To PG.
30 Oct. 1779: PG recommends rejection.
>House amends and refer to T.

4 Nov. 1779: T recommends rejection.
>House rejects.

**1073-P-†   Essex County—Citizens**
JHD: 25 Oct. 1779                                          Essex County

To allow Archibald M'Call, who left the country to educate his children in Great Britain in 1775, to return and become a citizen, and that his lands not be escheated.
25 Oct. 1779: To PG.
>Committee apparently did not report.
>See 943-P.

**1074-P-†   Pendleton, John**
JHD: 25 Oct. 1779                                          Hanover County

States that Hanover County court appointed him to provide provisions for Catherine Cameron, wife of a Continental soldier, and her family. The husband had died. Pendleton's accounts had not been approved by the auditor.
25 Oct. 1779: To T.
29 Oct. 1779: T recommends £134 13s.
>House agrees.

3 Nov. 1779: Senate agrees.

**1075-P   Graham, William and How, John**
JHD: 25 Oct. 1779                                          Not known

## Virginia Legislative Petitions

Compensation for impressed ship that was sunk and damaged to prevent capture by enemy. Her cargo was lost.

Manuscript unsigned, but has account and several depositions attached.
25 Oct. 1779: To T.
11 Dec. 1779: Carried over to next session of GA.
23 June 1780: T recommends rejection.
> House rejects.

### 1076-P-† Loudoun County—Citizens
JHD: 25 Oct. 1779                                                                     Loudoun County

To amend act regarding escheats of British subjects.
25 Oct. 1779: To committee to amend act concerning escheats.
> For amendment to general act in various particulars, see 10H153.

### 1077-P   Fluvanna County—Citizens
JHD: 25 Oct. 1779                                                                     Fluvanna County

Opposing sale of Saint Anne's glebe for benefit of Fluvanna Parish (see 981-P), and asking that incumbent minister be allowed to remain on the glebe now in Saint Anne's Parish, in Albemarle County (see 1017-P).

Manuscript signed by: Wilson Miles Cary, Rene Woodson, Joseph Woolling, William Williams, Jr., Stephen Peay, and twenty-seven others.
25 Oct. 1779: To R.
14 Dec. 1779: R recommends rejection of rights of incumbent to remain.
> House rejects.

14 Dec. 1779: House carried over to next session of GA the request that Fluvanna County's portion of sale be deposited in treasury until needed.
> No further record found.
> For act concerning sale of glebe, see 10H112.

### 1078-P   Fairfax County—Citizens
JHD: 25 Oct. 1779                                                                       Fairfax County

For dissolution of Fairfax Parish vestry and election of new one.

Manuscript signed by: Wm. Layne, Richd. Sandford, Thomas Triplett, G. Chapman, John Hunter, and twenty others. Dated 15 October 1779.
25 Oct. 1779: To R.
8 Nov. 1779: R reports as reasonable.
> House lays on table.
> No further record found.

## 25 – 26 October 1779

**1079-P-†  Baptist Association**
      JHD: 25 Oct. 1779                                                   Not known
For legalizing marriages performed by dissenting ministers.
25 Oct. 1779: To R.
8 Nov. 1779: R reports as reasonable and is directed to prepare a bill.
        Apparently no further action was taken at this session.
        For act allowing dissenting ministers to perform legal marriages, see 10H361.

**1079.1-P  de Sequeyra, John**
      JHD: 26 Oct. 1779                                                 Williamsburg
Asking compensation for his services as surgeon in mental hospital.
Manuscript unsigned, but name spelled as above.
26 Oct. 1779: To T.
30 Oct. 1779: T recommends £250 for weekly visits to year ending 17 December 1779.
        House agrees.
3 Nov. 1779: Senate agrees.
        See 857-M.

**1080-P  Hurt, John**
      JHD: 26 Oct. 1779                                                 Not known
For land certificates, the same as those issued to commissioned officers, to be allowed to chaplains.
Manuscript unsigned.
26 Oct. 1779: To PG.
30 Oct. 1779: PG recommends as reasonable and is directed to prepare a bill.
        This was incorporated in a general bill, also including surgeons and surgeons' mates, that was passed by House and Senate.
        For general act see 10H141.

**1081-P  Dunn, Lewis**
      JHD: 26 Oct. 1779                                                 Sussex County
For an act emancipating a mulatto slave, freed by the will of Dunn's father, Thomas Dunn.
Manuscript unsigned.
26 Oct. 1779: To PG.
30 Oct. 1779: PG recommends as reasonable.
        House agrees.

Virginia Legislative Petitions

This was incorporated in a general bill emancipating several slaves, which was approved by House and Senate.
For general act see 10H211.

## 1082-P-† College of William and Mary—President and Professors
JHD: 26 Oct. 1779                      Williamsburg
For assistance from the state in supporting the college.
26 Oct. 1779: To PG.
2 Nov. 1779: PG discharged. To SC.
    Committee apparently did not report.

## 1083-P    Wilkinson, Cary
JHD: 26 Oct. 1779                      Surry County
                                               James City County
                                               York County
As agent for John Paradise and his wife, Lucy, asks that their property be exempted from the escheat laws for British sympathizers. He is a native of Greece, and she is a native of this country.
    Manuscript unsigned.
26 Oct. 1779: To committee to amend escheat laws.
    For amendment to general act in various particulars, see 10H153.

## 1084-P    Birchill, Robert and Williams, Lessenby
JHD: 27 Oct. 1779                      Prince George County
For relief from payment for tobacco stolen from Blandford warehouse in Prince George County where they were inspectors.
    Manuscript signed by: Robt. Gilliam, John Shelton, John King, George Elliott, Gresset Davis, and five others.
27 Oct. 1779: To T.
11 Nov. 1779: T recommends rejection.
    House rejects.

## 1085-P-† Hart, George
JHD: 27 Oct. 1779                      Washington County
Additional compensation for work as a surgeon at Fort Patrick Henry in 1777.
27 Oct. 1779: To T.
4 Nov. 1779: T recommends rejection.
    House rejects, but on second reading agrees to an unspecified sum.
    Senate record not found, JS.

## 26 – 29 October 1779

**1086-P-†  Martin, Thomas Bryan**
JHD: 27 Oct. 1779                                           Hampshire County
Asking that a grant of 10,000 acres of land by Lord Fairfax to his nephew, Philip Martin, of Great Britain, who will become a resident of this state, not be escheated as British property.
27 Oct. 1779: To committee on escheats of British property.
   For a general act concerning British escheats, see 10H153.

**1087-P**
Eck–Not
found  **Augusta County—Citizens**
JHD: 27 Oct. 1779                                              Augusta County
Asking for passage of bill establishing religious freedom.
Manuscript signed by: Alexr. Long, David Henderson, Geo. Gray, Francis Long, John Brooking, and fifty-six others.
27 Oct. 1779: To committee of whole on religion.
   Committee apparently did not report.

**1088-P  Riddell, Susanna**
JHD: 29 Oct. 1779                                                 York County
For emancipation, for meritorious service, of a man slave.
Manuscript unsigned.
29 Oct. 1779: To PG.
30 Oct. 1779: PG reports reasonable.
   House agrees.
   This was incorporated in a general act emancipating several slaves, passed by House and Senate.
   For general act see 10H211.

**1089-P  Smith, Thomas**
JHD: 29 Oct. 1779                                                    Not known
For relief from act concerning importation rights.
Manuscript unsigned.
29 Oct. 1779: To PG.
   Committee apparently did not report.

**1090-P-†  Wallis, Hugh**
JHD: 29 Oct. 1779                                                    Not known
Asking that he be allowed to draw from public store as additional compensation for wound.

29 Oct. 1779: To T.
4 Nov. 1779: T recommends that he be allowed to draw from public store at same rate as soldiers in active service.
   House agrees.
9 Nov. 1779: Senate amends.
10 Nov. 1779: House agrees to Senate amendments.
   See 581-P-† and 1188-P under Wallace.

### 1091-P-† Dickenson, William
JHD: 29 Oct. 1779                                   Not known
Asking additional compensation for wound.
29 Oct. 1779: To T.
4 Nov. 1779: T recommends £26 for his present relief.
   House agrees.
5 Nov. 1779: Senate agrees.
   See 592-P-†.

### 1092-M-† Virginia State Garrison—Officers
JHD: 30 Oct. 1779                                   Not known
Asking for same pay as Continental officers, which has been withheld by governor and Council.
30 Oct. 1779: To SC.
   Committee apparently did not report.

### 1093-P-† Alexandria—Trustees
JHD: 30 Oct. 1779, for action                       Fairfax County
Asking for an act confirming sales and leases of parcels of land and water adjoining town.
Date unknown: To PG.
30 Oct. 1779: PG reports reasonable and is directed to prepare a bill.
11 Nov. 1779: PG presents a bill confirming sales and leases and enlarging town.
15 Nov. 1779: Recommitted to PG.
   PG presents an amended bill.
   House passes bill.
16 Nov. 1779: Senate passes amended bill.
   See 847-P and 848-P.
   For this act see 10H192.

## 29 October – 1 November 1779

**1094-P    Tobacco Owners—Wicomico Warehouse**
  JHD: 30 Oct. 1779                                    Northumberland County
  Asking that they be repaid for their tobacco, which was burned by the British on 14 June 1779.
  Manuscript unsigned.
  30 Oct. 1779: To PG.
  4 Nov. 1779: PG recommends rejection.
     House refers matter to committee on reviving warehouses.
     For act making public not liable for tobacco burned by enemy, see 10H275.

**1095-P    Anderson, John and Anderson, Mede**
  JHD: 30 Oct. 1779                                                Not known
  Asking to mine lead on a tract of unappropriated land belonging to the state, and that taxes paid thereon be paid by transferring to the state one-twentieth part of neat lead produced.
  Manuscript unsigned.
  30 Oct. 1779: To PG.
  4 Nov. 1779: PG finds reasonable and recommends that taxes be on land only.
     House agrees and directs PG to prepare a bill.
  5 Nov. 1779: Bill presented.
  8 Nov. 1779: Bill recommitted to PG.
  12 Nov. 1779: Bill amended.
  13 Nov. 1779: House passes bill.
  19 Nov. 1779: Senate amends bill.
  22 Nov. 1779: Senate recedes from amendments and passes bill.
     For this act, stipulating that one-fortieth part of lead be returned to state, see 10H193.

**1096-P    Godwin, Christopher**
  JHD: 1 Nov. 1779                                         Nansemond County
  To gain control over property fraudulently obtained from him by John Hamilton, who, as a British sympathizer, had fled the country, and his property has been escheated.
  Manuscript unsigned, but has attached the indenture or lease from Godwin to Hamilton.
  1 Nov. 1779: To PG.
  16 Nov. 1779: PG finds reasonable and is directed to prepare a bill.
  20 Nov. 1779: PG presents bill.
  25 Nov. 1779: House amends and passes bill.

30 Nov. 1779: Senate amends bill.
1 Dec. 1779: House rejects amendments, but Senate insists, and House finally agrees.
   For this act see 10H207.

### 1097-P  Edwards, Andrew
   JHD: 1 Nov. 1779                                       Stafford County
   To discontinue inspection of tobacco at Cave's warehouse.
   Manuscript unsigned.
1 Nov. 1779: To PG.
4 Nov. 1779: PG reports reasonable.
   Referred to special committee on warehouses.
   Not included in 1780 law.

### 1098-P
Eck–Not
found  **Amherst County—Citizens**
   JHD: 1 Nov. 1779                                       Amherst County
   Endorsing bill for religious freedom.
   Manuscript signed by: Henry Martin, Thos. Montgomery, John Murrill, Jr., John Murrill, John Hendricks, and fifty others.
1 Nov. 1779: To R.
   Committee apparently did not report.

### 1098 A-P
Eck–Not
found  **Amherst County—Citizens**
   JHD: 1 Nov. 1779                                       Amherst County
   Text is identical with 1098-P, which see.
   Manuscript signed by 106 persons.

### 1099-P  Hanover Parish, King George County—Vestry
   JHD: 1 Nov. 1779                                   King George County
   Asking permission to sell glebe.
   Manuscript signed by: Peter Jett, U. Boon, Geo. Marshall, John Lovell, Jeremiah Kirk, and four others.
1 Nov. 1779: To R.
14 Dec. 1779: Carried over to next session of GA.
   No further record found.

## 1 – 3 November 1779

**1100-P-†  Smith, William and Bressie, Henry**
    JHD: 1 Nov. 1779                        Not known
Compensation for blankets set aside in 1775 for use of state troops and plundered by British troops under Lord Dunmore.
1 Nov. 1779: To T.
4 Nov. 1779: T recommends £130 7s. 7d. in current Virginia money.
    House agrees.
10 Nov. 1779: Senate rejects.

**1101-P-†  Trent, Thomas**
    JHD: 2 Nov. 1779                        Not known
Additional compensation for loss of both arms in battle of Monmouth.
2 Nov. 1779: To T.
4 Nov. 1779: T recommends £50 in addition to pay as soldier.
    House agrees.
9 Nov. 1779: Senate agrees.

**1102-P  Henry County—Citizens**
    JHD: 2 Nov. 1779                        Henry County
For a division of the county.
Manuscript signed by: Lewis Jinkins, Robert Bolton, Wm. Law, Fred K. Rives, Burrell Rives, and 248 others. Contains a map of the proposed division.
2 Nov. 1779: To PG.
    Committee apparently did not report, but manuscript endorsement says "reasonable."
    No further record found.

**1103-P  Galt, John Minson and Prentis, Robert**
    JHD: 2 Nov. 1779                        Not known
As executors of the estate of Richard Charlton, ask that his property be divided among his children as he wished despite the fact his will left it to his heir-at-law.
Manuscript unsigned, but carries reference to John Barr.
2 Nov. 1779: House rejects by refusal to refer to a committee.
    See 385-P.

**1104-P  Littleton Parish, Cumberland County—Citizens**
    JHD: 3 Nov. 1779                        Cumberland County
Protesting the possible removal of Reverend Christopher MacRae, and asking that triple tax on those not taking loyalty oath be amended.

## Virginia Legislative Petitions

Manuscript signed by: Joseph Calland, Robt. Anderson, Jr., Permens. Coleman, Hesekiah Colquet, Edward Clemmons, and 166 others.
3 Nov. 1779: House lays on table.
No further record found.

### 1104 A-P  Littleton Parish, Cumberland County—Citizens
JHD: 3 Nov. 1779                                                       Cumberland County
Text is identical with 1104-P, which see.
Manuscript signed by 134 persons.

### 1105-P   Pickett, Martin
JHD: 3 Nov. 1779                                                                  Not known
Repayment of debt of John Goodrich, Sr., for hogshead of molasses sold to him, but debt not settled.
Manuscript not signed, but has statement of account of 30 July 1775, and receipt of Goodrich dated 5 August 1775 for the hogshead.
3 Nov. 1779: To T.
4 Nov. 1779: T recommends £473 17s. payment from escheated estate of
    Goodrich.
    House agrees.
9 Nov. 1779: Senate agrees under name of Martha Pickett.

### 1106-P-†  Charlotte County—Justices
JHD: 3 Nov. 1779                                                         Charlotte County
For payments of excess amounts to widows of soldiers, these amounts exceeding a recent law.
3 Nov. 1779: To T.
4 Nov. 1779: T recommends £162 10s. to be paid to claimants as follows: £63
    to James Abernathy, £47 to Edward Moseley, £52 10s. to John
    White, for provisions for support of Elizabeth Nichols, Elizabeth
    Whitlow, and Anne Heaton, whose husbands had died in the
    service.
    House agrees.
5 Nov. 1779: Senate agrees.
    For general act on this subject see 10H212.

### 1107-P   Holland, George
JHD: 3 Nov. 1779                                                                  Not known

## 3 November 1779

Compensation for surgeon's fees in treating Elizabeth Fisher, wife of a Continental soldier.
Manuscript unsigned.
3 Nov. 1779: To T.
11 Nov. 1779: T recommends rejection.
    House rejects.

### 1108-P    Lunenburg County—Citizens
    JHD: 3 Nov. 1779        Lunenburg County

Asking that if a bill for religious freedom is passed, an assessment be allowed to support reformed protestant religions.
Manuscript signed by: Wm. Taylor, Edward Broadnax, Benja. Tomlinson, John Manley, Richd Hight, and ninety-four others.
3 Nov. 1779: To committee of whole on religion.
    Committee apparently did not report.

### 1109-P    Ross, David
    JHD: 3 Nov. 1779        Not known

Expressing surprise that the governor and Council are considering rejecting his status as a citizen of Virginia.
Manuscript unsigned.
3 Nov. 1779: To PG.
10 Nov. 1779: PG recommends that all doubts concerning him as a citizen of Virginia be rejected.
    House agrees.
12 Nov. 1779: Senate agrees.

### 1110-P    West, Edward
    JHD: 3 Nov. 1779        Stafford County

For the establishment of a ferry across the Rappahannock River from his land in Stafford County to the land of Simon Miller in Culpeper County.
Manuscript unsigned.
3 Nov. 1779: To PG.
6 Nov. 1779: PG recommends as reasonable.
    This matter was incorporated in a general ferry bill passed by the House and Senate.
    For general ferry act see 10H196.

### 1111-P    Spotsylvania County—Citizens
    JHD: 3 Nov. 1779        Spotsylvania County

## Virginia Legislative Petitions

Protests removal of courthouse and asks for a division of the county.
Manuscript signed by: James Somerville, William Wiatt, Jno. Miller, Will. Craighill, Sr., S. Waddy, Jr., and 157 others.
3 Nov. 1779: To PG.
16 Nov. 1779: PG recommends rejection.
    House recommits to PG.
19 Nov. 1779: PG recommends rejection of division of Saint George and Norborne parishes to form new counties.
    House rejects.
    See 1130-P-† and 9H558.

**1112-P    Bowie, Sarah**
    JHD: 4 Nov. 1779                         Caroline County

States that ferriage rates set by county court are low, and asking that the act establishing the ferry be amended to allow her to charge for foot passengers. This ferry runs across Rappahannock River from Caroline County to King George County, and was formerly the property of James Bowie, deceased.
    Manuscript unsigned.
4 Nov. 1779: To PG.
9 Nov. 1779: PG reports as reasonable.
    Recommitted to PG in connection with bill for ferry across Kentucky River.
    A general ferry bill, including an amendment for foot passengers, was passed by House and Senate.
    For general ferry act see 10H196.

**1113-P    Virginia Continental Army—Officers**
    JHD: 4 Nov. 1779                              Not known

Asking for tax relief for their lands, which are unprofitable in their absence, and exemptions from military duty for their managers and overseers.
    Manuscript signed by: Dudley M. Woodford, P. Muhlenberg, James Wood, Wm. Russell, Nathal. Gist, and 122 others.
4 Nov. 1779: To PG.
22 Nov. 1779: PG recommends rejection.
    House rejects.

**1114-P    Petersburg, Blandford, and Pocahontas—Citizens**
    JHD: 4 Nov. 1779                       Dinwiddie County
                                                   Chesterfield County
Asking that these towns be consolidated and incorporated into one

## 4 November 1779

borough, with adjacent lands, and that the corporation be allowed to send a delegate to the General Assembly.
    Manuscript signed by: Robert Bolling, Jr., David Black, Will. Hill, Richd. Bate, Thos. Armistead, and 150 others. Manuscript dated 11 October 1779.
4 Nov. 1779: To PG.
6 Nov. 1779: PG recommends incorporation as reasonable, but that provision for delegate be rejected.
        House amends and agrees. Bill to be prepared.
        This bill was apparently not submitted.
        A similar petition was presented in June 1782, but incorporation did not become effective until 1784. See 11H382 and 1701-P.

**1115-P**    **Rockbridge County—Citizens**
        JHD: 4 Nov. 1779        Rockbridge County
    For repeal of tax on enumerated commodities.
    Manuscript signed by: Williamson Moore, George Weir, Alexander Moore, James Eken, George Campbell, and thirty-two others. Manuscript dated 11 October 1779.
4 Nov. 1779: To PG.
9 Nov. 1779: PG recommends rejection.
        House rejects.

**1116-P-†**  **Barksdale, Peter**
        JHD: 4 Nov. 1779        Not known
    Compensation for expenses for illness contracted on military duty.
4 Nov. 1779: To T.
11 Nov. 1779: T recommends £90.
        House agrees.
15 Nov. 1779: Senate agrees.

**1117-P-†**  **Dabney, James**
        JHD: 4 Nov. 1779        Not known
    Reimbursement for excess expenditures in furnishing necessaries for wife and children of James Boyd who had been drafted into service.
4 Nov. 1779: To T.
19 Nov. 1779: T recommends rejection.
        House rejects.

**1118-P**    **Ashlock, John**
        JHD: 4 Nov. 1779        Halifax County

## Virginia Legislative Petitions

Compensation for surgeon's fees for himself, he being old and infirm, and one son having been killed in service, and another still in service.
Manuscript unsigned. Dated 15 October 1779.
4 Nov. 1779: To T.
11 Nov. 1779: T recommends rejection.
   House rejects.

**1119-P   Will (Slave)**
JHD: 4 Nov. 1779                                    King William County
Asking for emancipation under the will of Mrs. Anne Colvin, deceased.
Manuscript unsigned.
4 Nov. 1779: To lie on table.
   House directs this be added to bill emancipating several slaves. This apparently was not done because his name does not appear in the act. See 10H211 and 1384-P.

**1120-P-†   Elizabeth City County and Warwick County—Citizens**
JHD: 6 Nov. 1779                                    Elizabeth City County
                                                    Warwick County
Compensation for damage done from overflow of milldam on the property of the heir of Booth Armistead, deceased.
6 Nov. 1779: House carries over to next session of GA.
9 Nov. 1779: A petition asking for action on this petition in the present session was presented on 9 November 1779 (1131-P).
   No further record found.

**1121-P   Riddell, James**
JHD: 6 Nov. 1779                                    Goochland County
Claims he entered into an agreement with Samuel Martin to oversee his estate in Virginia, but the property has been escheated since Martin was a British sympathizer. Asks remedy for breach of contract.
Manuscript unsigned.
6 Nov. 1779: To T.
18 Nov. 1779: T, after considerable inquiry, determines that Riddell had been paid in full by Richard Squire Taylor, attorney in fact for Martin. Recommends rejection.
   House rejects.

**1122-P   Quarles, John**
JHD: 6 Nov. 1779                                    King William County

## 4 – 6 November 1779

For payments of excess amounts to widows and children of Continental soldiers, these amounts exceeding a recent law.

Manuscript unsigned, but has attached a list of payments.

6 Nov. 1779: To T.

11 Dec. 1779: T recommends £230, being balance after auditors had deducted £12 each for Betty Edwards, Frances Crittendon, Molly Gaby, Nancy Cook, Sukey Langston, Sukey Frales, Sarah Mush, Lucy Skipper, Nancy Sampson, Sarah Howard, Nanny Major, and Sarah Major.

House agrees.

14 Dec. 1779: Senate agrees.

For general act on overpayment to widows and children, see 10H212.

### 1123-P-† Coles, John
JHD: 6 Nov. 1779             Albemarle County

For payments of excess amounts to widows and children of Continental soldiers, these amounts exceeding a recent law.

6 Nov. 1779: To T.

11 Nov. 1779: T recommends £157 above £12 allowed Mary Simmons.

House agrees.

15 Nov. 1779: Senate agrees.

For general act on overpayment to widows and children, see 10H212.

### 1124-P Wylly, Alexander
JHD: 6 Nov. 1779             Williamsburg

Asks for reappointment as keeper of Capitol building and salary for past year.

Manuscript unsigned, but has attached a statement by Alexander Blair that Wylly was appointed by governor and Council to keep Capitol in order.

6 Nov. 1779: To T.

11 Dec. 1779: T recommends reappointment and salary of £30 a year.

House agrees.

14 Dec. 1779: Senate agrees.

### 1125-P-† Lapsley, John
JHD: 6 Nov. 1779             Not known

Compensation for military wound received in 1777, and six months bounty.

## Virginia Legislative Petitions

6 Nov. 1779: To T.
11 Nov. 1779: T recommends rejection of bounty, but recommends half pay as lieutenant for life.
House rejects bounty.
House agrees to half pay.
12 Nov. 1779: Senate agrees to half pay.

**1126-P-†  Virginia Commissioners to Settle Claims for Unpatented Lands in Yohogania, Monongalia, and Ohio Counties**
JHD: 8 Nov. 1779                      Yohogania County
                                      Monongalia County
                                      Ohio County

Asking for an explanation of how they are to proceed under an act for adjusting and settling the titles of claimers to unpatented lands.
8 Nov. 1779: To SC.
No further action found.
See 10H35.

**1127-P**
Eck–Not
found  **Bedford County—Citizens**
JHD: 8 Nov. 1779                      Bedford County

Relief for refusal to take oath on value of property assessments because of religious scruples. Are willing to affirm.

Manuscript signed by: William Curniat, David Curniat, James Curniat, Jr., Reuben Curniat, John Bastian, and fourteen others. Affidavits of their character are attached.
8 Nov. 1779: To T.
9 Nov. 1779: T recommends that relief from fine of £100 be rejected.
House rejects.

**1128-P  Virginia Directors of Public Buildings—Richmond**
JHD: 8 Nov. 1779                      Henrico County

Asks that a committee of General Assembly be appointed to aid them in relocating Capitol and other state buildings in Richmond.

Manuscript signed by: Archibald Cary, Turner Southall, Robert Goode, and James Buchanan. Manuscript dated 3 November 1779.
8 Nov. 1779: House lays on table.
No further action found.

## 8 – 9 November 1779

**1129-M  Ballendine, John and Reveley, John**
  JHD: 9 Nov. 1779  Henrico County
  Buckingham County

Asking for an inquiry into their claims, legal and equitable, for their interest in land and improvements in Buckingham County and Westham.

Manuscript unsigned, but has attached a statement from Turner Southall as to completion of dam and lock at Westham. Apparently this was considered along with a letter from the governor.

9 Nov. 1779: To PG

18 Nov. 1779: PG says (1) they cannot adjudicate matters of law, (2) that governor and Council follow resolution of 25 June 1779, (3) recommends that commissioners proceed to settle accounts and report back to GA, and (4) that commissioners settle balances in regard to pig iron contract.
  House agrees to (3) and (4).

26 Nov. 1779: Senate agrees to (3) and (4).
  See 1174-R-†.

**1130-P-†  Spotsylvania County—Citizens**
  JHD: 9 Nov. 1779  Spotsylvania County

Opposing a division of the county and removal of courthouse and asking that act be repealed.

9 Nov. 1779: To PG.

16 Nov. 1779: PG reports as reasonable.
  Recommitted to PG.

19 Nov. 1779: PG again reports as reasonable.
  House agrees.
  See 1111-P and 9H558.

**1131-P  Curle, William Roscow Wilson**
  JHD: 9 Nov. 1779  Elizabeth City County

To require present General Assembly to take up petition of Elizabeth City County citizens for damage done by flooding of milldam (1120-P-†).

Manuscript unsigned, but has attached appeal of Curle to court and a certificate of Warwick County court dated 29 April 1779.

9 Nov. 1779: To PG.

12 Nov. 1779: PG recommends rejection.
  House rejects.

Virginia Legislative Petitions

**1132-P Henry, William; Burton, Jesse; Thompson, Roger; and Cobbs, John**
JHD: 9 Nov. 1779      Fluvanna County
As justices and clerk for Fluvanna County court they were accused by Fluvanna citizens of bribery and corruption in their election in October 1777, and having been found innocent by the General Court they seek reimbursement of costs.
Manuscript unsigned, but has minutes of General Court showing expenses of £185 10s.
9 Nov. 1779: To PG.
    PG finds reasonable. Recommends £62 8s., equally divided, for clerk's, sheriff's, and witnesses' fees; also £175 10s. for lawyer's fees; also £188 10s. for travel expenses.
    House agrees.
25 Nov. 1779: Senate agrees.
    See 405-P and M-†, and 623-P.

**1133-P-† James City County—Citizens**
JHD: 9 Nov. 1779      James City County
To have ferry across James River at Jamestown moved to land of Mrs. Ambler.
9 Nov. 1779: To PG.
23 Nov. 1779: PG reports as reasonable.
    House refers it to committee of PG to draw bill for ferry across Kentucky River.
    Apparently not included in general ferry act.

**1134-P**
Eck–
A1669 **Bedford County—Citizens**
JHD: 9 Nov. 1779      Bedford County
To form a new county from parts of Bedford and Henry counties.
Manuscript signed by: Thomas Arthur, Thos. Doggett, William Walton, William Wright, John Underwood, and ninety-five others.
9 Nov. 1779: To PG.
19 Nov. 1779: PG reports as reasonable.
    House rejects on second reading.

**1135-P Rockingham County—Citizens**
JHD: 9 Nov. 1779      Rockingham County

## 9 November 1779

To repeal tax on certain enumerated commodities.
Manuscript signed by: Leonard Herring, Joseph Rutherford, Joseph Dietom, Richard Ragan, Petr. Hog, and 128 others.
9 Nov. 1779: To PG.
18 Nov. 1779: PG recommends rejection.
>House rejects.

### 1136-P-† Bedford County—Citizens
>JHD: 9 Nov. 1779 Bedford County

For a division of the county into two distinct counties.
9 Nov. 1779: To PG.
12 Nov. 1779: Carried over to next session of GA.
6 Dec. 1780: PG reports as reasonable and is directed to prepare a bill.
9 Dec. 1780: Bill presented.
12 Dec. 1780: Bill passed and sent to Senate.
>Senate apparently did not act.
>Bedford County was not divided until 1781 (10H447).

### 1137-P-† Bland, William
>JHD: 9 Nov. 1779 Williamsburg

For additional salary as ordinary of Newgate.
9 Nov. 1779: To T.
13 Nov. 1779: T recommends £200 for year ending 1 October 1779.
>House agrees.

17 Nov. 1779: Senate agrees.
>See 777-P.

### 1138-P-† Johnson, Benjamin
>JHD: 9 Nov. 1779 King George County

For payment of excess amounts to widows and children of Continental soldiers, these amounts exceeding a recent law.
9 Nov. 1779: To T.
13 Nov. 1779: T recommends £11 16s. 8d., after deducting £12 10s. for provisions furnished Sarah Berryman, widow of Benjamin Berryman.
>House agrees.

17 Nov. 1779: Senate agrees.
>For general act on overpayment to widows and children, see 10H212.

## Virginia Legislative Petitions

**1139-P-† Boyd, George**
JHD: 10 Nov. 1779                                      Not known
For surgeon's fees for attending ten sick state soldiers.
10 Nov. 1779: To T.
16 Nov. 1779: T recommends £265 2s.
       House agrees.
19 Nov. 1779: Senate agrees.

**1140-P**
Eck–
A841    **Gilbert, George**
JHD: 10 Nov. 1779                               Amherst County
For additional compensation, by special levy, for building a prison in Amherst County, he and his apprentices having gone into military service in 1774, and prices having greatly increased.
    Manuscript signed by: John Bias, Obed. Bias, Wm. Stewart, James Stewart, Foray Slater, and eighty-two others.
10 Nov. 1779: To T.
19 Nov. 1779: T recommends rejection.
       House rejects.

**1141-P**   **Jeffreys, Barnett**
JHD: 10 Nov. 1779                                 Norfolk County
Compensation for his horse that died while he was in military service in May 1779.
    Manuscript attested by Richard Booker.
10 Nov. 1779: To T.
11 Dec. 1779: T recommends rejection.
       House rejects.

**1142-P-† Davis, Nicholas**
JHD: 10 Nov. 1779                                      Not known
Asking assistance in establishing, for charitable purposes, a free school, hospital, and church on Mount Bethel.
10 Nov. 1779: To T.
19 Nov. 1779: T recommends (1) rejection of proposal to free Davis from taxes, and (2) rejection of proposal to divide property between his heirs and charity.
       House rejects (1) and (2).

## 10 November 1779

T also recommends approval of proposal to raise funds by lottery.
House amends proposal and agrees.
No Senate action found.

**1143-P  Bellini, Charles**
   JHD: 10 Nov. 1779                                    Williamsburg
Additional salary as clerk of foreign correspondence.
Manuscript unsigned.
10 Nov. 1779: To T.
19 Nov. 1779: T recommends £600 a year for the future.
   House agrees.
26 Nov. 1779: Senate agrees.

**1144-P  Chew, Larkin**
   JHD: 10 Nov. 1779                                Spotsylvania County
Additional compensation above £40 a year allowed him for wound received on frontier.
Manuscript unsigned.
10 Nov. 1779: To T.
13 Nov. 1779: T recommends £100 for current relief.
   House agrees.
17 Nov. 1779: Senate agrees.

**1145-P  Carter, Theodorick; Guthrey, Alexander; Hendrick, William; and Fendley, David**
   JHD: 10 Nov. 1779                                Cumberland County
Additional compensation for aiding sheriff in transporting a criminal to public jail.
Manuscript unsigned.
10 Nov. 1779: To T.
19 Nov. 1779: T recommends rejection.
   House rejects.

**1146-P  Mahon, John**
   JHD: 10 Nov. 1779                                       Not known
Compensation for illness (rheumatism) contracted while in military service.
Manuscript unsigned.
10 Nov. 1779: To T.

## Virginia Legislative Petitions

19 Nov. 1779: T recommends rejection.
    Recommitted to T.
    Apparently no further action taken.

**1147-P-†  Witt, Jesse**
    JHD: 10 Nov. 1779        Bedford County
Compensation for illness (paralysis) contracted while in military service.
10 Nov. 1779: To T.
16 Nov. 1779: T recommends £50 for present relief.
    House agrees.
19 Nov. 1779: Senate agrees.

**1148-P**
Eck–
A840    **Amherst County—Citizens**
    JHD: 10 Nov. 1779        Amherst County
Opposing division of Amherst and Lexington parishes, and asking for commissioners to determine the number of tithables in each.
    Manuscript signed by: David Shepherd, Benj. Rucker, Richard Gatewood, John Bigge, Ambrose Rucker, and thirty-seven others.
10 Nov. 1779: To PG.
14 Dec. 1779: PG recommends as reasonable and is directed to prepare a bill.
18 Dec. 1779: Bill presented but House rejects on second reading.

**1149-P    Hanover County and Henrico County—Citizens**
    JHD: 10 Nov. 1779        Hanover County
                                            Henrico County
To establish more clearly the line between the two counties along the Chickahominy River, which overflows.
    Manuscript signed by: Richard Anderson, Peter Winston, Elisha Owen, Josiah Parsons, John Smith, and twenty-three others.
10 Nov. 1779: To PG.
23 Nov. 1779: PG recommends that appointment of commissioners to run the line be rejected.
    House rejects.
    See 1164-P-†.

**1150-P    M'Harg, Ebenezer**
    JHD: 10 Nov. 1779        Mecklenburg County

## 10 November 1779

For confirmation of citizenship, he having been accused of being a British sympathizer.

Manuscript unsigned, but has report of committee attached.

10 Nov. 1779: To PG.

15 Nov. 1779: PG recommends that he should be considered a citizen.

    House agrees.

17 Nov. 1779: Senate agrees.

**1151-P    Fisher, John**
    JHD: 10 Nov. 1779                        Halifax County

For confirmation of citizenship, he having been accused of being a British sympathizer.

Manuscript unsigned.

10 Nov. 1779: To PG.

15 Nov. 1779: PG recommends he be continued as a citizen after taking loyalty oath.

    House agrees.

17 Nov. 1779: Senate agrees.

**1152-P    Gratz, Bernard; Simmons, Joseph; Mills, Edmund; and Gratz, Michael**
    JHD: 10 Nov. 1779                        Western Lands

For confirmation to claims for land purchased from George Croghan, who had purchased it from the Indians.

Manuscript unsigned.

10 Nov. 1779: To PG.

25 Nov. 1779: PG recommends rejection since the matter should be determined in court of law.

    House rejects.

**1153-P    Raine, John**
    JHD: 10 Nov. 1779                        Cumberland County

Additional compensation, as sheriff, for conveying a criminal to public jail.

Manuscript unsigned.

10 Nov. 1779: To special committee to regulate fees.

    Apparently no action taken.

**1154-P-†  May, John**
    JHD: 10 Nov. 1779                        Williamsburg

Asking for a law to provide for a salary as clerk of General Court since fees are insufficient.

10 Nov. 1779: To special committee to regulate fees.
10 Dec. 1779: Committee recommends salary be that of predecessor and that paper be furnished.
      House agrees. Also increases fees for certificates and escheats.
14 Dec. 1779: Senate agrees.

**1155-P**
Eck–Not
found   **Amherst County—Citizens**
    JHD: 10 Nov. 1779                           Amherst County
To have a general assessment for all protestant religions, and to debar Roman Catholics, Jews, Turks, and infidels from public office.
    Manuscript signed by: Robert Wright, William Alford, John Alford, Joseph Hollings North, Thomas Beard, and 119 others.
10 Nov. 1779: To SC.
    Apparently no action taken.

**1156-P-†** **Amherst County—Citizens**
    JHD: 10 Nov. 1779                           Amherst County
For relief from raising the required quota of men for Continental service.
10 Nov. 1779: To SC.
    Apparently no action taken.

**1157-P**   **Tobacco Inspectors—Rocky Ridge Warehouse and Cary's Warehouse**
    JHD: 10 Nov. 1779                         Chesterfield County
Relief from law for discontinuing salaries and substituting a tax on tobacco.
Manuscript unsigned, but has a note by James Baker.
10 Nov. 1779: To committee of PG on reviving warehouses.
    Apparently no action taken.
    Salaries of inspectors were revised in 1780 (10H355).

**1158-P**   **Meriwether, Francis**
    JHD: 10 Nov. 1779                         Spotsylvania County
To secure title to land purchased from Cochran, Cunningham, and Company, of Glasgow, in 1773.
    Manuscript unsigned.

## 10 – 22 November 1779

10 Nov. 1779: Rejected by refusal to refer to a committee.
    See 547-P.

**1159-P    Campbell, Gilbert**
    JHD: 10 Nov. 1779                          Westmoreland County
  For payment of balance of his salary, £62 4s. 5d., due him as customs officer of Great Britain for the Port of South Potomac, up to the time of independence.
  Manuscript unsigned, but account and certificates attached.
10 Nov. 1779: Rejected by refusal to refer to a committee.

**1160-M    Mental Hospital—Directors**
    JHD: 16 Nov. 1779                                Williamsburg
  For additional financial support for the hospital, necessary because of depreciation of currency.
  Manuscript unsigned.
16 Nov. 1779: To PG for consideration in connection with bill reviving
              hospital.
23 Nov. 1779: House passes bill.
26 Nov. 1779: Senate passes bill.
              For this act, including extra allowances, see 10H204.

**1161-P-†  Dick, Alexander**
    JHD: 22 Nov. 1779, for action                  Not known
  For expenses incurred as a prisoner in Great Britain, and for voyage home.
Date unknown: To PG.
22 Nov. 1779: PG recommends £2,730, exclusive of pay.
              House agrees.
24 Nov. 1779: Senate agrees.
              See manuscript letter from Dick to Speaker of the House in petition file, 18 December 1780.

**1162-P-†  Ballendine, John**
    JHD: 22 Nov. 1779                                 Henrico County
  Asking that proposals be considered for continuing his canal from Westham to Richmond.
22 Nov. 1779: To PG.
25 Nov. 1779: PG recommends it be carried over to the next session of GA.
              House agrees.
              No further action found.

## Virginia Legislative Petitions

### 1163-M   Botetourt County—Citizens
JHD: 22 Nov. 1779                                      Botetourt County
Asking for amendment to act establishing land office; they find the act to be oppressive.
Manuscript signed by: William Ward, Samuel Walker, Jr., James Hearn, William McEckean, Andrew Woods, and ninety-seven others.
22 Nov. 1779: To PG.
24 Nov. 1779: PG recommends rejection.
   House rejects.

### 1164-P-† Hanover County and Henrico County—Citizens
JHD: 23 Nov. 1779, for action                          Hanover County
                                                       Henrico County
Opposing the establishment of a new boundary between the counties.
Date unknown: To PG.
23 Nov. 1779: PG recommends as reasonable.
   No action required.
   See 1149-P.

### 1165-M   Pelham, Peter
JHD: 23 Nov. 1779                                      Williamsburg
For adjustment of compensation for keeping public jail.
Manuscript unsigned.
23 Nov. 1779: Rejected by refusal to refer to a committee.

### 1166-M-† Harrison, Charles
JHD: 24 Nov. 1779                                      Not known
For bounty and other advantages for members of the artillery forces because they are not included in provisions for state forces.
24 Nov. 1779: To SC.
   For act concerning bounty land see 10H159.

### 1167-P-† Kentucky County—Citizens
JHD: 24 Nov. 1779, for action                          Kentucky County
Asking for extension of time in making payment for lands under preemption warrants.
Date unknown: To PG.
24 Nov. 1779: PG recommends that time be extended.
   House refers to committee on lands.
   For act extending time see 10H177.

## 22 November – 1 December 1779

### 1168-C-† Pollard, William
JHD: 1 Dec. 1779, for action          Amherst County
Asks £11 for boarding widow and children of Reuben Nevil. This amount is apparently for excess payment not allowable under a recent law.
Date unknown: To T.
1 Dec. 1779: T recommends approval.
   House agrees.
2 Dec. 1779: Senate agrees, JS.
   For general act on overpayment to widows and children, see 10H212.

### 1169-C-† Rose, Hugh
JHD: 1 Dec. 1779, for action          Amherst County
Asks £30 10s. for provisions to Mary Burnett, widow of John Burnett. This amount is apparently for excess payment not allowable under a recent law.
Date unknown: To T.
1 Dec. 1779: T recommends approval.
   House agrees.
2 Dec. 1779: Senate agrees, JS.
   For general act on overpayment to widows and children, see 10H212.

### 1170-C-† Layne, John
JHD: 1 Dec. 1779, for action          Amherst County
Asks £55 for provisions furnished Mary Burnett under direction of Hugh Rose. This amount is apparently for excess payment not allowable under a recent law.
Date unknown: To T.
1 Dec. 1779: T recommends approval.
   House agrees.
2 Dec. 1779: Senate agrees, JS.
   For general act on overpayment to widows and children, see 10H212.

### 1171-C-† Thomas, James
JHD: 1 Dec. 1779, for action          Culpeper County
Asks £44 for provisions furnished Elizabeth Maddox, a widow of a soldier. This amount is apparently for excess payment not allowable under a recent law.
Date unknown: To T.

## Virginia Legislative Petitions

1 Dec. 1779: T recommends approval.
    House agrees.
2 Dec. 1779: Senate agrees, JS.
    For general act on overpayment to widows and children, see 10H212.

### 1172-C-† Brown, Hezekiah
JHD: 1 Dec. 1779, for action             Culpeper County

Asks £117 10s. for provisions furnished Catherine Garriott, a widow of a soldier. This amount is apparently for excess payment not allowable under a recent law.

Date unknown: To T.
1 Dec. 1779: T recommends approval.
    House agrees.
2 Dec. 1779: Senate agrees, JS.
    For general act on overpayment to widows and children, see 10H212.

### 1173-C-† Brown, William
JHD: 1 Dec. 1779, for action             Culpeper County

Asks £73 1s. 4d. for provisions furnished widow of Burrass Moore, who died in Continental service. This amount is apparently for excess payment not allowable under a recent law.

Date unknown: To T.
1 Dec. 1779: T recommends approval.
    House agrees.
2 Dec. 1779: Senate agrees, JS.
    For general act on overpayment to widows and children, see 10H212.

### 1174-R-† Virginia—Board of War
JHD: 3 Dec. 1779, for action             Not known

Recommending (1) that foundry at Westham be continued, and (2) that David Ross be contracted with for 250 tons of pig iron.

Date unknown: To PG.
3 Dec. 1779: PG recommends that Westham foundry be continued and that the contract with David Ross for 250 tons of pig iron be carried out by the executive.
    House agrees.
6 Dec. 1779: Senate agrees.

## 1 – 14 December 1779

8 Dec. 1779: PG further recommends (1) that the executive be empowered to contract for clothing and necessaries for workmen and slaves at Westham foundry, (2) that expenses and clothing for past year be charged to public, (3) that John Reveley be paid £1,200 for management of foundry and that he be continued as manager for next year, and (4) that justices of Henrico County appoint viewers for opening road from foundry to Belvidera gate.

11 Dec. 1779: Senate agrees.

PG further resolves that commissioners be appointed to settle accounts of Richard Adams, Turner Southall, and Nathaniel Wilkinson, former trustees of Westham foundry.

House agrees.

Senate agrees.

See 1129-M.

### 1175-P-† Taylor, Richard

JHD: 6 Dec. 1779                                                  Not known

Compensation for surgeon's fees for wound he received while an officer in the navy.

6 Dec. 1779: To T.

11 Dec. 1779: T recommends £992 3s. for Dr. Wellford's services, and £122 for Dr. Tennent's services, and for such other services as are necessary to save his life.

House agrees.

14 Dec. 1779: Senate agrees.

### 1176-C-† Bibb, William

JHD: 14 Dec. 1779                               Prince Edward County

For settlement of his claim for pay as a member of the House because dispute had arisen over pay he received for ten days during which he did not attend the session.

14 Dec. 1779: To PE.

22 Dec. 1779: PE recommends the pay for those ten days be returned to the state.

Carried over to next session of GA so that Bibb could then offer his defense. Mr. [Thomas] Flournoy (the other member of the House of Delegates from Prince Edward County) agreed to repay the money.

Mr. Bibb served in 1780, but no further record found.

## Virginia Legislative Petitions

### 1177-M   Webb, George
JHD: 16 Dec. 1779                                      Williamsburg
Asking, as treasurer of the state, for an increase in salary.
Manuscript unsigned, but has attached a long statement concerning increase of business in his office.
16 Dec. 1779: To PG.
18 Dec. 1779: PG recommends (1) that increase of his percentage for business of land office and sale of British property is reasonable, and (2) that increase in salary be rejected.
   House recommits to PG.
21 Dec. 1779: PG again recommends increases for his percentage and pay for more than three clerks.
   House agrees to percentage and is directed to prepare a bill.
23 Dec. 1779: House and Senate pass bill.
   For this act and other salaries see 10H219.

### 1178-M   Virginia Auditors of Public Accounts
JHD: 17 Dec. 1779                                      Williamsburg
Asking for increases in salaries.
Manuscript unsigned.
17 Dec. 1779: To PG.
22 Dec. 1779: PG recommends £1,500 a year over present salary.
   To SC.
   SC amends and prepares bill.
23 Dec. 1779: House and Senate pass bill.
   For this act and other salaries see 10H219.

### 1179-P
### Eck–A9   de la Croix, Peter
JHD: 17 Dec. 1779, for action                     Accomack County
Recompense for imprisonment for not paying wages of his ship's crew, which had deserted. Also declares Accomack County court has no jurisdiction over French vessels.
Manuscript unsigned, but translation certified by Charles Bolling.
17 Dec. 1779: House resolves that depositions of witnesses shall be taken and matter brought before next session of GA.
20 Dec. 1779: Senate agrees.
   No further action found.

## 16 - 20 December 1779

**1180-Misc. Claims-†**

The following miscellaneous claims were not presented separately, and apparently went to T without a prior reading on the floor of the House. They are listed as they were approved in the journals and are indexed under name and subject.

    JHD: 20 Dec. 1779, for action                Not known

Date unknown: To T.

20 Dec. 1779: T recommends approval of 1180.1, 1180.2, 1180.3, and 1180.4. House agrees.

21 Dec. 1779: Senate agrees.

1180.1    That the claim of George Dabney, for provisions furnished by an order of Hanover County court, dated 3 September 1779, to the widows, wives, and children of sundry soldiers in the service of the United States and of this state, is reasonable; and that the claimant ought to be allowed the amount of his claim, being £249. 11s. 7d.; a particular account whereof, is as follows, to wit:

| | |
|---|---|
| For provisions furnished the widow of Charles Gregory, deceased, late a soldier in the Continental service, | £145   8s. 7d. |
| For provisions furnished the widow of John Camron, deceased, late a soldier in the same service, | £    3   0s. 0d. |
| For provisions furnished the wife and child of Peter Wilson, a soldier in the same service, | £    1   0s. 0d. |
| For provisions furnished the wife of John Alvis, a soldier in the same service, | £ 60   0s. 0d. |
| For provisions furnished the widow Cawthorn, who has a son in the same service, | £ 27 15s. 0d. |
| For provisions furnished Hannah King, who has a son in the service of this state, | £ 12   8s. 0d. |
| | £249 11s. 7d. |

1180.2    That the claim of Bowler Hall, for rent of a house twelve months, £40, and the milk of a cow, £5, for the use of the widow and family of Joseph Nunnally, late a soldier in the Continental service, an account whereof has been presented to and approved of by the court of the county of Amelia, 25 November 1779, is reasonable; and that the claimant ought to be allowed the sum of £45 for the same.

1180.3    That the claim of Richard Jones, Jr., for necessaries furnished the widow and family of Joseph Nunnally, late a soldier in the service of the United States, an account of which was presented to and approved of by the county court of Amelia, 25 November 1779, is reasonable; and that the claimant ought to be allowed the amount of his claim, being £163 4s.; a particular account whereof is as follows, to wit:

|  |  |  |
|---|---|---|
| 20 January 1779 | To cash paid for four barrels of corn, at £5 per barrel, | £ 20 0s. 0d. |
| | To ditto for 320 pounds pork, at £12 per hundred, | £ 38 8s. 0d. |
| | To ditto for 122 pounds beef, at 2s. per pound, | £ 12 4s. 0d. |
| 14 July | To ditto for forty-three and a half pounds bacon, at 12s., | £ 26 2s. 0d. |
| 22 July | To ditto for four and a half bushels corn, at £6 per bushel, | £ 27 0s. 0d. |
| 21 August | To a bushel of wheat, £10; 4 October, a bushel of ditto, £10, | £ 20 0s. 0d. |
| 20 October | To a peck of salt, | £ 7 10s. 0d. |
| 10 November | To three bushels corn, | £ 12 0s. 0d. |
| | | £163 4s. 0d. |

1180.4 That the claim of Thomas Bolling Munford, for provisions furnished by order of Amelia County court to the wives and children of John Brogan and Hugh Roke, poor soldiers in the Continental army, is reasonable; and that the claimant ought to be allowed the amount of his claim, being £165 7s. 6d.

1180.5 That the order of the court of Lunenburg County, of the 9th of this month, for a draft of £475 on the treasury, to be laid out in the purchase of provisions for the subsistence of the wife and children of John Boaz, a soldier in the Continental service, be rejected.

1180.6 That the allowance of £244 10s. granted to Jerriad Willingham by the county court of Lunenburg, November 1779, to supply Betty Wilkerson, a poor woman, whose husband died in the Continental service, with necessary provisions, be rejected.

## 20 December 1779 – 10 May 1780

1180.7   That the allowance of £357 10s. granted to Lodowick Farmer by the county court of Lunenburg, 11 November 1779, to be laid out in the purchase of provisions for the support of Anne Pailer, a poor woman who has two sons in the Continental service, and of Catharine Gradey, whose husband is likewise in the said service, be rejected.

**1181-P-†  Harvey, William**
    JHD: 10 May 1780                      Middlesex County
Contesting the election of Thomas Moore as a delegate to the House of Delegates from Middlesex County since he was not a resident of the county.
10 May 1780: To PE.
2 June 1780: PE finds Harvey not a resident, and he was unduly elected.
    House orders a new writ of election.

**1182-P   Batte, Thomas, Jr.**
    JHD: 10 May 1780                      Chesterfield County
To discontinue old ferry (Batte's) across Appomattox River and to establish new ferry across Appomattox River from Batte's land to town of Broadway in Prince George County.
    Manuscript signed by: Richd. Baugh, Blackman Moseley, Henry Archer, John Marshall, Baxter Folkes, and thirteen others.
10 May 1780: To PG.
    Carried over to next session of GA.
19 Dec. 1780: PG finds reasonable and is directed to prepare a bill.
    This matter was incorporated in a general ferry act passed by House and Senate.
    For general ferry act including this, see 10H365.

**1183-P   York Town—Citizens**
    JHD: 10 May 1780                      York County
For the incorporation and enlargement of town of York.
    Manuscript signed by: Wm. Cary, John May, Lawe. Smith, Matt. Pope, John Gibbs, and forty-nine others.
10 May 1780: To PG.
12 May 1780: PG finds reasonable and is directed to prepare a bill.
22 June 1780: Bill presented.
    House carries over to next session of GA.
    No further record found.
    Yorktown was not incorporated until 1786. See 11H473.

## Virginia Legislative Petitions

### 1184-P  Spotsylvania County—Magistrates
JHD: 10 May 1780                          Spotsylvania County

Asks that court be allowed to vacate Fredericksburg and meet at home of John Holladay until new courthouse is constructed.

Manuscript signed by: Joseph Brock, Mann Page, Jr., Geo. Thornton, Thomas Colson, and Willm. Smith.

10 May 1780: To PG.
12 May 1780: PG finds reasonable and is directed to prepare a bill.
25 May 1780: House passes bill.
27 May 1780: Senate passes bill.
    For this act see 10H228.

### 1185-P  Tobacco Inspectors—Quantico Warehouse and Dumfries Warehouse
JHD: 10 May 1780                        Prince William County

For increase in salaries because of depreciation of paper money.

Manuscript signed by: Wm. Brent, Simon Luttrell, John Chancellor, and M. Harrison.

10 May 1780: To PG.
    This matter was taken care of in a general law regarding inspection fees.
    For this act see 10H273.

### 1186-P-† Criddle, William
JHD: 10 May 1780                                Not known

Additional compensation for military wound; additional compensation necessary because of depreciation of paper currency.

10 May 1780: To T.
20 May 1780: T recommends £26 for current relief.
    House agrees.
30 May 1780: Senate agrees.

### 1187-P  Williams, James
JHD: 10 May 1780                                Williamsburg

Additional compensation for military wound; additional compensation necessary because of depreciation of paper currency.

Manuscript unsigned, but certificate on back.
10 May 1780: To T.

10 - 12 May 1780

20 May 1780: T recommends rejection.
>Disagreed to by House.
>Williams presented a new petition on 5 December 1780.
>See 1365-P-†.

**1188-P  Wallace, Hugh**
>JHD: 10 May 1780                                   Not known

Additional compensation for military wound; additional compensation necessary because of depreciation of paper currency.

Manuscript unsigned.

10 May 1780: To T.

20 May 1780: T recommends (1) that right to draw from public store be rejected, and (2) that he be allowed £250 for his present relief.
>House agrees to (2).

30 May 1780: Senate agrees to (2).

**1189-P  Chew, Larkin**
>JHD: 10 May 1780                                   Not known

Additional compensation for military wound; additional compensation necessary because of depreciation of paper currency.

Manuscript unsigned.

10 May 1780: To T.

20 May 1780: T recommends rejection of request to draw from public store.
>House rejects.

**1190-P  Archer, William and Goodwyn, Stephen**
>JHD: 10 May 1780                              Dinwiddie County

Asking relief for tobacco stolen from Bolling Brook warehouses. They, as inspectors, are obliged to pay the proprietors.

Manuscript unsigned. Depositions of Archer and Goodwyn attached.

10 May 1780: To T.

25 May 1780: T recommends rejection.
>House rejects.

**1191-P  De Klauman, Charles**
>JHD: 12 May 1780                                   Not known

Asking pay and benefits as captain in the state regiment of artillery and as major in additional battalion.

Manuscript unsigned. Attached certificate for appointment as major and accounts as captain, signed by Patrick Henry, 6 February 1779. Attached

355

## Virginia Legislative Petitions

certificate to inspect arms, signed by Thomas Jefferson. Attached certificate to aid in recruiting, signed by James Innes of Board of War.
12 May 1780: To T.
15 May 1780: T recommends that he be allowed £3,087 for pay and benefits.
   House agrees.
30 May 1780: Senate agrees.

**1192-P  Welsh, John**
   JHD: 12 May 1780                                                    Not known
Additional compensation for military wound; additional compensation necessary because of depreciation of paper currency.
   Manuscript unsigned.
12 May 1780: To T.
18 May 1780: T recommends rejection.
   House rejects.

**1193-P  Clarkson and Davis**
   JHD: 12 May 1780                                                Richmond Town
Asking that they continue to be public printers, their salary increased, and that additional time be given to procure a proper printing house in Richmond.
   Manuscript unsigned.
12 May 1780: To PG.
13 May 1780: Rejected by action of House appointing Messrs. Dixon and
   Nicholson as printers to the commonwealth.

**1194-P  Amelia County—Citizens**
   JHD: 12 May 1780                                                 Amelia County
Asks dissolution of present vestries and election hereafter by voice of the people, and that marriages solemnized by dissenting ministers be declared lawful.
   Manuscript signed by: Jeremiah Walker, Simeon Walton, Joseph Fowlkes, John Green, Henry Anderson, and seventy-seven others.
12 May 1780: To R.
8 June 1780: R finds reasonable and is directed to prepare bill or bills.
27 June 1780: Bill "for dissolution of vestries, and appointing overseers of the
   poor" presented and read twice. Committed to committee of the
   whole.
4 July 1780: Bill "declaring what shall be a lawful marriage" presented and
   read first time.

## 12 – 15 May 1780

6 July 1780: Amended vestries bill presented and read twice.
    Marriage bill read second time and committed to PG.
7 July 1780: House agrees to vestries bill.
    House agrees to marriage bill.
10 July 1780: Senate amends vestries bill.
11 July 1780: House amends Senate amendments to vestries bill.
    Senate agrees.
    No further action found in this session of GA.
    For act concerning marriages see 10H361.

**1195-P   Tobacco Inspectors—Royston's (Roiston's) Warehouse and Fredericksburg Warehouse**
    JHD: 13 May 1780                  Spotsylvania County
 For increase in salaries.
 Manuscript signed by: Michael Robinson, John Steward, Thos. Bartlet, and Jn. Holladay. Dated 1 May 1780.
13 May 1780: To PG.
    This matter was taken care of in a general law regarding inspection fees.
    For this act see 10H273.

**1196-P-†  Compton, Archibald**
    JHD: 13 May 1780                           Not known
 Additional compensation for military wound; additional compensation necessary because of depreciation of paper currency.
13 May 1780: To T.
20 May 1780: T recommends £100 for current relief.
    House amends and agrees.
30 May 1780: Senate agrees.

**1197-P   Thomas, Rees**
    JHD: 15 May 1780                    Spotsylvania County
 Compensation for a horse and the harnesses for four other horses, impressed for public service in 1777.
 Manuscript unsigned.
15 May 1780: To T.
20 June 1780: Carried over to next session of GA.
    Rees presented a new petition 12 December 1780.
    See 1388-P-†.

## Virginia Legislative Petitions

**1198-P Harrison, Thomas**
JHD: 15 May 1780            Rockingham County

Asks that a town be established on the fifty acres he has laid off into lots adjoining the courthouse of Rockingham County.

Manuscript unsigned.

15 May 1780: To PG.
17 May 1780: PG finds reasonable and is directed to prepare bill.
23 May 1780: Bill presented and read first time.
24 May 1780: Bill read second time and recommitted to PG.
14 June 1780: PG to receive clause or clauses relevant to bill.
20 June 1780: House passes bill establishing the town of Louisville in Kentucky County and the town of Harrisonburg in Rockingham County.
23 June 1780: Senate passes bill.
    See petition from Kentucky County on 8 June 1780 (1252-P).
    For this act see 10H293.

**1199-P Rockingham County—Citizens**
JHD: 15 May 1780            Rockingham County

Extension of time for surveying and returning entries to land under preemption rights.

Manuscript signed by: Good. Herring, Robert Dickey, Nathl. Harrison, Engle Boyer, James Bosher, and eighty-eight others.

15 May 1780: To PG.
17 May 1780: PG finds reasonable and is directed to prepare bill.
25 May 1780: Bill presented and read first time.
26 May 1780: Bill read second time and committed to SC.
14 June 1780: House passes bill.
17 June 1780: Senate amends bill.
19 June 1780: House amends Senate amendments.
20 June 1780: Senate agrees.
    For general act including preemption certificate, see 10H237.

**1200-P Mitchell, William**
JHD: 16 May 1780            York County

Asks reimbursement for medical expenses of £494 10s. paid to discharge account incurred by the late Captain John Shield who died and left no estate.

Manuscript unsigned.

16 May 1780: To T.

## 15 – 16 May 1780

18 May 1780: T finds reasonable and recommends payment of £494 10s.
  House agrees.
26 May 1780: Senate agrees.

### 1201-P-† Murdaugh, James
  JHD: 16 May 1780 　　　　　　　　　　　　　　　　Not known
Asks compensation for his slave, shot by mistake by a detachment of light horse belonging to the state.
16 May 1780: To T.
18 May 1780: T recommends rejection.
  House rejects.

### 1202-P King, Michael
  JHD: 16 May 1780 　　　　　　　　　　　　　　　　Not known
Asks compensation for his horse, killed while King was on duty as a captain with the militia.
  Manuscript unsigned.
16 May 1780: Rejected by refusal to refer to a committee.

### 1203-P Orange County—Citizens
  JHD: 16 May 1780 　　　　　　　　　　　　　　　Orange County
For division of the county into two districts due to inconvenience of battalion duty in general muster.
  Manuscript signed by: Robt. Thomas, Robt. Dannill, Fras. Moore, Jr., Richd. Carr, Caleb Able, and twenty-five others.
16 May 1780: To committee appointed to prepare and bring in a bill, "for the better regulation and discipline of the militia."
  Apparently no further action taken.

### 1204-P Prince William County—Citizens
  JHD: 16 May 1780 　　　　　　　　　　　　　Prince William County
Opposing a petition praying for the removal of their courthouse.
  Manuscript signed by: Hen. Westall, Richard Sampson, Joseph Johnson, Lawrence Southard, William Drury, and seventy-three others.
16 May 1780: To PG.
17 May 1780: House declares petition in opposition to removal to be reasonable.

### 1204 A-P Prince William County—Citizens
  JHD: 16 May 1780 　　　　　　　　　　　　　Prince William County

Text is identical with 1204-P, which see.
Manuscript signed by fifty-nine persons.

### 1204 B-P Prince William County—Citizens
JHD: 16 May 1780                      Prince William County
Text is identical with 1204-P, which see.
Manuscript signed by fifty-two persons.

### 1205-P    Cropper, John, Jr.
JHD: 17 May 1780                          Accomack County
Contesting the election of Thomas Bayley to serve as a delegate in the General Assembly.
Manuscript unsigned.
17 May 1780: To PE.
19 May 1780: PE resolves that persons who voted at the said election, whose freeholds or right of voting are questioned either by the petitioner or sitting member, be examined before James Arbuckle, Charles Bagwell, and John Teagle, or any two of them.
No further action found.

### 1206-P-† Ramsbottom, Isaac
JHD: 17 May 1780                                   Not known
Compensation for leg wound received while a soldier in the Continental army.
17 May 1780: To T.
20 May 1780: T recommends rejection.
     House recommits to T.
6 July 1780: T recommends £100 for present relief.
     House agrees.
7 July 1780: Senate agrees.

### 1207-P-† Willson, Willis
JHD: 17 May 1780                                   Not known
Asks compensation to John Phipp for horse impressed by Willson, who was acting under orders.
17 May 1780: To T.
25 May 1780: T recommends £150 in compensation.
     House agrees.
30 May 1780: Senate agrees.

## 16 – 17 May 1780

**1208-P  Berkeley County—Citizens**
JHD: 17 May 1780                    Berkeley County
Asks establishment of a ferry crossing the Potomac River, from the land of Joseph Mitchell to the land of Leaken Dorsey.
Manuscript signed by: John Brown, Robt. Vance, Joseph Sommerville, Jacob Fink, John West, Jr., and ten others.
17 May 1780: To PG.
    No further action found.

**1209-P**
Eck–
A460    **Alexandria—Merchants and Traders**
JHD: 17 May 1780                    Fairfax County
Asks amendment of law that requires merchants and traders to render, on oath, an account of all goods, wares, and merchandise sold within the last twelve months preceding the time of their assessment, and also amendment of other parts of the law.
Manuscript signed by: Hooe and Harrisons, of Alexandria, who originated it. Also has signatures of merchants from Richmond, Portsmouth, Falmouth, Alexandria, Petersburg, Blandford, and the Eastern Shore.
17 May 1780: To PG.
20 May 1780: PG declares reasonable such parts of the petition that relate to
    the tax of 2½ percent on the amount of all goods, wares, and
    merchandise, sold by retail, and the tax of 2½ percent ad valorem
    upon the amount of such sales.
    Referred to committee of ways and means, which prepared bill.
    Bill passed by House and Senate.
    See 1210-P.
    For this act see 10H271.

**1209.1-P  Chesterfield County—Merchants and Traders**
JHD: Not found [17 May 1780]        Chesterfield County
Asks amendment of law that requires merchants and traders to render, on oath, an account of all goods, wares, and merchandise sold within the last twelve months preceding the time of their assessment, and also amendment of other parts of the law
Manuscript signed by: James Lyle, James Buchanan, James Somersville, John Hall, Ross and Shore, and nine others.
17 May 1780: To PG.

## Virginia Legislative Petitions

20 May 1780: PG declares reasonable such parts of the petition that relate to the tax of 2½ percent on the amount of all goods, wares, and merchandise, sold by retail, and the tax of 2½ percent ad valorem upon the amount of such sales.
Referred to committee of ways and means, which prepared bill.
Bill passed by House and Senate.
See 1209-P.
For this act see 10H271.

**1210-P Winchester—Traders and Retail Dealers**
JHD: 17 May 1780                    Frederick County
Asks amendment of law that requires merchants and traders to render, on oath, an account of all goods, wares, and merchandise sold within the last twelve months preceding the time of their assessment, and also amendment of other parts of the law.
Manuscript signed by: James Dowdd, Sr., Willm. Holliday, John Kaine, James Holliday, John Reynolds, and seven others.
17 May 1780: To PG.
20 May 1780: PG declares reasonable such parts of the petition that relate to the tax of 2½ percent on the amount of all goods, wares, and merchandise, sold by retail, and the tax of 2½ percent ad valorem upon the amount of such sales.
Referred to committee of ways and means, which prepared bill.
Bill passed by House and Senate.
See 1209-P.
For this act see 10H271.

**1211-P Ege, Dorothy**
JHD: 18 May 1780                    Not known
Asks compensation for horse stolen by Drury Hodges and shot by persons who apprehended Hodges.
18 May 1780: To T.
25 May 1780: T recommends rejection.
House rejects.

**1212-P Stewart, Jane**
JHD: 18 May 1780                    Norfolk County
Asks compensation and return of slave taken from Portsmouth by state troops and sent to the lead mines.
Manuscript unsigned, but deposition attached.

## 17 – 18 May 1780

18 May 1780: To T.
25 May 1780: T recommends return of slave and payment of £800 for his hire. House agrees.
30 May 1780: Senate agrees.

**1213-P    Greenbrier County—Citizens**
JHD: 18 May 1780                                          Greenbrier County
Increase in allowance to spies from the militia.
Manuscript signed by: Andw. Donnally, John Archer, David Workman, Matthew Arbuckle, John Erwin, and eighteen others.
18 May 1780: To PG.
23 May 1780: House refers it to committee appointed to prepare and bring in a bill, "for the better regulation and discipline of the militia."
Apparently no further action taken.

**1214-P    Montgomery County—Citizens**
JHD: 18 May 1780                                          Montgomery County
Asks amendment of law "for adjusting and settling the titles of claimers to unpatented lands and limiting the time for establishing preemption rights" and of law "laying a tax, payable in certain enumerated commodities."
Manuscript signed by: Samuel Drake, John Mcfarland, George W. Nutt, John M. Mcfarland, Chas. Lynch, and fifty-one others.
18 May 1780: To PG.
Apparently no further action taken.
For general law see 10H237.

**1215-P**
Eck–
A843    **Amherst County—Citizens**
JHD: 18 May 1780                                          Amherst County
Asks extension of time in order to comply with the act "laying a tax, payable in certain enumerated commodities."
Manuscript signed by: John Montgomery, Thos. Matthews, Peter Bibee, Wm. Hansborough, John Rose, and sixty-five others.
18 May 1780: To lie on table.
23 May 1780: To committee of ways and means.
14 June 1780: Leave given to bring in a bill "to give further time to delinquent counties to pay their specific tax."
20 June 1780: Bill presented and read first time

## Virginia Legislative Petitions

22 June 1780: Bill passed by House and Senate.
    For act extending time see 10H292.

**1216-P**
Eck-A842
[Wrong date]
### Amherst Parish, Amherst County—Citizens
JHD: 18 May 1780                        Amherst County
  Asks alteration in division line between Amherst and Lexington parishes.
  Manuscript signed by: James Higginbotham, John Rose, James Nevill, John Dawson, Lucas Powell, and fifty-one others.
18 May 1780: To R.
    Carried over to next session of GA.
6 Dec. 1780: R finds reasonable and is directed to prepare a bill.
12 Dec. 1780: Bill presented.
15 Dec. 1780: House passes bill.
18 Dec. 1780: Senate passes bill.
    See 1026-P.
    For act changing line see 10H369.

**1217-P**   Galloway, David and Ashton, Burdit
JHD: 19 May 1780                      Westmoreland County
  Asking that trustees be appointed to act in regard to certain land of James Blair, deceased, that descended to his daughters.
  Manuscript unsigned.
19 May 1780: House rejects by refusal to refer to a committee.

**1218-P**   Rockbridge County—Justices
JHD: 19 May 1780                        Rockbridge County
  Authority to appoint commissioners to execute the act, "laying a tax, payable in certain enumerated commodities."
  Manuscript signed by: Wm. McGee, Jos. Buchanon, John Greenlee, John Lyle, David Gray, and three others.
19 May 1780: To PG.
23 May 1780: PG finds reasonable.
    House refers to committee of ways and means.
    For act extending time see 10H292.

**1219-P**   Thornton, Jeremiah
JHD: 19 May 1780                                  Not known

## 18 – 20 May 1780

Additional compensation for military wound; additional compensation necessary because of depreciation of paper currency.
Manuscript unsigned.
19 May 1780: To T.
        No further action found.
        Manuscript says not taken up by committee.

**1220-P   Cooper, Charles**
      JHD: 20 May 1780                                 Norfolk County
Compensation for house he had almost completed for James Guy in Norfolk. House was burned by order of convention, and James Guy joined the enemy.
Manuscript unsigned.
20 May 1780: To PG.
        Carried over to next session of GA.
8 Dec. 1780: PG recommends £250.
        House agrees.
        Senate action not found.

**1221-P   Martinsburg—Citizens**
      JHD: 20 May 1780                                 Berkeley County
Additional time to improve their lots in the said town.
Manuscript signed by: Michl. Bowland, Jacob Fink, Jeremiah Ong, Hugh Black, Patrick Ternan, and thirteen others.
20 May 1780: To PG
        No further action found.

**1222-P   Rockingham County—Court**
      JHD: 20 May 1780                               Rockingham County
Asks that late sheriff of Augusta pay to commissioners of tax of Rockingham County the quitrents received from that part of Augusta now in Rockingham County and that same be credited for their tax for the ensuing year.
Manuscript unsigned.
20 May 1780: To PG.
        Committee apparently did not report.

**1223-P   Daniel, George; Smith, Maurice; and Montague, Philip**
      JHD: 20 May 1780                                 Middlesex County

## Virginia Legislative Petitions

Asks compensation and return of two slaves sent to work in lead mines.
Manuscript unsigned.
20 May 1780: To T.
25 May 1780: T finds reasonable. Recommitted to T.
29 May 1780: T recommends return of slaves and compensation of £350.
House agrees.
3 June 1780: Senate agrees.

**1224-P   Rockbridge County—Justices**
JHD: 20 May 1780                                             Rockbridge County
Asks authority to provide for the poor.
Manuscript signed by: Sal. Lyle, John Tremble, Jas. Bucchanan, and Archd. Campbell.
20 May 1780: To R.
This matter was taken care of in a general law regarding vestries. For act see 10H288.

**1225-P   Manning, Mary**
JHD: 20 May 1780                                             Berkeley County
Asks increase in rents of leased land; increase necessary because of depreciation of paper currency.
Manuscript unsigned.
20 May 1780: To lie on table.
Apparently no further action taken.

**1226-P   Wylly, Alexander**
JHD: 22 May 1780                                             Williamsburg
Asks compensation for services as keeper of the Capitol and for transferring records from Williamsburg to Richmond.
Manuscript unsigned.
22 May 1780: To T.
29 May 1780: T recommends compensation of £270.
House agrees.
2 June 1780: Senate agrees.

**1227-P   Fox, John**
JHD: 23 May 1780                                             Gloucester County
To establish a ferry from his land in Gloucester County across York River to land of John Tabb.

## 20 - 23 May 1780

Manuscript signed by: John Buckner, Mordecai Throckmorton, John Whiting, George Green, James Nuttall, Jr., and 156 others.
23 May 1780: To PG.
> Carried over to next session of GA.
12 Dec. 1780: PG finds reasonable and is directed to prepare bill.
15 Dec. 1780: Bill presented.
16 Dec. 1780: Bill recommitted to PG.
21 Dec. 1780: Bill amended.
22 Dec. 1780: House passes bill.
26 Dec. 1780: Senate amends bill.
27 Dec. 1780: House agrees to Senate amendments.
> For general ferry act, including this one, see 10H365.

**1228-P**
Eck–
A1670  **Bedford County—Citizens**
JHD: 23 May 1780                                    Bedford County
Asks formation of new county from parts of Bedford and Henry counties.
Manuscript signed by: John Divarse, William Martain, Sr., William Martain, Jr., Brittan Scruggs, John Harris, and twenty-five others.
23 May 1780: To PG.
> No further action found.
> For act dividing Bedford County see 10H447.

**1229-P-†** **Henry County—Citizens**
JHD: 23 May 1780                                    Henry County
Asks formation of new county from parts of Bedford and Henry counties.
23 May 1780: To PG.
> No further action found.
> For act dividing Bedford County see 10H447.

**1230-P**
Eck–
A1671  **Bedford County—Citizens**
JHD: 23 May 1780                                    Bedford County
Opposing the formation of a new county from parts of Bedford and Henry counties.
Manuscript signed by: Jesse Burton, Wm. Burton, Henry Tate, Christo. Linch, Joseph Blankenship, Sr., and fifty-two others.

23 May 1780: To PG.
> Carried over to next session of GA.

6 Dec. 1780: PG recommends rejection.
> House rejects.
> For act dividing Bedford County see 10H447.

### 1230 A-P
Eck–
### A1672    Bedford County—Citizens
JHD: 23 May 1780                                        Bedford County

Text is identical with 1230-P, which see.
Manuscript signed by twenty-seven persons.

### 1231-P    Milmer, Thomas
JHD: 23 May 1780                                       Nansemond County

Asks that his lease to Cumings, Warwick, and Company be terminated and that he be authorized to receive rents and profits.

Manuscript unsigned. Dated 3 May 1780.

23 May 1780: To PG.
> No further action found.

### 1232-P-†    Dickerson, William
JHD: 23 May 1780                                            Not known

Additional compensation for military wounds; additional compensation necessary because of depreciation of paper currency.

23 May 1780: To T.

25 May 1780: T recommends £150 for current relief.
> House agrees.

30 May 1780: Senate agrees.

### 1233-P-†    Stafford County—Citizens
JHD: 24 May 1780                                          Stafford County

Asks that disinterested gentlemen of adjacent counties be appointed to move the courthouse to a place near the center of the county.

24 May 1780: To PG.
> Carried over to next session of GA.

21 Nov. 1780: PG finds reasonable and is directed to prepare bill.

29 Nov. 1780: Bill presented.

30 Nov. 1780: Bill recommitted to PG.

1 Dec. 1780: PG presents amended bill.

## 23 – 26 May 1780

2 Dec. 1780: House passes bill.
7 Dec. 1780: Senate amends bill.
    House agrees to Senate amendments.
    For this act see 10H370.

### 1234-M   Prince William County—Citizens
    JHD: 25 May 1780                          Prince William County

Asks consideration of whether an inquiry should not be made into the conduct of Meriwether Smith, one of the Virginia delegates to Congress.

Manuscript signed by: Thos. White, Alex. Brown, Alex. Lithgow, W. Harrison, William Tebbs, and fifteen others.
25 May 1780: To PG.
14 June 1780: PG recommends rejection.
    House rejects.
    See JHD, 14 June 1780, for discussion and rejection of memorial.

### 1235-P-†   Pitcher, Mason and Dickinson, Edward
    JHD: 25 May 1780                                    Stafford County

Compensation as inspectors at Falmouth warehouses for money paid into public treasury from sale of tobacco, and request for increase in salaries.
25 May 1780: To committee appointed to prepare and bring in a bill "to amend the act, for reviving several public warehouses, for the inspection of tobacco."
2 June 1780: Committee recommends (1) that compensation be rejected, and (2) that augmentation of salaries is reasonable.
    House agrees.
    No further action found for (2).

### 1236-P   Northampton County—Citizens
    JHD: 26 May 1780                                Northampton County

Complains that present mode of taxing lands by assessment is unequal and unjust and asks more equal way be found.

Manuscript signed by: Isaac Avery, Littl. Savage, Curtis Kendon, Henry Harmanson, Edward Robins, and ninety-four others.
26 May 1780: To committee of ways and means.
    Apparently no further action taken.

### 1237-P   Charlotte County—Citizens
    JHD: 26 May 1780                                        Charlotte County

## Virginia Legislative Petitions

Asks that a more just and equal mode of taxation by assessment of property be adopted.
Manuscript signed by: Ja. Speed, Thomas Rodgers, Dudley Barksdale, Joshua Morris, Rubn. Johnson, and 138 others.
26 May 1780: To committee of ways and means.
    Apparently no further action taken.

### 1238-M   Princess Anne County—Citizens
JHD: 26 May 1780                        Princess Anne County

Asks exchange for John Hancock, Charles Williamson, and John Smith, who were made prisoners by the enemy and carried to New York.
Manuscript signed by: Jacob Keeling, Henry Keeling, John Chapel, Edward G. Storm, Matthew Puttett, and forty-four others.
26 May 1780: To PG.
    Apparently no further action taken.
    (Entered incorrectly as Prince William County in JHD.)

### 1239-P   Northumberland County—Citizens
JHD: 26 May 1780                       Northumberland County

Compensation for tobacco carried to warehouses at North and South Wicomico. Considerable loss sustained by enemy's burning these warehouses.
Manuscript signed by: Richd. Hudnall, William Barrett, and Thos. Cuthb. Harum.
26 May 1780: To PG.
2 June 1780: PG finds reasonable.
    Recommitted to PG.
20 June 1780: PG recommends rejection.
    House rejects.

### 1240-P
Eck–
A1112   **Poage, John**
JHD: 26 May 1780                               Augusta County

States that deputy sheriff, Mr. Graham, was robbed while on his way to Williamsburg with tax collection of Augusta County. Asks mitigation of public proceedings and suspension of judgment.
Manuscript unsigned.
26 May 1780: To PG.
27 May 1780: PG recommends rejection.
    House rejects.

## 26 – 30 May 1780

**1241-P**
Rob–13  **Clark, George Rogers**
JHD: 27 May 1780                                          Kentucky County
Asks that land conveyed by deed to him from the Indians be confirmed. Manuscript unsigned.
27 May 1780: To PG.
30 June 1780: PG recommends (1) that upon payment of £7,000 a special warrant is to be directed to the surveyor of Kentucky County to lay off and survey the said tract of land, and (2) that said tract is to be exempted from payment of taxes until adjacent lands are settled and taxes imposed.
House rejects both resolutions.

**1242-P-†  Alexandria—Citizens**
JHD: 27 May 1780                                          Fairfax County
Asks amendment of law laying a 2½ percent tax upon goods, and other items, imported and retailed.
27 May 1780: To committee of ways and means.
No further action found.
For general act, including this tax, see 10H271.

**1243-P-†  Newman, John**
JHD: 30 May 1780                                          Not known
Compensation for loss of right arm while a soldier involved in the taking of Savannah.
30 May 1780: To T.
2 June 1780: T recommends £150 for current relief and half pay of a soldier, from 29 December 1778, during life.
House agrees.
7 June 1780: Senate agrees.

**1244-P-†  Stewart, Alexander**
JHD: 30 May 1780                                          Not known
Annuity formerly allowed him for wounds he received has expired. Asks further relief.
30 May 1780: To T.
20 June 1780: T recommends £200 for current relief.
House agrees.
22 June 1780: Senate agrees.

## Virginia Legislative Petitions

**1245-P    Triplett, James and Smith, William**
    JHD: 30 May 1780                               Westmoreland County
Ask compensation for tobacco stolen from the warehouses at Leedstown where they are inspectors.
    Manuscript unsigned, but has list attached.
30 May 1780: To PG.
        Carried over to next session of GA.
14 Nov. 1780: PG recommends payment of £2,389.
        House agrees.
5 Dec. 1780: Senate agrees.

**1246-P    Norfolk Borough and Portsmouth—Merchants and Traders**
    JHD: 1 June 1780                                   Norfolk Borough
                                                            Portsmouth
Asks repeal of law laying a 2½ percent tax upon goods, and other items, imported and retailed.
    Manuscript signed by: Henry and Tho. Brown, William North and Company, Zach. Rowland, John Kearnes, William Andrews, and twenty-six others.
1 June 1780: To committee of ways and means.
        No further action found.
        For general act, including this tax, see 10H271.

**1247-P-†  Lawson, Anthony**
    JHD: 1 June 1780                                         Not known
Asks compensation for public hire and value of his slave captured by the enemy.
1 June 1780: Rejected by refusal to refer to a committee.

**1248-P    Botetourt County—Citizens**
    JHD: 2 June 1780                                   Botetourt County
Asks relief concerning laws whose promulgation has been delayed, and also laws with which they cannot comply or by which they are aggrieved.
    Manuscript signed by: Thomas Mcfaron, Jams. Walker, Jr., Malcom Allen, Jessy Robinet, Wm. Davidson, and 103 others.
2 June 1780: To PG.
        Apparently no further action taken.

**1249-P    Carlyle, John**
    JHD: 3 June 1780                                      Fairfax County
Asks removal of warehouses at Hunting Creek inspection, in the town of

## 30 May – 8 June 1780

Alexandria, to lands of Baldwin Dade or heirs of John Alexander.
Manuscript unsigned.
3 June 1780: Rejected by refusal to refer to a committee.

### 1250-P   Cole, Walter King
JHD: 3 June 1780                                    Henry County

Asks for his interest in his reputed father's estate, sold for public benefit under the act "for sequestering British property."

Manuscript unsigned.
3 June 1780: To PG.
16 June 1780: PG finds reasonable and is directed to prepare bill.
30 June 1780: Bill presented.
6 July 1780: House passes bill.
7 July 1780: Senate passes bill.
        For this act see 10H300.

### 1251-P   Baptist Association
JHD: 5 June 1780                            Spotsylvania County

Asks for passage of act declaring marriages solemnized by dissenting ministers to be lawful.

Manuscript signed by: John Wallore and Joseph Anthony.
5 June 1780: To R.
8 June 1780: R finds reasonable and is directed to prepare bill.
4 July 1780: Bill presented.
7 July 1780: House passes bill.
        No further action found in this session of GA.
        For act concerning marriages see 10H361.

### 1252-P
### Rob-11   Kentucky County—Citizens
JHD: 8 June 1780                                  Kentucky County

For establishment of a town (Louisville) at falls of Ohio River.

Manuscript signed by: John Hawkins, Nicholas Meriwether, William Jesse, John Helm, Benjn. Roberts, and thirty-four others.
8 June 1780: To PG.
        For action see 1198-P.
        For this act see 10H293.

Virginia Legislative Petitions

**1253-P**
Rob–12    **Kentucky County—Citizens**
       JHD: 8 June 1780            Kentucky County
For a division of the county into three counties.
    Manuscript signed by: William Pope, Andw. Hyner, William Helm, Cyrus McCraskin, Joseph Roberts, and sixteen others.
8 June 1780: To PG.
10 June 1780: PG finds reasonable and is directed to prepare a bill.
12 June 1780: Bill presented.
        Recommitted to PG.
16 June 1780: PG presents amended bill.
20 June 1780: House passes bill.
23 June 1780: Senate passes bill.
        For this act, establishing the counties of Jefferson, Fayette, and Lincoln, and disestablishing Kentucky County, see 10H315, effective 1 November 1780.

**1253 A-P**
Rob–12
[Dated 1 May 1780 in error]
       **Kentucky County—Citizens**
       JHD: 8 June 1780            Kentucky County
For a division of the county.
Manuscript signed by eleven persons living south of the falls.
For action see 1253-P.

**1253 B-P**
Rob–12
[Dated 1 May 1780 in error]
       **Kentucky County—Citizens**
       JHD: 8 June 1780            Kentucky County
For a division of the county.
Manuscript signed by forty-five persons living north of the falls.
For action see 1253-P.

**1254-M**
Eck–
A1113    **Tandy, Smyth**
       JHD: 12 June 1780            Augusta County

## 8 – 12 June 1780

Relief for loss of £4,375 lent by individuals of the county to the public and for which he can in no way account.

Manuscript unsigned.

12 June 1780: To T.
14 June 1780: T recommends rejection.
    Recommitted to T.
20 June 1780: T recommends rejection.
    Laid on table.
27 June 1780: Taken from table and amended.
    House rejects.

### 1255-P
Eck–
A169     **Saratoga Convention Troops—Officers**
         JHD: 12 June 1780                          Albemarle County

Asks that more adequate provision be made for officers and soldiers who were raised to guard prisoners in Albemarle barracks. Cites lack of clothing and provisions, depreciation of money, and ineligibility for bounty land.

Manuscript signed by: Fras. Taylor, John Roberts, James Burton, Thos. Porter, G. Burnley, and seven others. Dated 3 June 1780.

12 June 1780: To PG.
16 June 1780: PG recommends that troops be given all the privileges of other troops in the Continental quota.
    House lays on table asking that PG confer with Colonel Wood, commandant of the post.
7 July 1780: PG, after conference, recommends (1) that governor and Council be given authority to raise a sufficiency of livestock from neighboring counties to supply the post, paying by certificate; (2) that Congress should give credit to state for money and specifics for support of troops; (3) that $200 reward be given to every person apprehending deserters found more than ten miles from the post; (4) that officers be allowed to keep horses assigned to them, but if they are moved, the horses shall remain in the state; and (5) that auditors make reasonable allowance to Colonel Wood for travel to Richmond.
    House agrees on (2)–(5) and requests that (1) be incorporated in bill to give governor and Council certain powers.
10 July 1780: Senate agrees.
    For act giving governor and Council certain powers, see 10H309.

Virginia Legislative Petitions

### 1256-P-† Tobacco Inspectors—Byrd's Warehouse and Shockoe Warehouse
JHD: 13 June 1780          Richmond Town

Asks relief of penalty for nonattendance at petty musters, and for relief from liability for goods lost or damaged during their absence on military service.

13 June 1780: To committee to whom the bill, "to amend the act, for reviving several public warehouses for the inspection of tobacco," was committed.

Apparently no further action taken.

For act concerning liability and militia duty, see 10H272.

### 1257-P-† Selser, Matthias
JHD: 16 June 1780          Not known

Asks compensation for medical expenses, wages, clothing, and rations for illness.

16 June 1780: To T.

20 June 1780: T recommends (1) £623 for surgeon's fee and expenses, and (2) that auditors make allowance for pay, rations, and clothing from 6 May 1778 to 27 March 1780, to be charged to the United States in account with this commonwealth.

House agrees.

24 June 1780: Senate agrees.

### 1258-P-† Pankie, Stephen, Jr.
JHD: 16 June 1780          Not known

Asks compensation for impressed horse, lost in public service in 1779.

16 June 1780: Rejected by refusal to refer to a committee.

### 1259-P-† Thorp, John
JHD: 17 June 1780          Not known

Compensation for military wound.

17 June 1780: To T.

20 June 1780: T recommends £300 for present relief.

House agrees.

22 June 1780: Senate agrees.

### 1260-M Virginia Directors of Public Buildings—Richmond
JHD: 19 June 1780          Richmond Town

Asks interposition of legislature to prevent sale of certain lots not valued, agreeable to the law of escheat and forfeiture.

## 13 – 20 June 1780

Manuscript signed by: Archibald Cary, Turner Southall, and James Buchanan.

19 June 1780: Rejected by refusal to refer to a committee, but see House journal entry for 11 July 1780 for some resolution concerning the directors

### 1261-P  Duckwall, Henry
JHD: 20 June 1780      Berkeley County

Asks compensation for clothing due him, he not having received enough.
Manuscript unsigned.

20 June 1780: To T.

24 June 1780: T recommends that auditors of public accounts make allowance for a suit of clothes.

House agrees.

29 June 1780: Senate agrees.

### 1262-P  Combs, George
JHD: 20 June 1780      Not known

Asks compensation for clothing due him, he not having received enough.
Manuscript unsigned.

20 June 1780: To T.

24 June 1780: T recommends that auditors of public accounts make allowance for one pair of breeches and one shirt.

House agrees.

29 June 1780: Senate agrees.

### 1263-P  Sullivant, Clement
JHD: 20 June 1780      Not known

Asks compensation for clothing due him, he not having received enough.
Manuscript unsigned.

20 June 1780: To T.

24 June 1780: T recommends that auditors of public accounts make allowance for one pair of breeches.

House agrees.

29 June 1780: Senate agrees.

### 1264-P-† Moore, John
JHD: 20 June 1780      Not known

Asks compensation for clothing due him, he not having received enough.

20 June 1780: To T.

## Virginia Legislative Petitions

24 June 1780: T recommends that auditors of public accounts make allowance for two hats, one waistcoat, three pairs of breeches, one pair of stockings, and two blankets.
House agrees.
29 June 1780: Senate agrees.

### 1265-P   Dixon, John
JHD: 20 June 1780                                                  Culpeper County

Asks redress for his escheated estate. General Court and court of chancery are unable to relieve him.
Manuscript unsigned.
20 June 1780: To CJ.
14 July 1780: CJ recommends that escheator of Culpeper County be directed to stay the sale of lands claimed by John Dixon, which have been escheated in the name of Susanna Anne Godwin, until Dixon's right thereto can be determined.
House agrees.
Senate agrees.

### 1266-P   Crutchfield, Fortunatus
JHD: 21 June 1780                                                  Hanover County

Asks to be exempted from military duty as long as he continues to be engaged as a purchasing commissary for the public.
Manuscript unsigned.
21 June 1780: Rejected by refusal to refer to a committee.

### 1267-M-† Virginia Continental Line—Officers
JHD: 22 June 1780                                                          Not known

This memorial for relief as British prisoners of war in New York, text not extant, was originally transmitted to the governor.
22 June 1780: To T.
23 June 1780: T recommends that governor and Council arrange to have 10,000 pounds of tobacco transmitted to each officer and volunteer. (They are named.)
House amends and recommits to T.
24 June 1780: T recommends 5,000 pounds of tobacco be sent to each, and if a flag of truce cannot be obtained, that the tobacco be sold for specie and the money transmitted or other steps taken.
House agrees.

## 20 – 23 June 1780

29 June 1780: Senate amends.
> House amends Senate amendments.
> Senate agrees to new amendments of House.

### 1268-M  Harmar, George
JHD: 23 June 1780                                                Williamsburg

Asks return of money arising from sale of lands belonging to John Harmar, his brother. There were properly executed deeds for the estate, but the lands were sold under the acts of escheat and forfeiture.

Manuscript unsigned.
23 June 1780: To PG.
27 June 1780: PG finds reasonable.
> PG ordered to bring in a bill, "respecting the estate of Walter King Cole" to receive a clause or clauses pursuant to the resolution.

30 June 1780: Bill presented.
6 July 1780: House passes bill.
7 July 1780: Senate passes bill.
> For this act see 10H300.

### 1269-P  Marks, Isaiah
JHD: 23 June 1780                                                  Not known

Asks relief for clothes, money, and papers, lost while he was a British prisoner of war.

Manuscript unsigned.
23 June 1780: To T.
24 June 1780: T recommends (1) that clothing due him should be furnished by commissary, and (2) that a new bounty payment for recruiting be issued under oath.
> House agrees.

29 June 1780: Senate agrees.

### 1270-C-† Todd, John, Jr.
JHD: 23 June 1780, for action                                      Not known

Compensation for money advanced for public use and reimbursed after considerable depreciation had taken place. Also asks payment of salary as commandant of the Illinois [Regiment] and allowance for loss of clothing and other effects that were captured by enemy on their removal from the Illinois [Regiment].

Date unknown: To PG.

## Virginia Legislative Petitions

23 June 1780: PG recommends (1) that governor and Council be authorized to settle and adjust the accounts of the said Todd and make such allowance for monies advanced and his salary, and (2) that governor and Council be authorized to make allowance as they deem reasonable for the apparel and other effects captured by the enemy.
House agrees to (1).
House rejected (2).
29 June 1780: Senate amends (1).
30 June 1780: House agrees to Senate amendments.

### 1271-M    Mental Hospital—Directors
JHD: 28 June 1780                                          Williamsburg

Ask that further provision be made because of depreciation of paper currency.

Manuscript signed: Thos. Nelson.
28 June 1780: To PG.
1 July 1780: PG recommends that directors have power to draw from public stores such clothing and other necessaries as may be wanted in hospital, and to draw upon the auditors for so much money as may be necessary. Half-yearly accounts to be rendered to the auditors.
House agrees.
Recommitted to PG to prepare a bill.
Apparently no further action taken.
For continuation of act to provide for mental hospital, see 10H424.

### 1272-P-† Gun Factory, Fredericksburg—Mechanics
JHD: 28 June 1780                                          Spotsylvania County

Ask increase in wages.
28 June 1780: To PG.
30 June 1780: PG recommends that wages be increased to £7 10s. per day, to continue until the end of next session of GA.
House agrees.
10 July 1780: Senate agrees.

### 1273-M
Eck–
A844    **Amherst County—Court Justices**
JHD: 30 June 1780                                          Amherst County

Asks relief wherein the court certified an allowance for the expense of

## 28 June – 12 July 1780

supporting the widow and child of a soldier before knowing of a later law. The amount was £56, authorized for Adam Brown who boarded the widow and child of Reuben Nevill, who had been killed in Continental service.
   Manuscript unsigned.
30 June 1780: To T.
3 July 1780: T recommends as reasonable.
      House agrees.
5 July 1780: Senate agrees.

**1274-P-† Du-Val, Samuel, Sr.; Ronald, William; Du-Val, William; and Du-Val, Samuel, Jr.**
    JHD: 4 July 1780                                             Not known
Ask relief in that impressment of their wagons and teams into public service will bring great injury and distress and oblige them to discontinue working their coal pits.
4 July 1780: To PG.
10 July 1780: PG finds reasonable. Samuel Du-Val, Sr., allotted five wagons and teams, William Ronald allotted ten wagons and teams, William Du-Val and Samuel Du-Val, Jr., allotted eight wagons and teams.
      House agrees.
      Apparently no further action taken.

**1275-P   White, Ambrose**
    JHD: 11 July 1780                                                  Not known
Asks compensation for clothing due him that he has not received since the field officers of his regiment are prisoners.
   Manuscript unsigned.
11 July 1780: To T.
12 July 1780: T finds reasonable. Auditor of public accounts empowered to make the usual allowance in money for the clothing allowance due in 1777.
      House agrees.
13 July 1780: Senate agrees.

**1276-P-† Coleman, James**
    JHD: 12 July 1780, for action                            Not known
Asks compensation for wounds received while a soldier in Colonel Buford's regiment.
Date unknown: To T.

## Virginia Legislative Petitions

12 July 1780: T recommends £150.
    House agrees.
    Apparently no further action taken.

### 1277-M   Buckingham County—Citizens
JHD: 7 Nov. 1780                  Buckingham County

Asks act to silence nonjuring preachers of every denomination and deprive them of their benefits, to prohibit those who refuse to give assurance of fidelity to the state the exercise of the professions of law or medicine, and to impose double taxes on nonjurors.

Manuscript signed by: Noah Lacy, Richard Ridgway, Archibald Hatcher, Jno. Liggan, John Druen, and ninety-three others.
7 Nov. 1780: To R.
20 Dec. 1780: Carried over to next session of GA.
    No further action found.

### 1277 A-M   Buckingham County—Citizens
JHD: 7 Nov. 1780                  Buckingham County

Text is similar to 1277-M, which see.
Manuscript signed by twenty-nine persons.

### 1277 B-M   Buckingham County—Citizens
JHD: 7 Nov. 1780                  Buckingham County

Text is similar to 1277-M, which see.
Manuscript signed by fifteen persons.

### 1277 C-M   Buckingham County—Citizens
JHD: 7 Nov. 1780                  Buckingham County

Text is similar to 1277-M, which see.
Manuscript signed by twenty-seven persons.

### 1278-P   Brunswick County—Citizens
JHD: 7 Nov. 1780                  Brunswick County

Opposing bill "to revise and amend the several tender laws which have been passed in this Commonwealth."

Manuscript signed by: William Hill, David Vaughan, Alexander Dugger, Charles Abernathy, Jno. Fisher, and nineteen others.

## 7 November 1780

7 Nov. 1780: To lie on table.
  For general tender act see 10H321.

### 1279-P Brunswick County—Citizens
  JHD: 7 Nov. 1780           Brunswick County
 Asks repeal of act "for emitting and funding a sum of money agreeable to the resolutions of Congress of the 18th of March last."
 Manuscript signed by: Chas. Collier, John C. Robinson, Buckner Ezell, Francis Eyers, Christopher Thrower, and eighty-one others.
7 Nov. 1780: To lie on table.
  For general tender act see 10H321.

### 1279 A-P Brunswick County—Citizens
  JHD: 7 Nov. 1780           Brunswick County
 Text is similar to 1279-P, which see.
 Manuscript signed by 175 persons.

### 1279 B-P Brunswick County—Citizens
  JHD: 7 Nov. 1780           Brunswick County
 Text is similar to 1279-P, which see.
 Manuscript signed by 417 persons.

### 1280-P
Eck–
### A1114 Augusta County—Citizens
  JHD: 7 Nov. 1780           Augusta County
 Asks that their settlement in that part of Augusta County called Tygart's Valley be added to Monongalia County.
 Manuscript signed by: Benj. Wilson, Abraham Little, Peter Springstone, Robert Clark, Franklin Smith, and seventy-six others.
7 Nov. 1780: To PG.
10 Nov. 1780: PG finds reasonable and is directed to prepare bill.
21 Nov. 1780: Bill presented.
23 Nov. 1780: House passes bill.
25 Nov. 1780: Senate passes bill.
  For this act see 10H351.

### 1281-P-† King George County and Westmoreland County—Citizens
  JHD: 7 Nov. 1780           King George County
                      Westmoreland County

## Virginia Legislative Petitions

Asks reestablishment of tobacco inspection at Machodack warehouses in King George County.

7 Nov. 1780: To PG.

21 Nov. 1780: PG finds reasonable and that the same should be united with inspection at Gibson's warehouse.

House agrees and orders PG to prepare bill or bills.

22 Nov. 1780: PG to whom was referred a bill "for reviving the inspection at Machodack" is instructed to receive a clause or clauses for increasing the salaries of inspectors at the different inspections by law established.

For general act on salaries, see 10H355.

For general act including the reviving of Machodack, see 10H474.

### 1282-P  Militia, Goochland County—Field Officers
JHD: 7 Nov. 1780                                    Goochland County

Asks relief from additional service for those militiamen who were in the late defeat of General Gate's army in the South and who have returned home and have incurred the penalty of an act by which they are deemed Continental soldiers for eight months.

Manuscript signed by: John Woodson, Jno. Hopkins, Jolley Parrish, and John Curd.

7 Nov. 1780: To PG.

14 Nov. 1780: PG recommends rejection.

House agrees.

See 1302-P.

### 1283-P-† Sharp, Thomas
JHD: 7 Nov. 1780                                             Not known

Compensation for suffering lack of clothing and other necessaries due to protraction of time of service as guard to the commissioners running the boundary line with North Carolina.

7 Nov. 1780: To PG.

10 Nov. 1780: PG recommends the lieutenant of the guard be allowed at rate of £500 per month, each sergeant allowed £300 per month, and each soldier allowed £200 per month for the time they acted as guards.

House agrees.

17 Nov. 1780: Senate agrees.

## 7 – 8 November 1780

**1284-P-†  Consolver, John**
JHD: 7 Nov. 1780                                                                 Not known
Compensation for loss of right arm and left hand in defeat of Colonel Buford's regiment in the South.
7 Nov. 1780: To T.
15 Nov. 1780: T recommends £150 for present relief.
       House agrees.
18 Nov. 1780: Senate agrees.

**1285-P-†  King, John**
JHD: 7 Nov. 1780                                                                 Not known
Compensation for loss of both arms in the defeat of Colonel Buford's regiment in the South.
7 Nov. 1780: To T.
15 Nov. 1780: T recommends £500 for present relief.
       House agrees.
18 Nov. 1780: Senate agrees.

**1286-P  Albemarle Parish, Sussex County—Vestry**
JHD: 8 Nov. 1780                                                                 Sussex County
For dissolution of the vestry.
Manuscript signed by: George Booth, Nath. Dunn, George Rives, Robt. Jones, Mich. Blord, and four others.
8 Nov. 1780: To R.
27 Nov. 1780: R finds reasonable and is directed to prepare bill.
2 Dec. 1780: Bill presented.
5 Dec. 1780: House passes bill.
8 Dec. 1780: Senate passes bill.
       For this act see 10H366.

**1287-P  Charles City County—Citizens**
JHD: 8 Nov. 1780                                                                 Charles City County
Asks amendment of acts of last session respecting the money emitted, agreeable to the resolutions of Congress of 18 March last, and for emitting and funding money on the credit of the state.
Manuscript signed by: William Merry, Benja. Mountcastle, Charles Holdsworth, Joseph Vaiden, Major Willcox, and 154 others.
8 Nov. 1780: To PG.
       For general tender act see 10H321.

## Virginia Legislative Petitions

**1288-P    Mayo, John**
JHD: 8 Nov. 1780                                    Chesterfield County
To establish a ferry across James River from Mayo's land in Chesterfield County to Mayo's lot in Richmond.
Manuscript signed by: David Parkinson, Levi Newby, Ben. Thomas, Jno. Wilson, William Turner, Jr., and fifty-nine others.
8 Nov. 1780: To PG.
5 Dec. 1780: PG finds reasonable.
      Recommitted to PG.
12 Dec. 1780: PG recommends deferral to next session of GA.
      Recommitted to PG.
18 Dec. 1780: Carried over to next session of GA.
      Apparently no further action taken until October 1781 session when it was presented as a new petition (1487-P).

**1289-P-†  Amelia County—Citizens**
JHD: 8 Nov. 1780                                            Amelia County
To establish a ferry across James River from John Mayo's land in Chesterfield County to Mayo's lot in Richmond.
8 Nov. 1780: To PG.
5 Dec. 1780: PG finds reasonable.
      Recommitted to PG.
12 Dec. 1780: PG recommends deferral to next session of GA.
      Recommitted to PG.
18 Dec. 1780: Carried over to next session of GA.
      Apparently no further action taken until October 1781 session when it was presented as a new petition (1487-P).

**1290-P    Cary, Archibald**
JHD: 8 Nov. 1780                                    Chesterfield County
To establish a ferry across James River from Cary's land in Chesterfield County to the Sandy Bar in Richmond.
Manuscript unsigned.
8 Nov. 1780: To PG.
12 Dec. 1780: PG recommends deferral to next session of GA.
      Recommitted to PG.
18 Dec. 1780: Carried over to next session of GA.
      Apparently no further action taken until October 1781 session when it was presented as a new petition (1487-P).

## 8 November 1780

**1291-P Veale, Samuel**
  JHD: 8 Nov. 1780            Norfolk County
As executor of George Veale, deceased, asks compensation from sales of the estate of John Goodrich and Company, who joined the British enemy, for goods sold to said company without receiving bar iron in return, as agreed.
 Manuscript unsigned.
8 Nov. 1780: To PG.
11 Nov. 1780: PG recommends payment sufficient to purchase or be equal to
   three tons of bar iron.
   House agrees.
   PG directed to prepare bill.
21 Nov. 1780: Bill presented.
22 Nov. 1780: Bill recommitted to PG.
   Apparently no further action taken.

**1292-P Armstrong, Andrew**
  JHD: 8 Nov. 1780            Botetourt County
Compensation for loss of three of his horses that died at Haus Meadows after conveying a load of powder while employed by Thomas Madison at the direction of the governor.
 Manuscript unsigned. Manuscript petition asks for £4,300 and includes attached depositions of William Johnson and John Henry.
8 Nov. 1780: To PG.
8 Dec. 1780: PG finds reasonable.
   House agrees. (Amount not stated.)
14 Dec. 1780: Senate agrees.

**1293-P Richmond County—Citizens**
  JHD: 8 Nov. 1780            Richmond County
Asks revival of the tobacco inspection at Glascock's warehouses in Richmond County.
 Manuscript signed by: William Colston, Thomas Williams, Jno. Sydnor, Edwd. Jones, Roger Peachey, and 112 others.
8 Nov. 1780: To PG.
8 Dec. 1780: PG finds reasonable.
   Read twice and amended.
   House agrees and orders that the committee to whom a bill "to
   amend the act for reviving several public warehouses for the

## Virginia Legislative Petitions

inspection of tobacco" was committed receive a clause or clauses pursuant to said resolution.

For general act including revival of Glascock's, see 10H474.

### 1294-P  Louisa County—Citizens
JHD: 8 Nov. 1780                               Louisa County

Opposing the bill to revise the tender laws.

Manuscript signed by: Robt. Anderson, Joseph Boxley, Benjamin Terrell, John Pulliam, James Beadels, and 104 others.

8 Nov. 1780: To lie on table.

For general tender act see 10H321.

### 1295-P  Mecklenburg County—Citizens
JHD: 8 Nov. 1780                               Mecklenburg County

Opposing the bill to revise the tender laws.

Manuscript signed by: Bennett Goode, Ben Ferrell, John Baskerville, Jacob Bugg, Nat. Moss, and 133 others.

8 Nov. 1780: To lie on table.

For general tender act see 10H321.

### 1296-P  Goochland County—Citizens
JHD: 8 Nov. 1780                               Goochland County

Asks repeal of act passed at last session of GA "for calling in and redeeming the money now in circulation, and for emitting and funding new bills of credit."

Manuscript signed by: Wm. Holman, John Ware, Benjamin East, William Purkins, David Webster, and 129 others.

8 Nov. 1780: To lie on table.

For general tender act see 10H321.

### 1297-P  Louisa County—Citizens
JHD: 8 Nov. 1780                               Louisa County

Asks repeal of act passed at last session of GA "for calling in and redeeming the money now in circulation, and for emitting and funding new bills of credit."

Manuscript signed by: William White, Jr., Edward Edwards, P. Phillips, John Winter, Ezekiel East, and 169 others.

8 Nov. 1780: To lie on table.

For general tender act see 10H321.

## 8 – 9 November 1780

**1298-M Baptist Association**
JHD: 8 Nov. 1780                                                Charlotte County
Asks relief from present vestry law and condition whereby marriages solemnized by dissenting ministers are not confirmed and sanctioned by law.
Manuscript signed by: Sam Harris and John Williams.
8 Nov. 1780: To R.
21 Nov. 1780: R recommends (1) that parts of the memorial asking that marriages solemnized by dissenting ministers may be declared lawful are reasonable, and (2) that parts of the memorial asking that the vestries in the several parishes throughout this state may be dissolved are reasonable.
House agrees to (1) and directs R to prepare bill.
(2) is laid on table.
2 Dec. 1780: Bill for (1) presented.
4 Dec. 1780: Bill for (1) recommitted to R.
15 Dec. 1780: R presents amended bill for (1).
18 Dec. 1780: House passes bill for (1).
28 Dec. 1780: Senate amends bill.
House agrees to some amendments and disagrees with others.
29 Dec. 1780: Senate adheres to amendments not agreed to by House.
30 Dec. 1780: House recedes from disagreement with Senate amendments.
For act relating to all dissenters, see 10H361.

**1299-P McCauley, Campbell**
JHD: 9 Nov. 1780                                                            Not known
Compensation for wounds received in the defeat of Colonel Buford's regiment in the South. The wounds have disabled him so that he cannot obtain a livelihood.
Manuscript unsigned, but name in petition spelled "Camel."
9 Nov. 1780: To T.
15 Nov. 1780: T recommends £300 for present relief.
House agrees.
18 Nov. 1780: Senate agrees.

**1300-P-† Davis, Charles**
JHD: 9 Nov. 1780                                                            Not known
Compensation for wounds received in the defeat of Colonel Buford's regiment in the South. The wounds have disabled him so that he cannot obtain a livelihood.
9 Nov. 1780: To T.

14 Dec. 1780: T recommends £500 for present relief and to draw a full suit of clothes from the public store.
    House agrees.
16 Dec. 1780: Senate agrees.

### 1301-P-† Nettles, Abraham
    JHD: 9 Nov. 1780                                             Not known

Compensation for illness contracted in service, resulting in paralysis.
9 Nov. 1780: To T.
15 Nov. 1780: T recommends £300 for present relief.
    House agrees.
18 Nov. 1780: Senate agrees.

### 1302-P
Eck–
A845    **Militia, Amherst County**
    JHD: 9 Nov. 1780                                       Amherst County

Asks relief from additional service for those militiamen who were in the late defeat of General Gate's army in the South where they lost all their clothing and came home for a supply thereof. On return to camp they were informed they had incurred the penalty of an act by which they are deemed Continental soldiers for eight months.

Manuscript signed by: Samuel Dinwiddie, Landon Carter, John Lobban, Simon Ramsden, Edw. Bybee, and sixteen others.
9 Nov. 1780: To PG.
14 Nov. 1780: PG recommends rejection.
    Recommitted to PG.
    Apparently no further action taken.
    See 1282-P.

### 1303-P Meacom, Ann; Meacom, Thomas; Meacom, Samuel; Meacom, John; Meacom, Sylvia; and Meacom, James
    JHD: 9 Nov. 1780                                Southampton County

For relief from the forfeiture of the estate of her husband, John Meacom, deceased, who was executed for the murder of one of his own slaves. Under the law the estate was sold for the benefit of the commonwealth and his widow and children (named above) were left destitute.

Manuscript unsigned.
9 Nov. 1780: To PG.

## 9 – 10 November 1780

11 Nov. 1780: PG recommends that money received from the sale of the estate be restored to petitioners.
PG directed to prepare a bill.
21 Nov. 1780: Bill presented.
23 Nov. 1780: House passes bill.
24 Nov. 1780: Senate passes bill.
For this act see 10H350.

**1304-P-† Lancaster County—Citizens**
JHD: 9 Nov. 1780                         Lancaster County
Asks reestablishment of tobacco inspection at Dymer's warehouses in Lancaster County.
9 Nov. 1780: To PG.
8 Dec. 1780: PG finds reasonable.
House amends and agrees, and orders that the committee to whom a bill "to amend the act for reviving several public warehouses for the inspection of tobacco" was committed receive a clause or clauses pursuant to said resolution.
Apparently no further action taken.

**1305-P King and Queen County—Citizens**
JHD: 9 Nov. 1780                    King and Queen County
Asks reestablishment of tobacco inspection at Turner's warehouse in King and Queen County.
Manuscript signed by: James Mitchell, Richd. Leigh, Thomas Burk, James Campbell, Jas. Henry, and seventy-one others.
9 Nov. 1780: To PG.
Apparently no further action taken.

**1306-P Powhatan County—Citizens**
JHD: 9 Nov. 1780                         Powhatan County
Opposing the bill to revise the tender laws.
Manuscript signed by: Wm. Clarke, John Hyde Saunders, Samuel Rice, Jacob McGehee, Henry Cox, Jr., and ninety-seven others.
9 Nov. 1780: To lie on table.
For general tender act see 10H321.

**1307-P-† Wilkins, Nathaniel**
JHD: 10 Nov. 1780                              Not known
Compensation for loss of right hand and part of his right arm in the defeat of

Colonel Buford's regiment in the South, which losses have rendered him incapable of obtaining a livelihood.
10 Nov. 1780: To T.
15 Nov. 1780: T recommends £300 for present relief.
>House agrees.
18 Nov. 1780: Senate agrees.

**1308-P de Sequeyra, John**
JHD: 10 Nov. 1780             Williamsburg
Asks continuance of salary for his attendance as physician to the mental hospital.
Manuscript unsigned.
10 Nov. 1780: To T.
15 Nov. 1780: T recommends £600 for year ending 17 December 1780.
>House agrees.
18 Nov. 1780: Senate agrees.

**1309-P-† Wallis, Hugh**
JHD: 10 Nov. 1780             Not known
Additional compensation for wounds received while a soldier in service to the commonwealth.
10 Nov. 1780: To T.
15 Nov. 1780: T recommends £400 for present relief.
>House agrees.
18 Nov. 1780: Senate agrees.
>See 581-P-† under Wallace.

**1310-P Long, Dorothy**
JHD: 10 Nov. 1780             Louisa County
Asks relief as she has lost her husband and two sons in the service of this state and had another son also enlisted in the Georgia service from which he was lately discharged and returned home in a weak state, and she is too poor to pay the expense of a doctor.
Manuscript unsigned. Manuscript endorsement says rejected 17 November 1780. Thomas Johnson's name is attached.
10 Nov. 1780: To T.
17 Nov. 1780: House rejects.

**1311-P Cumberland County—Citizens**
JHD: 10 Nov. 1780             Cumberland County

## 10 November 1780

Opposing the bill to revise the tender laws.
Manuscript signed by: Geo. Kuling, Maurice Langhorn, Chs. Ballone, Wm. Hudson, James Glenn, Sr., and 180 others.
10 Nov. 1780: To lie on table.
    For general tender act see 10H32L.

### 1312-P-* Prince Edward County—Citizens
    JHD: 10 Nov. 1780                       Prince Edward County
Asks act to silence nonjuring preachers of every denomination and deprive them of their benefits, to prohibit those who refuse to give assurance of allegiance to the state the exercise of the professions of law or medicine, and to impose double taxes on nonjurors.
10 Nov. 1780: To R.
20 Dec. 1780: Carried over to next session of GA.
    No further action found.

### 1313-P Cumberland County—Citizens
    JHD: 10 Nov. 1780                       Cumberland County
Asks act to silence nonjuring preachers of every denomination and deprive them of their benefits, to prohibit those who refuse to give assurance of allegiance to the state the exercise of the professions of law or medicine, and to impose double taxes on nonjurors.
Manuscript signed by: Lancer Anderson, Martin Blake, David Winniford, Robt. Walton, Creed Haskins, and fifty-seven others.
10 Nov. 1780: To R.
20 Nov. 1780: Carried over to next session of GA.
    No further action found.

### 1313 A-P Cumberland County—Citizens
    JHD: 10 Nov. 1780                       Cumberland County
Text is similar to 1313-P, which see.
Manuscript signed by twenty-nine persons.

### 1313 B-P Cumberland County—Citizens
    JHD: 10 Nov. 1780                       Cumberland County
Text is similar to 1313-P, which see.
Manuscript signed by 110 persons.

## Virginia Legislative Petitions

**1314-P**  Norfolk County and Nansemond County—Citizens
JHD: 10 Nov. 1780          Norfolk County
                            Nansemond County
Asks exemption from taxation on their lots in Norfolk and Portsmouth, which were exempted by act of convention in 1776, but now liable due to law of last session.
Manuscript signed by: Paul Loyall, Charles Thomas, Geo. Abyvon, Max. Calvert, Cornelius Calvert, and six others.
10 Nov. 1780: To PG.
   Apparently no further action taken.

**1315-P**  Charlotte County—Citizens
JHD: 10 Nov. 1780          Charlotte County
Asks formation of an invalid company of militia in every county.
Manuscript signed by: Matt. Flournoy, Tho. Spencer, Jr., Lew. Jones, Ja. Speed, Wood Bouldin, and fifty-four others.
10 Nov. 1780: To PG.
   Apparently no further action taken.

**1316-P**  Bilberry, Benjamin
JHD: 11 Nov. 1780          Richmond Town
Asks act to protect his wife, Kate, a Negro, and her increase from slavery after his death.
Manuscript unsigned.
11 Nov. 1780: To PG.
20 Nov. 1780: PG discharged from proceeding on petition and the committee to whom the bill "for the manumission of Ned, a negro man slave, the property of Henry Delony" was committed was instructed to receive clause or clauses for the manumission of Kate, late the property of Abraham Cowley, deceased.
22 Nov. 1780: PG presents amended bill "for the manumission of Ned. . . ."
23 Nov. 1780: House passes bill.
24 Nov. 1780: Senate passes bill.
   For this act, including Kate, see 10H372.

**1317-P**
Eck–
A1673  **Ross, David**
JHD: 11 Nov. 1780          Bedford County

## 10 – 13 November 1780

To establish a ferry over James River from Ross's land in Bedford County to Robert Bolling's land in Amherst County.
Manuscript unsigned. Dated 10 November 1780.
11 Nov. 1780: To PG.
19 Dec. 1780: PG finds reasonable.
>Read twice and PG ordered to receive clause or clauses pursuant to said resolution.
>For general ferry act, including this ferry, see 10H365.

**1318-P  Brunswick County—Citizens**
>JHD: 11 Nov. 1780　　　　　　　　　　　　　　Brunswick County
Asking passage of bill to revise the tender law.
Manuscript signed by: Joseph Kidd, Eras. Moore, Charles Portlock, Arthur Emmerson, W. Stark, and seventeen others.
11 Nov. 1780: To lie on table.
>For general tender act see 10H321.

**1318 A-P  Brunswick County—Citizens**
>JHD: 11 Nov. 1780　　　　　　　　　　　　　　Brunswick County
Text is similar to 1318-P, which see.
Manuscript signed by twenty-four persons.

**1319-P  Jones, John, Jr.**
>JHD: 13 Nov. 1780　　　　　　　　　　　　　　Dinwiddie County
Compensation for horse, impressed into the service of the Maryland brigade, for which no certificate was given to Jones.
Manuscript unsigned, but has depositions attached.
13 Nov. 1780: To T.
16 Nov. 1780: T recommends £3,000.
>House agrees.
12 Dec. 1780: Senate agrees.

**1320-P-†  Banks, John**
>JHD: 13 Nov. 1780　　　　　　　　　　　　　　　　　Not known
Compensation for accident that injured him while he was in military service.
13 Nov. 1780: To T.
1 Dec. 1780: T recommends £300 for present relief.
>House agrees.
5 Dec. 1780: Senate agrees.

### Virginia Legislative Petitions

**1321-P  Selden, Miles**
    JHD: 13 Nov. 1780                                         Elizabeth City County
Compensation for tract of land with houses near the town of Hampton; tract was seized in 1777 and houses were converted into a hospital for smallpox and remained such until last spring.
  Manuscript unsigned. Deposition of George Muter attached.
13 Nov. 1780: To T.
28 Dec. 1780: Carried over to next session of GA.
       No further action found.

**1322-P  Brunswick County—Citizens**
    JHD: 14 Nov. 1780                                              Brunswick County
Asking division of Brunswick County into two counties.
  Manuscript signed by: George Hicks, William Fogg, John Hicks, Jack Pennington, Asa Gresham, and thirty-eight others.
14 Nov. 1780: To PG.
16 Nov. 1780: PG finds reasonable that division be into two counties by a line
       to begin two miles above Chapman's Ford and running thence a due south course to the county line.
       PG rejects other part of petition asking a division of the county by Meherrin River.
       House agrees and directs PG to prepare a bill.
22 Nov. 1780: Bill presented.
25 Nov. 1780: House passes bill.
28 Nov. 1780: Senate amends bill.
       House agrees to Senate amendments.
       For this act establishing Greensville County, effective 1 February 1781, see 10H363.

**1322 A-P Brunswick County—Citizens**
    JHD: 14 Nov. 1780                                              Brunswick County
Text is similar to 1322-P, which see.
Manuscript signed by seventy-three persons.

**1322 B-P Brunswick County—Citizens**
    JHD: 14 Nov. 1780                                              Brunswick County
Text is similar to 1322-P, which see.
Manuscript signed by 118 persons.

## 13 – 15 November 1780

### 1322 C-P Brunswick County—Citizens
JHD: 14 Nov. 1780     Brunswick County
Text is similar to 1322-P, which see.
Manuscript signed by eighty-two persons.

### 1323-P Southampton County—Citizens
JHD: 14 Nov. 1780     Southampton County
Asks that the upper part of Southampton County be added to a part of Brunswick County to form one distinct county.
Manuscript signed by: Thos. Turner, Edw. Morgan, Colin Person, Samuel Clifton, Joshua Harvey, Jr., and thirty-three others.
14 Nov. 1780: To PG.
15 Nov. 1780: PG recommends rejection.
    House rejects.

### 1323 A-P Southampton County—Citizens
JHD: 14 Nov. 1780     Southampton County
Text is similar to 1323-P, which see.
Manuscript signed by five persons.

### 1323 B-P Southampton County—Citizens
JHD: 14 Nov. 1780     Southampton County
Text is similar to 1323-P, which see.
Manuscript signed by thirty persons.

### 1324-P Hix, Daniel
JHD: 14 Nov. 1780     Richmond Town
Asks relief for warrant obtained for wages as doorkeeper to the House and since lost without his having received payment.
Manuscript unsigned.
14 Nov. 1780: To T.
18 Nov. 1780: T finds reasonable and directs auditor of public accounts to
    renew the said warrant.
    House agrees.
23 Nov. 1780: Senate agrees.

### 1325-P Sutton, John
JHD: 15 Nov. 1780     Fairfax County
Asks return of estate bequeathed to him by the will of James Connell, his

## Virginia Legislative Petitions

uncle, late of the town of Alexandria, and which has been escheated to the commonwealth.

Manuscript unsigned.

15 Nov. 1780: To PG.

18 Nov. 1780: PG finds reasonable.

House amends and directs PG to prepare a bill.

21 Nov. 1780: Bill presented.

23 Nov. 1780: House passes bill.

28 Nov. 1780: Senate passes bill.

For this act see 10H372.

**1326-P  Tobacco Inspectors—Byrd's Warehouse and Shockoe Warehouse**

JHD: 15 Nov. 1780                                    Richmond Town

Asks for increase in salary equal to what they had received in 1774.

Manuscript unsigned.

15 Nov. 1780: To PG.

22 Nov. 1780: PG finds reasonable.

PG, to whom bill "for reviving the inspection at Machodack" was referred, is instructed to receive clause or clauses for increasing the salaries of inspectors at the different inspections by law established. For general act, including these two, see 10H355.

**1327-P  Tobacco Inspectors—Page's Warehouse and Crutchfield's Warehouse**

JHD: 15 Nov. 1780                                    Hanover County

Asks for increase in salary equal to what they had received in 1774.

Manuscript signed by: Clarke and Tally (of Page's warehouse) and Clarke and Wingfield (of Crutchfield's warehouse).

15 Nov. 1780: To PG.

22 Nov. 1780: PG finds reasonable.

PG, to whom bill "for reviving the inspection at Machodack" was referred, is instructed to receive clause or clauses for increasing the salaries of inspectors at the different inspections by law established. For general act, including these two, see 10H355.

**1328-P  Richmond—Merchants**

JHD: 15 Nov. 1780                                    Richmond Town

Asks for increase in salaries for tobacco inspectors, equal to that allowed in 1774.

## 15 – 16 November 1780

Manuscript signed by: Marsden and Smyth, John Hay, Wm. Hay, Charles Irving, James Buchanan, and eleven others.

15 Nov. 1780: To PG.

22 Nov. 1780: PG, to whom bill "for reviving the inspection at Machodack" was referred, is instructed to receive clause or clauses for increasing the salaries of inspectors at the different inspections by law established.

For general act see 10H355.

**1329-P-† Murphey, James**
  JHD: 15 Nov. 1780             Not known

Compensation for loss of right arm in defeat of Colonel Buford's regiment in the South.

15 Nov. 1780: To T.

23 Nov. 1780: T recommends £500 for present relief and a full suit of clothes from the public store.

  House agrees.

28 Nov. 1780: Senate agrees.

**1330-M Lynch, Charles**
  JHD: 16 Nov. 1780             Bedford County

Payment of services to superintend the lead mines. He has discharged the duty for one year and the Board of Trade, which hired him, has been discontinued.

Manuscript unsigned. Manuscript says not taken up by order of Mr. Talbot.

16 Nov. 1780: To T.

  Apparently no further action taken.

**1331-P-† Terry, Stephen**
  JHD: 16 Nov. 1780             Not known

Additional compensation for wounds received at the battle of Brandywine.

16 Nov. 1780: To T.

23 Nov. 1780: T recommends £500 for present relief.

  House agrees.

28 Nov. 1780: Senate agrees.

**1332-P**
Eck–
A1115  **Kilpatrick, Alexander**
    JHD: 16 Nov. 1780            Augusta County

## Virginia Legislative Petitions

Compensation for maintenance of criminals and others while he served as jailor of Augusta County. He was ignorant of the fees allowed by law, and the court made a considerable deduction from his account.
Manuscript unsigned. Account attached.
16 Nov. 1780: To PG.
    Apparently no further action taken.
    A similar petition was presented on 17 December 1781; see 1558-P.

**1333-P**    **Culpeper County—Citizens**
    JHD: 18 Nov. 1780        Culpeper County
Opposing the bill to revise the tender laws.
Manuscript signed by: Thos. Ashford, Daniel Pritman, John Breedlove, H. Davis, John Mennefee, and thirty-nine others. Letter of transmittal from B. French Strother and Henry Hill.
18 Nov. 1780: To lie on table.
    For general tender act see 10H321.

**1334-P**
Eck–
A168    **Albemarle County—Citizens**
    JHD: 18 Nov. 1780        Albemarle County
Opposing the bill to revise the tender laws.
Manuscript signed by: John Hudson, Alexander Gordon, Willm. McCord, Thos. Stockton, Charles Smith, and seventy-five others.
18 Nov. 1780: To lie on table.
    For general tender act see 10H321.

**1335-C-†**  **Claiborne, Richard**
    JHD: 18 Nov. 1780        Not known
Asks compensation for clothing that he should have received but did not, and a bounty of lands for service as a deputy quartermaster general to the Continental army.
18 Nov. 1780: To T.
24 Nov. 1780: T finds that requisitions are provided for by two acts of assembly passed at sessions of May and October 1779.
    Read second time and recommitted to T.
    Apparently no further action taken.

## 18 – 20 November 1780

**1336-P   Doggins, John**
JHD: 18 Nov. 1780                                                Dinwiddie County
Compensation for his horse that died after receiving an injury from one of the public horses, which Doggins was employed to convey to Petersburg.
Manuscript unsigned. Manuscript endorsement says £150 was paid to Doggins.
18 Nov. 1780: To T
20 Dec. 1780: T recommends £1,200.
       House agrees.
       Senate action not found.

**1337-P   Berkeley County—Citizens**
JHD: 18 Nov. 1780                                                Berkeley County
Asks a more equal method of recruitment for the army.
Manuscript signed by: Wm. Patterson, Anthy. Noble, John Dark, Hugh Varner, James McCalester, and fifty-six others.
18 Nov. 1780: To committee appointed to prepare and bring in a bill "for recruiting the army."
       For general act see 10H326.

**1338-M-†   Stafford County—Justices**
JHD: 20 Nov. 1780                                                Stafford County
Opposing the removal of their courthouse from the place where it now stands.
20 Nov. 1780: To PG.
       This petition is in opposition to 1233-P-†.

**1339-P-†   Stafford County—Citizens**
JHD: 20 Nov. 1780                                                Stafford County
Opposing removal of the courthouse from the place where it now stands.
20 Nov. 1780: To PG.
       This petition is in opposition to 1233-P-†.

**1340-P**
Eck–
**A1674   Bedford County—Citizens**
JHD: 20 Nov. 1780                                                Bedford County
Opposing the bill to revise the tender laws.
Manuscript signed by: Moses McIlvain, Samuel McIlvain, Joseph Goff, John Burford, Chas. Lambert, and seventy others.

## Virginia Legislative Petitions

20 Nov. 1780: To lie on table.
        For general tender act see 10H321.

### 1341-P-† Chambers, James
    JHD: 20 Nov. 1780                              Not known

Compensation for wounds received in the defeat of Colonel Buford's regiment in the South.
20 Nov. 1780: To T.
23 Nov. 1780: T recommends £500 for present relief.
        House agrees.
28 Nov. 1780: Senate agrees.

### 1342-P-† Tipton, William
    JHD: 20 Nov. 1780                              Not known

Compensation for wounds received at the battle of Savannah.
20 Nov. 1780: To T.
23 Nov. 1780: T recommends £500 for present relief and suit of clothes from
        public store.
        House agrees.
28 Nov. 1780: Senate agrees.

### 1343-P
Eck–
A1675    **Meade, John**
    JHD: 21 Nov. 1780                            Bedford County

Compensation for maintenance of prisoners while he served as jailor of Bedford County. Court made a considerable deduction in his account by refusing to allow him more than fees given by law.

Manuscript unsigned. Includes many names of those imprisoned, which are also found in JHD.
21 Nov. 1780: To PG.
29 Nov. 1780: PG discharged from proceeding on petition.
        Referred to T.
5 Dec. 1780: T recommends £6,480.
        Recommitted to T.
21 Dec. 1780: T recommends £5,400.
        House amends and agrees.

## 20 – 22 November 1780

28 Dec. 1780: Senate amends.
>House agrees to Senate amendments.
>Meade petitioned on 7 December 1781 to correct an error; see 1523-P.

### 1344-P-† Stevens, Smyth
JHD: 21 Nov. 1780                                              Not known

Compensation for loss of leg while a soldier in the 11th Virginia Regiment
21 Nov. 1780: To T.
14 Dec. 1780: T recommends £500 for present relief and a full suit of clothes from the public store.
>House agrees.

16 Dec. 1780: Senate agrees.

### 1345-P Mitchell, William
JHD: 21 Nov. 1780                                                York County

Asks reimbursement of judgment and costs rendered against him by York County court. As quartermaster of garrison at Yorktown, Mitchell had purchased sundry oak trees for use in the fortifications, and a detachment of artificers by mistake or neglect had cut down some pine trees.

Manuscript unsigned. Attached is statement of trespassing charge and fine.
21 Nov. 1780: To T.
25 Nov. 1780: T recommends £189 3s.
>House agrees.
>No Senate action found.

### 1346-P Roy, Richard and Catlett, John
JHD: 22 Nov. 1780                                           Caroline County

Asks increase in salaries as inspectors of tobacco at Roy's warehouse since present salaries allowed are insufficient for their trouble and expense.

Manuscript unsigned.
22 Nov. 1780: To lie on table.
>For general act see 10H355.

### 1347-P Pointer, William
JHD: 22 Nov. 1780                                        Charles City County

Compensation for his mare, impressed by an express rider. Horse was killed by severity of usage.

Manuscript unsigned. Deposition attached.
22 Nov. 1780: To T.

## Virginia Legislative Petitions

28 Dec. 1780: T recommends £3,000.
        House agrees.
29 Dec. 1780: Senate agrees.

### 1348-P Littleton Parish, Cumberland County—Citizens
JHD: 23 Nov. 1780                               Cumberland County

Opposing the petition of other inhabitants of the county asking that nonjuring clergymen of every denomination may be silenced, that nonjurors pay double taxes and be precluded from the exercise of the professions of law or medicine.

Manuscript signed by: Nathan Glen, William Coleman, William Glenn, Baron Guthrey, James Wright, and ninety-one others.
23 Nov. 1780: To R.
20 Dec. 1780: Carried over to next session of GA.
        No further action found.

### 1348 A-P Littleton Parish, Cumberland County—Citizens
JHD: 23 Nov. 1780                               Cumberland County

Text is similar to 1348-P, which see.
Manuscript signed by twenty-four persons.

### 1348 B-P Littleton Parish, Cumberland County—Citizens
JHD: 23 Nov. 1780                               Cumberland County

Text is similar to 1348-P, which see.
Manuscript signed by fifty-eight persons.

### 1348 C-P Littleton Parish, Cumberland County—Citizens
JHD: 23 Nov. 1780                               Cumberland County

Text is similar to 1348-P, which see.
Manuscript signed by thirty-three persons.

### 1349-P Crowley, Elizabeth
JHD: 23 Nov. 1780                                         Henry County

Additional compensation, necessary because of depreciation of currency, for support of herself and five small children in consideration of the death of her husband who was killed in service.

Manuscript unsigned.
23 Nov. 1780: To T.
28 Nov. 1780: T recommends £500 for present relief.
        House agrees.

30 Nov. 1780: Senate amends.
1 Dec. 1780: House agrees to Senate amendments.

**1350-P    Armstrong, James**
JHD: 23 Nov. 1780                                           Henry County
Compensation for his horse, stolen from him by tories during an expedition to suppress them.
Manuscript unsigned. Endorsement shows no action. Certificate attached.
23 Nov. 1780: To T.
> Apparently no further action taken.

**1351-P    Buckingham County—Citizens**
JHD: 23 Nov. 1780                                      Buckingham County
Asks repeal of act setting definite time to be served by soldiers.
Manuscript signed by: Hawkins Sanderson William Gibson, Richard West, John Cox, Boaz Ford, and fifty-one others.
23 Nov. 1780: To PG.
> Apparently no further action taken.

**1352-P-†  Dunlap, John and Hayes, James**
JHD: 24 Nov. 1780                                              Not known
Asks compensation for costly printing apparatus and materials taken by the enemy when the ship *Bachelor* was driven ashore by stress of weather. Shipment was made in consequence of an application made to them by the governor to establish a press and undertake the public printing business.
24 Nov. 1780: To special committee.
> Committee of whole discharged from proceeding on letters and papers of the governor to them referred, as respects the engagement made by the governor with Dunlap and Hayes. Same was referred to the committee on the foregoing petition.

14 Dec. 1780: Committee recommends (1) that Dunlap and Hayes ought to be compensated by the public for their loss, and the governor, with advice of Council, authorized to adjust and settle with the petitioners the amount of their loss and order payment from the public treasury; and (2) that an inquiry be made whether the printing press at Williamsburg is public property, and if so, the governor should direct its removal to Richmond for use by Dunlap and Hayes.
> House agrees.

16 Dec. 1780: Senate agrees.

## Virginia Legislative Petitions

### 1353-M-† Winchester—Mechanics
JHD: 24 Nov. 1780                  Frederick County

Asks that no apprentice be permitted to enlist into the army of the United States or of the commonwealth without his master's consent.

24 Nov. 1780: To PG.
5 Dec. 1780: PG finds reasonable.
    House rejects.

### 1354-P-† Bentley, William
JHD: 25 Nov. 1780                 Gloucester County

Compensation for a slave who ran away, was outlawed, pursued, and killed.

25 Nov. 1780: To T.
25 Dec. 1780: T recommends £6,000.
    House agrees.
28 Dec. 1780: Senate agrees.

### 1355-P-† Andrews, William
JHD: 25 Nov. 1780                         Not known

Compensation for wound received in the attack on Stony Point.

25 Nov. 1780: To T.
28 Nov. 1780: T recommends £500.
    Recommitted to T.
15 Dec. 1780: T recommends £500 for present relief and a full suit of clothes from the public store.
    House agrees.
18 Dec. 1780: Senate agrees.

### 1356-P-† Murray, Richard
JHD: 25 Nov. 1780                         Not known

Compensation for wounds received in the defeat of Colonel Buford's regiment in the South.

25 Nov. 1780: To T.
28 Nov. 1780: T recommends £500 for present relief.
    House agrees.
30 Nov. 1780: Senate agrees.

### 1357-M Western Frontier—Citizens
JHD: 27 Nov. 1780                 Montgomery County
                                                Washington County

## 24 – 29 November 1780

Greenbrier County
Kentucky Area

Asking that some plan may be devised for their better security from the depredations and incursions of the Indian enemy.

Manuscript, which is long and dramatic, is signed by: Ad. Smyth, Wm. Keelly, Andw. Armstrong, Daniel McNiell, Moses Dunlap, and ninety-seven others.

27 Nov. 1780: To PG.
    Apparently no further action taken.
    For general act, relating in part to defense of frontier, see 10H386.

### 1358-P-† Davis, Abraham

JHD: 29 Nov. 1780                        Not known

Compensation for wounds received while a soldier in the defeat of Colonel Buford's regiment at Hanging Rock.

29 Nov. 1780: To T.
1 Dec. 1780: T recommends £500 for present relief.
    House agrees.
5 Dec. 1780: Senate agrees.

### 1359-P    Quakers—Mecklenburg County

JHD: 29 Nov. 1780                 Mecklenburg County

Asks that citizens be legally authorized to manumit their slaves in such manner as will prevent injury to the community.

Manuscript signed by: James Ladd and endorsed by Md. Munford.

29 Nov. 1780: To PG.
5 Dec. 1780: PG finds reasonable and recommends (1) that manumission of certain slaves who have been declared free by last wills and testaments of their owners under certain restrictions and limitations, and (2) that all slaves heretofore manumitted under hand and seal of their owners shall be declared free.
    PG rejects granting a general license to society of Quakers for emancipating all their slaves.
    House agrees. PG to prepare bill pursuant to (1) and (2).
8 Dec. 1780: Bill presented.
9 Dec. 1780: Bill committed to committee of whole.
16 Dec. 1780: Carried over to second Monday in May 1781.
    No further action found.

## Virginia Legislative Petitions

### 1360-P Crayton, William
JHD: 29 Nov. 1780                                        Not known

Compensation for wounds received while a soldier at the defeat of Colonel Buford's regiment.

Manuscript unsigned.

29 Nov. 1780: To T.

5 Dec. 1780: T recommends £300 for present relief.
      House agrees.

8 Dec. 1780: Senate agrees.

### 1361-P Telford, Andrew and Telford, James
JHD: 1 Dec. 1780                                   Botetourt County
                                                                                    Amherst County

Asks exemption for themselves, their apprentices, and workmen from military service so that they may establish a factory of firearms.

Manuscript unsigned.

1 Dec. 1780: To PG.
      Apparently no further action taken.
      For general act exempting persons in ironworks, see 10H397.

### 1362-P Northumberland County—Citizens
JHD: 2 Dec. 1780                            Northumberland County

Asks that magistrates be appointed by annual or triennial election of the people.

Manuscript signed by: Catesby Jones, David Boyd, Abra. Beacham, Kenner Cralle, Thomas Edwards, and 113 others.

2 Dec. 1780: House lays on table.
      No further action found.

### 1363-P O'hara, Mary
JHD: 2 Dec. 1780                                      York County

Asks relief since her husband and two sons were killed in the defeat of Colonel Buford's regiment in the South.

Manuscript unsigned. Endorsed by Wm. Reynolds, delegate from York County.

2 Dec. 1780: To T.

12 Dec. 1780: T recommends £150 for present relief.
      House rejects.

408

## 29 November – 5 December 1780

**1364-P**
Eck–A1676
[Wrong date]
### Terrill, Harry
JHD: 2 Dec. 1780                           Bedford County

Asks additional compensation for expenses incurred while he and a guard conveyed to the public jail a number of persons accused of treason.

Manuscript unsigned. Includes names of members of guard.

2 Dec. 1780: To T.

20 Dec. 1780: T recommends rejection.
     House apparently rejects, as petition is so endorsed.

**1365-P-†** **Williams, James**
JHD: 5 Dec. 1780                                   Not known

Asks compensation since he became blind in his left eye and sorely afflicted in the sight of the other while a soldier in service of the commonwealth.

5 Dec. 1780: To T.

20 Dec. 1780: T recommends £300 for present relief.
     House agrees.

22 Dec. 1780: Senate agrees.
     See 1187-P.

**1366-P**   **Day, James**
JHD: 5 Dec. 1780                                   Not known

Asks assistance to recover from wound suffered while a soldier in Colonel Buford's regiment.

Manuscript unsigned.

5 Dec. 1780: To T.

12 Dec. 1780: T recommends that petitioner be allowed to remain in the public hospital until cure of his leg can be effected and that he draw a full suit of clothes from the public store.
     House agrees.

16 Dec. 1780: Senate agrees.

**1367-C**   **Nathan, Simon**
JHD: Not found [5 Dec. 1780]                   Philadelphia

Claim for a protested bill of exchange against Penet, de Costa et Frères, of Bordeaux, France.

Manuscript dated 5 December 1780.

409

## Virginia Legislative Petitions

5 Dec. 1780: To C.
>This claim was carried over to 30 September 1788. See *Calendar of State Papers*, 4:492, 585; 5:259-260.

### 1368-P  Coutts, Reuben
JHD: 5 Dec. 1780                              Richmond Town

Opposing establishment of ferry across the James River from John Mayo's land on the south side to the land of Coutts on the north side.

Manuscript unsigned.

5 Dec. 1780: To PG.
18 Dec. 1780: Carried over to next session of GA.
>No further action found.

### 1369-P  Greenbrier County—Citizens
JHD: 5 Dec. 1780                              Greenbrier County

Asks authorization to institute suits upon all claims in which they have been aggrieved by execution of the act for establishing land office, and also requests opening of a wagon road from the courthouse to the eastern waters.

Manuscript signed by: Thos. Edgar, John Davis, John Stewart, George Davidson, Robt. Johnston, and 158 others.

5 Dec. 1780: To C.
>This claim was carried over to 30 September 1788. See *Calendar of State Papers*, 4:492, 585; 5:259-260.

7 Dec. 1780: House passes bill.
9 Dec. 1780: Senate amends bill.
>House agrees to Senate amendments.

8 Dec. 1780: PG finds request to institute suits reasonable and is directed to prepare bill.
>A general bill was passed by the House and Senate.
>For act concerning wagon road, see 10H367.
>For general bill on suits or caveats, see 10H354.

### 1370-P-† Morgan, John
JHD: 6 Dec. 1780                              Not known

Compensation for wounds received in the defeat of Colonel Buford's regiment in the South.

6 Dec. 1780: To T.
12 Dec. 1780: T recommends £300 for present relief.
>House agrees.

16 Dec. 1780: Senate agrees.

## 5 - 6 December 1780

**1371-P  Sayers, Robert**
JHD: 6 Dec. 1780                                                        Montgomery County
Compensation to members of a troop of cavalry recruited by him in Montgomery County. They were on constant duty suppressing insurgents in this state and North Carolina and also furnished their own arms and horses.
Manuscript unsigned.
6 Dec. 1780: To T.
18 Dec. 1780: T recommends that auditor of public accounts be directed to allow officers and men the same pay while on duty as was allowed the troop of cavalry ordered to be raised by virtue of an act passed at the last session of GA.
House agrees.
20 Dec. 1780: Senate agrees.

**1372-P  Campbell, Isaac**
JHD: 6 Dec. 1780                                                        Montgomery County
Compensation to members of a troop of cavalry recruited by him in Montgomery County. They were on constant duty suppressing insurgents in this state and North Carolina and also furnished their own arms and horses.
Manuscript unsigned.
6 Dec. 1780: To T.
18 Dec. 1780: T recommends that auditor of public accounts be directed to allow officers and men the same pay while on duty as was allowed the troop of cavalry ordered to be raised by virtue of an act passed at the last session of GA.
House agrees.
20 Dec. 1780: Senate agrees.

**1373-M  Finley, Samuel; Pendleton, Nathaniel; and Bedinger, Henry**
JHD: 6 Dec. 1780                                                                Not known
Asks compensation to discharge debts and to equip themselves to join their respective regiments. As officers of the Virginia line, they have been confined for four years within the enemy's lines at New York as prisoners of war and necessarily constrained to contract debts.
Manuscript unsigned.
6 Dec. 1780: To T.
7 Dec. 1780: T recommends (1) that petition is reasonable; (2) that the governor, with advice of Council, take proper measures to discharge the several debts out of tobacco due them; and (3) that £15,000 be advanced by the public to each of the memorialists,

## Virginia Legislative Petitions

upon account, for deficiency of clothing and pay due them.
House agrees to (1) and (2).
House recommits (3) to T.
9 Dec. 1780: T recommends for (3) that warrants be granted to memorialists for such money as will procure clothing due them and that £4,000 be advanced to each, upon account, for deficiency of pay due them.
House agrees to (3).
12 Dec. 1780: Senate amends.
House agrees to Senate amendments.

**1374-P   McKinney, John**
JHD: 6 Dec. 1780                                                   Not known
Additional compensation for wounds received while a soldier in the service of the commonwealth.
Manuscript unsigned, but has certificate attached.
6 Dec. 1780: To T.
20 Dec. 1780: T recommends £300 for present relief.
House agrees.
22 Dec. 1780: Senate amends.
23 Dec. 1780: House agrees to Senate amendments.

**1375-P**
Eck–
A1116   **Moffett, George**
JHD: 6 Dec. 1780                                                 Augusta County
Asks increase in the number of districts, and that he, as sheriff, be relieved from penalty of the law for failing to collect the public taxes in due time.
Manuscript signed by: Alex. Robertson and Joseph Bell.
6 Dec. 1780: To PG.
Apparently no further action taken.

**1376-P   Dandridge, Nathaniel West**
JHD: 6 Dec. 1780                                                Hanover County
Asks that the act respecting the rebuilding of mills may be explained and amended so as to afford relief to the petitioner whose mill on Mill Creek is affected by another mill on the same stream of water.
Manuscript signed by: John Richardson, Richd. Richardson, Jno. Anderson, John Mayo, Joseph Watson, and fourteen others.
6 Dec. 1780: Rejected by refusal to refer to a committee.

## 6 – 8 December 1780

**1377-P** **Moorman, James; Johnson, Benjamin; Venable, John; and Taylor, James**
JHD: 8 Dec. 1780                                                     Louisa County
Asks that certain slaves to be manumitted by the will of Charles Moorman, deceased, not be manumitted since the petitioners conceive themselves entitled to a fee simple estate in them.
Manuscript signed by petitioners.
8 Dec. 1780: To lie on table.
   Apparently no further action taken.

**1378-P** **Bledsoe, Anthony**
JHD: 8 Dec. 1780                                                     Orange County
Asks compensation for considerable sums advanced by him as commissary to the commissioners and their guard who ran the boundary line between this state and North Carolina.
Manuscript unsigned.
8 Dec. 1780: To PG.
21 Dec. 1780: PG recommends that auditors of public accounts make allowance for his services, as well as reasonable expenses, as they think just and right, and to draw their warrant upon the treasurer for payment thereof.
   House agrees.
22 Dec. 1780: Senate agrees.

**1379-P**
Eck–
A846    **Campbell, Archibald**
JHD: 8 Dec. 1780                                                     Amherst County
Compensation for his slave, condemned for a felony, but who escaped from jail.
Manuscript unsigned.
8 Dec. 1780: To T.
23 Dec. 1780: T recommends £3,500.
   Carried over to next session of GA.
   No further action found.

**1380-P-†** **Hughes, John**
JHD: 8 Dec. 1780                                                     Not known
Additional compensation for loss of his eyesight while a soldier in the service of the commonwealth.

## Virginia Legislative Petitions

8 Dec. 1780: To T.
12 Dec. 1780: T recommends £500 for present relief and that he be allowed to draw a full suit of clothes from the public store.
   House agrees.
14 Dec. 1780: Senate agrees.

### 1381-P  Reveley, John
JHD: 9 Dec. 1780                                                                 Henrico County

Asks payment of salary as manager of the public foundry since 19 October 1779, at which time his former salary was paid.

Manuscript unsigned. Manuscript has attached certificate of John Beckley.
9 Dec. 1780: To T.
20 Dec. 1780: T recommends 15,000 pounds of crop tobacco or an equivalent in money.
   House agrees.
22 Dec. 1780: Senate agrees.

### 1382-P  Carter, William
JHD: 9 Dec. 1780                                                                       Not known

Compensation for wounds received while a dragoon in Colonel Baylor's regiment of cavalry.

Manuscript unsigned.
9 Dec. 1780: To T. (Manuscript endorsement says not reported.)
   Apparently no further action taken.

### 1383-P  Hanover County, King William County, and New Kent County—Citizens
JHD: 9 Dec. 1780                                                                 Hanover County
                                                                             King William County
                                                                                New Kent County

Asks revival of inspection at Meriwether's warehouse in Hanover County.

Manuscript signed by: Elisha Meredith, John Meredith, Samuel Grantland, Edward Cooke, John Clopton, and 130 others. Manuscript says reasonable and to be incorporated in tobacco law.
9 Dec. 1780: To PG.
   For general act including Meriwether's, see 10H474.

### 1384-P  Bennet, Anne
JHD: 9 Dec. 1780                                                                       Not known

Asks that a slave, Will, to be manumitted by the last will of Anne Colvin,

## 9 – 12 December 1780

deceased, not be manumitted since by the death of her sister, Elizabeth Bennet, the petitioner is entitled to a fee simple estate in the slave.
Manuscript unsigned.
9 Dec. 1780: To lie on table.
> Apparently no further action taken.
> See 1119-P for petition of Will.

**1385-P  Cross, Samuel**
JHD: 11 Dec. 1780                                     Hanover County
Compensation for lock chain, tongue chain, and seven new twilled bags, lost when his wagon and team were pressed into the service of the United States on 15 February last.
Manuscript unsigned.
11 Dec. 1780: To T.
> Apparently no further action taken.

**1386-P  Chesterfield County—Citizens**
JHD: 11 Dec. 1780                                     Chesterfield County
Asks passage of act that would allow horse racing under proper restrictions.
Manuscript signed by: Henry Delony, Robt. Goode, Thomas Randolph, Francis Goode, Josiah Tatum, and eighty-one others.
11 Dec. 1780: To PG.
> Apparently no further action taken.

**1387-P  West, Drury**
JHD: 12 Dec. 1780                                     Henrico County
Compensation for his horse that died during the petitioner's service as a volunteer dragoon.
Manuscript unsigned, but has attached certificate of value. The name of Nat. Wilkinson, a member of House from Henrico County, is attached.
12 Dec. 1780: To T.
20 Dec. 1780: T recommends £1,500.
> House agrees.
> Probably approved by Senate, but no record found.

**1388-P-† Thomas, Rees**
JHD: 12 Dec. 1780                                     Spotsylvania County
Compensation for his wagon and team, impressed into the service of the United States by a Continental officer in 1777.
12 Dec. 1780: To T.

## Virginia Legislative Petitions

20 Dec. 1780: Carried over to next session of GA.
    No further action found.
    See 1197-P.

### 1389-P-† Smith, Thomas
JHD: 12 Dec. 1780                                                    Not known

    Asks relief in that he imported a number of indentured servants into the commonwealth and was entitled to fifty acres of land for each servant. He was absent from the state on public service and upon returning found himself precluded from his rights by an act limiting the time to prove them.
12 Dec. 1780: To PG.
    Apparently no further action taken.

### 1390-M
Eck–

**A1118**   **Matthews, Sampson**
JHD: 12 Dec. 1780                                                   Augusta County

    Asks interposition of the legislature in that a number of militiamen were lately called into service from Augusta County without any field officers of their county to command them. The officers consider it as a degradation.

    Manuscript signed by: George Moffett, Wm. Bowyer, Alexr. Robertson, Thos. Hughart, John McCreery, and Andr. Lockridge.
12 Dec. 1780: To PG.
    Apparently no further action taken.

### 1391-M
Eck–

**A1117**   **Matthews, Sampson**
JHD: 12 Dec. 1780                                                   Augusta County

    Asks relief in that he obtained a considerable sum of money from the people of Augusta County, on loan to the public and upon an assurance from the memorialist to see them repaid. The money was put into the hands of proper persons to be conveyed to the public treasury, and they lost a part thereof in the amount of £4,000 and more.

    Manuscript unsigned.
12 Dec. 1780: To T.
28 Dec. 1780: T recommends rejection.
    House agrees.

## 12 – 14 December 1780

**1392-P   King and Queen County—Citizens**
JHD: 12 Dec. 1780                                        King and Queen County
Asks that the three present parishes, Saint Stephen's, Stratton Major, and Drysdale, be divided and formed into two parishes agreeable to certain boundaries.
Manuscript signed by: Geo. Lyne, Christopher Harwood, Wm. Courtney, Wm. Flech, Jos. Harwood, and twenty-two others.
12 Dec. 1780: To R.
20 Dec. 1780: Carried over to next session of GA.
   No further action taken.

**1393-P   Saint Margaret's Parish, Caroline County—Citizens**
JHD: 12 Dec. 1780                                        Caroline County
Asks that vestry be dissolved since it is not the choice of the people and is an unconstitutional one.
Manuscript signed by: Benja. Tompkins, L. Temple, Roger Quarles, Ro. Tompkins, Joel Higgin, and twenty-seven others.
12 Dec. 1780: Carried over to next session of GA.
   No further action found.

**1393 A-P Saint Margaret's Parish, Caroline County—Citizens**
JHD: 12 Dec. 1780                                        Caroline County
Text is similar to 1393-P, which see.
Manuscript signed by forty-three persons.

**1394-P   Booth, Thomas**
JHD: 14 Dec. 1780                                        Henrico County
Additional compensation for three acres of his land, adjoining John Ballendine's land at Westham, that were taken for public use.
Manuscript unsigned.
14 Dec. 1780: To T.
28 Dec. 1780: Carried over to next session of GA.
   No further action found.

**1395-P-†  Wellburn, William**
JHD: 14 Dec. 1780                                        Not known
Compensation for wound received in the defeat of Colonel Buford's regiment in the South.
14 Dec. 1780: To T.

## Virginia Legislative Petitions

20 Dec. 1780: T recommends £300 for present relief.
        House agrees.
22 Dec. 1780: Senate agrees.

**1396-P**
Eck–Not
found    **Bruce, Richard**
        JHD: 14 Dec. 1780                      Albemarle County
Asks reimbursement for £164 advanced to Judith Epperson, widow of David Epperson, deceased, late a soldier in the Continental service.
Manuscript unsigned.
14 Dec. 1780: To T.
28 Dec. 1780: T recommends that auditor of public accounts be directed to grant a warrant for £164 to petitioner.
        House agrees.
29 Dec. 1780: Senate agrees.

**1397-P**   **Cross, Samuel**
        JHD: 14 Dec. 1780                             Not known
Compensation for horses sold to the state quartermaster.
Manuscript unsigned.
14 Dec. 1780: To T.
        Apparently no further action taken.

**1398-P-†**  **Black, William**
        JHD: 14 Dec. 1780                      Chesterfield County
Asks act to enable him to enlarge the town of Manchester by laying off sixty-five acres of his land adjoining that town.
14 Dec. 1780: To PG.
18 Dec. 1780: Carried over to next session of GA.
        No further action found.

**1399-P**   **Ashton, Burdit**
        JHD: 14 Dec. 1780                      Westmoreland County
Asks act to permit sale of undivided fourth part of three tracts of land descended to his daughters from the estate of James Blair through Sarah, their mother and his wife.
Manuscript unsigned.
14 Dec. 1780: To PG.

## 14 December 1780

18 Dec. 1780: PG recommends rejection.
    House rejects.
    See 1217-P.

**1400-P  Culpeper County—Citizens**
    JHD: 14 Dec. 1780                    Culpeper County

Asks that Landon Carter be compelled to open a ferry at Norman's ford on the Rappahannock River, or that Isaac Herron be empowered to that effect.

Manuscript signed by: John Camp, Chs. Porter, Jno. Bramham, Alexn. Deale, Saml. Baird, and thirty-seven others.

14 Dec. 1780: To PG.
19 Dec. 1780: PG recommends (1) that the part of the petition asking establishment of a public ferry at Norman's ford is reasonable, and (2) that the part of petition asking passage of an act to empower Isaac Herron to keep a public ferry in case Landon Carter refused to do so be rejected.
    House agrees to (1) and (2).
    PG to prepare a bill relevant to (1). This was included in a general ferry act passed by House and Senate.
    For general ferry act see 10H365.

**1401-P  Harmer, George**
    JHD: 14 Dec. 1780                             Not known

Asks restoration to him of slaves purchased by the public under the escheat and forfeiture act or that he may receive a slave boy named Ned now in public employment at Manchester. Slaves were part of his estate sold under the act, and he cannot draw the amount of the sales from the public treasury.

Manuscript unsigned.

14 Dec. 1780: To PG.
18 Dec. 1780: PG recommends (1) that slaves conveyed to George Harmer by John Harmer and sold be restored to him; and (2) that Ned, one of the said slaves sold, be immediately restored to the petitioner by 10 January next.
    House agrees.
    PG directed to prepare bill.
21 Dec. 1780: Bill presented.
23 Dec. 1780: House passes bill.
26 Dec. 1780: Senate passes bill.
    For this act see 10H371.

## Virginia Legislative Petitions

**1402-P  King William County—Citizens**
JHD: 14 Dec. 1780                                  King William County
Asks revival of the Piping Tree inspection.
Manuscript signed by: John Pomfrett, Robin King, Richd. King, John King, Wm. King, and eighteen others.
14 Dec. 1780: To lie on table.
      Apparently no further action taken.

**1403-P**
Eck–Not
found  **Nottoway Parish, Amelia County—Vestry**
JHD: 14 Dec. 1780                                  Amelia County
Asks that Thomas Wilkinson, the present incumbent minister of Nottoway Parish, be removed from his position.
Manuscript signed by: Stephen Cocke, Saml. Sherwin, Richard Jones, Jr., Will. Fitzgerald, Peter Lamkin, Stith Bolling, John Goode, and J. Henderson.
14 Dec. 1780: To R.
      Apparently no further action taken. Manuscript endorsement states, "Nothing to be done with this Petition by order of Mr. Pride who presented it."

**1404-P  Tobacco Warehouse Proprietors**
JHD: 15 Dec. 1780                                  Spotsylvania County
                                                          and others
Asks increase in allowance for the rent of their warehouses, or that the warehouses be taken for public use and the petitioners paid their reasonable valuation.
Manuscript signed by: Mann Page for Page's and Crutchfield's, James Miller for Roy's, William Bankhead for Matton's, Fra. Conway for Gibson's, Thos. Jett for Leed's, Thos. Bridgeforth for Layton's, William McWilliams for Royston's, John Richards for Falmouth and Dixon's, and William Todd for Todd's.
15 Dec. 1780: To PG.
      Apparently no further action taken, but see general act increasing allowance, 10H355.

**1405-P  Manchester—Trustees**
JHD: 15 Dec. 1780                                  Chesterfield County
Asks that petition of John Mayo for a public ferry be suspended until a suit is determined between the two parties.

## 14 – 15 December 1780

Manuscript signed by: James Lyle, Alexr. Trent, Robt. Goode, Archibald Cary, and Richd. Adams.
15 Dec. 1780: To PG.
18 Dec. 1780: Carried over to next session of GA.
    Apparently no further action taken.

### 1406-P   Byras, John
JHD: 15 Dec. 1780                         Louisa County

Compensation for horse, impressed by the forage master and lost while the petitioner commanded a company of militia that marched to South Carolina.

Manuscript unsigned, but certificate of value attached.
15 Dec. 1780: To T.
20 Dec. 1780: T recommends £1,500.
    House agrees.
22 Dec. 1780: Senate agrees.

### 1407-P   Riddick, Josiah
JHD: 15 Dec. 1780                      Nansemond County

Compensation for horse, impressed into service when the petitioner was part of a reconnoitering party taken by the enemy.

Manuscript unsigned, but certificate of value attested to by three persons is attached.
15 Dec. 1780: To T.
20 Dec. 1780: T recommends £2,000.
    House agrees.
25 Dec. 1780: Senate agrees.

### 1408-P   Macon, William
JHD: 15 Dec. 1780                            Not known

Compensation for his horse, which died while the petitioner was a volunteer in General Lawson's legion.

Manuscript unsigned.
15 Dec. 1780: Rejected by refusal to refer to a committee.

### 1409-P   Dameron, Jacob
JHD: 15 Dec. 1780                   Northumberland County

Asks for bounty lands to which he is entitled under the royal proclamation of 1763.

Manuscript unsigned, but certificate attached.

## Virginia Legislative Petitions

15 Dec. 1780: Carried over to next session of GA.
    No further action found.

**1410-P    East, David**
    JHD: 15 Dec. 1780            Isle of Wight County
Compensation for wounds received in the surprise of Colonel Washington's regiment at Lenew's ferry on Santee River.
    Manuscript unsigned.
15 Dec. 1780: To T.
    Apparently no further action taken.

**1411-P**
Eck-A1677
[Wrong date]
    **Ward, John**
    JHD: 16 Dec. 1780            Bedford County
Asks compensation from the auditors of public accounts who have refused to allow payment of certificates from officers to whom the petitioner furnished provisions to certain detachments of troops marching south.
    Manuscript unsigned.
16 Dec. 1780: To T.
28 Dec. 1780: T recommends that auditors of public accounts be directed to examine and settle the petitioner's account against the public. House agrees.
30 Dec. 1780: Senate agrees.

**1412-P-†    Middlesex County—Citizens**
    JHD: 16 Dec. 1780            Middlesex County
Asks that courthouse be moved to the place where their old courthouse stood.
16 Dec. 1780: Carried over to next session of GA.
    No further action found.
    See 1413-P.

**1413-P    Middlesex County—Citizens**
    JHD: 16 Dec. 1780            Middlesex County
Opposing the removal of the courthouse to the place where the old courthouse stood.
    Manuscript signed by: Thos. Montague, Robert Daniel, Benjamin Judd, Griffen Tuggle, Jacob Owin, and eighty-six others.

## 15 – 21 December 1780

16 Dec. 1780: Carried over to next session of GA.
   No further action found.
   See 1412-P-†.

### 1414-M  Woodson, Tarlton
JHD: 20 Dec. 1780                                    Not known

Compensation for deficiency of pay and clothing in that he has been a prisoner with the enemy on Long Island nearly three years, during which time he has received no clothing and only a small proportion of his pay.

Manuscript unsigned.
20 Dec. 1780: To T.
23 Dec. 1780: T recommends £8,000.
   House agrees.
26 Dec. 1780: Senate agrees.

### 1415-M  Willis, John
JHD: 21 Dec. 1780                                    Not known

Compensation for deficiency of pay and clothing in that he is just exchanged after suffering nearly three years captivity on Long Island, during which time he received only a small proportion of pay and clothing.

Manuscript unsigned.
21 Dec. 1780: To T.
23 Dec. 1780: T recommends £8,000.
   House agrees.
26 Dec. 1780: Senate agrees.

### 1416-P-†  Fredericksburg—Citizens
JHD: 21 Dec. 1780                                    Spotsylvania County

Asks incorporation of the town since they suffer great inconvenience by the moving of the courthouse.

21 Dec. 1780: Carried over to next session of GA.
24 Nov. 1781: Bill presented by leave.
   House and Senate passed this bill.
   See 1417-P.
   For act incorporating town of Fredericksburg in Spotsylvania County, see 10H439.

### 1417-P  Fredericksburg—Citizens
JHD: Not found [21 Dec. 1780]                        Spotsylvania County

423

## Virginia Legislative Petitions

Against incorporation of Fredericksburg, but for the establishment of a jail there.

Manuscript signed by: Thos. Brown, Nathaniel Gray, Willim. Smith, Richard Kenny, Sam Reddy, and 100 others. Dated 25 May 1780. Endorsed October [1779?].

(This petition was apparently not referred to a committee. It is placed under this date since it is in opposition to 1416-P-†.)

> For act incorporating town of Fredericksburg in Spotsylvania County, see 10H439.

### 1418-M  Selden, Miles, Jr.
JHD: 22 Dec. 1780                                           Richmond Town

Compensation for his houses, used for the reception and storage of public records, the care of which he has declined.

Manuscript unsigned.

22 Dec. 1780: To CJ.

29 Dec. 1780: T recommends £1,000 and that governor and Council be directed to take proper measures to oblige the clerks of the Supreme Court and executive boards to remove said records to their respective offices.
> House agrees.
> Probably agreed to by Senate.

### 1419-P  Stephen, Adam and Noble, Anthony
JHD: 23 Dec. 1780                                                Not known

Compensation for manufacture of fifteen stand of arms delivered for public use and for which the governor and Council wish a price determined.

Manuscript unsigned. Only part of manuscript extant. Includes attestation by Thomas Jefferson.

23 Dec. 1780: To T.

28 Dec. 1780: T recommends £10 for each stand of arms, amounting to £150.
> House agrees.
> Senate probably agrees.

### 1420-M-†  College of William and Mary—President and Professors
JHD: 30 Dec. 1780                                             Williamsburg

Relevant to the appropriation and exchange of sundry Negro slaves belonging to the public.

30 Dec. 1780: Carried over to next session of GA.
> No further action found.

## 22 December 1780 – 7 March 1781

**1421-P    Cumberland County—Citizens**
JHD: 5 March 1781                                          Cumberland County

Asking for repeal or amendment of the act of the last session of the GA that imposed a 2 percent tax for the purpose of raising funds to supply the state's quota for the Continental army.

Manuscript signed by: William Guthrey, Pesmith Hill, Thomas Scott, Jonas Bradley, Samuel Gordon, Jr., and 170 others.

5 March 1781: To SC.
13 March 1781: SC discharged. To special committee that had been directed to prepare a bill on inconveniences arising from two acts of the last GA.
   Bill presented and postponed.
19 March 1781: Committee amends bill and House amends bill.
20 March 1781: House passes bill.
21 March 1781: Senate amends bill and House eventually agrees to Senate amendments.
   For this act see 10H393.

**1422-P-†  Augusta County—Citizens**
JHD: 5 March 1781                                               Augusta County

Asking for repeal or amendment of an act of the last session of the GA that imposed a 2 percent tax for the purpose of raising funds to supply the state's quota for the Continental army.

   For action on this petition see 1421-P.

**1423-M    Gill, Erasmus**
JHD: 6 March 1781                                                    Not known

Asks for clothing and subsistence following his stay as a prisoner of war on Long Island. He is returning to his unit.

Manuscript unsigned.
6 March 1781: Carried over to next session of GA.
   No further action found.

**1424-M-†  Morrow, Charles**
JHD: 7 March 1781                                                    Not known

Compensation for considerable sum advanced by him for the purchase of forage for public use.

7 March 1781: Carried over to next session of GA.
   No further action found.

## Virginia Legislative Petitions

### 1425-M  Berkeley County—Citizens
JHD: 7 March 1781                                Berkeley County

Asks that future demands of the legislature in regard to recruiting for the army and operation of the act for supplying the army with provisions may be adapted to the ability and circumstances of the people to pay and that the mode of supplying recruits be by voluntary enlistment instead of drafting.

Manuscript signed by: Mich. McKewn, Sam. Duncan, John Lyle, Matthew Duncan, William Pettenson, and twenty-two others.

7 March 1781: Carried over to next session of GA.
> No further action found, but see a new memorial presented 4 December 1781 (1518-M).

### 1426-P  Elizabeth City County—Citizens
JHD: 8 March 1781                             Elizabeth City County

Asks relief from liability to certain penalties. They were members of the militia of the county, which opposed an attack by the enemy during the present invasion upon Hampton, and being unsupported by militia of adjacent counties, were made prisoner and discharged on parole.

Manuscript signed by: William Hawkins, George Hope, Robt. Armistead, Robert Bright, Geo. Latimer, and twenty others. Manuscript attested by justices of peace of Elizabeth City County.

8 March 1781: To a special committee.
9 March 1781: Committee finds requests of certain of the petitioners to be reasonable and that the governor should be desired to have them exchanged.
> Committee also recommends that the governor appoint commissioners to inquire into the conduct of other petitioners.
> House lays on table.

13 March 1781: House amends, recommending (1) that requests of William Hawkins, Pennuel Crook, Robert Armistead, John Paul, Samuel Ship, John Banks, William Gooch, Francis Ballard, William Cunningham, Richard Bart, John Seymour, William Harper, Howard Skinner, Michael Counsel, William Rosun, Wilson Curl, and Amiger Webb are reasonable, and that the governor be desired to have them exchanged; and (2) that the governor appoint commissioners to inquire into the conduct of Robert Bright, George Latimer, Thomas Latimer, Thomas Allen, George Hope, William Dunn, and William Armistead, and report findings to next session of GA.
> House agrees.

## 7 – 14 March 1781

19 March 1781: Senate amends.
>House disagrees.
>Senate insists on amendments.
>House disagrees.

20 March 1781: Senate insists on amendments.
>House disagrees.
>No further action found.

**1427-M    Call, Richard**
>JHD: 9 March 1781                                              Not known

Asks that the lack of horses for recruits for Colonel Washington's corps of dragoons be made up by the legislature.

Manuscript unsigned.

9 March 1781: To SC.

17 March 1781: SC recommends (1) that the governor with advice of Council take speediest measures by purchase or otherwise to remount such of the dragoons of the 1st and 3rd regiments of cavalry as are now dismounted, and (2) that the governor with advice of Council be empowered to appoint a person with authority to receive all horses purchased by the state or turned over to quartermaster's department, except such retained for the southern army and related responsibilities.
>House agrees.

19 March 1781: Senate agrees.

**1428-P    Rockbridge County—Citizens**
>JHD: 9 March 1781                                         Rockbridge County

Asks that they be permitted to discharge the term of duty in the shorter time of three months for which they are required by the draft law to serve.

Manuscript signed by: Robert Tedford, James Campbell, Robt. Hays, Charles Hays, James Canon, and ninety others.

9 March 1781: To lie on table.
>No further action found.

**1429-P    Orange County—Citizens**
>JHD: 14 March 1781                                            Orange County

Asks that time of service for the drafts to be raised by the act for recruiting this state's quota of troops for the Continental army may be shortened to three months.

427

## Virginia Legislative Petitions

Manuscript signed by: Johnny Scott, James Wayte, James Connolly, William Lucas, John Willhoit, and 131 others.
14 March 1781: Rejected by refusal to refer to a committee.

### 1430-P
Eck-A10  **Accomack County—Citizens**
JHD: 14 March 1781                                         Accomack County

Asks relief, in that by operation of the embargo law they cannot dispose of their grain to procure money for discharging their public taxes.

Manuscript signed by: Geo. Corbin, Thos. Lillaston, Charles Bagwell, John Hunter, Nath. Beaucamp, and sixty-six others.
14 March 1781: To lie on table.
   No further action found.

### 1431-R  Ross, David
JHD: 17 March 1781                                                Not known

Asks for certain powers in his capacity as commercial agent. (This representation was transmitted by the governor.)

Manuscript unsigned.
17 March 1781: To SC.
21 March 1781: SC discharged and special committee appointed to prepare and bring in a bill.
   Committee presents bill.
   House passes bill.
22 March 1781: Senate amends.
   House disagrees.
   Senate insists on amendments.
   House postpones action until 10 May next.
   No further action found.

### 1432-P
Eck–
A848  **Amherst County—Citizens**
JHD: 29 May 1781                                             Amherst County

Asks amendment of the militia laws in regard to pay and tour of duty.

Manuscript signed by: Wm. Loving, Lucas Debrell, James Nevil, Gabl. Penn, Richard Ballinger, and eight others.
29 May 1781: To lie on table.
   To committee appointed to prepare a bill for regulation of the militia.

14 June 1781: Special committee to prepare a bill.
15 June 1781: Bill presented.
   To SC.
18 June 1781: SC amends bill.
19 June 1781: House passes bill.
20 June 1781: Senate amends bill.
   House agrees to some Senate amendments and disagrees with others.
22 June 1781: Senate disagrees with House amendments and adheres to its own amendment.
   House recedes and agrees with Senate amendment.
   For this act see 10H416.

**1433-M  Poage, Robert; Wallace, Caleb; Rice, David; Read, William; Holt, John H.; and Early, Joshua**
   JHD: 30 May 1781                                         Not known
Asks that state be divided into equal districts for recruiting.
Manuscript unsigned.
30 May 1781: To lie on table.
   Apparently no further action taken.

**1434-P-†  Augusta County—Citizens**
   JHD: 31 May 1781                                      Augusta County
Asks relief in that the requisition of men from their county under the late draft law is unequal and unjust.
31 May 1781: To SC.
   Apparently no further action taken.

**1435-M  Pendleton, Edmund and Taylor, John**
   JHD: 1 June 1781                                       Caroline County
Asks interference and legislation on their behalf relevant to their claim to certain lands in North Carolina that were supposed to be in this state before the extension of the boundary line.
Manuscript in Pendleton's handwriting and signed by Pendleton and Taylor.
1 June 1781: To CJ.
9 June 1781: CJ finds (1) that representation to General Assembly of North Carolina is reasonable, and (2) that other parts of memorial are

reasonable, and that governor with advice of Council should be authorized and required to appoint such an agent.
(1) to CJ to prepare.
(2) laid on table.
11 June 1781: CJ presents representation (1).
    House amends and agrees.
14 June 1781: Senate agrees to (1).
    House considers (2) and agrees.
16 June 1781: Senate agrees.

**1436-P   Talley, Nathaniel**
    JHD: 1 June 1781                                Hanover County
    Asks relief since as executor of John Tate, deceased, and guardian to his orphans, he leased lands for the term of eight years on consideration of £24 per annum and now depreciation and taxes presently imposed will produce ruin to the orphans.
    Manuscript unsigned.
1 June 1781: To CJ.
    Apparently no further action taken.
    Petition resubmitted on 24 November 1781 (1489-P).

**1437-P   Caroline County—Citizens**
    JHD: 2 June 1781                                Caroline County
    Asks that some mode may be devised by which persons tolerating toryism shall be discriminated against and compelled to leave the state.
    Manuscript signed by: Edmd. Pendleton, Edmd. Pendleton, Jr., Jno. Hoomes, Ph. Johnston, Eusebeous Hone, and 312 others.
2 June 1781: To lie on table.
    Apparently no further action taken, but see 10H413.

**1438-P   Page, Mann**
    JHD: 7 June 1781                             Prince William County
    Asks pardon of Will, a Negro man slave (accused of treason, a crime for which a slave was not liable), the property of the estate of John Tayloe, deceased. Thomas Jefferson had issued a reprieve until 30 June 1781.
    Manuscript unsigned, but has attached the proceedings of the Prince William County court.
7 June 1781: To CJ.
9 June 1781: CJ finds reasonable and is directed to prepare a bill or bills.
14 June 1781: Senate agrees in form of a resolution. There is no act.

1 – 19 June 1781

**1439-P    Henry County—Citizens**
JHD: 8 June 1781                                                    Henry County
Asks relief in that they are greatly injured by the present mode for regulating impresses.
Manuscript signed by: John Connaway, Jno. Stuart, Thomas Walker, Silas Williams, Reuben Nance, and sixty others.
8 June 1781: To CJ.
18 June 1781: CJ finds reasonable and is directed to prepare bill or bills.
For general act concerning impressment see 10H437.

**1440-P**
Eck–Not
found    **Poage, John**
JHD: 14 June 1781                                                   Augusta County
Asks relief for a judgment obtained against him as high sheriff of Augusta County for default of his deputy who was robbed.
Manuscript unsigned.
14 June 1781: To a special committee.
16 June 1781: Committee finds reasonable but resolves that final determination be postponed to next session of GA.
House agrees.
19 June 1781: Senate agrees.
12 Dec. 1781: Motion made that it be resolved that John Poage be given a full acquittance against a judgment entered in the General Court upon his paying £35,345 5s. into the public treasury on or before 1 March 1782.
House agrees.
17 Dec. 1781: Senate agrees.

**1441-P    Rockbridge County—Citizens**
JHD: 14 June 1781                                                 Rockbridge County
Asks amendment of the law for drafting soldiers for the Continental army.
Manuscript signed by: John Moore, Thos. Steel, Andrew Moore, Robert Taylor, Saml. Moore, and 200 others. Manuscript has attached list of names.
14 June 1781: To lie on table.
No further action found.

**1442-P    Pittsylvania County—Citizens**
JHD: 19 June 1781                                                 Pittsylvania County

## Virginia Legislative Petitions

Asks relief from execution of the law of 1780 for drafting soldiers for the Continental army for eighteen months.

Manuscript signed by: Hugh Reynolds, Joshua Cantrall, Thomas Lackay, Joseph Ballinger, Matthew Morleaise, and ninety-nine others.
19 June 1781: To lie on table.
  No further action found.

### 1443-R-† Prince William County—Commissioners of the Escheated Property

JHD: 21 June 1781, for action          Prince William County

Relevant to the estate, late the property of Robert Bristow, a British subject.
Date unknown: To CJ.
21 June 1781: CJ resolves (1) that commissioners be directed not to confirm the sales of the said estate unless they are bound by law to do so, (2) that the treasurer receive on account any money that may be offered him by Henry Peyton, late sheriff of Prince William County, and (3) that commissioners in the meantime receive the profits of the said estate and give account annually at the treasury office.
  House agrees.
22 June 1781: Senate agrees.

### 1444-P-† Kirkpatrick, Samuel

JHD: 21 June 1781          Not known

Compensation for wounds received at battle of Guilford.
21 June 1781: To a special committee.
  Committee recommends £1,000 for present relief and £15 per year in specie, or value thereof in paper money, during his life.
  House agrees.
23 June 1781: Senate agrees.

### 1445-P Hall, Lyman

JHD: 21 June 1781          Not known

Asks extension of term for which they were exempted from payment of taxes as exiled citizens from Georgia and South Carolina. The law allowing the exemption has expired.

Manuscript unsigned.
21 June 1781: Carried over to next session of GA.
22 Nov. 1781: To PG.
  No further action found.

## 21 June – 20 November 1781

### 1446-P-† Fayette County—Citizens
    JHD: 21 June 1781                        Fayette County
For establishment of town of Lexington in Fayette County.
21 June 1781: Carried over to next session of GA.
    Similar petitions presented again on 22 November 1781 and 7 December 1781 (1483-P-† and 1525-P).
    For act establishing town of Lexington in Fayette County in 1782, see 11H100.

### 1447-R-† Matthews, George
    JHD: 22 June 1781                            Not known
Representation of sundry matters on behalf of himself and the officers of the 9th Virginia Regiment.
22 June 1781: Carried over to next session of GA.
    Representation made again on 22 November 1781 (1484-R-†).

### 1448-M-† Page, Mann and Triplett, Francis
    JHD: 20 Nov. 1781                            Not known
Asks that the public pay for caps supplied to a company of horse raised by Triplett.
20 Nov. 1781: To T.
27 Nov. 1781: T reports resolution.
    House lays on table.
27 Dec. 1781: Senate agrees to resolution for paying a sum of money to Mann Page and Francis Triplett.

### 1449-P Mosby, William
    JHD: 20 Nov. 1781                          Henrico County
Compensation for horse, saddle, and bridle, taken by the enemy in the defeat of General Gates at Camden.
Manuscript unsigned, and the endorsement says rejected. Certificates are attached.
20 Nov. 1781: To T.
    No further action found.

### 1450-P Greenbrier County—Citizens
    JHD: 20 Nov. 1781                      Greenbrier County
Asks repeal or amendment of the act for opening a road from their courthouse to the Warm Springs in Augusta County.

## Virginia Legislative Petitions

Manuscript signed by: Israel Meadow, William Lacey, Thomas Gully, Moses Turpin, Nathanal Gartener, and 143 others.
20 Nov. 1781: To PG.
21 Nov. 1781: PG recommends (1) that operation of act ought to be suspended for two years, and (2) that petition be rejected.
    To lie on table.
26 Nov. 1781: House agrees after consideration.
    PG directed to prepare bill pursuant to (1).
27 Nov. 1781: Bill presented.
30 Nov. 1781: House passes bill.
1 Dec. 1781: Senate passes bill.
    For this act see 10H444.

### 1450 A-P Greenbrier County—Citizens
JHD: 20 Nov. 1781                                  Greenbrier County
Text is similar to 1450-P, which see.
Manuscript signed by 134 persons.

### 1451-P
Eck-
A847    **Amherst County—Citizens**
JHD: 20 Nov. 1781                                    Amherst County
Asks passage of act laying county off into districts with each district compelled to furnish a tent and a wagon. Asks also that measures be taken for supplying the militia with arms and ammunition.
Manuscript signed by: Abram Warwick, Thos. Hawkins, John Bibb, Hezekiah Hargrove, Zach. Taliaferro, and forty-three others.
20 Nov. 1781: To lie on table.
    Apparently no further action taken.

### 1452-P-† Littlepage, John Carter
JHD: 21 Nov. 1781                                    Bedford County
Asks compensation, as one of the tenants in common, for use of the lead mines in Bedford County that were taken for public use in 1776. Asks also that the proprietors be permitted to work the mines for their private advantage.
21 Nov. 1781: To PG.
26 Nov. 1781: PG recommends as reasonable and is directed to prepare a bill.
7 Dec. 1781: Bill presented to empower the proprietors of the lead mines to work them.
8 Dec. 1781: Bill recommitted to PG.

## 20 – 21 November 1781

3 Jan. 1782: PG discharged from consideration of bill concerning the lead mines.
    House passes resolution that governor and Council be directed to appoint three persons to examine and settle the accounts of the managers of the lead mines and report the same to the next GA.
5 Jan. 1782: Senate agrees.

### 1453-P
Eck–
A1679    **Bedford County—Citizens**
    JHD: 21 Nov. 1781                                  Bedford County
Asks division of the county agreeable to certain boundaries.
  Manuscript signed by: James Kasey, Elisha Hurt, John Starr, Isaac Hibbs, Wm. Thornhill, and forty-six others.
21 Nov. 1781: To PG.
22 Nov. 1781: PG recommends as reasonable and is directed to prepare a bill.
23 Nov. 1781: Bill presented.
    To lie on table.
26 Nov. 1781: Bill recommitted to PG.
1 Dec. 1781: Bill read third time and recommitted to PG.
8 Dec. 1781: House passes bill.
15 Dec. 1781: Senate amends bill.
    House agrees to Senate amendment.
    For this act establishing Campbell County as of 1 February 1782, see 10H447.

### 1453 A-P
Eck–
A1679    **Bedford County—Citizens**
    JHD: 21 Nov. 1781                                  Bedford County
Text is identical with 1453-P, which see.
Manuscript signed by eighty-six persons.

### 1453 B-P
Eck–
A1679    **Bedford County—Citizens**
    JHD: 21 Nov. 1781                                  Bedford County
Text is identical with 1453-P, which see.
Manuscript signed by forty-six persons.

## Virginia Legislative Petitions

**1453 C-P**
Eck-
A1679    **Bedford County—Citizens**                          Bedford County
         JHD: 21 Nov. 1781
    Text is identical with 1453-P, which see.
    Manuscript signed by thirty-seven persons.

**1453 D-P**
Eck-
A1679    **Bedford County—Citizens**                          Bedford County
         JHD: 21 Nov. 1781
    Text is identical with 1453-P, which see.
    Manuscript signed by 111 persons.

**1453 E-P**
Eck-
A1679    **Bedford County—Citizens**                          Bedford County
         JHD: 21 Nov. 1781
    Text is identical with 1453-P, which see.
    Manuscript signed by fifty-six persons.

**1453 F-P**
Eck-
A1679    **Bedford County—Citizens**                          Bedford County
         JHD: 21 Nov. 1781
    Text is identical with 1453-P, which see.
    Manuscript signed by thirty persons.

**1453 G-P**
Eck-
A1679    **Bedford County—Citizens**                          Bedford County
         JHD: 21 Nov. 1781
    Text is identical with 1453-P, which see.
    Manuscript signed by seven persons.

**1453 H-P**
Eck-
A1679    **Bedford County—Citizens**

## 21 November 1781

    JHD: 21 Nov. 1781                            Bedford County
Text is identical with 1453-P, which see.
Manuscript signed by nineteen persons.

### 1453 I-P
Eck–
A1679    **Bedford County—Citizens**
        JHD: 21 Nov. 1781                 Bedford County
Text is identical with 1453-P, which see.
Manuscript signed by sixty persons.

### 1453 J-P
Eck–
A1679    **Bedford County—Citizens**
        JHD: 21 Nov. 1781                 Bedford County
Text is identical with 1453-P, which see.
Manuscript signed by 110 persons.

### 1453 K-P
Eck–
A1679    **Bedford County—Citizens**
        JHD: 21 Nov. 1781                 Bedford County
Text is identical with 1453-P, which see.
Manuscript signed by sixty-nine persons.

### 1453 L-P
Eck–
A1679    **Bedford County—Citizens**
        JHD: 21 Nov. 1781                 Bedford County
Text is identical with 1453-P, which see.
Manuscript signed by forty-nine persons.

### 1453 M-P
Eck–
A1679    **Bedford County—Citizens**
        JHD: 21 Nov. 1781                 Bedford County
Text is identical with 1453-P, which see.
Manuscript signed by seventy-two persons.

## Virginia Legislative Petitions

**1454-P**
Eck-
A1678  **Bedford County—Citizens**
JHD: 21 Nov. 1781                  Bedford County
Opposing a division of the county.
Manuscript signed by: James Callaway, Charles Callaway, W. Read, Wm. Callaway, John Callaway, Bourne Price, and Fran. Thorp.
21 Nov. 1781: To PG.
22 Nov. 1781: PG recommends rejection.
    House rejects.

**1455-P**
Eck-
A727  **Amelia County—Commissioners of the Money Tax**
JHD: 21 Nov. 1781                  Amelia County
Asks relief from penalties for not discharging their duty due to the fact that one of the commissioners resigned.
Manuscript signed by: Richard Jones, Jr., and John Booker, Jr.
21 Nov. 1781: To PG.
26 Nov. 1781: PG recommends rejection.
    House rejects.

**1456-P-†  Cabell, Nicholas; Innes, Harry; and Cabell, Joseph**
JHD: 21 Nov. 1781                  Washington County
                                             Montgomery County
Asks that an additional allowance be made to them as commissioners, agreeable to the act "for ascertaining the titles of claimers to unpatented lands," in that the allowance made by law is inadequate.
21 Nov. 1781: To T.
    Apparently no further action taken.
    Petition appears to have been presented again on 29 May 1782 (1621-P).
    See also 1512-P.

**1457-P-†  Boatwright, Benoni**
JHD: 21 Nov. 1781                  Not known
Compensation for expense and inconvenience suffered after the enemy's incursion to Point of Fork, when two Continental soldiers went to the petitioner's house sick and remained there a considerable time.

## 21 November 1781

21 Nov. 1781: To T.
    No further action found.

### 1458-P-† Cunningham, Elizabeth
    JHD: 21 Nov. 1781                                              Not known

Asks relief in that she has reason to believe that her husband, Bartlet Cunningham, a Continental soldier, was killed or taken prisoner at the battle of Camden, and she and her three small children are in great distress.

21 Nov. 1781: To T.
    No further action found.

### 1459-P-† Buntain, Alexander
    JHD: 21 Nov. 1781                                      Rockbridge County

Compensation for wound received at the battle of Guilford.

21 Nov. 1781: To T.

27 Dec. 1781: T recommends allowance of one year's pay for present relief and further allowance of half pay during life, to be charged to the United States in account with this commonwealth.
    House agrees.

29 Dec. 1781: Senate agrees.

### 1460-P Gilliam, John
    JHD: 21 Nov. 1781                                         Brunswick County

Compensation for two mares, impressed into public service, for which he has not received payment, and for allowance in their appraisal due to the depreciation of money.

  Manuscript unsigned.

21 Nov. 1781: To T.

20 Dec. 1781: T recommends that it be carried over to next session of GA.
    House lays on table.
    No further action found.
    Manuscript endorsement says that this matter was laid before the court of claims in Brunswick County, and was allowed.

### 1461-P-† Caldwell, John
    JHD: 21 Nov. 1781                                        Rockbridge County

Compensation for wound received at the defeat of Colonel Tarleton.

21 Nov. 1781: To T.

## Virginia Legislative Petitions

27 Dec. 1781: T recommends allowance of one year's pay for present relief and further allowance of half pay during life, to be charged to the United States in account with this commonwealth.
House agrees.
29 Dec. 1781: Senate agrees.

### 1462-P-† Nettles, Abraham
JHD: 21 Nov. 1781                                   Not known

Additional compensation for wounds received while a soldier in the public service.
21 Nov. 1781: To T.
18 Dec. 1781: T recommends allowance of one year's pay for present relief and further allowance of half pay during life, to be charged to the United States in account with this commonwealth.
House agrees.
Messrs. Richard Lee, Jefferson, and Henry to prepare bill.
For general act making payments in specie to pensioners and survivors, see 10H461.

### 1463-P-† Fisher, Frederick
JHD: 21 Nov. 1781                              Washington County

Compensation for wound received at the battle of Kings Mountain.
21 Nov. 1781: To T.
24 Dec. 1781: T recommends allowance of one year's pay for present relief and further allowance of half pay for three years, to be charged to the United States in account with this commonwealth.
House agrees.
27 Dec. 1781: Senate agrees.

### 1464-P-† Moore, William
JHD: 21 Nov. 1781                              Washington County

Compensation for wound received at the battle of Kings Mountain.
21 Nov. 1781: To T.
24 Dec. 1781: T recommends allowance of two years pay for present relief and further allowance of half pay during life, to be charged to the United States in account with this commonwealth.
House agrees.
27 Dec. 1781: Senate agrees.

## 21 November 1781

**1465-P-†  Cusick, John**
JHD: 21 Nov. 1781                                             Washington County
Compensation for wound received while in the militia under the command of General Campbell on their march to reinforce General Greene.
21 Nov. 1781: To T.
24 Dec. 1781: T recommends allowance of two years pay for present relief, to be charged to the United States in account with this commonwealth.
House agrees.
27 Dec. 1781: Senate agrees.

**1466-P  Brumley, John**
JHD: 21 Nov. 1781                                                        Not known
Reparation for loss caused by General Nelson's brigade of militia encamped on his plantation in May when they burned his fences and destroyed his wheat.
Manuscript unsigned.
21 Nov. 1781: Rejected by refusal to refer to a committee.

**1467-P  Wylly, Alexander**
JHD: 21 Nov. 1781                                                   Richmond Town
Compensation for the service of affixing the seal of the commonwealth to patents for land.
Manuscript unsigned. Dated 15 November 1781.
21 Nov. 1781: Rejected by refusal to refer to a committee.

**1468-P  Hargrove, John**
JHD: 21 Nov. 1781                                                Greensville County
Compensation for horse, saddle, and bridle, lost when he was taken by the enemy while employed by the commanding officer of Greensville County to ride express on public service.
Manuscript unsigned.
21 Nov. 1781: Rejected by refusal to refer to a committee.

**1469-P  Patrick, John**
JHD: 21 Nov. 1781                                                 Brunswick County
Compensation for a slave, the property of the petitioner, who ran away and, after being duly outlawed, was shot to death.
Manuscript unsigned.
21 Nov. 1781: Rejected by refusal to refer to a committee.

## Virginia Legislative Petitions

**1470-P   Richmond County—Citizens**
JHD: 21 Nov. 1781                                       Richmond County
Asks revival of inspection of tobacco at Glascock's warehouse in Richmond County.
Manuscript signed by: Rawleigh Downman, Jonathan Williams, Samford Jones, Wm. Peachey, John Smith, Jr., and 108 others.
21 Nov. 1781: To lie on table.
11 Dec. 1781: To PG.
19 Dec. 1781: PG recommends as reasonable.
> Referred to committee of the whole on the bill "to continue and amend the several acts of Assembly, respecting the inspection of tobacco."

24 Dec. 1781: Committee amends bill.
26 Dec. 1781: House passes bill.
29 Dec. 1781: Senate amends bill.
> House agrees to some Senate amendments, amends some Senate amendments, and disagrees with some Senate amendments.

31 Dec. 1781: Senate recedes from the amendments to which the House disagreed.
> For general act including Glascock's see 10H474.

**1471-M   North Carolina—Speakers of the Two Houses of Assembly**
JHD: 21 Nov. 1781                                       North Carolina
Respecting the navigation of Ocracoke Inlet.
Manuscript signed by: Alex. Martin and Thos. Binbury.
21 Nov. 1781: To lie on table.
> Apparently no further action taken.

**1472-P-†  Peachey, Thomas Griffin**
JHD: 22 Nov. 1781                                       Amelia County
Asks compensation for his storehouses at Rocky Run in Amelia County that were seized and possessed by the public commissaries and quartermasters and were burned by the enemy on 12 July last.
22 Nov. 1781: To PG.
26 Nov. 1781: PG finds reasonable and recommends that the auditors of public accounts do allow such a sum of money as they think just and right and issue a warrant upon the treasurer for payment. To lie on table.
16 Nov. 1782: Report and petition referred to PG.
> No further action found.

## 21 – 22 November 1781

**1473-P-†  Harrison, William**
  JHD: 22 Nov. 1781                                              Yohogania County
                                                      (That part now in Pennsylvania)
  Asks relief in that he was appointed by governor and Council to furnish provisions and boats for the expedition against Detroit, and a sum of money was sent to him for that purpose. He made contracts, but the insufficiency of the sum and delay of further supplies produced so great a depreciation that the people with whom he contracted refused to receive the money due them, and the petitioner remains liable for the same.
  22 Nov. 1781: To PG.
  26 Nov. 1781: PG finds reasonable and recommends that commissioners from Virginia who live close to the Pennsylvania line should be appointed to adjust and settle the account and report to the next session of GA.
  House agrees.
  5 Dec. 1781: Senate amends.
  House agrees to Senate amendment.

**1474-P   Stafford County—Citizens**
  JHD: 22 Nov. 1781                                              Stafford County
  Asks that the courthouse remain in its present location.
  Manuscript signed by: Jonathan Finnall, Bartho. Barrett, Jos. Spilman, Elijah Hinson, Benja. Berry, and thirty-seven others. Also report of commissioners to ascertain center of county, signed by Joseph Brock, Fra. Thornton, and James Lewis.
  22 Nov. 1781: To PG.
  26 Nov. 1781: PG recommends as reasonable.
  House agrees.
  No further action found.

**1474 A-P Stafford County—Citizens**
  JHD: 22 Nov. 1781                                              Stafford County
  Text is identical with 1474-P, which see.
  Manuscript signed by sixty persons.

**1474 B-P Stafford County—Citizens**
  JHD: 22 Nov. 1781                                              Stafford County
  Text is identical with 1474-P, which see.
  Manuscript signed by 198 persons.

# Virginia Legislative Petitions

**1475-P Venable, Samuel**
JHD: 22 Nov. 1781  Prince Edward County
Compensation for his horse, taken when he was captured by the enemy after he had joined the army and was detached on a reconnoitering party.
Manuscript unsigned. Endorsement says rejected as being allowed by court of claims in Prince Edward County.
22 Nov. 1781: To T.
20 Dec. 1781: T recommends referral to next session of GA.
>To lie on table.
>No further action found.

**1476-P Smith, Richmond**
JHD: 22 Nov. 1781  Prince Edward County
Compensation for his horse, taken when he was captured by the enemy after he had joined the army and was detached on a reconnoitering party.
Manuscript unsigned. Endorsement says rejected as being allowed by the court of claims in Prince Edward County.
22 Nov. 1781: To T.
20 Dec. 1781: T recommends referral to next session of GA.
>To lie on table.
>No further action found.

**1477-P-† Cunningham, James**
JHD: 22 Nov. 1781  Augusta County
Compensation for wound received at battle of Guilford.
22 Nov. 1781: To T.
18 Dec. 1781: T recommends allowance of one year's pay for present relief and further allowance of half pay during life, to be charged to the United States in account with this commonwealth.
>Special committee to prepare bill.
22 Dec. 1781: By motion, House resolves that petitioner ought to be allowed one year's pay in specie for present relief and half pay during life to be charged to the United States.
>House agrees.
>Apparently no further action taken.
>For general act making payments in specie to pensioners and survivors, see 10H461.

**1478-P-† Martin, Alexander**
JHD: 22 Nov. 1781  Augusta County

## 22 November 1781

Compensation for wound received at battle of Guilford.
22 Nov. 1781: To T.
24 Dec. 1781: T recommends allowance of two years pay for present relief and full pay for two years to come, to be charged to the United States in account with this commonwealth.
House agrees.
27 Dec. 1781: Senate agrees.

**1479-P  Antrim Parish, Halifax County—Churchwardens and Vestry**
JHD: 22 Nov. 1781                                           Halifax County
Asks dissolution of the vestry and that glebe be sold or disposed of for the use of the parish.
Manuscript unsigned.
22 Nov. 1781: To R.
15 Dec. 1781: R recommends (1) that vestry be dissolved and a new vestry chosen, and (2) that sale or rental of glebe lands ought to be referred to next session of GA.
House agrees to (1) and directs R to prepare bill.
House lays (2) on table.
21 Dec. 1781: R presents bill for (1).
House orders second reading of bill on the second Monday in May next.
This appears to have been considered on 8 June 1782 and subsequently enacted.
See 1671-P.
For this act see 11H73.

**1480-P  Prince Edward County—Citizens**
JHD: 22 Nov. 1781                                      Prince Edward County
Asks passage of act that would dissolve now acting vestries throughout the state and reelect others.
Manuscript signed by: Thomas Scott, Ro. Lawson, Wm. Watts, Will. Bibb, Philp. Holcombe, and six others. Endorsement says referred to next session on 21 December 1781 and rejected 9 June 1782.
22 Nov. 1781: To T.
21 Dec. 1781: Carried over to next session of GA.
Unable to locate in May 1782 minutes of General Assembly.

445

## Virginia Legislative Petitions

### 1481-P  Daniel, Walker
JHD: 22 Nov. 1781                                          Halifax County

Compensation for his horse, impressed by an officer of General Greene's army for the use of the army and detained a considerable time in the service, after which he was returned to the petitioner greatly injured.

Manuscript unsigned.

22 Nov. 1781: Rejected by refusal to refer to a committee.

### 1482-P  Frederick County—Citizens
JHD: 22 Nov. 1781                                   Frederick County

Asks repeal of the impress and embargo laws and that all present money taxes cease, and in lieu thereof that specific and specie taxes be imposed.

Manuscript signed by: Robt. White, Gerd. Briscoe, John Kercheval, Alex. White, Marquis Caloner, and thirty-one others.

22 Nov. 1781: To lie on table.

    Apparently no further action taken.

### 1483-P-†  Fayette County—Citizens
JHD: 22 Nov. 1781                                      Fayette County

Asks that the town of Lexington in Fayette County may be established as a town by act of assembly.

22 Nov. 1781: To PG.

    Apparently no further action taken.

    Similar petitions were presented 21 June 1781 and 7 December 1781 (1446-P-† and 1525-P).

    For act establishing town of Lexington in Fayette County in 1782, see 11H100.

### 1484-R-†  Mathews, George
JHD: 22 Nov. 1781                                                   Not known

Representation of sundry matters on behalf of himself and the officers of the 9th Virginia Regiment.

22 Nov. 1781: To PG.

19 Dec. 1781: PG resolves (1) that at the appointment of six additional battalions in 1776 when the officers were to take rank from time of appointment, no neglect was intended to officers of the nine battalions before directed to be raised who were not to take rank until called into actual service, but the assembly "being incompetent to the settlement of rank between their officers, the same ought to be referred to a board of general officers"; and (2) that the

446

## 22 – 24 November 1781

commercial agent ought to furnish officers of the Virginia line on Continental establishment, who from captivity or otherwise have not drawn clothing allowed by law, with such clothing and at same price as other officers of said line were charged.

House agrees to (1).
House lays (2) on table.
22 Dec. 1781: Senate agrees to (1).
Apparently no further action taken on (2).
See 1447-R-†.

### 1485-P   Swan, John
JHD: 24 Nov. 1781                                                   Monongalia County

Asks relief in that he has been prevented from confirming his right, agreeable to the land laws passed during his absence, to purchase 5,000 acres of land due for services agreeable to the Proclamation of 1763.

Manuscript unsigned, but dated 13 March 1781.
24 Nov. 1781: To PG.
27 Nov. 1781: Carried over to next session of GA.
Apparently no further action taken.

### 1486-P   Tobacco Warehouse Proprietors
JHD: 24 Nov. 1781                                                     Stafford County

Asks increase in allowance for the rent of their warehouses or that the warehouses be taken for public use and the petitioners paid their valuation.

Manuscript signed by: Thos. Jett, Wm. McWilliams, John Richards, Fras. Conway, James Miller, Archibald Ritchie, Thos. Bridgforth, and Will. Bankhead.
24 Nov. 1781: To PG.
No further action found.
See 1623-P.
For general act see 10H474.

### 1487-P   Mayo, John
JHD: 24 Nov. 1781                                                  Chesterfield County

To establish ferry across James River from Mayo's land in Chesterfield County to Mayo's lot in town of Richmond.

Manuscript unsigned.
24 Nov. 1781: To PG.
30 Nov. 1781: PG recommends rejection.
House rejects.

## Virginia Legislative Petitions

### 1488-P Henrico County—Citizens
JHD: 24 Nov. 1781            Henrico County

To establish ferry across James River from Mayo's land in Chesterfield County to Mayo's lot in town of Richmond.

Manuscript signed by: John Harris, Wm. Cunningham, Jos. Tayler, John Deane, Nath. Venable, and fourteen others.

24 Nov. 1781: To PG.

30 Nov. 1781: PG recommends rejection.

    House rejects.

### 1489-P Talley, Nathaniel
JHD: 24 Nov. 1781            Hanover County

Text is identical with 1436-P, which see.

Manuscript unsigned.

24 Nov. 1781: To PG.

    Apparently no further action taken.

### 1490-P-† Brown, John; Wade, Richard; and Morton, John
JHD: 24 Nov. 1781            Not known

Asks compensation for the time they, as soldiers, were in captivity, and also that their rights of preemption as settlers in Kentucky be confirmed to them.

24 Nov. 1781: To T.

28 Dec. 1781: T recommends (1) that auditors of public accounts settle the pay due to them in specie, and (2) that the request that a proportion of land be allotted to them for their services and sufferings while in captivity be rejected.

    House agrees to (1) and (2).

31 Dec. 1781: Senate agrees to (1).

### 1491-P-† Smith, James
JHD: 24 Nov. 1781            Not known

Compensation for wound received at the battle of Guilford.

24 Nov. 1781: To T.

20 Dec. 1781: T recommends same allowances as have been made to other wounded soldiers in similar circumstances.

    House lays on table.

    Apparently no further action taken.

    For general act making payment in specie to pensioners and survivors, see 10H461.

## 24 November 1781

**1492-P**
Eck–
A1119  **M'Kinny, John**
JHD: 24 Nov. 1781                                             Augusta County
Additional compensation for wounds received while serving as a soldier in the service of his country.
Manuscript unsigned.
24 Nov. 1781: To T.
18 Dec. 1781: T recommends allowance of £10 specie per annum during life to be discharged in current money at such difference of exchange as may be settled by the grand jury next preceding the time of receiving the same.
House agrees.
Apparently no further action taken.
For act concerning payment in specie to pensioners and survivors, see 10H461.

**1493-P**  **Turberville, John**
JHD: 24 Nov. 1781                                          Westmoreland County
Compensation for wagon, team, and Negro driver, impressed for the purpose of attending a party of drafted soldiers from this state to join the Continental army, then in Pennsylvania.
Manuscript unsigned.
24 Nov. 1781: To T.
27 Nov. 1781: T recommends (1) that compensation for loss of wagon, team, and driver be rejected, and (2) that the request that delegates from this state in Congress may be directed to apply to that body for compensation is reasonable.
House rejects entire petition.

**1494-P**
Eck–
A1680  **Tate, Caleb**
JHD: 24 Nov. 1781                                              Bedford County
Compensation for whiskey and writing paper, impressed for the use of General Steven's brigade of militia, then in South Carolina.
Manuscript unsigned. Endorsement says reported.
24 Nov. 1781: To T.
No further action found.

449

## Virginia Legislative Petitions

**1495-P  Savage, Nathaniel Littleton**
JHD: 24 Nov. 1781                                             New Kent County
Compensation for considerable injury done to his estate in New Kent County by the armies of the United States, militia, and others, which have destroyed a great part of his crops, laid waste his fields and pastures, and burned his fencing.
Manuscript unsigned.
24 Nov. 1781: House rejects by refusal to refer to a committee.

**1496-M-† Gibson, John**
JHD: 26 Nov. 1781                                                      Not known
Compensation for a quantity of goods furnished for the expedition under General Clarke, for which General Clarke engaged on the part of the public to pay the memorialist a certain sum in hard money and gave him a draft on the executive, and for which he cannot obtain payment.
26 Nov. 1781: To SC.
5 Dec. 1781: SC comes to several resolutions.
   House recommits to SC.
8 Dec. 1781: SC recommends (1) that the petition is reasonable, (2) that £1,425 16s. 9d. ought to be paid petitioner with interest from the time it became due, and (3) that the petitioner be allowed reasonable expenses in traveling to and from the assembly on this business.
   House amends (1) to reject it.
   House disagrees to (2) and (3).

**1497-P  King George County and Westmoreland County—Citizens**
JHD: 26 Nov. 1781                                          King George County
                                                         Westmoreland County
Asks revival of inspection of tobacco at Machodack warehouse.
Manuscript signed by: William Bonnard, F. Thornton, Thacker Washington, Wm. Washington, Thomas Chancellor, and forty-one others.
26 Nov. 1781: To lie on table.
11 Dec. 1781: To PG.
19 Dec. 1781: PG finds reasonable.
   House agrees.
   Referred to the committee of the whole on the bill "to continue and amend the several acts of Assembly, respecting the inspection of tobacco."
For general act, including Machodack, see 10H474.

## 24 – 29 November 1781

**1498-P**    **Baine, Robert**
     JHD: 27 Nov. 1781                         Henrico County

Asks that his estate or the sales thereof may be made good to him and that he may be admitted to the rights of citizenship. He left this state in 1775 for the West Indies upon indispensable private business, but with a fixed determination to return. During his absence his estate was taken and sold for public use under the law of escheat and forfeiture.

   Manuscript unsigned.

27 Nov. 1781: To PG.

30 Nov. 1781: PG recommends (1) that petition is reasonable; (2) that the property sold under the law and purchased by the public ought to be restored with compensation for use thereof, upon his taking the oath of allegiance to this state; (3) that restitution be made for property sold to individuals; and (4) that compensation be made for any timber taken off the land for public use.

          House agrees to all resolutions.

6 Dec. 1781: PG presents bill.

8 Dec. 1781: Recommitted to PG.

12 Dec. 1781: House passes bill.

15 Dec. 1781: Senate passes bill.

          For this act see 10H452.

**1499-P-†**    **Harris, John**
     JHD: 29 Nov. 1781                              Not known

Compensation for thirty-nine head of cattle, taken from him in July last for the use of the troops under the command of Major General Lafayette.

29 Nov. 1781: To T.

3 Dec. 1781: T comes to a resolution.

          House lays on table.

          A similar petition may have been presented on 25 May 1782 (1609-P-†).

**1500-P-†**    **Chew, John, Jr.**
     JHD: 29 Nov. 1781                              Not known

Compensation for wounds received while serving as a lieutenant in Colonel Stubblefield's regiment of militia at the battle of Camden.

29 Nov. 1781: To T.

18 Dec. 1781: T recommends allowance of one year's pay for present relief and further allowance of half pay of a lieutenant during life, to be

## Virginia Legislative Petitions

charged to the United States in account with this commonwealth.
House lays on table.
2 Jan. 1782: House agrees.
Senate agrees.

**1501-P  Rose, Duncan**
JHD: 29 Nov. 1781                                        Gloucester County
Asks payment for several sums of money and quantities of tobacco advanced for public use, and also for an arrearage of pay due him as a member of the Board of Trade.
Manuscript unsigned.
29 Nov. 1781: To T.
15 Dec. 1781: T recommends (1) payment of 145,749 pounds of tobacco, and
(2) that as much of the aforesaid tobacco as respects the trading department ought to be paid to the petitioner by the agent of that department as soon as circumstances will admit, with interest until paid.
House agrees.
18 Dec. 1781: Senate agrees.

**1502-P-† Flood, Elizabeth**
JHD: 29 Nov. 1781                                             Essex County
Asks that Archibald M'Caul and his daughter, Catherine, be permitted to return to Virginia, and that their estates be restored to them.
29 Nov. 1781: To PG.
1 Dec. 1781: PG discharged from proceeding on this petition.
A new petition on behalf of Catherine M'Caul was presented on 18 May 1782 (1580-P).

**1503-P-† Cary, Archibald**
JHD: 30 Nov. 1781                                       Chesterfield County
To establish ferry across James River from his land on south side of James River to Steger's Island on the north side.
30 Nov. 1781: To PG.
7 Dec. 1781: PG recommends rejection.
House lays on table.
No further action found.

**1504-P  Dixon, John**
JHD: 30 Nov. 1781                                            Richmond Town

## 29 – 30 November 1781

Compensation for a Loan Office certificate in the amount of £600 and upwards that was destroyed along with other papers and books during the incursion of General Arnold.

Manuscript unsigned, but a docket thereon for 21 May 1782 says reasonable upon taking oath and putting up bond. Attached is a certificate of Foster Webb.

30 Nov. 1781: To PG.
      Apparently no further action taken.

### 1505-M  Virginia Continental Line—Officers
JHD: 30 Nov. 1781                               Not known

Asks relief in that they have suffered from depreciation of their pay, considerable arrearages of which are now due them, that supplies of clothing and other necessaries have been very lacking, and that they are aggrieved by a preclusion of the rights of denization, in common with other citizens.

Manuscript unsigned.
30 Nov. 1781: To a special committee.
6 Dec. 1781: Committee presents resolutions.
      Amended by House to read (1) that the whole pay of the troops be made good from 1 January 1777, according to their times of service; (2) that the auditor acquainted with the business of the army be appointed to liquidate and adjust the accounts of the officers and soldiers of the Virginia line in Continental service and that certificates, equal to specie, be given individually for the respective balances; (3) that in the meantime, like certificates be given for the amount of two years' pay to all officers now of the line who were in service prior to 1 May 1777, and to those who have since come into service similiar certificates shall be issued for one year, provided that they have been in service one year; (4) that the wages of the officers and soldiers in the future ought to be paid once in every quarter of a year at least; (5) that where it shall appear to the auditors that from captivity or other circumstances, officers had sufficient reasons why their accounts were not settled, or where it shall be manifest that there has been no misapplication on their part of the public monies that may have been in their hands, then in such cases no depreciation shall be charged; and that where it shall be made to appear that officers have advanced their own monies for public service, they shall be allowed the depreciation; (6) that the tract of land included within the Mississippi, Ohio, and Tennessee rivers and the North Carolina line be substituted in lieu

## Virginia Legislative Petitions

of such part of the country formerly allotted for the troops, which since has been taken within the North Carolina boundary, excluding such lands as are actually located therein, and the several apportionments be made by surveyors to be appointed for that purpose, when the executive shall think proper, and the lands be appropriated by lot and be free from taxation during continuance of the present war, subject, however, to revert to the state on resignation or forfeiture of commission respectively; and (7) that reduced officers on half pay ought to be eligible as members of the General Assembly.

House agrees.

Special committee to prepare bill or bills.

Motion was made that the reasonable expenses of the officers, deputed on behalf of the officers of this state in the Continental line to attend the General Assembly on the subject of their memorial, ought to be paid by the public treasurer.

House agrees.

14 Dec. 1781: Committee presents bill "to adjust and regulate the pay and accounts of the officers and soldiers of this State on continental establishment."

24 Dec. 1781: Bill read third time and clause offered, by way of rider, "that all tobacco arising from the sale of confiscated estates, be appropriated to the payment and redemption of the certificates, to be granted to the officers and soldiers."

House passes bill and rider.

29 Dec. 1781: Senate amends bill.

House agrees to some Senate amendments and disagrees with others.

31 Dec. 1781: Motion was made that the House resolve that the auditors be directed to settle the account of Colonel Russell for his expenses in attending this assembly, on behalf of the other officers, to the day on which the bill "for regulating their pay" passed the House.

House agrees.

1 Jan. 1782: Senate amends resolution relevant to Colonel Russell.

House agrees to Senate amendment to resolution relevant to Colonel Russell.

Senate insists on their amendments to the bill "to adjust and regulate. . . ."

## 30 November – 1 December 1781

2 Jan. 1782: House recedes from its disagreement to amendments insisted on by Senate to bill "to adjust and regulate. . . ."

For this act see 10H462.

### 1506-P-† Browder, William
JHD: 30 Nov. 1781                                   Dinwiddie County

Compensation for mare, taken by the enemy in Petersburg while it was being used to remove public stores.

30 Nov. 1781: To T.

18 Dec. 1781: T recommends £40 specie.

    House agrees.

19 Dec. 1781: Senate agrees.

### 1507-P Tobacco Inspectors—Hobb's Hole Warehouses
JHD: 30 Nov. 1781                                   Essex County

Asks reimbursement by the public for the loss of tobacco when the warehouses were twice broken open, without the default of the petitioners, and tobacco stolen.

Manuscript unsigned. Attested by Essex County court.

30 Nov. 1781: To T

1 Jan. 1782: Carried over to next session of GA.

    Carried over several times and not acted on until 5 June 1783.

### 1508-P Kinkeade, John
JHD: 1 Dec. 1781                                     Washington County

Compensation for opening a road through the Cumberland Mountains to Kentucky.

Manuscript unsigned.

1 Dec. 1781: To PG.

14 Dec. 1781: PG recommends £25 specie.

    House agrees.

18 Dec. 1781: Senate agrees.

### 1509-P Hanover County—Citizens
JHD: 1 Dec. 1781                                     Hanover County
                                                              King William County

Asks revival of inspection of tobacco at Meriwether's warehouse in Hanover County.

Manuscript signed by: J. Syme, Jno. Jones, Jno. Cunningham, Wm. John-

## Virginia Legislative Petitions

son, Geo. Earnest, and thirty others. Manuscript docket notes referred to committee on tobacco law.
1 Dec. 1781: To PG.
    No further action found.
    For general law including Meriwether's see 10H474.

### 1510-P   Aston, Esther
JHD: 1 Dec. 1781                       Yohogania County

Asks for bounty land on the basis of the service of her deceased husband, George Aston, as a captain during the last war.
Manuscript unsigned.
1 Dec. 1781: To PG.
    Apparently no further action taken.

### 1511-P   Washington County—Citizens
JHD: 1 Dec. 1781                       Washington County

Asks that an act be passed to explain the land laws so that their claims to vacant lands will be made legal agreeable to law. The said lands are claimed by the Loyal Company under illicit surveys.

Manuscript signed by: Robert Edmondson, Moses Buchanan, John Kelly, John Edmiston, John Jones, and fourteen others.
1 Dec. 1781: To PG.
    No further action found.
    For act concerning county courts deciding land cases, see 10H484.

### 1511 A-P Washington County—Citizens
JHD: 1 Dec. 1781                       Washington County
Text is similar to 1511-P, which see.
Manuscript signed by 161 persons.

### 1512-P   Cabell, Joseph; Innes, Harry; and Cabell, Nicholas
JHD: 1 Dec. 1781                       Washington County
                                                          Montgomery County

Asks explanation and amendment of the land laws as they relate to the Loyal Company. The petitioners are commissioners for settling the titles of claimers to unpatented lands within the district of Washington and Montgomery.
Manuscript unsigned.

## 1 – 3 December 1781

1 Dec. 1781: To PG.
> No further action found.
> See 1456-P-† and 1621-P.
> For act concerning county courts deciding land cases, see 10H484.

### 1513-P-† Jones, William
JHD: 3 Dec. 1781     Not known

Compensation for wound received at the battle of Brandywine.

3 Dec. 1781: To T.
> No further action found.
> This petition may have been presented again in May 1782, but the record is not clear.
> See 1597-P-†.

### 1514-P-† Simster, John
JHD: 3 Dec. 1781     Not known

Compensation for wound received at the defeat of Colonel Buford.

3 Dec. 1781: To T.

1 Jan. 1782: T recommends one year's pay for present relief and further allowance of half pay during life, to be charged to the United States in account with this commonwealth.
> House agrees.
> Senate agrees.

### 1515-P Surry County—Citizens
JHD: 3 Dec. 1781     Surry County

Asks establishment of inspection of tobacco at Low Point in Surry County since the destruction of the warehouses at Cabin Point has produced great disadvantages.

Manuscript signed by: Jn. Lee, James Rae, Stephen Sorsby, William Collins, Wm. Maget, and six others. Dated 7 November 1781.

3 Dec. 1781: To PG.

19 Dec. 1781: PG finds reasonable.
> Referred to committee of the whole on the bill "to continue and amend the several acts of Assembly, respecting the inspection of tobacco."
> For general act, including discontinuance of Cabin Point and establishment of Low Point, see 10H474.

## Virginia Legislative Petitions

### 1516-P    Dunlop, Archibald
JHD: 3 Dec. 1781                                    Surry County
Asks establishment of inspection of tobacco on his land in Surry County at Low Point, commonly called Guilford.
Manuscript unsigned.
3 Dec. 1781: To PG.
    See 1515-P.
    For general act see 10H474.

### 1517-M    Virginia State Battalion—Officers
JHD: 3 Dec. 1781                                    Not known
Asks relief in that they have suffered great inconveniences by the depreciation of their pay and the arrearages due to them, as well as by their failure to receive clothing also due to them.
Manuscript signed by: Thomas Marshall, George Minter, and E. Read.
3 Dec. 1781: To a special committee.
12 Dec. 1781: Committee recommends (1) that officers of state battalions and corps are entitled to half pay during life; (2) that a return of all state officers ought to be made to the next assembly; (3) that the whole pay of state troops be made good from the first of January 1777; (4) that bounty land given to officers of the Virginia line, in Continental service, ought to be extended to state officers; (5) that state officers, reduced and on half pay, ought to be eligible as members of the General Assembly; (6) that state cavalry is entitled to same indulgences and advantages as the infantry; (7) that the same allowances should be made to state officers that have attended this assembly on the business of the officers and soldiers of the state, for their expenses, that is made to the officers of the Virginia Continental line; and (8) that state officers in actual service ought to receive the same advances of pay for their present relief as officers in Continental service.
House lays (1) on table.
House amends (2) and (3) and agrees to them.
House agrees to (4)–(8) and bill or bills are to be brought in by special committee.
14 Dec. 1781: Committee presents bill "to adjust and regulate the pay and accounts of the officers and soldiers of this State on continental establishment." (This bill appears to have included officers and soldiers of the state line.)
15 Dec. 1781: Senate agrees to (7).

458

## 3 – 5 December 1781

24 Dec. 1781: Bill read third time and clause offered, by way of rider, "that all tobacco arising from the sale of confiscated estates, be appropriated to the payment and redemption of the certificates, to be granted to the officers and soldiers."

24 Dec. 1781: House passes bill and rider.

29 Dec. 1781: Senate amends bill.
>House agrees to some Senate amendments and disagrees with others.

1 Jan. 1782: Senate insists on their amendments to the bill "to adjust and regulate. . . ."

2 Jan. 1782: House recedes from its disagreement to amendments insisted on by Senate to bill "to adjust and regulate. . . ."
>For general act see 10H462.

### 1518-M  Berkeley County—Citizens
JHD: 4 Dec. 1781                                        Berkeley County

Asks relief from the laws of impress, which they conceive to be impolitic and unjust.

Manuscript unsigned.

4 Dec. 1781: To SC.
>No further action found.
>See 1425-M.
>For general act concerning impressment see 10H468.

### 1519-P  Thompson, Anne
JHD: 5 Dec. 1781                                        Louisa County

Compensation for the great expense and inconvenience caused her when a wounded soldier of General Wayne's brigade was left at her house and remained for five months.

Manuscript signed: George Harrison. Attached is a certificate of Thomas Johnson.

5 Dec. 1781: To T.

18 Dec. 1781: T recommends rejection.
>House rejects.

### 1520-P  Loudoun County—Citizens
JHD: 5 Dec. 1781                                        Loudoun County

Asks division of the county into two distinct counties, agreeable to certain boundaries.

## Virginia Legislative Petitions

Manuscript signed by: Wm. Stanhope, John Minor, John Gess, Alex. Chisholm, Sturman Chilton, and thirty-one others.
5 Dec. 1781: Carried over to next session of GA.
>(Loudoun County was never divided.)
>These may have been the petitions referred to PG on 4 June 1782. See 1654-P-†.

### 1520 A-P Loudoun County—Citizens
JHD: 5 Dec. 1781      Loudoun County
Text is similar to 1520-P, which see.
Manuscript signed by forty-two persons.

### 1520 B-P Loudoun County—Citizens
JHD: 5 Dec. 1781      Loudoun County
Text is similar to 1520-P, which see.
Manuscript signed by ten persons.

### 1520 C-P Loudoun County—Citizens
JHD: 5 Dec. 1781      Loudoun County
Text is similar to 1520-P, which see.
Manuscript signed by sixteen persons.

### 1520 D-P Loudoun County—Citizens
JHD: 5 Dec. 1781      Loudoun County
Text is similar to 1520-P, which see.
Manuscript signed by thirty-three persons.

### 1520 E-P Loudoun County—Citizens
JHD: 5 Dec. 1781      Loudoun County
Text is similar to 1520-P, which see.
Manuscript signed by 318 persons.

### 1520 F-P Loudoun County—Citizens
JHD: 5 Dec. 1781      Loudoun County
Text is similar to 1520-P, which see.
Manuscript signed by seventeen persons.

## 5 – 7 December 1781

**1520 G-P   Loudoun County—Citizens**
    JHD: 5 Dec. 1781                              Loudoun County
    Text is similar to 1520-P, which see.
    Manuscript signed by thirty-five persons.

**1521-P   Loudoun County—Citizens**
    JHD: 5 Dec. 1781                              Loudoun County
Opposing a division of the county into two distinct counties, agreeable to certain boundaries.
    Manuscript signed by: William George, Joseph Calwall, Noble Leonard, Robert Fitzpatrick, John Neilson, and 128 others. Manuscript list of tithables attached.
5 Dec. 1781: Carried over to next session of GA.
        (Loudoun County was never divided.)
        These may have been the petitions referred to PG on 4 June 1782. See 1655-P.

**1521 A-P   Loudoun County—Citizens**
    JHD: 5 Dec. 1781                              Loudoun County
    Text is similar to 1521-P, which see.
    Manuscript signed by 127 persons.

**1522-P   Black, William**
    JHD: 6 Dec. 1781                        Chesterfield County
To establish ferry across James River from Black's land in Chesterfield County to the public landing at Rockett's in Henrico County.
    Manuscript unsigned.
6 Dec. 1781: To PG.
7 Dec. 1781: PG finds reasonable.
        House agrees and directs PG to prepare a bill.
20 Dec. 1781: PG presents bill.
        House passes bill.
27 Dec. 1781: Senate agrees.
        For general ferry act including this one see 10H459.

**1523-P**
Eck–
A1681   **Meade, John**
    JHD: 7 Dec. 1781                             Bedford County
As jailor of Bedford County, asks payment of £300, together with the

## Virginia Legislative Petitions

depreciation thereupon, for claim presented to a former assembly and allowed, but in which there was an error.

Manuscript unsigned. Endorsement shows that on 21 June 1782 this matter was referred to next session of GA.

7 Dec. 1781: To T.

> Meade presented the same petition on 16 November 1782. See also 1343-P.

### 1524-P-† Conner, John
JHD: 7 Dec. 1781                                                  Not known

Compensation for wound received at the battle of Camden.

7 Dec. 1781: To T.

18 Dec. 1781: T recommends allowance of one year's pay for present relief and further allowance of half pay during life, to be charged to the United States in account with this commonwealth.
House agrees.
Special committee to prepare a bill. (See 1539-P-†.)
(This bill probably relates to an act paying pensions in specie.)
No Senate action is found on this particular petition.
For act paying pensions in specie, see 10H461.

### 1525-P
Rob–14  **Fayette County—Citizens**
JHD: 7 Dec. 1781                                              Fayette County

Asks that Lexington, in Fayette County, may be established as a town by act of assembly.

Manuscript signed by: Levi Todd, R. Patterson, B. Netherland, David Vance, David Mitchell, and forty-five others. Endorsement says to be heard on 14 June 1782. Reported reasonable on 15 June 1782. Manuscript has survey map of Lexington by John Todd, Jr., and others.

7 Dec. 1781: To PG.

> Apparently no further action taken in this session. Similar petitions were presented 21 June 1781 and 22 Nov. 1781 (1446-P-† and 1483-P-†).
>
> For act establishing town of Lexington in Fayette County, see 11H100, May 1782 session.

### 1526-P-† Conner, John
JHD: 8 Dec. 1781                                                  Not known

Asks compensation for considerable advances for the service of this state in

## 7 – 8 December 1781

the Illinois and western country. He has received paper money in part for one claim and the said money has depreciated and his other claims are as yet unsatisfied.

8 Dec. 1781: To T.
    No further action found.

**1527-P-† Morgan, John**
    JHD: 8 Dec. 1781                                                         Not known
Compensation for wounds received at the defeat of Colonel Buford.
8 Dec. 1781: To T.
18 Dec. 1781: T recommends six months pay for present relief and further allowance of half pay during life, and also to be furnished with a blanket and suit of clothes, to be charged to the United States in account with this commonwealth.
    House agrees.
1 Jan. 1782: Senate agrees.

**1528-P-† Godwin, Lemuel (Administrator of Thomas Fisher, deceased)**
    JHD: 8 Dec. 1781                                       Chesterfield County
Compensation to heirs of Thomas Fisher for horse and accoutrements lost to the enemy when Fisher, a volunteer in the Chesterfield militia, fell while opposing the enemy near Manchester.
8 Dec. 1781: To T.
20 Dec. 1781: T recommends referral to next session of GA.
    House lays on table.
    Apparently no further action taken.

**1529-P-† Branch, William**
    JHD: 8 Dec. 1781                                                         Not known
Compensation for his horse, disabled after it was furnished for service of the cavalry on the approach of the British army to Petersburg.
8 Dec. 1781: To T.
20 Dec. 1781: T recommends referral to next session of GA.
    House lays on table.
    Apparently no further action taken.

**1530-P Norfolk County and Norfolk Borough—Citizens**
    JHD: 8 Dec. 1781                                       Norfolk County
                                                                             Norfolk Borough

## Virginia Legislative Petitions

Asks relief in that the losses sustained by the depredations of the enemy will, they fear, render them unable to pay the usual taxes for the support of government.

Manuscript signed by: Matthew Godfrey, Tho. Nash, Saml. Portlock, Matthew Portlock, Mathias Portlock, and twenty-nine others.
8 Dec. 1781: To PG.
10 Dec. 1781: PG recommends rejection.
> House rejects.

**1531-M**
Eck–
A1120 **Bowyer, William**
JHD: 8 Dec. 1781                      Augusta County

Asks that he be allowed the same advantages as Continental officers while he continues as a prisoner upon parole, and compensation to those men under his command who lost their horses to the enemy.

Manuscript unsigned, but endorsement thereon notes referred to next session of GA.
8 Dec. 1781: To PG.
10 Dec. 1781: PG presents resolutions, amended to read (1) that request for same advantages as Continental officers be rejected, and (2) that compensation for loss of horses is reasonable and like proceedings should be had for adjusting the same, as shall be provided in cases of impressment.
> House agrees.
> No further action found.

**1532-P and**
Remonstrance
    **Prince William County—Citizens**
    JHD: 10 Dec. 1781              Prince William County

Asks amendment or repeal of the acts vesting extraordinary powers in the executive: authorizing impresses, laying an embargo, and making paper money a legal tender.

Manuscript signed by: T. Blackburn, John Pope, Peter Evans, Hy. Hampton, Geo. N. Brown, and fifty-three others.
10 Dec. 1781: To SC.

## 8 - 10 December 1781

22 Dec. 1781: Speaker lays before the House a letter from Thomas Nelson, Jr., late governor, respecting his conduct. (Not extant in petition file.)
    SC presents resolution.
    House agrees.
26 Dec. 1781: Bill presented "to legalize the measures taken by Thomas Nelson, jun. Esq. late Governor of this Commonwealth, for supplying the Allied army and militia, employed in the siege of York."
27 Dec. 1781: Read second time and committed to committee of the whole.
28 Dec. 1781: Committee amends.
    House agrees.
29 Dec. 1781: House passes bill.
31 Dec. 1781: Senate amends bill.
    House agrees to Senate amendments.
    For this act see 10H478.

### 1533-P   Richmond—Merchants and Traders
    JHD: 10 Dec. 1781                            Richmond Town

Asks for establishment of inspection of tobacco at Rockett's landing near town of Richmond.

Manuscript signed by: Steph. Tankard, Robt. Boyd, Jesse Rosser, Wm. White, Jacob Cohan and Isaacs, and fifteen others.

10 Dec. 1781: To PG.
17 Dec. 1781: PG finds reasonable.
    House agrees.
    Ordered that PG, to whom it was referred to bring in a bill "to revive and amend the several acts for the inspection of tobacco," do receive a clause or clauses pursuant thereto.
    House and Senate pass this bill.
    See 1536-P.
    For general act including Rockett's see 10H474.

### 1534-P-†  Lee, Richard Evers
    JHD: 10 Dec. 1781                                  Not known

Compensation for his one-fourth interest in the sloop *Warwick* that was burned at Osborne's by orders of Baron von Steuben and Commodore Lewis on the approach of the British.

10 Dec. 1781: To T.
1 Jan. 1782: T finds reasonable.
    House lays on table.
    No further action found.

## Virginia Legislative Petitions

**1535-M    General George Rogers Clark's Regiment—Officers**
JHD: 11 Dec. 1781                                                                 Not known

Asks that they be assigned a quantity of land equal to that reserved for distribution among them in the cession made by this state to the United States since they believe that Congress has refused that cession.

Manuscript unsigned.

11 Dec. 1781: To PG.

18 Dec. 1781: Motion made that House resolve that Captain John Rogers, and
       the officers and light dragoons of his corps, shall be entitled to their
       due proportion of the lands allowed and granted to the officers and
       soldiers of the regiment commanded by Colonel George Rogers
       Clark.
       House agrees.

20 Dec. 1781: Senate agrees.

**1536-P    Richmond—Merchants and Traders**
JHD: 11 Dec. 1781                                                                 Richmond Town

Opposing establishment of inspection of tobacco at Rockett's landing.

Manuscript signed by: David Ross and Company, Hunter Banks and Company, Thomas M. Randolph, David Ross, Wm. Hay, Charles Irving, and Dan. L. Hylton.

11 Dec. 1781: To PG.

17 Dec. 1781: PG recommends rejection.
       House rejects.
       See 1533-P.
       For act establishing warehouse at Rockett's landing, see 10H474.

**1537-P-†    Richmond—Citizens Who Suffered from Arnold's Invasion**
JHD: 11 Dec. 1781                                                                 Richmond Town

Compensation for houses taken for public service prior to the invasion by General Arnold and burned by the enemy.

11 Dec. 1781: To T.
       Apparently no further action taken.

**1538-P    Newton, Thomas and Bowdoin, Preston**
JHD: 12 Dec. 1781                                                                 Norfolk County
                                                                                                                  Portsmouth

Compensation to the estate of Robert Tucker, deceased, for land taken for public use in the defense of the town of Portsmouth.

Manuscript unsigned.

11 – 14 December 1781

12 Dec. 1781: To T.
20 Dec. 1781: T finds reasonable.
        Court of Norfolk County to ascertain such damages and report to next session of GA.
        House agrees.
24 Dec. 1781: Senate agrees.
        Report not found.

### 1539-P-† King, John
        JHD: 12 Dec. 1781                               Not known

Compensation for wounds received at the defeat of Colonel Buford.

12 Dec. 1781: To T.
18 Dec. 1781: T recommends two years pay for present relief and further allowance of half pay during life, to be charged to the United States in account with this commonwealth.
        House agrees.
        Special committee to prepare a bill. (See 1524-P-†.)
        No further action found.

### 1540-P-† Trabue, James
        JHD: 12 Dec. 1781                             Kentucky County

Asks allowance for depreciation on certificates given to various persons by him as purchasing commissary for the public in Kentucky County. He was taken prisoner in 1780, and the said certificates were not given until his release.

12 Dec. 1781: To T.
20 Dec. 1781: T recommends that the governor with the advice of Council ought to appoint commissioners to adjust and settle the said claims.
        House agrees.
29 Dec. 1781: Senate agrees.

### 1541-P-† Conan, John Francis
        JHD: 14 Dec. 1781, for action               Not known

Compensation for supplies and services as a surgeon at the instance of General Clark.

Date unknown: To T.
14 Dec. 1781: T discharged from proceeding.

## Virginia Legislative Petitions

1 Jan. 1782: Motion made that the treasurer be directed to advance Conan $1,000, as part of his demand, for his present support and maintenance.
House agrees.
4 Jan. 1782: Senate agrees.

### 1542-M   Clarke, Daniel
JHD: 14 Dec. 1781                                             Not known

Asks that the House make payment now or at a future date for money he advanced for the western service, and that the agreement to make payment be absolute and unconditional. If paid at a future date, interest should be included. Memorialist had agreed to accept part of the payment in tobacco but its price is now greatly disadvantageous to the memorialist.
Manuscript unsigned.
14 Dec. 1781: To T.
18 Dec. 1781: T discharged from proceeding.
Referred to PG.
25 Dec. 1781: PG finds reasonable.
Amended to read that David Ross is to state the claim of Daniel Clarke and return the same to next session of GA.
29 Dec. 1781: Senate amends.
House agrees to Senate amendments.
Further action not found.

### 1543-P   Clarke, Daniel, on behalf of Oliver Pollock
JHD: 14 Dec. 1781                                             Not known

Asks that the House make payment in the same manner as Congress has done in similar cases for sums advanced to the state of Virginia by Pollock for the prosecution of the war and for which he has not been repaid.
Manuscript unsigned.
14 Dec. 1781: To T.
18 Dec. 1781: T discharged from proceeding.
Referred to PG.
25 Dec. 1781: PG finds reasonable.
Amended to read that David Ross is to state the claim of Daniel Clarke and return the same to next session of GA.
29 Dec. 1781: Senate amends.
House agrees to Senate amendments.
Further action not found.
See 1542-M and 1553-P.

## 14 December 1781

**1544-P    M'Millian, John**
JHD: 14 Dec. 1781                                                Prince William County
Compensation for three horses, stolen after they were impressed into the public service.
Manuscript unsigned. Docket says rejected 14 June 1782, the court of claims of Prince William County having taken care of it.
14 Dec. 1781: To T.
20 Dec. 1781: T recommends referral to next session of GA.
    House lays on table.
    Apparently no further action taken.

**1545-P-†    Williams, Elisha**
JHD: 14 Dec. 1781                                                                    Not known
Compensation for his horse, shot dead by a sentinel belonging to General Nelson's brigade of militia.
14 Dec. 1781: To T.
18 Dec. 1781: T recommends rejection.
    House rejects.

**1546-P    Washington County and Montgomery County—Citizens**
JHD: 14 Dec. 1781                                                Washington County
                                                                   Montgomery County
Asks amendment of the land laws so as to give the commissioners of the district the power to hear and determine in all such cases.
Manuscript signed by: W. Ingles, Jacob Kittering, Nathaniel Morgan, Lorton Steel, Dvd. Beetie, and fifty-one others. Endorsement says rejected 21 June 1782.
14 Dec. 1781: To PG.
    No further action found.
    For act concerning county courts deciding land cases, see 10H484.

**1547-P    Inglis, William**
JHD: 14 Dec. 1781                                                Montgomery County
Asks amendment of the land laws so as to give the commissioners of the district the power to hear and determine in all such cases.
Manuscript unsigned.
14 Dec. 1781: To PG.
    No further action found.
    For act concerning county courts deciding land cases, see 10H484.

Virginia Legislative Petitions

**1548-P-†  Lincoln County, Fayette County, and Jefferson County—Citizens**
JHD: 14 Dec. 1781
Lincoln County
Fayette County
Jefferson County

Asks that provision be made for their future good government since from their detached and remote situation they do not participate in the common benefits of government as it is now administered.

14 Dec. 1781: To a special committee.
18 Dec. 1781: Committee finds reasonable and is directed to prepare bill.
19 Dec. 1781: Bill presented "for dividing the Commonwealth into districts, and establishing a subordinate executive for the western district," and also bill "for establishing Supreme Courts in the western district."
20 Dec. 1781: Both bills committed to a committee of the whole on the second Monday in May next.

There were new petitions in May 1782 (1629-P and 1640-P).

**1549-P  Chesterfield County—Court Justices**
JHD: 15 Dec. 1781
Chesterfield County

Asks that they be enabled to rebuild, at public expense, their courthouse and prisons that were taken by order of the executive and converted into storehouses for public use; that being so applied they were burned by the enemy.

Manuscript signed by: Jos. Royall, Blackman Moseley, Thos. Bolling, George Woodson, John Archer, Thos. Worsham, Benja. Branch, Geo. Robertson, David Holt, Bernd. Markham, and Jno. Bott. Attached is manuscript deposition signed by Thomas Burfoot, quartermaster, and Colonel William Davies.

15 Dec. 1781: To PG.

Apparently no further action taken.

**1550-P-†  Vaughan, John**
JHD: 15 Dec. 1781
Not known

Asks relief in that being detached on command with a party of British prisoners, he drew £2,000 for their support, which was so expended, but he lost the vouchers for the application thereof.

15 Dec. 1781: To PG.

Apparently no further action taken.

## 14 – 15 December 1781

**1551-P   Holmes, Christian**
JHD: 15 Dec. 1781                                                Not known
   Compensation for an accident that happened to him while in service and that prevents him from serving out his commission as major in Colonel Harrison's regiment.
   Manuscript unsigned.
15 Dec. 1781: To PG.
         Apparently no further action taken.

**1552-P-†   Wilkins, Nathaniel**
JHD: 15 Dec. 1781                                                Not known
   Compensation for loss of his right hand at the battle of Waxhaw, which prevents him from procuring a livelihood by labor.
15 Dec. 1781: To T.
18 Dec. 1781: T recommends one year's pay for present relief and further
         allowance of half pay during life.
         House agrees.
         Special committee to prepare bill. (This bill probably relates to an act paying pensions in specie.)
         No further action found.
         For act paying pensions in specie, see 10H461.

**1553-P   Achen, Thomas**
JHD: 15 Dec. 1781                                                Not known
   Asks payment for bill of exchange on the treasurer for £2,162 he advanced to Oliver Pollock, agent for this state, for use of the western department.
   Manuscript unsigned.
15 Dec. 1781: To T.
18 Dec. 1781: T discharged from proceeding.
         Referred to PG.
         No further action found.
         See 1543-P.

**1554-P-†   Williams, James**
JHD: 15 Dec. 1781                                                Not known
   Compensation for loss of eyesight while a soldier in the last and present war.
15 Dec. 1781: To T.
18 Dec. 1781: T recommends six months pay for present relief and further
         allowance of half pay during life.
         House agrees.

## Virginia Legislative Petitions

Special committee to prepare a bill. (This bill probably relates to an act paying pensions in specie.)
No further action found.
Petition appears to have been presented again 5 June 1782 (1659-P) and rejected 7 June 1782.
For an act paying pensions in specie, see 10H461.

### 1555-P-† M'Cabe, Henry
JHD: 17 Dec. 1781      Not known

Asks that he may be authorized to dispose of part of estate of his father, Henry M'Cabe, Sr., to which he is presumptive heir.
17 Dec. 1781: To PG.
19 Dec. 1781: PG finds reasonable.
    House agrees and directs PG to prepare bill.
24 Dec. 1781: PG presents bill.
25 Dec. 1781: House passes bill.
29 Dec. 1781: Senate amends.
    House agrees to Senate amendment.
    For this act see 10H488.

### 1556-P    Manchester—Merchants and Citizens
JHD: 17 Dec. 1781      Chesterfield County

Asks that the warehouses in the town that were burned by the enemy may be reestablished and the inspection of tobacco continued there.

Manuscript signed by: James Lyle, Alex. Banks, John Murchie, Robert Donald, David Leitch, Jacob Rubsamen, Alex. Trent, A. Love, and Lemuel Godwin.
17 Dec. 1781: To PG.
    For authorization for renting houses for tobacco inspection in Manchester, see 10H474.

### 1557-P    Louisa County—Commissioners of the Money Tax
JHD: 17 Dec. 1781      Louisa County

Asks relief in that they collected the tax in the county and paid it into the public treasury, but part of it has been returned as counterfeit.

Manuscript unsigned, but the endorsement says rejected 14 June 1782.
17 Dec. 1781: To T.
20 Dec. 1781: Carried over to next session of GA.

## 17 – 18 December 1781

**1558-P**
Eck–
A1121   **Kilpatrick, Alexander**
   JHD: 17 Dec. 1781                                   Augusta County
   Asks relief in that he, as appointed jailer in Augusta County, sustained great loss by the insufficiency of fees collected for the support of prisoners.
   Manuscript unsigned. Endorsement says reported 24 December 1782 and rejected 12 June 1783.
17 Dec. 1781: To T.
   Carried over to next session of GA.
16 Nov. 1782: To T.
27 Dec. 1782: Carried over to next session of GA.
12 June 1783: C recommends rejection.
   House recommits.
25 June 1783: House agrees to fees.
27 June 1783: Senate agrees.
   See 1332-P.

**1559-P-†  Brooke, Robert**
   JHD: 18 Dec. 1781                                         Not known
   Compensation for his horse and accoutrements, kept by the enemy after he was taken prisoner while serving as a volunteer in a corps of horse.
18 Dec. 1781: To T.
20 Dec. 1781: T recommends referral to next session of GA.
   House lays on table.
   No further action found.

**1560-P   New Kent County—Citizens**
   JHD: 18 Dec. 1781                                   New Kent County
   Asks that inspection of tobacco may be established at Waddy's, in the said county, since the warehouses at Brickhouse and Littlepage's were burned by the enemy.
   Manuscript signed by: John Wilkinson, Edward Waddill, William Moses, Daniel Moses, Chas. Howleson, and twelve others.
18 Dec. 1781: To PG.
      For general warehouse act see 10H474. This establishes inspection at Waddy's and discontinues Brickhouse unless rebuilt at owner's expense.

473

## Virginia Legislative Petitions

**1561-P  Haskins, Edward and Markham, Vincent**
JHD: 18 Dec. 1781                                    Powhatan County
   Asks relief in that they, as sheriffs of Powhatan County, collected the taxes due, and Markham went to the auditors' office to settle the same, but the auditors not having time to settle the accounts and Markham being taken with smallpox, a judgment has gone against them in General Court.
   Manuscript unsigned.
18 Dec. 1781: To PG.
   No further action found.

**1562-M  Smith, Thomas**
JHD: 18 Dec. 1781                                             Not known
   Compensation for past and future services due to his appointment by the governor and Council in 1779 to settle the accounts of this state against the United States.
   Manuscript unsigned.
18 Dec. 1781: To a special committee.
21 Dec. 1781: Committee recommends payments in specie, or the value thereof in tobacco, to Smith and to his clerk.
   Recommitted to same committee.
24 Dec. 1781: Committee presents resolution.
   House lays on table.
25 Dec. 1781: House takes resolution from table and amends it to allow Smith £300 specie per annum, or the value thereof in tobacco, deducting therefrom $2,000 in paper dollars or £10 specie and also value of rations. Clerk to be paid £100 specie per annum, or the value thereof in tobacco.
   House agrees.
29 Dec. 1781: Senate amends.
   House agrees to Senate amendments.

**1563-M-† Carrington, Edward**
JHD: 18 Dec. 1781                                             Not known
   Asks legislative provision to procure wagons, provisions, and horses for use of the southern army.
18 Dec. 1781: To committee appointed to bring in a bill "to regulate impresses."
26 Dec. 1781: Committee resolves (1) that delinquent counties be immediately compelled to make up wagons and teams required of them,

## 18 December 1781 – 16 May 1782

and (2) that persons of credit be appointed to have power and authority to give receipts for such horses.
House agrees.
Special committee to prepare bill.
27 Dec. 1781: Committee presents bill.
28 Dec. 1781: Bill committed to PG.
31 Dec. 1781: PG reports bill without amendments.
House passes bill.
3 Jan. 1782: Senate amends.
House agrees to Senate amendment.
For general impressment act see 10H468.

**1564-P-†  Selden, Miles, Jr.; Prosser, Thomas; Buckanan, James; Lyle, James; Buckanan, James for Thompson Mason; Adams, Richard; and Nicholas, George**
JHD: 24 Dec. 1781, for action      Henrico County
Compensation for sundry houses, the property of the petitioners, that were appropriated for public use and, in consequence, destroyed by the enemy.
Date unknown: To T.
24 Dec. 1781: T recommends amended resolution that the court of Henrico County ascertain the value of the said houses and return the same, together with the proofs relative thereto, to the next session of GA.
House agrees.
29 Dec. 1781: Senate agrees.

**1565-P    Prince Edward County—Citizens**
MHD: 16 May 1782      Prince Edward County
Opposing tender law. Asks that instead of specie, paper money be redeemed to pay taxes and that fines be heavier for absentee members of General Assembly.
Manuscript signed by: John Blair Smith, John Nash, Thos. Haskins, Benj. Haskins, Henry Watkins, and 126 others. Dated 15 March 1782.
16 May 1782: To SC.
No further action found.

**1566-M    Virginia Directors of Public Buildings—Richmond**
MHD: 16 May 1782      Richmond Town
States that buildings in Richmond are secured for the government. Asks that General Assembly investigate lapse of contract for enlarging public jail by Wood and Price.

## Virginia Legislative Petitions

Manuscript unsigned. Manuscript endorsement says that directors have done their duty.
16 May 1782: To PG.
    No further action found.
    See 1567-P.

### 1567-P   Wood, Drury and Price, Barret
MHD: 16 May 1782            Richmond Town

Asks release from contract to build a public jail. Cites loss of materials to troops and impressment of horse and wagon.

Manuscript unsigned. Manuscript endorsement says rejected, and jail to be finished.
16 May 1782: To PG.
    Rejected.
    See 1566-M.

### 1568-P   Cary, Archibald
MHD: 16 May 1782            Chesterfield County

To establish a ferry across the James River from the coal landing in Manchester to Sandy Bar in town of Richmond.

Manuscript unsigned. Manuscript endorsement says rejected.
16 May 1782: To PG.
    Rejected.

### 1569-P
Eck–
A728   **Amelia County—Citizens**
MHD: 16 May 1782            Amelia County

Asks redress of certain grievances concerning contracts, judgments, and tax law.

Manuscript signed by: Jesse Watson, Francis Tucker, John Morgan, James Fowlkes, John Rogers, and eighty-seven others.
16 May 1782: To SC.
    No further action found.

### 1570-P-†   Amelia County—Citizens
MHD: 16 May 1782            Amelia County

Text and subject not known.
16 May 1782: To R.
    No further action found.

## 16 – 17 May 1782

**1571-P  Hughes, James**
MHD: 16 May 1782                                              Richmond Town
Asks pardon from sentence of death for high treason, which consisted of bearing arms and associating with Cornwallis's troops when in Richmond.
Manuscript signed by: Robt. Rawlings, Anty. Geoghigan, Francis Graves, Gabriel Galt, Robt. Mitchell, and twenty-three others. Manuscript endorsement says reasonable.
16 May 1782: To PG.
>Found reasonable.

For act pardoning Hughes see 11H21.

**1572-P  Smith, Robert**
MHD: 16 May 1782                                              Not known
Asks pardon from sentence of death by General Court. He had taken arms with a group to protest heavy taxes, but being advised it was not proper, he had laid down his arms and reported himself.
Manuscript unsigned. Manuscript endorsement says reasonable.
16 May 1782: To PG.
>Found reasonable.

For act pardoning Smith see 11H21.

**1573-P  Brunswick County—Citizens**
MHD: 17 May 1782                                              Brunswick County
Opposing the tender law.
Manuscript signed by: W. Stith, Absalom Bennitt, John Hicks, Tom. Haynes, George Hicks, and seventy-four others.
17 May 1782: To SC.
>No further action found.

**1574-P  Brunswick County—Citizens**
MHD: 17 May 1782                                              Brunswick County
Asks adjustment of taxation on commodities, and notes opposition to the tax law of November 1781.
Manuscript signed by: W. Stith, Will. Stith, Jr., John Stith, Thos. Haynes, John Gadkins, and fifty-eight others.
17 May 1782: To SC.
>No further action found.

For law modifying tax on commodities, see 11H9.

## Virginia Legislative Petitions

**1575-P   Mayo, John**
MHD: 17 May 1782                                          Chesterfield County
To establish a ferry across James River from Chesterfield County to Henrico County.
Manuscript unsigned. Manuscript endorsement says rejected.
17 May 1782: To PG.
   Rejected.

**1576-P   Boggess, John**
MHD: 17 May 1782                                             Norfolk Borough
Asks that state treasurer be required to accept collected taxes for Norfolk despite the fact that two invasions of the British prevented him from presenting them on time.
Manuscript signed by: Cornelius Calvert, Jr., George Kelly, and Paul Loyall. Manuscript endorsement says reasonable.
17 May 1782: To PG.
   Found reasonable.

**1577-C-†   County Claims**
MHD: 17 May 1782                                                   Not known
Text and subject not known.
17 May 1782: To T.
   No further action found.

**1578-P-†   Pemberton, ———**
MHD: 17 May 1782                                                   Not known
Text and subject not known.
17 May 1782: To T.
   No further action found.

**1579-P-†   Greenway, ———**
MHD: 17 May 1782                                                   Not known
Text and subject not known.
17 May 1782: To PG.
21 May 1782: PG discharged from proceeding.

**1580-P   Flood, Elizabeth and McCaul, George**
MHD: 18 May 1782                                                Essex County
Asks restoration of estate of Catherine McCaul, born in Virginia but now in

478

## 17 – 18 May 1782

Great Britain, and daughter of Archibald McCaul, accused of being a British sympathizer.

Manuscript unsigned. Manuscript says first part rejected but second part reasonable.

18 May 1782: To PG.

>For earlier petitions on this subject, see 934-P, 1073-P-†, and 1502-P-†. See also 5 December 1783 for further petitions, and see 12H261.
>
>For this act see 12H261.

**1581-P  Rust, Benjamin and Clement, Anne**
MHD: 18 May 1782                                                Richmond County

To establish a ferry across the Rappahannock River from Richmond County to Essex County.

Manuscript unsigned. Manuscript endorsement says referred to next session of GA.

18 May 1782: To PG.

>Referred to next session of GA.

16 Nov. 1782: To PG.

>Carried over to next session of GA

**1582-P  Conner, Charles**
MHD: 18 May 1782                                                Norfolk County

Asks for escheated property of Alexander Montgomery, who fled to England, as payment of debt for goods purchased.

Manuscript unsigned. Account attached.

18 May 1782: To PG.

>No further action found.

**1583-P-†  Bruce, ———**
MHD: 18 May 1782                                                Not known

Text and subject not known.

18 May 1782: To PG.

>No further action found.

**1584-P-†  Cox, ———**
MHD: 18 May 1782                                                Not known

Text and subject not known.

18 May 1782: To PG.

>No further action found.

## Virginia Legislative Petitions

**1585-P-† Beckham, ———**
     MHD: 20 May 1782              Not known
Text and subject not known.
20 May 1782: To T.
     No further action found.

**1586-P   Winchester—Hustings Court**
     MHD: 20 May 1782              Frederick County
  Asks that licenses for ordinaries be issued by the town of Winchester rather than by the county court of Frederick County.
  Manuscript signed by: Fred. Conrad, Philip Burr, Edwd. Smith, Edward McGuire, and Joseph Holmes.
20 May 1782: To PG.
     House and Senate pass bill.
     For this act see 11H34.

**1587-P**
Eck–
A1682   **Ready, Isaac**
     MHD: 20 May 1782              Bedford County
  Compensation for wound received at battle at Guilford Courthouse.
  Manuscript unsigned. Manuscript endorsement says reported.
20 May 1782: To T.
     Carried over to next session of GA.
16 Nov. 1782: Carried over to next session of GA.

**1588-P   Brunswick County—Citizens**
     MHD: 21 May 1782              Brunswick County
  Asks payment of their considerations for recruiting for the Continental army.
  Manuscript signed by: Henry Nicolson, John Short, John Stead, Nat. Robinson, and Xpher Thrower. Manuscript endorsement says rejected, but later reported.
21 May 1782: To PG.
     No further action found.

**1589-M-† Wood, ———**
     MHD: 21 May 1782              Not known
Text and subject not known.

21 May 1782: House lays on table.
No further action found.

**1590-P-† Hodges, ———**
MHD: 21 May 1782                                   Not known
Text and subject not known.
21 May 1782: To T.
No further action found.

**1591-P-† Campbell, ———**
MHD: 21 May 1782                                   Not known
Text and subject not known.
21 May 1782: To T.
No further action found.

**1592-P   Bernard, William**
MHD: 21 May 1782                          King George County
To establish a ferry across the Machodack Creek in King George County.
Manuscript unsigned. Manuscript endorsement says rejected.
21 May 1782: To PG.

**1593-P   Keeling, Robert; Langley, Robert; and Stone, Simon**
MHD: 22 May 1782                          Princess Anne County
Asks return of slaves from lead mines.
Manuscript unsigned.
22 May 1782: To PG.
No further action found.

**1594-P   Chesterfield County—Citizens**
MHD: 22 May 1782                             Chesterfield County
Asks repeal of the stay of execution of the debt law since those who are able to afford payment are now ignoring debts and buying up property.
Manuscript signed by: Jno. Archer, Chars. Cogbill, Womack Blankinship, Jos. Wells, Blackman Moseley, and twenty-one others.
22 May 1782: To committee on tax bill.
No further action found.
For change in debt law in 1783 see 11H349.

## Virginia Legislative Petitions

**1595-P-† Chesterfield County—Citizens**
    MHD: 22 May 1782                                     Chesterfield County
Text and subject not known.
22 May 1782: To CJ.
    No further action found.

**1596-P-† Holding, ———**
    MHD: 22 May 1782                                                 Not known
Text and subject not known.
22 May 1782: To T.
    No further action found.

**1597-P-† Jones, ———**
    MHD: 22 May 1782                                                 Not known
Text and subject not known.
22 May 1782: To T.
    No further action found.
    See 1513-P-†.

**1598-P Lunenburg County—Citizens**
    MHD: 23 May 1782                                         Lunenburg County
Asks removal of county courthouse from the lands of Joseph Smith.
    Manuscript signed by: N. Hobson, Stephen E. Broadner, Anthy. Street, Christopher Billups, Edwd. Jordan, and nine others. Dated March 1782.
23 May 1782: To PG.
    House and Senate pass bill.
    For this act see 11H31.

**1599-P Georgia—Citizens**
    MHD: 23 May 1782                                          State of Georgia
Asks that taxes on enumerated commodities not apply to them since they will be taxed again in Georgia should they succeed in returning there.
    Manuscript signed by: Edw. Davies, Js. Twigs, Lyman Hall, Saml. Burley, and Lyman Hall for the estate of Samuel Miller. Dated 12 April 1782.
23 May 1782: To committee on tax law.
    No further action found.

**1600-P Harrison, Benjamin**
    MHD: 23 May 1782                                       Prince George County

## 22 – 24 May 1782

Asks revaluation of acreage and value for tax purposes of certain property in Brandon Parish.

Manuscript unsigned. Noted as rejected. Recommitted and found reasonable.

23 May 1782: House lays on table.
Date unknown: To PG.
    Carried over to next session of GA.
12 Nov. 1782: To PG.
14 Nov. 1782: Recommitted to PG.
21 Nov. 1782: PG recommends (1) that relief from unequal assessment is reasonable, and (2) that it be referred to commissioners of Prince George County.
    House agrees.
22 Nov. 1782: Senate agrees.

### 1601-P    Tomlin, Walker
MHD: 24 May 1782                       King William County

To establish a ferry across the Pamunkey River from King William County to Hanover County.

Manuscript unsigned. Manuscript endorsement says reasonable and bill to be drawn, but not found in Hening.

24 May 1782: To PG.
    Carried over to next session of GA.
14 Nov. 1782: To PG.
12 Dec. 1782: PG recommends rejection.
    Recommitted to PG.
    No further action found.

### 1602-M-†    Washington, ———
MHD: 24 May 1782                                 Not known

Text and subject not known.
24 May 1782: To PG.
    No further action found.

### 1603-P    Hughes, John
MHD: 24 May 1782                                 Not known

Asks pension for an unidentified soldier who lost his sight by smallpox.

Manuscript unsigned. Manuscript endorsement says rejected on 30 May.
24 May 1782: To T.
30 May 1782: Rejected.

## Virginia Legislative Petitions

**1604-P  Montgomery County—Citizens**
MHD: 24 May 1782                                 Montgomery County
Asks relief since they are against paying taxes in commodities. No specie is available and time is too short for payment by May.
Manuscript signed by: Daniel Hone, John Nash, Henry Begley, Joseph Polly, William Polly, and seventy-seven others.
24 May 1782: To committee on tax bill.
For act extending time to 1 September 1782, see 11H9.

**1605-P  Hanover County—Citizens**
MHD: 24 May 1782                                      Hanover County
Opposing the draft of militia for Continental service.
Manuscript signed by: J. Syme, John Pendleton, Owen Dabney, Thos. Mallory, Edward Bullock, and 111 others. Manuscript says referred to committee on delinquencies of militia law.
24 May 1782: To committee on recruiting bill.
No further action found.

**1606-M  Virginia Continental Army—Officers**
MHD: 25 May 1782                                           Not known
Asks that a committee be appointed to confer with them over the act passed at the last session that equalized pay but did not allow for depreciation of certificates.
Manuscript signed by: P. Muhlenberg, Chs. Scott, William Davies, and O. Towles. Endorsement says reasonable.
25 May 1782: To PG.
   House and Senate pass bill.
   For this act see 11H81.

**1607-P  Carter, Charles**
MHD: 25 May 1782                                           Not known
Asks relief in that there is a scarcity of wood at the lead mines.
Manuscript unsigned.
25 May 1782: To PG.
   No further action found.

**1608-P  Parberry, James**
MHD: 25 May 1782                                           Not known
For use of wood on land adjacent to the lead mine.

## 24 – 27 May 1782

Manuscript in handwriting of Patrick Henry, from whom Parberry had purchased a share of the lead mines.
25 May 1782: To PG.
    No further action found.

**1609-P-†  Harris, ———**
    MHD: 25 May 1782                    Not known
Text and subject not known.
25 May 1782: To T.
    No further action found.
    See 1499-P-†.

**1610-P-†  Askew, ———**
    MHD: 25 May 1782                    Not known
Text and subject not known.
25 May 1782: To T.
    No further action found.

**1611-P  Watkins, George**
    MHD: 27 May 1782                    Elizabeth City County
Compensation for part of his wages, earned on board a ship taken by the British, where he was imprisoned and later paroled.
Manuscript unsigned, but endorsement says rejected 21 June 1782. Certificate of ship's captain attached.
27 May 1782: To T.
21 June 1782: Rejected.

**1612-P  Fairfax County—Citizens**
    MHD: 27 May 1782                    Fairfax County
Asks reduction of unjust taxes.
The text is printed and signed by: Michael Thorn, Andw. Wales, John Bird, John Finley, John Fitzgerald, and 100 others.
27 May 1782: To committee on tax law.
    For revision of tax laws see 11H66.

**1613-P  Prince William County—Citizens**
    MHD: 27 May 1782                    Prince William County
Asks that there be no further emission of paper money because of its depreciation.
Manuscript signed by: T. Blackburn, William Carr, Thos. Bird, Jno. Law-

son, Geo. Graham, and 141 others. Notes surrender of British at Yorktown.
27 May 1782: To committee on tax law.
>No further action found.

**1614-P**
Eck-
A462 **Alexandria—Citizens**
MHD: 27 May 1782 Fairfax County
To establish a ferry across the Potomac River from Alexandria to Hawkins's, Addison's, or Rozier's in Maryland. Also asks for representation in the General Assembly.
Manuscript signed by: Oliver Price, Robert Lyle, Wm. Payton, Jacob Cox, John Harper, and fifty-two others. Manuscript endorsement says reasonable in part, and bill to be drawn.
27 May 1782: To PG.
>PG finds reasonable in part, and bill to be drawn.
>Not found in Hening.

**1615-P** **Northampton County—Citizens**
MHD: 27 May 1782 Northampton County
Asks that salt be used for payment of taxes.
Manuscript signed by: Littl. Savage, John Harmans, Jr., G. Kendall, William Harmanson, Nelson Robins, and sixteen others.
27 May 1782: To committee on tax bill.
>No further action found.

**1616-P** **Richmond Town—Citizens**
MHD: 28 May 1782 Henrico County
Asks incorporation of the town.
Manuscript signed by: Isaac Youngblood, John Beckley, Gabriel Galt, Step. Tankard, Robt. Boyd, and sixty-one others. Manuscript endorsement says reasonable and bill drawn.
28 May 1782: To PG.
>House and Senate pass bill.
>For this act see 11H45.

**1617-P** **Ball, John**
MHD: 28 May 1782 Not known

## 27 – 29 May 1782

Compensation for loss of impressed ships and cargo of tobacco captured by the British.
Manuscript unsigned.
28 May 1782: To T, then to PG.
    No further action found.

### 1618-P  Goode, Robert
MHD: 28 May 1782            Chesterfield County

Asks relief in that as sheriff of Chesterfield County he was delayed by the public auditors and county commissioner of taxes, due mainly to Arnold's raid, from transmitting the tax payments, including many commodity certificates, to the auditors for warrants. Since all taxes had not been certified, General Court had entered judgment against him.

Manuscript unsigned. Manuscript endorsement says reasonable and reported.
28 May 1782: To PG.
    Found reasonable and reported.
    For general act including unavoidable delays, see 11H77.

### 1619-P-†  Hunt, ——
MHD: 28 May 1782            Not known

Text and subject not known.
28 May 1782: To T.
    No further action found.

### 1620-P  Western Lands—Citizens
MHD: 29 May 1782            Western Lands

Asks for free navigation of the Mississippi River.
Manuscript signed by: John May, John Tabb, Squire Boone, Jas. Speed, Jno. Mosby, and six others.
29 May 1782: To committee to instruct delegates of Congress.
    No further action found.

### 1621-P  Cabell, Joseph; Innes, Harry; and Cabell, Nicholas
MHD: 29 May 1782            Washington County
                                          Montgomery County

Asks additional funds as commissioner for settling land titles in Washington and Montgomery counties. The business is still unfinished.

Manuscript unsigned. Manuscript endorsement says reasonable. Report of committee attached with recommendation of £12,240.

## Virginia Legislative Petitions

29 May 1782: To T.
    Found reasonable and £12,240 recommended.
    This may be 1456-P-†, which see.
    No further action found.
    See also 1512-P.

**1622-P**   **Fluvanna County—Citizens**
    MHD: 29 May 1782                           Fluvanna County
Asks delay of tax payments on commodities.
Manuscript signed by: George Butler, Thos. Tindall, Joseph Mayo, Thos. Mayo, John Tollers, and forty-three others.
29 May 1782: House lays on table.
    House and Senate pass bill.
    For general act granting delay see 11H9.

**1623-P**   **Tobacco Warehouse Proprietors—Bowling's Warehouse and Boyd's Warehouse**
    MHD: 29 May 1782                           Stafford County
                                                      Spotsylvania County
                                                      Hanover County
Asks increase in tobacco warehouse rents.
Manuscript signed by: Neill Buchanan (Bowling's) and Christopher McConnie (Boyd's). (This is an addition to 1486-P, which see.)
29 May 1782: To CJ.
    No further action found.

**1624-P-†**   **Campbell, ———**
    MHD: 29 May 1782                               Not known
Text and subject not known.
29 May 1782: To T.
    No further action found.

**1625-P**   **Quakers**
    MHD: 29 May 1782                               Not known
Asks protection of emancipated slaves. Protests slavery in general.
Manuscript signed: Edw. Stabler (clerk).
29 May 1782: To PG.
    For act concerning manumission of slaves, see 11H39.

## 29 – 30 May 1782

**1626-P  Bradley, William**
MHD: 30 May 1782                                              Culpeper County
To establish the town of Stevensburg on his land in Culpeper County.
Manuscript unsigned.
30 May 1782: To PG.
> House and Senate pass this bill.
> For this act see 11H36.

**1627-P  Cooper, Leonard**
MHD: 30 May 1782                                              Not known
Additional compensation for military wound.
Manuscript unsigned, but endorsement says rejected 30 May 1782.
30 May 1782: To T.
> Rejected.

**1628-P**
Eck–
A730  **Jones, Daniel**
MHD: 30 May 1782                                              Amelia County
Compensation for his house and mill, taken from him by officers provisioning the army and burned by the British.

Manuscript unsigned, but endorsement says deferred to next session of GA on 14 June, reported 12 December 1782, deferred to next session, and rejected 13 June 1783.
30 May 1782: To T.
14 June 1782: Carried over to next session of GA.
12 Dec. 1782: Carried over to next session of GA.
16 June 1783: House rejects.

**1629-P**
Rob–15  **Jefferson County, Fayette County, and Lincoln County— Citizens**
MHD: 30 May 1782                                              Jefferson County
                                                              Fayette County
                                                              Lincoln County
Relevant to land grants and the district court for the three counties.

Manuscript signed by: Francis Dove, Thomas Parker, John Wood, John Anderson, William Whittery, and thirty-eight others. Manuscript has report of committee attached.

## Virginia Legislative Petitions

30 May 1782: To CJ.
> For act on this court see 11H85.

### 1630-M  Fredericksburg—Mayor and Council
> MHD: 30 May 1782                                                Spotsylvania County

Asks that the size of the town be increased and that the hustings court be made a court of record. Also requests certain taxing powers and representation in General Assembly.

Manuscript signed by: Ch. Mortimer, mayor, and Henry Armistead, clerk. Endorsement says reasonable in part and rejected in part.

30 May 1782: To PG.
> For a general act, including some provisions for Fredericksburg, see 11H45.

### 1631-P  Wodrow, Andrew
> MHD: 30 May 1782                                                     Stafford County

Asks that he be authorized to execute deeds for the sale of property belonging to the estate of Alexander Wodrow.

Manuscript unsigned. Endorsement says reasonable. Manuscript has will of Alexander Wodrow attached.

30 May 1782: To PG.
> Carried over to next session of GA.

4 Dec. 1782: PG recommends approval.
7 Dec. 1782: House passes bill.
9 Dec. 1782: Senate passes bill.
> For this act see 11H150.

### 1632-P  Turpin, Thomas
> MHD: 30 May 1782                                                      Henrico County

Asks for use for private purposes certain portions of land and buildings appropriated by the director of public buildings for state use.

Manuscript unsigned. Endorsement says reasonable.

30 May 1782: To T.
> Reasonable.
> No further action found.

### 1633-P  Campbell, John and Henderson, Samuel
> MHD: 30 May 1782                                                            Not known

## 30 - 31 May 1782

Compensation for depreciation not allowed for claim for sale of beef to the state in 1780.
Manuscript unsigned. Dated 22 May 1782.
30 May 1782: To committee of the whole on claims bill.
    No further action found.

**1634-P-†  Matthews, ———**
    MHD: 30 May 1782      Not known
Text and subject not known.
30 May 1782: To PG.
    No further action found.

**1635-P**
Eck-
A1122     **Augusta County—Citizens**
    MHD: 30 May 1782      Augusta County
Protests against the draft law.
Manuscript signed by: Jas. Steel, James Anderson, John McKenney, Jas. Seawright, Joseph Bell, and eight others.
30 May 1782: To committee on recruitment laws.
    For revision of laws on recruitment see 11H14.

**1636-P-†  Woods, ———**
    MHD: 31 May 1782      Not known
Text and subject not known.
31 May 1782: To T.
    No further action found.

**1637-P-†  Cooper, ———**
    MHD: 31 May 1782      Not known
Text and subject not known.
31 May 1782: To T.
    No further action found.

**1638-P-†  Vaughan, ———**
    MHD: 31 May 1782      Not known
Text and subject not known.
31 May 1782: To T.
    No further action found.

## Virginia Legislative Petitions

**1639-P** **Wilson, Joseph, and Company**
MHD: 1 June 1782                                Not known

Compensation for loss of ship and cargo, sunk to avoid capture by the British.

Manuscript unsigned. Endorsement says first part rejected and second part reasonable.

1 June 1782: To PG.
        First part rejected and second part found reasonable.
        No further action found.

**1640-P**
Rob–16   **Jefferson County, Fayette County, and Lincoln County— Citizens**
MHD: 1 June 1782                               Jefferson County
                                                                  Fayette County
                                                                  Lincoln County

Relevant to cultivation of lands and a court for the district.

Manuscript signed by: J. Hite, Jos. Hite, Jacob Holsclaw, Wm. McBrayers, James McAfee, and thirty-five others.

1 June 1782: House lays on table.
        For act on court see 11H85.

**1641-P-†** **Collins, ———**
MHD: 1 June 1782                                Not known

Text and subject not known.

1 June 1782: House rejects.

**1642-P** **Stafford County—Citizens**
MHD: 1 June 1782                                Stafford County

Asks consolidation of Dixon's and Falmouth's tobacco warehouses.

Manuscript signed by: Jno. Anderson, William Wiatt, Wm. Anderson, Eliezer Callender, David Henderson, and seventy others. Endorsement says referred to committee on bill on tobacco.

1 June 1782: To CJ(?).
        No further action found.

**1643-P** **Botetourt County—Citizens**
MHD: 3 June 1782                                Botetourt County

Protests against taxation of land and commodities and the lack of specie.

Manuscript signed by: Geo. Skillum, Rd. Smyth, Thos. Rowland, Wm.

## 1 – 3 June 1782

McNeelly, Thos. Madison, and 188 others. Endorsement shows sent to committee of the whole and not reported.
3 June 1782: To committee of the whole.
    For act granting delay of payment of tax on commodities, see 11H9.

**1644-P-† Harmanson, ———, and others**         Not known
    MHD: 3 June 1782
Text and subject not known.
3 June 1782: To T.
    No further action found.

**1645-P-† Hampshire, ———**         Not known
    MHD: 3 June 1782
Text and subject not known.
3 June 1782: To PG.
    No further action found.

**1646-P**
Rob–
17(?)   **Jefferson County—Citizens**         Jefferson County
    MHD: 3 June 1782
Asks confirmation of marriages by magistrates and citizens.
Manuscript signed by: W. Pope, Merth. Price, Daniel Sullivan, Ben Pope, Leond. Helm, and thirty others. Endorsement notes reasonable and bill to be brought in. Dated at Louisville, 2 April 1782.
3 June 1782: To R.
    Found reasonable and bill to be drawn.
    Robertson notes a similar petition from Lincoln County, No. 17, which became law as below.
    For this act see 11H281 in 1783.

**1647-P Maury, James**         Not known
    MHD: 3 June 1782
Compensation for loss of ship to the British.
Manuscript unsigned. Endorsement says rejected.
3 June 1782: To PG.
    Rejected.

## Virginia Legislative Petitions

**1648-P Amox, Matthew**
MHD: 3 June 1782 Botetourt County
Compensation for military wound and medical expenses.
Manuscript signed by: Henry Bowling, Tho. Poage, Tolever Craig, Joseph Richardson, Thomas Rowland, and eleven others. Endorsement says reasonable. Allowed half pay for life and £10 for medical expenses.
3 June 1782: To T.
> Found reasonable, allowed half pay for life and £10 for medical expenses.

**1649-M Baptist Association**
MHD: 3 June 1782 Not known
Asks that dissenters be eligible for vestries and that dissenter marriages be recognized.
Manuscript signed by: Elijah Craig and Reuben Ford. Endorsement shows that it may have been rejected and later referred to next session of GA.
3 June 1782: To R.
> Rejected, then referred to next session of GA.

30 May 1783: A new memorial on this subject was presented.

**1650-P**
Eck–A11 **Accomack County—Citizens**
MHD: 3 June 1782 Accomack County
Against the manumission of slaves.
Manuscript signed by: Wm. Williams, William Joyner, Gilbert Bailes, William Gibb, Abel Upshur, and fifty-seven others.
3 June 1782: To PG.
> No further action found.

**1651-P-† Tobacco Inspectors—Port Royal**
MHD: 3 June 1782 Caroline County
Text and subject not known.
3 June 1782: House rejects.

**1652-P**
Eck–
A1684 **Lynch, John**
MHD: 3 June 1780 Bedford County
Asks repeal of the act that discontinued the ferry across the Fluvanna

## 3 – 4 June 1782

(James) River from the petitioner's land in Bedford County to his land in Amherst County.

Manuscript unsigned.

3 June 1780: To PG.
> House and Senate pass bill.
> For this act see 11H38.

**1653-P**
Eck–
A1683   **Russell Parish, Bedford County and Campbell County—Citizens**
MHD: 3 June 1782                                          Bedford County
                                                          Campbell County

Asks division of the parish along county lines.

Manuscript signed by: Richard Stith, John Quarles, W. Mead, W. Leftwich, John Callaway, Arch. Moon, John Caffery, Robert Alexander, G. R. Lewis, and David G. Talbot. Endorsement says reasonable, 6 June 1782, and bill to be brought in.

3 June 1782: To R.
6 June 1782: Found reasonable and bill to be drawn.
> No further action found.

**1654-P-†  Loudoun County—Citizens**
MHD: 4 June 1782                                          Loudoun County

Text and subject not known.

4 June 1782: To PG.
> No further action found in this session.
> This may have been 1520-P, carried over from the session of October 1781.

**1655-P  Loudoun County—Citizens**
MHD: 4 June 1782                                          Loudoun County

Opposing division of the county.

Manuscript signed by: William George, Joseph Calwall, Noble Leonard, Robert Fitzpatrick, John Neilson, and 128 others. Certificate of number of tithables attached.

4 June 1782: To PG.
> No further action found in this session.
> This may have been the petition, 1521-P, carried over from the session of October 1781. Loudoun County was never divided.

## Virginia Legislative Petitions

**1655 A-P Loudoun County—Citizens**
    MHD: 4 June 1782      Loudoun County
Text is similar to 1655-P, which see.
Manuscript signed by 127 persons.

**1656-P-† Bentley, ———**
    MHD: 4 June 1782      Not known
Text and subject not known.
4 June 1782: To PG.
    No further action found.

**1657-P Punter, Henry**
    MHD: 4 June 1782      Henrico County
Relevant to the salary of a clerk of the commissioner of the navy.
Manuscript unsigned. Has certificate of service attached.
4 June 1782: To PG.
    No further action found.

**1658-P-† Taylor, ———**
    MHD: 5 June 1782      Not known
Text and subject not known.
5 June 1782: To PG.
    No further action found.

**1659-P Williams, James**
    MHD: 5 June 1782      Not known
Additional compensation for loss of eyesight due to this and previous wars.
Manuscript unsigned. Endorsement says rejected 7 June 1782.
5 June 1782: To T.
7 June 1782: Rejected.

**1660-P-† Mercer's Executors**
    MHD: 6 June 1782      Not known
Text and subject not known.
6 June 1782: To PG.
    No further action found.

**1661-P Réné, Bryson, and Company**
    MHD: 6 June 1782      Not known
Protests duty charges made by naval office on a vessel with a cargo of sugar

## 4 – 8 June 1782

that they salvaged after it had been forced ashore on the North Carolina coast by the British.

Manuscript unsigned. Certificate of the manifest of cargo attached.

6 June 1782: To committee on shipwrecked property.
        No further action found.

**1662-P-†  Porterfield, ———**
    MHD: 6 June 1782                         Not known
Text and subject not known.
6 June 1782: To PG.
        No further action found.

**1663-P  Freeland, Mace**
    MHD: 7 June 1782                      Buckingham County

Asks for division of escheated estate of Robert Williams among himself and others.

Manuscript unsigned.
7 June 1782: To PG.
        House and Senate pass bill.
        For this act see 11H65.

**1664-P  Anderson, Mary**
    MHD: 7 June 1782                        Hanover County

Asks that the estate of Samuel Gist, a British subject, be vested in her, the daughter of the said Gist.

Manuscript unsigned. Endorsement says referred to PG.
7 June 1782: To PG.
        House and Senate pass bill.
        For this act see 11H54.

**1665-P  Henry County—Citizens**
    MHD: 8 June 1782                          Henry County

Asks that part of Henry County on Yadkin River, called Hollow, be added to Montgomery County

Manuscript signed by: Jos. Jones, Daniel Cave, William Hawke, Cornelius Keith, Matthew Laffoon, and thirty-two others. Endorsement says to PG and referred to next session of GA.

## Virginia Legislative Petitions

8 June 1782: To PG.
> Referred to next session of GA.
> No further action found.
> See 1677-P.

**1666-P  Surry County—Citizens**                     Surry County
> MHD: 8 June 1782

Opposing the tender law of 1780.

Manuscript signed by: William Browne, Jacob Faulcon, Wm. Spratley, Lemuel Cocke, Willis Wilson, and 123 others. Dated 10 May 1782.

8 June 1782: To PG.
> No further action found.

**1667-P  Ballendine, Thomas**                     Buckingham County
> MHD: 8 June 1782

Relevant to the settlement of the estate of his father, John Ballendine, and debts owed by him to the state.

Manuscript unsigned. Endorsement says referred to next session of GA.

8 June 1782: To PG.
> Carried over to next session of GA.

16 Nov. 1782: Carried over to next session of GA.

31 May 1783: Thomas Ballendine presents a new petition.
> Settlement was finally made by the Buckingham County court.

**1668-P  Blair, John**                     Richmond Town
> MHD: 8 June 1782

Asks that salaries of judges of the High Court of Chancery not be paid partially in paper money.

Manuscript unsigned. Endorsement says taken account of in May 1782 act, but act not found.

8 June 1782: To T.
> Apparently carried over to next session of GA.

16 Nov. 1782: Carried over to next session of GA.

**1669-P-† Liggons, ———**                     Not known
> MHD: 8 June 1782

Text and subject not known.

8 June 1782: To T.
> No further action found.

498

## 8 June 1782

**1670-P-†  Fairfax, ———**
    MHD: 8 June 1782                                              Not known
  Text and subject not known.
  8 June 1782: To PG.
        No further action found.

**1671-P   Antrim Parish, Halifax County—Citizens**
    MHD: 8 June 1782                                          Halifax County
  Asks dissolution of the vestry and the sale of glebe lands.
  Manuscript signed by: Wm. Wright, William Owen, Nathl. Hunt, Simon Jackson, Hatcher Owen, and 107 others. Endorsement says dissolution of vestry reasonable, but sale of glebe rejected.
  8 June 1782: To R.
        Dissolution of vestry found reasonable, but sale of glebe rejected. This may have been 1479-P, carried over from the October 1781 session of GA.
        For act dissolving Antrim Parish and Westover Parish, see 11H73.

**1672-P   Vestal, Ann and Vestal, Hannah**
    MHD: 8 June 1782                                          Berkeley County
  Asks relief from impoverishment due to collection of a bond on Thomas Speake, once sheriff of Frederick County.
  Manuscript unsigned.
  8 June 1782: To PG.
        No further action found.

**1673-P**
Eck-
A1123   **Staunton—Citizens**
    MHD: 8 June 1782                                          Augusta County
  Asks permission to raise hogs and let them run at large in the streets, and to repeal an earlier act forbidding this.
  Manuscript signed by: Robert Reid, Daniel Kidd, Robert Burns, Th. Hughes, Francis Mara, and nineteen others. Manuscript notes bill drawn.
  8 June 1782: To PG.
        For this act see 11H60, repealing the earlier act.

**1674-P   Obanion, Bryan, III**
    MHD: 8 June 1782                                          Fauquier County
  Asks repeal of the act passed in October 1778 whereby 257 acres of land

## Virginia Legislative Petitions

belonging to the estate of Bryan Obanion were escheated and sold.
Manuscript unsigned.
8 June 1782: To PG.
>See 798-M.
>For the repealing act see 11H60.

**1675-P-†  Monongalia County**
>MHD: 8 June 1782                                                    Monongalia County
Text and subject not known.
8 June 1782: To PG.
>No further action found.

**1676-P   Henry County—Citizens**
>MHD: 8 June 1782                                                    Henry County
Asks formation of a new county from parts of Henry and Bedford counties.
Manuscript signed by: Thos. Poole, William Menefee, Sr., Richard Newport, George Menefee, Wm. Conner, and 173 others. Endorsement says to PG.
8 June 1782: To PG.
>No further action found.

**1677-P   Henry County—Citizens**
>MHD: Not found [no date]                                            Henry County
Opposing a division of the county, except that they would allow that part of the county called Hollow to become part of Montgomery County.
Manuscript signed by: Geo. Waller, Wm. Lovell, Thos. Nunn, Thos. Cooper, Josiah Turner, and fifty-nine others.
Date unknown: Probably to PG.
>No further action found.
>See 1665-P and 1676-P.

**1677 A-P Henry County—Citizens**
>MHD: Not found [no date]                                            Henry County
Text is similar to 1677-P, which see.
Manuscript signed by forty-seven persons.

**1677 B-P Henry County—Citizens**
>MHD: Not found [no date]                                            Henry County
Text is similar to 1677-P, which see.
Manuscript signed by 184 persons.

## 8 June 1782

**1678-P**    **Henrico County—Citizens**
MHD: 8 June 1782            Henrico County
Relevant to control of slaves let out for hire.
Manuscript signed by: John Mayo, Jr., Wm. Gathright, Hobson Owen, Tho. Prosser, Adam Craig, and twenty-eight others. Endorsement says referred to PG.
8 June 1782: To PG.
     Bill to be drawn.
     At least two acts of this session deal with the control and emancipation of slaves, 10H23 and 39.

**1679-P**
Eck–
A729    **Hutcheson, Ambrose**
MHD: 8 June 1782            Amelia County
Asks permission to sell 217 acres of land left to the petitioner's son by Joseph Ferguson.
Manuscript unsigned. Endorsement says rejected 14 June 1782.
8 June 1782: To PG.
14 June 1782: House rejects.

**1680-P**    **Poythress, Peter**
MHD: 8 June 1782            Dinwiddie County
Compensation for execution of two slaves.
Manuscript unsigned. Endorsement says rejected. Court minutes and deposition of sheriff attached.
8 June 1782: To PG.
     Carried over to next session of GA.
16 Nov. 1782: To PG.
14 Dec. 1782: House agrees to £250.
21 Dec. 1782: Senate agrees.

**1681-P**
Eck–
A1685    **Bedford County—Citizens**
MHD: 8 June 1782            Bedford County
Asks that the county be divided.
Manuscript signed by: Jacob Early, Jesse Tate, Con. Noell, Simon Miller, Benj. Roberson, and twenty-six others.

## Virginia Legislative Petitions

8 June 1782: To PG.
    No further action found.

### 1681 A-P
Eck–
A1685    **Bedford County—Citizens**
    MHD: 8 June 1782        Bedford County
  Text is identical with 1681-P, which see.
  Manuscript signed by thirty-eight persons.

### 1681 B-P
Eck–
A1685    **Bedford County—Citizens**
    MHD: 8 June 1782        Bedford County
  Text is identical with 1681-P, which see.
  Manuscript signed by 316 persons.

### 1681 C-P
Eck–
A1685    **Bedford County—Citizens**
    MHD: 8 June 1782        Bedford County
  Text is identical with 1681-P, which see.
  Manuscript signed by eighty-five persons.

### 1682-P    **Campbell County—Citizens**
    MHD: 8 June 1782        Campbell County
Asks that an opening be made for passage of fish around or through a dam on Falling River.
  Manuscript signed by: John Cock, Thomas Jones, Thomas Lewis, Geo. Cock, Wm. Cock, and forty-three others. Endorsement says rejected.
8 June 1782: To PG.
    Rejected.

### 1683-P    **Louisa County—Citizens**
    MHD: 10 June 1782        Louisa County
Asks that the militia be kept armed and trained, which is not now the case.
  Manuscript signed by: Jas. Dabney, John Parker, John Todd, Christn. Johnson, John Fretwell, and sixteen others.

## 8 – 10 June 1782

10 June 1782: To committee on militia bill.
>No further action found.
>Militia law were altered in October session of 1782, 10H173.

**1684-P   Briscoe, Reuben**
>MHD: 10 June 1782                     Westmoreland County

Compensation for express riders for the tax commissioner.
   Manuscript unsigned. Attached certificate of auditor shows tobacco was delivered by express rider, but his expenses, by law, could not be paid.
10 June 1782: To T.
>No further action found.

**1685-P   Jett, Thomas**
>MHD: 10 June 1782                                     Not known

Asks payment of commission for purchasing horses for use of the army.
   Manuscript unsigned. Endorsement says referred to next session of GA.
10 June 1782: To T.
>Referred to next session of GA.
16 Nov. 1782: To T.
>No further action found.

**1686-P   Daniel, George**
>MHD: 10 June 1782                        Middlesex County

Asks relief from judgment against him for nonpayment of taxes collected in the form of certificates that were taken by General Arnold. Daniel has been unable to obtain duplicates in time to submit them before the law was passed making such payments illegal.
   Manuscript unsigned. Manuscript has deposition of Maurice Smith.
10 June 1782: To committee of the whole on claim bill.
>>For act granting delay of payment of tax on commodities, see 11H9.

**1687-P-†   Princess Anne County**
>MHD: 10 June 1782                        Princess Anne County

Text and subject not known.
10 June 1782: To committee on common lands.
>No further action found.

## Virginia Legislative Petitions

**1688-P-† Maclin, ———**
    MHD: 11 June 1782          Not known
Text and subject not known.
11 June 1782: To PG.
    This may have been the petition considered 21 November 1782, which was rejected.

**1689-P-† Morgan, ———**
    MHD: 11 June 1782          Not known
Text and subject not known.
11 June 1782: To PG.
    This may have been the petition considered 21 November 1782 and laid on table 12 December 1782.

**1690-P-† Brubecker, ———**
    MHD: 11 June 1782          Not known
Text and subject not known.
11 June 1782: "Read & Leave to appoint Trustees—Zane." (Minutes.)
    No further action found.

**1691-P-† Seldon, ———**
    MHD: 11 June 1782          Not known
Text and subject not known.
11 June 1782: To PG.
    This may have been the petition considered 16 November 1782.

**1692-P-† Mayo, ———**
    MHD: 11 June 1782          Not known
Text and subject not known.
11 June 1782: To PG.
    This may have been the petition considered 19 December 1782 and laid on table.

**1693-P-† Ramsdell, ———**
    MHD: 11 June 1782          Not known
Text and subject not known.
11 June 1782: To PG.
    No further action found.

## 11 June 1782

**1694-M  Märck, Ulric**
MHD: 11 June 1782                                    Dinwiddie County
Compensation for goods sold to the state and not paid for, as well as a horse lost in action to the British. Also adjustment of his Loan Office certificate with which he was to be paid for goods sold. He wishes to become a citizen.
Manuscript unsigned, but originated at Blandford. Endorsement says reasonable, and Loan Office certificate to be adjusted.
11 June 1782: To PG.
Found reasonable and Loan Office certificate to be adjusted.
No further action found.

**1695-P-†  Cocke, ———**
MHD: 11 June 1782                                    Not known
Text and subject not known.
11 June 1782: To PG.
No further action found.

**1696-P-†**
Eck–
A169  **Taylor, Francis**
MHD: 11 June 1782                                    Albemarle County
Asks increase in the pay of officers and soldiers at Albemarle barracks because of depreciation of paper money.
Manuscript unsigned.
11 June 1782: To PG.
No further action found.

**1697-P-†  Brown, ———**
MHD: 11 June 1782                                    Not known
Text and subject not known.
11 June 1782: To PG.
No further action found.

**1698-P-†  Seawell, ———**
MHD: 11 June 1782                                    Not known
Text and subject not known.
11 June 1782: House rejects.

## Virginia Legislative Petitions

### 1699-P-† Brunswick County
MHD: 11 June 1782            Brunswick County
Text and subject not known.
11 June 1782: To PG.
>This may have been the petition considered 4 December 1782 for changing location of courthouse, which was passed.
>For act changing location of courthouse, see 11H256.

### 1700-P Richardson, George
MHD: 11 June 1782            Henrico County
Wishes to keep horses captured by the army, but by a late act of the assembly the former owners must be found.
Manuscript unsigned.
11 June 1782: To PG.
>No further action found.

### 1701-P Petersburg—Citizens
MHD: 11 June 1782            Petersburg
                                                   Dinwiddie County
                                                   Chesterfield County
Asks consolidation of the towns of Petersburg, Blandford, and Pocahontas.
Manuscript signed by: John Thomson, Edwd. Stabler, Saml. Davies, D'Osmont, Jno. Grammar, and seventy-three others. Dated 10 May 1782. Endorsement says referred to next session, 14 June 1782; referred to next session, 21 November 1782; referred to next session, 6 December 1782.
11 June 1782: To PG.
14 June 1782: Referred to next session of GA.
21 Nov. 1782: Referred to next session of GA.
6 Dec. 1782: Referred to next session of GA.
>See 1114-P.
>For consolidation act in 1784 see 11H382.

### 1702-P Louisa County—Citizens
MHD: 11 June 1782            Louisa County
Asks that those convicted of excessive gaming serve for one year in the army.
Manuscript signed by: John Fox, Jno. Jackson, Jesse Paulett, Tho. White, Joseph Thomson, and sixty-two others. Endorsement says referred to next session, found reasonable, and a bill drawn.
11 June 1782: To PG.
>Referred to next session of GA.

## 11 – 17 June 1782

16 Nov. 1782: To PG.
27 Nov. 1782: Found reasonable and PG to prepare a bill.
30 Nov. 1782: Bill presented.
2 Dec. 1782: Bill rejected by House.

1703-P-† Allen, ———            Not known
       MHD: 11 June 1782
Text and subject not known.
11 June 1782: To PG.
       No further action found.

1704-P   Copeland, Peter          
       MHD: 11 June 1782        Charles City County
Compensation for a slave executed for a felony.
Manuscript unsigned. Endorsement says reported as reasonable. Certificate of Wm. Christian, sheriff, attached. Slave was valued at £3,000.
11 June 1782: To PG.
14 Dec. 1782: Found reasonable and to be allowed £30(?).
       House agrees.
21 Dec. 1782: Senate agrees.

1705-P
Eck–
A170   Jouett, John
       MHD: 11 June 1782        Albemarle County
                                                        Charlottesville
Compensation for damage to his house in fitting it up for use of the legislature at the May session 1781.
   Manuscript unsigned.
11 June 1782: To PG.
       No further action found.

1706-P   Lamb, James
       MHD: 17 June 1782        Princess Anne County
Asks clemency for conviction of treason.
   Manuscript unsigned.
17 June 1782: House lays on table.

## Virginia Legislative Petitions

15 Nov. 1782: To SC.
    SC recommends pardons for Lamb, Joshua Hopkins, and John Caton.
    House and Senate pass bill.
    For act pardoning Lamb and others see 11H129.

**1707-P-†  Payne, ———**
    MHD: 21 June 1782                    Not known
Text and subject not known.
21 June 1782: To T.
    No further action found.

# Index to Petitioners and Signers

These index entries, for petitioners and signers of general petitions, refer to the serial numbers assigned to petition abstracts, not to page numbers.

## A

Aaron, Abraham, 775
Abbott, Ishmael, 722
Abell, James, 567.8
Abernathy, Charles, 1278
Able, Caleb, 1203
Abyvon, Geo., 1314
Accomack County, citizens of, 81, 1430, 1650
Achen, Thomas, 1553
Adair, John, 404.62, 567.54
Adam, Robert, 348
Adams, Anne, 499
Adams, James, 893, 981
Adams, Richard, 1564
Adams, Richd., 1405
Adams, Robert, 27
Adams, Thos., 750
Adcock, Robt., 984
Admiralty Court, justices of, 1031
Aimes, John, 480
Albemarle County, citizens of, 272, 1014, 1025, 1334
Albemarle Parish (Sussex Co.), vestry of, 1286
Alden, Archer, 199
Alden, Saml., 199
Alexander, James, 317
Alexander, Robert, 1653
Alexandria: citizens of, 237, 902, 903, 1069, 1242, 1614; merchants and traders of, 1209; trustees of, 348, 1093
Alford, John, 1155
Alford, William, 1155
Allan, William, 984
Allen, ———, 1703
Allen, Charles, 636
Allen, Jas., 1050
Allen, Malcom, 1248
Allen, Richd., 981
Allen, Richmond, 930
Allen, Samuel, 661
Allen, William, 1024, 1025
Allen, Wm., 906
Alley, James, 440
Allison, Charles, 324
Allison, John, 308
Allphin John, 806
Ambler J., 1005
Ambler, Jacquelin, 251
Amelia County. See also Nottoway Parish
citizens of, 534, 534 A, 534 B, 579, 579 A-579 D, 666, 958, 1194, 1289, 1569, 1570
and militia of, 62
tax commissioners of, 1455
Amherst County: citizens of, 132, 153, 292, 293, 651.1, 651.2, 799, 865, 1024, 1025, 1026, 1032, 1098, 1098 A, 1148, 1155, 1156, 1215, 1432, 1451; court justices of, 1273; militia of, 1302. See also Amherst Parish
Amherst Parish (Amherst Co.), citizens of, 153, 551.1, 1216
Amox, Matthew, 1648
Anderson, Edward, 1027
Anderson, Henry, 1194
Anderson, Jacob, 404.59
Anderson, James, 1635
Anderson, Jno., 1376, 1642
Anderson, John, 913, 1095, 1629
Anderson, Lancer, 1313
Anderson, Mary, 1664

Anderson, Matthew, 522
Anderson, Mede, 913, 1095
Anderson, Natl., 522
Anderson, Nickolas, 105
Anderson, Richard, 1149
Anderson, Robt., 1294
Anderson, Robt., Jr., 1104
Anderson, William, 269, 404.27
Anderson, Wm., 522, 1642
Andrew, Ephraim, 337
Andrew, James, 836
Andrews, Eleck, 1053
Andrews, William, 1246, 1355
Angel, Rodham, 932
Angella, Barlet, 265
Angle, Barren, 265
Anglican Church. *See* Church of England
Anthony, Joseph, 1251
Antrim Parish (Halifax Co.): churchwardens and vestry of, 1028, 1479; citizens of, 1671
Apperson, Richard, 651
Appleberry, Thos., 981
Arbuckle, James, 380
Arbuckle, Matthew, 1213
Archer, Edward, 84, 544, 870, 1005
Archer, Henry, 1182
Archer, Jno., 1594
Archer, John, 429, 1213, 1549
Archer, William, 1190
Armistead, C., 914
Armistead, Henry, 1630
Armistead, Robt., 1426
Armistead, Thos., 1114
Armstrong, Andrew, 1292
Armstrong, Andw., 1357
Armstrong, James, 1350
Armstrong, John, 345
Arnold, James, 404.90
Arthur, Thomas, 1134
Ashford, Thos., 1333
Ashlock, John, 1118
Ashton, Burdit, 1018, 1217, 1399
Askew, ———, 1610
Aston, Esther, 1510
Atkinson, Matthew, representative of, 836
Auditors of Public Accounts. *See* Virginia Auditors of Public Accounts

Augusta County. *See also* Back Creek lands; Buckanan River lands; Bullpasture River lands; Cowpasture River lands; Jackson River lands; Monongalia River lands; Potomac River lands
   citizens of, 428, 444, 500, 685, 694, 826, 826 A, 943, 945, 959, 959 A, 959 B, 960, 966, 966 A, 1050, 1087, 1280, 1434, 1635
   committee of, 12, 221
   militia of, 933
Austin, William, 906
Avell, Richard, 1069
Avery, Billy Haley, 376
Avery, Isaac, 1236
Aylett, James, 368
Aylett, William, 69, 566, 773

### B

Bachelor, Thomas (Norfolk borough), 61
Bachelor (Batchelor?), Thomas (Norfolk Co.), 14
Back Creek lands, citizens of, 899
Backley, John, 102
Badgett, Thomas, 575
Bagwell, Charles, 1430
Bailes, Gilbert, 1650
Bailey, Edmund, 136
Bailey, Ezekiah, 292
Bailey, James Wallace, 459
Bailey, John, 1051
Bailey, Joshua, 434
Baine, Robert, 1498
Baird, Saml., 1400
Baker, Benjamin, 531
Baker, Christopher, 295
Baker, Saml., 124
Baker and Hardy, 282
Ball, David, 534
Ball, James, Jr., 1051
Ball, Jas., 1051
Ball, John, 567.10, 1617
Ball, Richard, 504
Ballard, William, 374
Ballendine, John, 4, 24, 78, 469, 474, 606, 619, 990, 1129, 1162
Ballendine, Thomas, 1667

Ballenger, Wm., 879
Ballinger, Joseph, 1442
Ballinger, Richard, 1432
Ballone, Chs., 1311
Bankhead, Will., 1486
Bankhead, William, 1404
Banks, Alex., 1556
Banks, Hunter and Company, 1536
Banks, John, 1320
Banks, Thomas, 191
Bannerman, Benjamin, 381
Bannester, Isaac, 865
Baptist Association, 1079 1251, 1298, 1649
Baptist church (Prince William Co.). See Prince William County
Barber, Charles, 121
Barbour, Jas., 984
Baremore, George, 879
Barksdale, Dudley, 1237
Barksdale, Peter, 1116
Barnabas, Arthur, 952
Barnaby, Elias, 357
Barnes, Isaiah, 538
Barnes, John Barker, 81
Barnes, N. B., 156
Barnes, Thomas, 90, 345
Barnett, Robert, 368
Barnett, Wm., 981
Barran, Jas., 713
Barrett, Amy, 762
Barrett, Bartho., 1474
Barrett, William, 1239
Bartec, William, 953
Bartlet, Thos., 1195
Bartlett, Thomas, 960
Bartley, John, 984
Baskervill, William, 645
Baskerville, John, 1295
Bastian, John, 1127
Batchelor, Thomas. See Bachelor, Thomas
Bate, Richd., 1114
Batt, Benjamin, 936
Batte, Thomas, Jr., 1182
Baugh, Richd., 1182
Baxter, Alexander, 426
Baylor, John, 1042
Beacham, Abra. 1362

Beadels, James, 1294
Beaker, Robert, 438
Beale, Isaac, 72
Bean, Richard, 200
Beard Thomas, 1155
Beasley, Thomas, 567.3
Beatey, John, 438
Beaty, John, 368
Beaucamp, Nath., 1430
Becket, George, 94
Beckford Parish (Dunmore Co.), vestry of, 411
Beckham, ———, 1585
Beckley, John, 1616
Bedford County, citizens of, 132, 311 312, 445, 607, 649, 707, 865, 951, 951 A-951 D, 952, 969, 1127, 1134, 1136, 1228, 1230, 1230 A, 1340, 1453, 1453 A-1453 M, 1454, 1681, 1681 A-1681 C. See also Russell Parish
Bedinger, Henry, 1373
Beeler, B., 1020
Beets, James, 404.123
Begley, Henry, 1604
Bell, John, 651, 687, 1065
Bell, Joseph, 1375, 1635
Bell, Thos., 1049
Bellini, Charles, 1143
Bennet Anne, 1384
Bennett, James, 513
Bennitt, Absalom, 1573
Bennitt, William, 567.43
Benson, Benjamin, 415
Bentley, ———, 1656
Bentley, William, 1354
Benton Lazarus, 518
Berkeley County: citizens of, 973, 973 A-973 E, 1020, 1208, 1337, 1425, 1518; citizens of (Warm Springs area), 193
Bernard, J., 686
Bernard, William, 1592
Berry, Benj., 973
Berry, Benja., 1474
Berry, Francis, 404.26
Berry, George, Jr., 395
Berry, James, 404.76, 630, 1030
Berry, John, 437
Berry, Thomas, 394, 404.95, 611, 790

Bettie, Dvd., 1546
Beuford, Ambrose, 957
Bias, John, 1140
Bias, Obed., 1140
Bibb, John, 1451
Bibb, Will., 1480
Bibb, William, 1176
Bibee, Peter, 292, 293, 1215
Bigge, John, 1148
Bilberry, Benjamin, 1316
Bilbo, James, 280
Billups, Christopher, 1598
Billups, Humphrey, 219
Billups, Joseph, Sr., 914
Binbury, Thos., 1471
Binn, Charles, 919
Birchill, Robert, 1084
Birchill, Robt., 927
Bird, John, 1612
Bird, Thos., 1613
Bittle, Kirby, 771
Black, David, 1114
Black, Hugh, 1221
Black, James, 440
Black, Jno., 437
Black, Thomas, 567.11
Black, William, 992, 1047, 1398, 1522
Blackburn, Arthur, 388
Blackburn, Benjamin, 463
Blackburn, Geo., 448
Blackburn, George, 75
Blackburn, T., 189, 1039, 1532, 1613
Blackman, Moses, 54
Blackwell, Saint, 711
Blair, John, 168, 787, 1002, 1668
Blair, John, and Associates, 819
Blake, Martin, 1313
Blake, Richard, 381
Blakely, William, 122
Blakey, Smith, 567.4
Bland, William, 777, 1137
Blandford (Prince George Co.), citizens of, 1114
Blandford warehouse, 603, 927
Blankenship, Joseph, Sr., 1230
Blankinship, Womack, 1594
Blanks, David, 700
Blanton, Charles, 1033

Blanton, William, 317
Bledsoe, Anthony, 45, 552, 567.89, 1378
Bleuw, John, Sr., 809
Blizzard, Thomas, 845
Blood, Amos, 54
Blord, Mich., 1286
Blunt, Washer, 1069
Blunt, Wm., 771
Boatwright, Benoni, 1457
Bogard, Abraham, 889
Boggess, John, 1576
Boggs, Robert, 404.53
Bohannan, Arm., 918
Bohon, Benjamin, 406
Boling, Anne, 407
Bolling, Robert, Jr., 1114
Bolling, Stith, 1403
Bolling, Thos., 1549
Bollingbrooke warehouse, 487
Bolling's warehouse, 603. *See also* John Bolling's warehouse
Bolton, Robert, 1102
Boney, Mich., 221
Bonnard, William, 1497
Booker, Edward, 958
Booker, James, 1056
Booker, John, Jr., 958, 1455
Booker, Richd., 711
Booker, Wm., 676
Boon, Squire, 895
Boon, U., 1099
Boon, Will, 140 A
Boone, Daniel, 470, 498
Boone, Squire, 1620
Boonesborough (Kentucky Co.), citizens of, 1030
Boonesfort. *See* Boonesborough
Boot, Joseph, 98
Booth, George, 1286
Booth, Thomas, 1394
Booth, William, 260
Boram, John, 755
Bosher, James, 1199
Botetourt County: citizens of, 324, 428, 429, 430, 430 A–430 E, 650, 974, 1163, 1248, 1643; citizens of (western waters), 80. *See also* Botetourt Parish

Botetourt Parish (Botetourt Co.), vestry of, 167
Bott, Jno., 1549
Bott, Miles, 1072
Bott, William, 1072
Bottom, John Side, 879
Bouldin, Wood, 1315
Boulding, Wood, 651
Bouram, John, 129
Bourn, Eleanor, 843
Boush, Arthur, 9, 43
Boush, Goodrich, 1, 8
Boush, Samuel, 7, 8
Bousman, Jacob, 257
Bowdoin, Preston, 212, 276, 1538
Bowen, Charles, 324
Bowen, Leanor. See Bourn, Eleanor
Bowie, Sarah, 1112
Bowland, Michal, 278
Bowland, Michl., 1221
Bowles, Hen., 760
Bowling, Henry, 1648
Bowling's warehouse, 1623
Bowman, Abrm., 941
Bowman, Wm., 906
Bowyer, William, 1531
Bowyer, Wm., 948, 1390
Boxen, W., 193
Boxley, Joseph, 1294
Boyd, David, 1362
Boyd, George, 1028, 1044, 1139
Boyd, John, representative of 817
Boyd, Robt., 1533, 1616
Boyd, Spencer, 92
Boyd's warehouse, 603, 927, 1623
Boyer, Engle, 1199
Boykin, John, 648
Bozwell, Reuben, 906
Braden, Joseph, 768
Bradford, Joseph, 1043
Bradley, James, 404.103
Bradley, Jonas, 1421
Bradley, William, 1626
Braggs, David, 937
Bramham, Jno., 1400
Bramham, Spencer Thaddeus, 540
Branch, Benja., 1549
Branch, Daniel, Jr., 760

Branch, William, 1529
Brandon, David, 165
Brannum, John, 381
Bransteter, Andrew, 567.66
Bratton, Robert, 966
Breedlove, John, 1333
Bremer, Sackville, 1022
Brent, George, 178
Brent, Robert, 178
Brent, Wm., 946, 1185
Bressie, Henry, 325, 1100
Brett, George, 620
Brett, John, 879
Brickell, Jno., 844
Bridgforth, Thos., 1404, 1486
Bright, Robert, 1426
Brink, Hybert, 404.7
Briscoe, Gerd., 1482
Briscoe, Reuben, 1684
Bristow, William, 432
Britt, John, 658
Broaddus, Thomas, 479
Broadnax, Edw., 942
Broadnax, Edward, 1108
Broadner, Stephen E., 1598
Brock, Joseph, 1184
Brooke, John, 750
Brooke, Robert, 1559
Brooking, John, 1087
Brooking, Vivion, 62
Brooks, Littleton, 567.46
Brooks, William, 203
Broskin, Wm., 672
Browder, William, 1506
Brown, ———, 1697
Brown, Aaron, 1053
Brown, Alex., 1234
Brown, Benjamin, 1037
Brown, Eleanor. See Bourn, Eleanor
Brown, Elict, 923
Brown, Elizabeth, 202
Brown, Geo. N., 1532
Brown, Henry, 1246
Brown, Hezekiah, 1172
Brown, James, 293, 498
Brown, John, 179, 301, 410, 588, 906, 1208, 1490
Brown, Robert, 567.13

513

Brown, Sarah, 881
Brown, Tho., 1246
Brown, Thomas, 631
Brown, Thos., 1417
Brown, William, 567.75, 923, 1173
Browne, John, 1038
Browne, William, 1666
Brubecker, ———, 1690
Bruce, ———, 1583
Bruce, Richard, 1396
Bruce, William, 185
Brumley, John, 1466
Brummet, William, 906
Brumstreter, Andrew, 887
Brunswick County, 1699; citizens of, 236, 633, 1053, 1278, 1279, 1279 A, 1279 B, 1318, 1318 A, 1322, 1322 A–1322 C, 1573, 1574, 1588; tax commissioners, assessors, and sheriff of, 1013
Bruton Parish (James City and York cos.), wardens and vestry of, 314
Bryan, Battaley, 1065
Bryant, Thomas, 621
Bucchanan, Jas., 1224
Buchanan, James, 948, 1128, 1209.1, 1260, 1328
Buchanan, Moses, 1511
Buchanan, Neill, 1623
Buchanan, Robert, 602.1
Buchanan, William, 859
Buchanon, Jos., 1218
Buck, Diana, 551
Buckanan, James, 1564
Buckanan River lands, citizens of, 852
Buckingham County, citizens of, 292, 522, 538, 627, 695, 696, 1024, 1025, 1135, 1277, 1277 A–1277 C, 1351. *See also* Tillotson Parish
Buckles, James, 644
Buckles, William, 644
Buckner, John, 1227
Buckner, John, Jr., 793
Bucktrout, Benjamin, 23, 460
Buford, James, 404.39
Buford, John, 634
Bugg, Jacob, 1295
Bullitt, Cuth., 1007, 1039

Bullitt, Cuthbert, 758
Bullock, Edward, 1605
Bullock, James, 907.16
Bullock, John, 1030
Bullock, Leonard Henley, 97
Bullpasture River lands, citizens of, 899
Bunch, James, 831
Buntain, Alexander, 1459
Burden, Archibald, 906
Burford, John, 1340
Burges, Jno., 648
Burges, Wm., 683
Burgess, William, 64
Burgoyne, Joseph, 739
Burk, Thomas, 1305
Burley, Saml., 1599
Burnett, Mary, 381
Burnett, Thomas, 879
Burnley, G., 1255
Burns, Robert, 1673
Burr, Philip, 1586
Burroughs, Geo., 936
Burton, J., 272
Burton, James, 651, 1255
Burton, Jesse, 623, 1132, 1230
Burton, Jno., 81
Burton, William, 404.18
Burton, Wm., 1230
Burwell, Anne, 486
Burwell, Lewis, Jr., 161, 962
Butcher, John, 847
Butler, Alexander, 567.73
Butler, George, 1622
Butt, Arthur, 545
Bybee, Edw., 1302
Bybee, Joseph, 761
Bybee, Thomas, 906
Byras, John, 1406
Byrd's warehouse, 1256, 1326

## C

Cabell, Joseph, 60, 1456, 1512, 1621
Cabell, Nicholas, 1456, 1512, 1621
Cabin Point warehouse, 42, 560
Caffery, John, 1653
Cage, William, 404.10

Caldwell, George, 567.70 597
Caldwell, John, 1461
Call, Richard, 1427
Calland, Jos., 549
Calland, Joseph, 1104
Callaway, Charles, 1454
Callaway, James, 1454
Callaway, John, 880, 1454, 1653
Callaway, Richard, 1071
Callaway, Wm., 1454
Callender, Eliezer, 1642
Calmes, Marquis, 925
Caloner, Marquis, 1482
Calvert, Christopher, 51, 52
Calvert, Cornelius, 729, 1314
Calvert, Cornelius, Jr., 1576
Calvert, John, 159
Calvert, Max., 1314
Calvert, Maximillian, 1016
Calvert, William, 567.15
Calwall, Joseph, 1521, 1655
Calwell, Samuell, 317
Camden, William, 651.2
Cameron, James, 567.56
Cammock, Henry, 508
Camp, John, 1400
Camp, Mary, 1063
Campbell, ———, 1591, 1624
Campbell, Aaron, 1026
Campbell, Alexander, 102
Campbell, Archd., 1224
Campbell, Archibald, 1379
Campbell, Arthur, 315
Campbell, Colin, 127
Campbell, Dougall, 164
Campbell, Elias, 918
Campbell, George, 1115
Campbell, Gilbert, 1159
Campbell, Isaac, 1372
Campbell, James, 404.49, 701, 1305, 1428
Campbell, John, 277, 448, 1633
Campbell, Joshua, 64
Campbell, Robert, 419
Campbell, Saml., 498
Campbell, Samuel, 567.36, 907.7
Campbell, William, 45, 54
Campbell, William, Jr., 632
Campbell, Wm., 448

Campbell County, citizens of, 1682. *See also* Russell Parish
Canon, James, 1428
Cantrall, Joshua, 1442
Cantrell, Christopher, 507
Card-makers, 571
Cardar, Jno., 337
Carlock, Hanhrist, 404.92
Carlyle, John, 586, 1249
Carmack, John, 511
Carmicx, Geo., 54
Carney Onsbey, 404.116
Caroline County, citizens of, 56, 83, 479, 520 520 A, 520 B, 1023, 1437. *See also* Drysdale Parish; Saint Margaret's Parish
Carpenter, Andreas, 157
Carr, Garland, 149
Carr, Richd., 1203
Carr, William, 567.39, 1613
Carrel, Bartholomew, 404.20
Carrington, Edward, 1563
Carrington, Geo., Jr., 549
Carrington, Joseph, 250
Carrington, Luke, 1056
Carrington, P., 1009
Carson, David, 567.53
Carter, Ch., 937
Carter, Charles, 1607
Carter, Hezekiah, 261
Carter, Jeduthen, 119
Carter, John Jarret, 270
Carter, Landon, 1302
Carter, Shadrick, 261
Carter, Theodorick, 1145
Carter, William, 1382
Cartwright, Joseph, 907.13
Cary, Archibald, 1128, 1260, 1290, 1405, 1503, 1568
Cary, Wilson Miles, 87, 272, 1077
Cary, Wm., 1183
Cary's warehouse, 487, 1157
Casaday, John, 433
Casaday, Wm., 433
Cassity, Peter, Jr., 139
Casson, Charles, 517
Catlett, John, 275, 1346
Cave, Daniel, 1665
Cave, David, 939

Cave, William, 949
Cedar Point warehouse, 603
Chambers, James, 1341
Chambers, Wm., 1020
Chamblis, William, 488
Chancellor, John, 1185
Chancellor, Thomas, 1497
Chapel, John, 1238
Chapin, Benja., 1069
Chapman, G., 1078
Chapman, Richa., 715
Chapman, William, 30
Chappell, Thos., Jr., 273
Chappell, Thos., Sr., 273
Charles City County, citizens of, 1287
Charlotte County: citizens of, 267, 273, 1022, 1237, 1315; justices of, 1106
Charlottesville, citizens of, 928
Charters, Thomas, 951
Cheatham, Matthew, 760
Chesterfield County. *See also* Manchester Parish
    citizens of, 3, 11, 958, 1386, 1594, 1595
        committee of, 55
        court justices of, 1549
        merchants and traders of, 1209.1
Chew, John, Jr., 1500
Chew, Larkin, 1144, 1189
Chew, Thos., 526
Childress, Joseph, 931
Childress, Robt., 931
Chiles, Micajah, 928
Chiles, Thomas, 496
Chiles, William, 230
Chilton, Jesse, 567.12
Chilton, Sturman, 1520
Chincoteague Island, citizens of, 81
Chisholm, Alex., 1520
Chowning, John, 779
Christ Church Parish (Lancaster Co.), 504, 504 A–504 D, 505
Christian, Samson, 899
Christian, William, 109, 346
Churchill, William, 89
Church of England, clergy of, 218
Cincade, John, 317
Claiborne, Aug., 488

Claiborne, Richard, 1335
Clapham, Josias, 735, 915
Clark, George Rogers, 150, 1241; officers in regiment of, 1535
Clark, John, 906
Clark, Joseph, 923
Clark, Robert, 1280
Clarke, Daniel, 1542, 1543
Clarke, John, 1057
Clarke, Thomas, 830
Clarke, Wm., 1306
Clarke and Tally, 1327
Clarke and Wingfield, 1327
Clarkson, David, 766
Clarkson, John, 911
Clarkson and Davis, 1193
Clay, Charles, 1017
Clement, Anne, 1581
Clemmons, Edward, 1104
Clifton, Samuel, 1323
Clopton, John, 1383
Cobbs, John, 623, 1132
Cochran, John, 404.35
Cochran, William, 973
Cock, Geo., 1682
Cock, John, 1682
Cock, Wm., 1682
Cockburn, George, 292, 293
Cockburn, Robt., 278
Cocke, ———, 1695
Cocke, Anne, 107, 404.4
Cocke, James, 950
Cocke, Lemuel, 1666
Cocke, Stephen, 1403
Cocke, William, 371
Cockeral, John, 1037
Cocks, Charles, 567.29
Cogar, Jacob, 449
Cogbill, Chars., 1594
Cohan, Jacob, and Isaacs, 1533
Coke, Sarah, 279
Cole, Abraham, 907.1
Cole, Jno., 183
Cole, John, 651
Cole, Walter King, 1250
Coleburn, Robert, 516
Coleman, Daniel, 663
Coleman, James, 673, 949, 1276

Coleman, Permens., 1104
Coleman, Rebecca, 403
Coleman, Thos., 961, 1059
Coleman, William, 1348
Coles, Isaac, 1028
Coles, John, 155, 1123
Coles, Walter, 1028
Coles, William, 559
Coleville, Andrew, 75
Collard, Benja., 928
Collicot, James, 579
Collier, Chas., 1279
Collier, Lockey, estate of, 907.17
Collins, ———, 1641
Collins, James, 242
Collins, John, 673, 949
Collins, William, 1515
Collis, Thomas, 348
Colquet, Hesekiah, 1104
Colson, Thomas, 1184
Colston, William, 1293
Combs, George, 1262
Compton, Archibald, 703, 1196
Conan, John Francis, 1541
Connaway, John, 1439
Conner, Charles, 1582
Conner, Chas., 676
Conner, John, 1524, 1526
Conner, Wm., 438, 1676
Connolly, James, 1429
Conrad, Fred., 1586
Conrad, Frederick, 925
Consolver, John, 1284
Continental army. *See also* Military officers
  captains, 1st and 2d Regiments of, 114
  officers of, 1113, 1267, 1505, 1606
    field, 529
  and soldiers, 557
Convention troops. *See* Saratoga convention troops
Conway, Fra., 1404
Conway, Francis, 56
Conway, Fras., 1486
Conway, Henry, 651
Conway, Richd., 848
Cooke, Adam, estate of, 558
Cooke, Edward, 1383
Cooke, John, 793, 1038

Cocn, George, 404.144
Cocper, ———, 1637
Cocper, Charles, 1220
Cocper, John, 362
Cooper, Leonard, 1627
Cooper, Thomas, 102
Cooper, Thos., 1677
Copeland, Peter, 1704
Cope Parish (Westmoreland Co.), citizens of, 628
Corbin, Geo., 1430
Corbin, John Tayloe, 5, 118
Cormack, Daniel M., 567.61
Corrick, Joel, Jr., 191
Cornick, Lemuel, 191
Cornwell, Samuel, 434
Corrick, Dim, 778
Corrick, Horatio, 778
Cottrell, Anne, 287
Coulter, John, 34 A
Coulter, Michael, 40
County claims, 1577
Courtney, Wm., 1392
Coutts, Reuben, 1368
Cowan, Andrew, 567.52
Cowden, Robert, 567.80
Cowley, Abraham, 184
Cowpasture River lands, citizens of, 899
Cowper, Edward, 101
Cowper, Roe, 713
Cox, ———, 1584
Cox, Charles, 199
Cox, Henry, Jr., 1306
Cox, Jacob, 1069, 1614
Cox, John, 145, 622.8, 1351
Crabtree, James, 602.1
Craig, Adam, 149, 1678
Craig, Elijah, 1649
Craig, John, 53, 143, 230, 567.32, 874
Craig, Tolever, 1648
Craig, William, 317
Craighill, Will., Sr., 1111
Cralle, Kenner, 1362
Crane, John, 404.119
Crane, Lewis, 404.118
Cranstone, Jas., 57
Crawford, John, 906
Crawford, William, 404.38

517

Crawley, John, 170
Crayton, William, 1360
Crews, Gideon, 931
Criddle, William, 2, 576, 1186
Criminals. *See* Public jail (Williamsburg)
Crocket, Walter, 45
Crockett, James, 899
Croghan, George, 985, 988
Crookshanks, John, 88
Cropper, John, Jr., 1205
Cross, Samuel, 1385, 1397
Crowley, Elizabeth, 1349
Crutcher, Leonard, 296
Crutchfield, Fortunatus, 1266
Crutchfield's warehouse, 487, 515, 718, 926, 1327
Cruze, Jno., 922
Cullens, Daniel, 879
Cullins, John, 595
Culpeper, Henry, 545
Culpeper County: citizens of, 217, 242, 426, 482, 672, 673, 673 A, 806, 918, 918 A, 939, 984, 984 A, 1043, 1045, 1055, 1333, 1400; Lutheran church [Hebron] in, members of, 157
Cumberland County, citizens of, 199, 199 A, 199 B, 261, 261 A–261 E, 265, 265 A–265 E, 266, 320, 527, 530, 1311, 1313, 1313 A, 1313 B, 1421. *See also* Littleton Parish
Cumberland Parish (Lunenburg Co.), vestry of, 318
Cummings, Charles, 75
Cummins, Peter, 794
Cunes, Jacob, 126
Cunningham, Elizabeth, 1458
Cunningham, James, 1022, 1477
Cunningham, Jno., 1509
Cunningham, Natha., 922
Cunningham, Wm., 1488
Curd, John, 1282
Cureton, James, 744
Cureton, John, Jr., 942
Curle, William Roscow Wilson, 1131
Curniat, David, 1127
Curniat, James, Jr., 1127
Curniat, Reuben, 1127
Curniat, William, 1127

Currants, Wm., 433
Cusick, John, 1465
Custis, Henry, 81
Cutchin, Joseph, 39

## D

Dabney, George, 1180.1
Dabney, James, 1117
Dabney, Jas., 1683
Dabney, Owen, 1605
Dalton, David, 404.16
Dameron, Jacob, 1409
Damron, George, 627
Dancey, Benjamin, 567.6
Dandridge, Nathaniel West, 1376
Daniel, George, 344, 1223, 1686
Daniel, James, 479
Daniel, Reuben, 465
Daniel, Robert, 1413
Daniel, Walker, 1481
Dannill, Robt., 1203
Dark, John, 1337
Darke, William, 72
Daugherty, James, 567.48
Daugherty, Michael, 875
Davenport, James, 591
Davenport, R., 1014
Davenport, William, 446
Davidson, George, 1369
Davidson, Thomas, 667
Davidson, Wm., 1248
Davies, Azariah, 498
Davies, David, 182
Davies, Edw., 1599
Davies, Saml., 1701
Davies, William, 1606
Davis, Abraham, 1358
Davis, Augustine, 911
Davis, Charles, 1300
Davis, Gresset, 1084
Davis, H., 1333
Davis, James, 883, 959
Davis, John, 1369
Davis, Nicholas, 1142
Davis, Richard, 906
Davis, William, 879
Davis's warehouse, 603, 927

Dawson, John, 1216
Dawson, Jonathan, 622.6
Day, James, 1366
Deale, Alexn., 1400
Dean, John, 1060
Deane, Daniel, 138
Deane, John, 1488
Debo, Philip, 119
Deborax, Charles, 391
Debrell, Lucas, 1432
Decamp, John, 907.6
DeGraffenreid, Wm., 13 942
Dehaven, Jacob, 739
De Klauman, Charles, 1191
De la Croix, Peter, 1179
Delony, Henry, 1386
Depart, James, 438
De Sequeyra, John, 857, 1079.1, 1308
Devore, James, 509
Dick, Alexander, 1161
Dick, Chas., 815, 929
Dickenson, Arthur, 618
Dickenson, William, 582, 1091
Dickerson, John, 906
Dickerson, William, 1232
Dickeson, Elijah, 650
Dickey, Michaell, 1050
Dickey, Robert, 1199
Dickie, Jno., 1028
Dickinson, Arthur, 622.4
Dickinson, Edward, 1235
Dietom, Joseph, 1135
Dillard, Geo., 92
Dillard, John, 132
Dillon, William, 834
Dinwiddie, Samuel, 1302
Dissenters, 141, 164 A; of Albemarle Co., 155, 155 A, 183; of Amherst Co., 155, 155 A, 183; of Berkeley Co. (Tuscarora congregation), 164; of Buckingham Co., 155, 155 A; of Prince Edward Co., 124
Divarse, John, 1228
Dix, John, 342
Dixon, Jane, 158, 268
Dixon, John, 793, 910, 1265, 1504
Dixon, John, Jr., 15
Dixon, Robert, 13
Dixon's warehouse, 926, 1064

Doggett, George, 587
Doggett, Thos., 1134
Doggins, John, 1336
Donald, Robert, 1556
Doniphan, Joseph, 1030
Donnally, Andw., 1213
Donnan, David, 421
Doran, James, 567.68
D'Osmont, ————, 1701
Dougherty, Henry, 622.11
Doughten, John, 953
Douglas, Samuel, 398
Douglass, Edward, 842
Douglass, Margaret, 416
Dove, Francis, 1629
Dowdd, James, Sr., 1210
Downey, Darby, 637
Downman, Raleigh, 400
Downman, Rawleigh, 1470
Downs, Henry, 787
Dowsing, Everard, 318
Drake, Benjamin, 404.122
Drake, Ephraim, 860
Drake, Jonathan, 511
Drake, Margaret, 858
Drake, Samuel, 1214
Drake, William, 951
Driver, John, 844
Druen, John, 1277
Drysdale Parish (Caroline and King and Queen cos.), citizens of, 961, 1027, 1027 A–1027 C, 1033, 1033 A, 1033 B, 1059
Drury, William, 1204
Dualey, John, 484
Duckwall, Henry, 1261
Dudley, Thomas, 689
Dugger, Alexander, 1278
Dugger, Eleck, 1053
Duke, Sarah, 837
Dumfries warehouse, 1185
Duncan, George, 272
Duncan, James, 420
Duncan, Matthew, 1425
Duncan, Sam., 1425
Duncom, Elizabeth, 373
Dunkin, John, 437
Dunlap, John, 1352

Dunlap, Moses, 1357
Dunlop, Alexander, 787
Dunlop, Archibald, 1516
Dunlop, Ephraim, 368, 404.46
Dunlop, John, 899
Dunmore County: citizens, committee of, 142. *See also* Beckford Parish
Dunn, James, 423
Dunn, Lewis, 1081
Dunn, Nath., 1286
Dunn, Wm., Sr., 488
Durham, Amos, 743
Durley, Mary, 556
DuVal, Samuel, Jr., 1070, 1274
Du-Val, Samuel, Sr., 1274
Du-Val, William, 1274
Duval, Wm., 793
Dyer, James, 845
Dyer, Roger, 845

### E

Early, Jacob, 600, 1681
Early, Joshua, 1433
Earnest, Geo., 1509
Eason, Samuel, 567.21
East, Benjamin, 1296
East, David, 1410
East, Ezekiel, 1297
Eaton, Amos, 368
Edgar, Thos., 1369
Edmidson, Wm., 437
Edmiston, John, 1511
Edmondson, James Powell, 598
Edmondson, Robert, 1511
Edmondson, William, 315
Edmonson, F., Jr., 941
Edmonson, Willm., 1056
Edmundson, William, 567.51
Edwards, Andrew, 197, 936, 1097
Edwards, Edward, 1297
Edwards, James, 778
Edwards, John, 656
Edwards, Nicholas, 404.129, 567.62
Edwards, Thomas, 1362
Edwin, James, 787
Egbert, Lawrence, 949
Ege, Dorothy, 1211

Eggleston, Joseph, 1072
Eggleston, William, 1072
Ekew, James, 1115
Elam, John, 13
Eldridge, He., 1013
Elizabeth City County, citizens of, 1120, 1426
Elizabeth River Parish (Norfolk Co.), citizens of, 677
Ellegood, Jacob, 864
Elligood, Mary, 67
Elliot, Elizabeth, 340
Elliott, George, 1084
Elliott, John, 725
Ellis, John, 322, 991
Emery, William, 223
Emmerson, Arthur, 1318
English, David, 567.22
Epperson, Richard, 470, 896
Eppes, Peter, 1029
Eppes, William, 651
Erwin, John, 1213
Essex County, citizens of, 365, 1056, 1073. *See also* Saint Anne's Parish
Estes, Elijah, 756
Estill, James, 1011
Etheridge, Amos, 43
Eustace, J., 375
Evans, Peter, 1532
Everard, Thos., 950
Ewell, Ja., 189
Ewell, Jas., 1051
Ewell, John, 189
Ewers, Thomas, 906
Ewin, Samuel, 450, 567.81
Ewing, Alexander, 651
Eyers, Francis, 1279
Ezell, Buckner, 1279

### F

Fair, Samuel, 567.71
Fairfax, ———, 1670
Fairfax County, citizens of, 338, 847, 1068, 1078, 1612
Falkner, Ralph, 651
Falmouth, trustees of, 937
Falmouth warehouse, 926, 1064

Fambrough, Thomas, 238
Faris, Gideon, 404.80
Farley, Francis, Jr., 722
Farley, Francis, Sr., 722
Farley, Nat, 722
Farley, Seth, 273
Farmer, Lodk., 942
Farmer, Lodowick, 13, 318, 1180.7
Faulcon, Jacob, 1666
Fawley, John, 739
Fayette County, citizens of, 1446, 1483, 1525, 1548, 1629, 1640
Feagan, Wm., 879
Fear, Hamner, 299
Fearn, Thomas, 77
Fendley, David, 1145
Ferebee, James, 64
Ferrell, Ben, 1295
Feston, John, 720
Field, Ezekiel, 850
Field, Henry, 802
Field, Henry, Jr., 259
Figg, Sarah, 551
Fincastle County
   citizens of
      Pendleton District of, 34, 34 A
      western part of, 75. 76, 115
      committee of, 116
Fink, Jacob, 1208, 1221
Finley, John, 401, 1612
Finley, Robert, 404.55
Finley, Samuel, 1373
Finn, Jno., 931
Finnall, Jonathan, 1474
Finnie, William, 28
Finnill, Thomas, 417
Fischer, Wm., 181
Fisher, Frederick, 1463
Fisher, Jno., 1278
Fisher, John, 1151
Fisher, Stephen, 652
Fitzgerald, Jarret, 392
Fitzgerald, John, 847, 1612
Fitzgerald, Will., 1403
Fitzhugh, Henry, 140
Fitzhugh, John, 954
Fitzhugh, Thomas, 954
Fitzhugh, William, 954

Fitzpatrick, Robert, 1521, 1655
Flech, Wm., 1392
Flee-, Henry, 706
Fleming, Thomas, 848
Fleming, William, 769
Flood, Elizabeth, 934, 1502, 1580
Florence, William, 879
Flournoy, Matt., 1315
Floyd, Mitchell, 301
Fluvanna County, citizens of, 405, 493, 494, 682, 682 A–682 C, 683, 683 A–683 C, 981, 1077, 1622
Fogg, William, 1322
Folkes, Baxter, 1182
Ford, Boaz, 1351
Ford, Reuben, 1649
Ford, Richd., 522
Forman, William, representative of, 753
Forqueren, Peter, 884
Forquesan, Peter, Sr., 865
Fortune, Benjamin, 906
Foster, Elizabeth, 207
Fowler, John, 760
Fowler, John, Jr., 760
Fowler, Thomas, 404.138
Fowlkes, James, 1569
Fowlkes, John, 534
Fowlkes, Joseph, 1194
Fox, John, 528, 793, 914, 987, 1227, 1702
Fraily, Frederick, 567.50
Francis, William, 702
Franciscoe, Michael, 567.17
Franklin, James, 132
Franklin, Thomas, 813
Frazer, William, 464, 706
Frederick County. *See also* Frederick Parish
   citizens of, 941, 973, 973 A–973 E, 996, 1482
   committee of, 100
Frederick Parish (Frederick Co.), church-wardens and vestrymen of, 925
Fredericksburg: citizens of, 815, 929, 1416, 1417; gun factory, mechanics of, 1272; mayor and council of, 1630
Fredericksburg warehouse, 926, 1195
Freeland, Mace, 1663
Freelander, Solomon, 628
French, John, 879

Fretwell, John, 1683
Frogg, William, 404.86
Fry, Benjamin, 577
Fulgham, Charles, 537
Fuller, Edward, 787
Fuqua, Randolph, 442
Furhran, John, 404.84
Furlong, John, 261
Furnis, John, 415

## G

Gaar, Adam, 157
Gadkins, John, 1574
Gaines, Benjamin, 1043
Gaines, Dan, 117
Gaines, Dan., 651.1
Gaines, Humphrey, 242
Gaines, James, 426
Gaines, Richard, Jr., 1022
Galbraith, Chas., 57
Galloway, David, 1018, 1217
Galt, Gabriel, 1571, 1616
Galt, James, 728
Galt, John Minson, 1103
Galt, Patrick, 241
Gambel, Margaret, 413
Gambell, Robert, 567.59
Gannaway, Wm., 627
Garbert, Jacob, 309
Garland, Edward, 206
Garland, George, 120
Garland, Griffin, 121
Garland, Nath., 1014
Garland, Peter, 651
Garner, Joseph, 271
Garnett, James, 567.2
Garrett, Hum., 92
Gartener, Nathanal, 1450
Gasking, Henry, 778
Gaskins, Thos., 375
Gass, David, 765, 876, 1011
Gatewood, Jos., 961
Gatewood, Richard, 1148
Gathright, Wm., 1678
Gautier, Nicholas, 789
Gay, Samuel, 404.71
Gayle, Matthew, 961

Gender, Jacob, 404.58
Geoghigan, Anty., 1571
George (slave), 805
George, William, 1034, 1521, 1655
Georgia (state), citizens of, 1599
Gess, John, 1520
Getgood, David, 404.69
Getwood, David, 368
Gibb, William, 1650
Gibbons, John, 932
Gibbs, John, 624, 1183
Gibson, Abraham, 536
Gibson, John, 567.45, 1496
Gibson, William, 1351
Gilbert, George, 1140
Gilbert, Henry, 1026
Gilder, Zachariah, 672
Giles, William, 958
Gill, Erasmus, 1423
Gillenwaters, Thos., 132
Gilliam, John, 1460
Gilliam, Robt., 1084
Gillock, Lawrence, 653
Gilmer, Geo., 183
Gilmore, John, 354
Gilmore, Robert, 102
Girty, Simon, 297
Gist, Nathal., 1113
Gist, Nathaniel, 471, 523
Glass, Vincent, 561
Glassell, Andrew, 926
Glaze, Windle, 809
Gleaves, Michael, 567.31
Glen, Nathan, 265, 549, 1348
Glenn, James, Sr., 1311
Glenn, William, 1348
Godfrey, Matt., 1
Godfrey, Matthew, 1530
Godwin, Christopher, 1096
Godwin, Lemuel, 1528, 1556
Goff, John, 616
Goff, Joseph, 1340
Goldsby, Thomas, 567.86
Gooch, Wade, 715
Goochland County, citizens of, 683, 683 A–
 683 C, 785, 788, 900, 901, 1296;
 militia of, field officers of, 1282
Goode, Bennett, 280, 1295

Goode, Francis, 1386
Goode, John, 751, 1403
Goode, Robert, 626, 1128, 1618
Goode, Robt., 1386, 1405
Goodell, Parke, 750
Goodrich, Dorothy, 963
Goodrich, John, Jr., 162
Goodrich, John, Sr., 458
Goodrich, Margaret, 65, 712
Goodwin, Thomas, 907.5
Goodwyn, Stephen, 1190
Gordon, Alexander, 1334
Gordon, James, 806
Gordon, John, 567.84, 622.2
Gordon, Samuel, Jr., 1421
Gorman, William, 452
Gould, David, 548
Gouret, Stephen, 627
Graham, Alexander, 22
Graham, Archibald, 404.88
Graham, Geo., 1613
Graham, George, 22
Graham, Reginald, 946
Graham, Richd., 189, 946
Graham, William, 1075
Grammar, Jno., 1701
Grammer, William, 927
Grantland, Samuel, 1383
Gratz, Bernard, 1152
Gratz, Michael, 1152
Graves, Francis, 1571
Gray, David, 1218
Gray, Geo., 1087
Gray, Nathaniel, 1417
Grayson, Spence, 253
Grayson, William, 946, 1039
Great Britain: natives of, 57, 104; merchants' assistants of, 57
Greathouse, Jacob, representative of, 817
Green, George, 1227
Green, John, 1194
Green, Thomas, 809
Greenbrier County, citizens of, 1213, 1369, 1450, 1450 A
Greenlee, John, 1218
Greenway, ———, 1579
Greer, James, 567.79
Gresham, Asa, 1322

Gretter, Mich., 903
Grider, John, 866
Grider, Martin, 866
Griffin, James, 404.8
Griffin, Jno., 320
Griffin, John Tayloe, 497
Griffin, Mary, 497
Griffith, James, 966
Grills, William, 420
Grimes, Phillip, 338
Grindstaff, Jacob, representative of, 817
Gripson, William, 627
Grubb, James, 376
Gully, Thomas, 1450
Gun factory (Fredericksburg), mechanics of, 1272
Guthrey, Alexander, 1145
Guthrey, Baron, 1348
Guthrey, William, 1421
Guttery, John, 301
Gwatkins, Charles, 882
Gwin, James, 317

# H

Habit, Richard, 137
Hack, James, 141
Hackett Goldsbury, 727
Haff, Peter, 567.47
Haislip, Spencer, 683
Hale, John, 650
Halifax County, citizens of, 59, 128, 166, 555, 573, 693, 811, 922, 922 A. See also Antrim Parish
Hall, Bowler, 1180.2
Hall, James, Jr., 488
Hall, Jas., 922
Hall, John, 1209.1
Hall, Lyman, 1445, 1599
Hall, William, 404.63, 922
Halsy, Rodger, 806
Hambleton, John, 594
Hamilton, Andw., 966
Hamilton, Francis, 567.42
Hamilton, James, 404.139
Hamilton, Jessee, 139
Hamilton, John, 57
Hamilton, Margrett, 550

Hamilton, Patr., 852
Hamilton, Thos., 308
Hammond, Griffion, 739
Hammond, John, 156
Hammond, Thomas, 622.3
Hampden-Sidney (Hampden-Sydney) Academy, trustees of, 244
Hampshire, ———, 1645
Hampshire County, citizens of, 336
Hampton, citizens of, 713
Hampton, Hy., 1532
Hampton, John, 105
Hancock, John, 331
Hancock, Stephen, 1011
Hancock, William, 1030
Handley, Archld., 317
Handley, William, 141
Hanewinkel, Alexander, 169
Hanks, Luke, 1012
Hanley, James, 317
Hanover County, citizens of, 36, 37, 1149, 1164, 1383, 1509, 1605. *See also* Saint Paul's Parish
Hanover Parish (King George Co.): citizens of, 686; vestry of, 1099
Hanover Presbytery. *See* Presbyterian church
Hansborough, Peter, 341
Hansborough, Wm., 1215
Hansford, Edward, 33, 584
Hardaway, Stith, 958
Hardway, Daniel, 1072
Hardwick, Robert, 567.74
Hargrove, Hezekiah, 1451
Hargrove, John, 1468
Harmans, John, Jr., 1615
Harmanson, ———, 1644
Harmanson, Henry, 1236
Harmanson, William, 1615
Harmer, George, 1268, 1401
Harness, Isaac, representative of, 753
Harper, John, 1614
Harris, ———, 1609
Harris, Charles, 294
Harris, James, 404.121, 907.8
Harris, John, 1228, 1488, 1499
Harris, John, Jr., 404.140
Harris, John, Sr., 404.120

Harris, Matthew, 651.1
Harris, Robert, 404.2, 1014
Harris, Sam, 1298
Harris, William, 786
Harrison, Benjamin, 1600
Harrison, Burr, 366
Harrison, Charles, 329, 1166
Harrison, George, 1519
Harrison, M., 1185
Harrison, Nathl., 1199
Harrison, Thomas, 1198
Harrison, W., 1234
Harrison, William, 1473
Harriss, He., 1013
Harrocks, Richard, 404.30
Harrup, Elizabeth, 767
Hart, David, 97
Hart, George, 396, 1085
Hart, Nathaniel, 97
Hart, Thomas, 97
Harum, Thos. Cuthb., 1239
Harvey, Joshua, Jr., 1323
Harvey, Mungo, 1060
Harvey, William, 1181
Harvie, John, 262
Harvie, Richd., 928
Harwell, Richard, 869
Harwood, Christopher, 629, 1392
Harwood, James, 45
Harwood, Jos., 1392
Haskins, Benj., 1565
Haskins, Creed, 1313
Haskins, Edward, 1561
Haskins, Thos., 1565
Hatcher, Archibald, 1277
Hatcher, Fredk., 549
Hatcher, Joel, 567.91
Hawke, William, 1665
Hawkins, John, 1252
Hawkins, Joshua, 659
Hawkins, Thos., 1451
Hawkins, William, 811, 1426
Hay, Charles, 301
Hay, John, 1328
Hay, Wm., 1328, 1536
Hayes, James, 1352
Hayes, Winkfield, 922
Haynes, John, 610

Haynes, Joseph, 112, 239
Haynes, Thos., 1574
Haynes, Tom., 1573
Haynes, William, 191, 404.81
Haynie, John, 932
Hays, Ann, 490
Hays, Charles, 1428
Hays, Robt., 1428
Hazard, Ebenezer, 367
Hazleky, Samuel, 879
Hearn, James, 1163
Heath, William, 673
Heaton, Amos, 404.97
Hedges, Ezekiel, representative of, 836
Helm, John, 1252
Helm, Leonard, 567.77
Helm, Leond., 1646
Helm, Lynarigh, 812
Helm, William, 1253
Helphinstine, Peter, 187
Henderson, Daniel, 404.94
Henderson, David (of Augusta Co.), 1087
Henderson, David (of Stafford Co.), 1642
Henderson, J., 1403
Henderson, Nathaniel, 563, 783, 888
Henderson, Richard, and Company, 976
Henderson, Robert, 97, 906
Henderson, Samuel, 1633
Hendrick, John, 320
Hendrick, Solomon, 567.25
Hendrick, William, 1145
Hendrick, Zach., 320
Hendricks, Humphrey, 16
Hendricks, John, 1098
Henley, Charles, 133
Henley, John, 331
Henrico County
    citizens of, 21, 1046, 1149, 1164, 1488, 1678
    committee of, 228
Henry, Jas., 1305
Henry, W., 272
Henry, William, 623, 1132
Henry County, citizens of, 311, 312, 607, 615, 675, 707, 708, 953, 965, 969, 1102, 1229, 1439, 1665, 1676, 1677, 1677 A, 1677 B
Henson, Jesse, 404.110

Henson, William, 404.104
Herbert, William, 45
Herndon, Joseph, 230
Herndon, Zack, 806
Herrin, Jonathan, Sr., 833
Herring, Good., 1199
Herring, Leonard, 1135
Heth, Will, 529
Hewitt, Richard, 186
Hiatt, John, 673, 949
Hibbs, Isaac, 1453
Hickman, George, 285
Hicks, George, 1322, 1573
Hicks, John, 1322, 1573
Hicks, Thomas, 845
Hicks, William, 404.67
Higgin, James, 256
Higgin, Joel, 1393
Higginbotham, Benjamin, 906
Higginbotham, Frederick, 1032
Higginbotham, James, 1032, 1216
Higginbotham, John, 1032
Higginbotham, Moses, 1032
Hight, Richd., 1108
Hill, Pesmith, 1421
Hill, Will., 1114
Hill, William, 1278
Hinson, Elijah, 1474
Hite, Abraham, 404.14
Hite, Abraham, Jr., 98, 115, 116
Hite, Isaac, 907.2, 989, 1015, 1021
Hite, J., 1640
Hite, Jos., 1640
Hite, Thomas, 798
Hix, Daniel, 1001, 1324
Hobb's Hole warehouse, 1507
Hobday, John, 205.1, 248
Hobson, Adcock, 549
Hobson, N., 1598
Hobson, Nichs., 942
Hodges, ———, 1590
Hodges, Ferebee, 381
Hodges, Martha, 443
Hog, Petr., 1135
Hogan, William, 1012
Hoge, Jno., 941
Hogg, James, 97
Hogg, Richard, 1046

525

Hoggar, James, 193
Hoggins, Humphrey, 404.34
Holcombe, Philp., 1480
Holden, Sam., 534
Holding, ———, 1596
Holdsworth, Charles, 1287
Holladay, Jn., 1195
Holland, George, 651, 1107
Holliday, Hezekiah, 224
Holliday, James, 1210
Holliday, Willm., 1210
Holman, Tandy, 906
Holman, Wm., 1296
Holmes, Christian, 1551
Holmes, Joseph, 1586
Holsclaw, Jacob, 1640
Holstein, Stephen, 404.43
Holstein River, citizens on, 35
Holt, David, 1549
Holt, Jas., 1
Holt, John H., 1433
Holt, Joseph, 1009
Holtsclaw, Nathan, 879
Hommel, Peter, 477
Hone, Daniel, 1604
Hone, Eusebeous, 1437
Hooe, Gerard, 572
Hooe, John, 812
Hooe, William, 140
Hooe and Harrisons, 1209
Hook, John, 829, 865
Hoomes, Jno., 1437
Hope, George, 1426
Hopkins, Jno., 1282
Hopkins, Jonathan, 535
Hord, Mordecai, 965
Hore, Elias, 186
Horner, John, 957
Horrell, James, 906
Horrell, Wm., 906
Horsley, Robert, 301
Horton, Beverly, 879
Hounshel, John, 567.64
How, John, 1075
Howard, Richard, 29
Howleson, Chas., 1560
Howse, Lawrence, 983
Hubard, Jno., 914

Hubbard, Hannah, 404.22
Hubbard, Joseph, 504
Hudgins, Mary, 219
Hudgins, William, 219
Hudnall, Richd., 1239
Hudson, John, 1334
Hudson, William, 651
Hudson, Wm., 1311
Hugart, William, 404.44
Hughart, Thos., 1390
Hughes, James, 1571
Hughes, John, 879, 1036, 1380, 1603
Hughes, Th., 1673
Hughes, Thomas, 110
Hughes, William, 977
Hume, Charles, 672
Humphrey, Josa., 948
Humphreys, Joshua, 309
Humphreys, Sarah, 823
Hungate, William, 650
Hunt, ———, 1619
Hunt, Eli, 811
Hunt, George, 932
Hunt, Nathl., 811, 1671
Hunter, Dave, 1020
Hunter, David, 404.152
Hunter, Jam., 975
Hunter, James, 198, 213, 386, 938, 954
Hunter, James, Jr., 938
Hunter, John, 713, 1078, 1430
Hunter, William, 912
Hurall, John, 927
Hurly, Samuel, 119
Hurst, John, 338
Hurt, Elisha, 1453
Hurt, John, 1080
Husband, Thomas, 694
Hutcheson, Ambrose, 1679
Hutchings, John, 746
Hutchings, Leanna, 764
Hutchingson, William, 879
Hutson, Eleanor, 1052
Hyland, Frances, 1000
Hylton, Dan. L., 1536
Hyner, Andw., 1253

## I

Indiana Company, 904; proprietors of, 384
Ingles, W., 1546
Inglis, William, 1547
Ingraham, Richard, 942
Ingram, Samuel, 567.37, 691
Ingram, William, 404.72, 906
Innes, Harry, 1456, 1512, 1621
Irion, Lewis, 952
Irion, Phil. Jacob, 952
Irvine, Margaret, 453
Irving, Charles, 1328, 1536
Irwin, Andrew, 567.82
Irwin, Christopher, 404.33
Irwin, David, 404.128
Isle of Wight County: citizens of, 131; court justices of, 106. See also Newport Parish

## J

Jackman, John, 637
Jackson, Francis, 137
Jackson, Jno., 1702
Jackson, Philip, 903
Jackson, Simon, 1671
Jackson, William, 787
Jackson River lands, citizens of, 899
Jacobs, Thomas, 136
Jaeger, Johannes, 157
James, Henry, 975
James, Jn., 140
James, John, 29
James, John, Jr., 778
James, Richard, 698
James City County, citizens of, 1133. See also Bruton Parish
Jameson, William, 899
Jamison, Edward, 602.1
Jamison, John, 602.1
Jarrett, John, 774
Jarvis, Richd., 677
Jefferson County, citizens of, 1548, 1629, 1640, 1646
Jeffreys, Barnett, 1141
Jenkins, Daniel, 338
Jenkins, William, 651

Jennings, Jonathan, 567.63
Jennings, Wm., 711
Jerdone, Sarah, 1041
Jesse, William, 1252
Jett, Edgar, 939
Jett, Peter, 1099
Jett, Thomas, 359, 1685
Jett, Thos., 1404, 1486
Jinkins, Lewis, 1102
Jinnings, James, 677
John Bolling's warehouse, 487, 603
Johnson, Benjamin, 952, 1138, 1377
Johnson, Christn., 1683
Johnson, Daniel, 879
Johnson, Gideon, 711
Johnson, James, 91, 754
Johnson, John, 906
Johnson, Joseph, 1204
Johnson, Phil. Bud, 446
Johnson, Richard, 782
Johnson, Rubn., 1237
Johnson, Samuel, representative of, 753
Johnson, Tandy, 179
Johnson, Thomas, Jr., 418, 569, 832
Johnson, William, 86, 97, 301, 682, 944
Johnson, Winniford, 968
Johnson, Wm., 1509
Johnston, Ph., 1437
Johnston, Philip, 1027
Johnston, Richd., 1027
Johnston, Robt., 1369
Johnston, William, 56
Johnston, Wm., 181, 1027, 1050
Jones, ———, 1597
Jones, Catesby, 1362
Jones, Catlet, 470, 662
Jones, Daniel, 1628
Jones, Edwd., 1293
Jones, Jas., 1005
Jones, J. G., 116
Jones, Jr., 520
Jones, Jno., 928, 1509
Jones, John, 22, 56, 404.3, 1002, 1511
Jones, John, Jr., 1319
Jones, John Gabriel, 150
Jones, Jos., 1665
Jones, Joseph, 64
Jones, Joshua, 397

Jones, Lew., 1315
Jones, Mary, 331
Jones, Minetree, 504
Jones, Philip, 62
Jones, Richard, Jr., 1180.3, 1403, 1455
Jones, Robt., 1286
Jones, Samford, 1470
Jones, Solomon, 753
Jones, Thomas, 1682
Jones, William, 643, 1513
Jordan, Edwd., 1598
Jordan, Saml., 942
Jordan, Thomas, Jr., 891
Jouett, John, 1705
Joyner, Liam, 1650
Judd, Benjamin, 1413

### K

Kaine, John, 1210
Kasey, James, 1453
Katharine, Francis, 404.93
Kaufman, Jacob, 119
Kearnes, John, 1246
Keeling, Henry, 1238
Keeling, Jacob, 192, 1238
Keeling, Robert, 1593
Keeling, William, 331
Keeling, William, Jr., 331
Keelly, Wm., 1357
Keeney, John, 387
Keesell, George, 742
Keith, Cornelius, 1665
Kelley, James, 404.133
Kelley, Wm., 918
Kelly, George, 1576
Kelly, John, 1511
Kendall, G., 1615
Kendon, Curtis, 1236
Kennedy, William, 601
Kenny, Richard, 1417
Kent, Samuel, 504
Kentucky County, citizens of, 435, 498, 604, 1011, 1167, 1252, 1253, 1253 A, 1253 B
Kercheval, John, 1482
Kerr, David, 498
Kidd, Daniel, 539, 1673

Kidd, Joseph, 1318
Kidd, Samuel, 683
Kidd, William, 479
Kilpatrick, Alexander, 1332, 1558
Kincade, Wm., 941
Kincannon, James, 368
Kinder, Peter, 899
King, Jno., 1050
King, John, 1084, 1285, 1402, 1539
King, Michael, 1202
King, Miles, 713
King, Richd., 1402
King, Robin, 1402
King, Wil., 648
King, Wm., 1402
King and Queen County, citizens of, 1305, 1392. *See also* Drysdale Parish; Stratton Major Parish
King George County, citizens of, 56, 140 A, 332, 364, 466, 467, 1281, 1497. *See also* Hanover Parish
King William County, citizens of, 863, 1383, 1402
Kinkade, Robert, 975
Kinkead, John, 437
Kinkeade, John, 1508
Kirk, James, 726, 770
Kirk, Jeremiah, 1099
Kirkpatrick, Samuel, 1444
Kittering, Jacob, 1546
Knibb, John, 246, 247
Knight, Wm., 847
Kreggar, William, 429
Kuling, Geo., 1311
Kyle, Joseph, 1034

### L

Lacey, William, 1450
Lackay, Thomas, 1442
Lacy, Elliott, 785
Lacy, Noah, 1277
Ladd, James, 1359
Laffoon, Matthew, 1665
Lafong, George, 1003
Lamb, James, 1706
Lambert, Chas., 1340
Lambert, Jonathan, 295

Lamkin, Peter, 1403
Lancaster County, citizens of, 1051, 1304. *See also* Christ Church Parish
Lane, Gilman, 757
Lane, Lambert, 404.106
Lane, William, 404.105, 404.146, 622.10
Langhorn, Maurice, 1311
Langhorne, Jno., 549
Langley, Lemuel, 677
Langley, Robert, 330, 1593
Lanibrand, John, 923
Lankey, Rich., 124
Lapsley, John, 1125
Larkin, Robert, 337
Lashbrooks, John, 879
Latham, John, 399, 404.98
Latimer, Geo., 1426
Laurel Hill, citizens of, 54
Laury, Thomas, 961
Law, Wm., 1102
Lawless, Wm., 261
Lawrence, Wm., 280
Lawson, Anthony, 1247
Lawson, Daniel, 120
Lawson, Henry, 567.1
Lawson, Jno., 1613
Lawson, Ro., 529, 1480
Lawson, Thomas, 245
Lawson, Will, 484
Lawson, William, 424
Layne, John, 1170
Layne, Wm., 1078
Leak, Mask, 1014
Lebo, Isaac, 867
Lee, Hancock, 1065
Lee, Jn., 1515
Lee, Lewis, 478
Lee, Richard Evers, 1534
Leftwich, W., 1653
Leg, Wm., 879
Leigh, Richd., 1305
Leitch, David, 1556
Leland, John, 375
Lello, John, 545
Lenox, Walter, 1004
Leonard, Noble, 1521, 1655
Leslie, Patrick, 70
Lester, Dionysius, 240

Lester, Thomas, 338
Leston, Edward, 809
Lewis, Aaron, 602.1
Lewis, Addison, 149
Lewis, Andrew, 68
Lewis, Charles, 183
Lewis, Charles, Jr., 183
Lewis, Charles L., 155
Lewis, Edward, 475
Lewis, Fielding, 815, 929
Lewis, G. R., 1653
Lewis, Jacob, 644
Lewis, John, 404.19, 772, 785
Lewis, Jona., Jr., 155
Lewis, Joseph, 750
Lewis, Thomas, 300, 1682
Lewis, Thos., 221
Lewis, William, 473
Lewis, Z., 446
Liggan, Jno., 1277
Liggons, ———, 1669
Light, Peter, 188
Lightburne, Henry, 56
Lightburne, Richard, 56
Lillaston, Thos., 1430
Lilly, Armiger, 981
Linch, Christo., 1230
Lincoln County, citizens of, 1548, 1629, 1640
Lindsay, Isaac, 404.124
Lindsay, John, 151
Linthicum, Thos., 682
Lithgow, Alex., 1234
Lithgow, Alexander, 172
Little, Abraham, 1280
Little, Andrew, 898
Little, Valentine, 567.69, 622.9
Littlepage, John Carter, 1452
Littleton Parish (Cumberland Co.): citizens of, 1104, 1104 A, 1348, 1348 A–1348 C; vestry of, 549
Livingston, Samuel, 661
Liviston, John, 117
Lobban, John, 1302
Lockett, Pleasant, 436
Lockridge, Andr., 1390
Logan, Benjamin, 567.78
Logan, Hugh, 1034

Logan, John, 75
Logwood, Thomas, 404.54, 562, 840, 865
Long, Alexr., 1087
Long, Dorothy, 1310
Long, Francis, 1087
Long, John, 1027
Long, Robert, 303
Long, William, 484
Longest, Anne, 219
Lonsdale, William, 19
Looney, John, 511
Loudoun County, citizens of, 70, 546, 739, 1037, 1037 A, 1076, 1520, 1520 A–1520 G, 1521, 1521 A, 1654, 1655, 1655 A
Louisa County: citizens of, 920, 1294, 1297, 1683, 1702; tax commissioners of, 1557
Love, A., 1556
Love, Alexander, 995
Love, Philip, 567.19
Love, Phillip, 345
Love, William, 937
Lovell, John, 1099
Lovell, Wm., 1677
Loving, William, 292, 293
Loving, Wm., 651.1, 1432
Lowery, Samuel, 753
Lowry, Patrick, 404.9
Loyal, Paul, 746
Loyall, Paul, 1314, 1576
Loyd, John, 650
Lucas, John, 29
Lucas, Robert, 49
Lucas, William, 29, 1429
Lumpkin, Thomas, 132
Lumsdon, George, 583
Lunenburg County: citizens of, 13, 181, 236, 273, 318, 553, 1108, 1598; court of, 318, 1180.5. *See also* Cumberland Parish
Lush, Andrew, 58
Lutheran church ([Hebron], Culpeper Co.), members of, 157
Luttrall, John, 97
Luttrell, Simon, 1185
Lyell, Fenwick, 108
Lyle, Hugh, 164

Lyle, James, 1070, 1209.1, 1405, 1556, 1564
Lyle, John, 41, 355, 1218, 1425
Lyle, Robert, 1614
Lyle, Sal., 1224
Lyle, William, 861
Lynch, Charles, 25, 323, 792, 1330
Lynch, Chas., 1214
Lynch, John, 1652
Lyne, Edmd., 965
Lyne, Geo., 92, 1392
Lyne, Henry, 965
Lyne, John, 92
Lynn, Adam, 847
Lyon, James, 567.7
Lyons, Peter, 997

## M

McAfee, James, 1640
McBrayers, Wm., 1640
M'Cabe, Henry, 1555
McCalester, James, 1337
McCarty, Charles, 678
M'Carty, James, 890
M'Carty, Robert, 906
McCaul, George, 1580
McCauley, Campbell, 1299
M'Clain, Joseph, representative of, 817
M'Clanahan, Absalom, 404.87
M'Clanahan, John, 404.83
M'Clannahan, William, 302
McClean, John, 479
McClennedain, Alexander, 694
M'Clern, James, 404.137
McClintog, Wm., 959
M'Cockle, James, 404.64
McConnie, Christopher, 1623
McCord, Willm., 1334
M'Cormick, Joseph, 404.61
McCraskin, Cyrus, 1253
McCreery, John, 1390
M'Cue, William, 351
M'Donald, James, 567.27
McDowell, Saml., 221
McEckean, William, 1163
M'Elheney, Robert, 567.87
McElheny, John, 484

M'Farland, James, 404.153
Mcfarland, John, 404.125, 1214
Mcfarland, John M., 1214
McFarley, Wm., 1069
M'Farlin, William, 214
Mcfaron, Thomas, 1248
M'Farren, Martin, 1034
M'Gaffock, James, 368
M'Gahey, Manasses, 74
McGary, Hugh, 514
McGee, Wm., 1218
McGehee, Jacob, 1306
M'Gregor, Walter, 879
M'Grew, Robert, representative of, 753
McGuire, Edward, 1586
M'Guire, John, 177
M'Harg, Ebenezer, 1150
McIlvain, Moses, 1340
McIlvain, Samuel, 1340
M'Kain, James, 567.55
M'Kay, Jonathan, 389
McKenney, John, 1635
McKenny, Francis, 54
M'Kenny, John, 281
M'Kenzie, Daniel, 404.31
MacKenzie, Wm., 626, 1070
McKeund, Jno., 626
McKewn, Mich., 1425
M'Kinney, Charles, 613
McKinney, John, 1374
M'Kinny, John, 1492
M'Knight, William, 906
McLane, Daniel, 138
M'Lane, James, 906
McLane, John, 138
Maclin, ———, 1688
M'Millian, John, 1544
McNeelly, Wm., 1643
McNees, James, Sr., 117
McNiell, Daniel, 1357
M'Nutt, Robert, 567.35
Macon, William, 1408
M'Reynolds, Joseph, 567.76
M'Roberts, Alexander, 978, 1034
M'Roberts, Samuel, 1034
McWilliams, William, 1404
McWilliams, Wm., 1486
Madison, James, 1002

Madison, John, 680
Madison, Thomas, 608
Madison, Thos., 1643
Magann, Merritt, 301
Maget, Wm., 1515
Mahon, John, 1146
Mallory, Thos., 1605
Maloney, Daniel, 70
Manchester
  citizens of, 626, 1070
    and merchants of, 1556
  trustees of, 229, 1405
Manchester Parish (Chesterfield Co.),
  citizens of, 760
Manley, John, 1108
Mann, Field, 1072
Mannefee, Jones, 1043
Manning, Mary, 1225
Mara, Francis, 1673
Marable, Matthew, 690
Marchant, Daniel, 210, 219
Marchant, Elisha, 210, 219
Märck, Ulric, 1694
Markham, Bernd., 1549
Markham, Vincent, 1561
Markland, William, 404.60
Marks, Isaiah, 1269
Marks, John, 183
Marrs, Henry Munday, 431
Marsden and Smyth, 1328
Marshall, Geo., 1099
Marshall, Henry, 711
Marshall, John, 1182
Marshall, Thomas, 1517
Marshall, Wm., 520
Martain, William, Jr., 1228
Martain, William, Sr., 1228
Martin, Alex., 1471
Martin, Alexander, 1478
Martin, Benjamin, 682
Martin, Charles, 1065
Martin, Geo., 438
Martin, Henry, 1098
Martin, Hugh, 852
Martin, James, 1033
Martin, John, 686, 877, 907.12
Martin, Jonathan, 404.68
Martin, Joseph, 567.5

Martin, Samuel, 404.131
Martin, Thomas Bryan, 1086
Martin, William, 567.9, 852
Martinsburg, citizens of, 278, 1221
Marys, Joseph, 132
Mason, George, 871
Mason, James, 567.20
Mason, Thompson, 1564
Masten, Thos., 448
Masters, Benja., 230
Masters, Edward, 906
Masters, James, 906
Masters, William, 230
Mathews, George, 694, 1484
Mathews, Samp., 948
Matthews, ———, 1634
Matthews, Anne, 489
Matthews, Beverly, 879
Matthews, George, 1447
Matthews, Samp., 221
Matthews, Sampson, 369, 1390, 1391
Matthews, Thos., 1215
Mattocks, Notley, 1024, 1025
Maupin, Gabriel, 154, 795
Maury, James, 1647
Maxey, Josiah, 128
Maximillian, John, 812
Maxwell, James, 361
May, John, 141, 1154, 1183, 1620
May, Sam., 941
Mayle, Lydia, 304
Mayo, ———, 1692
Mayo, John, 225, 1054, 1288, 1376, 1487, 1575
Mayo, John, Jr., 1678
Mayo, Joseph, 1622
Mayo, Thos., 1622
Mays, David, 1053
Meacom, Ann, 1303
Meacom, James, 1303
Meacom, John, 1303
Meacom, Samuel, 1303
Meacom, Sylvia, 1303
Meacom, Thomas, 1303
Mead, W., 1653
Meade, John, 1343, 1523
Meade, William, 404.40
Meador, Jesse, 951

Meadow, Israel, 1450
Meads, Ebenezer, 567.30
Mecklenburg County, citizens of, 29, 66, 181, 236, 280, 337, 422, 922, 922 A, 1295. See also Quakers
Mecklenburg Town (Shepherdstown), citizens of, 647
Meenes, Benjamin, 117
Menefee, George, 1676
Menefee, William, Sr., 1676
Mennefee, John, 1333
Mental hospital (Williamsburg), directors of, 749, 982, 1160, 1271
Mercer, ———, executors of, 1660
Mercer, Hugh, trustees of, 938
Mercer, J. S., 815
Meredith, Elisha, 1383
Meredith, John, 1383
Meredith, S., 715
Meriwether, Francis, 547, 1158
Meriwether, Nicholas, 1252
Meriwether, Thos., 308
Meriwether's warehouse, 487, 515, 718
Merry, William, 1287
Methodist church, 173
Micou, Paul, 151
Middlesex County, citizens of, 1412, 1413
Milby, Ellinah, 491
Miles, Joseph, 274, 599
Military officers, 565, 759. See also Continental army
 army, 310
 artillery, 711, 986
  and infantry, 484
 marine corps, 308
 navy, 862
 state battalion, 1517
 state garrison, 1092
Militia. See names of counties
Miller, Alexander, 852
Miller, Anthony, 753
Miller, George, 404.132
Miller, James, 381, 1404, 1486
Miller, Jean, 714
Miller, Jno., 1111
Miller, Samuel, estate of, 1599
Miller, Simon, 665, 1681
Miller, Simon, Jr., 865

Miller, William, 1034
Mills, Edmund, 1152
Millyard, Sarah, 158
Milmer, Thomas, 1231
Milum, William, 404.89
Minefee, John, 953
Minefee, William, 953
Minor, John, 70, 520, 736, 1520
Minter, George, 1517
Miskell, Newman, 156
Miskell, William, 156
Mitchell, David, 1525
Mitchell, James, 1305
Mitchell, Joseph, 146
Mitchell, Mildred, 921
Mitchell, Robt., 1571
Mitchell, Thomas, 975
Mitchell, Thos., 280
Mitchell, William, 404.102, 1200, 1345
Moffat (Moffett?), George, 50
Moffatt, Geo., 1050
Moffett, George, 1375, 1390
Moffett, Josiah, 745
Monongalia County, 1675; court of, 807
Monongalia River lands, citizens of, 852
Montague, John, 939
Montague, Philip, 1223
Montague, Thos., 1413
Montague, William, 776
Montgomerie, Samuel, 567.33
Montgomery, Alexr., 440
Montgomery, David, 1025
Montgomery, James, 448, 975
Montgomery, John, 1215
Montgomery, Thos., 1098
Montgomery County, citizens of, 324, 326, 427, 437, 437 A, 437 B, 438, 438 A, 441, 604, 974, 1214, 1546, 1604
Moody, Edward, 484
Moody, Hannah, 543
Moody, James, 484
Moody, Matthew, 967
Moody, Thomas, 181
Moody, William, 234
Moon, Arch., 1653
Moon, Gideon, 457
Moon, Jacob, 646
Moon, Joseph, 440

Moor, Edward, 937
Moor, George, 465
Moore, Alexander, 1115
Moore, Andrew, 1441
Moore, Elijah, 1012
Moore, Eras., 1318
Moore, Fras., Jr., 1203
Moore, Henly, 907.9
Moore, James, 836
Moore, John, 354, 1033, 1264, 1441
Moore, Saml., 1441
Moore, William, 1464
Moore, Williamson, 1115
Moorefield, Richard, 960
Moorman, James, 1377
Moreton, John, 947
Morgan, ———, 1689
Morgan, Daniel, 220, 855
Morgan, Danl., 973
Morgan, Edw., 1323
Morgan, John, 1370, 1527, 1569
Morgan, Nathaniel, 1546
Morleaise, Matthew, 1442
Morret, Nicholas, 627
Morris, Gideon, 404.70
Morris, Joshua, 1237
Morris, Richard, 540
Morrow, Charles, 1424
Morson, Arthur, 937
Mortimer, Ch., 1630
Morton, John, 1490
Morton, Richard, 408
Morton, Sarah, 855
Morton, Wm., 1009
Mosby, Jno., 1620
Mosby, Littlebury, 564
Mosby, William, 1449
Moseley, Basett, 677
Moseley, Bassett, 43
Moseley, Blackman, 1182, 1549, 1594
Moseley, Edward Hack, Jr., 148
Moses, Daniel, 1560
Moses, William, 1560
Moss, Frederick, 754, 755
Moss, Hugh, 785
Moss, Nat., 1295
Motley Edwin, 1059
Mottley, Joel, 579

Mountcastle, Benja., 1287
Mountjoy, Alvin, 936
Mountjoy, John, 1038
Mugg, Notley, representative of, 836
Muhlenberg, P., 1113, 1606
Muhollen, Thomas, 959
Muir, John, 848
Muldrough, John, 567.14
Mulhey, Jonathan, 404.114
Mulhey, Philip, Jr., 404.112
Mulhey, Philip, Sr., 404.111
Munford, Edw., 579
Munford, Md., 1359
Munford, Thomas Bolling, 1180.4
Murchie, John, 1070, 1556
Murdaugh, James, 1201
Murphey, James, 1329
Murphey, Lewis, 879
Murphey, Michael, 894
Murphey, Patrick, 404.45
Murray, Abraham, 651
Murray, John, 1007
Murray, Richard, 1356
Murrill, John, 1098
Murrill, John, Jr., 1098
Muse, James, 628
Muse, James, Jr., 628
Muse, Nicholas, 628
Muter, George, 732
Myatt, Peter, 137
Myler, James, 190

# N

Nance, Reuben, 1439
Nansemond County, citizens of, 716, 1314. *See also* Upper Parish
Napier, Thos., 155
Nash, John, 1565, 1604
Nash, Tho., 1530
Nash, Thomas, 549
Nathan, Simon, 1367
Neaville, Joseph, 262
Neil, Stephen, 404.24
Neilson, John, 1521, 1655
Nelson, Edward, 1030
Nelson, John, 1008
Nelson, Thomas, 481

Nelson, Thos., 1271
Nelson, William, 686
Netherland, B., 1525
Nettles, Abraham, 1301, 1462
Nettles, William, 404.134
Nevil, James, 1432
Nevill, James, 1216
Nevill, John, 529
Newby, Levi, 1288
Newel, Saml., 75
Newell, Elizabeth, 334
Newell, James, 335, 907.11
Newell, James, Jr., 567.40
Newell, Samuel, estate of, 622.1
New Kent County, citizens of, 1383, 1560
Newman, Abner, 639
Newman, Edmond, 879
Newman, John, 1243
Newman, Jonathan, 1034
Newport, Richard, 1676
Newport Parish (Isle of Wight Co.), citizens of, 77
Newton, Thomas, 1538
Nicholas, George, 1564
Nicholson, Thomas, 910
Nicolson, Henry, 1053, 1588
Nixon, Robert, 1043
Noble, Anthony, 697, 1419
Noble, Anthy., 1337
Noe, Bazil, 803
Noell, Con., 1681
Norfolk (borough): citizens of, 243, 350, 1530; mayor, aldermen, and councilmen of, 243; merchants and traders of, 1246
Norfolk County. *See also* Elizabeth River Parish; Portsmouth Parish
  citizens of, 43, 716, 1314, 1530
  committee of, 1
Norris, John, 676
North, John, 637
North, Joseph Hollings, 1155
North, William, and Company, 1246
Northampton County, citizens of, 1236, 1615
North Carolina (state), 1471
North Farnham Parish (Richmond Co.): citizens of, 156; wardens of, 678

534

Northumberland County, citizens of, 375, 1239, 1362. *See also* Wicomico Parish
Nottoway Parish (Amelia Co.), vestry of, 1403
Nowland, John, 404.142
Nowland, Thomas, 735
Nowlen, David, 232
Nunn, Thos., 1677
Nutt, George W., 1214
Nutt, Willson, 375
Nuttall, James, Jr., 1227

## O

Obanion, Bryan, III, 1674
O'Cannon, Bryant, 404.5
Ocheltre, Michael, 404.45
O'Connor, John, 280
Oelschlagel, John Erhardt, 426
Ogle, Jacob, representative of, 836
Ogle, Joseph, 836
Ogleby, Thomas, 906
Oglesby, Wm., 272
Ohair, Michael, 567.18
O'Hara, Charles, 429
O'hara, Mary, 1363
Ohio Company, 849
Oldham, Saml., 1020
Oliver, Drury, 651
Omohundro, Richd., 683
Ong, Jeremiah, 1221
Onsby, Arthur, 404.127
Orange County, citizens of, 171, 291, 415, 415 A, 465, 526, 673, 673 A, 806, 923, 949, 1049, 1203, 1429
Osborne's warehouse, 487
Owen, Elisha, 1149
Owen, Hatcher, 1671
Owen, Hobson, 1678
Owen, John, 372
Owen, Richardson, 980
Owen, William, 372, 952, 1671
Owens, Charles, 879
Owens, John, 524
Owin, Jacob, 1413
Owin, Robert, 966

## P

Packer, Augustine, 85
Page, Mann, 926, 1404, 1438, 1448
Page, Mann, Jr., 1184
Page, William, 906
Page's warehouse, 487, 515
Palmoni, Fleming, 261
Pankie, Stephen, Jr., 1258
Paradise, John, 140 A
Parberry, James, 1608
Parham, Lewis, 29
Parishes. *See* names of parishes
Park, Edwd., 1046
Parker, George, 567.65
Parker, John, 1683
Parker, Nicholas, 525
Parker, Robert, 580
Parker, Thomas, 1629
Parkinson, David, 1288
Parramore, Thomas, 748
Parrish, Jolley, 1282
Parrot, Robert, 219
Parry, Joshua, 309
Parsons, James, 208
Parsons, Josiah, 1149
Passons, Edw., 722
Pate, Anthony, 951
Pate, Matthew, 1005
Pate, Thomas, 404.29
Patrick, John, 1469
Patterson, James, 725
Patterson, R., 1525
Patterson, Wm., 164, 1337
Paulett, Jesse, 1702
Payne, ———, 1707
Payne, Archer, 570
Payne, John, Jr., 617
Payton, Wm., 1614
Peachey, Roger, 1293
Peachey, Thomas G., 62
Peachey, Thomas Griffin, 1472
Peachey, Wm., 1470
Peak, James, 105
Peak, John, 105
Pearson, Joseph, 907.3
Pearson, Moses, 533
Peatt, Robert, 836

Peay, Stephen, 1077
Peck, Benjamin, 216
Peebles, Jesse, 488
Peed, John, 456
Peed, Philip, 210, 219
Pelham, Peter, 1165
Pemberton, ———, 1578
Pemberton, John, 415
Pendleton, Edmd., 1437
Pendleton, Edmd., Jr., 1437
Pendleton, Edmund, 301, 997, 1435
Pendleton, Henry, 657
Pendleton, John, 1074, 1605
Pendleton, Nathaniel, 1373
Pendleton, Philip, 190
Penet, Wendel, and Company, 979
Penn, Gabl., 1026, 1432
Penn, John, 651.2
Pennington, Jack, 1322
Penticost, Dorsey, 554
Peoples, William, 567.67
Perkins, William, 1056
Perrin, Joseph, 567.60
Person, Colin, 1323
Petersburg, citizens of, 1114, 1701
Peterson, Edward, 809; representative of, 753
Petit, George, 699
Pettenson, William, 1425
Petters, Junis, 739
Peyton, Craven, 671, 1067
Peyton, Ephraim, 103
Peyton, Henry, 189
Phelps, John, 404.85
Philips, Thomas, 353
Phillips, P., 1297
Phripp, Matthew, 746, 824
Pickens, Samuel, 661
Pickett, Jeremiah, 1033
Pickett, Martin, 1105
Pigg, James, 141
Pigg, William, 141
Piner, John, 939
Pinkney, John, 226
Piper, Wm., 686
Pitcher, Mason, 1235
Pitman, William, 932
Pitney, Nathll., 973

Pittsylvania County, citizens of, 119, 119 A, 506, 602, 675, 957, 1442
Pleasants, Thomas, Jr., 750
Poage, John, 1240, 1440
Poage, Robert, 1433
Poage, Tho., 1648
Poage, William, 907.14
Pocahontas (Chesterfield Co.), citizens of, 1114
Pointer, William, 651, 1347
Pollard, Ben., 308
Pollard, George, 320
Pollard, John, 959
Pollard, William, 1168
Pollock, Oliver, 1543
Polly, Joseph, 1604
Polly, William, 1604
Pomfrett, John, 1402
Poole, Thos., 1676
Pope, Ben, 1646
Pope, John, 1532
Pope, Matt., 1183
Pope, W., 1646
Pope, William, 1253
Porch, Solomon, 404.1
Porter, Ben., 526
Porter, Chs., 1400
Porter, David, 676
Porter, Hugh, 124
Porter, Samuel, 1035
Porter, Thos., 1255
Porterfield, ———, 1662
Porterfield, Charles, 177
Portlock, Charles, 1318
Portlock, Mathias, 1530
Portlock, Matthew, 1530
Portlock, Saml., 1530
Portlock, Samuel, 669
Port Royal (Caroline Co.): citizens of, 56; tobacco inspectors of, 1651
Portsmouth, merchants and traders of, 1246
Portsmouth Parish (Norfolk Co.), citizens of, 676
Poston, Elias, 944
Potomac River lands, citizens of, 845
Potter, Thomas, 73
Powell, Abraham, 753

Powell, Ambrose, 242
Powell, Anne, 609
Powell, Benjamin, representative of, 753
Powell, Henry, 210
Powell, James, 672
Powell, Jeremiah, 609
Powell, John, 1010
Powell, Lucas, 1216
Powell, Seymour, 382
Powell, Thomas, 651.2
Power, James Collins, 903
Power, Samuel Simmons, 903
Powers, John, 287
Powhatan County, citizens of, 1306
Poythress, Peter, 1680
Prentis, Robert, 1103
Presbyterian church (Hanover Presbytery), members of, 160, 377
Presbyterians, 745
Preston, Robert, 404.56
Preston, William, 31, 731
Price, Barret, 567
Price, Bourne, 1454
Price, Elisha, 1046
Price, James, 1046
Price, Joseph, 522
Price, Merth., 1646
Price, Oliver, 614
Price, Thomas 63, 313, 567.44
Prichard, Samuel, 113
Priggett, Edward, 890
Prince Edward County, citizens of, 1312, 1480, 1565. *See also* Saint Patrick's Parish
Princess Anne County, 1687; citizens of, 716, 778, 1238
Prince William County: Baptist church (Occoquan), members of, 105; citizens of, 189, 812, 1012, 1039, 1204, 1204 A, 1204 B, 1234 1532, 1613; commissioners of the escheated property of, 1443; militia (court-martial) of, 201; tax commissioners of, 1007
Prisoners of war. *See* Saratoga convention troops
Pritchard, Samuel, 144
Pritchett, Lucretia, 89
Pritman, Daniel, 1333

Procter, George, 1049
Proctor, Uriah, 673
Prosser, Tho., 1678
Prosser, Thomas, 1564
Public jail (Williamsburg), criminals in, 196
Pugh Jacob, representative of, 753
Pugh, Joseph, 142, 637
Puller, John, 626
Pulliam, John, 1294
Punter, Henry, 1657
Purcel, Thomas, 879
Purdie, Alexander, 503, 723
Purdie, George, 816
Purkins, William, 1296
Puttett, Matthew, 1238

## Q

Quakers, 818, 1625; of Mecklenburg County, 1359
Quantico warehouse, 1185
Quarles, James, 308, 484
Quarles, John, 705, 1122, 1653
Quarles, Roger, 520, 1393

## R

Rachel, 385
Rachel, Jr., 385
Radors, Jonathan, 725
Rae, Jacob W., 713
Rae, James, 1515
Ragan, Richard, 1135
Ragdale, John, 13
Ragsdale, John, 318
Raine, John, 1153
Raines, John, 822
Rakestraw, Ro., 1022
Ramsay, William, 404.101
Ramsay, Wm., 848
Ramsbottom, Isaac, 1206
Ramscell, ———, 1693
Ramscen, Simon, 1302
Ramsey, Edward, 847
Ramsey, Thomas, 404.135, 841
Randall, Abel, 944
Randolph, Beverley, 578

Randolph, Edm., 1002
Randolph, Edmund, 168
Randolph, Harrison, 149
Randolph, Thomas, 1386
Randolph, Thomas M., 1536
Randolph, Thomas Mann, 993, 1048
Ravenhill, Francis, 142
Rawlings, Margaret, 512
Rawlings, Pemberton, 1011
Rawlings, Robt., 1571
Read, E., 1517
Read, W., 1454
Read, William, 1433
Ready, Isaac, 1587
Records, Charles, 725
Reddy, Sam, 1417
Reed, Cornelius, 430
Reed, Thomas, 903, 1009
Reeves, Richard, 420
Reid, Robert, 1673
Reinhart, George, representative of, 817
Reins, Meredy, 567.28, 907.10
Renard, Richard, 246
Réné, Bryson, and Company, 1661
Rentfre, Joseph, 650
Rentfro, Joshua, 404.42
Reverley, John, 20, 24, 469, 483, 655, 1129, 1381
Reynolds, Hugh, 1442
Reynolds, John, 1210
Rice, Benjamin, 404.125
Rice, Charles, 404.107
Rice, David, 1433
Rice, Henry, 404.99
Rice, John, 404.108
Rice, Nicholas, 404.130
Rice, Samuel, 1306
Rice, Tandy, 682
Rice, William, 404.109
Rice, William, Sr., 404.147
Richards, John, 926, 1404, 1486
Richardson, Abel, 368
Richardson, George, 1700
Richardson, Henry, 404.151
Richardson, James, 404.136
Richardson, John, 1376
Richardson, Joseph, 1648
Richardson, Richd., 1376

Richardson, William, 715
Richey, Charles, 124
Richmond (town)
 citizens of, 1537, 1616
 merchants of, 1328
 and traders of, 1333, 1536
Richmond County, citizens of, 1293, 1470.
 *See also* North Farnham Parish
Ricketts, Stephen, 906
Riddell, James, 1121
Riddell, Susanna, 1088
Riddick, Constantine, 328
Riddick, Henry, 844
Riddick, Josiah, 844, 1407
Riddick, Willis, 844
Riddle, Isaac, 404.73
Ridgway, Richard, 1277
Rigdon, John, 836
Riley, Patrick, 661
Ripley, Andrew, 372
Ripley, Thomas, 372
Ritchie, Archibald, 1058, 1486
Ritchie, William, 1034
Ritson, Thomas, 99
River, Henry, representative of, 753
Rives, Burrell, 1102
Rives, Fred K., 1102
Rives, George, 1286
Roane, Sarah, 343
Roberson, Benj., 1681
Roberts, Benjn., 1252
Roberts, John, 1255
Roberts, Joseph, 1253
Roberts, Pleasant, 62
Roberts, William, 255
Robertson, Alex., 1375
Robertson, Alexander, 694
Robertson, Alexr., 1390
Robertson, Geo., 1549
Robertson, George, 710
Robertson, William, 755, 821
Robertson, William, Jr., 821
Robinet, Jessy, 1248
Robins, Edward, 1236
Robins, Nelson, 1615
Robinson, James, 404.28, 404.65
Robinson, John, administrators of, 868
Robinson, John C., 1279

Robinson, Michael, 1195
Robinson, Nat., 1588
Robinson, William, 960
Rockbridge County: citizens of, 1115, 1428, 1441; justices of 1218, 1224. *See also* Back Creek lands
Rockingham County: citizens of, 998, 999, 1199; court justices of, 684, 1222
Rocky Ridge warehouse, 437, 1157
Rodgers, John, 324, 429, 745
Rodgers, Thomas, 1237
Rogers, Benjamin, 836
Rogers, Hamilton, 745
Rogers, John, 1569
Rogers, Ulysses, 668
Roiston's warehouse. *See* Royston's warehouse
Rollin, James, 356
Ronald, William, 1274
Ronaldson, Patrick, 709
Rose, Dun., 950
Rose, Duncan, 1501
Rose, Hugh, 1169
Rose, John, 289, 1215, 1215
Ross, David, 1109, 1317, 1431, 1536
Ross, David, and Company, 1536
Ross, Edward, 404.78
Ross, John, 809
Ross, William, 567.16
Ross and Shore, 1209.1
Rosser, Jesse, 1533
Roswell, Nehemiah, 465
Rounceval, David, 404.100
Rounceval, Isaac, 404.150
Row, Frances, 485
Rowe, Geo., 918
Rowe, Hansford, 321
Rowland, James, 345
Rowland, Michael, 404.96
Rowland, Thomas, 345, 390, 1648
Rowland, Thos., 1643
Rowland, Zach., 1246
Roy, Richard, 275, 1346
Roy, Richd., 479
Royall, John, 128
Royall, Jos., 1549
Royston, John, 793
Royston's warehouse, 926, 1195

Rozer, Henry, Jr., 193
Rubsamen, Jacob, 626, 1070, 1556
Rucker, Ambrose, 117, 651.2, 1032, 1148
Rucker, Benj., 1148
Ruffin, Edmund, Jr., 454
Ruffing, Benjn., 648
Russel, Joseph, 404.66
Russell, William, 45, 622.7
Russell, Wm., 1113
Russell Parish (Bedford and Campbell cos.), citizens of, 897, 940, 1653
Rust, Benjamin, 1581
Rust, Jeremiah, 567.72
Rutherford, Joseph, 1135
Rutherford, Robert, 260

S

Sadler, Benjamin, Jr., 835
Saint Anne's Parish (Essex Co.), citizens of, 358
St. George, Hamilton Usher, 264
Saint Margaret's Parish (Caroline Co.), citizens of, 1393, 1393 A
Saint Patrick's Parish (Prince Edward Co.), vestry of, 412
Saint Paul's Parish (Hanover Co.), citizens of, 715, 715 A
Salmon, John, 796, 965
Sampson, Richard, 1204
Samuel, Henry, 961
Samuel, John, 57, 806
Sanderson, Hawkins, 1351
Sandford, Daniel, 176
Sandford, Danl., 1
Sandford, Richd., 1078
Sandford, Robert, 415
Sandidge, Joseph, 635
Saratoga convention troops, officers of, 1255
Saunders, John Hyde, 1306
Savage, Littl., 1236, 1615
Savage, Nathaniel Littleton, 211, 252, 674, 1495
Savage, William, 231
Savidge, Mourning, 541
Sawyers James, 404.36
Sawyers William, 368

Sayer, Charles, 378
Sayers, Robert, 1371
Schofield, William, 692
Scott, Chas., 529
Scott, Chs., 1606
Scott, George, 436, 567.58
Scott, James, 872
Scott, John, 381, 507
Scott, Johnny, 1429
Scott, Joseph, 507
Scott, Matthew, 404.51
Scott, Saml., 436
Scott, Thomas, 1421, 1480
Scruggs, Brett, 906
Scruggs, Brittan, 1228
Seabrook, Nich., 1046
Seary, Bartlett, 878
Seawell, ———, 1698
Seawright, Jas., 1635
Seayers, Frances, 1062
Seddon, Thos., 1065
Selden, Elizabeth, 924
Selden, Joseph, 174
Selden, Miles, 149, 1321
Selden, Miles, Jr., 1418, 1564
Seldon, ———, 1691
Selser, Matthias, 1257
Shackelford, John, 811
Shadborne, Amos, 879
Shadford, Geo., 173
Shank, James, 111
Sharp, Thomas, 1283
Shaw, Thomas, 879
Shaw, Thos., 1043
Sheen, John, 637
Shelby, Evan, 46, 368
Shelby, Evan, Jr., 436
Shelden, Thomas, 301
Shelton, John, 1084
Shelton, Richd., 1024, 1025
Shelton, Spencer, 957
Shenandoah County, citizens of, 637
Shepherd, Abraham, 625
Shepherd, Andrew, 1049
Shepherd, David, 1148
Shepherdstown. *See* Mecklenburg Town
Shepperd, William, representative of, 817
Sherwin, Saml., 1403

Shields, Jacob, 70
Shinn, Levi, 283
Shipley, John, 210, 219
Shipley, Joseph, 210, 219
Shipley, Ralph, 219
Shivers, Elisha, representative of, 753
Shockoe warehouse, 1256, 1326
Short, John, 957, 1588
Short, William, Sr., 633
Shouse, Adam, 70
Shultz, Christian, 567.34
Siling, An., 278
Simmons, Joseph, 1152
Simms, Charles, 404.12, 828, 1028.1
Simpson, Alexander, 309
Simpson, John, 567.41
Simpson, Southey, 347, 784
Sims, Mathew, 1028
Simster, John, 1514
Sinclair, Alexander, 369, 694
Sinclair, Alexd., 948
Sinclair, Henry, 22
Singleton, Elizabeth, 853
Singleton, Henry, 908
Singleton, Robt., 181
Skean, Jonathan, 102
Skillideay, George, 124
Skillum, Geo., 1643
Skinker, J., 140 A
Slater, Foray, 1140
Slaughter, George, 30
Slaughter, John, 426
Slaughter, Robert, 787
Slaughter, Thomas, 125
Smelly, John, 39
Smith, Charles, 1334
Smith, Conrod, 404.21
Smith, Daniel, 112, 404.79
Smith, David, 404.75
Smith, Edward, 324
Smith, Edwd., 1586
Smith, Ezekiel, 511
Smith, Franklin, 1280
Smith, Griffin, 534
Smith, Isaac, 205, 212, 276
Smith, James, 352, 404.143, 532, 1491
Smith, John, 44, 112, 404.77, 925, 973, 1149; representative of, 817

Smith, John, Jr., 1470
Smith, John Blair, 1565
Smith, Johnston, 906
Smith, Lawe., 1183
Smith, Maurice, 1223
Smith, Nicholas, 404.6
Smith, Richmond, 1476
Smith, Robert, 1572
Smith, Robt., 931
Smith, Thomas, 301, 404.141, 1089, 1389, 1562
Smith, Thoroughgood, 212, 472
Smith, Thoroughgood, and Company, 284
Smith, William, 10, 307, 325, 1100, 1245
Smith, Willim., 1417
Smith, Willm., 1184
Smith, Wm., 156
Smyth, Ad., 1357
Smyth, Adam, 222
Smyth, Rd., 1643
Snickers, Ed., 925
Snickers, Edward, 855
Snodgrass, Jn., Sr., 164
Somersville, James, 1209.1
Somerville, James, 1111
Sommerville, Joseph, 1208
Sorsby, Stephen, 1515
South, John, 860
South, John, Sr., 1011
Southall, Turner, 233, 1128, 1260
Southampton County, citizens of, 648, 771, 1323, 1323 A, 1323 B
Southard, Benja., 338
Southard, Lawrence, 1204
South Quay warehouse, 717
Speed, Ja., 1022, 1237, 1315
Speed, Jas., 1620
Spencer, Edward, 787
Spencer, Tho., Jr., 1315
Spilman, Jos., 1474
Spivy, Benja., 771
Spotsylvania County: citizens of, 82, 230, 230 A–230 F, 446, 447, 455, 476, 1065, 1065 A, 1065 B, 1111, 1130; magistrates of, 1184
Spratley, Wm., 1666
Springer, Joab, 404.113
Springstone, Peter, 1280

Stabler, Edw., 1625
Stabler, Edwd., 1701
Stadler, John, 734
Stafford County: citizens of, 140, 468, 936, 954, 955, 972, 1038, 1065, 1065 A, 1065 B, 1233, 1339, 1474, 1474 A, 1474 B, 1642; justices of, 1338
Stanhope, William, 916
Stanhope, Wm., 1520
Stark, W., 1318
Starke, Johne, 715
Starke, Joseph, 585
Starr, John, 1453
Staunton, citizens of, 846, 948, 1673
Stead, John, 1588
Steel, Francis, 906
Steel, James, 567.57
Steel, Jas , 1635
Steel, Lorton, 1546
Steel, Thos., 1441
Stephen, Adam, 697, 1419
Stephen, Andrew, 526
Stephen, Robert, 1020
Stephens, John, 48
Stephens, Richard, Jr., 502
Stephenson, Robert, 567.85
Stephinson, Charles, 836
Sterneighter, Henry, representative of, 836
Sterns, Jacob, 567.38
Stevens, James, 651.1, 906
Stevens, Munford, 242
Stevens, Smyth, 1344
Stevenson, William, 465
Steward, John, 1195
Steward, Walter, 135
Stewart, Alexander, 18, 1244
Stewart, James, 1140
Stewart, Jane, 1212
Stewart, John, 429, 519, 1369
Stewart, Raleigh, 138
Stewart, Ralph, 492, 852
Stewart, Robert, 404.74
Stewart, Wm., 1140
Stith, John, 1574
Stith, Richard, 1653
Stith, W., 1573, 1574
Stith, Will., Jr., 1574
Stockton, Thos., 1334

541

Stoff, Benjamin, 430
Stokes, Hy., 942
Stokes, Hy., Jr., 942
Stone, Simon, 1593
Storey, Stephen, 430
Storm, Edward G., 1238
Stout, Daniel, 960
Strange, John, 682
Stratton, John, 688
Stratton Major Parish (King and Queen Co.), citizens of, 92
Street, Anthy., 1598
Strother, John, 426
Stroud, Joseph, 461
Stuart, Jno., 1439
Stubblefield, Beverly, 651
Sturdivant, Daniel, 927
Suffolk, citizens of, 425
Suggett, James, 175
Sullivan, Daniel, 1646
Sullivant, Clement, 1263
Sullivant, Thomas, 730
Summervill, R., 57
Surmerman, George, 661
Surry County, citizens of, 1515, 1666
Sussex County, citizens of, 180, 488. *See also* Albemarle Parish
Suttle, William, 879
Sutton, John, 1325
Swan, John, 1485
Swearenger, John, Sr., 567.90
Swearingen, Sarah, 970
Swearingen, Thomas, Jr., 1019
Sydebotham, Will., 193
Sydnor, Giles, 360
Sydnor, Jno., 1293
Sydnor, John, 678
Sydnor, Wm., 1051
Syme, J., 1509, 1605

### T

Tabb, John, 1620
Tabb, Thomas, 318
Talbot, David G., 1653
Talbot, Isham, 404.47
Talbot, Thomas, 43
Talbot, William, 79
Taliaferro, John, 772
Taliaferro, Richard, 906
Taliaferro, Samuel, 928
Taliaferro, Walker, 520
Taliaferro, Zach., 1451
Talley, Nathaniel, 1436, 1489
Tambrough, Thomas, 404.23
Tandy, Smyth, 195, 1254
Tanford, Patr., 628
Tankard, Step., 1616
Tankard, Steph., 1533
Tankard, Stephen, 824
Tankersley, Richd., 292, 293, 1024, 1025, 1026
Tankey, Richd., 377
Tarny, Tho., 1038
Tate, Caleb, 953, 1494
Tate, Henry, 1230
Tate, Jesse, 1681
Tatum, Josiah, 1386
Tayler, Jos., 1488
Taylor, ———, 1658
Taylor, Francis, 1696
Taylor, Fras., 1255
Taylor, George, 787
Taylor, Henry, 725
Taylor, Isaac, 278
Taylor, James, 349, 526, 746, 1377
Taylor, John, 504, 1435
Taylor, Richard, 651, 1175
Taylor, Robert, 1441
Taylor, Wm., 318, 375, 960, 1108
Tebbs, Foushee, 812, 946, 1007, 1039
Tebbs, William, 1234
Tedford, Robert, 1428
Telford, Andrew, 1361
Telford, James, 1361
Temple, John, 590
Temple, L., 1393
Ternan, Patrick, 1221
Terrell, Benjamin, 1294
Terrell, Robt., 939
Terrell, William, 414
Terrill, Harry, 1364
Terrill, John, 526
Terrill, Robert, 672
Terry, Stephen, 521, 679, 1331
Terry, William, 6

Terry, Wm., 811
Thilman, Paul, 804
Thomas, Ben., 1288
Thomas, Benjamin, 404.5
Thomas, Charles, 1314
Thomas, Isaac, 263, 370
Thomas, James, 1171
Thomas, John, 923
Thomas, Joseph, 641
Thomas, Rees, 1197, 1388
Thomas, Richard, 567.83
Thomas, Robt., 1203
Thomas, Rowland, 465
Thomas, Wm., 1037
Thomasson, William, 654
Thompson, A., 221
Thompson, Anne, 1519
Thompson, Isaac, 381
Thompson, Ja., 436
Thompson, Roger, 1061, 1132
Thompson, Samuel, 119
Thompson, William, 731
Thomson, John, 1701
Thomson, Joseph, 1702
Thomson, Moses, 139
Thomson, Robert, 317
Thomson, Roger, 623
Thorn, Michael, 1612
Thornburg, Benjamin, 646
Thornhill, Wm., 1453
Thornton, Bartholomew, 498
Thornton, Daniel, 642
Thornton, F., 140, 1497
Thornton, Fra., 929
Thornton, Geo., 929, 1184
Thornton, George, 854
Thornton, James, 780, 781
Thornton, Jeremiah, 1219
Thornton, John, 140 A
Thornton, William, 324
Thorp, Fran., 1454
Thorp, John, 1259
Threlkeld, Elijah, 1038
Throckmorton, Mordecai, 1227
Thrower, Christopher, 1279
Thrower, Xpher, 1588
Thunley, Richard, 1012

Tillotson Parish (Buckingham Co.), citizens of, 931
Timberlake, Philip, 574
Tincher, Francis, 317
Tindall, Thos., 1622
Tinsley, William, 651.2
Tinsly, Joshua, 664
Tipton, William, 1342
Tobacco
    inspectors for, 42, 71, 487, 515, 560, 603, 717, 718, 926, 927, 1064, 1157, 1185, 1195, 1256, 1326, 1327, 1507, 1651
    planters and merchants of, 750
    warehouses for (*see also* names of warehouses)
        proprietors of, 1094, 1404, 1486, 1623
Todd, John, 160, 1683
Todd, John, Jr., 1270
Todd, Levi, 907.15, 1525
Todd, Samuel, 151
Todd, William, 935, 1404
Tollers, John, 1622
Tolly, Daniel, 661
Tomer, Thomas, 381
Tomkins, Francis, 914
Tomlin, Walker, 1601
Tomlinson, Benja., 942, 1108
Tomlinson, Samuel, representative of, 817
Tompkins, Benja., 1393
Tompkins, Bennett, 38, 721
Tompkins, John, 721
Tompkins, Ro., 1393
Towles, O., 446, 1606
Towles, Thomas, 446
Townes, W., 199
Trabue, James, 1540
Transylvania, citizens of, 26
Traverse, Daniel, 954
Travis, Champion, 96
Trebell, William, 234
Tredley, Michael, 381
Tremble, John, 1224
Trent, Alex., 1556
Trent, Alexr., 1405
Trent, Thomas, 1101
Triplett, Francis, 1448

Triplett, James, 1245
Triplett, Thomas, 1078
Trucker, William, 651
Truss, Gideon, 305
Truss, Josiah, 306
Tucker, Francis, 1569
Tucker, Joanna, 747
Tucker, Matthew, Jr., 579
Tucker, Robert, 605, 892
Tucker, St. George, 917
Tucker, Travis, 971, 994
Tuggle, Griffen, 1413
Tunstall, Will, 965
Turberville, John, 1493
Turbyfill, John, Sr., 633
Turner, James, 6
Turner, John Farbush, 740
Turner, Josiah, 1677
Turner, Robt. Armstrong, 959
Turner, Thomas, 77
Turner, Thos., 1323
Turner, William, 77
Turner, William, Jr., 1288
Turney, Peter, 567.88
Turpin, Moses, 1450
Turpin, Thomas, 1632
Tuttle, James, 567.25, 886
Twigs, Js., 1599
Tyger's (Tygart's) Valley, citizens of, 138, 139, 433, 852
Tyler, Charles, 906
Tyler, Daniel, 906
Tyler, John, 906
Tyler, John, Jr., 1039
Tyler, Thomas G., 1040
Tyler, William, 801
Tyson, Nathaniel, 249

## U

Underhill, William, 568
Underwood, John, 1134
Unwon, William, 137
Upper Parish (Nansemond Co.), citizens of, 844
Upshur, Abel, 1650
Upshur, Arthur, 204, 254

Urie, William, 1006
Urquhart, Willm., 648

## V

Vaiden, Joseph, 1287
Vanbibber, Abraham, 462
Vance, David, 1525
Vance, Jacob, 890
Vance, Robt., 1208
Varner, Hugh, 164, 1337
Vaughan, ———, 1638
Vaughan, Bland, 1033
Vaughan, Craddock, 942
Vaughan, David, 1278
Vaughan, John, 1550
Vaughan, Thomas, 128
Vaughan, Thos., 771
Veale, Saml., 676
Veale, Samuel, 1291
Veale, Thomas, 545, 873
Venable, John, 1377
Venable, Nath., 1488
Venable, Nathaniel, 439
Venable, Samuel, 1475
Vestal, Ann, 1672
Vestal, Hannah, 1672
Viney, Bartholomew, representative of, 753
Virginia Auditors of Public Accounts, 950, 1178
Virginia Board of War, 1174
Virginia Commissioners of the Navy, 596
Virginia commissioners to settle claims for unpatented lands, 1126
Virginia Continental line. *See* Continental army; Military officers
Virginia Directors of Public Buildings, 1128, 1260, 1566
Voss, Edward, 298, 660, 907.4
Vowle, Tho., 936

## W

Waddill, Edward, 1560
Waddy, S., Jr., 1111
Wade, Andrew, 128
Wade, James, 957
Wade, Pearce, 301

Wade, Richard, 1490
Waggoner, Andrew, 215
Wales, Andw., 1612
Walker, Charles, 415
Walker, James, 567.49
Walker, Jams., Jr., 1248
Walker, Jeremiah, 534, 810, 958, 1194
Walker, John, 440, 567.24, 885
Walker, Samuel, 1034
Walker, Samuel, Jr., 1163
Walker, Thomas, 724, 738, 1439
Walker, Thomas, Jr., 1066
Walker, William, 265
Wallace, Andrew, 404.32
Wallace, Caleb, 160, 1021, 1433
Wallace, David, 404.41
Wallace, Hugh, 581, 1188. See also Wallis, Hugh
Waller, Edw., 337
Waller, Geo., 1677
Wallis, Hugh, 1090, 1309. See also Wallace, Hugh
Wallore, John, 1251
Walton, George, 813
Walton, Henry, 1013
Walton, Joseph, 813
Walton, Robt., 1313
Walton, Sherwood, 813
Walton, Simeon, 1194
Walton, William, 813, 1134
Ward, Jacob, 242
Ward, John, 797, 1411
Ward, William, 1163
Ware, Edward, 906
Ware, John, 1296
Ware, Nelson, 1012
Warner, Daniel, 288
Warrasqueake Bay warehouses, 71
Warwick, Abram, 1451
Warwick County, citizens of, 1120
Washburn, Charles, 286
Washington, ———, 1602
Washington, Bailey, 956
Washington, Chas., 815, 929
Washington, John, 140, 686
Washington, Samuel, 260, 772
Washington, Thacker, 1497
Washington, Wm., 1497

Washington County: citizens of, 324, 327, 363, 427, 436, 436 A–436 C, 437, 437 A, 437 B, 438, 438 A, 602.1, 602.1 A, 602.1 B, 604, 1511, 1511 A, 1546; court, members of, 409, 448
Washington Parish (Westmoreland Co.), citizens of, 686
Waterson, Henry, 47
Watkins, George, 130, 1611
Watkins, Henry, 1565
Watkins, Joseph, 612
Watkins, Robert, 235
Watkins, Thomas, 814
Watkins, William, 593
Watson, Christopher, 379, 393
Watson, Jesse, 1569
Watson, Joseph, 1376
Wattaugh River, citizens owning land on, 35
Watts, John, 81, 927
Watts, William, 951
Watts, Wm., 1480
Wayland, Adam, 157
Wayte, James, 1429
Webb, Edmund, 1013
Webb, Geo., 1002
Webb, George, 1177
Weber, Johannes, 157
Webley, Mary, 123
Webster, David, 1296
Weedon, G., 938
Weir, George, 1115
Weldie, William, 839
Wellburn, William, 1395
Wells, Abner, 273
Wells, Jos., 1594
Welsh, John, 1192
Welt, George, 301
Wertmiller, John, 845
West, Drury, 1387
West, Edward, 1110
West, John, Jr., 194, 1208
West, Richard, 1351
Westall, Hen., 1204
West Augusta District: citizens of, committee of, 163
Western lands, citizens of, 440, 722, 1357, 1620

Westfall, George, 138, 139, 433
Westfall, Wm., 433
Westmoreland County, citizens of, 56, 332, 719, 1281, 1497. *See also* Cople Parish; Washington Parish
Weylie, John, 1037
Whalen, James, 1059
Whaley, John, 1037
Wharton, John, 1014
Wheeler, Benjamin Dodd, 404.15
White, Alex., 925, 1482
White, Ambrose, 1059, 1275
White, Chilion, 1059
White, Epa., 128
White, Geo., 140 A
White, James, 879
White, John, 434, 733, 851
White, Robert, 827
White, Robt., 1482
White, Tho., 1702
White, Thos., 1234
White, William, 567.26
White, William, Jr., 1297
White, Wm., 1533
Whitehead, Grizzel, 589
Whiting, John, 914, 1227
Whiting, Kemp, 209
Whitlock, Josiah, 273
Whitner, Henry, 404.148
Whitner, Lewis, 404.149
Whitsitt, William, 117
Whittery, William, 1629
Wiatt, John, 651.1
Wiatt, William, 1111, 1642
Wicomico Parish (Northumberland Co.), citizens of, 932
Wicomico warehouse, 1094
Wiggonton, Abraham, 879
Wiggonton, John, 879
Wilcox, Edmund, 495
Wilder, George, 879
Wiley, John, 404.25
Wilkins, Douglass, Jr., 1013
Wilkins, Nathaniel, 1307, 1552
Wilkins, Willis, 290
Wilkinson, Cary, 339, 1083
Wilkinson, Edward, 905
Wilkinson, John, 1560

Wilkinson, Mills, 319
Will (slave), 1119
Willcox, Major, 1287
Willhoit, John, 1429
William and Mary, College of: president and professors of, 1082, 1420; rector, visitors, and governors of, 333, 791
Williams, Edward, 105
Williams, Elisha, 1545
Williams, Evan, 201, 812, 875, 946
Williams, James, 404.145, 1187, 1365, 1554, 1659
Williams, John, 97, 661, 1298
Williams, Jonathan, 1470
Williams, Joseph, 813
Williams, Karliel, 926
Williams, Lessenby, 927, 1084
Williams, Mildred, 542
Williams, Philip, 404.115
Williams, Remembrance, 809
Williams, Richard, Sr., 809
Williams, Robert, 771
Williams, Silas, 1439
Williams, Thomas, 451, 1293
Williams, William, Jr., 1077
Williams, Wm., 1650
Williamsburg mental hospital. *See* Mental hospital (Williamsburg)
Williamson, Alex., 193
Willingham, Jerriad, 1180.6
Willis, John, 787, 1415
Willis, Lewis, 1049
Willoughby, John, Jr., 383
Wills, Sam., 579
Wills, Samuel, 77
Wills, William, Jr., 404.57
Wills, Willis, 77
Willson, Willis, 1207
Wilson, Alexd., 745
Wilson, Archer, 614
Wilson, Benj., 1280
Wilson, Benja., 549
Wilson, Benjamin, 139
Wilson, Jno., 1288
Wilson, John, 1, 43, 62, 430, 592, 745, 752, 753, 838
Wilson, Joseph, and Company, 1639
Wilson, Joshua, 430

Wilson, Matthew, 32
Wilson, Peter, 95
Wilson, Robt., 975
Wilson, Thomas, 741
Wilson, William, 134
Wilson, Willis, 1666
Winchester: citizens of, 820, 964; hustings court of, 1586; mechanics of, 1353; traders and retail dealers of, 1210
Window, John, 219
Window, Thomas, 219
Winniford, David, 1313
Winslow, Ben, 1049
Winslow, Benjamin, 825
Winston, Peter, 1149
Winter, John, 1297
Winters, Moses, 404.117
Wire-drawers, 571
Wise, Tugley R., 81
Witt, Jesse, 1147
Wodrow, Andrew, 1631
Wollenback, George, 278
Womack, Jesse, 404.82
Wonycutt, Aphia, 670
Wood, ———, 1589
Wood, Drury, 1567
Wood, Isaac, 404.17
Wood, James, 404.11, 404.13, 763, 1113
Wood, John, 404.52, 1629
Wood, Leighton, Jr., 800
Wood, Robt., 925
Woodford, Dudley M., 1113
Woodford, William, 772
Woodford, Wm., 529
Woodie, James, 316
Wooding, Robert, 152
Wooding, Victor, 155
Woodroof, Cliffinden, 320
Woodroof, David, 1024, 1025
Woodroof, John, 301
Woodruff, John, 179
Woods, ———, 1636
Woods, Andrew, 1163
Woodson, George, 1549
Woodson, Isham, 785
Woodson, John, 1282
Woodson, John Stephen, 785
Woodson, Miller, 265

Woodson, Rene, 1077
Woodson, Stepn., 199
Woodson, Tarlton, 1414
Woodward, Chesley, 402
Woodward, Lance, 404.91
Woody, William, 683
Woolfolk, John George, 147
Woolford, Frederick, 227
Woolling, Joseph, 1077
Workman, David, 1213
Wormeley, Ralph, Jr., 17
Worsham, Thos., 1549
Worthington, Edward, 661
Wray, George, 22, 909
Wright, Austin, 337
Wright, James, 1348
Wright, John, 966
Wright, Robert, 1155
Wright, Thos., 181
Wright, William, 1134
Wright, Wm., 1671
Wroe, William, 704
Wylden, James, 677
Wylly, Alexander, 124, 1226, 1467
Wynne, Norman, 633
Wynne, Peter, 633
Wynne, Stith, 633

### XYZ

Yancey, Phil., 984
Yates, Chs., 815
Yohogania County: citizens of, 501, 725; court of, 808
York County, citizens of. *See* Bruton Parish
Yorktown, citizens of, 1183
Young, Adam, 622.5
Young, John, 404.37
Young, W., 1056
Youngblood, Isaac, 1616
Yowell, John, 918
Zane, Isaac, 258
Zenesburg, citizens of, 510

# Index to Subjects

Subject entries refer to the serial numbers assigned to petition abstracts, not to page numbers.

## A

Abingdon, establishment of, 448
Accomack County: contested General Assembly election in, 1205; saltworks in, 380
Admiralty court, continuing sessions at Williamsburg, 1031
Akins, Thomas, 495
Albemarle barracks. *See* Prisoners of war (British and Hessian)
Albemarle County: addition of land to, 682, 682 A–682 C; division of, 272; Fluvanna (James) River ferry in, 292; Rockfish River ferry in, 292, 293. *See also* Saint Anne's Parish (Albemarle Co.)
Albemarle Parish (Sussex Co.), vestry of, 1286
Alcom, James, 390
Alexander, John, 847
Alexandria: election of trustees in, 726; enlargement of, 847; flour and grain trade in, 70; fortification of, 237; incorporation of, 902, 903, 964; land and water in, 1093; officers of, 902; Potomac River ferry in, 1614; property rights in, 848; representation of, in General Assembly, 1614
Alvis, John, 1180.1
Ambler, Mrs., 1133
Amelia County: division of, 534, 534 A, 534 B, 579, 579 A–579 D, 666; tax commissioners in, 1072, 1455; vestries in, 1194. *See also* Nottoway Parish (Amelia Co.)

Amherst County: Fluvanna (James) River ferry in, 132, 865, 1652; James River ferry in, 1317; military districts established in, 1451; prison construction in, 1140; Rockfish River ferry in, 292, 293. *See also* Amherst Parish; Lexington Parish
Amherst Parish (Amherst Co.): division of, 651.1, 1026, 1148, 1216; vestry of, 153
Anderson, Thomas, 292
Antigua, 15
Antrim Parish (Halifax Co.): sale of glebe lands in proposed, 1028, 1479, 1671; vestry of, 1028, 1479, 1671
Apprentices, compensation to masters for, 481, 546
Arbuckle, James, 1205
Arbuckle, Thomas, 390
Armistead, Booth, 1120
Armistead, John, 930
Arnold, Benedict, 1504, 1537, 1618, 1686
Assateague Island, 81
Astin, William, 390
Aston, George, 1510
Atkinson, John, 169
Atkinson, Matthew, 838
Augusta County: appointment of field officers in, 1390; boundaries of, 163, 694; citizens of, 1391; division of, 163, 428, 433, 444, 500, 685, 826, 826 A, 845, 899, 899 A, 943, 945, 959, 959 A, 959 B, 960, 966, 966 A, 998, 999, 1280; deputy sheriff of, 1240, 1440; jailor of, 1332, 1558; militia of, 60, 1390; public buildings valued in,

549

Augusta County *(continued)* 684; sheriff of, 1440; tax collection districts in, 1375; tobacco levies in, 684. *See also* Augusta Parish

Augusta Parish (Augusta Co.): sale of glebe land in, 684; vestry of, 428

Aylett, William, 800

## B

*Bachelor* (ship), 1352
Badgett, John, 575
Bagwell, Charles, 1205
Baker, James, 1157
Baker, Martin, 390
Ballendine, John, 979, 1394; settlement of estate of, 1667
Bankes, Mrs. Joseph, 805
Barr, John, 385, 1103
Barr, Zachariah, 385
Barrett, Jonathan, 762
Bath (Berkeley Co.): establishment of, 193; lots in, 586
Bath County, formation of, 959, 959 A, 959 B
Batte, Richard, 993, 1048
Batte's ferry, 1182
Battery Creek (Bedford Co.), 865
Beckford Parish (Dunmore and Shenandoah cos.): levy for, 411; vestry of, 637
Beckley, John, 623, 1381
Bedford County: division of, 311, 312, 445, 607, 615, 649, 650, 707, 708, 951, 951 A–951 D, 952, 953, 969, 1134, 1136, 1228, 1229, 1230, 1230 A, 1453, 1453 A–1453 M, 1454, 1676, 1681, 1681 A–1681 C; Fluvanna (James) River ferry in, 132, 865, 1652; jailor of, 1343, 1523; James River ferry in, 1317; militia of, 60; prisoner guards for, 1364; property assessment in, 1127; Staunton River ferry in, 797. *See also* Russell Parish
Bennet, Elizabeth, 1384
Bennett, Henry, 194
Bennett, William, 116
Benton, Jesse, 405

Berkeley County, Potomac River ferry in, 625, 970, 1019, 1020, 1208
Bermudians, food for, 917
Berry, Bradley, 790
Berryman, Benjamin, 1138
Berryman, Sarah, 1138
Birdwell, Robert, 390
Bishop, Adam, 72
Blackburn, T., 201
Blair, Anne, 1018
Blair, Elizabeth, 1018
Blair, James, 1018, 1217, 1399
Blair, John, 72
Blair, Margaret, 1018
Blair, Samuel, 390
Blair, Sarah, 1018
Blandford (Prince George Co.), 1114, 1701
Blankenship, Joseph, 450
Bledsoe, Anthony, 315
Boaz, John, 1180.5
Bohon, Benjamin, 406
Bohon, John, 406
Bohon, William, 406
Boling, Jesse, 407
Boling, John, 407
Boling, Thornsberry, 407
Boling, William, 407
Bolling, Charles, 1179
Bolling, Robert, 1317
Booker, Richard, 1141
Boonesborough (Kentucky Co.): battle of, 896, 989, 1015; establishment of, 1030; express rider from, 563; Kentucky River ferry in, 1071
Botetourt County, 116; care of poor of, 769; citizens of, 1248; confirmation of land titles in, 429; division of, 428, 429, 430, 430 A–430 E, 650, 974; election of delegates from, 80; militia of, 60; town to be established in, 758. *See also* Botetourt Parish
Botetourt Parish (Botetourt Co.): division of, 116; rector of, 222; vestry of, 167, 345, 428
Bourn, John, 843
Boush, Randolph, 754, 755
Bowdoin, John, 212
Bowdoin and Eyre, firm of, 205

Bowie, James, 1112
Bowler's warehouse, 365
Bowman, John, 116
Bowman, Joseph, 116, 262
Bowyer, Thomas, 390
Boyd, James, 1117
Boyd, Wm. David, 385
Boyle, James, 861
Bramham, Spencer, 640
Brandon Parish (Prince George Co.), 1600
Brickhouse warehouse, 1560
Bridges, toll, 771, 958
Briggs, Jesse, 656
Bristow, Robert, 1443
Broadway (Prince George Co.), 1182
Brogan, John, 1180.4
Brown, Adam, 1273
Brown, Coleman, 202
Brunswick County: division of, 1322, 1322 A–1322 C, 1323, 1323 A, 1323 B; taxes collected in, 1013
Bryan, Frederick, 234
Bryant, James, 390
Bryant, Josiah, 390
Bryant, William, 390
Buck, John, 551
Buckingham County: blast furnace in, 24, 606, 619; claims of, 1129; debts of, 1667; division of, 522, 538, 627, 695, 696; Fluvanna (James) River ferry in, 292; grants to, 469; Rockfish River ferry in, 292. See also Tillotson Parish; Westham
Bullitt, George, 481
Burks, John, 390
Burnett, John, 1169
Burnett, Mary, 1169, 1170
Burns, James, 495

## C

Calbert, William, 390
Cabin Point warehouse, 1515, 1516
Camden Parish (Henry and Pittsylvania cos.), division of, 651.1, 675
Cameron, Catherine, 1074
Cameron Parish (Loudoun Co.), rector of, 253

Campbell, Alexander, 1060
Campbell, Arthur, 109
Campbell, Daniel, 1060
Campbell, Neil, 292
Campbell County, formation of, 1453, 1453 A–1453 M. See also Russell Parish
Camron John, 1180.1
Carbin, Edward, 390
Caroline County: Pamunkey River ferry in, 804; public fishing rights in, 479; Rappahannock River ferry in, 56, 1112. See also Drysdale Parish; Saint Asaph's Parish; Saint Margaret's Parish
Carrington, George, 469, 578
Carrington, Joseph, 578
Carrol, Joseph, 390
Carter, Charles, 121
Carter, Landon, 121, 1400
Cartmill, Henry, 390
Cary, Wilson Miles, 493
Cave's warehouse, 197, 198, 1097
Cawthorn, Mrs., 1180.1
Chapman, John, 404.24
Charlotte County, division of, 273. See also Cornwall Parish
Charlottesville, lots in, 928
Charlton, Richard, estate of, 1103
Chesterfield County: Appomattox River ferry in, 1182; courthouse and prison in, 1549; James River ferry in, 992, 993, 1047, 1048, 1054, 1288, 1289, 1290 1368, 1405, 1487, 1488, 1503, 1522 1568, 1575; sheriff of, 1618. See also Manchester Parish
Chickahominy River, 1149
Chincoteague Island, 81
Christ Church Parish (Lancaster and Middlesex cos.), vestry of, 77, 504, 504 A–504 D, 505
Church of England: abolition of vestry law for, 1298; continuation of, 218, 320, 337, 528; disestablishment of, 124, 141, 155, 155 A, 160, 164, 164 A, 183, 553; salaries of clergy of, 863. See also names of parishes; Parishes
Clapham, Josiah, 916
Clapham's ferry, 735

Clark, Daniel, compensation to, 1542, 1543
Clark, George Rogers, 115, 116, 1535
Clarke, Benajah, 1057
Cloyd, James, 390
Cobbs, John, 405
Cochran, Cunningham, and Company (Glasgow), 547, 1158
Cocke, William, 315
Cole, Walter King, 1268
Coles, Walter, 1044
Colland, Samuel, and Company, 232
Colville, John, 194
Colvin, Anne, 1119, 1384
Connell, James, 1325
Connoway, Cornelius, 72
Continental army: bounty for enlisting in, 360; deserters from, 809, 814, 983; deputy quartermaster general for, 1335; draft law for, 1635; recruitment for, 645, 1421, 1422, 1425, 1518, 1588; volunteers in, 799. *See also* Military officers; Military service; Militia
Continental Congress, 12, 68, 680; investigation of member of, 1234
Convention troops. *See* Prisoners of war (British and Hessian)
Cook, Benjamin, 145
Cook, Nancy, 1122
Cook (Cooke) family, counterfeiters, 122, 145, 376
Coon, Philip, 72
Cornick, Joel, 389
Cornwall Parish (Charlotte Co.), 273
County courts: clerks of, 149; cryer of, 967. *See also* names of counties
Cowen, John, 116
Cowley, Abraham, 233, 1316
Crabtree, Abraham, 841
Crawford, John, 390
Crawford, William, 390
Crimes: breach of peace, 121; bribery and corruption, 291, 315, 405, 623, 1132; burglary, 73; counterfeiting, 122, 145, 376, 593, 705, 1034, 1557; gaming, penalties for, 1045, 1702; horse stealing, 73, 238, 404.23, 442, 502, 656, 733, 754, 755, 895, 1046, 1211, 1350, 1544; murder, 73, 74, 239, 1303; neglect of public duties, 1043; preaching, 810; refusal to take oaths, 1127; robbery, 73, 159, 249, 277, 360, 634, 915, 916, 1240, 1254, 1391, 1440; treason, 1571, 1572, 1706
Criminals: clemency for, 821; clothing and blankets furnished to, 196; hanging of, 1438; transportation of, 232, 238, 239, 567.8–567.13, 656, 754, 755, 1145, 1153, 1364; trials of, to be expedited, 73, 74, 196
Crittenden, John, 116
Crittendon, Frances, 1122
Croghan, George, 828, 1152
Crutchfield's warehouse, 1404
Culp, Daniel, 72
Culpeper County: division of, 482, 918, 918 A, 984, 984 A; Rappahannock River ferry in, 1110, 1400
Cumberland County: contested General Assembly election in, 578; courthouse in, 493, 527, 530; division of, 199, 199 A, 199 B, 261, 261 A–261 E, 265, 265 A–265 E, 266, 522, 538, 627, 695, 696; sheriff of, 698; transportation of criminals in, 1145, 1153. *See also* Littleton Parish; Southam Parish
Cumberland Parish (Lunenburg Co.), 273, 318
Cumings, Warwick, and Company, 1231
Cummins, John, 861
Cunningham and Company. *See* Cochran, Cunningham, and Company
Currency, 21, 280; depreciation of, 69, 939, 973, 973 A–973 E, 1185, 1613; lack of, 1604, 1643; laws for, 278, 1279, 1279 A, 1279 B, 1287, 1294, 1295, 1296, 1297, 1306, 1311, 1318, 1318 A, 1333, 1334, 1340, 1532, 1565, 1573, 1666; loss of, 113, 203, 366

# D

Dailey, Zadock, 752
Darke, William, 72
Davidson, John, 861

Davies, Nicholas, 132
Davis, Nicholas, 865
De Klauman, Charles, 711
DeLoyent, William, 621
Debts: how settled, 189; law for, 1594. *See also* Public debts
Dillon, Jesse, 834
Dissenters: authenticity of their petitions questioned, 553; confirmation of marriages of, 1079, 1194, 1251, 1298, 1649; eligibility for vestries of, 1649; exemption from support of established church by, 157, 221, 377, 549; privileges of, 105, 320, 1050; imprisonment of, 810
Dixon, James, estate of, 268
Dixon, John, 319, 389
Dixon's warehouse, 1404, 1486
Douglass, George, 416
Douglass, John, 842
Drysdale Parish (Caroline and King and Queen cos.): division of, 1027, 1027 A–1027 C, 1033, 1033 A, 1033 B, 1059, 1392; vestry of, 961
Dumfries, 946, 1012
Dunmore, fourth earl of, 58, 109, 127, 262; confiscation of property by, 87, 107, 191, 192, 225, 254, 328, 389, 544; creditors of, 84, 144, 205, 234, 258, 284, 339; desertion of slaves to, 8, 9, 38, 44, 52, 110, 136, 148, 321, 330, 331, 343, 344, 361, 362, 378, 383, 400, 454, 748, 764, 776; estate of, 168, 260
Dunmore County, name changed, 428. *See also* Beckford Parish
Dunn, Thomas, 1081
Dymer's warehouses, 1304

E

Eagnew, Thomas, 390
East Augusta District, 138, 139
Edwards, Betty, 1122
Effingham (Cumberland Co.), disestablishment of, 493, 527
Elizabeth City County, defense of, 22. *See also* Milldams

Elizabeth River Parish (Norfolk Co.), vestry of, 677
Elligood, Jacob, 67
Embargo law, 1430, 1482, 1532
Epperson, David, 1396
Epperson, Judith, 1396
Escheated property, 798, 1260, 1265, 1268, 1303, 1325, 1663, 1674. *See also* Great Britain
Espey, James, 390
Essex County, Rappahannock River ferry in, 1581. *See also* Saint Anne's Parish (Essex Co.)
Evans, James, 477
Evans, John, 861

F

Fairfax, George William, 1067
Fairfax, Thomas (sixth baron Fairfax), 121, 193, 259, 941, 1086
Fairfax County: Potomac River ferry in, 1614; justices of, 902. *See also* Fairfax Parish
Fairfax Parish (Fairfax Co.), vestry of, 1078
Falmouth, Rappahannock River ferry in, 929, 936, 937, 938, 1065, 1065 A, 1065 B
Falmouth warehouse, 1404, 1486
Fayette County: cultivation of land in, 1640; district court in, 1629, 1640; formation of, 1253, 1253 A, 1253 B; land grants in, 1629
Fees: for county officers, 171, 217; for witnesses, 404.11
Fenley, Robert, 390
Ferguson, Joseph, 1679
Ferries, tolls on, 572. *See also* names of counties
Ferryboats, 223, 240
Ferry-house, 161, 962
Field, John, 850
Figg, James, 551
Fincastle County: delegates to revolutionary conventions from, 115, 116; division of, 75, 115, 116; incorporation as part of Virginia colony of, 34, 34 A; militia of, 60

553

Finnill, John, 417
Finnill, Reuben, 417
Firebricks, manufacture of, 483, 655
Fisher, Elizabeth, 1107
Fisher, Thomas, 1528
Fishing rights, public, 479
Fitzhugh, William, 936
Flanagin, Samuel, 73
Fleming, Thomas, 654
Flood, Nicholas, 934
Fluvanna County: clerk of, 623, 1132; courthouse in, 493, 494; dissolution of, 682, 682 A–682 C, 683, 683 A–683 C; division of, 785, 788; formation of, 272; officers of, 405, 623, 1132. *See also* Fluvanna Parish
Fluvanna Parish (Fluvanna Co.): formation of, 272; glebe land in, 981, 1077
Foreign correspondence, clerk of, 1143
Fort Pitt, 215
Fort Randolph, 861
Foster, John, 207
Fragor, John, 390
Frayles, Sukey, 1122
Frederick County: Shenandoah River ferry in, 941; sheriff of, 1672. *See also* Frederick Parish
Frederick Parish (Frederick Co.), 411; vestry of, 925
Fredericksburg, 82, 230, 815, 1184; enlargement of, 1630; establishment of jail in, 1417; hustings court of, 1630; incorporation of, 1416, 1417; Rappahannock River ferry in, 929, 1065, 1065 A, 1065 B; representation of, in General Assembly, 1630; taxation in, 1630
Fredericksburg warehouse, 926

### G

Gaby, Molly, 1122
Galt, James, 982
Galt, Patrick, 472
Gambel, James, 413
Garrard, William, 955
Garriott, Catherine, 1172
Gaunt, James, 390

General Assembly, 1705
  absentee members of, 1565
  acts of, 811, 812, 1051
  authority of Senate questioned, 418, 569
  chairs for Senate, 404.30
  doorkeeper for House of Delegates, 1000, 1001, 1002, 1003, 1004, 1005, 1006, 1324
  elections to
    contested, 291, 315, 578, 1181, 1205
    legality of questioned, 930
    new, 338
  pay of, 811, 812, 1176
  petitions to, printed, 628, 1612
  representation in, 80, 1114, 1614, 1630
General Court, clerk of, 1154
Gibson's warehouse, 1404, 1486
Gist, Samuel, estate of, 1664
Givens, George, 390
Glascock's warehouses, 1293, 1470
Gloucester County: saltworks in, 205.1, 721; York River ferry in, 528, 793, 914, 1227
Godwin, Susanna Anne, 1265
Goochland County: addition of land to, 682, 682 A–682 C; division of, 682, 682 A–682 C, 683, 683 A–683 C, 785, 788, 900, 901
Goodrich, Bridger, 296; creditors of, 1291
Goodrich, John, Jr.: accounts paid to, 162; creditors of, 1291; wife and children of, 963
Goodrich, John, Sr.: creditors of, 64, 1105, 1291; imprisonment of, 65, 458, 496, 589, 617, 632, 829; property of, in Virginia, 537, 712; shipping business of, 254, 296
Goodrich, William, 254
Goods and services: compensation for, 325, 370, 1694; affixing seal of commonwealth to land patents, 1467; axe, 567.82; bills of exchange, 1367; chair and harness, 617; clothing, 1270; construction work, 567.79; crops, 219, 371, 399, 1495; depositions, 404.13, 404.14; express riders, 215, 404.10,

554

404.12, 548, 563, 567.85, 601, 907.11, 1347, 1684; ferriages, 404.4 567.12; furniture, 747; hoes, 567 82; molasses, 252; physicians, 241, 472, 857, 1079.1, 1085, 1308, 1541; post-riders, 267; threshing machine, invention of, 248; timber, 51, 391; transportation, 347; wagonage, 33; writing paper, 1494. *See also* Liquor; Military stores
Gradey, Catharine, 1180.7
Graham, James, 1240
Gray, David, 861
Gray, George, 442
Gray, William, 738
Great Britain
citizens of (*see also* Prisoners of war [British and Hessian])
allowance to, 499
escheated property of, 1023, 1076, 1086, 1250, 1443, 1582
estates of, in Virginia, 194, 1664
return to England of, 57, 104
customs officer of, 1159
merchants of, 280
debts owed to, 671, 1060
land sold by, 547, 1153
sympathizers with (*see also* Goodrich, John, Jr.; Goodrich, John, Sr.; Loyalty; M'Caul, Archibald; M'Caul, Catherine; Oaths)
escheated property of, 57, 1029, 1041, 1042, 1067, 1083, 1096, 1121, 1498
expulsion from country of, 710, 716, 1437
fines for, 204
imprisonment of, 5, 17, 65, 118, 133, 458, 580, 864, 866, 867
return to Virginia of, 920, 921
trial of, 264, 567.90
Greenbrier County: confirmation of land titles in, 317; formation of, 428; road building in, 1369, 1450, 1450 A. *See also* Greenbrier Parish
Greenbrier Parish (Greenbrier Co.), formation of, 428
Greensville County, formation of, 1322, 1322 A–1322 C

Gregory, Charles, 1180.1
Guilford warehouse. *See* Low Point (Guilford) warehouse
Gulliford Edward, 390
Gunnery, instruction in art of, 621
Guttery, John, 495
Guy, Cy., 118
Guy, James, 1220
Gwynn's Island, 210, 362

## H

Hadley, Joseph, 502
Halifax County: courthouse in, 59, 128, 129, 130, 152; Dan River ferry in, 165, 166, 255; division of, 555, 573, 693; recruitment of soldiers in, 1044; Roanoke River ferry in, 922, 922 A; transportation of criminals from, 754. *See also* Antrim Parish
Hamilton, David, 550
Hamilton, John, 1096
Hampden-Sydney Academy, 244
Hampshire County: clerk to tax commissioners of, 944; commissary for provisions in, 98; division of, 428, 500
Hampton, 22, 713, 1426
Hampton River, blockade of, 22
Hancock, John, 1238
Hanover (town), 382
Hanover County: boundaries of, 1149, 1164; county committee elected in, 36; division of, 900, 901; Pamunkey River ferry in, 804, 1601. *See also* Saint Paul's Parish
Hanover Parish (King George Co.): altering boundaries in, 686; sale of glebe land in, 1099
Harbinson, David, 390
Hardin, John, 262
Harland, Silas, 116
Harmer, John, 1268
Harris, Samuel, 517
Harrisonburg, establishment of, 1198
Hays, Daniel, 490
Heaton, Anne, 1106
Henderson, Richard, and Company, 26, 404.11 404.13, 404.14

Henrico County: boundaries of, 1149, 1164; James River ferry in, 992, 993, 1047, 1048, 1503, 1522, 1575
Henry, John, 1292
Henry, Patrick: governor, 452, 646, 705; lead mine shareholder, 1608
Henry, William, 390, 405
Henry County: division of, 311, 312, 445, 607, 615, 649, 650, 707, 708, 953, 965, 969, 1102, 1134, 1228, 1229, 1230, 1230 A, 1665, 1676, 1677, 1677 A, 1677 B; formation of, 119. *See also* Camden Parish
Herrin, Jonathan, Jr., 833
Herrod, James, 116
Herron, Isaac, 1400
Higgins, Benjamin, 73
High Court of Chancery, judges of, 1668
Hite, Isaac, 116
Hoalston, Stephen, 390
Hodges, Drury, 1211
Hodges, John, 71
Hodges, Martha, 403
Holstein River, 471
Hooe's ferry, 572
Horse racing, legalization of, 1386
Horses
    capture of, 1700
    compensation for, 50, 404.32, 404.33, 404.38–404.96, 404.153, 548, 567.16–567.26, 567.28–567.71, 567.80, 567.81, 567.83, 567.84, 567.88, 567.89, 622.1, 622.6, 622.8–622.11, 861, 907.1
    death of, 47, 49, 143, 145, 175, 187, 215, 283, 355, 392, 404.35, 404.37, 414, 431, 460, 540, 583, 622.2, 632, 657, 680, 858, 889, 1061, 1141, 1202, 1211, 1292, 1336, 1347, 1387, 1408, 1545
    hire of, 390, 404.22–404.25, 404.38–404.41, 404.43, 561, 562, 567.8, 567.9, 567.10, 567.11, 567.13, 567.33, 567.87, 610, 622.5, 622.7
    impressment of, 287, 589, 597, 613, 616, 755, 768, 829, 854, 860, 882, 884, 890, 893, 894, 898, 1207, 1319, 1407, 1460
    injury to, 122, 232, 238, 239, 473, 496, 629, 796, 1481, 1529
    loss of, 103, 135, 335, 396, 404.20, 404.21, 404.28, 404.31, 404.36, 564, 567.5, 567.7, 567.14, 567.15, 585, 600, 609, 610, 622.3, 656, 802, 803, 842, 859, 860, 874, 876, 877, 878, 885, 886, 887, 907.2, 907.7–907.10, 907.12–907.15, 1258, 1449, 1468, 1475, 1476, 1528, 1531, 1559, 1694
    pasturage of, 404.9
    purchase of, 563, 1685
    sale of, to state, 1397
    stealing of, 733, 895, 1211, 1350, 1544
    deficiency of, in cavalry, 1427
    and harness
        compensation for, 567.81, 622.6, 622.11, 837
        impressment of, 838, 875, 883, 1197,
        loss of, 404.31, 404.36, 404.37, 567.47, 567.48, 567.54–567.56, 567.89
    public, 608, 1336
    and wagons
        compensation for, 402
        hire of, 552, 880
        impressment of, 439, 443, 766, 822, 1388, 1493
        procurement of, 1563
Houses. *See* Property
Howard, Benjamin, 292
Howard, Sarah, 1122
Howard, William, 292, 293
Howell, Mary, 73
Howell, Thomas, 390
Hughes, Ashford, 738
Humphreys, John, 823
Hunting Creek warehouses, 1249
Hutchings, Joseph, 746
Hutchinson, George, 390
Hysaw, Henry, 861
Hyser, John, 72

## I

Illinois Regiment. *See* Military officers
Impress law, 1439, 1482, 1518, 1532
Indentured servants: compensation to masters for, 357, 478, 480, 780; land grants for importation of, 872
Indiana Company, 404.13, 404.14
Indians
    Cherokees, 392, 450, 514
        communications with, 334, 601
        enlistment of, in American army, 523
        land purchased from, 26, 97, 115, 471, 1152, 1241
        treaties with, 97, 471, 523
    depredations of, 384, 1357
        compensation for, 277, 283, 334, 335, 370, 388, 394, 395, 435, 510, 518, 558, 559, 837, 838, 842, 858, 859
    intelligence against, 263
    interpreter for, 297
    plunder from towns of, 262
    protection against, 80, 125, 427
    purchase of land from, 25, 384, 828, 904, 988
    treaties with, 26, 384
Ingles, John, 72
Ingles, William, 72, 90
Iron manufacture, 188, 606, 655
Iron ore, prospecting for, 386
Ironworks, 404.29, 980; slaves used in, 4
Irvine, Abraham, 453
Isle of Wight County, courts to be held in, 106. *See also* Newport Parish
Israel, Isaac, 72

## J

James City County: care of poor of, 314; James River ferry in, 240, 1133
Jamestown, James River ferry in, 240, 1133
Jefferson, Peter, 738
Jefferson, Thomas, 1438
Jefferson County: cultivation of land in, 1640; district court in, 1629, 1640;
formation of, 1253, 1253 A, 1253 B; land grants in, 1629
Johnson, John, 239, 968
Johnson, William, 1292
Johnston, Aaron, 798
Johnston, Frances, 798
Johnston, Richard, 118
Jones, Jn., 118
Jones, John, 390
Jones, John Gabriel, 115, 116

## K

Kemp's landing, 778
Kentucky County: defense of, 125, 150, 1011; division of, 1253, 1253 A, 1253 B; formation of, 115, 116; Kentucky River ferry in, 1071; land law established in, 604; preemption warrants for land in, 1167; purchasing commissary in, 1540; road opened to, 1508 saltworks in, 498. *See also* Land law
Kimerland, Jacob, 390
King, Hannah, 1180.1
King and Queen County, Mattaponi River ferry in, 706. *See also* Drysdale Parish; Saint Asaph's Parish; Saint Stephen's Parish; Stratton Major Parish
King George County: boundaries of, 140, 140 A; division of, 322, 364, 466, 467; Machodack Creek ferry in, 1592; military quotas in, 466, 468; Rappahannock River ferry in, 56, 1112. *See also* Hanover Parish
King William County: Mattaponi River ferry in, 706; Pamunkey River ferry in, 1601
Kyles, Joseph, 390
Kyles, William, 390

## L

Lancaster County, Rappahannock River ferry in, 779. *See also* Christ Church Parish
Land: army deserters to forfeit, 1022; bounty, 1409, 1485, 1510; certificates,

Land (continued)
1021; entailed, 935, 987; inherited, 497, 798, 1018, 1103, 1325, 1555, 1674; leased, 1096, 1225; lottery for, 786; in North Carolina, 1435; purchased from the Indians, 26, 97, 115, 384, 471, 828, 904, 988, 1152, 1241; rights to, 507; sale of, 772, 1679; settlement of, 1014; surveyors of, 438, 438 A; taken for public use, 1063, 1394, 1632; titles, 429, 501, 737

Land companies, 26, 324, 404.11–404.14, 440, 737, 828, 985, 988, 1511, 1511 A, 1512; land grants to, 97, 384, 440, 724, 849, 904

Land law: amendment of, 1511, 1511 A, 1512, 1546, 1547; establishment of, 604

Land office, 722, 1163, 1369

Land patents and grants, 507, 868, 980, 1011, 1629; confirmation of, 722, 731, 738, 825, 850, 871, 985, 988, 1028.1; extension of time for surveying and claiming of, 819, 1167, 1199; importation rights to, 872, 1037, 1037 A, 1038, 1039, 1058, 1089, 1389; for military service, 759, 1490, 1535; relief from burden of, 26, 976; seal of commonwealth affixed to, 1467; surveying of, 738, 787, 813; unpatented, claimants to, 1126, 1214, 1456, 1511, 1511 A, 1512

Langston, Sukey, 1122
Lawrence, David, 390
Lawrence, Isaac, 390
Lawrence, Patrick, 390
Layton's warehouse, 1404, 1486
Lead mines: compensation for public use of, 1452; private use of state-owned, 913, 1095; slaves used in, 25, 136, 178, 212, 224, 276, 330, 331, 343, 344, 378, 400, 423, 712, 748, 776, 1212, 1223, 1593; superintendent of, 1330; wood for, 391, 1607, 1608
Leatherdale, James, 390
Leatherdale, William, 390
Lee, Benja., 623
Lee, William, 322, 991

Leeds (Westmoreland Co.), 359
Leed's warehouse, 1404, 1486
Leesburg, 726
Lewis, Andrew, 758
Lewis, Charles, 992, 1047, 1066
Lewis, Fielding, 936, 937, 938
Lewis, John, 95
Lewis, Thomas, 758
Lexington (Fayette Co.): establishment of, 1446, 1483, 1525; map of, 1525
Lexington (Rockbridge Co.), establishment of, 428
Lexington Parish (Amherst Co.), division of, 1026, 1148, 1216
Liberty (brig), 732
Lightfoot, Armistead, 497
Lightfoot, John, 497
Lightfoot, Philip, 497
Lincoln County: cultivation of land in, 1640; district court in, 1629, 1640; formation of, 1253, 1253 A, 1253 B; land grants in, 1629
Liquor
  compensation for
    destruction of distilleries for, 252, 674
    furnishing, 172, 174, 205.1, 517, 770, 1494
  prohibition of distilleries for, 995
  sale to military of, 242
Littlepage's warehouse, 1560
Littleton Parish (Cumberland Co.), 265, 265 A–265 E; rector of, 1104, 1104 A
Livestock. *See also* Horses
  compensation for
    death of, 245, 418, 569, 774, 832
    herding of, 511, 608
    loss of, 349, 514
    pasturage for, 567.90
    purchase of, 208
    removal of, from Eastern Shore, 81
    use of, 404.7, 1499
  running at large, 647, 948, 1070, 1673
Loan Office certificates, 1504, 1694
Lockhart, Patrick, 390
Long Island (Holstein River), 393, 396, 397, 399, 401
Loudoun County: clerk of, 919; division

of, 1520, 1520 A–1520 G, 1521, 1521 A, 1655, 1655 A; land taxes in, 70; Potomac River ferry in, 735, 739; sheriff of, 736. See also Cameron Parish

Louisa County: addition of land to, 682, 682 A–682 C; division of, 900, 901

Louisville (Kentucky Co.), establishment of, 1198, 1252

Low Point (Guilford) warehouse, 1515, 1516

Loyal Company, 737, 1511, 1511 A, 1512; land grants to, 724

Loyalty, of citizens questioned, 1109, 1150, 1151

Lunenburg County: courthouse in, 1598; division of, 273; juries and witnesses in, 942. See also Cumberland Parish

Lyle, John, 861

Lyle, Samuel, 861

## M

McCall, James, 450
M'Caul (M'Call), Archibald, 934, 1073, 1502, 1580
M'Caul, Catherine, 1502, 1580
M'Clure, Samuel, 390
M'Cluskey, Elizabeth, 73
M'Cluskey, Thomas, 73
McConnel, Andrew, 116
McConnel, William, 116
M'Cuown, James, 390
M'Elheny, Robert, 861
M'Farran, Samuel, 390
M'Farrin, John, 390
M'Farrin, Martin, 390
M'Gahey, Manasses, 73
McGary, Hugh, 116, 548
Machodack warehouse, 1281, 1497
Mackey, Mary, 861
M'Lure, Alexander, 861
M'Lure, Moses, 861
M'Mullen, John, 861
McRae, Christopher, 1104, 1104 A
M'Roberts, Samuel, 390
Maddox, Elizabeth, 1171
Major, Nanny, 1122
Major, Sarah, 1122

Malone, James, 861
Manchester, 267; enlargement of, 1398; hogs in, 1070; James River ferry in, 1054, 1288, 1289, 1368, 1405, 1487, 1488, 1568; removal of buildings in, 229; trustees of, 626
Manchester Parish (Chesterfield Co.), vestry of, 760
Manchester warehouses, 1556
Maritime law, 1179, 1661
Marriage, legalizing of, 1079, 1194, 1251, 1298, 1646
Martin, Philip, 1086
Martin, Samuel, of Whitehaven, 1121
Martin, Thomas Bryan, 941
Martin, William, 623
Martinsburg (Berkeley Co.): establishment of, 278; improvement of lots in, 1221
Maryland (state), 849; ferries to, 625, 739, 970, 1019, 1020, 1208, 1614
Mason's Hall (Norfolk borough), 746
Matthews, Owen, 489
Matton's warehouse, 1404, 1486
Maxwell, John, 116
Mayle, Charles, 304
Mayo, John, 296; ferry of, 1405
Meacom, John, 1303
Mecklenburg County: juryman in, 690; Roanoke River ferry in, 422, 922, 922 A. See also Saint James's Parish
Mecklenburg Town (Shepherdstown), hogs in, 647
Mental hospital (Williamsburg): appropriations for, 749, 1160, 1271; caretaker and matron at, 728, 982; physicians at, 857, 1079.1, 1308
Meriwether, Thomas, 738
Meriwether's warehouse, 1383, 1509
Mickleburrough, Robt., 118
Middlesex County: contested General Assembly election in, 1181; courthouse in, 1412, 1413; Rappahannock River ferry in, 779; sheriff of, 1686. See also Christ Church Parish
Milby, James, 491
Military officers
appointment of, 1390
better medical treatment for, 763

559

Military officers (continued)
  bounty land for, 1517
  clothing for, 1517
  in Continental line
    adjustment of taxation on, 1113
    bounty land for, 1505
    clothing allowance for, 1447, 1484, 1505
    expenses for, 1505
    pay for, 1505, 1606
    rank of, 1447, 1484, 1505
  opposition to election of, 711
  pay for, 30, 31, 32, 45, 46, 862, 1092, 1517, 1696
    army engineers, 68
    commandant of the Illinois [Regiment], 1270
  rank of, 114, 308, 310
  redress of grievances of, 986
Military service
  appointment of field officers for, 1390
  bounty for, 360, 879, 906, 1166, 1255
  compensation for, 109, 111, 214, 235, 286, 288, 295, 346, 352, 354, 356, 404.26, 449, 513, 554, 644, 765
    accidents during, 700, 1551
    advances made for, 1526
    allowance for, 741
    blindness caused by smallpox during, 667, 730, 1036, 1603
    boarding men in, 88, 227
    bounty and subsistence for, 915, 916
    chaplains in, 1080
    clothing for, 1255, 1261, 1262, 1263, 1264, 1275, 1283, 1366
    commissioner to pay claims for, 60
    death during, 202, 207, 334, 373, 413, 453, 485, 489, 490, 491, 518, 525, 541, 542, 543, 550, 551, 762, 767, 823, 968, 1052, 1062
    hospital care during, 1366
    illness during, 48, 270, 372, 379, 432, 533, 594, 636, 638, 702, 757, 891, 1116, 1146, 1147, 1257, 1301
    messenger sent to locate soldier in, 611
    nursing care during, 206, 406, 407, 408, 416, 417, 512, 532, 574, 575, 640, 641, 642, 653, 654, 658, 743, 751, 781, 801, 833, 834, 841, 843, 1310, 1457, 1519
    pay for, 6, 48, 50, 95, 112, 200, 262, 404.5, 404.8, 404.97–404.152, 557, 879, 906, 1191, 1255, 1696
      assistant commissary in, 90
      butcher in, 85
      carpenter in, 40
      deserters from, 262
      drover in, 41
      packhorse master in, 111
      rangers in, 102
    physician's care during, 58, 79, 147, 179, 206, 241, 256, 301, 404.15–404.17, 472, 495, 704, 835, 839, 989, 1015, 1035, 1057, 1085, 1175, 1200, 1541, 1648
    prisoners of war during, 177, 462, 1161, 1267, 1269, 1373, 1414, 1415, 1423, 1531, 1611
    provisions for, 1255
      families of soldiers in, 881, 1074, 1180.1–1180.7
    rations, 879, 906
      and lodging during, 285
    recruitment into, 91, 250, 879, 906, 923
    support of soldiers in, 72
    suppressing insurgents during, 1371, 1372
    travel expenses in, 393, 639, 651, 734, 783, 790, 794
    widows of soldiers in
      excess payments to, 1106, 1122, 1123, 1138, 1168, 1169, 1170, 1171, 1172, 1173
      to educate children of, 1062
      support for, 529, 1180.1–1180.3, 1180.6, 1273, 1310, 1349, 1363, 1396, 1458
    wives of soldiers in, 856, 1107, 1117
    wounds received during, 2, 18, 19,

63, 93, 94, 117, 134, 262, 271, 274, 281, 294, 299, 300, 303, 351, 388, 394, 395, 397, 398, 401, 419, 435, 452, 456, 457, 470, 475, 477, 508, 519, 521, 576, 577, 581, 582, 587, 588, 590, 591, 592, 595, 598, 599, 612, 614, 630, 631, 635, 643, 652, 659, 662, 668, 679, 691, 692, 699, 701, 703, 720, 744, 756, 761, 827, 830, 831, 896, 977, 1090, 1091, 1101, 1125, 1144, 1186, 1187, 1188, 1189, 1192, 1196, 1206, 1219, 1232, 1243, 1244, 1276, 1284, 1285, 1299, 1300, 1307, 1309, 1320, 1329, 1331, 1341, 1342, 1344, 1355, 1356, 1358, 1360, 1365, 1366, 1370, 1374, 1380, 1382, 1395, 1410, 1444, 1459, 1461, 1462, 1463, 1464, 1465, 1477, 1478, 1491, 1492, 1500, 1513, 1514, 1524, 1527, 1539, 1552, 1554, 1587, 1627, 1648, 1659

disposition of plunder from Indian towns for, 262
exchange of prisoners of war in, 1238, 1426
exemption from, 1361
    for apprentices, 1353, 1361
    for card-makers and wire-drawers, 571
    for iron manufacturers and apprentices, 100, 142, 1361
    for Menonists, 100, 142, 818
    for overseers, 11, 13, 29, 62, 83 and managers, 1113
    for postal workers, 367
    for purchasing commissary, 1266
    for Quakers, 100, 142, 818
    for cotton manufacturers, 434
length of time in, adjustment of
    for draftees, 1428, 1429, 1442
    for Continental line, 1282, 1302, 1351
recruitment for, 1044
    Continental troops in, 1425, 1518

division of state into districts for, 1433
equalization of, 1337, 1434, 1441
relief from, 1156
substitutes in, law for, 996
Military stores. *See also* Liquor
    armorer for, 126
    assistant commissary for, pay of, 90
    commissary for
        at Fort Randolph, 861
        in Hampshire Co., 98
    commissary general for, 69, 566, 800
    commissioners to purchase, 681
    compensation for, 15, 249, 462
    arms, 28
    beef, 516, 1633
    biscuits, 172
    blankets, 567.74, 753, 836, 1100
    cannons, 249, 313, 729
    caps, 1448
    clothing, 420, 565
    drum, 782
    firearms, 727, 1419
    flour, 567.27
    forage, 484, 782, 1424
    goods, 1496
    gunpowder, 55, 78, 463, 792, 1473
    guns, 353, 404.88, 567.72, 567.73, 567.75, 567.76, 567.86, 634, 661, 753, 775, 836, 837, 855
    lead, 347
    linen, 539
    lumber, 374, 391
    provisions, 366, 404.6, 451, 1411, 1473
    rations, 172, 282, 285, 410, 567.77, 567.78, 879, 906
    rifles, 16, 420, 697, 817
    sails, 231
    salt, 99, 687
    tomahawk, 567.86
    trees, 1345
    wagon, 424
    wagon chains and bags, 1385
    wheel timber, 535
    keeper of (Williamsburg), 154
    provision of
        cannons, 237

Military stores (continued)
    powder mill, 23
    salt, iron, and wool cards, 1053
    subsidies for manufacture of
        firearms, 309
        gunpowder, 323
        linen, 27, 182, 195, 369
        rope, 169
        sailcloth, 27
        sail duck, 369
        woolen cloth, 182
    rope works, 316
    saltpeter, 25, 146, 507
    saltworks
        in Accomack Co., 380
        in Gloucester Co., 205.1, 721
        in Kentucky Co., 498
        in York Co., 205.1
    warehouses for naval stores, 197, 198
Militia. See also Continental army; Military service; names of counties
    appointment of
        county officers for, by governor, 501
        field officers in, 1390
    arming and training of, 1683
    drafted into Continental service, 1605
    fines for, 201, 1426
    invalid corps of, formation of, 1315
    laws for, 1432
    musters, 3, 82, 230, 230 A–230 F
    pay for adjutant of, 127
    raising of, for defense of frontier, 933
Milldams: on Banister River, 957; in Elizabeth City Co., 1120, 1131; on Falling River, 1682; on Meherrin River, 181; on Nottoway River, 180; on Rapidan River, 673, 673 A, 806; on Robertson River, 673, 673 A, 806; in Warwick Co., 1120, 1131
Miller, Alexander, 714
Miller, Simon, 1110
Mills, John, Jr., 390
Mississippi River, navigation of, 1620
Mitchell, Thomas, 920, 921
Moffat, George, 18, 19
Money. See Currency
Money bills, 418, 569

Monongalia County: court of, 807; division of, 960, 1280; formation of, 163; unpatented lands in, 1126
Montgomery, Alexander, 1582
Montgomery County: boundaries of, 326, 327, 436, 436 A–436 C, 437, 437 A, 437 B, 602.1, 602.1 A, 602.1 B; division of, 428, 441, 974, 1665, 1677, 1677 A, 1677 B; formation of, 115, 116; land law established in, 604; settling land titles in, 1621; unpatented lands in, 1456
Moody, Samuel, 543
Moor, John, 390
Moore, Burrass, 1173
Moore, Conrad, 336
Moore, Thomas, 1181
Moorefield (Hampshire Co.), establishment of, 336
Moorman, Charles, 1377
Morehead, Charles, 502
Morton, Edmond, 856
Morton, Jarot, 408
Mount Bethel: church, hospital, and school at, 1142
Murray, John. See Dunmore, fourth earl of
Murray, William, 344
Mush, Sarah, 1122
Muter, George, 1321

### N

Nansemond County. See Upper Parish
Naval defense, inadequacy of, 1068
Naval office, removal of, 1069
Navy Board, shipbuilding for, 620, 784
Ned (slave), 1401
Nelson, Arthur, 735
Nelson, Thomas, 413, 551, 1271
Nelson, Thomas, Jr., 1532
Nevil, Reuben, 1168
Nevill, Reuben, 1273
Newell, Samuel, 334, 335
New Orleans, La., 452
Newport Parish (Isle of Wight Co.), vestry of, 77
New Town (Princess Anne Co.), 778
New York (state), 1267

Nicholas, James, 390
Nichols, Elizabeth, 1106
Norborne Parish (Frederick Co.), 411
Norfolk (borough): destruction in, 33, 44, 51, 61, 123, 158, 243, 252, 605, 669, 670, 674, 746, 747, 824, 870, 892, 908, 924, 971, 994, 995, 1220; ferryboat in, 223; laying out of, 350; rebuilding in, 350, 746; taxes in, 1314, 1530, 1576
Norfolk County: courthouse destroyed in, 1; election to revolutionary convention from, 1; removal of inhabitants from, 43, 316; taxes in, 1530. *See also* Elizabeth River Parish; Portsmouth Parish
*Norfolk's Revenge* (galley), 159
North Farnham Parish (Richmond Co.), vestry of, 156, 678
Northampton County, citizens of, 1615
Northern Neck Proprietary, 193, 1086; collection of quitrents in 259; surveys in, 121
Northumberland County, magistrates appointed for, 1362. *See also* Wicomico Parish
Nottoway Parish (Amelia Co.), rector of, 1403
Nottoway Parish (Southampton Co.), vestry of, 648
Nowland, Thomas, 735
Nunnally, Joseph, 1180.2, 1180.3

O

Oaths
 how taken, 745
 loyalty, 133
  fines for not taking
   imposed on clergymen, 1104, 1104 A, 1277, 1277 A–1277 C, 1312, 1313, 1313 A, 1313 B, 1348, 1348 A–1348 C
   relief from, 633, 663, 664, 665, 852, 975, 1007, 1008, 1009, 1010
  for property assessment, 646, 1127
Obanion, Bryan (the elder), 798, 1674

Ocracoke Inlet, N.C., 64, 1471
O'Hara, James, 277
Ohio Company, 440
Ohio County: division of, 363; formation of, 163; unpatented lands in, 1126
Ohio River, 427
Orange County: contested General Assembly election in, 291; division of, 465, 476, 482; military districts in, 949 1203
Ordinaries, licensing of, 1586
Ordinary of Newgate, 777, 1137
Ormston, Robert, 1000
Otter Creek (Amherst Co.), 865

P

Pace, William, 623
Page's warehouse, 1404
Pailer, Anne, 1180.7
Paradise, John, 339, 1083
Paradise, Lucy, 1083
Parishes, 651.2, 1194, 1480, 1649. *See also* names of parishes
Parker Nicholas, Jr., 525
Patesfield (Isle of Wight Co.), 131
Patterson, Turner, 636
Patton James, 731
Payne, Robert, 342
Peage, Thomas, 390
Pendergrass, Garret, 116
Pendleton District, 34, 34 A
Penet, de Costa et Frères, 1367
Penet, Wendel, and Company, 979
Penticost, Dorsey, 501
Petersburg: enlargement of, 1114, 1701; representation of, in General Assembly, 1114
Phelps's Creek, blast furnace on, 24
Phipp, John, 1207
Piping Tree warehouse, 1402
Pittsburgh, 215, 452; Monongahela River ferry in, 257
Pittsylvania County: courthouse in, 506, 602; Dan River ferry in, 342, 524; division of, 119, 119 A; militia of, 60; Staunton River ferry in, 797. *See also* Camden Parish

Pocahontas (Chesterfield Co.), 1114, 1701
Pollock, John, 741
Pollock, Oliver, 1543, 1553
Porter, Charles, 291
Port Royal (Caroline Co.), 56
Portsmouth, land taxes in, 1314
Portsmouth Parish (Norfolk Co.): poor of, 14; vestry of, 676
Potter, Thomas, 72, 238, 404.23, 754, 755
Powhatan County: formation of, 265, 265 A–265 E; sheriffs of, 1561
Presbyterians, 377
Preston, William, 34 A
Price, Barret, 1566
Pride, Habakkuk, 73
Prince Edward County: commissioners of, 978; sheriff of, 947. See also Saint Patrick's Parish
Prince George County: Appomattox River ferry in, 1182; jail fire in, 421. See also Brandon Parish
Princess Anne County: courthouse in, 778; removal of inhabitants from, 43, 316
Prince William County, courthouse in, 1012, 1204, 1204 A, 1204 B
Printing. See Public printer
Prisoners of war (British and Hessian): clothing for, 137; guarding of, 1255, 1696; rations and lodging for, 285; restrictions on, 709; wood for, 184, 233. See also Military service (for American prisoners of war)
Pritchett, Joseph, 89
Property. See also Slaves; Tobacco
  destroyed, damaged, or seized
    compensation for, 170, 226, 368, 387, 661, 688, 747, 908, 971, 1466, 1472, 1495, 1538
    houses, 33, 44, 51, 61, 96, 101, 158, 170, 176, 209, 210, 211, 243, 251, 252, 279, 304, 305, 306, 307, 322, 348, 381, 382, 425, 510, 536, 545, 605, 669, 670, 824, 870, 873, 909, 924, 994, 995, 1220, 1321, 1537, 1564, 1628, 1705
    mills, 892, 1376, 1628

  ships, 22, 64, 87, 99, 216, 231, 254, 296, 302, 328, 473, 544, 556, 732, 740, 1016, 1075, 1473, 1534, 1617, 1639, 1647
  oath for assessment of, 646, 1127
  sold, compensation for, 151
Public buildings, 1128, 1260, 1566; Capitol (Richmond), 1128; Capitol (Williamsburg), keeper of, 1124, 1226; director for, 1632; jail (Richmond), 1566, 1567; jail (Williamsburg), 196, 777, 1137, 1165; magazine (Williamsburg), keeper of, 28, 795
Public debts: adjustment of, 1068, 1270; loss of money advanced for the public, 1044, 1254, 1391; money advanced for western service, 1542, 1543
Public printers, 1193; appointment of, 910, 911, 912, 1193; compensation to, 503, 723, 1352
Public records, 404.11, 1040, 1226, 1418
Public store. See Aylett, William; Military stores
Purdie, Alexander, 910, 911, 912

**R**

Ramsey, Elizabeth, 1029
Ramsey, Patrick, 1029
Ramsey, William, 861
Randolph, Edmund, 705
Ray, Joseph, 232
Reid, Elizabeth, 861
Reid, Joseph, 861
Religion. See also Church of England; Dissenters; Presbyterians
  non-Protestants barred from public office, 1155
  support of, 141, 520, 1108
    Protestant, 1155
  taxation for, 1051
Religious freedom: act for, 1051; opposition to, 1055, 1056; support of, 155, 155 A, 501, 520, 1087, 1098, 1098 A, 1108. See also Oaths, loyalty, fines for not taking
Reveley, John, 619, 1174

Richardson, Isaac, 390
Richmond (town): canal to, 1162; incorporation of, 1616; James River ferry in, 1054, 1288, 1289, 1290, 1368, 1405, 1487, 1488, 1522, 1568; lots in, 1260; notary in, 789
Richmond County: Rappahannock River ferry in, 1581; surveyors of, 121. *See also* North Farnham Parish
Ritchey, William, 390
Robertson, John, 861
Robinson, James, 390
Robinson, John, estate of 868, 997
Rockbridge County: division of, 899, 899 A; formation of, 428; poor of, 1224. *See also* Rockbridge Parish
Rockbridge Parish (Rockbridge Co.), 428
Rockett's landing warehouse, 1533, 1536
Rockingham County: boundaries of, 684, 694; division of, 945, 998, 999; formation of, 428; tobacco levies in, 684. *See also* Rockingham Parish
Rockingham Parish (Rockingham Co.), 428
Rogers, John, 1535
Roke, Hugh, 1180.4
Rootes, John, 987
Rootes, Sarah, 987
Ross, David, 1174, 1542, 1543
Ross, William, 390
Row, Benjamin, 485
Roy's warehouse, 1404, 1486
Royston's warehouse, 1404, 1486
Russell, Colonel, 1505
Russell Parish (Bedford and Campbell cos.): division of, 1653; sale of glebe land in, 897, 940
Rutledge, George, 390

## S

Saint Anne's Parish (Albemarle Co.), glebe land in, 981, 1017, 1077
Saint Anne's Parish (Essex Co.), vestry of, 358
Saint Asaph's Parish (Caroline and King and Queen cos.), formation of, 1027, 1027 A-1027 C
Saint Eustatia Island, 15, 254, 462

Saint James Southam Parish (Cumberland Co.). *See* Southam Parish
Saint James's Parish (Mecklenburg Co.), 66
Saint John's Church (Richmond), 228
Saint Margaret's Parish (Caroline Co.), vestry of, 1393, 1393 A
Saint Patrick's Parish (Prince Edward Co.), glebe land in, 412
Saint Paul's Parish (Hanover Co.), vestry of, 715, 715 A
Saint Stephen's Parish (King and Queen Co.), division of, 1392
Saltworks, 174, 205.1, 216. *See also* Military stores
Sampson, Nancy, 1122
Saratoga convention troops. *See* Prisoners of war (British and Hessian)
Savidge, Philip, 541
Seayers, John, 1062
Seayers, Mrs., 529
Sheldon, Thos., 495
Shenandoah County, name changed to, 428. *See also* Beckford Parish
Shepherd, Abraham, 970, 1019
Shepherdstown. *See* Mecklenburg Town
Shield, John, 1200
Ships, 151, 1179, 1661. *See also* Property
Simmons, Mary, 1123
Skipper, Lucy, 1122
Slaves
  compensation for
    death of, 7, 8, 9, 10, 38, 89, 213, 264, 321, 341, 349, 361, 370, 421, 486, 492, 567.91, 570, 618, 660, 742, 752, 783, 888, 1201, 1354, 1469
    defection of, 38, 44, 52, 110, 148, 362, 378, 383, 454, 776
    employment of, 52, 178
    execution of, 269, 298, 404.1-404.3, 404.18, 404.19, 404.27, 567.1-567.4, 567.6, 622.4, 624, 907.3-907.6, 907.16, 907.17, 1680, 1704
    loss of, 86, 319, 816, 1247, 1379
    seizure of, 87, 107, 191, 192, 225, 389, 544
  emancipation of, 385, 805, 1066, 1081,

Slaves (continued)
 1088, 1119, 1316, 1359, 1377, 1384, 1650
 employment of, 52, 216, 323, 1678
  in canal construction, 4
  in ironwork, 4
  in lead mines, 25
  in public work, 1401
  in saltpeter mines, 25
 pardoning of, 1438
 public, 1401, 1420
 return of, 764, 1401
  employees of lead mines, 25, 136, 212, 224, 276, 330, 331, 343, 344, 378, 400, 423, 712, 748, 776, 1212, 1223, 1593
 taxation on, 1051
Smallpox, 338, 595, 667, 730, 1036, 1561, 1603; hospital for, 1321; inoculation for, 329
Smith, Adam, 390
Smith, Henry, 390
Smith, John, 1238
Smith, Meriwether, 1234
Smith, Thomas, 495
Smith, William, 698
Southall, Turner, 1129
Southam Parish (Cumberland Co.), 265, 265 A–265 E
Southampton County, division of, 1323, 1323 A, 1323 B. *See also* Nottoway Parish (Southampton Co.)
South Quay warehouse, 531
Speake, Thomas, 1672
Spies, 558, 559, 1213
Spotsylvania County: courthouse in, 446, 447, 455, 815, 1111, 1130, 1184; division of, 476, 1111, 1130; Rappahannock River ferry in, 929, 936, 937, 938, 1065, 1065 A, 1065 B
Sprowle, Andrew, 362, 584
Stadler, John, 68
Stafford County: boundaries of, 140, 140 A; courthouse in, 954, 955, 956, 972, 1233, 1338, 1339, 1474, 1474 A, 1474 B; division of, 364, 466; military quotas in, 466, 468; Rappahannock River ferry in, 936, 937, 938, 1065, 1065 A, 1065 B, 1110; transcription of records of, 1040
Stanhope, William, 915
Staunton: hogs in, 948, 1673; street repair in, 846, 948; taxes for improvements in, 846, 948
Stevensburg (Culpeper Co.), establishment of, 1626
Stone, Caleb, 623
Stone, Elijah, 623
Stratton Major Parish (King and Queen Co.): division of, 1392; vestry of, 77, 92
Sussex County. *See* Albemarle Parish
Swearingen, Thomas, 625
Swearingen, Thomas, Jr., 970

## T

Taliaferro, Walker, 118
Tamboro, Andrew, 507
Tappahannock, 934
Tate, John, orphans of, 1436, 1489
Taxes. *See also* names of counties; names of parishes
 adjustment of, 1032, 1049, 1072, 1236, 1237, 1600, 1612
  law for, 1051, 1209, 1209.1, 1210, 1242, 1246, 1421, 1422, 1425, 1482, 1532, 1569, 1574, 1594
  on enumerated commodities, 1025, 1115, 1135, 1214, 1215, 1218, 1574, 1604
  on land and commodities, 1643
 delay of payment of, 1622
 exemption from, 1314
  for exiles to Virginia from Georgia and South Carolina, 1445
 imposition of, 236, 415, 415 A, 426, 939
 payment of, 21, 318, 1222, 1615
 relief from, 37, 70, 1113, 1430, 1455, 1530, 1561, 1604, 1618, 1686
Tayloe, John, 1438
Taylor, Isaac, 72
Taylor, Richard, 1121
Taylor, William, 623
Teagle, John, 1205

Tennent, Dr., 1175
Thomasson, Turner, 654
Thompson, Roger, 405
Thornton, Jeremiah, 781
Thornton, Jesse, 642
Thornton, John, 772, 805
Tillotson Parish (Buckingham Co.), vestry of, 931
Titus, Joseph, 390
Tobacco
    compensation for loss of, 39, 71, 120, 185, 186, 190, 246, 247, 275, 289, 560, 689, 1084, 1094, 1190, 1239, 1245, 1507, 1617
    disposition of, 42
    inspectors for, 750, 1402
        salaries of, 487, 515, 603, 717, 718, 926, 927, 1064, 1157, 1185, 1195, 1235, 1326, 1327, 1328, 1346
    laws for, 750, 1024
    levies on, 684
    rates on, 736
    restraint of growing of, 526
    taxes on, 1157
    warehouses for
        changing location of, 359, 464
        compensation for burning of, 340, 1239, 1556
        consolidation of, 1642
        establishment of, 365, 375, 531
        inspections at, 719, 1097, 1281, 1293, 1304, 1305, 1383, 1402, 1470, 1497, 1509, 1515, 1516, 1533, 1536, 1560, 1556
        removal of, 1249
        rent on, 1404, 1486, 1623
Todd's warehouse, 1404
Towns, establishment of, 427, 758. See also names of towns
Transylvania, 53, 97, 115, 116
Trent, Henry, 132
Trigg, Abraham, 34 A
Tucker, Robert, 1538
Turnbull, John, 997
Turner's warehouse, 1305
Twisdel, William, 406
Tyger's (Tygart's) Valley, 1280

Tyler, Henry, 1040

## U

Upper Parish (Nansemond Co.), 844

## V

Vallendigham, George, 262
Veale, George, 1291
Vinsant, Elijah, 390
Virginia, British invasion of, 1504, 1529, 1537, 1564, 1618, 1686
Virginia Auditors of Public Accounts
    salaries of, 1178
    clerks to, 950
Virginia Board of Trade, 1330, 1501
Virginia Commissioner of the Navy, salary of clerk to, 596, 1657
Virginia–North Carolina boundary, 1283, 1378, 1435
Virginia–Pennsylvania boundary, 54
Virginia State Treasurer: duties of, 1576; salary of, 1177

## W

Waddy's warehouse, 1560
Walker, Henry, 390
Walker, Hugh, 89
Walker's Company, 440
Wallace, David, 390
Wallop's Island, 81
Ware, John, 623
Warwick (Chesterfield Co.), 316
*Warwick* (sloop), 1534
Warwick County. See Milldams
Washington, George, 329
Washington County: boundaries of, 326, 327, 436, 436 A–436 C, 437, 437 A, 437 B, 602.1, 602.1 A, 602.1 B; contested General Assembly election in, 315; courthouse in, 436, 436 A–436 C, 437, 437 A, 437 B, 448; court meetings in, 409; division of, 363; formation of, 115, 116; land law established in, 604; road building in, 1508; settling land titles in, 1621; unpatented lands in, 1456

Washington District, 34
Washington Parish (Westmoreland Co.), altering boundaries of, 686
Waspar, Absolum, 512
Wellford, Dr., 1175
Wells, Elias, 623
Wells, Willis, 623
West Augusta District, 138, 146
Western frontiers: government of, 1548; land on, 76; military service on, 1526; protection from Indians of, 80, 125, 427, 933, 1357; to be part of Virginia, 34, 34 A, 35; townships to be established on, 427. *See also* Indians; Kentucky County; Military officers; Military service; Militia; Public debts
Westham, 1129, 1394; blast furnace at, 24; boring mill at, 990; canal at, 4, 474, 979, 990, 1162; forge and slitting mill at, 606; foundry at, 20, 483, 619, 655, 979, 1174, 1381; pig iron produced at, 606, 655
Westmoreland County: division of, 332, 364, 467; express riders for, 1684. *See also* Washington Parish
Wharton, J. Thomas, 384
Whitlow, Elizabeth, 1106
Wicomico Parish (Northumberland Co.), vestry of, 932
Wicomico River warehouses, 375
Wilkerson, Betty, 1180.6
Wilkinson, Thomas, 1403
Will (slave), 1384
William and Mary, College of: financial assistance to, 333, 791, 1082; rent for leased land of, 488
Williams, Lewis, 542
Williams, Robert, 1663
Williamsburg, court "writers" in, 149. *See also* Mental hospital (Williamsburg)
Williamson, Charles, 1238
Williamson, Robert, 754, 755
Willoughby, John, Sr., 383
Wills, William, 390
Wilson, John, 238
Wilson, Peter, 1180.1
Wilson, Samuel, 71
Winchester, 809; incorporation of, 820, 902, 964; ordinary licenses in, 1586
Witt, George, 495
Wodrow, Alexander, estate of, 1631
Wonycutt, Nicholas, 670
Wood, Drury, 1566
Wood, Ebenezer, 563
Wood, John, 390
Wood, Jonathan, 390
Woods, Robert, 390
Woodstock (Dunmore Co.), 227
Woodward, Benjamin, 376
Wright, Francis, 609

## XYZ

Yancey, Charles, 418, 569, 832
Yeager, Henry, 72
Yohogania County: court in, 808; division of, 725; formation of, 163; land title disputes in, 501; militia officers in, appointment of, 501; Monongahela River ferry in, 257, 509; unpatented lands in, 1126
York County: care of poor in, 314; saltworks in, 205.1; York River ferry in, 528, 793, 914, 1227
Yorktown: garrison at, 1345; incorporation and enlargement of, 1183
Young, Ridley, 404.22

# Geographic Index

Index entries for counties or localities named at the upper right of the petition abstracts refer to the serial numbers assigned to petition abstracts, not to page numbers, and are printed in roman face. Serial numbers printed in italic face (e.g., *618*) indicate noteworthy references to geographic areas within the texts of the petition abstracts.

Accomack County, 81, 136, 204, 216, 254, 285, 380, 472, 515, 580, 748, 784, 1179, 1205, 1430, 1650

Albemarle County, 155, 155 A, 183, 272, *292, 293, 682,* 682 A–682 C, 724, 738, 928, *981,* 1014, 1017, 1025, 1066, *1077,* 1123, 1255, 1334, 1396, 1696, 1705

Alexandria, *70,* 237, *726, 847,* 848, 902, 903, *1209, 1242*

Amelia County, 62, *250,* 534, 534 A, 534 B, 579, 579 A–579 D, 663, 666, 958, 1072, 1194, 1289, 1403, 1455, 1472, 1569, 1570, 1628, 1679

Amherst County, 117, 132, 153, 155, 155 A, 183, 292, 293, 301, 495, 651.1, 651.2, 799, 865, 1024, 1025, 1026, 1032, 1098, 1098 A, 1140, 1148, 1155, 1156, 1168, 1169, 1170, 1215, 1216, 1273, 1302, *1317,* 1361, 1379, 1432, 1451

Augusta County, 12, 60, 95, *112,* 195, 221, 428, 433, 444, 449, 500, 502, 507, 509, *684,* 685, 694, 714, 731, 826, 826 A, 828, 845, 846, 852, 899, 899 A, 933, 943, 945, 948, 959, 959 A, 959 B, 960, 966, 966 A, 985, 988, 1028.1, 1050, 1087, 1240, 1254, 1280, 1332, 1375, 1390, 1391, 1422, 1434, 1440, 1477, 1478, 1492, 1531, 1558, 1635, 1673

Bedford County, 25, 60, 132, 311, 312, 323, 402, 445, 454, 552, 589, 607, 615, *650,* 705, 707, 708, 786, 792, 797, 829, 865, 880, 883, 884, 893, 894, 897, 940, 951, 951 A–951 D, 952, *953,* 969, 1127, 1134, 1136, 1147, 1228, *1229,* 1230, 1230 A, 1317, 1330, 1340, 1343, 1364, 1411, 1452, 1453, 1453 A–1453 M, 1454, 1494, 1523, 1587, 1652, 1653, *1676,* 1681, 1681 A–1681 C

Berkeley County, 146, 164, 188, 193, 260, 278, 586, 625, 644, 646, 647, 649, 697, 798, 970, 973, 973 A–973 E, 1019, 1020, 1208, 1221, 1225, 1261, 1337, 1425, 1518, 1672

Botetourt County, 60, 80, 167, 222, 324, 345, 390, 428, 429, 430, 430 A–430 E, 632, 650, 758, 769, 974, 1034, 1163, 1248, 1292, 1361, 1643, 1648

Brunswick County, 236, 497, 633, 656, 767, 1010, 1013, 1053, 1278, 1279, 1279 A, 1279 B, 1318, 1318 A, 1322, 1322 A–1322 C, 1460, 1469, 1573, 1574, 1588, 1699

Buckingham County, 4, 24, 155, 155 A, 292, 469, 522, 538, 606, 619, 627, 695, 696, 931, 1024, 1025, 1129, 1277, 1277 A–1277 C, 1351, 1663, 1667

Campbell County, 1653, 1682

Caroline County, 56, 83, 86, 118, 147, 275, 479, 496, 520, 520 A, 520 B, 772, 782, *804,* 961, 1023, 1027, 1027 A–1027 C, 1033, 1033 A, 1033 B, 1042,

Caroline County *(continued)*
1059, 1112, 1346, 1393, 1393 A,
1435, 1437, 1651
Charles City County, 79, 1287, 1347,
1704
Charlotte County, 267, 273, 451, 790,
1008, 1009, 1022, 1106, 1237, 1298,
1315
Charlottesville, *928*, 1705
Chesterfield County, 3, 11, 55, 229, *250*,
487, 603, 626, 760, 810, 917, 958,
992, 1047, *1048*, 1054, 1070, 1114,
1157, 1182, 1209.1, 1288, 1290, 1386,
1398, 1405, 1487, 1503, 1522, 1528,
1549, 1556, 1568, 1575, 1594, 1595,
1618, 1701
Culpeper County, 157, 217, 242, 259,
303, 426, 482, 657, 660, 672, 673,
673 A, 803, 806, 821, 918, 918 A,
939, 984, 984 A, 1043, 1045, 1055,
*1110*, 1171, 1172, 1173, 1265, 1333,
1400, 1626
Cumberland County, 199, 199 A, 199 B,
*250*, 261, 261 A–261 E, 265, 265 A–
265 E, 266, 269, 320, 527, 530, 549,
578, *695*, *696*, 1104, 1104 A, 1145,
1153, 1311, 1313, 1313 A, 1313 B,
1348, 1348 A–1348 C, 1421
Delaware (state), 687
Dinwiddie County, 421, 593, 822, 1114,
1190, 1319, 1336, 1506, 1680, 1694,
1701
Dunmore County, 142, 227, 411
East Augusta District, 138, 139
Elizabeth City County, 22, 174, 713, 1016,
1120, 1131, 1321, 1426, 1611
Essex County, 358, 365, 664, 665, 1056,
1058, 1073, 1502, 1507, 1580, *1581*
Fairfax County, 182, 194, 338, 726, 847,
848, 871, 902, 903, 1068, 1069, 1078,
1093, 1209, 1242, 1249, 1325, 1612,
1614
Fauquier County, 259, 481, 1674
Fayette County, 1446, 1483, 1525, 1548,
1629, 1640
Fincastle County, 31, 34, 34 A, *49*, 60, 75,
76, 90, 109, 115, 116, *390*
Fluvanna County, *272*, 405, 493, 494, 527,
623, 682, 682 A–682 C, 683, 683 A–
683 C, 766, *785*, *788*, 981, 1077, 1132,
1622
France, 979
Frederick County, 100, 420, 820, 855,
925, 941, 964, 973, 973 A–973 E, 996,
1210, 1353, 1482, 1586
Fredericksburg, *82*, 169, *230*, *815*, *1065*,
*1184*, *1416*, *1417*
Georgia (state), 1599
Gloucester County, 205.1, 207, 209, 210,
219, 248, 528, 721, 793, 914, 987,
1227, 1354, 1501
Goochland County, 570, 617, 682, 682 A–
682 C, 683, 683 A–683 C, 785, 788,
900, 901, 1121, 1282, 1296
Great Britain, 57
Greenbrier County, 314, 441, 1213, 1357,
1369, 1450, 1450 A
Greensville County, 1468
Halifax County, 6, 59, 73, 128, 129, 130,
152, 165, 166, 238, 239, 255, 393,
424, 555, 573, 693, 754, 755, 811,
922, 922 A, 1028, 1044, 1118, 1151,
1479, 1481, 1671
Hampshire County, *98*, 208, 336, 507,
592, 595, 753, 809, 944, 1086
Hampton, *22*, 101, 713, 909, *1426*
Hanover County, 36, 37, 328, 487, 515,
715, 715 A, 804, *900*, *901*, 926, 1074,
1149, 1164, 1266, 1327, 1376, 1383,
1385, 1436, 1489, 1509, *1601*, 1605,
1623, 1664; and surroundings, 160,
377
Henrico County, 4, 21, 78, 228, 246, 247,
474, 483, 606, 619, 655, 789, 990,
*992*, 993, 1000, 1002, 1046, *1047*,
1048, 1128, 1129, 1149, 1162, 1164,
1381, 1387, 1394, 1449, 1488, 1498,
*1522*, 1564, *1575*, 1616, 1632, 1657,
1678, 1700
Henry County, 311, 312, 445, 607, 615,
*650*, 675, 707, 708, 953, 965, 969,
1102, *1228*, 1229, *1230*, 1250, 1349,
1350, 1439, 1665, 1676, 1677,
1677 A, 1677 B
Isle of Wight County, 39, 71, 77, 106,
131, 816, 1410

James City County, 161, 240 314, 962, 1083, 1133
Jamestown, 96, 107
Jefferson County, 1548, 1629, 1640, 1646
Kentucky area, 125, 150, 1357
Kentucky County, 435, 470. 498, 514, 548, 604, 652, 662, 783, 376, 877, 878, 882, 888, 895, 1011, 1030, 1071, 1167, 1241, 1252, 1253, 1253 A, 1253 B, 1540
King and Queen County, 77, 92, 190, 706, 935, 961, 1027, 1027 A-1027 C, 1033, 1033 A, 1033 B, 1059, 1305, 1392
King George County, 56, 140, 140 A, 185, 332, 364, 466, 467, 468, 572, 686, 1018, 1099, 1112, 1138. 1281, 1497, 1592
King William County, 459, 464, 706, 863, 1119, 1122, 1383, 1402 1509, 1601
Lancaster County, 504, 504 A-504 D, 505, 776, 779, 1051, 1304
Lexington (Fayette Co.), 1483, 1525
Lincoln County, 1548, 1629, 1640
Loudoun County, 70, 74, 194, 253, 546, 735, 736, 739, 915, 916, 919, 1037, 1037 A, 1076, 1520, 1520 A-1520 G, 1521, 1521 A, 1654, 1655, 1655 A
Louisa County, 418, 569, 575, 583, 682, 682 A-682 C, 832, 900, 901, 920, 921, 1294, 1297, 1310, 1377, 1406, 1519, 1557, 1683, 1702
Lunenburg County, 13, 91, 181, 236, 273, 318, 475, 553, 942, 1108, 1598
Mecklenburg County, 29, 56, 91, 181, 236, 280, 337, 422, 457, 690, 922, 922 A, 1150, 1295, 1359
Middlesex County, 77, 779, 1181, 1223, 1412, 1413, 1686
Monongalia County, 807, 960, 1126, 1280, 1485, 1675
Montgomery County, 324, 326, 391, 427, 437, 437 A, 437 B, 438, 438 A, 441, 602.1, 602.1 A, 602.1 B 604, 859, 974, 980, 1214, 1357, 1371, 1372, 1456, 1512, 1546, 1547, 1604, 1621, 1665, 1677, 1677 A, 1677 B
Nansemond County, 712, 716, 300, 531, 844, 1096, 1231, 1314, 1407

New Kent County, 930, 1383, 1495, 1560
Norfolk (borough), 1, 33, 44, 51, 52, 61 99, 123, 158, 223, 243, 252, 268, 313, 350, 605, 669, 670, 674, 729, 746, 747, 824, 870, 892, 908, 924, 971, 994, 995, 1246, 1314, 1530, 1576
Norfolk County, 1, 7, 8, 9, 14, 43, 176, 290, 304, 305, 306, 307, 316, 325, 340, 349, 362, 374, 378, 383, 414, 584, 605, 609, 676, 677, 716, 752, 1141, 1212, 1220, 1291, 1314, 1530, 1538, 1582
Northampton County, 212, 249, 688, 1236, 1615
North Carolina (state), 1283, 1435, 1471
Northumberland County, 170, 375, 385, 473, 932, 1094, 1239, 1362, 1409
Ohio County, 363, 817, 1126
Ohio River lands, 384
Orange County, 171, 291, 406, 407, 408, 415, 415 A, 416, 417, 465, 482, 526, 654, 673, 673 A, 806, 825, 923, 949, 1049, 1203, 1378, 1429
Petersburg, 1114, 1701
Philadelphia, Pa., 1367
Pittsylvania County, 60, 119, 119 A, 122, 145, 232, 342, 376, 506, 524, 533, 602, 675, 775, 797, 957, 1442
Port Royal (Caroline Co.), 56
Portsmouth, 58, 381, 517, 536, 545, 873, 1246, 1314, 1538
Powhatan County, 265, 265 A-265 E, 564, 1306, 1561
Prince Edward County, 124, 244, 412, 439, 947, 978, 1176, 1312, 1475, 1476, 1480, 1565
Prince George County, 927, 1084, 1182, 1600
Princess Anne County, 43, 133, 316, 535, 716, 752, 778, 864, 1238, 1593, 1587, 1706
Prince William County, 105, 172, 189, 201, 245, 259, 348, 794, 812, 872, 946, 1007, 1012, 1039, 1185, 1204, 1204 A, 1204 B, 1234, 1438, 1443, 1532, 1544, 1613
Richmond (town), 184, 228, 233, 789, 1031, 1162, 1193, 1256, 1260, 1288,

*1289, 1290,* 1316, 1324, 1326, 1328, 1368, 1418, 1467, *1487, 1488,* 1504, 1533, 1536, 1537, 1566, 1567, 1571, 1668
Richmond County, 120, 121, 156, 360, 678, 934, 1060, 1293, 1470, 1581
Rockbridge County, 899, 899 A, 975, 1115, 1218, 1224, 1428, 1441, 1459, 1461
Rockingham County, 684, 68*5,* 6*94,* 742, 998, 999, 1135, 1198, 1199, 1222
Shenandoah County, 637
Southampton County, 648, 658, 771, 1303, 1323, 1323 A, 1323 B
Spotsylvania County, 82, 230, 230 A–230 F, 298, 446, 447, 455, 476, 547, 815, 926, 929, 938, 1065, 1065 A, 1065 B, 1111, 1130, 1144, 1158, 1184, 1195, 1197, 1251, 1272, 1388, 1416, 1417, 1623, 1630; and others, 1404
Stafford County, 140, 178, 186, 197, 198, 341, *364,* 386, 466, 468, 926, 936, 937, 954, 955, 956, 972, 1038, 1040, 1064, 1065, 1065 A, 1065 B, 1097, 1110, 1233, 1235, 1338, 1339, 1474, 1474 A, 1474 B, 1486, 1623, 1631, 1642
Staunton, *195,* 369
Suffolk, 425, 8*44*
Surry County, 42, 541, 542, 543, 560, 774, 1083, 1515, 1516, 1666
Sussex County, 180, 488, 599, 1081, 1286
Virginia (state), 141
Virginia–Pennsylvania boundary, 54
Warwick County, 1120
Washington County, 315, 324, 327, 363, 409, 419, 427, 436, 436 A–436 C, 437, 437 A, 437 B, 438, 438 A, 448, 602.1, 602.1 A, 602.1 B, 604, 630, 867, 1085, 1357, 1456, 1463, 1464, 1465, 1508, 1511, 1511 A, 1512, 1546, 1621
West Augusta District, *138, 146,* 163, 554
Western frontier, 35
Western lands, 440, 722, 737, 787, 813, 819, 849, 850, 904, 976, 1152, 1620; south of Ohio River, 26, 53, 97
Westmoreland County, *56,* 332, 359, *364,* 628, 686, 719, 1159, 1217, 1245, 1281, 1399, 1493, 1497, 1684
Williamsburg, 23, 28, 149, 154, 168, *196,* 322, 333, 367, 460, 503, 723, 728, 749, 777, 791, 795, 857, 910, 911, 912, 950, 982, 1003, 1004, 1005, 1031, 1063, 1079.1, 1082, 1124, 1137, 1143, 1154, 1160, 1165, 1177, 1178, 1187, 1226, 1268, 1271, 1308, 1420
Yohogania County, 257, 501, 509, 554, 725, 741, 808, 1126, 1473, 1510
York County, 38, 205.1, 211, 251, 314, 443, 453, 618, *793, 914,* 1083, 1088, 1200, *1227,* 1345, 1363
Yorktown, *211, 251,* 382, 1183

**Virginia Legislative Petitions**
was set in Goudy type by Composition Division, of Richmond,
and printed by Braceland Brothers Printing Company,
of Philadelphia, on 75 lb. Curtis Rag white laid text,
an acid-free permanent/durable paper.

929.1  C562v  1984

Church, Randolph W. 1907-

Virginia legislative
petitions :
  LIBRARY USE ONLY

**MAINE STATE LIBRARY**
929.1 C562v, 1984, LIBRARY, USE ONLY
Church, Randolph W.
Virginia legislative petitions

3 5081 00098731 2

WITHDRAWN